Romania & Moldova

Steve Kokker, Cathryn Kemp

Contents

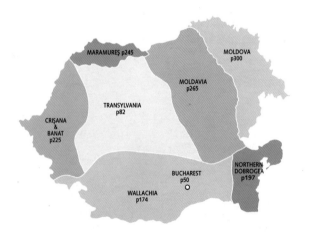

MARAMUREŞ p245

MOLDOVA p300

MOLDAVIA p265

TRANSYLVANIA p82

CRIŞANA & BANAT p225

BUCHAREST p50

NORTHERN DOBROGEA p197

WALLACHIA p174

Destination: Romania & Moldova

Students of European history know the scene well, an image of the continent as it once was: a bucolic paradise of rolling fields tended by lonely shepherds; horses' hooves on cobblestoned roads; a pace of life as unhurried as a farmer chewing a piece of hay. Rural Europe – a space and time that's increasingly looked back upon nostalgically as the race quickens towards a superpower future.

Alas! It's a lost way of life, gone in the grinding mesh of modernity! But wait...

Romania and Moldova are among the last bastions of Europe's traditional heart and soul. Here, its pastoral heart beats on in unspoiled countryside. Isolated villages nestled in lush valleys carry on traditions long relegated to tourist attractions just a few hundred kilometres west: yes, gentle shepherds tend to their flock – only they'll be talking on their mobile phone as they do.

And that's the kicker; these 'final frontier' countries may be a living museum to Europe's lost ways, but they're also defiantly modern and boldly strutting into the future. The nightlife in stylish Bucharest, Cluj-Napoca and Chişinău can hold its own against any found further west; Romania and Moldova are very much with the times even as they harbour a time gone by.

There's so much for travellers to bite into here: some of Europe's best skiing and hiking, breathtaking landscape, friendly locals offering swigs of delicious homemade wine, sun-drenched coastal resorts, picturesque castles (Romania isn't Dracula country for nothing!) and painted monasteries, plus plush hotels and snazzy restaurants – all affordably priced.

From Transylvania to Transdniestr (the country that doesn't exist), there are wall-to-wall discoveries here awaiting travellers looking for exciting, surprising, welcoming and breathtakingly beautiful destinations.

RHONDA GUTENBERG

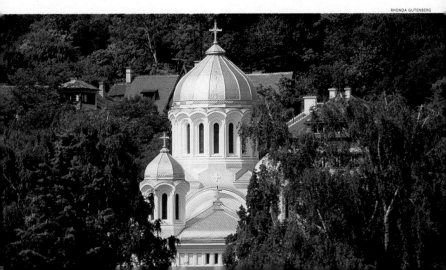

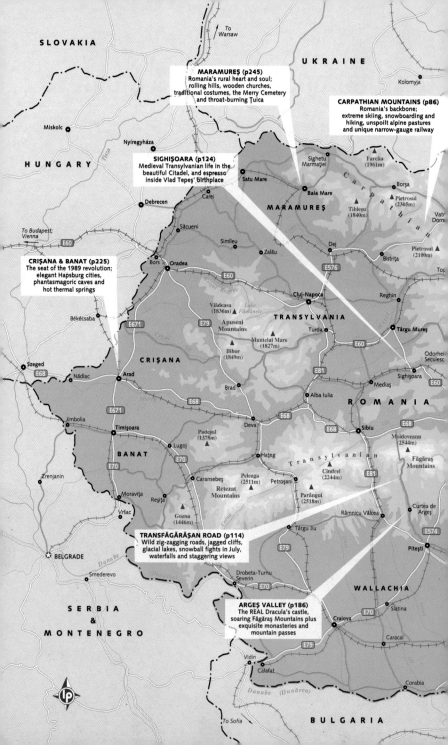

SLOVAKIA

To Warsaw

UKRAINE

Kolomyja

MARAMUREȘ (p245)
Romania's rural heart and soul;
rolling hills, wooden churches,
traditional costumes, the Merry Cemetery
and throat-burning Țuica

CARPATHIAN MOUNTAINS (p86)
Romania's backbone;
extreme skiing, snowboarding and
hiking, unspoilt alpine pastures
and unique narrow-gauge railway

Miskolc

Nyíregyháza

HUNGARY

Sighetu
Marmaţiei

Farcău
(1961m)

Borşa

SIGHIȘOARA (p124)
Medieval Transylvanian life in the
beautiful Citadel, and espresso
inside Vlad Tepeș' birthplace

Satu Mare

Baia Mare

Pietrosul
(2305m)

Vatra
Dorn

Debrecen

Carei

MARAMUREȘ

Tibleşu
(1840m)

To Budapest;
Vienna

E60

Săcueni

Simleu

Zalău

Dej

Pietrosul
(2100m)

Bistrita

Top

Borş

Oradea

E60

Tisul Repede

E576

CRIȘANA & BANAT (p225)
The seat of the 1989 revolution;
elegant Hapsburg cities,
phantasmagoric caves and
hot thermal springs

Cluj-Napoca

Reghin

Békécsaba

E671

E79

Vlădeasa
(1836m)

Lake
Fântânele

Apuseni
Mountains

TRANSYLVANIA

Turda

E60

Târgu Mureş

Szeged

E68

Nădlac

CRIȘANA

Bihor
(1849m)

Muntelui Mare
(1827m)

E81

Odorheii
Secuiesc

Arad

Brad

Alba Iulia

Mediaş

Sighişoara

E60

Jimbolia

E671

E68

E68

Deva

E68

Sibiu

E68

R O M A N I A

Timişoara

E70

Padeşul
(1378m)

Moldoveanu
(2544m)

BANAT

Lugoj

E70

Haţeg

Transylvanian

Făgăraş
Mountains

Zrenjanin

Caransebeş

Peleaga
(2511m)

Petroşani

Cindrel
(2244m)

E81

Moraviţa

Reşiţa

Retezat
Mountains

Parângul
(2518m)

Curtea de
Argeş

Vršac

Gozna
(1446m)

Râmnicu Vâlcea

BELGRADE

Danube

TRANSFĂGĂRĂȘAN ROAD (p114)
Wild zig-zagging roads, jagged cliffs,
glacial lakes, snowball fights in July,
waterfalls and staggering views

Târgu Jiu

E79

E574

Piteşti

Smederevo

Drobeta-Turnu
Severin

E70

WALLACHIA

**S E R B I A
&**

ARGEȘ VALLEY (p186)
The REAL Dracula's castle,
soaring Făgăraş Mountains plus
exquisite monasteries and
mountain passes

Craiova

E70

Slatina

M O N T E N E G R O

E79

Caracal

Vidin

Corabia

Calafat

Danube (Dunărea)

To Sofia

B U L G A R I A

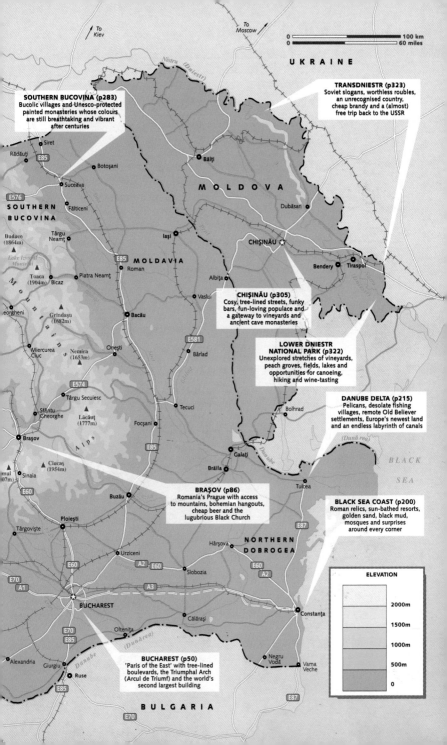

To Kiev

To Moscow

100 km
60 miles

UKRAINE

SOUTHERN BUCOVINA (p283)
Bucolic villages and Unesco-protected painted monasteries whose colours are still breathtaking and vibrant after centuries

TRANSDNIESTR (p323)
Soviet slogans, worthless roubles, an unrecognised country, cheap brandy and a (almost) free trip back to the USSR

Nistru (Dniestr)

Siret
Rădăuți
E85
Botoșani
Bălți
M O L D O V A
Suceava
E576
SOUTHERN BUCOVINA
Fălticeni
Dubăsari
Budaen (1864m)
Târgu Neamț
Iași
CHIȘINĂU
Lake Izvorul Muntelui
Toaca (1904m)
Bicaz
Piatra Neamț
M O L D A V I A
E85
Roman
Bendery
Tiraspol
Mountains
Grindușu (1682m)
eorgheni
Albița

CHIȘINĂU (p305)
Cosy, tree-lined streets, funky bars, fun-loving populace and a gateway to vineyards and ancient cave monasteries

Miercurea Ciuc
Nemira (1653m)
Onești
Vaslui
Bacău
E581
Bârlad

LOWER DNIESTR NATIONAL PARK (p322)
Unexplored stretches of vineyards, peach groves, fields, lakes and opportunities for canoeing, hiking and wine-tasting

E574
Târgu Secuiesc
Sfântu Gheorghe
Lăcăuț (1777m)
Tecuci
Focșani
Bolhrad

DANUBE DELTA (p215)
Pelicans, desolate fishing villages, remote Old Believer settlements, Europe's newest land and an endless labyrinth of canals

Brașov
Alps
E85
Galați
(Dună rea)
Ciucaș (1954m)
Brăila
B L A C K
mul 07m)
Sinaia
Danube
Tulcea
S E A

BRAȘOV (p86)
Romania's Prague with access to mountains, bohemian hangouts, cheap beer and the lugubrious Black Church

E60
Buzău

BLACK SEA COAST (p200)
Roman relics, sun-bathed resorts, golden sand, black mud, mosques and surprises around every corner

Ploiești
Târgoviște
E87
Hârșova
N O R T H E R N
Urziceni
D O B R O G E A
A2
E60
E70
Slobozia
E60
A1
A3
A2
BUCHAREST
E70
Călărași
Constanța
E85
Oltenița
(Dunărea)
BUCHAREST (p50)
'Paris of the East' with tree-lined boulevards, the Triumphal Arch (Arcul de Triumf) and the world's second largest building

Alexandria
Giurgiu
Danube
Negru Vodă
Vama Veche
Ruse
E85
E87
B U L G A R I A
E70

ELEVATION

2000m
1500m
1000m
500m
0

Romania is blessed with a splendid variety of simply beautiful natural sites. Visits to these and other places will definitely be the highlights of your trip.

No trip to Romania would be complete without acquainting yourself with the mighty, majestic Carpathian Mountains. There are many access points, from the cable car lifts at **Sinaia** (p107) and **Buşteni** (p104), to the quieter **Paltiniş** (p122), the busy ski hills at **Predeal** (p102) and **Poiana Braşov** (p96), and the less-touristy **Retezat** (p172) mountain chain and the **Ceahlău massif** (p281). When you're all hiked and skied out, set your sights on such eye-candy as the beautiful **Iron Gates National Park** (p192) or the dizzying **Bicaz gorges** (p282). There are also some of Europe's largest, most fantastic **caves** (p232) that dazzle with their unexpected mysteries. For wildlife, you can see some of Europe's last groups of large **carnivores** (p101) or thousands of birds from around the world who temporarily call the **Danube Delta** home (p215) – even pelicans!

Scărişoara Ice Caves (p232)

COLIN DAVID SHAW

COLIN DAVID SHAW

Vidraru Dam and
Transfăgărăşan road (p114)

Danube Delta (p215)

DIANA MAYFIELD

DIANA MAYFIELD

Suceviţa Monastery (p291)

COLIN DAVID SHAW

Bicaz Gorge (p282)

Bucegi Mountains (p106)

COLIN DAVID SHAW

Romania also offers all the comforts and charms of the city – both big and small. Whether you're having cocktails in **Bucharest** (p50) or checking out its great museums (or the monstrous **Palace of Parliament**, p57), going from one hot nightclub to another in hopping, stylish **Cluj-Napoca** (p144) or slinging back cheap, delicious beer in the bohemian paradise of medieval **Braşov** (p86), you're guaranteed a good time. You can check out fabulous monasteries in the heart of the country's second-biggest city, **Iaşi** (p268). In cosy **Timişoara** (p236) you can follow the heroic trail of the 1989 revolution, and in **Craiova** (p193) the **Art Museum** (p193) will let you peek at the great works of Brancuş after you see yourself a million times over in its surreal mirrors! Never a dull moment!

Braşov council house (p86)

Palace of Parliament, Bucharest (p57)

All Saints Church, Chişinău, Moldova (p305)

Getting Started

Thanks to Romania's grand diversity – enjoy baking under the sun on golden sands, shivering on a mountain top, lazing about in timeless, remote villages, or shaking it in hip nightclubs – there is something for all tastes and budgets here. Getting around should be no problem, with options running the gamut from renting a car and driver to hitchhiking – and if all else fails, hop a ride on a horse-drawn cart full of hay!

WHEN TO GO

Romania is a year-round destination, and the best time to go depends on what you're most interested in doing there. There is much variation in its climate: the average annual temperature in the south is 11°C, 7°C in the north and only 2°C in the mountains. In the summer months, temperatures have risen to above 40°C in recent years in Bucharest and along the Black Sea Coast, while winter chills of below -35°C are not unknown in the Braşov depression and around Miercurea Ciuc. In general, Romania's climate is transitional between temperate regions (the southeast can feel positively Mediterranean) and the more extreme weather characteristics of the continental interior. The average annual rainfall is 660mm, yet in the mountains that figure is usually over twice that amount, while in the Danube Delta it's often half that.

See Climate Charts (p335) for more information.

Summer (June to August) is an obvious time to visit for beach fun on the coast and for sunny hiking and mountain biking in the Carpathians; all tourist facilities are open then and the weather is usually great, but you will have to share the sites with more tourists. These months are best for bird-watching in the Danube Delta. Spring in Romania is a pastiche of wildflowers, melting snow and melodious bird song. At higher elevations, snow lingers as late as mid-May, and the hiking season doesn't begin in earnest until mid-June. The best months for skiing are December to March, though the season extends either way some winters.

DON'T LEAVE HOME WITHOUT...

Though most forgotten items can be picked up in Romania's urban centres, bring your own gear if you plan to hike or camp. Supplies and equipment aren't hard to find, but they can be prohibitively expensive. See also p332. Otherwise, remember:

- Extra tissues or toilet paper
- First-aid kit
- Swiss army knife
- Torch (flashlight)
- Universal sink plug
- Sun block lotion
- Insect repellent
- Extra video tapes or memory cards
- Contact lens solution
- Souvenir flag pins of your home country (to give as gifts!)
- Checking the latest visa regulations (p342) – especially for Moldova (p342)

Moldova is best to visit from spring to autumn, as skiing is almost non-existent and winter sports are not well-developed there. October's Wine Festival (with its visa-free regime; see p342) is an especially tempting time to visit, though spring and summer are best for city strolling and hiking in remote areas.

COSTS & MONEY

Romania and Moldova are among the most affordable destinations in Europe; for relatively little money, you can extract maximum pleasure from all they have to offer. While transportation and food, even in decent restaurants, is very affordable, accommodation is likely to take the biggest bite out of your daily budget.

As anywhere, however, it's possible to travel on a variety of budgets here, anywhere from scraping by on the bare minimum to living it up and feeling like royalty for a fraction of the price it would take to do so in western Europe. In Romania, backpackers staying at grotty camp grounds, hostels or cheap hotels near train and bus stations and filling up on kebabs, pastries and cheap eats can scrape by on €10 to €14 a day, including museum visits but not inter-city travel which in any case is inexpensive by any standards (when travelling by bus, expect to pay about €1 per hour of travel). For those who wish to stay in mid-priced hotels, dine out once or twice a day and perhaps hire the occasional guide or go on guided tours, expect to pay €25 or €35 per day, excluding travel.

In Moldova, because of the undeveloped hostel infrastructure, you'll likely pay more for accommodation than in Romania. Also, while prices are lower than in Romania, you'll most likely make more use of services such as hired guides or drivers here which might make your stay slightly more expensive than in Romania. Still, backpackers can get by on $15 a day, using public transport for trips outside Chişinău and if willing to hike or hitchhike. Anyone on a larger budget, who can hire drivers for excursions and stay in rented flats or mid-priced hotels can expect to pay at least $30 to $45 a day.

TRAVEL LITERATURE

Much of the travel literature about Romania deals with historical or topical social issues. Olivia Manning's *Balkan Trilogy* (1987, reprinted 1998) is a colourful portrait of Bucharest at the outbreak of WWII that has long been considered the classic work on Romania. Serialised on British TV as *The Fortunes of War*, it has reached a large audience with its details about life in the capital in the late 1930s.

A well-known book is Petru Popescu's *The Return* (1997), chronicling the well-known author's return to his Romanian homeland after defecting in the 1970s and after years living the life of a California bestseller (including a vampire novel) and screenwriter. He returns with his wife, a daughter of a Holocaust survivor, and has much to say about life after dictatorship. His observations are intriguing, though his inflated ego gets in the way much of the time.

Similar in many ways but by far better written is Norman Manea's *The Hooligan's Return: A Memoir* (2003). This accomplished author's return to his homeland in the late 1990s unleashes not only a search for identity and a flood of memories (of having lived in a Transdniestrian transit camp), but also many memorable observations on contemporary life in Romania.

Dominique Fernandez' *Romanian Rhapsody: An Overlooked Corner of Europe* (2000) is a good bet. This French author made four trips through

TOP TENS

TOP 10 ACTIVITIES TO LOOK FORWARD TO

Aside from all the outdoor activities listed throughout the chapters, here are some of the more subtle but equally memorable activities you can anticipate revelling in:

- Downing a bottle of local wine, champagne or brandy with newfound friends
- Picnicking by a sunflower field in Moldova and slicing up a plump, juicy watermelon
- Hopping a ride on a horse-drawn cart
- Hiking from one monastery to another in Moldavia
- Creeping in Dracula's footsteps
- Slapping on some smelly curative mud on the Black Sea Coast (p209)
- Going underground to a cave or salt mine in Transylvania, Crişana or Banat
- Braving a session of ţuica or pălinkă (p45)
- Trying some innards with your soup with ciorbă de burtă (p43)
- Hang out with a shepherd

TOP 10 MOVIES FILMED IN ROMANIA

Romania has its own film industry (p35), but these might be easier to find at your local video store – most under the category Cheap Horror Films (now, why go to Romania to film horror and vampire movies...?)

- *Amen* (Costa Gavras, 2003)
- *Wild Dogs* (Thom Fitzgerald, 2003)
- *Cold Mountain* (Anthony Minghella, 2003)
- *My Giant* (Michael Lehmann, 1998)
- *Elvira's Haunted Hills* (Sam Irvin, 2002)
- *Witchouse 1 and 2* (Jack Reed, 1999 & JR Bookwalter, 2000)
- *Straight to Darkness* (Jeff Burr, 2001)
- *Serpent's Lair* (Jeffrey Reiner, 1995)
- *Beowulf* (Graham Baker, 1999)
- *Asylum* (Gregory Gieras, 2001)

TOP 10 FESTIVALS

Every part of Romania has some kind of festival going on throughout the year, from international film festivals to country get-togethers where shepherds meet and locals sell their wares. Here are our favourites:

- Snow Festival, April, Păltiniş (p122)
- Juni Pageant, May, Braşov (p91)
- Tânjaua de pe Mara Folk Festival, May, Hoteni (p259)
- Bucharest Carnival, late May/early June, Bucharest (p68)
- Medieval Festival of the Arts, July, Sighişoara (p125)
- International Folk Music and Dance Festival of Ethnic Minorities in Europe, August, Cluj-Napoca (p151)
- Mountain Festival, August, Fundata (p101)
- Sâmbra Oilor, September, Bran (p100)
- Wine Festival, October, Chişinău (p338)
- De la Colind la Stea, December, Braşov (p91)

Romania and Moldova and beautifully interweaves history, culture and art with everyday people's stories and in the process shakes up some distorted notions the West has of Romania and Eastern Europe in general. His personal politics take the foreground at times, but this is a writer who knows the field well.

One of the more intriguing titles is Alan Ogden's 2000 book *Romania Revisited: On the Trail of English Travellers 1602–1941*. The author travelled the country in 1998, following in the footsteps of historical travellers, from the first motorists to romantics like Leigh Fermor. Dacian, Byzantine and Saxon Romania are beautifully evoked in this gripping series of tales.

Isabel Fonseca's *Bury Me Standing – the Gypsies and their Journey* (1996) is unique. The author spent several months travelling with the Roma in Eastern Europe between 1991 and 1995. The chapter covering Romania looks at racial attacks against Roma in Transylvania. This will give you a deep understanding of the Roma and their culture, one you're unlikely to get travelling on your own and listening to the average Romanian's disparaging comments about them.

Highly recommended is Stephen Henighan's *Lost Province: Adventures in a Moldovan Family* (2003). One of the best travelogues about Moldova, it follows a Canadian's experiences teaching English in this forgotten country and is humourous and touching while bringing up astute, even disturbing points about Soviet cultural colonisation and the inter-ethnic tension he finds there. Incredibly insightful, it will help you make the most of your trip there.

There are very few English-language accounts of travelling through Moldova, but Tony Hawks' *Playing the Moldovans at Tennis* provides a witty but respectful travelogue account of the author's exploits pursuing members of the Moldovan football team for a game of tennis – all to win a bet. It's chock-full of sardonic observations and quirky anecdotes.

INTERNET RESOURCES

All Moldova (www.allmoldova.com) An excellent source of information, with lots of tourist-related links for Moldova, and breaking news and stories too.

Lonely Planet (www.lonelyplanet.com) Listings, up-to-date traveller's reports, helpful hints and news items. The subwwway section has loads of helpful links.

Moldovan Ministry of Tourism (www.turism.md) Not the most easily navigable site ever, this state site is extremely helpful with news bulletins, the latest visa regulations, festival information and all forms of helpful travel advice.

Romania.com (www.romania.com) An excellent, well-represented site featuring everything from the latest sports scores to up-to-date news items and travel tips.

Romania.org (www.romania.org) A useful portal to links about everything you wanted to know about the coutry.

Tourism in Romania (www.turism.ro) Ministry of Tourism's official site has detailed descriptions of every region in Romania, good photos and some practical information.

Itineraries

Romania's greatest asset is its diversity, offering tourists who want to stray off the beaten track as much to do and see as those who want to stay well and truly on it. The routes presented are merely suggestions; travellers are encouraged to mix and match as they please!

CLASSIC ROUTES

SHARP FANGS & MOUNTAIN PEAKS   10 Days / Bucharest to Sighişoara

This is the classic route for travellers whose time is limited but who still want to experience a real Romanian sampler tour. You start off in **Bucharest** (p50). Most visitors take the first train heading to Braşov, but if you've read our chapter, you'll probably decide to stay at least a day or two in the capital. Next, head to **Sinaia** (p107) en route to Braşov. You'll want a minimum of two days to explore Sinaia and **Buşteni** (p104), checking out the **Peleş Castle** (p109) and getting in some hiking, biking or skiing at the dizzying top of these towns' cable cars.

When you feel like crowds, happening bars and urban delights again, move on to **Braşov** (p86), a bohemian paradise wrapped in a medieval cloak. Still bloodthirsty? Then get your neck over to **Bran** (p98) to buy your Dracula paraphernalia at the supposed Dracula's Castle. Don't miss the nearby castle at **Râşnov** (p95). There are hiking options here, but you really must get to **Sighişoara** (p124). Here you can have an espresso in **Vlad Tepeş' birthplace** (p127) and wander around the gorgeous medieval old town. Cursing for having only given yourself 10 days in Romania, head back to Bucharest and home.

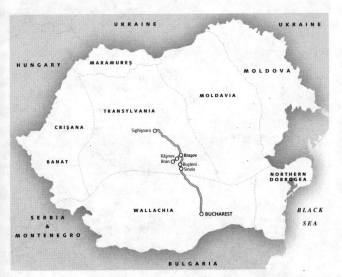

Head from Bucharest to Sinaia by train or maxitaxi (minibus), check out Buşteni before going to Braşov, and the castles at Bran and Râşnov. Visit Sighişoara before heading back to Bucharest. You'll have travelled about 600km.

ROADS LESS TRAVELLED

EUROPE'S COUSIN ONCE REMOVED
Seven – 10 Days / Ţipova to Lower Dniestr National Park

With fewer than 20,000 foreign tourists each year, just visiting Moldova will put you truly off the beaten track. Arrive in **Chişinău** (p305) and let yourself be surprised by how cosy, friendly and relentlessly swinging it is. After checking out the sites and hitting the tireless club and bar scene, you'll be ready to make several day trips.

First up should be the mind-blowing cave monastery at **Orheiul Vechi** (p320). There's another equally stunning one further north at **Ţipova** (p321). Nature-loving travellers can see all that this flat country has to offer in the **Lower Dniestr National Park** (p322), where you can hike and canoe but also lie in sunflower fields and picnic on the fruits of the land, indulging in fresh peaches and watermelons as well as grapes in either their original or liquid fermented form!

Next, revisit the Soviet era by visiting **Transdniestr** (p323), a country that doesn't officially exist but which has its own currency, hymn and flag, and lots of men in uniform running around. To wind down, spend at least two days happily floating along the **Wine Route** (p317) in some of the continent's largest wine cellars, sampling what made Moldova famous throughout the USSR.

Chişinău is conveniently located in the middle of Moldova, making it easy to use as a base for several interesting day trips. Covering all the locations, you'll travel some 700km over a week or more.

TAILORED TRIPS

UNESCO HERITAGE SITES   Three Weeks

For all you Unesco fetishists out there, here is a demanding tour of Romania and its seven World Heritage sites. This will take you around the country in a roughly anticlockwise direction, but you'll need at least 20 days to cover some 2500km in your own transportation. From **Bucharest** (p50), go to Tulcea and from there explore the fantastic canals of the **Danube Delta** (site No 1; p215). Travel north via Galaţi to Suceava (p284), the gateway to the unforgettable **painted monasteries** (site No 2; p288) near Târgu Neamţ in Southern Bucovina (p277). After scraping your jaw from the ground, continue west to Surdeşti, in Maramureş, for its famous **wooden churches** (site No 3; p254). Treat yourself with a few days in one of the region's villages where time seems to have stopped a century ago. Venture into Transylvania next. First stop is **Sighişoara** (p124) to wander around its historic citadel (site No 4), then to the nearby **Biertan Saxon fortified church** (site No 5; p129). Others are close by – check them out too. Next are the **Dacian fortresses** near Hunedoara (site No 6; p170). You can hike in the mountains of the **Retezat National Park** (p172) before arriving at the riveting monastery of **Horezu** (site No 7; p188), where you can give thanks for having the energy to complete the trip!

TAKE THE KIDS ALONG   Two Weeks

This is a high-energy 12- to 15-day trip that covers approximately 1300km of Wallachia, Transylvania and Crişana – a journey that is sure to keep a wide smile on your kids' faces. Start off in Bucharest and either go boating on **Herăstrău Lake** (p65) or pretend to travel the whole way round Romania in a day at the **Village Museum** (p64). Then head to Poienari (via Piteşti and Curtea de Argeş), where you'll find the 'real' **Dracula's castle** (Poienari castle; p186) – all 1480 steps to reach it. From there, keep heading north along the fantastic, ever-twisting **Transfăgărăşan road** (p114). Once on Hwy 1, head west to Hunedoara and visit some ancient **Roman strongholds** (p171). Then get ready for some heady caving in Crişana province, north of Hunedoara, in the **Bear Cave** (p232) and the famous **Ice Cave** (p232), both located near Chiscău. Keep heading north to Oradea where you can check out an ace **puppet show** (p228) or splash around in a **thermal pool** in Băile Felix (p231) before heading to Cluj-Napoca, stopping for some **horse riding** (p150) on the way. Just south of here is the Turda **salt mine** (p155), where you can enjoy a game of table tennis in the depths of the cave. If the young 'uns have any energy left, head northeast to Bistriţa and beyond to the **Hotel Castel Dracula** near the town of Piatra Fântânele (p163) and see what surprise lies in the basement, before returning to Bucharest.

The Authors

STEVE KOKKER   Coordinating Author

Steve is a die-hard Eastern European lover, having spent most of his time since 1996 living away from his native Montreal, basing himself in his father's home town of Tallinn, Estonia, and trekking through the Baltic region, Russia, Belarus and the Ukraine (including a memorable night in Chornobyl). Despite having developed a feel for the heart and soul of the area, Steve's experience drinking *samagon* (moonshine) in Russia no doubt was the best preparation for the onslaught of knock-your-block-off Romanian *ţuica* and rivers of delicious Moldovan wine, which sweetened the research for this book. Steve has been writing and photographing for Lonely Planet since 1998, and has also directed several documentary films. He was responsible for the Transylvania, Northern Dobrogea, Moldavia, Moldova, introductory and concluding chapters.

MY FAVOURITE TRIP

The trip that (just!) nudges out the (stiff) competition is my excursion to Orheiul Vechi (p320) in Moldova. After driving along a highway and pot-holed, dusty side roads we arrived at this massive, ancient site of worship and refuge, an enormous limestone ridge, pock-marked with openings leading to tiny rock chambers where, over the centuries, monks have meditated in utter, deafening tranquillity. I was given a brief tour of the chapel, itself a sombre, elegant hall embedded inside the mountain, by a bearded monk who chortled 'Who needs the Internet when you have all of this!?' Later, a small village funeral procession began arriving down the stone steps, locals from a nearby village. I stood at the back. The young tykes in the crowd stared at me and my digital camera the whole time; the others were immersed in chanting, gesticulating and crossing themselves repeatedly. The atmosphere, especially in such a locale, was dizzying; the intimacy and informality of the ritual unforgettable.

CATHRYN KEMP

Experienced Eastern Europe author Cathryn Kemp discovered the outer reaches of Romania for her latest Lonely Planet adventure. She rode on the back of horse-drawn carts and gasped at the bejewelled ancient monasteries in Wallachia, hiked up rolling cartoon-like hills in Maramureş and waded in thermal mud in spa resorts across this wild, fantastical nation to bring you the best, the worst, the treasures and the traumas of travelling in Romania.

MY FAVOURITE TRIP

It has to be the time travel back to medieval ways of living in Maramureş. Dubbed the 'heart and soul' of Romania by people who know, this enclave of earlier, better civilisation was an unmissable pleasure. The land in the north of Romania has the last peasant culture in Europe after centuries of being cut-off from modern 'progress' by the awesome Carpathian Mountains. People really do wear traditional dress, they really do farm the land, sing ancient folk songs and pray daily in their incredible wooden churches. I've never found anything quite like it before – and it's left an indelible mark on me.

NICOLA WILLIAMS

France-based travel writer Nicola Williams made her first trip to Romania in 1991 when she trucked it to Transylvania with 10 Welsh policemen as part of an international aid convoy. Today a confirmed Eastern Europe addict, she has travelled the length and breadth of Romania and Moldova, not to mention most neighbouring countries. Nicola researched and wrote the first edition of this guide in 1997.

CONTRIBUTING AUTHORS

The Health chapter was adapted from material written by Dr Caroline Evans, a GP specialising in travel medicine.

Snapshot

One of the most exciting aspects of travel is being plunged, temporarily, into the issues and concerns of the inhabitants of the country you're visiting. In Romania and Moldova, both struggling to improve their standard of living, there is no shortage of topical issues you'll likely hear about from the people you meet on the road.

In Romania, the government's drive toward integration and membership in the EU is topic *numǎral unu* in the newspapers and sometimes in the bar rooms of the nation. Watching all the horse-drawn carts pass by in the villages, towns and even cities of Romania, it's easy to think that the country's goal of accession by 2007 is just a tad optimistic, but the government is forging full-steam ahead in adjusting its laws to adhere to EU conventions and a majority of the urban populace is enthusiastic about joining.

Still, the European aspirations of the government remain beyond the realm of most ordinary Romanians, foremost on whose minds is how to improve their daily lot. You're likely to hear about searching for job opportunities or about fantastic ideas which only need sponsors and financing to become real.

Also on the minds of Romanians are the putative lingering tensions with the Hungarian population (some say there's no problem, others will be less polite, but everyone has an opinion about it), and the so-called 'Roma question'. Romanians like to bring up their supposed Roman ancestry and highly resent foreign assumptions that Romanians are Roma or are related to them in any way. For a guaranteed dynamic (if not explosive) conversation, dip into that one.

In Moldova, as EU integration is a far-off dream for the moment, it's not brought up much in conversation. There are way too many other problems to deal with beforehand, especially Moldova's own unsettled problems with internal integration, namely with the breakaway region of Transdniestr. The contentious possibility of Moldova becoming a federation of several autonomous regions has not been completely abandoned. Until these issues are cleared up, it will be hard to deal with other major issues of a backwards economy, lack of foreign investment, corruption and unemployment, to name just a few.

Expect one of the first topics of conversations to be about Moldova's biggest pride and joy: wine (p45). To avoid having to answer 'no' when asked if you've had any, enjoy a bottle or two upon arrival! You're also likely to hear about relatives of the people you meet working in the country you're from – it's an unofficial fact that a good part of Moldova's economy has been sustained by the astounding 25% of working-age Moldovans who are working in other countries and the money they send back.

QUICK FACTS

Romania/Moldova

Population (millions):
21.7/4.43

Area (sq km):
238,391/33,700

GDP growth (mid-2003):
4.5%/5.4%

Yearly inflation rate
(2002-3): 15%/7.5%

Official unemployment
rate: 8.9%/8%

Average monthly salary:
€117/$70

Life expectancy (male-
female): 69-75/60-69

Adult male-female
smokers:
62-25%/46-18%

Moldova's world rank
for length of its prison
sentences: 2

€ needed to repair all
of Romania's roads:
28.7 billion

History

ANTIQUITY

Ancient Romania was inhabited by Thracian tribes. The Greeks called them the Getae, the Romans called them Dacians, but they were actually a single Geto-Dacian people. Their principal religion was the cult of Zalmoxis; when people died, they went to him. The Geto-Dacians communicated with their god through meditation, ritual sacrifice and shunning bodily desires.

From the 7th century BC the Greeks established trading colonies along the Black Sea at Callatis (Mangalia, p211), Tomis (Constanţa, p200) and Histria (p215). In the 1st century BC, a strong Dacian state was established by King Burebista to counter the Roman threat. The last Dacian king, Decebal (r AD 87–106), consolidated this state but was unable to stave off attacks led by the Roman emperor Trajan in 101–02. Further attacks ensued in 105–06, leading to the Roman victory at the Dacian capital of Sarmizegetusa and the final Roman conquest of the region. Dacia thus became a province of the Roman Empire.

The Romans recorded their expansion north of the Danube (most of present Romania, including the Transylvanian plateau, came under their rule) on two famous monuments: Trajan's Column in Rome, and the 'Tropaeum Trajani' at Adamclisi (p214), on the site of their victory in Dobrogea. The slave-owning Romans brought with them a superior civilisation and mixed with the conquered tribes to form a Daco-Roman people speaking Latin.

Faced with Goth attacks in AD 271, Emperor Aurelian (r 270–75) decided to withdraw the Roman legions south of the Danube, meaning that Rome governed the region for under 175 years. Romanised peasants remained in Dacia and mixed with the locals; hence the Roman heritage of contemporary Romanians.

The Illustrated History of Romania (http://domino.kappa.ro/guvern/istoria-e.html) is one of the best places to get the ins and outs of the political vicissitudes of this fascinating country.

THE MIDDLE AGES

Waves of migrating peoples, including the Goths, Huns, Avars, Slavs, Bulgars and Magyars (Hungarians), swept across this territory from the 4th to the 10th centuries, each leaving their mark on local culture, language and the gene pool. Romanians survived in village communities and gradually assimilated the Slavs and other peoples who settled there. By the 10th century a fragmented feudal system ruled by a military class appeared.

A NICE PLACE TO VISIT...

The Latin poet Ovid was exiled to Tomis (Constanţa) on the Black Sea by the Roman emperor Augustus in AD 9. In the works that he wrote there, Ovid complained of local tribes, barbarians who attacked him with poisoned arrows, of wild warriors whose hairy faces were covered with icicles in winter, of regular sword fights between neighbours in the city forum, and of the horrific human sacrifices that the Tomisans practised.

650 BC	AD 106
Dacians are first recorded in the area of present-day Transylvania from their trade with Greeks.	Dacia becomes a Roman province (until 271).

From the 10th century the Magyars expanded into Transylvania, north and west of the Carpathian Mountains, and by the 13th century all of Transylvania was an autonomous principality under the Hungarian crown.

Written from a Hungarian perspective, Transyl- vanian History (http: //members.fortunecity .com/magyarhun/magyar /id3.html) offers a detailed and informative history of the Magyars in Transylvania.

Following devastating Tartar raids on Transylvania in 1241 and 1242, King Bela IV of Hungary persuaded German Saxons to settle in Transylvania with free land and tax incentives. He wanted to defend the crown's south-eastern flank. He also granted the Székelys (p132) – a Hungarian ethnic group who had earlier migrated to the region with the Magyars – autonomy in return for their military support.

In the 14th century, Prince Basarab I (r 1310–52) united various political formations in the region south of the Carpathians to create the first Romanian principality – Wallachia, dubbed Țara Românească (Romanian Land). It's indigenous peasantry became known as Vlachs.

Peasants dominated the populations of these medieval principalities. In Wallachia and Moldavia peasants were subjugated as serfs to the landed aristocracy (*boyars*), a hereditary class. There were some free, land-owning peasants (*moșneni*) too. The two principalities were ruled by a prince who was also the military leader. Most noblemen were Hungarian; the peasants were Romanians. After a 1437 peasant uprising in Transylvania, Magyar nobles formed a political alliance with the Székely and Saxon leaders. This Union of the Three Nations became the constitutional basis for government in Transylvania in the 16th century.

OTTOMAN EXPANSION

Throughout the 14th and 15th centuries Wallachia and Moldavia offered strong resistance to the Ottoman's northward expansion. Mircea cel Bătrân (Mircea the Old; r 1386–1418), Vlad Țepeș ('The Impaler'; r 1448, 1456–62, 1476), and Ștefan cel Mare (Stephen the Great; r 1457–1504) were legendary figures in this struggle.

The Balkan Vlachs: Born to Assimilate? is an essay worth reading at www.farsarotul.org/nl18 _1.htm for greater understanding of the origins of the Vlachs, considered modern Romanians' ancestors.

When the Turks conquered Hungary in the 16th century, Transylvania became a vassal of the Ottoman Empire, retaining its autonomy by paying tribute to the sultan. Catholicism and Protestantism were recognised as official state religions; the Orthodox faith of many Romanians remained an unofficial religion. Later, attempts were made to force them to convert to Catholicism.

After the Ottoman victory in Transylvania, Wallachia and Moldavia also paid tribute to the Turks but maintained their autonomy (this indirect control explains why the only Ottoman buildings seen in Romania today are in Northern Dobrogea).

In 1600 Wallachia and Moldavia were briefly united with Transylvania under Mihai Viteazul (Michael the Brave; r 1593–1601) at Alba Iulia. In order to fight Ottoman rule, he joined forces in 1594 with the ruling princes of Moldavia and Transylvania against the Turks, attacking strongholds and massacring Turks. In 1595 the Turks called a truce with Viteazul.

The Transylvanian prince, Andrew Báthory, subsequently turned against the Wallachian prince and, on 28 October 1599, Mihai Viteazul defeated and killed Báthory's troops near Sibiu. Viteazul declared himself the new prince of Transylvania, then in spring 1600 invaded Moldavia where he was also crowned prince. This first political union of the three

896	1241
The Magyars settle in the Carpathian Basin; a century later Stephen I, their king, integrates Transylvania into his Hungarian kingdom.	The Mongols invade Transylvania and go on a year-long rampage, plundering the region and slaying much of the local populace.

Romanian principalities lasted just over a year: Viteazul was defeated by a joint Habsburg-Transylvanian noble army just months later and in August 1601 he was captured and beheaded.

In 1683 the Turks were defeated at the gates of Vienna and in 1687 Transylvania came under Habsburg rule.

The 18th century marked the start of Transylvanian Romanians' fight for political emancipation. Romanian peasants constituted 60% of the population yet continued to be excluded from political life. In 1784 three serfs called Horea, Cloşca and Crişan led a major uprising. It was quashed, and its leaders were crushed to death on what is today a favoured tourist site (p165). But on 22 August 1785 the Habsburg emperor, Joseph II, abolished serfdom in Transylvania.

The 17th century in Wallachia was marked by the lengthy reign of Constantin Brâncoveanu (r 1688–1714), a period of relative peace and prosperity characterised by a great cultural and artistic renaissance. In 1775 part of Moldavia's northern territory – Bucovina – was annexed by Austria-Hungary. This was followed in 1812 by the loss of its eastern territory – Bessarabia (most of which is in present-day Moldova) – to Russia. After the Russo-Turkish War of 1828–29, Wallachia and Moldavia became Russian protectorates while remaining in the Ottoman Empire.

The web site for Constantin Roman's excellent book *Blouse Roumaine* (www.blouseromaine .com), an incredible compendium of notable female personalities in Romania's history, contains many fascinating excerpts.

ONE STATE

In Transylvania the revolutionary spirit which gripped much of Europe in the years leading up to 1848 was entangled with the Hungarian revolution, which in Transylvania was led by Hungarian poet Sándor Petőfi. Hungarian revolutionaries sought an end to Habsburg domination of Hungary. Concurrently, Romanian revolutionaries demanded their political emancipation, equality and the abolition of serfdom.

The Austrian authorities struck a deal with Transylvania's Romanians, promising them national recognition in return for joining forces with them against the Hungarian revolutionaries in Transylvania. Thus Transylvanian Romanians fought against and enacted revenge upon Transylvanian Hungarians for what was seen as centuries of mistreatment. Russian intervention finally quashed the Hungarian revolutionaries, ending a revolution that had shocked all sides by its escalation into civil war.

In its aftermath, the region fell under direct rule of Austria-Hungary from Budapest. Ruthless 'Magyarisation' followed: Hungarian was established as the official language and any Romanians who dared oppose the regime – such as the Memorandumists of 1892, a group of intellectual and political figures who voiced their opposition to Austro-Hungarian rule in a memorandum – were severely punished.

By contrast Wallachia and Moldavia prospered. In 1859, with French support, Alexandru Ioan Cuza was elected to the thrones of Moldavia and Wallachia, creating a national state known as the United Romanian Principalities on 11 December 1861. This was renamed Romania in 1862.

The reform-minded Cuza was forced to abdicate in 1866 by mutinous army officers, and his place was taken by the Prussian prince Carol I. With Russian assistance, Romania declared independence from the Ottoman Empire in 1877. After the 1877–78 War of Independence,

If you're bringing the kids along to Moldova pick up Patricia Sheehan's *Moldova* (2000), the 20th in the *Cultures of the World* series. Written for 9th to 12th graders, it contains lots of historical facts.

1431	1453
Vlad Tepeş (Vlad the Impaler) is born. He becomes the ruler of Wallachia, and is famous for impaling his victims on wooden spikes.	The fall of Constantinople. The Ottomans block trade on the Black Sea and Romania's isolation deepens.

THE WARRIOR QUEEN

'There is only one man in Romania and that is the queen.' That is how a French diplomat described Queen Marie of Romania whose diplomatic experience at the Paris Peace Conference in 1919 bolstered Romania's flagging image abroad, raised its political profile and assured her legendary status.

Queen Marie (1875–1938), the granddaughter of Britain's Queen Victoria, married Ferdinand I (1865–1927), heir to the Romanian throne, in 1892 when she was 17. Despite widespread horror in Britain at her mismatch to a prince of a 'semibarbaric' country, Marie developed a strong kinship with Romania, declaring, 'My love for my country Romania is my religion'.

Following an alleged love affair with American aristocrat Waldorf Astor, she knuckled down to twisting her tongue around the Romanian language and acquainting herself with Romanian politics.

During the second Balkan War (1913) the princess ran a cholera hospital for Romanian soldiers on the Bulgarian side of the Danube. In 1914 Ferdinand I was crowned king and Marie became queen.

Despite proving herself to be a 'viable political force', Queen Marie remained the 'people's princess' throughout her reign. At the outbreak of WWI she wrote her first book, *My Country*, to raise funds for the British Red Cross in Romania.

Prior to her evacuation to Iaşi in 1916, she worked in hospitals in Bucharest, distributing food and cigarettes to wounded soldiers. In Iaşi she set about reorganising the appallingly makeshift hospitals.

After she represented Romania at the peace conference in Paris, the French press dubbed her the 'business queen'. A mother of six, she wrote over 100 diaries from 1914 until her death in 1938. During her lifetime 15 of her books were published. Her autobiography, *The Story of My Life*, appeared in two volumes in 1934–35.

Queen Marie is buried in Curtea de Argeş (p185). Her heart, originally encased in a gold casket and buried in Balcic (in today's Bulgaria) is safeguarded in Bucharest's National History Museum.

Dobrogea became part of Romania. Under the consequent Treaty of San Stefano and the Congress of Berlin in 1878, Romanian independence was recognised. In 1881 it was declared a kingdom and on 22 May 1881 Carol I was crowned the first king of Romania.

Lucian Pintilie's 1994 film *An Unforgettable Summer* is set in 1925 in a disputed area near the Romanian-Bulgarian border. Romance and intrigue reign in this great little film.

WWI & GREATER ROMANIA

Through shrewd political maneuvering, Romania greatly benefited from WWI. Despite Romania having formed a secret alliance with Austria-Hungary in 1883, it began WWI with neutrality. In 1916, the government under Ion Brătianu, declared war on Austria-Hungary. Its objective was to seize Transylvania from Austria-Hungary.

The defeat of Austria-Hungary in 1918 paved the way for the formation of modern Romania. Bessarabia, the area east of the Prut River which had been part of Moldavia until 1812 when it was taken by the Russians, was joined to Romania. Likewise Bucovina, which had been in Austrian-Hungarian hands since 1775, was also reunited with Romania. Part of the Austrian-Hungarian Banat which had been incorporated in Romania, was also handed over. Furthermore, Transylvania was finally united with Romania. Hence, at the end of WWI Romania – now known as Greater

1467	1600
Stephen the Great defeats the Hungarian army at Baia; it is Hungary's last attempt to conquer Moldova.	Wallachia, Transylvania and Moldavia are united for 15 months under Mihai Viteazul.

Romania – more than doubled its territory (from 120,000 to 295,000 sq km) and its population (from 7.5 to 16 million). The acquisition of this new territory was ratified by the Triple Entente powers in 1920 under the Treaty of Trianon.

WWII

In the years leading up to WWII, Romania, under the able guidance of foreign minister Nicolae Titulescu, sought security in an alliance with France and Britain, and joined Yugoslavia and Czechoslovakia in the Little Entente. Romania also signed a Balkan Pact with Yugoslavia, Turkey and Greece, and later established diplomatic relations with the USSR. These efforts were weakened by the Western powers' appeasement of Hitler and by Romania's own King Carol II.

Carol II succeeded his father Ferdinand I to the throne. Extreme right-wing parties opposed to a democratic regime emerged, notably the anti-Semitic League of the National Christian Defense which consequently gave birth to the Legion of the Archangel Michael in 1927. This notorious breakaway faction, better known as the fascist Iron Guard, was led by Corneliu Codreanu and by 1935 dominated the political scene.

Finding himself unable to manipulate the political parties, Carol II declared a royal dictatorship in February 1938. All political parties were dissolved and laws were passed to halve the size of the electorate. Between 1939 and 1940 alone, Romania had no less than nine different governments.

In 1939 Carol II clamped down on the anti-Semitic Iron Guard, which until 1937 he had supported. Codreanu and 13 other legionaries were arrested, sentenced to 10 years imprisonment, then assassinated. In revenge for their leader's death, Iron Guard members murdered Carol II's prime minister, Armand Călinescu, leading to the butchering of 252 Iron Guard members by Carol II's forces. In accordance with the king's wishes, the corpses were strung up in public squares. Only with the collapse of the Axis powers at the end of WWII did the Iron Guard disintegrate (in 1999, Codreanu's nephew Nicador Zelea Codreanu tried unsuccessfully to revive the reviled group).

Romania was isolated after the fall of France in May 1940, and in June 1940 Greater Romania collapsed in accordance with the Molotov-Ribbentrop Pact. The USSR re-occupied Bessarabia. On 30 August 1940 Romania was forced to cede northern Transylvania to Hungary by order of Nazi Germany and Fascist Italy. In September 1940 Southern Dobrogea was given to Bulgaria.

Not surprisingly, the loss of territories sparked widespread popular demonstrations. Even Carol II realised he could not squash the increasing mass hysteria and on the advice of one of his councillors, the king called in General Marshall Ion Antonescu. To defend the interests of the ruling classes, Antonescu forced King Carol II to abdicate in favour of the king's 19-year-old son Michael. Antonescu then imposed a fascist dictatorship with himself as *conducător* (supreme leader).

German troops were allowed to enter Romania in October 1940, and in June 1941 Antonescu joined Hitler's anti-Soviet war. One of Antonescu's aims in joining forces with Hitler was to recover Bessarabia and this was

DID YOU KNOW?

The first ton of oil worldwide was extracted from Romania (the second was from the USA, the third from Russia).

Radu Ioanid's *The Holocaust in Romania* (2000) chronicles how Romania used other brutal methods aside from organised murder to try and rid itself of Roma and Jews during WWII.

1812	1819–34
Treaty of Bucharest grants Russia control of eastern Moldavia and the Ottoman Empire gains control of western Moldavia.	Wallachia and Moldavia were occupied by Russia. Between 1835-56 the two principalities were Russian protectorates.

achieved in August 1941. The results of this Romanian-Nazi alliance were gruesome, with over 200,000 Romanian Jews – mainly from newly regained Bessarabia – and 40,000 Roma (Gypsies) deported to transit camps in Transdniestr and murdered in Auschwitz. After the war, Antonescu was turned over to the Soviet authorities who condemned him to death in a show trial. Bessarabia fell back into Soviet hands.

As the war went badly and the Soviet army approached Romania's borders, a rare national consensus was achieved. On 23 August 1944 an opportunistic Romania suddenly changed sides again, capturing the 53,159 German soldiers who were stationed in Romania at the time, and declared war on Nazi Germany. By this dramatic act, Romania salvaged its independence and shortened the war. By 25 October the Romanian and Soviet armies had driven the Hungarian and German forces from Transylvania, replacing the valued territory back under Romanian control. The costs, however, were appalling: 500,000 Romanian soldiers died fighting for the Axis powers, and another 170,000 died after Romania joined the Allies.

THE COMMUNIST ERA

Prior to 1945 Romania's Communist Party had no more than 1000 members. Its post-war ascendancy, which saw membership soar to over one million, was a consequence of backing from Moscow. The Soviet-engineered return of Transylvania greatly enhanced the prestige of the left-wing parties, which won the parliamentary elections in November 1946. A year later Prime Minister Petru Groza forced King Michael to abdicate (allegedly by holding the queen mother at gunpoint), the monarchy was abolished, and a Romanian People's Republic proclaimed.

A period of terror ensued in which all the prewar leaders, prominent intellectuals and suspected dissidents were imprisoned or interned in hard-labour camps. The most notorious prisons were in Piteşti, Gherla, Sighetu Marmaţiei and Aiud. Factories and businesses were nationalised, and in 1953 a new Slavicised orthography was introduced to obliterate all Latin roots of the Romanian language, while street and town names were changed to honour Soviet figures. Braşov was renamed Oraşul Stalin.

Romania's loyalty to Moscow continued only until the late 1950s. Soviet troops were withdrawn from Romania in 1958, and street and town names were changed once more to emphasise the country's Roman heritage. After 1960 Romania adopted an independent foreign policy under two 'national' communist leaders, Gheorghe Gheorghiu-Dej (leader from 1952 to 1965) and his protégé Nicolae Ceauşescu (from 1965 to 1989), both of whom had been imprisoned during WWII. Under these figures the concept of a great Romanian socialist state was flaunted.

Romania never broke completely with the USSR, but Ceauşescu refused to assist the Soviets in their 1968 'intervention' in Czechoslovakia. His public condemnation of it earned him praise and economic aid from the West. In 1975 Romania was granted 'most favoured nation' status by the USA, which yielded more than US$1 billion in US-backed credits in the decade that followed. And when Romania condemned the Soviet invasion in Afghanistan and participated in the 1984 Los Angeles

1864

Romanian Jews forbidden to practise law.

1945

Following secret talks between Stalin, Churchill and Roosevelt, Romania falls under the Soviet 'sphere of influence'.

Olympic Games despite a Soviet-bloc boycott, Ceauşescu was officially decorated by Britain's Queen Elizabeth II.

Meanwhile, Romanians suffered painfully during the 25-year dictatorship of Nicolae Ceauşescu and his family. Thousands were imprisoned or repressed by the much-feared secret police (Securitate), huge amounts of money were squandered on megalomaniacal, grandiose projects and the population lived in abject poverty.

THE 1989 REVOLUTION

In late 1989, as the world watched the collapse of one communist regime after another, it seemed only a matter of time before Romania's turn would come. The Romanian revolution was carried out with Latin passion and intensity. The spark that ignited Romania came on 15 December 1989, when Father László Tökés publicly condemned the dictator from his Hungarian church in Timişoara, prompting the Reformed Church of Romania to remove him from his post. Police attempts to arrest demonstrating parishioners failed and within days the unrest had spread across the city, leading to some 115 deaths. Ceauşescu proclaimed martial law in Timiş County and dispatched trainloads of troops to crush the rebellion. The turning point came on 19 December, when the army in Timişoara went over to the side of the demonstrators.

On 21 December in Bucharest, an address made by Ceauşescu during a mass rally was cut short by anti-Ceauşescu demonstrators in the 100,000-strong crowd who booed the dictator and shouted 'Murderer', 'Timişoara' and other provocations. These demonstrators later retreated to the wide boulevard between Piaţa Universităţii and Piaţa Romană – only to be brutally crushed hours later by police gunfire and armoured cars. Drenched by ice-cold water from fire hoses, the demonstrators refused to submit and began erecting barricades under the eyes of Western journalists in the adjacent Hotel Inter-Continental. At 11pm the police began their assault on Piaţa Universităţii, using a tank to smash the barricades. By dawn the square had been cleared and the bodies of those killed removed. Estimates vary, but at least 1033 were killed.

DID YOU KNOW?
Romania's foreign debt was estimated in 2002 at $11.6 billion.

For more of the dirt (there's a lot) on the Ceauşescu clan's crimes against its own people, try Ion Mihai Pacepa's engaging *Red Horizons* (1990).

THE DICTATOR'S BRIGHT IDEAS

In his attempts to eliminate foreign debt and look good in front of the world, in the 1980s Nicolae Ceauşescu exported Romania's food while his own people were forced to ration even staple goods (meat was all but unattainable by the mid-1980s) and instituted power cuts to save money. His opponents were at best harassed, at worst killed by experimental methods of torture. One such method was known as Radu, used by Ceauşescu on his political opponents, especially Hungarian nationalists, whom he despised. Radu consisted of bombarding the body with low-level radiation and allowing cancer to settle. Many of those he had arrested eventually died of strange forms of cancer.

In March 1987, Ceauşescu embarked on a rural urbanisation program that would see the total destruction of 8000 villages (mainly in Transylvania) and the resettlement of their (mainly Hungarian) inhabitants. After having bulldozed one-sixth of Bucharest to build his House of the People (p57), no one doubted he'd proceed with his plans. Several dozen villages were razed, but thankfully the project went uncompleted.

1989	1992
Nicolae Ceauşescu and money-squandering wife Elena are found guilty of genocide by a makeshift tribunal and executed.	After Moldova's declaration of independence, civil war breaks out between Moldovan authorities and the region of Transdniestr.

The following morning thousands more demonstrators took to the streets, and a state of emergency was announced. At noon Ceauşescu reappeared on the balcony of the Central Committee building to try to speak again, only to be forced to flee by helicopter from the roof of the building. Ceauşescu and his wife, Elena, were arrested in Târgovişte, taken to a military base and, on 25 December, condemned by an anonymous court and executed by a firing squad. Footage of the Ceauşescu family's luxury apartments broadcast on TV showed pure gold food scales in the kitchen and rows of diamond-studded shoes in Elena's bedroom.

While these events had all the earmarks of a people's revolution, many scholars have advanced the notion that they were just as much the result of a coup d'etat as well: the Communist Party, tired of having to bow down to Ceauşescu as royalty, had been planning an overthrow for months before the events of December 1989.

ATTEMPTS AT DEMOCRACY

The National Salvation Front (FSN) took immediate control of the country. In May 1990, it won the country's first democratic elections since 1946, placing Ion Iliescu, a Communist Party member since the age of 14 at the helm as president. Protests ensued, but Iliescu graciously sent in 20,000 coal miners to violently squash them. Iliescu was nonetheless re-elected in 1992 as the head of a coalition government under the banner of the Party of Social Democracy. New name, same policies. Market reforms remained nowhere in sight. In 1993 subsidies on food, transportation and energy were scrapped, prompting prices to spiral sky-high and employment to plummet to an all-time low. Iliescu, meanwhile, personally benefitted from shady deal-making (p145).

Iliescu was finally ousted in the 1996 presidential elections by an even more embittered, impoverished and desperate populace who ushered in Emil Constantinescu, leader of the right-of-centre election alliance Democratic Convention of Romania (CDR), as president.

Constantinescu's reform-minded government made entry into NATO and the European Union (EU) its top priorities, together with fast-paced structural economic reform, the fight against corruption and improved relations with Romania's neighbours, especially Hungary.

Scandal and corruption surrounded the November 2000 electoral race. In May of that year, the National Fund for Investment (NFI) collapsed. Thousands of investors – mainly pensioners who'd deposited their life savings into the government fund – took to the streets to demand their cash back (US$47.4 million, long squandered by the NFI). Police used tear gas to dispel rioters in Bucharest.

After Contantinescu refused to run in the 2000 'Mafia-style' elections, 70 year-old Iliescu re-took the helm as the country's president. His Social Democrat Party today forms a minority government. The notoriously nationalist, xenophobic Greater Romania Party led by Corneliu Vadim Tudor is the country's second party, having won 21% of the votes. Adrian Nastase is head of government as prime minister.

Romania's 1991 constitution provides for a parliamentary system of government. Its two-chamber parliament – comprising the Chamber of

1994	1997
Romania is the first country to sign up for NATO's Partnership for Peace program in the hopes of eventually joining the organisation.	The number of stray dogs in Bucharest reaches between 150,000 and 200,000.

Deputies (lower house) and Senate (upper house) – is elected every four years. The next general elections are scheduled for December 2004.

The government's main goals, aside from domestic issues, is integration with the EU and other international bodies. In 2002, Romania was invited to join NATO. During the American war against Iraq in 2003, Romania was one of the first countries to guarantee access to airfields and allowed Americans to set up military bases on their soil.

MOLDOVA SINCE 2000

For details on Moldova's earlier history, see p303.

Visitors are surprised to hear that there is a Communist government in power in Moldova – after all the tiny country has suffered through after declaring independence from the USSR. Vladimir Voronin is president of the republic, and also the president of the parliamentary Communist Party. He has strong Russian sympathies and has taken steps to dissociate Moldova from its Romanian roots, focusing instead on the separateness of the Moldovan identity and language, but ones fashioned very much under its Soviet and Russian history of dominance. In his inaugural address in April 2001, he described Moldova as a European Cuba which needed to guard itself against 'imperialist predators' in Europe, just as Cuba had against the USA.

The president is elected by parliamentary assembly. The prime minister is Vasile Tarlev.

These officials have become highly unpopular. In 2002, several thousands took to the streets in Chişinău to protest a government plan to force school children to learn Russian. The government backed down but refused to step down, as the crowds were demanding. In November 2003, up to 50,000 took to the capital's streets in a peaceful protest demanding the government's resignation; they were incensed that Russian troops remain on Moldovan soil (in the breakaway region of Transdniestr) and about a Russian plan to change Moldova to a federation, giving self-rule to Transniestr. Placards read: Down with Communists! and We Want to Join NATO!

In 2003, Russian troops started to honour their years-old agreement of pulling out of Transdniestr; by the end of the year, they had removed some 20,000 tons of weapons, ammunition and equipment – about half of all that had remained on the territory since the Communist era.

The government under Voronin has been both trying to buddy up to the EU and international bodies (they joined the WTO in 2001), signing a Partnership and Cooperation Agreement with the EU in 1999, as well as snuggling up to the Russian and Ukrainian governments. If the government survives until elections in 2004, a major change in government is expected.

DID YOU KNOW?

Moldova ranks second in the world for the percentage of its population living under the official poverty line: 80% (2002).

Nicholas Dima's *Moldova and the Transdnestr Republic* (2001) offers the most complete analysis of Moldova's odd political positioning, and explores Russia's interest in the area.

DID YOU KNOW?

Moldova is ranked second in the world for the percentage of female professionals in its population: 67% (2002).

2002	2004
Romanian artist Constantin Brancusi's (1867–1957) bronze and gold leaf *Danaide* sells for $18,159,500 at Christie's in London.	Romania joins NATO

The Culture

THE NATIONAL PSYCHE

Nearly all travellers are impressed with the general friendliness of the Romanians they meet on the road. And after the few rounds of Ţuica (p45) usually offered to guests, the level of friendliness increases exponentially! Often freely giving of their time and energy (outside the capital, the concept of 'rushing' is an alien one), Romanians tend to take kindly, even protectively, to travellers; especially to those who show an interest in, and some understanding of, Romania. In villages, it's common to be invited into someone's home.

Romanians tend to be down-to-earth, don't waste time on false niceties, and like people who are open but also pragmatic and forthright. They have a Latin temperament and are often strong-minded, charming, stubbornly proud and staunchly aware of their roots. Most take great pride in their country's rich natural heritage and folk culture. Befriend any Romanian and within hours an expedition to the mountains will be mapped out for you.

However, many Romanians may seem formal and initially stiff by North American or even European standards. They have a natural reserve and shyness which, when trespassed upon, can transform into brusque behaviour. Their natural cautiousness can impede openness and showing curiosity, and you might get the sense that they're 'checking you out' before deciding to open themselves up to friendship.

Moldovans, though they are ethnically related to Romanians, have almost none of the reserve, shyness or formality of their cousins, thanks to generations of Slavic influence under Soviet and Russian rule. Highly approachable people, they will happily enter into conversation, extend genuine offers of help and show unbounded curiosity about you. Moldovans like to mix being productive with having a good time and will easily throw away plans to enjoy time with newfound friends. With a keen intelligence leaning towards the philosophical, they have no illusions about where their country stands in relation to the world but aren't self-pitying about it.

LIFESTYLE

Romania and Moldova are jigsaws of economics and attitude as much as of ethnicity. This has given rise to tension between minority groups, but most people today are united in their struggle to make a decent living. While pensioners are often the ones to have had the hardest time adapting to recent social changes, the younger generation is full of beans. In the cities, a sizable chunk of it drives fast cars and sports mobile phones; another chunk is driven by the dream of doing the same. Still others have embarked on a more difficult route: questioning where their country is headed and defining values and priorities. Sometimes it's easier to just head off into the mountains where no social issue matters much!

Romania wasted time in the 1990s stumbling through often ineffectual economic reforms and has only relatively recently found its footing and a sense of direction. This has led to optimism, but has left the country with a host of lingering social issues to contend with. The problem of its high number of orphanages was complicated by a ban on foreign adoptions in 2001 in an effort to stem a system of auctioning babies to

A great way to find out what Romanians are like is chatting with them! Check out the chat rooms at www.protv.ro and http://forum.taifas.ro, or get a list of others at www.scribens.polymtl.ca/~ureche/ziare/chat.

YOU KNOW YOU ARE IN ROMANIA WHEN...

Otopeni airport loudspeaker announcement: 'Ladies and gentlemen, for security reasons you are kindly required not to carry firearms in your hand luggage. Thank you for your understanding'.

DID YOU KNOW?

Moldova is ranked first in the world for total spending on education: 10.3% of the government budget (2002).

the highest bidder and to please EU directives. Only in the last days of 2001 did Romania finally repeal the criminalisation of homosexuality, becoming one of the last European countries to do so; any women's or feminist movement is barely nascent. There's also the question of what to do with all those forlorn stray dogs!

You are likely to see homeless or destitute children, perhaps begging for money or food, perhaps just trying to eke out a living on the streets. **The Information and Cooperation Centre for Homeless Children** (http://members .tripod .com/cicfa; %21 212 6176)) in Bucharest works in association with the Save the Children association (www.copii.ro) and City Hall to disseminate information and regroup related charities to combat this sad social issue. Interested parties are welcome to contact them for more information.

POPULATION

Romania's urbanisation was slow in coming: it remained largely a rural country until well after WWII when nearly three-quarters of its population lived in villages. Modernisation, industrialisation and Ceauşescu's attempts to urbanise and centralise Romania saw the urban population rise from 23.4% in 1948 to 55% today, still low by European standards. Moldova's figure of 41% makes it the second-least urbanised country in Europe. Romania's overall population is decreasing by 0.21% a year, while Moldova's is increasing at a snail-paced 0.09%.

Romanians make up 89% of their population; Hungarians are the next largest ethnic group (6.6%), followed by Roma (2.5%), Ukrainian and German (each 0.3%). Russians and Turks each take up but 0.2%. Germans and Hungarians live almost exclusively in Transylvania, while Ukrainian and Russians live mainly near the Danube Delta, and Turks are found along the Black Sea Coast.

Moldovans comprise but 64.5% of their population, followed by Ukrainians (13.8%), Russians (13%), Gagauz (4.5%), Bulgarian (2%), and Jewish (1.5%).

MULTICULTURALISM
Germans

The German population in Romania peaked in the 1930s when there were 800,000 Saxons in Transylvania. Numbers have dwindled to no more than 65,000 today. During WWII, 175,000 Romanian Germans were killed or left the country. After Romania switched sides to join the Allies against Hitler's Nazi Germany, 70,000 Germans were accused of Nazi collaboration and sentenced to five years hard labour. Survivors returned to find their land and property confiscated by the newly installed communist regime.

Under Ceauşescu, Germans, like all other inhabitants, were not allowed to freely leave Romania. Instead Ceauşescu charged West Germany about $8000 for each exit permit it issued. In the 1980s, some 70,000 exit permits were 'bought'. Unsurprisingly, between 1989 and 1995 an estimated 100,000 Germans left the country. Today's remaining Saxon community in Transylvania is served by state-run German schools and represented politically by the German Democratic Forum (Demokratisches Forum der Deutschen).

Roma

The government estimates that only 420,000 Roma (Gypsies) live in Romania, although the community itself and the Budapest-based European

DID YOU KNOW?
Romania is usually in the top five countries in the world for having the highest marriage rates.

Rodica Botoman's *Discover Romanian* (1995) is one of the best books of its kind to learn Romanian, as it's full of cultural insights and linguistic 'tricks'.

85% of the Tatar and Turkish population of Romania live in Constanţa county.

Roma Rights Centre (http://errc.org) believes it to be at least 1.8 million, making it the largest such community in the world.

The Mongols and Tartars brought the first enslaved Roma to Romania in 1242. Nomadic Roma *(corturari)* from India settled in Romania from the 15th century onwards.

For lots more information about the Roma and their culture, check out these helpful sites:
www.rroma .ro;
www.romanothan.ro;
www.divers.ro;
www.romanews.ro.

Around 50% of the world's Roma population was wiped out by the Holocaust. They were persecuted under communism and are still widely reviled today, blamed for crime and social instability and harassed by the authorities. The remaining nomadic Roma number anywhere from 2500 to 10,000. They are split between 40 different clans comprising 21 castes, each of which has its own traditional costume, superstitions and taboos.

Politically, Roma are represented by the Alliance for Romany Unity, the Romany Christian Centre, the Community of Roma Ethnicity and the Roma Party (Partida Romilor), headed by Madalin Voicu.

Hungarians

Under Ceauşescu, all Hungarian-language newspapers and magazines in Romania were closed down, and very few Hungarian schools and cultural centres existed. Since 1989, however, the rights of Romania's 1.7 million Hungarians have been recognised. They are represented politically in parliament and have their own publications, schools and cultural centres.

Though calmer relations exist between Romanians and Hungarians – and between Romania and Hungary, there is still a palpable level of distrust and tension, fueled by historical injustices on both sides. Despite attempts to assimilate the Hungarians into local culture, they have retained a distinct identity; in Székely Land, it sometimes feels as if the population has no idea they're actually living in Romania!

Moldova

Despite the brutal civil war which erupted here in 1992 due to the breakaway Ukrainian- and Russian-dominated Transdniestr region, and though there is great disagreement between the Moldovan government and the Transdniestrian administration, very little inter-ethnic tension is felt between Moldovans and any of their minority groups.

MEDIA

After an initial explosion in print media after the fall of communism, the situation has stabilised in Romania, despite a continued tendency towards sensationalism in its news reporting. Among today's most influential papers are *Evenimentual zilei, Adevarul, Cronica Româna* and *Ziua*. You can watch Romanian TV and hear live radio broadcasts at http://www.cefta.org/memberstates/romania/romedia/romedia.htm.

Moldova has had a serious problem with freedom of expression in its media since gaining independence. The government has restricted journalists' access to and the right to publish information about material deemed sensitive. All six major newspapers are under some form of state control. The government also suspended the broadcasting of the hugely popular Romanian TV·1 channel (replacing it with a Ukrainian station) and of Russian ORT (which broadcast independent and locally-produced news reports). In 2003, the Council of Europe blasted Moldova for excessive control of its media, for inappropriate legislation and official harassment of reporters.

RELIGION

The majority of Romania's population (87%) is Eastern Orthodox Christian. The rest is split between Protestant (6.8%), Catholic (5.6%), Muslim (0.4%), plus there are some 39,000 Jehovah's Witnesses and 14,000 Jews. The Muslims mainly live in Northern Dobrogea, and the Protestants are mostly made up of Transylvanian Germans. In Moldova, 98% of the population is Eastern Orthodox, 1.5% are Jewish, and there are some 18,000 Jehovah's Witnesses.

Sport

Football has a huge following in both Romania and Moldova. Romania's national team made impressive showing in the World Cups throughout the 1990s when their biggest star was Gheorghe Hagi. Two most popular teams are Steaua Bucuresti (www.steauafc.com) and Dinamo (www.fcdinamo.ro). Top club Steaua Bucharest forged itself a formidable international reputation by winning the European Champions' Cup in 1986. Since then, it has suffered from bribery scandals and match-fixing allegations. Dinamo, formed in 1948, has won nine Romanian Cups and won the national championships 16 times. Steaua Bucharest's home ground is **Steaua Stadium** (☎ 21-410 7710; B-dul Ghencea 35). **Ştefan cel Mare Stadium** (☎ 21-210 3519; Şoseaua Ştefan cel Mare 7-9), and **Rapid Stadium** (☎ 21-220 2149; Calea Giuleşti), are other notable stadiums in the capital. Tickets are sold at the stadium gates.

One of the biggest names in Romania's sport world is gymnast Nadia Comaneci, born in Oneşti. In 1976, at the age of 15, she stunned the world by receiving the first perfect 10 in Olympic history (plus five medals) for her dazzling feats on the compulsory bars at the Montreal Olympics. She later emigrated to the USA and has written several memoirs.

See p304 for an amusing account of Moldova's infamous underwater hockey team. For more information on sports in Moldova, see www .ournet.md/~sportmd. Moldova won three medals at the 2000 Sydney Summer Olympics.

ARTS
Folk & Roma Music & Art

Traditional Romanian folk instruments include the *bucium* (alphorn), the *cimpoi* (bagpipes), the *cobză* (a pear-shaped lute) and the *nai* (a pan-pipe of about 20 cane tubes). Many kinds of flute are used, including the ocarina (a ceramic flute) and the *tilinca* (a flute without finger holes). The violin is today the most common folk instrument.

The *doină* is an individual, improvised love song, a sort of Romanian blues with a social or romantic theme. The *baladă* (ballad), on the other hand, is a collective narrative song steeped with feeling. Couples may dance in a circle, a semicircle or a line. In the *sârbă*, males and females dance quickly in a closed circle with their hands on each other's shoulders. The *hora* is another fast circle dance. In the *brâu* (belt dance), dancers form a chain by grasping their neighbour's belt.

Modern Roma or Tzigane (Gypsy) music has absorbed many influences. Roma musicians circulate through the village inviting neighbours to join in weddings, births, baptisms, funerals and harvest festivals. Improvised songs are often directed at a specific individual and are designed to elicit an emotional response (and a tip). To appeal to older people, the musicians sing traditional *baladă*, or epic songs in verse, often recounting the exploits of Robin Hood-style outlaws who apply

Number of medals Romania has won in all the Winter Olympics: one (world ranking: last place).

Number of medals Romania has won in all the Summer Olympics: 265 (world ranking: 10th).

justice through their actions. *Muzică lătărească* is the term to describe the music you're likely to see performed with violin and accordion in restaurants. It is a variant of traditional Roma music played during special events or gatherings inside homes or inns in the 17th to 20th centuries. Professional Roma ensembles include the famous Taraf de Haiduci (The Outlaws' Ensemble).

Painting on glass and wood remains a popular folk art today. Considered to be of Byzantine origin, this traditional peasant art was widespread in Romania from the 17th century onwards. Superstition and strong religious beliefs surrounded these icons which were painted, not for decorative reasons but to protect a household from evil spirits. Well-known 19th-century icon painters include Dionisie Iuga, Maria Chifor and Tudor Tocariu. The glass icons of contemporary artist Georgeta Maria Uiga from Baia Mare are exhibited worldwide.

Literature

Romanian literature draws heavily on the country's rich folkloric heritage coupled with its turbulent history as an occupied country inhabited by a persecuted people. In 15th-century medieval society, when writings were still scripted in Slavonic, an oral epic folk literature emerged. The *miorița* was a simple folk tale detailing life in the fields or on the mountainside.

Writings in Romanian, initially religious, took shape around 1420. Modern literature emerged in the mid-19th century in the shape of romantic poet Mihai Eminescu (1850–89), who captured the spirituality of the Romanian people in his work (see p33). Eminescu's grand disillusionment with love, interwoven with folk myths and historical elements, characterised his major works.

During the latter half of the 19th century the influential Junimea literary society (1863), of which Eminescu was a member, was founded by Titu Maiorescu (1840–1917) in Iași. Maiorescu was a literary critic who condemned the growing influence of foreign literature on Romanian writers. Perhaps the Romanian writer best known internationally is the playwright Eugene Ionesco (1912–94), a leading exponent of the 'theatre of the absurd', who lived in France after 1938.

The quest for 'national values' ensued in the prewar period with novelists like Cezar Petrescu (1892–1961), Liviu Rebreanu (1885–1944), and Mihail Sadoveanu (1880–1961).

Romanian literature became a tool of the Communist Party from 1947 onwards, with few works of note emerging and much repression of dissident voices. Andrei Codrescu was exiled to the USA in 1966 and went on to write numerous books about Romanian-related issues.

Contemporary Romanian literature looks to the future as much as the past. The energy of today's writers is epitomised in the two poetry volumes, *Young Poets of a New Romania,* translated by Brenda Walker, and *An Anthology of Contemporary Romanian Poetry* translated by Andrea Deletant.

Popular Music, Classical Music & Opera

Pop music in Romania is alive and well, pumped out on the nation's radios and on maxitaxi dusty cassette players. Radio stations have a tendency of playing the same few songs repeatedly through the day; you may think the stations only have five CDs to choose from – and two of those are by tacky 1980s holdouts. Two of the most internationally-recognised Romanians are Michael Cretu, writer and producer for Enigma and Sandra, and Gheorghe Zamfir, a pan-flautist whose wispy music often inspires groans.

A DACIAN'S PRAYER (EXCERPT)

Be curses on the fellow who would my praise acclaim,
But blessings upon him who does my soul defame;
Believe no matter whom who slanders my renown,
Give power to the arm that lifts to strike me down;
Let him upon the earth above all others loom
Who steals away the stone that lies upon my tomb.

Hunted by humanity, let me my whole life fly
Until I feel from weeping my very eyes are dry;
Let everyone detest me no matter where I go,
Until from persecution myself I do not know;
Let misery and horror my heart transform to stone,
That I may hate my mother, in whose love I have grown;
Till hating and deceiving for me with love will vie,
And I forget my suffering, and learn at last to die.

Mihai Eminescu

Hip-hop is fast gaining in popularity, and is well represented by local bands like Paraziţi, Moromeţi, The Family, and Bustaflex. The R&B queen of Romania is Nico. Pashaman is a mildly popular singer doing something akin to reggae. Sadly, a pop style termed *Manele* has overtaken the airwaves recently; it's a suspicious mix of dance, hip-hop, reggae and homemade techno with wild flourishes of pseudo-Turkish and Middle Eastern-influenced wailings to boot. Cassettes of the stuff line the windows of train station kiosks, and is either loved or despised.

Several 1960s folk and rock bands remain very popular: Phoenix plays haunting and melodic folk that's close to the Romanian heart, while Iris still manages to rattle the roof with its hard guitar riffs. Pasărea Colibri is a contemporary, extremely popular band with great folk-inspired soft rock pop tunes; if there's a chance to see the band live, do so! Two popular, guitar-oriented pop groups from Moldova are Zdob si Zdup and Gândul Mâţei.

The Romanian classical music world is nearly synonymous with George Enescu (1881–1955), whose *Romanian Rhapsodies Nos 1 & 2* and opera *Odeipe* are considered classics. He was as accomplished a violinist as composer, studied under Fauré in Paris and was also a conductor, cellist and pianist. Other figures of note include composer Ciprian Porumbescu (1853–83) whose haunting, melodic works reflected links with traditional Romanian folk music; his lovely Baladă and operetta *Crai Nou* are among his most popular works. Paul Constantinescu (1909–63) was a state-sponsored popular composer of film scores, opera *(O noapte furtunuosa)* and concertos.

Transylvania was an important European centre of classical music from the 16th century. Most of the activity centred in Sibiu, where one of Europe's first organ schools was founded, where Romanian composer Ion Caianu worked and where Liszt, Johann and Richard Strauss and Johannes Brahms visited and played.

In Moldova, two of the most prolific modern composers are Arkady Luxemburg and Evgeny Doga, who have both scored films and multimedia projects as well as written songs, concertos, suites and symphonies. Dimitrie Gagauz has for over three decades been the foremost composer of songs reflecting the folklore of the Turkic-influenced Gagauz population of southern Moldova. Working in Comrat, he has tried to keep old

The best introduction to Romanian classical music is *Romantic Walk Through Romanian Music*, a compilation of lovely pieces by Porumbescu, Enescu, Dimitrescu and others.

traditions alive, teaching about forgotten instruments like the faul and kaval and founding the popular band Fisiu.

Architecture

Travelling through Romania, you're likely to notice a variety of styles: arched Byzantine porches and windows in Northern Dobrogea; ornamental, wooden gates in Székely Land; lavish villas in areas with rich Roma; gothic and baroque structural masterpieces in Transylvania; traditional folk-styled homes in small villages; and endless stretches of functionalist concrete block apartment buildings outside – and sometimes in – most city centres. This is aside from the unique Saxon fortified churches in Transylvania, and Moldavia's fortified and painted monasteries. Bucharest is a fascinating blend of grand, florid buildings, French ecclecticism and Rococo. The Brancovan style, incorporating Oriental and Baroque elements was developed under Wallachian ruler Romanian Constantin Brâncoveanu.

One of the best articles about the particularities of modern Romanian architecture and of the peculiarities of the Soviet experiments in design (and their influence on the look of today's Bucharest) is Ioan Augustin's *The Post Communist/Monumental Junk Space* at www.anuc.ro /junkspace_e.html.

Visual Arts

Medieval painting was marked by a strong Byzantine influence. It expressed itself through frescoes depicting scenes from the Bible on outside walls as a means of educating illiterate peasants (they were the first in the world to be painted in this way), on the iconostasis inside churches, and in miniature form as a decorative frame for religious manuscripts.

The paintings of Nicolae Grigorescu (1838–1907) absorbed French impressionism and created canvasses alive with the colour of the Romanian peasantry. He broke the prevailing strict academic mould, heralding the emergence of modern Romanian painting. His work is popular with international collectors, and sells for up to $50,000 each.

Modernism was further embraced by Gheorghe Petraşcu (1872–1949), whose paintings also drew on the world around him. The symbolist movement was represented by Ion Ţuculescu (1910–62), who incorporated elements of Romanian folk art such as the decorative motifs of Moldavian carpets in his work.

Romania's most famous sculptor is Constantin Brancusi (1876–1957), whose polished bronze and wood works display a refined subtlety which belie the great passion and depth of thought which has gone into them. His work is held at the Pompidou Centre in Paris (across the street from which is a replica of his Paris studio), the Guggenheim, New York's MOMA, the Philadelphia Museum of Art, the Australian National Gallery in Canberra and in Romania at the Museum of Art in Craiova and Bucharest's National Museum of Art.

Since 1989, Romanian painting has undergone an explosion of exploration, with artists experimenting with a variety of styles and themes which either beforehand were discouraged or repressed. These styles, of varying effectiveness, replaced a prior emphasis on introspection so evident in Communist-era painting.

The biggest name in Moldovan painting is Mihai Grecu (1916–98), who co-founded the National School of Painting and was also a poet and free love advocate. His works range from the formally classical to a

Donald Leroy Dyer has written seminal books about Moldovan culture and language issues. Try *Studies in Moldovan* (1996) and *The Romanian Dialect of Moldova* (1999).

folk-styled art naive. In sculpture, Anatol Coseac today produces some highly original woodworks.

Theatre

The first theatre on Romanian soil was reputedly in the ancient city of Histria, as archeological digs attest. The first Romanian-language theatre opened in 1817, and the literary cultural boom of the following decade gave rise to talented playwrights and stage actors. Today, there are theatres in every major city and town, and several respected theatre schools.

A Jewish theatre has been established in Bucharest since 1948, and the first-ever Jewish professional theatre in the world was formed in 1876 in Iași. The Hungarian minority have established theatres in Cluj-Napoca, Timișoara and Târgu Mures.

Cinema & Television

Mircea Daneliuc has been a major name in Romanian cinema since his debut in 1975 with *The Long Drive*, an unusual road movie in which two men and a woman work out their differences in the context of an intolerant world. Later films such as *Glissando* (1980) and *Fed Up* (1994) have focused on the realities of the Romanian experience using unexpected, at times psychedelic, cinematic techniques.

Romanian cinema blossomed in 1994 with Lucian Pintilie's *Unforgettable Summer*, which made a small splash at Cannes that year. Other notable films to look out for include Daneliuc's *Senator of the Snails* and Radu Gabrea's *The Tragic Love Story of Rosenemil*. As more foreign films get filmed in Romania, more funding is finding its way into the industry, whose output has slowly increased in recent years.

Some recent shining examples of films popular on the international film festival circuit are Sinisa Dragin's *Every Day God Kisses Us on the Mouth* (2001), a dark, unusual tale of a serial killer, Radu Munteanu's *Rage* (2002), a surreal look at the peculiarities of modern Romania, and Cristi Puiu's *Stuff and Dough* (2001), a tension-filled thriller.

In Moldova, a separate film industry came into being with Kruschev's thaw, when works emerged combining unabashed romance mixed with Soviet realism (known as 'Moldovan poetic film') and became popular throughout the USSR. Moldova's films continued to be more lyrical and nostalgic than Romania's, which have tended to prefer realistic depictions of life. One of the most famous Soviet films ever was a Moldovan masterpiece from 1976: Emil Loteanu's *The Gypsy Camp Vanishes Into Heaven*, which blends hauntingly beautiful music with sweeping landscapes and impassioned love between a gypsy horse thief and a young girl.

Very few films are made in Moldova today, as the government has failed to protect its domestic industry and funding is rare (save for occasional co-productions). Add to that the fact that Moldova has the world's second-lowest cinema attendance rate, and it's an uphill battle for the movie industry!

Environment

THE LAND

Covering 237,500 sq km, oval-shaped Romania is made up of three main geographical regions, each with its particular features. The mighty Carpathian Mountains form the shape of a scythe swooping down into the country's center from the Ukraine and curling up northwards. West of this are large plateaus where bucolic villages and towns lie among the hills and valleys. East of the mountains are the low-lying plains (where most of the country's agricultural output comes from) which end at the Black Sea and Europe's second-largest delta region where the Danube spills into the sea.

Moldova couldn't look more different. Tiny (33,843 sq km) and land-locked, it's a flat country of gently rolling steppes, with a gradual sloping towards the Black Sea. With one of the highest percentages of arable land in the world, Moldova is blessed with rich soil. Fields of grains, fruits and sunflowers are characteristic of the countryside. Mineral and rock deposits are typically lignite, gypsum and limestone. A great effort has been made by environmental groups to protect Moldova's wetland regions along the lower Prut and Dniestr rivers.

See the difference!
Highest elevation in Romania: 2543m (Mt Moldoveanu); highest elevation in Moldova: 430m (Mt Balaneşti).

WILDLIFE
Animals

The highest concentration of large carnivores anywhere in Europe is found in the Romanian Carpathians. See p101 for information on how to see some of these creatures.

Romania's splendid nature teems with enough life to keep enthusiasts busy for quite a while: there are 33,792 species of animals here (707 of which are vertebrates; 55 of these are endangered) as well as 3700 species of plants (39 of which are endangered).

Birdlife in the Danube Delta is a never-ending treat (p216). It is a major migration hub for numerous bird species and home to 60% of the world's small pygmy cormorant population.

Moldova counts some 16,500 species of animals (460 of which are vertebrates) as its citizens.

Proportion of forested land in Romania/Moldova: 28.1/9.5%.

Proportion of agricultural land in Romania/Moldova: 39/64%.

Plants

Both Romania and Moldova are home to 6600 plant species. Typical alpine flora species include yellow poppy, Transylvanian columbine, saxifrage and, in the southern Carpathians, the protected edelweiss.

The Carpathian Mountains are among the least-spoilt mountains in Europe, with alpine pastures above and thick beech, fir, spruce and oak forests below. About 1350 floral species have been recorded there. Typical alpine species include yellow poppy, Transylvanian columbine, saxifrage and, in the southern Carpathians, the protected edelweiss.

DID YOU KNOW?

Half of Europe's bear population (some 5400), a third of its wolves (some 3500) and a third of its lynx (about 2000) roam Romania freely.

NATIONAL PARKS

Romania has over 500 protected areas, including 12 national parks, three biosphere reserves and one World Natural Heritage site (the Danube Delta), totalling over 12,000 sq km. Most of these are in the Carpathians.

Except for the Danube Delta Biosphere Reserve (DDBR), none of the reserves or national parks have organised visitor facilities. Some are accessible by public transport; others are not. More information on many reserves and parks are included in the relevant regional chapters.

Moldova has five scientific reserves and 30 protected areas, but has only recently designated one area as a national park, the 500-sq-km Lower Dniestr National Park (p322).

Following is a run-down of Romania's major parks and reserves.

Bucegi Nature Reserve

The Bucegi Nature Reserve protects the entire 300 sq km of the Bucegi Mountain Range. The reserve contains a variety of forests and abundant botanic species including edelweiss. It is also home to the woodpecker. The Bucegi Nature Reserve Museum is located in Sinaia (p110).

Retezat National Park

The Retezat Mountains encompass Romania's first national park, established in 1935 on 130 sq km. Today it has been declared a Unesco Biosphere Reserve and expanded to 544 sq km. It has some 300 plant species and its wilds are roamed by black mountain goats, bears, foxes and stags. Come migration season, the monk eagle is known to pass by.

Piatra Craiului

The Piatra Craiului range, a staggering wall of mountains 25km long, stretches from Zărneşti in the north to Podu Dâmboviţei in the south. Since 1939 the area has been protected but it was only declared a national park in 1990. Since 1999 it has been administered under guidance from the European Ecological Network (Eeconet). Its treasures include mountain cocks, black goats, wolves, stags and unusual hazel-coloured bears.

Ceahlău Massif

The 52-sq-km area of the Ceahlău Massif has been protected since 1941 as the Ceahlău Massif National Park (Parcul Naţionale Muntele Ceahlău). Among its many treasures are countless flower species and rare fauna such as the cliff butterfly and mountain cock. You can also spy deer, black mountain goats and bears.

Iron Gates Natural Park

This phenomenal park (Porţile de Fier; p192; www.portiledefier.ro) takes up a staggering 1156.55 sq km of spectacular scenery at the area where the Danube first enters Romania at the most impressive stretch of the great river's entire course. The park comprises of a series of stunning gorges 134km long, several lakes (including a glacial lake above the Tarcu peak) and views of an enormous dam.

Apuseni Mountains

The Apuseni Mountains were recognised as a geological reserve in 1938. At their centre is a karst plateau with an extensive cave system lying beneath. Wild boars, deer, stags and bears continue to inhabit the region's pine forests, but their future survival is jeopardised by uncontrolled hunting in these parts. The Apuseni Mountains have been earmarked for the creation of a future national park.

Todirescu Flower Reservation

The crowning glory of the Rarău Massif is the glorious Todirescu Flower Reservation (Fâneţele Montane de la Plaiul Todirescu; 1933), which sprawls for 44 hectares across Todirescu Mountain on the southern edge of the Slătioara Reservation. In July its meadows are ablaze with colour. Tulips, bluebells, daffodils, daisies, chrysanthemums and the poisonous omagul (aconitum anthora) are just some of the many floral delights found here.

Frank Carter and David Turnock's *Environmental Problems in East-Central Europe* (2002) is the place to turn for the specific ecological problems – and solutions – for this area.

Number of tons collected and disposed of during the first year of clean up at the Retezat National Park: 50

DID YOU KNOW?

29% of the current energy production in Romania comes from hydropower stations; the second-most used source is geothermal energy.

ENVIRONMENTAL ISSUES

Ah, the beauty of the landscape, the majesty of the high peaks and waterfalls, and the deep serenity of the picture-perfect fields and valleys! But... argh, what are all those plastic bottles doing there at the foot of the mountain?

It's a sad and distressing scenario that repeats itself throughout Romania: you'll be in the middle of nearly incomprehensible beauty when you suddenly stumble upon a dozen crushed beer cans or spot a pile of garbage floating in a creek. For NGOs like Pro Natura (www.pronatura.ro) and the Transylvania Ecological Club (p147; www.greenagenda.org), sensitising an apathetic public about how to diminish the impact of tourism on the environment are main priorities.

It's also a battle that has just begun. Under the Communist regime, the government tried aggressively to harness natural resources, regardless of the ecological costs. Posting signs saying 'Please remove your trash' would have been anachronistic when rivers were being diverted and ecosystems destroyed nearby (it should be noted that plastic bottles, a main culprit, did not exist in Communist times – people used recyclable glass bottles; in a way, Westernisation has been a step backwards!). Still today, even in protected areas, guidelines and enforcement are rare.

The government-sponsored Pro Natura started a conservation program in 1992 at the Retezat National Park and a year later on the Cerna Valley.

Despite their valiant efforts, much needs to be done. You can do your part by being respectful to nature even in places where you see lack of respect or by contacting or going on organised activities with the eco-groups and established tour guides mentioned throughout this book.

> The Romanian government's goal is that by 2010, one third of total energy production will come from renewable sources.

Cleanup Since 1990

Much has been done since 1990, including cleaning up a chemical and nuclear waste-pit at Sulina, where European countries dumped waste in exchange for hard currency; building new smoke stacks at Baia Mare, Romania's largest non-ferrous metal centre; closing industrial plants in Giurgiu and Copşa Mică and outfitting others with special filters.

Though the pollution bellowing out of Romania's factories has been halved, air pollution still exceeds acceptable levels in some areas, and the Danube Delta has a long way to go before it can be pronounced a healthy environment (especially after the gold-mine disaster in Baia Mare in 2000, when 100,000 cubic metres of cyanide-contaminated water spilled into the Tisa and Danube rivers). The DDBR has worked hard to 'ecologically reconstruct' large areas of land in the Delta (p200), but the drive to develop tourism and build resorts and sports facilities in or near bird and animal breeding grounds there is threatening one of the planet's most delicate ecosystems.

Change in Moldova has been even slower. Never heavily industrial, it faces more issues of protection and conservation than pollution. A majority of its 3600 rivers and rivulets were drained, diverted or dammed, threatening ecosystems.

> **DID YOU KNOW?**
>
> 10% of the current energy production in Moldova is from hydro-power stations, 90% from fossil fuels. Moldova imports 1.2 billion kWh of energy a year.

UNESCO WORLD HERITAGE SITES IN ROMANIA

- Danube Delta
- Villages with Fortified Churches in Transylvania
- Monastery of Horezu
- Churches of Moldavia
- Historic Centre of Sighişoara
- Dacian Fortresses of the Orastie Mountains
- Wooden Churches of Maramureş

Activities

While there are many beautiful and interesting sites to see in Romania, the diverse landscape lends itself so perfectly to active vacationing it would be a shame not to take advantage of it. See the castles and painted monasteries, but get in a few days of hiking! Hit those funky bars and take part in a village festival with shepherds but take a deep breath of fresh mountain air and jump off a cliff paragliding or go caving or mountain biking...the list of things to do here is endless!

For more precise information on these activities, where to find guides, maps and other resources, refer to the corresponding areas in the chapters. For activities in Moldova, see the Lower Dniestr National Park (p322) section in the Moldova chapter.

SKIING & SNOWBOARDING

Romania is fast becoming recognised across Europe as one of the continent's best – and certainly among the most affordable – ski and snowboard centres. Each year sees more ski tourists arrive – and certainly not leave disappointed! Thanks to the Carpathian Mountains, Romania has scenery that rivals Switzerland's and full-service resorts like Sinaia (p107), Predeal (p102) and Poiana Braşov (p96), all near Braşov. Sinaia offers the best downhill skiing, Poiana Braşov is the best resort, and Predeal is good for beginners. The Făgăraş Mountains are your best bet for longer distance ski treks.

The ski season runs from December to mid-March. You can hire gear for about €10 per day from all the major hotels in the resorts, plus at some shops like Sinai's super-helpful Snow (p109), which doubles as a ski school. Ski passes for the three major resorts are sold on a point system; for ten trips up a chairlift, count on paying €8 to €13. Five- to seven-day ski courses usually cost €60 to €80 for adults and €40 to €60 for children. The equipment and services are not at Western European levels, but that doesn't stop skiers from having a great time. For proof, check out the forum at www.ski-in-romania.com, which also posts snowfall information and other listings.

Suntours (suntours_ro@hotmail.com) in Braşov is one of many agencies which organise ski vacations.

To get information on great skiing expeditions outside the main resorts, check out www.mountainguide.ro/en/ski.htm. You'll find some excellent options in some of Romania's most scenic spots.

Other sites posting travellers' reviews include the Lonely Planet's Thorn Tree section at www.lonelyplanet.com, and www.outdoorreview.com.

MOUNTAIN RESCUE

Emergency rescue is provided by **Salvamont** (www.salvamont.org, Romanian only), a volountary mountain rescue organisation with 21 stations countrywide. Its members are skilled climbers, skiers and medics. They are also an invaluable source for weather warnings and practical advice.

Contact Salvamont via the local hospital, mayor's office (primăria) or through its headquarters in Braşov. However, in an emergency dial ☎ 961.

Some of Salvamont's major contact points are as follows:

Braşov (☎ 268-471 517; County Council Service, Str Varga 23)
Buşteni (☎ 244-320 048, 320 006; Primărie, B-dul Libertăţii 91)
Sibiu (☎ 0745-140 144, 269-216 477; Str Nicolae Bălcescu 9)
Sinaia (☎ 0722-737 913; Primărie, B-dul Carol I; ☎ 244-311 094; Hotel Peştera)
Zărneşti (☎ 0722-737 919/16; opposite Cabana Plaiu Foii)

HIKING & CLIMBING

For great listings
of mountain bike,
snowboarding and
skiing events in Bucegi
mountains area, see
www.surmont.ro.

Along with skiing, hiking is without doubt the most popular sport in Romania and, as with skiing, Transylvania and Moldavia are where the action is. The Carpathians offer endless opportunities for hikers, the most popular areas being the Bucegi (p105) and Făgăraş (p112) ranges, south and west of Braşov. Other zones include the Retezat National Park (p172), northwest of Târgu Jiu; the Apuseni Mountains (p151), southwest of Cluj-Napoca; around Paltiniş, (p122) west of Sibiu; the less-frequented Rarău Mountains (p297); and the Ceahlău Massif (p281).

Trails are generally well marked, and a system of cabanas, huts, even hotels along the trails on the mountain tops and plateaus make even a several-day trek more than comfortable. For shorter treks, there are dozens of options: take the cable car up the rocksides at Sinaia (p109) or Buşteni (p105) and make your way to the Ialomiceora monastery; hike from Poiana Braşov to Râşnov castle (p95); or trek from one monastery to another in Moldavia.

Rock climbers look
no further than
www.romaniaclimb.com
for the absolute best info
on where, when, how
and with whom to scale
the Carpathian's rocky
heights.

Though individual hiking is more than possible, we also recommend going on organised treks in small groups or hiring a guide familiar with the area you choose to explore – this is partly a safety issue but also local guides' familiarity with the land can help you get the most out of the experience. Throughout the text, we offer suggestions for guided tours. Even some youth hostels (like the Retro Hostel in Cluj-Napoca, p152) offer fun, guided excursions. Another good source of guides can be found at www.alpineguide.ro.

For those who like to
organise hiking trips
from home (if your
home is in the UK, that
is!), try High Places
www.highplaces.co.uk
/treks/romania, based in
Sheffield.

Rock climbing is another obvious sport in Romania, and the best – though most challenging – place to do it is in and around the **Piatra Craiului National Park** (p101; www.pcrai.ro). The Bicaz Gorge (p281) offers spectacular challenges too. **Green Mountain Holidays** (p150; www.greenmountainholidays.ro) near Cluj-Napoca organises hiking, climbing and other tours.

Maps

Detailed hiking maps are available but are of varying quality. You'll more easily find maps in big city bookstores. They're sometimes found at tourist offices, but only the better ones, as found in Sibiu or Sinaia. You might also stumble upon Communist-era maps in shops and cable

---

SAFE & RESPONSIBLE TREKKING

The popularity of hiking and camping is placing great pressure on the natural environment. Please consider the following tips:

- Carry out all your rubbish. If you've carried it in, you can carry it out. Especially don't forget plastic bottles, sanitary napkins and condoms!

- Never bury your rubbish. This disturbs soil and ground cover, encourages erosion, may injure animals who dig it up and may take years to decompose.

- Minimise the waste you must carry out by taking minimal packaging and taking no more food than you will need

- Don't use detergents or toothpaste in or near watercourses, even if they are biodegradable.

- Stick to existing tracks – if you blaze a new trail, it will turn into a watercourse with the next heavy rainfall and eventually cause soil loss and scarring

- If you light a fire, use an existing fireplace rather than creating a new one. Don't surround fires with rocks as this creates a visual scar. Use only dead, fallen wood. Remember the adage 'the bigger the fool, the bigger the fire'. Use minimal wood, just what you need for cooking.

car stations; some are surprisingly helpful – some. Cartografica produces excellent maps and, to a lesser degree, some of Amco Press' publications might be of use.

Your best bet, however, are maps by **Bel Alpin** (☎ 21-684 0579; belalpin@fx.ro) which also publishes excellent books on hiking in the Făgăraş Mountains. The Transylvania Ecological Club in Cluj-Napoca (p147) publishes a map of the region.

MOUNTAIN-BIKING

Given Romania's ideal mountain-biking terrain, it is not surprising that the sport has taken off in a big way in recent years. The most active biking clubs are in Cluj-Napoca, Sibiu, Oradea and Târgu Mureş. The plateaus atop the mountains at Sinaia and Buşteni are also popular with bikers who like to ride on top of the world. Yet there are countless areas perfect for biking in Romania, and it makes an excellent (if sometimes challenging) method to see Transylvania, Moldavia, Maramureş and the Banat regions. If you're ready to head up steep inclines and are super-careful coming down them (narrow roads and ubiquitous horse-drawn carts can be obstacles), cycling is a thrilling way to experience the grandiose nature Romania has to offer.

Clubul de Cicloturism Napoca (p150) can offer the best advice for cycling in the region and organises summer tours. Transylvania Adventure (www.adventuretransylvania.com), located in Satu Mare, also offers good biking tours.

CAVING

Romania has over 12,000 caves (*peştera*) but only a few are open to tourism. The spectacular **Peştera Gheţarul de la Scărişoara**, an ice cave in the Apuseni Mountains (p151) and the 3566m-long **Peştera Muierii** (Women's Cave, p188) are the most popular. The former is unforgettable; the latter isn't particularly impressive but it's one of the most accessible. One of Romania's best caves, also open to tourists, is the impressive **Peştera Urşilor** (Bear Cave; p232), northwest of Oradea.

Though some caves can be explored by just showing up or via arrangements with travel agencies, your best bet is to get in touch with Romania's main speleological organisations. They can give practical details, help and advice and let you know the best way to visit the best caves. They sometimes organise trips of their own. The **Romanian Speleological Foundation** (www.frspeo.ro/prezentare, Romanian only) has its head office in Oradea (☎ 259-472 434; lifeapuseni@rdsor.ro) and branches in Bucharest (☎ 21-212 5784; bucuresti@frspeo.ro) and Cluj-Napoca (☎ 264-595 954; speo@mail.dntcj.ro). The **Emil Racoviţa Institute of Speleology** has offices in Bucharest (☎ 21-211 3874; sconstantin@pcnet.pcnet.ro) and Cluj-Napoca (☎ 264-595 954; bonac@bioge.ubbcluj.ro). **GESS** (☎ 241-756 422; gess@dial.kappa.ro) is an ecological group in Northern Dobrogea (p200) involved in marine and cave biology; a great bunch, they occasionally organise exploratory and diving trips to the famous Movile cave near Mangalia.

Most of Romania's caves are not open to the public, are dangerous to explore on your own and destructive to do so for the caves' delicate ecosystems.

HORSE-RIDING

As you'll seen soon after your arrival in the country, Romania is a country steeped in horse tradition. For centuries horses have been used to plough, pull logs, cart crops and provide transport. Rarely used for

Romanian Travel & Adventure (www.outdoor guides.go.ro) offers a dizzying array of hiking, trekking and mountain biking trips throughout the country.

Find out all you ever wanted to know about Emil Racoviţa, one of the world's premier speleologists at www.speleological -institute-cluj.org/about _us/about_us_en.

DID YOU KNOW?

In 2002, cavers found a 35,000 year-old human jawbone while digging around in the Peştera cu Oase (Cave with Bones) in the southwestern Carpathians that turned out to be the oldest known human fossil in Europe.

Looking for some fellow spelunkers? In addition to contacting the federations listed in the text, check out the caving trips offered at //www.green mountainholidays.ro /cavingtrip.html.

leisure, horses remain vital to the daily lives of villagers and some city-dwellers too.

Throughout the Carpathians a network of trails leading to some of the country's most beautiful and remote areas can be explored on horseback. The best on offer is the **Ştefan cel Mare Equestrian Centre** (p163; ☎ 263-378 470; www.riding-holidays.ro) near Bistriţa in the heart of Dracula country in small village of Lunca Ilvei. Another good bet is **Daksa** (p151; ☎ 0740-053 550; www.daksa.net) located just outside Cluj-Napoca. Both offer fun excursions which take in small villages and chats with shepherds.

Depending on the kind of excursion, prices usually range from €40 to €100 per person per day, including lodging, equipment and meals.

BIRD-WATCHING

Follow the links at www.dmoz.org /recreation/outdoors /speleology/organizations /europe/romania to find in-depth (pardon the pun) information about caving and caves in Romania.

Europe's greatest wetlands, the Danube Delta is the obvious destination for bird-watching travellers to Romania. Almost the entire world's population of red-breasted geese (up to 70,000) winter here, and in the summer, thousands of pygmy cormorants and white pelicans, along with birds from up to 300 other species can be seen here. Though you are guaranteed to see some birds on any of the boat excursions you take from Tulcea or inside the delta region on boats big or small, **Ibis Tours** (p218; ☎ 240-512 787; www.ibistours.net) can organise specialised tours guided by ornithologists. Otherwise, the **Information and Ecological Education Centre** (☎ 240-519 214; www.deltaturism.ro) can suggest other ways to spot the flying beauties. There are also bird-watching excursions in Transylvania's mountains. **Aventours** (p87; www.discoveromania.ro) in Braşov can organise such trips.

PARAGLIDING

The website www.uib .no/people/nglbn has general information about Romanian speleology and these associations.

This is still a burgeoning sport in Romania, despite the fantastic choices of jagged cliffs from which to throw yourself off. Some of the major tour operators and travel agencies might be able to hook you up with gliding clubs, but you're probably best going straight to the pilots themselves: try **Alexandru Balmus** (☎ 0722-520 123; alexandru_b@mccann.ro) and **Mircea Asanache** (☎ 0722-370 925; masanache@yahoo.com), both experienced gliders. They work out of **Eagle Air Sport** (www.paragliding.ro) which groups airborne enthusiasts and organises flights in many regions throughout Romania, including near Alba Iulia, Braşov, Suceava and Hunedoara.

Food & Drink

Let's leave the debate as to whether or not something called Romanian cuisine actually exists and plunge, mouth wide open, into a world of tasty, hearty, simple food: Romanian cooking. Incorporating all the fresh produce its varied and fertile land produces into uncomplicated recipes, the dishes produced across Romania have a home-made character to them. Relying heavily upon pork (at least half their traditional meals feature this meat in some form), staples like potatoes and cabbage, and liberal borrowings from the cultures which have traversed and occupied its land, Romanian and Moldovan cooking is not for those seeking to diet. Hearty meals fit for a Nordic explorer are the name of the game here. No point in fussing about calories and arteries – food, as with life itself, is meant to be enjoyed to the full here. It's easier to give in and enjoy...

STAPLES & SPECIALITIES
Food
Mămăligă is a word you'd better familiarise yourself with, and quick. You'll find it on every menu, and you're likely to be served it in guesthouses morning, noon or night. In short, it is a cornmeal mush similar to polenta, and can be boiled, baked or fried. Traditionally it is served with nothing more than a sprinkling of *brânză*, a salty sheep cheese. *Mămăligă* can be frightfully bland (and very filling), especially the kind served up in diners and bistros, but when home-made, warm, and served with fresh *smântână* (sour cream), it ranks up there as one of the world's best comfort foods. There's also a delicious variation called *bulz* – *mămăligă* layered with cheese and baked in the oven with butter.

Ciorbă (soup) is the other mainstay of the Romanian diet. It is tart, deliciously warming on cold winter days and often served with a dollop of *smântână*. Favourites include *ciorbă de perişoare* (spicy soup with meatballs and vegetables) and *ciorbă de legume* (vegetable soup cooked with meat stock). Often *bors* (a fermented liquid mixture of bran and water) is added to give a sour taste. The undisputed *ciorbă* king is *ciorbă de burtă*, a lightly garlicky soup made of tripe (that's cow innards for the less quaint); for flavour, a fatty piece of beef is often added. The idea alone is enough to send some running, but locals swear by it. Often, soup leftovers are transformed into *ghiveci* (vegetable stew) or *tocană* (onion and meat stew) for the following day's dinner.

Tochitură is likely to be found on most menus across both countries. There are regional variances (see Regional & Seasonal Cooking p44), but it's usually comprised of pan-fried pork, sometimes mixed with other meats, in a spicy pepper sauce served with *mămăligă* and topped with a fried egg. In cheaper restaurants, this can be horribly salty, the meat rubbery, but when done well, it's delicious. *Sarmale* (cabbage or vine leaves stuffed with spiced meat and rice), an inheritance from the days of Ottoman rule, is another popular dish; it's hard to go wrong with that one. Restaurants and beer gardens typically offer *mititei* or *mici* (*meech*; spicy grilled meatballs). Other common dishes are *muşchi de vacă/porc/ miel* (cutlet of beef/pork/lamb), *ficat* (liver), *piept de pui* (chicken breast) and *cabanos prajit* (fried sausages).

Typical desserts include *plăcintă* (turnovers), *clătite* (crepes) and *cozonac* (a brioche). *Saraillie* is a yummy almond cake soaked in syrup. *Papanaşi* are cheese-filled pastries covered with jam and sour cream.

Galia Sperber's *The Art of Romanian Cooking* is a great compendium of all of the country's best dishes. Imagine, now you can make your own *mămăligă* (corn mush) in the comfort of your own home!

Kuros kalacs are enormous round donuts with candied sprinkles or chocolate coating; arteries alert! For a Romanian snack attack while on the move, munch on *covrigi*, rings of hard bread speckled with salt crystals.

Romanian and Moldovan cuisines are very similar. In Moldova, some Russian influences have made pickled fruits and vegetables more popular there, as are Russian meals like *pelmeni* (similar to ravioli). A Turkic influence has arguably been stronger in Moldova; in the south you may find the delicious *gagauz sorpa*, a spicy ram soup.

Regional & Seasonal Cooking

You'll be surprised at how different the same dishes can taste depending on where you eat them; each historical region of Romania has its own culinary influences which you as a traveller can benefit from. There are some dishes that can only be found in specific areas.

What might run through your mind while watching locals feast on things like blood sausage: *gustul disputǎ n-are* (there's no accounting for taste).

Moldavia is the place to try *tochiturǎ* (where it's known as its original name *tochiturǎ moldoveneascǎ*). Here it's made with pig's livers and kidneys, wine, pepper and garlic, and it's served without *mǎmǎligǎ*. Moldavia is also famous for other meals guaranteed to make a vegetarian lose their cookies: *racituri* is a jelly made from pig's hooves, used primarily in winter folk celebrations, and their *ciorbǎ de potroace*, a soup made with chicken entrails, rice and vegetables is said to be a guaranteed cure for hangovers. Some may prefer aspirin.

Transylvania boasts a variety of flavours, plus German and Hungarian dishes. For those who find traditional Romanian dishes bland and devoid of spices, flavourful and hot Hungarian dishes like *gulash*, paprikas and *panierte* will be welcome. The usual Transylvanian diet relies on pork, smoked lard (sliced and eaten with onions on fresh bread) and vegetable soup. When in Cluj-Napoca, don't miss *varzǎ de la Cluj* (cabbage à la Cluj), a scrumptious mix of cabbage, minced meat and light spices baked and served with sour cream.

In Wallachia, you'll find lots of prunes on the menu, often mixed with meat in a stew. In the Banat region, you'll find food spicier than in the rest of Romania, as it's influenced by Serbian cuisine. *Coajǎ* is a unique type of cheese found only in the villages around Bran, which comes wrapped in (and tasting of) tree bark.

At Christmas in Transylvania, you will find *singeretta* – sausages made with pig's blood, liver, kidneys and fat. How perfect in Dracula country. They're a German inheritance.

In and around the Danube Delta region, fish and game figure largely on the menu; a local specialty is soup made from up to ten kinds of fish and vegetables (pieces of garlic are thrown in later), usually slowly simmered in a cast-iron kettle. Carp kebab is another goodie. People in this area, and in the Dobrogea and Wallachian plains, also eat a lot of grains, beets and maize, grown so plentifully in the region. In Dobrogea, mutton is cooked in sunflower oil, giving it a unique flavour, and plates like pickled fish, fillets, rolls, mincemeat balls, croquettes of zander, Danube herring, shoat fish, carp, pike or sturgeon are also very tasteful.

On All Saints Day (March 9), little *mucenici* (martyrs) are baked, in most of Romania they are pieces of unleavened dough in the form of the figure '8'. However, in Moldavia they're brushed with honey and sprinkled with walnuts, and in Wallachia they're boiled in water with sugar then covered with crushed walnuts and cinnamon. Easter meals revolve around lamb; especially tasty is lamb *stufat*, a stew made with green onions and garlic. A traditional Christmas cake, to coincide with carolling, is *cozonac* (a pound cake), walnut cake or pumpkin pie.

DRINKS

Wine is the first and last word in the drink world in both Romania and Moldova, which each produce excellent wines (and brandies, especially in Moldova). Among the best Romanian wines are Cotnari, Murfatlar, Odobeşti, Târnave and Valea Călugărească. In Moldova, the big names are Cricova, Ialoveni, Cojuşna and Străşeni. Red wines are called *negru* and *roşu*, white wine is *vin alb*, while *sec* means 'dry', *dulce* is 'sweet' and *spumos* translates as 'sparkling'. You'll find that Romanian semisweet is most people's idea of sweet, and dry is closer to semisweet. Wine is still categorised along the sweet-dry continuum more than by the kind of grape used (a legacy of the Communist era).

A common practice is to mix the sweeter wines with mineral water; this idea makes connoisseurs' skin crawl – until they taste how sweet it would be otherwise. A bottle of wine in a restaurant should cost no more than €4, and less in a wine shop or cellar *(vin* or *vinuri)* – the cheapest and most fun way to sample local wine.

The harder stuff is worth trying as well – if you're a male, you're bound to be offered this on social occasions, but beware of the wallop it packs. *Ţuica* is a once-filtered clear brandy made from fermented fruit (the tastiest and most popular is plum *Ţuica*), usually 30 proof. *Palincă* (called *Horinca* in Maramureş and *Jinars* in the Cluj-Napoca region) is similar, only it's filtered twice and is usually around 60 proof; the stuff can knock your socks off. Both of these are often made at home, where the resulting moonshine can either be much tastier than the store-bought versions or much stronger and wince-inducing. In northern Moldavia, moonshine is called *samahonca,* similar to the Russian word for it.

In Northern Dobrogea, you're likely to find cafés which make a mean Turkish coffee, with a thick sludge at the bottom and a generous spoonful of sugar. Unless you specifically ask, coffee and *ceai* (tea) are served black and with sugar. If you want it white ask for it *cu lapte* (with milk); without sugar, *fără zahăr.*

WHERE TO EAT & DRINK

In cities and towns in Romania, you'll usually have a wide range of dining choices, from cheap bistros to formal restaurants (which in the more remote towns might only be found in hotels). Most places, even bars, bistros or cafés will also serve food, even if it's a greasy filled pastry. In Moldova, outside of Chişinău, where the choice of eateries is astounding, you'll be lucky to find a decent restaurant and will be stuck with hotel dining rooms, bars or cafeterias. There are few restaurants which cater to children (it's rare to find a children's menu or booster chair), but staff are usually accommodating.

The cost of a restaurant or café main meal is almost always between €1 and €5 across the country, no matter the style of place. The vast majority charge €2 to €3. The final cost of the bill increases as you add an appetiser (usually no more than €1.50), drinks and dessert. Still, entire meals at medium-priced places rarely exceed €5 to €6 per person, or €10 at higher-priced venues. Of course, there are first-class restaurants where it's possible to wine and dine for €20 to €40 per person also, but generally eating out is an affordable treat in Romania and Moldova. Eating out in Bucharest and Chişinău tends to be more expensive than in other centres.

A tip of 10% is considered decent.

For a rundown on Romanian wines, visit http://romania-on-line.net/business/wines.htm.

Something you might be offered as you stagger out of your Romanian or Moldovan friends' house: *la botul calului* (literally 'horse's mouth'). It means 'one for the road'!

Aside from wine, vodka is the intoxicating drink of choice in Moldova, a Soviet legacy. But beware – local vodkas are distilled from sugar, which gives a not-so-sweet headache come morning.

VEGETARIANS & VEGANS

Thanks to the Orthodox diet, you can always find some vegetarian dishes, unexciting and repetitious as they will come to be. If a plate of *mămăligă* does not turn you on, try *cașcaval pâine* (cheese covered in breadcrumbs and fried), *salată roșii* (tomato salad), *salată castraveți* (cucumber salad) and *salată asortată* (mixed salad, usually just a mix of – guess what? – tomatoes and cucumbers). When you're really lucky, you'll find vegetable soup or stew, or a dish made from eggplant.

Otherwise, fresh fruits are easy to find (huge watermelons, yum), and whatever's grown locally is bound to have had less chemicals involved in its growth than the ones in your home country. The notion of 'organic' food doesn't exist here as much of the locally-grown produce is chemical-free to begin with. The notion of a vegetarian restaurant is far from being popular in these countries where a meal without meat isn't considered a meal at all.

> Romanians expect that every 'real' meal must have meat in it. There's even a proverb: *Cel mai bun pește este porcul* – The best fish is pork.

In this edition, care was taken to note which restaurants serve substantial vegetarian meals and go beyond the bare minimum.

Quick Eats

Self-catering is relatively simple in these countries. Every town has a central market *(piață centrală)*, piled high with fresh fruits and vegetables, sometimes fish and dried products. Pastries and cakes are sold everywhere in kiosks or shops for €0.10 to €0.25 a piece, a loaf of bread is about €0.20. In all cities and most towns there are 24-hour shops and/or Western-style supermarkets. If you're in small towns, you'll probably be stuck getting fresh, filled pastries from kiosks. Kebab kiosks are usually easy to find throughout the country, and unless you're in a really remote place, a pizza parlour is never too far away.

EAT YOUR WORDS

It's always best to know a little of the local language, especially in restaurants, where the vegetable soup you thought you'd ordered becomes tripe or chicken innards soup when served. To avoid having to mime the animal or vegetable of your choice, here are a few phrases and words to help you get by. See our Language chapter for more information (p357).

Useful Phrases

Please, bring me the ...
va rawg, sa·mee a·doo·che·tee ...   *Vă rog să·mi aduceti ...*
Where I can get a quick snack?
oon·de ash poo·te·a ga·see oon bar eks·pres?   *Unde aş putea găsi un bar expres?*
Do you know a cheap/good restaurant nearby?
koo·naw·ash·te·ti preen a·praw·pee·e·re   *Cunoaşteti prin apropiere un restaurant*
oon re·staw·ron ee·ef·tin/boon?   *ieftin/bun?*
Can you tell me what this is?
spoo·ne·tsi·mee va·rog che boo·ka·te soont a·ches·ta?   *Spuneţi·mi, vă rog, ce bucate sunt acesta?*

WHAT'S THAT?

barărie	bar/beer hall	*gogoşerie*	place selling donuts
brutărie	bakery	*patiserie*	patisserie
cafenea	cafeteria	*restaurant*	restaurant
cofetărie	confectionery	*tavernă*	tavern
crama	wine cellar	*terasă*	terrace

It's time to eat!
tre·boo·ye se man·kam

Trebuie să mâncăm

Keep the change.
fa·ra rest

Fără rest

Is this a vegetarian meal?
a·che·ste boo·ka·te soont deen le·goo·me?

Aceste bucate sunt din legume?

I don't want ketchup.
noo vre·a·oo ke·chup

Nu vreau ketchup

I don't eat ...
e·oo noo ma·nink ...

Eu nu mănânc ...

When in Székely Land, you might need to know that *vendeglo* and *etterem* mean 'restaurant' in Hungarian.

Romanian-English Menu Decoder
DRINKS

ap cald	hot water
ap mineral	mineral water
ap rece	cold water
berrie	beer house
cafea	coffee
ceai	tea
lapte	milk
suc de mere	apple juice
suc de portocale	orange juice
vin alba	white wine
vin rou	red wine

FRUITS & VEGETABLES

ardei	peppers
cartofi	potatoes
castravete	cucumber
ceap	onion
ciuperci	mushrooms
fruct	fruit
legume	vegetable
marcov	carrot
sfecl	beet
varz	cabbage
vinete	eggplant

MEATS & STAPLES

ardei umpluti	stuffed peppers
cacaval	cheese
carne de miel	lamb
carne de porc	pork
carne de vac	beef
creier	brains
orez	rice
ou	egg
pâine	bread
sup	soup
unc	ham

FISH

crap	carp
crevete	shrimp
morun	sturgeon

pete	fish
sardele	sardine
scrumbrie	herring
somon	salmon
ton	tuna
tuic	pike

OTHER

copti	baked
fiert	boiled
la frigare	roasted
la grtar	grilled
list	menu
not de plat	bill
prjit/pai	fried
usturoi	garlic

Romania

DAVID GREEDY

Bucharest

Forget Prague, forget Budapest – just forget them all, because Bucharest (Bucureşti) is where travellers are heading. This is Eastern Europe's secret – but it's about to get out.

Bucharest has a fascinating mix of architecture that maps Romania's chequered history. The ugly face of communism created by its bloody counterpart Nicolae Ceauşescu sits alongside the incredible beauty of Romania's elegant past and its Parisian pretensions. Down dingy side streets flanked by Soviet-style high-rises you'll find exquisite 18th-century monasteries, pretty gardens and ornate Orthodox churches. A lively bar life is flourishing, and the music scene is growing while optimism for the future mounts. Not bad for a city that only threw off Ceauşescu's stranglehold under two decades ago. Despite his crimes against architecture and the community (he bulldozed one-sixth of the city to build his vast House of the People folly in the 1980s), his attempts to create a grandiose Stalinist capital failed. The memories of the city's struggle for freedom are everywhere – from bullet-marked buildings to candles lit in memory of those who perished. Yet this city has soul – and the fun is in finding it.

TOP FIVE

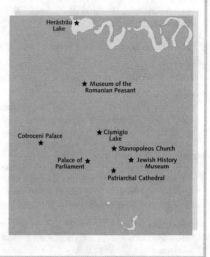

- Stumble across urban treasures such as **Stavropoleos Church** (p60), **Patriarchal Cathedral** (p57) and **Cotroceni Palace** (p63)

- Be astonished at the size of the monumental **Palace of Parliament** (p57)

- Pay tribute to Holocaust victims at the **Jewish History Museum** (p67) inside a stunning former synagogue

- Discover the only surviving paintings of Ceauşescu in the shocking **Communism Exhibition** (p63) at the Museum of the Romanian Peasant

- Soak up the city's Parisian feel in Bucharest's **parks** (p65), skate on **Cişmigiu Lake** in winter (p65) or sail across **Herăstrău Lake** (p65) in summer

- POPULATION: 2 MILLION   ■ AREA: 238 SQ KM   ■ AVERAGE MONTHLY WAGE: €74

BUCHAREST

HISTORY

Legend has it that Bucharest was founded by a shepherd named Bucur (*bucurie*; literally 'joy') who built a church on the right bank of the Dâmbovița River.

The city, which lies on the Wallachian plains between the Carpathian foothills and the Danube River, was settled by Geto-Dacians as early as 70 BC. By 1459 a princely residence and military citadel had been established under the chancellery of infamous Prince Vlad Țepeș. By the end of the 17th century, the city was the capital of Wallachia and ranked among southeastern Europe's wealthiest cities. Bucharest became the national capital in 1862, as it lay on the main trade route between East and West and offered a strategic base to defend Romania against marauding Turks.

The early 20th century was Bucharest's golden age. Large neoclassical buildings sprang up, fashionable parks were laid out and landscaped on Parisian models and, by the end of the 1930s, Bucharest was known throughout Europe as 'Little Paris'.

Bombing by the Allies during WWII, coupled with a 1940 earthquake measuring 7.4 on the Richter scale, destroyed much of Bucharest's prewar beauty. In March 1977 a second major earthquake claimed 1391 lives and flattened countless buildings. Ceaușescu's criminal redevelopment of the city marked the final death knell of Romania's elegant past.

The revolution of 1989 ripped the city to shreds. Although still haunted by its bloody history, Bucharest is recovering from its painful rebirth with contemporary building projects, the cull of snarling street dogs, care of street children who once roamed the city, crime prevention measures and an optimism born of hard-won freedom. Yet there's still much to do, and Bucharest's future is as uncertain as it is exciting.

ORIENTATION

Bucharest's international airport, Otopeni, is 17km north of the centre. Șoseaua Kiseleff runs south past Băneasa domestic airport (8km from the city) and Herăstrău Park to Piața Victoriei. Calea Victoriei cuts through the heart of the historic centre, connecting to the Romanian Athenaeum on Piața Revoluției (south).

The main train station, Gară de Nord, is 2km northwest of central Bucharest. B-dul General Magheru, the southern foot of which is called B-dul Nicolae Bălcescu, links Piața Romană (north) with Piața Universității (south); a central focal point close to the Ion Luca Caragiale National Theatre and Hotel Inter-Continental. Forming the eastern edge of the historic centre, B-dul IC Brătianu runs south from Piața Universității to Piața Unirii, the Civic Centre and the Palace of Parliament.

Maps

Find your bearings with Amco Press' bilingual *Bucharest City Plan* (1:15,000; €2), which is available at the bookshops of the Hilton and Marriott hotels. Its *Bucharest*

BUCHAREST IN...

Two Days

Breathe in the morning air atop the **Triumphal Arch**, getting a bird's-eye view of the urban anarchy you're about to embrace. Saunter down elegant Șoseaua Kiseleff to the **Village Museum**. Spend the morning stomping between Transylvania, Moldova and Maramures before leaving the museum and heading south. Indulge yourself with lunch at the historic **Athénée Palace Hilton** off Piața Revoluției and see the balcony on the **former Central Committee of the Communist Party building** (now the Senate), where Ceaușescu made his final speech. Head south down Calea Victoriei, Bucharest's bustling heart, to the **Palace of Parliament**. Finish off with an evening stroll and a lakeside beer in **Cișmigiu Garden**. Discover **Dracula's tomb** on the second day by rowing across **Snagov Lake**. Return via beautiful **Căldărușani Monastery**.

Four Days

Follow the same agenda, then peruse the **Museum of the Romanian Peasant** and **National Art Museum**. From culture to clubbing – dance away your last night at funky **EXIT** toe-tap to jazz at **Green Hours 22 Jazz Club** or enjoy a classical concert at the **Romanian Athenaeum**.

Public Ground Transport map (€1 from bus-ticket kiosks) is essential for anyone intent on exploring the city by bus, tram or metro.

Bucharest in your Pocket contains city centre maps, as does the Bucharest freebie *What?Where?When?*

INFORMATION
Bookshops
Librăria Noi (Map p60; ☎ 311 0700; B-dul Nicolae Bălcescu 18; ☽ 10am-8pm Mon-Sat, 11am-7pm Sun) Best bookshop in Bucharest by a mile. It stocks the only decent range of English-language novels in the city. Good selection of guidebooks and maps on Romania.
Salingers (www.salingers.ro) Calea 13 Septembrie (Map pp54-5; ☎ 403 3534; Calea 13 Septembrie 90, in Marriott Grand Hotel) Str Episcopiei (Map p60; ☎ 312 6746; Athénée Palace Hilton, Str Episcopiei 1-3) Stocks some English-language fiction and nonfiction, as well as Lonely Planet guides.

Cultural Centres
American Cultural Centre (Map p60; ☎ 210 1602; Str Jean Louis Calderon 7-9) Call for opening times.
British Council Library (Map pp54-5; ☎ 210 0314; Calea Dorobanţilor 14; ☽ 10am-5pm Mon-Fri, 10am-noon Sat) Offers English-language newspapers and Internet access.
French Institute (Map pp54-5; ☎ 210 0224; B-dul Dacia 77) Screens films and has an excellent bistro as well as Internet access.

Emergency
Operators of emergency numbers speak Romanian only.
Ambulance (☎ 961, 973)
Fire (☎ 981)
Police (☎ 955)
Police Station (Map p60; ☎ 311 2021; Calea Victoriei 17)

Internet Access
Internet cafés in Bucharest have sprung up like mushrooms. Rates vary from €0.30 to €1 per hour. Most offer overnight- and extended-use discounts.
Acces Internet (Map pp54-5; ☎ 650 7879; B-dul Lascar Catargiu 6; ☽ 24hr)
Brit C@fe (Map pp54-5; ☎ 210 0314; Calea Dorobanţilor 14; ☽ 9.30am-9.30pm Mon-Fri, 10am-2pm Sat)
CNET (Map p60; ☎ 311 2682; Calea Victoriei 25; ☽ 9am-7pm Mon-Sat, 9am-1pm Sun)
Cyber Espace (Map pp54-5; ☎ 211 3836; B-dul Dacia 77; ☽ 10am-10pm Mon-Sat)
eNET (Map p60; ☎ 315 4871; B-dul Nicolae Bălcescu 24; ☽ 10am-10pm Mon-Sat)

Left Luggage
At **Gară de Nord** (Map pp54-5; ☎ 223 2060; Piaţa Gară de Nord 1; ☽ 24hr) you can store handbags for €1 and backpacks/suitcases for €1.50. It's located at the counter in the centre of the hall.

Media
International press is found in the newsagents at the Grand Marriott and the Athénée Palace Hilton.
Expat Life Bizarre fanzine brimming with wisecracks.
Nine O'Clock Romania's only so-called English-language daily is known more for its hilarious attempts at English than its news content.
Vivid Best of the bunch.

Medical Services
Emergency Clinic Hospital (Map pp54-5; ☎ 230 0106; Calea Floreasca 8; ☽ 24hr) Bucharest's 'showcase' hospital.
Medicover (Map pp54-5; ☎ 310 4410/11, emergency ☎ 310 4040; www.medicover.ro; Calea Plevnei 96; ☽ 8am-8pm Mon-Fri, 8am-1pm Sat) Good private clinic.
Pro-Dental Care (Map p60; ☎ 313 4781; Str Hristo Botev 7; ☽ 9am-6pm Mon-Fri)
Puls (☎ 224 0187, emergency ☎ 242 1333; ☽ 7.30am-7.30pm Mon-Sat, 7.30am-1.30pm Sun) Private ambulance company with English-speaking medics.
Sensi-Blu Pharmacy B-dul Nicolae Bălcescu (Map p60; ☎ 212 4923; B-dul Nicolae Bălcescu 7) Excellent 24-hour pharmacy chain; Calea Victoriei (Map p60; ☎ 315 3160; Calea Victoriei 12A)
Unirea Medical Centre (Map pp54-5; ☎ 327 1190; B-dul Unirii 57)

Money
Currency exchanges are everywhere. Don't use the exchanges in the baggage claim hall of Otopeni airport as they offer the worst rates in the city.
Alliance Exchange (Map p60; B-dul Nicolae Bălcescu 30; ☽ 24hr)
IDM Exchange (Map pp54-5; Gară de Nord; ☽ 5.50am-11.10pm)
OK Exchange Nonstop (Map pp54-5; Str George Enescu; ☽ 24hr)

ATM machines are around every corner, including in **Unirea Shopping Centre** (Str Domniţa Anastasia 10-14); inside the main CFR office; and at **Teatrul Excelsior** (Map p60; Str Ion Câmpineanu & Calea Academei).

BUCHAREST

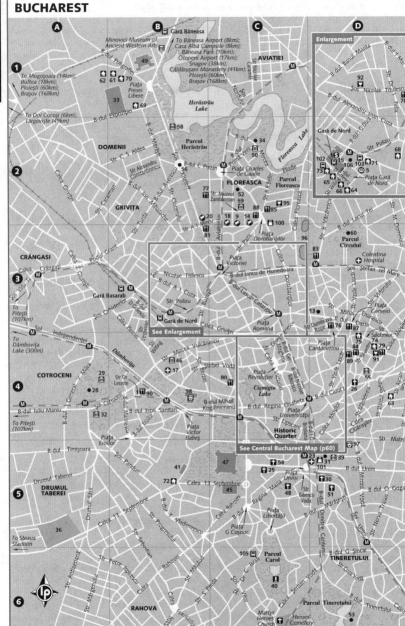

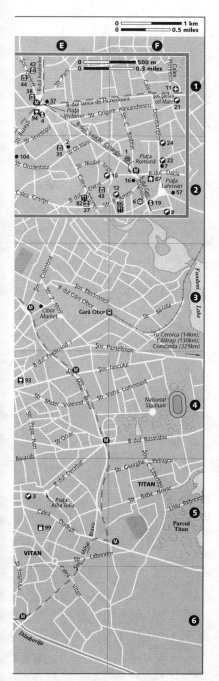

For cash transfers, travellers cheques and banking services:

Banca Comercială Română B-dul Regina Elisabeta (Map p60; B-dul Regina Elisabeta 5; ☻ 9am-4pm Mon-Fri); Calea Victoriei (Map pp54-5; Calea Victoriei 155; ☻ 9am-1pm Mon-Fri).

HVB Bank (Map p60; ☎ 203 2222; www.hvb.ro; Calea Victoriei 88; ☻ 9am-4pm Mon-Fri) It also has art exhibitions.

Post

Branch Post Offices Str Gării de Nord (Map pp54-5; Str Gării de Nord 6-8; ☻ 9am-5pm Mon-Fri); Str Ion Câmpineanu (Map pp54-5; ☎ 212 6389; Str Ion Câmpineanu 21; ☻ 7am-3pm Mon, Wed, Fri, 1-9pm Tue & Thu)

Central Post Office (Poşta Română Oficiul Bucureşti 1; Map p60; ☎ 315 9030; www.posta-romana.ro; Str Matei Millo 10; ☻ 7.30am- 8pm Mon-Fri, 8am-2pm Sat) Collect post-restante mail here.

Telephone

Chat away at Romanian prices using your very own mobile by investing in a local SIM card. Otherwise, card-operated orange telephones hug buildings or live in blue booths throughout the city. RomTelecom cards can be bought from kiosks in denominations of €4 to €6 and used for both national and international calls.

Connex (Otopeni airport baggage claim area; ☻ 9am-8pm) It has branches all over the city but you can swap SIMs here as you arrive. Rates are €1 per minute for international calls and €0.50 per minute for national calls. Text-messaging costs €0.15 per message.

Telephone Office (Map p60; cnr Calea Victoriei & Str Matei Millo; ☻ 24hr)

Tourist Information

Incredibly, Bucharest still has no official tourist information office, so independent ventures fill the gap. Ask at the reception of big hotels, eg the Hilton, about free maps and city tours.

Atlantic Tours (Map pp54-5; ☎ 212 9232; www.atlantic .ro; Calea Victoriei 202; ☻ 9am-6pm Mon-Fri, 9am-1pm Sat)

Cultural Tourism Institute/RoCultours (Map pp54-5; ☎ 223 2619; www.rotravel.com/cti; Str Grigore Alexandrescu 108; ☻ 10am-6pm) Best of the bunch for cultural tours with personalised itineraries. You must call or email at least a day ahead to arrange a time to visit.

Elvis Villa Tourist Information (Map pp54-5; ☎ 312 1653; platform 2 Gară de Nord; ☻ 7am-10pm) Friendly staff speak English, French, Italian and Japanese and organise city tours, Dracula tours and hand out free maps. They can also book you a bed, a taxi, an international bus or just point you in the right direction.

European Union Information Centre (Map p60; ☎ 315 3470; www.infoeuropa.ro; Piaţa Revoluţiei; ✆ 10am-5pm Mon-Fri) Based inside the Central University Library, it has English-speaking staff.

Lar Tours (Map p60; ☎ 201 1850; www.lartours.ro; Str Ştirbei Vodă 2-4; ✆ 9am-5pm Mon-Fri) Agent for rural homestay firm Antrec.

Marshal Turism (Map pp54-5; ☎ 223 1204; www.marshal.ro; B-dul General Magheru 43; ✆ 9am-6pm Mon-Fri, 9am-1pm Sat)

ONT Carpaţl (Map p60; ☎ 314 1922; www.ont.ro; B-dul General Magheru 7; ✆ 9am-6pm Mon-Fri, 9am-1pm Sat)

Wasteels (Map pp54-5; ☎ 222 7844; www.wasteels travel.ro; Gară de Nord; ✆ 9am-6pm Mon-Fri, 9am-2pm Sat)

DANGERS & ANNOYANCES

Bucharest is generally safer than most other Western European capitals but it suffers the same petty-crime problems. Safeguard your wallet and be vigilant when walking alone at night. Gară de Nord is still blighted by begging children and shifty-looking characters so be on your guard.

Mosquitoes are the scourge of summer so bring a heavy-duty repellent. The street dogs have been culled but there are still strays, so if threatened just bend down and look like you'll throw a stone and they'll run off.

Scams
FLIRTY TAXI DRIVER
He'll be a total charmer until you demand he switches on the meter or question why he's charging 10 times the proper price. Always check the meter is on. Do demand your change if you have larger notes than the fare or else the driver may keep it as a tip. Always sit in the back (unlike Romanian

passengers) if you are a woman alone, as it reduces the risk of being hassled.

TRUSTING TOURIST
The classic scam. People still keep falling for this one. Someone stops you on the street, asks to see a 100,000 lei note – then both the stranger and your wallet disappears in a flash.

FAKE TOURIST POLICE
A man wearing what looks like an official uniform demands to see your passport. You ask for ID and he flashes a card which you can't read anyway because it's in Romanian. If he persists, say you'll walk to the nearest police station. Never hand over your passport in the street.

FAKE TAXI DRIVERS OR HOSTEL REPS
Neither Villa Helga nor Elvis Villa send out taxis or reps to meet travellers at Gară de Nord. If someone says they're from either, they're lying. Insist on making your own way there and go outside the station to find a reputable taxi or ring a taxi company.

SIGHTS
Most of Bucharest's major attractions lie in a north-south axis through the heart of the city and inner suburbs. There's no actual focal point, so life and the attractions centre around each of the squares: Piaţa Unirii in the south, Piaţa Universităţii and Piaţa Revoluţiei in the centre, and Piaţa Romană and Piaţa Victoriei in the north.

Central Bucharest
PALACE OF PARLIAMENT   Map pp54–5
Bucharest's (and indeed Romania's) infamous star attraction, the **Palace of Parliament** (Palatul Parlamentului; Map pp54-5; ☎ 311 3611; cic@camera.ro; Calea 13 Septembrie 1; adult/student €3/1.50; ⊗ 10am-4pm) is the big mama of monstrous buildings. Conceived at the height of Ceauşescu's Communist fervour it was called, ironically, the House of the People (Casa Poporului) before 1989. The enormous showcase of Romanian craftsmanship with 12 floors now houses the chamber of deputies in its grandiose innards. The 45-minute tour (in English, French or Romanian) is a staggering insight into Ceauşescu's ego-driven vision (see the boxed text on p58).

CIVIC CENTRE
The urban wasteland that is **B-dul Unirii** was intended as the Champs Elysee–style axis for Ceauşescu's civic project that saw him destroy an entire suburb to build the Palace of Parliament and Piaţa Unirii.

It runs east for 3.2km from the square – built deliberately 6m longer than the Parisian boulevard. The 'Boulevard of the Victory of Socialism', as it was originally named, leads to a square at its western end, large enough to hold 300,000 people. Government ministries, the state prosecution office and the Romanian Intelligence Service (the successor to the Securitate) are housed in the vast civic centre buildings bordering the square. The once-elegant and expensive apartments at the western end lie half-empty and devoid of life.

Some 26 churches, two synagogues and a monastery in the city's most historic quarter were bulldozed to make way for this project, and about 70,000 people made homeless.

On the southern side of the Palace of Parliament is the huge, half-built **National Institute for Science & Technology** (Map pp54-5; Calea 13 Septembrie), of which Elena Ceauşescu was president. West is the new **Ministry of Defence** (Map pp54-5; Calea 13 Septembrie).

PIAŢA UNIRII
From Piaţa Unirii metro station, walk over to the large ornamental **fountain** in the middle of the square. On the northeastern side is the **Unirea Shopping Centre** (Map pp54-5; B-dul Unirii), and the main **city market** is a long block behind it – shop here for fresh fruit and vegetables.

The **Dâmboviţa River** snakes up to the northeastern corner before disappearing underground, beneath the square, on its journey to the southwest of the city. The natural twists and turns of the river were canalised between 1880 and 1883 and further enhanced with concrete in the 1980s.

A foundation stone laid in the centre of Piaţa Unirii in January 1999 marks the site of the proposed **Cathedral of National Salvation** (Catedrala Mântuirii Neamului). Realists insist the Romanian Orthodox Church will never raise the millions of euros needed to build their pipe-dream edifice.

Patriarchal Cathedral (Catedrala Patriahală; Map pp54-5; Str Dealul Mitropoliei) sits south of Piaţa

PALACE OF PARLIAMENT: FACT & FICTION

Controversy still rages around this massive edifice. More than a symbol of Ceauşescu's Communist vision – it stands today as a reminder of the price Romania paid to satisfy the egotistical whims of Nicolae and Elena. While people starved, hospitals suffered shortages of medicine, and industry ground to a halt, Ceauşescu embarked on building the world's second-largest building at an estimated cost of €3.3 billion.

The monument has attracted its own myths that, added to the facts, make the Palace of Parliament Bucharest's most fascinating architectural wonder.

Fact

■ It was built in 1984 to house the Central Committee, presidential office and state ministries. Today, it houses the Chamber of Deputies, Constitutional Court and an international conference centre.

■ One-sixth of Bucharest was bulldozed to accommodate the monstrous building, which stands 85m tall and has a surface area of 330,000 sq metres.

■ It is the world's second-largest building in surface (after the USA's Pentagon) and the third-largest in volume.

■ Over 700 architects and three shifts of 20,000 workers laboured on it 24 hours a day for five years.

■ It has 12 storeys and 3100 furnished rooms. Two of its 60-plus galleries are 150m long and 18m wide. Forty of its 64 reception halls are 600 sq metres; Union Hall is 3000 sq metres in size.

■ Beneath it is a vast nuclear bunker, plummeting 20m deep.

■ In the 1980s, when lit, the building consumed a day's electricity supply for the whole of Bucharest in four hours.

■ When Ceauşescu was toppled, building work was not complete. He had not yet decided on the roof design.

■ The carpet once coating the floor of Union Hall weighs 14 tonnes; today, it's rolled up.

■ The crystal chandelier in the Human Rights Hall weighs 2.5 tonnes.

■ It is still known locally by its former name, the House of the People (Casa Poporului).

■ In 2000 the halls of the palace were plastered with religious icons during the making of the movie *Amen*.

Fiction

■ The glass ceiling of the ballroom can open to allow a helicopter to land!

■ Michael Jackson stood on the balcony and said 'Hello Budapest, I'm so glad to be here' (he made the legendary error at the National Stadium).

■ The entire palace is decorated with pure gold.

Unirii, atop Patriarchy Hill. It's the majestic centre of the Romanian Orthodox faith. During the 15th century a small wooden church surrounded by vineyards stood on the hill. The cathedral consecrated the metropolitan centre of Wallachia in 1868, and was built between 1656 and 1658 by Wallachian prince Şerban Basarab. None of the original interior paintings or icons remain bar a single **icon** (1665) depicting Constantin and Helen, the cathedral's patron saints. The present-day frescoes were painted by Dimitrie Belizarie in 1923. To the west is a small **chapel**, linked by a balcony to the **Patriarchal Palace**, the southern wings of which date to 1932. Three beautifully carved, 16th- and 17th-century **stone crosses** flank the northern wall of the cathedral. Alongside is a **belfry** (1698) and a former parliament building dating from 1907.

Other surviving churches include the 16th-century **Prince Radu Monastery** (Mânăstirea Radu Vodă; Map pp54-5; Str Radu Vodă 24) and the nearby **Church of Bucur the Shepherd** (Biserica Bucur Ciobanul; Map pp54-5; Str Radu Vodă), dating from 1743 and dedicated to the city's legendary founder.

Tiny **St Apostles' Church** (Biserica Sfintii Apostoli; Map pp54-5; Str Apostoli 33a), built in 1636, survived systemisation to a degree. It was not moved but the surrounding parkland was ripped up and replaced with blocks of flats. Southwest is the surviving **Antim Monastery** (Mânăstirea Antim; Map pp54-5; Str Antim), a beautiful walled complex built in 1715 by the metropolitan bishop Antim Ivireanu.

Another impressive church that survived is the candy-striped **Princess Bălaşa Church** (Biserica Domnița Bălaşa; Map p60; off Spl Independenței). The church, just north of Piaţa Unirii, is named after Brâncoveanu's sixth daughter, who had a small wooden church built here in 1744. Widowed from 1745, the princess replaced the church with a stone structure in 1751 and set up a school and asylum. Damaged by an earthquake, the second church was replaced by a third church between 1838 and 1842, which was subsequently damaged by floods and replaced by a fourth church between 1881 and 1885.

Prince Mihai Monastery (Mânăstirea Mihai Vodă; Map p60; Str Sapienţei), built between 1589 and 1591 under the orders of Mihai Viteazul (r 1593–1601), was moved 279m east in 1985 to a patch of wasteland between apartment blocks.

PIAŢA UNIVERSITĂŢII
Some of the fiercest fighting took place here during the 1989 revolution. Journalists watched tanks roll over Romanian freedom fighters and soldiers shoot into crowds of protestors from their viewpoint inside Hotel Inter-Continental. Scour the area and you'll find bullet marks in buildings and 10 stone crosses commemorating those killed. A **black cross** (B-dul Nicolae Bălcescu 18) marks the spot where the first protestor, Mihai Gătlan, died at 5.30pm on 21 December 1989.

Piaţa Universităţii (Map p60; B-dul Regina Elisabeta) is the hub of Bucharest's intellectual and political life. The main **university building** (Map p60; B-dul Regina Elisabeta) – built between 1856 and 1868 and inaugurated in 1869 – is on the square's northwestern corner.

The onion domes of the **Student Church** (Map p60; B-dul Regina Elisabeta) peep out from the southeastern side of the square. This Russian Orthodox church dates from 1905–09. East from Piaţa Universităţii, heading along B-dul Carol I, you come to the alabaster **Armenian Church** (Map pp54-5; ☎ 313 9070; B-dul Carol I 43; ♥ 9am-6pm Mon-Sat, 8am-1pm Sun).

Theodor Pallady Museum (Muzeul Theodor Pallady; Map pp54-5; ☎ 211 4979; Str Spătarului 22; ♥ 10am-6pm Wed-Sun) is housed inside the exquisite 18th-century Casa Melik, a former merchant's house. It contains the private art collection of the Raut family (now part of the National Art Museum).

HISTORY & ART MUSEUM
The **museum** (Map p60; ☎ 315 6858; B-dul IC Brătianu 2; admission €0.50; ♥ 10am-6pm Tue-Sun) has displays of costumes and artefacts from 19th- and 20th-century Bucharest. Designed by two Austrian architects, the neo-Gothic palace was built between 1832 and 1834 for the Şuţu family, notorious for their high-society parties. The document, issued by Vlad Ţepeş in 1459, in which the city was chronicled for the first time, is also housed here.

HISTORIC CENTRE & CALEA VICTORIEI
Bucharest's historic heart sprang up around the **Old Princely Court** (Curtea Veche; Map p60) in the 15th century. Artisans and traders – whose occupations are still reflected in street names like Str Covaci (trough-makers street) and Str Şelari (saddle-makers street) – settled here in the 14th century, but it was not until the reigning prince of Wallachia, Vlad Ţepeş, fortified the settlement and built a **Prince's Palace** (Palatul Voievodal; Map p60) that it flourished as a commercial centre. At the end of the 18th century, heavily damaged by earthquakes, it was auctioned off to local merchants.

The **Old Princely Court Church** (Biserica Curtea Veche; Map p60; Str Franceză), built between 1546 and 1559 during the reign of Mircea Ciobanul (Mircea the Shepherd), is Bucharest's oldest church. The original 16th-century frescoes next to the altar remain well preserved. The carved stone portal

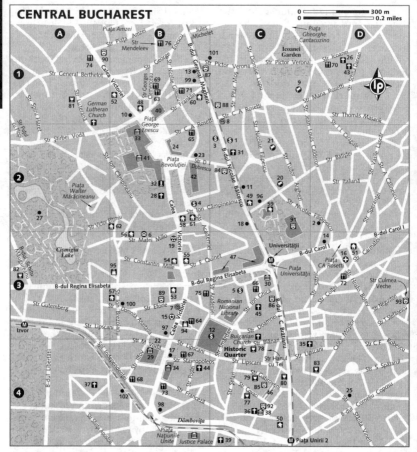

CENTRAL BUCHAREST

was added in 1715. Southeast of the church stands **Hanul lui Manuc** (see Sleeping p69), built to shelter travelling merchants.

Stavropoleos Church (Map p60; Str Stavropoleos), the street name of which literally translates to 'town of the cross', was built by Greek monk Ioanichie Stratonikeas in 1724 in late-Brâncoveanu style. Prominent Romanian architect Ion Mincu designed the courtyard and restored this little gem in 1899. Inside are richly ornate wood and stone carvings, coloured with paintings and frescoes.

The Wallachian prince Constantin Brâncoveanu (r 1688–1714) is buried in **New St George's Church** (Biserica Sfântul Gheorghe-Nou; Map p60; Str Lipscani), which was built in 1699.

Brâncoveanu was captured by the Turks in 1714 following his refusal to take part in the Russo-Turkish War (1711). He and his four sons were taken to Istanbul where they were tortured then decapitated. His wife smuggled his mutilated body back to Romania.

Str Lipscani is the centre of a bohemian nightlife, with small streets crowded with bars and clubs. In summer a pedestrianised cobbled pathway, appropriately called **Summer Street** (Map p60; off Str Covaci), is alive with music and party people.

At its western end, Str Lipscani crosses **Calea Victoriei**, Bucharest's most historic street. It was built under Brâncoveanu's orders in 1692 to link his summer palace in

Mogoșoaia, 14km northwest of Bucharest, with the heart of his capital city.

Bucharest's financial houses moved to the historic heart in the 19th century after the princely residence was moved to the north of the city. On the corner of Str Lipscani and Calea Victoriei stands the **Bucharest Financial Plaza** (Map p60), a mirrored building. Next door is the **Economic Consortium Palace** (Casa de Economii și Consemnațiuni, CEC; Map p60), designed by French architect Paul Gottereau between 1894 and 1900.

Casa Capșa (Map p60; Calea Victoriei 36) was an historic café dating from 1852 and the meeting place of Romania's eminent artists, literary figures and politicians of the 1930s. It's now a swanky hotel – Hotel Capșa (see Sleeping p70) – far removed from its bohemian roots.

NATIONAL HISTORY MUSEUM

The **museum** (Map p60; ☎ 311 3356; Calea Victoriei 12; adult/student/child €1/0.50/0.30; ☼ 9am-5pm Wed-Sun), in the former Post Office Palace, was built in a neoclassical style between 1894

and 1900. The 600,000 haphazardly arranged exhibits tell Romania's story from prehistoric times to WWI. The highlight is a treasury crammed with gold objects and precious stones. Allow a couple of hours to drift through the exhibits.

PIAȚA REVOLUȚIEI Map p60

The scene of Ceaușescu's infamous last speech was on the balcony of the former **Central Committee of the Communist Party** building on 21 December 1989. Amid cries of 'Down with Ceaușescu', he escaped in a helicopter from the roof. Meanwhile, the crowds were riddled with bullets, and many died.

On the front façade next to the entrance is a plaque dedicated to the 'young and courageous people' who 'drove out the dictator', thus 'giving the Romanian people back their freedom and dignity'. A statue of a man, broken but put back together again, dominates the small green area in front. The building now houses the Senate.

Crețulescu Church (1722) stands just south of the square. The red-brick structure was damaged in the 1989 revolution. To the side stands a **memorial bust** of Corneliu Coposu, who spent 17 years in prison for his anti-Communist activities and, prior to his death in 1995, was awarded the Légion d'Honneur by the French government. Behind the church is a **statue** of a headless torso in memorial to fallen revolutionaires.

The **Central University Library** (1895; Calea Victoriei 88) houses the European Union Information Centre, HVB bank and the university library. The **building shell** (cnr Str DI Dobrescu & Str Boteanu) was left as a poignant reminder of the revolution, it housed the hated Securitate and was destroyed by protestors. In 2003 the Romanian Architecture Union built a contemporary glass structure inside it to house its headquarters.

West of Piaţa Revoluţiei, the Roman Catholic red-brick **Italian Church** (B-dul Nicolae Bălcescu 28) holds services in Italian.

NATIONAL ART MUSEUM
Housed in the Royal Palace, the **National Art Museum** (Muzeul Naţional de Artă; Map p60; ☎ 313 3030; http://art.museum.ro; Calea Victoriei 49-53; adult €2, child & student €1; ☯ 10am-6pm Wed-Sun) has more than 700 icons, tapestries and carvings presented in funky purple and red rooms as part of the Treasures of Romanian Art section. The European Gallery boasts works by Rembrandt, El Greco and Breughel. Spend a day absorbing both collections. Tours in English or French (€4) must be booked in advance. Several branch museums of the National Art Museum are dotted around town.

Each spring, monarchists gather outside the Royal Palace to celebrate Romania's former national day (10 May). Built between 1812 and 1815 by Prince Dinicu Golescu, the palace became the official royal residence in 1834 during the reign of Prince Alexandru Ghica (r 1834–42). The current façade dates from the 1930s. Until 1989 it was the seat of the State Council and was called the Palace of the Republic.

ROMANIAN ATHENAEUM
This exquisite circular building is the majestic heart of Romania's classical-music tradition. **Romanian Athenaeum** (Ateneul Român; Map p60; ☎ 315 8798; Str Franklin 1; admission €1-5; ☯ 10am-4pm Mon, 2-10pm Tue Wed & Fri, 2-4pm Thu, 10am-10pm Sat & Sun) hosts prestigious concerts

and should not be missed. Scenes from Romanian history are featured on the interior fresco inside the Big Hall on the 1st floor, and the dome is 41m high. It was built in 1888 with mostly public funds. A huge appeal dubbed 'Give a Penny for the Athenaeum' saved it from disaster after the original patron's funds dried up. The peristyle is adorned with mosaics of five Romanian rulers, including Moldavian prince Vasile Lupu (r 1512–21), Wallachian Matei Basarab (r 1632–54) and King Carol I (r 1881–1914). The composer George Enescu made his debut here in 1898, followed five years later by the first performance of his masterpiece *Romanian Rhapsody*. Today, it's home to the **George Enescu Philharmonic Orchestra**.

ATHÉNÉE PALACE
Now home to the deliriously posh Hilton (see Sleeping p69), the **Athénée Palace** (Map p60; Str Episcopiei 1-3) is the grand dame of Bucharest, holding a particular place in the city's history. It was the first concrete building in Bucharest when designed and built in 1914 by French architect Téophile Bradeau. Sitting on the northern side of Piaţa Revoluţiei, it hosted political intrigue, scandals and high living when German officers used it as their base during WWII. It suffered heavy bombing during the war and was consequently rebuilt in 1945. A new wing was added in 1966. The hotel became notorious for being a den of iniquity with high-class prostitution in the interwar years, then suffered yet more damage from fire and bullets during the revolution.

OTHER MUSEUMS
The excellent **Art Collection Museum** (Muzeul Colecţiilor de Artă; Map pp54-5; ☎ 650 6132; Calea Victoriei 111; adult/student €1/0.50; ☯ 10am-6pm Wed-Sun) was formed from several private collections and is today part of the National Art Museum. There are many fine works by 19th-century Romanian painter Nicolae Grigorescu. It's worthwhile spending an afternoon here.

National composer George Enescu (1881–1955) lived for a short time in the former Cantacuzino Palace. The building was built in the early 1900s in a French-baroque style and features a wonderful clam-shaped portecochere above the main entrance. The **George**

Enescu Museum (Muzeul George Enescu; Map pp54-5; ☎ 659 6365; Calea Victoriei 141; admission €0.50; ☻ 10am-5pm Tue-Sun) exhibits the musician's manuscripts and personal belongings. A collection of Bach scores belonging to Queen Elizabeth of Romania is on display.

PIAȚA VICTORIEI & AROUND

The square is dominated by the **Government Building** (1938; Map pp54-5). On the northwestern side of the square is the interesting **Grigore Antipa Natural History Museum** (Muzeul de Istorie Naturală Grigore Antipa; Map pp54-5; ☎ 312 8826; Șos Kiseleff 1; adult/child €1/0.50; ☻ 10am-5pm Tue-Sun). Children will love the live reptile displays and collections of shocked-looking stuffed mammals.

A short walk southeast down B-dul Lascăr Catargiu is the **Piața Romană** (Map pp54-5). It has a statue of **Lupoaica Romei** (the wolf of Rome) and the abandoned children **Romulus and Remus**, whom the wolf fed and cared for, enabling them to found the city of Rome, which was a gift from Italy.

West of the square is the **Museum of Romanian Literature** (Muzeul Literaturii Române; Map pp54-5; B-dul Dacia 12; admission free; ☻ 10am-4pm). Close by is the **Church of the Icon** (Biserica Icoanei; Map p60; Str Icoanei), built by the monk and former privy secretary Mihail Babreanu between 1745 and 1750. Around the corner is pretty **St Slujbă's Monastery** (Mănăstirea Sfânta Slujbă; Map p60; Str Schitul Darvari 3), which is surrounded by a lush walled garden.

Western Bucharest   Map pp54–5

Cotroceni Palace (Șos Cotroceni 1) lies along the western bank of the Dâmbovița River. It was built between 1891 and 1893 as a gift from King Ferdinand to his wife, Marie, and housed the royal court from 1893 until 1947. Today it contains the charming 19th-century **Cotroceni Museum** (Muzeul Național Cotroceni; ☎ 221 1200; admission €1.50; ☻ 9.30am-5.30pm). Visits here must be prebooked.

Northwards is Bucharest's **Botanic Garden** (Șos Cotroceni; ☻ 9am-1pm Tue, Thu & Sun). Originally part of the palace's park, the gardens were replanted in the university grounds in the 1870s and relocated to the present site in 1884. The garden, spread across 17 hectares and home to some 20,000 plant species from all over Romania, houses the **Botanic Museum & Greenhouse** (admission €0.50;

☻ 9am-1pm Tue, Thu & Sun). It's especially good for children.

Visitors won't fail to notice the rather stagnant waters of the Dâmbovița. This was yet another of Ceaușescu's grand projects. He felt Bucharest lacked a great river like London and Moscow, so he rechannelled the river in an enormous engineering feat, building a massive dam in the west of the city and created **Dâmbovița Lake**. Crângași metro station is about 500m from the dam.

The **National Military Museum** (Muzeul Militar Național; ☎ 637 3830; Str Mircea Vulcănescu 125-127; admission €0.50; ☻ 9am-5pm Tue-Sun) recounts the bloody history of the Romanian army. There is an exhibition on the 1989 revolution; the names of 939 people who died during the bloodshed are engraved on a marble memorial cross. From here, bearing south along Calea Plevnei, you come to the **Opera House** (Opera Română; ☎ 314 6980; B-dul Mihail Kogălniceanu 70). A **statue** of George Enescu, whose opera *Oedipus* premiered here, stands in front of the building.

Northern Bucharest   Map pp54–5

MUSEUM OF THE ROMANIAN PEASANT

This joyful **museum** (Muzeul Țăranului Român; ☎ 212 9661; Șos Kiseleff 3; adult/child €2/0.50; ☻ 10am-6pm Tue-Sun) is the best museum in all of Romania. Amazingly, inside you'll find the carcass of an 18th-century Transylvanian wooden church among other rural treasures. It's a favourite for kids. Downstairs is the must-see **Communism Exhibition**, which has the only surviving portraits of Ceaușescu, several thoughtful Lenins and heart-rending accounts of those who objected to collectivisation. Set aside at least three hours for your visit.

MUSEUM OF GEOLOGY

Opposite the Museum of the Romanian Peasant is the **Museum of Geology** (Muzeul de Geologie; ☎ 650 5094; Șos Kiseleff; adult/child €1.50/0.50; ☻ 10am-3pm Mon-Fri), where you can while away an hour or two among Romania's finest rocks!

TRIUMPHAL ARCH

North along tree-lined Șoseaua Kiseleff is the **Triumphal Arch** (Arcul de Triumf). Based on Paris' namesake monument, it was a symbol of cultural ties prior to WWI.

The 11m-tall arch, constructed from reinforced concrete, and granite mined in Deva, was built between 1935 and 1936 to commemorate the reunification of Romania in 1918.

The sites of the WWI battles in which the Romanian front fought are inscribed inside the arch, and King Ferdinand and Queen Marie feature on its southern façade. A makeshift triumphal monument allegedly made from cardboard and wood had been erected on the site in 1878 to mark the achievement of Romanian independence the previous year. In 1922 a new wooden structure was hastily thrown up in time for King Ferdinand's triumphant entry into the city as the first king of a united Greater Romania. The arch was so ludicrous that composer George Enescu wrote to the city mayor, demanding to know when a 'real' triumphal arch would be erected. Visitors can now climb stairs to the top of the arch (from 10am to 4pm) and get a bird's-eye view of the city.

ŞOSEAUA KISELEFF AND AROUND

Home to some of the most luxurious villas of Bucharest, **Şoseaua Kiseleff** stretches from Piaţa Victoriei to Herăstrău Park. During the Communist era it was the most prestigious residential area in the city, reserved strictly for Communist Party officials (nomenklatura).

Nicolae and Elena Ceauşescu had their private residence, **Primăverii Palace** (B-dul Primăverii 50), nearby. The palace is heavily guarded and off-limits to everyone except state guests and personnel from NATO or the Cultural Tourism Initiative. Just across from the entrance to Ceauşescu's mansion is **Gheorghe Gheorghiu-Dej's former residence** (B-dul Mircea Eliade of), once the home of Romania's Communist ruler until 1965.

The **Romanian TV Headquarters** (Calea Dorobanţilor) had its daily air-time reduced to two hours in the late 1980s, one hour of which was devoted to broadcasting presidential activities. In December 1989 revolutionaries broke into the television building and announced the collapse of the government on air. In front of the building is a small **memorial** to those killed here.

The **Zambaccian Museum** (Muzeul Zambaccian; ☎ 230 1920; Str Muzeul Zambaccian 21a; admission €1; ☉ 10am-6pm Wed-Sun) boasts Romania's only

Cezanne. Art-loving Armenian businessman Krikor Zambaccian's (1889–1962) small collection includes works by Matisse and Picasso.

Northwest of the Zambaccian Museum is the **Exhibition Pavilion & Conference Centre** (B-dul Expoziţiei 2), home to the Romanian Expo. The modern **World Trade Centre**, housing a fashionable shopping mall and five-star Sofitel hotel, is just opposite the Exhibition Centre.

The famous **Village Museum** (Muzeul Satului; ☎ 222 9110; Şos Kiseleff 28-30; adult/child €1/0.50; ☉ 9am-7pm Tue-Sun) is a shadow of its former self after fires wrecked many exhibits in 1997 and 2002. It's still worth an afternoon, however, as there's a total of 50 complete homesteads, churches, windmills and even sunken houses from rural Romania. Built in 1936 by Royal Decree, it is one of Europe's oldest open-air museums and a must for children. Get here from the centre by taking bus No 131 or 331 from B-dul General Magheru or Piaţa Romană to the 'Muzeul Satului' stop.

At its northern end, Şoseaua Kiseleff splays out into Piaţa Presei Libere, which is dominated by the enormous **Press House** (Casa Presei Libere). It has a 1956 Stalinist, wedding-cake structure. The Press House gave a clear message to the citizens of Bucharest – Big Brother is watching you! A symbol of the powerful Communist regime, until 1990 the house was called the 'House of the Sparks' (Casa Scânteii); behind closed doors it was known as the 'House of Lies'. It's still home to the city's hacks.

A **statue of Lenin** that stood on the red marble pedestal in front of the building was moved in 1989 to Mogoşoaia (see p80).

City Cemeteries

Ghencea Military Cemetery (Cimitirul Militar Ghencea; Map pp54-5, Calea 13 Septembrie; ☉ 9am-6pm) is to the west of the civil cemetery (see boxed text p65). Propeller blades stand upright amid the sea of graves. **Belu Cemetery** (Cimitirul Belu; Calea Şerban Vodă), the main city cemetery, houses the tombs of Romania's most notable writers and poets, including comic playwright and humorist Ion Luca Caragiale (1852–1912), novelist Ion Liviu Rebreanu (1885–1944), Moldavian-born writer and historian Mihail Sadoveanu (1880–1961) and national poet Mihai Eminescu (1850–89).

Parks & Lakes

Escape the city heat or marvel at the wealth of greenery in Bucharest's urban oases.

Herăstrău Lake (Lacul Herăstrău) stretches from east to west, north of Piaţa Charles de Gaulle (metro Piaţa Aviatorilor), and is surrounded by a 2-sq-km pleasure park.

Băneasa Park (Parcul Băneasa), 10km north, is surrounded by lush forest. Take bus No 301 from Piaţa Romană for this park.

Strange **wooden sculptures**, called *Wooden Spirits*, live in **Circus Park** (Parcul Circului; Map pp54-5). They were carved by local artist Titi Teodorescu from the trunks of trees that died in the park.

Cişmigiu Garden (Grădina Cişmigiu; Map p60) is Bucharest's oldest park – and its most popular. Spend hazy, lazy afternoons strolling, people-watching and flirting (it's known as 'lovers park').

Cycling paths circle the lake at **Youth Park** (Parcul Tineretului; Map pp54-5), at the southern limits of the city centre. Sporting events, fashion shows, conferences and open-air concerts take place in the **Sports & Culture Palace**, in the east of the park.

Northwest of Youth Park, **Carol I Park** (Map pp54-5; Calea Şerban Vodă) was inaugurated in 1906. An eternal flame burns in memory of the unknown soldier, and bands play in the bandstand. Its centrepiece is a 20m-tall **mausoleum**, built in 1958 from black Norwegian granite and topped with five arches of red Swedish granite. It was put up in memory of the 'Heroes of the Struggle for

the People's and the Homeland's Liberty, for Socialism'.

ACTIVITIES
Boating

You can hire rowing boats (€1.50 per hour) from a small launch on the western side of **Cişmigiu Lake**. On the western shores of **Herăstrău Lake** there are two small landings, from where a boat cruises the vast lake (twice daily between May and October). A 30-minute trip costs €2 (from landing '*debarcaderul centrul*') or you can pay €1 for a return crossing (from landing '*traversări cu vaporul*')

Ice-skating

Winter brings this popular sport to **Cişmigiu Lake**, which freezes solid and brings out the Romanian Torvill and Deans and even more spectators.

People-watching

This is the beloved pastime of Bucharestians. Get yourself settled on one of **Cişmigiu Garden's** green metal benches and indulge in some serious staring. Or, you can always be a 'flaunter' and give them something to look at!

Swimming & Fitness

Splash about in style in the Marriott Grand Hotel's (p70) indoor pool or use the pool and gym at the Crowne Plaza Hotel Health Club (p70). The Hilton (p69) also boasts a

---

PAUPERS' GRAVES

Ghencea Civil Cemetery (Cimitirul Civil Ghencea; Map pp54-50; Calea 13 Septembrie; ☉ 9am-6pm) has two infamous inhabitants: Nicolae Ceauşescu and his wife Elena (who was dubbed Eva Peron).

The pair was secretly buried here on 30 December 1989, in hastily prepared graves. Nicolae lies in row 135, on the left of the cemetery. No stone tomb adorns his earth grave, dug into a pathway, but two crosses – one metal, the other stone – mark his body. The black steel cross is inscribed with his name, date of birth and death. A red marble cross bearing a picture of Nicolae and the inscription, 'A tear on your tomb from Romanian people' was erected in 2001 by the Communist Party, and he is visited each year by delegations from China and Russia. His own people have stayed away – and surprisingly there's no graffiti, just a lit candle and a motley collection of fresh flowers.

Elena was buried separately from him, in row H25, directly across the cemetery to the right. They weren't buried together as it was said they did too many bad things together so should stay apart. Her name is daubed with white paint across a black metal cross. The body of their playboy son Nicu, who died from liver cirrhosis in 1996, is buried nearby.

To get here, take bus No 385 or 173 from Piaţa Unirii; or bus No 203, 204, 214 or 303; or tram No 8, 47 or 58.

BUCHAREST

JEWISH BUCHAREST

'Our Museum should have a beneficial influence on the Romanian public – a daring project considering it is proposed by one of the smallest ethnic minorities in today's Romania,' said Professor Dr Nicolae Cajal, a Romanian Academy member.

It was not always so – Bucharest had a thriving Jewish community dating from the 16th century, when merchants and traders settled here. By 1861 more than 6000 Jews lived in the capital. There were around 30 synagogues at this time.

The 19th century brought anti-Semitism along with internal conflicts within the Jewish community, and many Jews left. Nevertheless, on the eve of WWII there were an estimated 95,000 Jews in Bucharest and 80 working synagogues. Today, there are only 4000 Jews in Bucharest (7000 in Romania).

The **Jewish History Museum** (Muzeul de Istorie al Comunitaţilor Evreieşti din România; Map pp54–5; ☎ 311 0870; Str Mămulari 3; admission €1; ☻ 9am–1pm Mon, Wed, Sun, 10am–6pm Thu) bears testimony to the city's once-thriving history. The museum, housed in the beautiful former tailor's synagogue, has been renovated and is now the city's showpiece lesson in Jewish culture. It dates from 1850 and is one of three surviving pre-WWII synagogues. The Holocaust Room shows horrific photographs and a sculpture of a shrouded man in memory of the 150,000 Jews who were deported to hard-labour camps in Transdniestr, Moldova, and the 200,000 from Transylvania who died in Auschwitz. You can hire an English-speaking guide for €1.25.

Little remains of the old **Jewish quarter** of Văcăreşti, northeast of Piaţa Unirii in Bucharest's historic heart. During the Iron Guard's fascist pogrom in 1941, entire streets of houses were burnt to the ground, synagogues looted and Jewish-run businesses razed. What remained was levelled by Ceauşescu in the mid-1980s.

The **Choral Temple** (Map p60; ☎ 315 5090; Str Sfânta Vineri 9), built in 1857, is the city's main working synagogue. It's visually stunning inside, but getting inside is hard as non-Jewish people are not permitted entry due to the tough security. Its magnificent Moorish turrets, choir loft and organ remain intact. A **memorial** to the victims of the Holocaust, put up in 1991, fronts the temple.

The **Sephardic Jewish Cemetery** (Cimitirul Evreisc de rit Sefard; Calea Şerban Vodă) lies opposite Belu Cemetery in the south of the city (metro Eroii Revoluţiei). Two rows of graves dated 21–23 January 1941 mark the Iron Guard's pogrom against the Jewish community in Bucharest, during which at least 170 Jews were murdered.

pool. Using any of these facilities will cost you €15 per day. Cheaper is Hotel Turist's (p69) pool and gym, where a swim costs €4 and the gym €3.

WALKING TOUR

This tour visits the main sites of the 1989 revolution and Bucharest's Communist legacy.

Start at the fountain on **Piaţa Unirii** (**1**; p57), one of Europe's largest public squares. Note the uniform architectural style beloved by Ceauşescu. Head down B-dul Unirii. You'll see how quickly the atmosphere changes to a ghost town the further west you travel. Cut through an alleyway to find **Antim Monastery** (**2**; p59), which survived the urban cull. Continue to the vast area fronting the **Palace of Parliament** (**3**; p57), which has space for 300,000 people, and the balcony intended for Ceauşescu's speeches. Visit the monstrous edifice!

Head north to Izvor metro station, cross over the bridge and head west alongside the still waters of the rechannelled Dâmboviţa River. Turn right at Str Constantin Noica towards the **National Military Museum** (**4**; p63) for the revolution exhibition. From here, head southeast to **Piaţa Universităţii** (**5**; p59) along B-dul Mihail Kogălniceanu and its continuation, B-dul Regina Elisabeta. Once in the square you're in the heart of the revolution struggle. Discover the 10 stone crosses dedicated to victims and spot the black cross at B-dul Nicolae Bălcescu 18. From the towering **Hotel Inter-Continental** (**6**; p70) was where journalists filmed the carnage.

Continue north along B-dul Nicolae Bălcescu for a short way, then turn left into Str Ion Câmpineanu and continue until Calea Victoriei. Turn right (northwards) at Calea Victoriei to **Piaţa Revoluţiei** (**7**; p61), where you'll see the **former Central Committee**

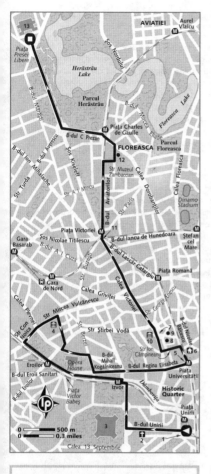

Start/Finish: Piaţa Unirii/Piaţa Presei Librere
Distance: 12km
Duration: About 3 hours

of the Communist Party building (8; p61) and the infamous balcony. This is where the revolution exploded in Bucharest, following the protests in Timişoara which started the wave of unrest. A speech from Ceauşescu (on the balcony) was the catalyst for the bloody and brutal events of the next hours. See bulletmarks around the square. The statue of a broken man, a headless torso with six thrashing arms and a simple metal cross frame the square. Feel the suffering of the people by seeing the stone memorial, and gasp at the

burned out **building shell (9; p62)**, which was targeted as the former Securitate (secret police) headquarters. The **Royal Palace (10; p62)** was also damaged by fire and bullets.

Head north along Calea Victoriei to **Piaţa Victoriei (11; p63)**, then north along B-dul Aviatorilor, turning off to the **Romanian TV Headquarters (12; p64)**, the scene of some of the fiercest fighting. The end of the Ceauşescu regime was broadcast from here on the night of 22 December 1989.

Continue northwest through Piaţa Charles de Gaulle, turning right up Şoseaua Kiseleff. Looming ahead is the ominous **Press House (13; p64)**; look for the remains of its huge hammer and sickle midway up the tower.

BUCHAREST FOR CHILDREN
The fabulous *In Your Pocket* guide has a section dedicated to entertaining your little darlings. Both **Cişmigiu Garden** (p65) and **Herăstrău Park** (p65) have play areas for children; the latter has a tennis court for teens, and they can also discover the Wooden Spirits and Big Top in **Circus Park** (p65) – shows are held nightly in summer.

Ţăndărică Puppet Theatre (Teatrul de Marionete şi Păpuşi Ţăndărică; Map pp54-5; ☎ 211 0829; Str Eremia Grigorescu 26; admission €2; box office 2-5pm Mon-Fri, 9am-noon Sat, 9am-3pm Sun) is a favourite, but shows are mostly in Romanian.

Bucureşti Mall (Map pp54-5; ☎ 327 6100; Calea Vitan 55) has a play area and an electronic games room for the older ones, and a multiplex cinema.

TOURS
Most travel agencies organise city tours and day trips (see p55).

The **Cultural Tourism Institute/RoCultours** (Map pp54-5; ☎ 223 2619; cti@com.pcnet.ro; B-dul Primăverii 50) organise cultural and academic tours in English, French, German and Japanese. Tours must be booked in advance.

The **Hilton** (Map p60; ☎ 303 3777; www.hilton.com) does daily city tours (€25 for three hours) which include drinks and admission fees. Or private guides, such as **Corneliu Serban** (☎ 0723 356 096), can organise you an itinerary for around €30 per day.

FESTIVALS & EVENTS
Dress up, get down or chill out at Bucharest's theatre and music festivals. Annual events worth the wait:

REVOLUTION: WITNESSING HISTORY

Ceauşescu stepped onto the balcony. He started talking about Timişoara, about stamping down the first wave of protest against him. He told us it would get better, 10,000 lei more for studying, crazy lies. First people were murmuring, the voices from the crowd around me started saying 'Down with Ceauşescu'. Then the voices got louder, I heard myself shout. The sounds of bullets shattered the air. We heard shooting and I ran, I didn't know where to. They had killed people. Troops were loading bodies into trucks. I escaped but later heard that they'd barricaded people into Piaţa Universităţii. Students sat down in front of the tanks but the tanks just rolled over them. They were hemmed in like animals, with no escape and gunned down. One thousand people perished in that square that night. It was our darkest hour.

Cornelui, eyewitness on the night of 21 December 1989

On the outskirts of Bucharest the tanks rolled towards the city centre, the crunch of their tracks and the heavy labouring of out-dated machinery adding to the menace that had filled the grey skies for days. When the gun-turrets lay still, the soldiers who defected over to their people stood out of the tanks and smiled. People threw flowers at the tanks and gave crews meagre offerings of food. The elation at having overthrown decades of oppression was hitting home – it was a humbling experience. People walked around wearing Romanian flags draped over their heads, the centre circle which bore an imperial crest cut out. Over the next few days I struck out from the journalists' enclave of the Hotel Inter-Continental to see the Paris of the East. But fear took a long time to subside. The TV station – perhaps unprepared for the first moments of liberty – played Charlie Chaplin's film *The Great Dictator*, followed by a Lisa Stansfield concert. It only added to the surreal feel of Bucharest.

Journalist Danny Buckland, who covered the revolution in Romania for London's Daily Star.

Bucharest Carnival (late May/early June) Week-long carnival with street and folk dancers, street theatre and live bands performing in Bucharest's historic heart.

Dreher Beer Festival (mid-June) Four-day beer festival with live bands and drinking contests in Herăstrău Park.

Open-Air Concerts (mid-June) Showcase for young classical musicians in Izvorani village (40km north of Bucharest).

Fête de la Musique (21 June) French-music festival organised by the French Institute.

Hora Festival (1 August) Three-day dance festival attracting traditional folk-dance troupes from all over the country; held in the Village Museum.

Craftsman's Fair (15 August) Local craft fair hosted by the Village Museum, with guest craftspeople from all over Romania.

George Enescu Music Festival (4-24 September) Held every odd-numbered year, attracting musicians from all over the world.

National Theatre Festival (October) Week-long theatre festival held in the National Theatre.

St Dumitru Day (last week of October) Two-day carnival celebrating Bucharest's patron saint, Dumitru.

SLEEPING

New hotels for mid-range and business travellers seem to be springing up overnight.

Budget backpackers aren't forgotten either. Aim for a room near the university or Piaţa Revoluţiei, which have some of the most characterful options. The cheapest (and grottiest) area is around Gară de Nord.

Note that there's a first-night tax of 3% on rooms in Bucharest.

Budget

HOSTELS

Elvis Villa (Map pp54-5; ☎ 312 1653; www.elvisvilla.ro; Str Avram Iancu 5; dm €12) A backpacker favourite. Bucharest character Elvis (an Aussie) struts around his clean, funky hostel offering free laundry facilities, free Internet use and even free beer. It's a party place and the rooms are small so don't expect an early night. Discounts are available for long-term stays.

Youth Hostel Villa Helga (Map pp54-5, ☎ 610 2214; Str Salcâmilor 2; dm €12) Centrally located, this place offers peace and quiet, a friendly atmosphere, and free laundry, breakfast and Internet access to guests. There are discounts for long-term stays.

Vila 11 (Map pp54-5; ☎ 0722 495 900/901; vila 11bb@hotmail.com; Str Institutul Medico Militar 11; dm/d

---

AUTHOR'S CHOICE

Athénée Palace Hilton (Map p60; ☎ 303 3777; www.hilton.com; Athénée Palace, Str Episcopiei 1-3; s/d €310/340, tr €430-560; 🖳) For glamour and style in sumptuous surroundings the Hilton surpasses them all. Yet it's the fusion of elegance with the building's fascinating and colourful history that makes this the top dog. The fairylight-lit terrace is the best in the city, while the brasserie is *the* meeting point for expats, tourists and business travellers. Indulge yourself and imagine the secret liaisons and political scandals that once simmered in these fabulous rooms.

Hanul lui Manuc (Manuc's Inn; Map p60; ☎ 313 1415; hmanuc@rnc.ro; Str Franceză 62-64; s/d €20/35) An infamous hotel housed in one of Bucharest's oldest buildings. Originally a 19th-century merchants' inn (caravanserai), it has a colourful guest list from its past, including prostitutes, criminals, rogues and merchants. Legend has it that the original owner was poisoned by a fortune-teller who had to murder him to make his prophecy (that the inn-keeper would die) come true.

Sculpted wooden balconies line the terrace overlooking the courtyard. As a budget choice it can't be beaten, but (and this is a big but) we found the restaurant service to be appallingly slow and surly. Despite this it remains the best-known and most popular option for travellers seeking Bucharest's flamboyant past.

€12.50/27) Brand new, family-owned *pensiune* near Gară de Nord where you'll find home comforts and a peaceful atmosphere. A gem.

HOTELS

Hotel Carpaţi (Map p60; ☎ 315 0140; www.carpatihotel.compace.ro; Str Matei Millo 16; s €11-16, d €29-40) A popular budget choice, so book in advance. It's central with an excellent free breakfast, gleaming reception and clean rooms.

Hotel Muntenia (Map p60; ☎ 314 6010; muntenia@dial.kappa.ro; Str Academiei 19-21; s/d/tr €16/25/33) Fabulously ugly, cavernous hotel with large rooms and faintly seedy air. Its excellent value and location make it a wise yet kitsch choice – especially with the Soviet-style receptionists' hairdos!

Hotel Turist (Map pp54-5; ☎ 224 4460; dht@parch.ro; B-dul Poligrafiei 3-5; s €24-28, d €33-38) Those Soviet architects have done it again – tall, ugly and concrete. But with free breakfast, private bathroom and friendly staff it's great value. The downside of being north of the centre is offset by the pool next door and gym guests can pay to use.

Hotel Bucegi (Map pp54-5; ☎ 212 7154; Str Witing 2; s €16, d €22-31, tr €28) It's the best of the fairly bad bunch near Gară de Nord. Saying that, its 57 rooms have prevented many an exhausted backpacker from a less-pleasant night in this grotty part of Bucharest.

Travellers arriving into the city by train will notice other hotels around Gară de Nord, including the OK **Hotel Marna** (Map pp54-5), bargain-basement **Hotel Cerna** (Map

pp54-5) and **Hotel Astoria** (Map pp54-5). Be warned, they're fine if you need a bed but the location is rundown and seedy.

Casa Albă (☎ 230 5203; Aleea Privighetorilor 1-3; huts €12-15, tents €3-5; 🕑 mid-Apr–Oct) You can pitch a tent or rent a two-bed wooden hut *(căsuţe)* in these well-maintained grounds. Take bus No 301 from Piaţa Romană to Şoseaua Bucureşti-Ploieşti; get off at the stop after Băneasa airport and head east along Aleea Privighetorilor. Bus 783 to/from Otopeni airport also stops here.

Snagov Lake has a complex that permits camping (see p78).

Mid-Range

HOTELS

Hotel Opera (Map p60; ☎ 312 4857; Str Ion Brezoianu 37; s/d €125/143; 🖳 💻) This hotel has benefited from a total refit and has a classical, though slightly overdone, music theme. It's in a central location, and rooms have TV.

Hotel Duke (Map pp54-5; ☎ 212 5344; www.hotelduke.ro; B-dul Dacia 33; s/d €100/130) A gorgeous little hotel in a lovely area. It's friendly, and staff will pamper you and put a choccie on your pillow – it's that kind of place.

Hotel Banat (Map p60; ☎ 313 1056; Piaţa CA Rosetti 5; s €65, d €65-75, t €105) A stunning haunted-house façade hides some good, clean rooms in the heart of the city.

Hotel Bulevard (Map p60; ☎ 315 3300; B-dul Regina Elisabeta 21; s/d/tr €66/79/96) A chintz-lover's paradise. It's a bit over-the-top glam but it's smack-bang in the centre and good value.

Hotel Capitol (Map p60; ☎ 315 8030; www.hotel capitol.ro; Calea Victoriei 29; s/d/tr €75/98/110) Its exterior has Parisian elegance by the bucketload, but inside we found a rather seedy atmosphere, which may vanish with ongoing renovation.

Best Western Parc Hotel (Map pp54-5; ☎ 224 2000; www.parch.ro; B-dul Poligrafiei 3-5; s/d €128/146; ✶) A stunning transformation of a rather bleak Soviet-style skyscraper. Rooms have amazing views – just ignore its blue-and-yellow exterior. It has a pool and gym and is child-friendly.

Hotel Central (Map p60; ☎ 315 5636; www.central hotel.ro; Str Ion Brezoianu 13; s/d/tr €80/90/120; ✶) This place has had a makeover, adding some of that 'could be anywhere in the world' feeling to this nice but impersonal hotel.

Near Gară de Nord there's an **Ibis Hotel** (Map pp54-5; ☎ 222 2722; Calea Griviţei 143; s & d €69).

APARTMENTS

You can stay in a luxury city pad that has the same laundry and cleaning services as hotels for upwards of €40 a night. Companies offering apartments include **Shannon Apartments** (☎ 222 9473; larkin@dnt.ro) and **Bucharest Comfort Suites** (Map p60; ☎ 310 2884; www.comfortsuites.ro; B-dul Nicolae Bălcescu 16).

Top End

Hotel Inter-Continental (Map p60; ☎ 310 2020; www .interconti.com; B-dul Nicolae Bălcescu 2-4; s €294, d €320-420; ✶) This place towers above Piaţa Universităţii, which was centre stage in the revolution. Inside it's a super-swanky, 22-floor, five-star wonder with a casino.

Marriott Grand Hotel (Map pp54-5; ☎ 403 1000; www.marriott.com; Calea 13 Septembrie 90; s €250, d €250-450; ✶) This hotel sits in the shadow of the Palace of Parliament, itself a monumental edifice that lay unfinished by Ceauşescu's timely demise. Today, it's sheer luxury, with snooty staff and incredible five-star rooms.

Hotel Capşa (Map p60; ☎ 313 4038; Calea Victoriei 36; s/d €231/300) It has a bohemian history and a charming façade, with beautiful rooms right at the centre of the action.

Hotel Sofitel (Map pp54-5; ☎ 224 3000; www .sofitel.ro; B-dul Expoziţiei 2; s/d €225/240; ✶) Adjoining the World Trade Centre, this place has 202 classy rooms with incredible views over the city and a pleasing, elegant air.

Crowne Plaza Bucharest (Map pp54-5; ☎ 224 0034; www.crownplaza.com; B-dul Poligrafiei 1; s/d €195/ 211; ✶) A sparkling haven of peace and luxury at the northern end of Bucharest. It boasts a leafy outdoor terrace bar which does great cocktails.

In the city centre there's also **Hotel Lido** (Map p60; ☎ 314 4930; www.lido.ro; B-dul General Magheru 5-7) and the landmark **Hotel Continental** (Map p60; ☎ 313 4114; www.continentalhotels.ro; Calea Victoriei 56; s/d €164/186). **Hotel Bucureşti** (Map p60; Calea Victoriei) was undergoing a multimillion euro face-lift at the time of writing and will emerge as a five-star hotel.

EATING

Bucharest is fast becoming a cosmopolitan city of international restaurants with prices to suit all budgets. Once the home of stodgy eastern European delights, now there are restaurants to rival London, with cuisines ranging from Spanish, French, American and Lebanese.

Be warned, don't rely on using your MasterCard or Visa as not all places accept them. Also, at first glance prices may appear cheap – until you realise they're per 100g – so you may have to double or triple the figure, depending on the size of your portion!

Restaurants

INTERNATIONAL

Basilicum (Map pp54-5; ☎ 222 6779; Str Popa Savu 7; mains €8) A delightful rustic Italian place with proper pasta dishes, mouthwatering salads such as avocado, smoked salmon and mango, and a candlelit back terrace. Just north of the centre. Very romantic.

Paradis (Map p60; ☎ 315 2601; Str Hristo Botev 10; mains from €1.50) Brilliant-value buffet lunch at this Lebanese joint. Aubergine stew, spicy rice and falafel for vegetarians, while carnivores can tuck into lamb stew with mounds of flat bread. A budget gem.

Trattoria Il Calcio (Map p60; ☎ 0722-134 299; Str Mendeleev 14; mains €6) Drool over fabulous antipasti or snack on a lunchtime salad. This Italian restaurant in the heart of Piaţa Amzei is a popular choice.

La Strada Terrace (Map p60; ☎ 303 3777; Athénée Palace Hilton; mains €5) Hugely popular for a light vegetarian lunch of falafel in pitta bread, or sophisticated night-time dining from an international menu on the leafy, beautifully lit terrace. An expat institution.

AUTHOR'S CHOICE

Balthazar (Map pp54-5; ☎ 212 1460; Str Dumbrava Rosie 2; mains €15) Bucharest's best and hippest restaurant. A dreamy, creamy interior with subtle lighting lures in hungry food aficionados. The exquisite French/Thai fusion menu boasts delicate prawns dished in banana leaves, and a divine wine list. Indulge yourself on the fairy-light lit terrace with the city's A-list guests.

Bistro Vilacrosse (Map p60; ☎ 315 4562; Pasajul Macca/Vilacrosse; mains €3) This place borrows its style from Parisian side streets, and has Edith Piaf warbling in the background, wood floors and gingham tablecloths. Escape the city heat and crowds in this glass-domed passage while sipping fresh coffee and eating a mozzarella salad with (French!) fries, a warm baguette of your choice, or steak. Bizarrely, a red English phone box is the entrance to the toilets!

Bistro Atheneu (Map p60; ☎ 313 4900; Str Episcopiei 3; mains €12) An old favourite. Its high-quality food and friendly, French-inspired atmosphere draws large crowds, as does its serenading musicians who play most evenings.

La Taifas (Map p60; ☎ 311 3204; Str Georges Clemenceau 6; mains €10) Gets glowing reports for its roast lamb with rosemary trimmings. Set in a central, shady area, the service is good and the atmosphere friendly.

Café de la Joie (Map p60; ☎ 315 0937; Str Bibliotecii 4; mains €5) A delightful culinary treasure hidden in the basement of a concrete office block off Piaţa Universităţii. The candlelit bistro oozes soul, with jazzy French classics playing in the background and a changing menu chalked up on the blackboard.

Mediterraneo (Map p60; ☎ 211 5308; Str Icoanei 18-20; mains €10) The home of the best Sunday lunch in Bucharest. It's an expat favourite, with Italian- and Mediterranean-inspired cooking.

Smart's (Map pp54-5; ☎ 211 9035; Str Alex Donici 14; mains €10) Serves European bar-style food such as meaty beef steaks doused in sauce, and giant salads. It's an institution in Bucharest, so book ahead.

Il Gattopardo Blu (Map pp54-5; ☎ 212 7886; Calea Victoriei 115; mains €15) It is named after Visconti's film *The Leopard* and is famous for its unique and historical setting inside the Writers' Union house (Uniunea Scriitorilor). It serves exquisite seafood dishes, juicy steaks and adventurous pastas.

Valencia (Map pp54-5; ☎ 312 8196; Str Dr Leonte 12; mains €7) Wash down fluffy *calamares*, hot spicy peppers, *patatas bravas* (Spanish dish of roasted potatoes, chilli sauce and mayonnaise) and tortilla, with jugs of authentic sangria in this lovely restaurant south of the centre (opposite the municipal hospital).

ROMANIAN

Boema (Map p60; ☎ 313 3783, Str CA Rosetti 10; mains €7) Swathed in sheepskin rugs, handsewn tapestries and plumes of dried plants, this Romanian restaurant is a rustic treat in the city centre. The *borş* (soup) is excellent and the menu is flexible.

Menuet (Map p60; ☎ 312 0143; Str Nicolae Golescu 12; mains €7) Featuring heavy, old-style furnishings, Menuet dishes up excellent Romanian cuisine, including the crispiest, gooiest and tastiest *caşcaval pane* (fried cheese) around.

Caru cu Bere (Map p60; ☎ 313 7560; Str Stavropoleos 3-5; mains €7) Bucharest's oldest beer hall (dating from 1875) and worth a visit for its lavish, Gothic-style decor if not for the average food and slow service. Roma bands play loudly most days from noon.

La Mama (Map pp54-5; ☎ 212 4086; Str B Văcărescu 3; mains €3-6) Deservedly packed every night because of its hearty Romanian dishes, lively atmosphere and super cheap prices. Tuck into fresh salads, steaming bowls of soup, and meat or fish mains.

Bureibista (Map pp54-5; ☎ 210 9704; Calea Moşilor 26; mains €6-9) Good-value traditional dining. Try the cheese croquettes and garlic mushrooms while brushing off the persistent roaming folk band.

Bureibista Pescăresc (Map pp54-5; ☎ 212 5429; B-dul Nicolae Titulescu 39-49; meals €15) There's live fish to choose from, as well as good fish *borş* and herb-crusted salmon, inside this fishermen-themed, dark-wood sister restaurant.

Casa Doina (Map pp54-5; ☎ 222 3179; Şos Kiseleff 4; mains €10) Its gorgeous terrace garden pulls in the great and good of Bucharest. Expensive but exquisite Romanian dishes are served by waiters in penguin suits in the garden adorned with tinkling fountains and serenading musicians.

Nicoreşti (Map pp54-5; ☎ 211 2480; Str Maria Ro-setti 40; mains €4) Another pleasant Romanian choice, with traditional Romanian dishes such as *sarmale* (stuffed cabbage or vine leaves), accompanied by *mămăligă* (Roma-nian polenta) and meat dishes.

Count Dracula Club (Map p60; ☎ 312 1353; Spl Independenţei 8a; mains €10) Only for kids or kitsch-lovers. Eat your Romanian staples – or exotic pheasant, venison or wild boar – surrounded by 'human skulls', pickled bats, and blood-dripping walls. Dine in the coffin-clad chapel for the full house-of-horror experience.

Cafés

Nova Brasilia (Map pp54-5; ☎ 231 5540; Str Radu Bel-ler 6; meals €3) This is the city's queen of cof-fee. Choose from frothy cappuccinos, cold iced coffees and indulgent mochaccinos. There are also divine cakes and pastries to torment you.

Picasso Café (Map p60; ☎ 312 1576; Str Franceză 2-4; mains €4) The art theme may be overdone but it's a nice city haven for reading the paper and drinking coffee. There's a small selection of salads and cakes.

Café & Latte (Map pp54-5; ☎ 314 3834; B-dul Schitu Măgureanu 35; mains €3) A friendly joint full of students and actors. Along with a decent latte you can munch on toasted sandwiches and cakes.

Quick Eats

Sandwich Factory (Map pp54-5; ☎ 230 3923; Piaţa Dorobanti 28; meals €1-3) Rejoice! From baguettes to bagels, sandwiches to salads, lunchtimes have been transformed!

Red Lion (Map p60; ☎ 315 1526; Str Academiei 1a; meals from €1) Ignore the delirious delights of the pretend outdoor terrace with plas-tic lawn, plastic sunflowers and wooden benches – focus instead on its pizzas.

Self-Catering

Piaţă Amzei (Amzei Market; Map pp54-5; Piaţa Amzei; ☼ sunrise-sunset) This open-air market has the juiciest selection of fresh fruit and veg in Bucharest.

Piaţa Gemeni (Map pp54-5) Another open-air market, within spitting distance of the Youth Hostel Villa Helga hostel, off B-dul Dacia.

Pâtisserie Parisienne Valerie (Map p60; Calea Victo-riei 63) A French-style bakery selling delicious cakes and pastries.

DRINKING

Bucharest's budding bar scene is liveliest in the **Lipscani** area, which now has a dedicated pedestrianised road called **Summer Street** which is lined with trendy pubs and outside tables. **Piaţa Universităţii** is alive with revellers at the weekend, and hosts free outdoor pop concerts in summer.

Other rocking venues include:

Amsterdam Grand Café (Map p60; ☎ 313 7580; Str Covaci 6; ☼ 10am-2am) It's like being at home – yet much nicer, funkier and with better-looking bar staff and better cooking. Get here early and feast on massive portions of excellent food (the vegetable fajitas are particularly good), then enjoy the beer and eclectic crowds.

La Ruine (Map p60; ☎ 312 3943; Str Lipscani 88; ☼ 11am-6am) This outdoor, bamboo-clad bar is brilliantly set up in the space left by a demolished building, hence the name.

Tipsy (Map p60; B-dul Schitu Măugureanu 13; ☼ 3pm-4am) Funky little bar with hip crowd, good tunes, regular DJs and a summer terrace. It also serves simple food.

Lăptăria Enache/La Motor (Map p60; B-dul Nicolae Bălcescu 2) Trendy joint on the 4th floor of the Ion Luca Caragiale National Theatre (with a rooftop bar another floor up). It's lined with one long bar, a lively student crowd, huge metal sculptures and a new wooden seating area. Enjoy live jazz at weekends, summer film screenings on the roof terrace and generally raucous behaviour. Enter via the unmarked entrance at the northern side of the theatre, to the side of Dominusart Gallery.

White Horse (Map pp54-5; ☎ 231 2795; Str George Călinescu 4; ☼ noon-3am) British pub with crazy, boozed-up patrons having fun every weekend. It's noisy, crowded and smoky – but a top night out.

Buddha Bar (Map pp54-5; Calea Moşilor 36) So trendy it hurts. Soak up the cool karma in this lush, red-painted bar within staggering distance of Bureibista restaurant and Youth Hostel Villa Helga.

Dubliner (Map pp54-5; ☎ 222 9473; Şos Titulescu 18; ☼ 9am-2am) A good, old-fashioned pub with simple grub, including Guinness and steak pie. The olde-worlde style is offset by Sky Sports, which draws in the footy crowd.

Opium Studio (Map pp54-5; ☎ 0722-505 066; Str Horei 5; ☼ 7pm-4am) Cool, collected and outrageously eclectic is the name of the game at this cellar bar, furnished in the most fabulously theatrical of manners.

Clubs

Show the locals how to boogie at the following venues:

Club A (Map p60; ☎ 315 6853; Str Blănari 14; ❂ 9pm-5am) Run by students, this club is a classic and beloved by all who go here. Indie pop/rock tunes rule the day at Club A.

Salsa 2 (Map p60; ☎ 0723-412 267; Str Luterană 9; ❂ 3pm-6am) Bongos, steel drums and lots of body-beat make this a sexy, upbeat taste of Cuba.

Twice (Map p60; ☎ 313 5592; Str Sfânta Vineri 4; ❂ 9pm-5am) Popular party place, with techno beats and classic '80s and '90s hits in one crazy club.

Fire Club (Map p60; ☎ 0722-390 946; Str Gabroveni 12; ❂ 10pm-6am) This club spins alternative sounds until the wee hours.

Vox Maris (Map pp54-5; ☎ 311 1994; Calea Victoriei 155; ❂ 10pm-4am) Big, cheesy, super club with lots of one-armed bandits.

ENTERTAINMENT

Şapte Seri (Seven Evenings) is a free, weekly entertainment listings magazine. Plug into the local scene with cinema, theatre and opera programmes; details of the week's sporting events; and information on live gigs and concerts in Bucharest's bars and clubs.

Posters advertising underground music nights and alternative-club DJs or live bands appear all over the city, so keep your eyes peeled.

Cinemas

Most films are shown in their original language with Romanian subtitles, and tickets cost between €1 and €3.

Hollywood Multiplex (Map pp54-5; ☎ 327 7020; Bucureşti Mall, Calea Vitan 55-59) Bucharest's only multiscreen cinema.

Cinemateca Eforie (Map p60; ☎ 313 0483; Str Eforie 2) Shows art-house and world films.

French Institute (Map pp54-5; ☎ 210 0224; B-dul Dacia 77) Screens a variety of foreign films.

Mainstream cinemas are clustered near B-dul Nicolae Bălcescu and B-dul Regina Elisabeta. They include **Cinema Scala** (Map p60; ☎ 211 0372; B-dul General Magheru 2-4), **Cinema Luceafărul** (Map p60; ☎ 315 8767; B-dul IC Brătianu

6) and **Cinema Patria** (Map p60; ☎ 211 8625; B-dul General Magheru 12-14).

Gay & Lesbian Venues

Bucharest's fledgling gay scene remains stilted by lingering homophobic attitudes across both the city and country. But there is some action.

Queens (Map p60; www.bucharestonline.ro/enclubs .html; Str Culmea Veche 2; ❂ noon-3am) is the only 'real' gay venue in Bucharest.

Live Music

There's some good live music in Bucharest – just follow your ears.

Green Hours 22 Jazz Club (Map p60; ☎ 314 5751; Calea Victoriei 120; ❂ 24hr) Hip cellar bar with live jazz, a weekend disco and even short theatre performances; the itinerary is posted inside. In summer hang out with the cool, bohemian crowd at the outside bar to the sound of smooth jazz.

Jukebox (Map p60; ☎ 314 8314; Str Sepcari 22; ❂ 8pm-3am Mon-Sat) Namesake band Jukebox gets this place jumping in the basement. It's heaving with fun-lovers at the weekend.

Backstage (Map p60; ☎ 312 3943; Str Gabroveni 14; ❂ 9pm-5am) Live rock in a sweaty red-brick vaulted cellar.

Art Jazz Club (Map p60; ☎ 0723-520 643; B-dul Nicolae Bălcescu; ❂ 8pm-3am) Toe-tapping live music weekly.

Romanian Athenaeum (Map p60; ☎ 315 8798; Str Franklin 1; tickets €1-3) Experience the George Enescu Philharmonic Orchestra.

Opera & Ballet

Opera House (Opera Română; Map pp54-5; ☎ 314 6980; onr@kappa.ro; B-dul Mihail Kogălniceanu 70; tickets €1-4). Soak up the cultural flavour of Romania's music scene with a refined night at the opera. See the **box office** (❂ 10am-1pm & 2-7.30pm Tue-Sun) for details of the shows and get warbling.

Sport

The team Steaua Bucureşti play at Steaua Stadium; fans can get kitted out in all the red-white-and-blue Steaua paraphernalia at the side's **club shop** (Map p60; ☎ 094 299 037; cnr Str Ion Zalomit & Str Ion Brezioanu).

Its rival side, Dinamo Bucureşti, play at **Dinamo Stadium** (Map pp54-5; ☎ 210 6974; Şos Ştefan cel Mare 7-9), which is also home to a club shop.

Theatre

Bucharest has many **theatres** (🕙 Sep-Jun), offering a lively mix of comedy, farce, satire and straight contemporary plays in a variety of languages. Tickets cost no more than €3.

Ion Luca Caragiale National Theatre (Teatrul Naţional Ion Luca Caragiale; Map p60; ☎ 614 7171, 615 4746; B-dul Nicolae Bălcescu 2) is named after the 20th-century playwright who kicked off his career here as a prompter. The theatre was built in the 1970s; the original theatre dating from 1852 was destroyed during WWII. The **box office** (🕙 10am-7pm) is on the southern side of the building.

The **Jewish State Theatre** (Teatrul Evreiesc de Stat; Map pp54-5; ☎ 323 4530; Str Iuliu Barasch 15) holds plays in Hebrew and Yiddish.

SHOPPING

For beautifully made woven rugs, table runners, national Romanian costumes, ceramics and other local crafts, don't miss the excellent folk art shop inside the **Museum of the Romanian Peasant** (Map pp54-5; ☎ 212 9661; Şos Kiseleff 3; 🕙 10am-6pm Tue-Sun).

Interesting art galleries and antique shops are clustered in 'embassy land' around Str Jean Louis Calderon, and north of Hotel Bucureşti along Calea Victoriei. Do not miss **Pasajul Villacros** (Map p60; Calea Victoriei 16), a covered passage topped with an ornate yellow-glass roof, which has some funky clothes and curiosities shops.

The narrow alleys and passages winding off Str Lipscani in the old part of the city

---

MAGIC POTION COMMOTION

No Romanian will let you leave their country without buying a pot of Gerovital face cream. This is one for the ladies. This so-called magic potion has caused a storm in Romania and with celebrities around the world since it was invented by leading Romanian scientist Dr Ana Aslan. The story goes that when she died she looked 20 years younger than her age! Good marketing or a skincare revelation? Who knows, but get a jar of this stuff that claims to slow the ageing process and see for yourself! Elizabeth Taylor, Pablo Picasso, Charlie Chaplin and John F Kennedy allegedly used the cream. Buy it at pharmacies across Bucharest.

---

are equally delightful to explore; wrought iron gates lead to Str Hanul cu Tei, an alley passage filled with tiny craft shops.

Bucureşti Mall (Map pp54-5; ☎ 327 6100; Calea Vitan 55; 🕙 9am-8pm) is a four-storey mall that houses a supermarket and international chain stores for American-style shopping.

Mario Plaza (Map pp54-5; Calea Dorobanţilor 172-178; 🕙 9am-8pm) is a swanky designer-label haven, and **Unirea Shopping Centre** (Map pp54-5; Piaţa Unirii 3; 🕙 9am-6pm) offers Bucharest's central department store.

GETTING THERE & AWAY
Air

International flights use **Otopeni airport** (☎ 201 4050, 204 1423; Şos Bucureşti-Ploieşti), 17km north of Bucharest on the road to Ploieşti. The airport has a lower-level floor for internal flight arrivals and departures.

Arrivals use terminal A and departures leave from the newer terminal B. The Otopeni airport **information desk** (☎ 204 1000; www.otp-airport.ro) in terminal B is opens 24 hours.

Tarom (☎ 337 0220; Spl Independenţei 17) has its head office at Otopeni airport (☎ 204 1355, 201 4979). Romania's national airline has four daily flights to Timişoara, two daily flights to Baia-Mare (except weekends), one flight daily to Oradea, one week to Constanţa, daily to Satu Mare (except weekends), daily to Sibiu (except weekends) and four weekly to Cluj. All Tarom flights use Otopeni airport.

One-way tickets to anywhere in the country cost US$75 plus tax (the tax differs depending on the destination airport) and returns cost between US$112 and US$124 plus tax.

International flights include daily flights (except weekends) to New York via Timişoara, daily flights to Athens, daily flights to London (except Thursday and Friday), one flight a week to Berlin, four a week to Brussels, five a week to Istanbul, twice a week to Madrid, and daily flights to Warsaw, Zurich and Vienna.

Air Moldova (Map p60; ☎ 312 1258; Str Batiştei 5) has three flights weekly to Chişinău from Otopeni.

Băneasa airport (☎ 232 0020; Şos Bucureşti-Ploieşti 40), 8km north of the centre, is used for internal flights and charter flights for package holidays. Domestic airline **Angel**

Airlines (☎ 211 1701) has twice-weekly flights to Arad, daily flights to Iasi (except weekends) and flights to Suceava from here.

Bus

Don't bother catching a bus unless it's a short trip through the city. The state buses are poor and they take ages.

The **central bus station** (Map pp54-5; Calea Griviței, opp Hotel Ibis) is a few paltry stops rather than a station. Services change regularly and it is wise to check the timetables stuck on the lamp posts first. There is no ticket office; hop aboard the bus and buy a ticket from the driver.

A bus journey in the city costs a mere €0.20. Services nationally go to/from Tulcea, Brașov, Constanța, Târgoviște and Ploiești.

Filaret bus station (Map pp54-5; ☎ 336 0692; Piața Gării Filaret 1) has daily buses to Mogoșoaia (€0.75, 19km), Buftea (€1, 24km), Giurgiu (€1.50, 62km), Ploiești (€1.50, 62km) and Calafat (€6, 327km).

Hurray for maxitaxis, which are part bus, part taxi. These speedy little devils have almost rendered the stuffy, slow and dirty buses obsolete. They leave mostly when they're full but do have timetables. C&I is the main private maxitaxi company. Its white maxitaxis leave from a spot in the centre of Piața Gară de Nord, opposite the Sensi Blu chemist. Services go to Brașov (€5, every 30 minutes, 6am to 7pm) and Craiova (€5.50, every half-hour, 5.30am to 8pm).

MOLDOVA

There are seven daily buses to Chișinău (€10, about 12 hours) which depart from Filaret bus station. Buy tickets in advance from **Filaret Tours** (Map pp54-5; ☎ 336 6780), which has an office inside the station.

TURKEY

Murat (Map pp54-5; ☎ 336 6215; B-dul D Golescu 31) runs a bus to Istanbul (one way/return €34/68, once a day at 4pm) from Filaret bus station. It runs a free shuttle bus from its office at the back of Gară de Nord to Filaret which leaves at 2.30pm. The buses are luxurious, with air-con and free tea and coffee.

Ortadoğu Tur (Map pp54-5; ☎ 312 2423; Str Gară de Nord 6-8) runs buses to Istanbul (one way/

return €37/74, 2.30pm and 3.30pm daily) leaving from outside its office opposite Gară de Nord. The buses are excellent and have air-con and free drinks and you get a free breakfast in Istanbul. In Istanbul you can change buses for its services to Iran, Syria, Moldova and Ukraine.

WESTERN EUROPE

Eurolines (Map pp54-5; ☎ 230 5489; www.eurolines.ro; Str Buzești 44) has buses to Frankfurt and Stuttgart (€50, once a day at 5am), Paris (€95, once a day at 6am), Madrid (€24, three per week at 6am) and Belgium (€114, three per week at 5am).

Double T (Map p60; ☎ 313 3642; doublet@fx.ro; Calea Victoriei 2) has daily buses to Germany.

Car & Motorcycle

Bucharest has some of Romania's worst potholes, which, combined with the daredevil driving skills of many Romanians, makes for a hair-raising ride. Petrol costs approximately €0.75 per litre and diesel is €0.50 per litre. There are plenty of 24-hour petrol stations around the city which sell oil and accessories.

Parking in Bucharest is problematic in the centre, much like any other capital. Parking a car in the centre, particularly off Piața Victoriei and Piața Universității, costs €0.30 – look for the wardens in yellow-and-blue uniforms.

CAR RENTAL

Car rental is pricey as it's geared towards the business traveller. The usual big names are based at Otopeni airport.

Avis Hilton (Map p60; ☎ 312 2043); Hotel Inter-Continental (Map p60; ☎ 314 1837); Otopeni airport (☎ 201 4783; www.avisworld.com; ☒ 8am-8pm) Charges upwards of €80 per day for cars.

Cars4Rent (☎ 0723-347 192, 0788-303 923; www.cars4rent.ro) A cheap option, with prices starting from €30 a day.

Europcar General Magheru (Map p60; ☎ 313 1540; B-dul General Magheru 7); Otopeni airport (☎ 312 7078)

Easy Rent A Car Otopeni airport (☎ 413 3379; easy_rentacar@yahoo.com) Cheap cars from €30 per day.

Train

Bucharest boasts a complex but comprehensive train network that links the capital to the regions and the rest of Europe and the East.

Gară de Nord (☎ 223 2060; Piaţa Gară de Nord 1) is the central station for national and international trains. It has two halls, one for 1st-class and international tickets, the other – much grottier and more crowded – is for 2nd-class tickets.

First class is always recommended, especially for women travelling on their own, as it's safer, cleaner and still relatively cheap. Tickets for local and national trains are only sold at the train station one or two hours before departure.

The ticket hall for international destinations, 1st-class tickets and sleeping compartments (marked 'casele de bilete Cl. 1') is on the right as you enter the station's main entrance. Window No 1 ('casa internaţionala') is for international tickets; window Nos 2 to 7 are for other 1st-class tickets; and window Nos 8 and 9 are for sleepers and couchettes on national trains ('vagon de dormit şi cuseta').

You must have a valid ticket to get onto the platforms. Guards have been posted at the entrance to stop undesirables, begging children and drunks who made Gară de Nord the hell-hole it used to be. Timetables are in the main aisle of the station building opposite the 1st-class ticket hall. Notice boards listing ticket prices are displayed in the 2nd-class ticket office. Prices change every month.

Some local trains to/from Cernica and Constanţa use **Gară Obor** (☎ 252 0204) station, east of the centre. Local trains to/from Snagov and a couple of seasonal *accelerat* trains to/from Mangalia on the Black Sea coast and Cluj-Napoca sometimes use **Gară Băneasa** (☎ 223 2060; Şos Bucureşti-Ploieşti) on the northern edge of town.

All advance tickets (up to 24 hours before departure) can be bought from the **Agenţie de Voiaj CFR office** (Map p60; ☎ 313 2643; www.cfr.ro; Str Domnita Anastasia 10-14). A seat reservation is compulsory if you are travelling with an Inter-Rail pass. International tickets must be bought in advance.

Domestic tickets are sold through the **Agentie de Voiaj CFR office** (☽ 7.30am-7.30pm Mon-Fri, 8am-noon Sat) on the ground (1st) floor of Gară de Nord; international tickets and rail passes can be purchased on the 2nd floor. Train timetables (€1) are sold at the ticket desks in the domestic ticket hall. Some staff speak English.

Daily international trains include two to Sofia (€24), one to Belgrade (€20), one to Moscow (€55), five to Budapest (€40), one to Chişinău and one each to Istanbul (€24) and Vienna.

GETTING AROUND
To/From the Airport
To get to Otopeni or Băneasa airports take bus No 783 from the city centre, which departs every 15 minutes between 5.37am and 11.23pm (every half-hour at weekends) from Piaţa Unirii and goes via Piaţa Victoriei.

Buy a ticket, valid for two trips, for €1 at any Régie Autonome de Transport de Bucureşti (RATB) bus-ticket booth near a bus stop. Once inside the bus remember to feed the ticket into the machine.

Băneasa is 20 minutes from the centre; get off at the 'aeroportul Băneasa' stop. Buses also link Băneasa with Piaţa Romană and Gară de Nord.

Otopeni is about 40 minutes from the city centre. The bus stops outside the departures hall (terminal B) then continues to the arrivals halls (terminal A).

Taking a reputable taxi from the centre to Otopeni airport should cost no more than €5.

To get to the centre from Otopeni, catch bus No 783 from the stop in front of terminal A. Tickets are sold at the booth next to the stop, or direct from the driver (the easier option). Avoid any officials who tell you not to take the bus, they are trying to get you into an expensive taxi.

This is the first scam you might experience in Bucharest – gangs of private taxis have a monopoly at the airport and will try to charge you €25 to the centre. The easiest way to avoid this rip-off is to ring a taxi and wait for it downstairs from the arrivals hall: exit the building, cross the street towards the car park and take the lift to the right down one floor. Even if you haven't called a taxi, there are dozens of 'real' taxis waiting there who will use their meter to take you into town.

Bicycle
Youth Hostel Villa Helga (p68) has bicycles to rent in summer for €10 a day.

Bus, Tram & Trolleybus
For buses, trams and trolleybuses buy tickets (€0.20) at any RATB street kiosk,

marked 'casa de bilete' or simply 'bilete'. Punch your ticket on board or risk a €10 on-the-spot fine if caught by an inspector. Single- and two-journey tickets (€0.40) are available as well as a 10-trip ticket (€1.50) or a monthly pass (€8) for unlimited bus, tram, trolleybus and metro use.

Public transport runs from 5am to approximately 11.30pm (reduced service on Sunday). Buy a timetable (Ghidul Mijoacelor de Transport În Comun; €1) from ticket booths or check www.ratb.ro.

Metro

Bucharest's metro dates from 1979 and has four lines and 45 stations. Line M4 is the newest. Trains run every five to seven minutes during peak periods and about every 20 minutes off-peak between 5.30am and 11.30pm.

To use the metro buy a magnetic-strip ticket at the subterranean kiosks inside the main entrance to the metro station. Tickets valid for either two/10 journeys cost €0.20/ 1.50. A one-month unlimited travel ticket costs €4.50. For routes see the Bucharest metro map below.

Metro stations are poorly signposted so sit near the front of the train to give yourself a better chance of seeing the station names. At platform level, the name of the station where you are is the one with a box around it. The others indicate the direction the train is going.

BUCHAREST METRO

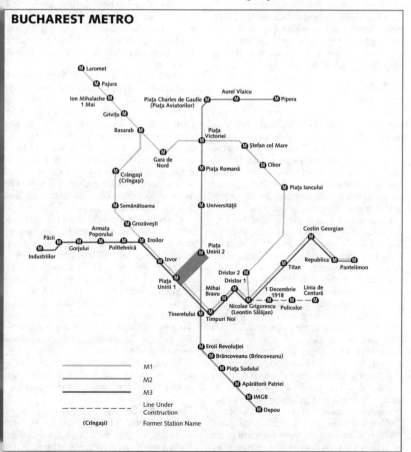

Taxi

Opt for a taxi with a meter. Reputable companies include **CrisTaxi** (☎ 9461), **Meridian** (☎ 9444) and **Prof Taxi** (☎ 9422).

Always check that the meter is switched on, as Bucharest is plagued by dodgy taxi drivers, and stand your ground if they charge too much or try to avoid giving you change. But the good news is that at €0.20 per km they're an absolute bargain – and quicker than taking a crowded, sweaty bus.

For longer journeys always negotiate a price before setting out.

AROUND BUCHAREST

Bloodcurdling delights such as Dracula's tomb, 'Lenin's graveyard' and breath-taking monasteries hidden among unspoilt forests and lakes are some of the sights within an easy day's reach of Bucharest.

SNAGOV

☎ 21 / pop 7000

The tomb of infamous tyrant Vlad Ţepeş lures visitors to this delightful spot – as much as the large lake and leisure complex. Devour the legend of Dracula by visiting the tomb where his headless torso is said to lie, buried in the famous 16th-century **church & monastery** (admission €1), which is tucked away on an island in Snagov Lake. So tiny is this pretty island that only elderly nun Maria and a priest inhabit it, giving small tours of the historic site. Deep forest surrounds the lake, which is estimated to be 576 hectares large and an impressive 18km long.

A simple wooden church was built on the island in the 11th century by Mircea cel Bătrân. A monastery was added in the late 14th century during the reign of King Dan I (r 1383–86), and in 1453 the wooden church was replaced by a stone edifice that later sank in the lake.

In 1456 Vlad Ţepeş (the Impaler) built fortifications around the monastery. He also built a bridge from the island to the mainland, a bell tower, a new church, an escape tunnel, and a prison and torture chamber. Nicolae Bălcescu, leader of the 1848 revolution in Wallachia, and other 1848 revolutionaries were imprisoned in Snagov prison for a short time. A mass grave for those who died in the prison was dug in the grounds. The remains of the prison can still be seen today behind the present-day church.

The present stone church, listed as a Unesco World Heritage site and currently under renovation for several years, dates from 1521. Some paintings date from 1563. The body of Vlad Ţepeş was reputedly buried below the dome, just in front of the church's wooden iconostasis. However, when the grave was opened in 1931 it was reported to be empty. Nevertheless, there is mounting credibility given to the presence of a headless torso, evidence that the unfortunate owner may have been killed by the Turks, as decapitation was a favourite Turkish execution method. Today, the humble grave inside the church, marked by a simple portrait of Vlad, is simply known as 'Dracula's tomb'. Daily services are held in the new, wooden church that stands close to the old, stone church.

The early-20th-century **Snagov Palace**, just across the lake from the island, was built by Prince Nicolae, brother of King Carol II, in the Italian Renaissance style. During the Ceauşescu era the palace was used for meetings of high-level government officials, and today houses a restaurant, conference centre and hotel reserved exclusively for state guests. Ceauşescu had a summer home on Snagov Lake, **Villa No 10**, now occasionally rented to rich and famous tourists.

You can hire a boat to row yourself to the island from Complex Astoria (see Sleeping & Eating p78). It costs €6 per hour. Alternatively, you can call upon the services of the burly Ana, who will row you there and back for €1.50 per person from the village of Silestru on the northern lakeshore – go to the end of the small wooden jetty at the foot of the radio mast and call out 'Ana'. To get to Silestru, continue north along the E60 past the 'Snagov Sat 11km' turn-off and turn right in Ciolpani.

Some winters, in December and January, it is often possible to walk or ice-skate across the frozen lake to the monastery.

Sleeping & Eating

Complex Astoria (☎ 313 6782; tent sites €5, 2-room villas €120), a 10-minute walk from Snagov Plajă train station on the southern side of

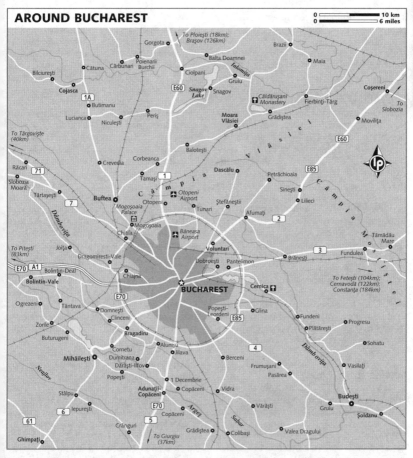

AROUND BUCHAREST

0 —————— 10 km
0 —————— 6 miles

the lake, is a large wooded complex with plenty of space to pitch your tent. It also has wooden huts and villas to rent, and there's a hotel on site with singles/doubles for €34/50 a night.

To get to here by car, turn east off the E60 (signposted 'Snagov Sat 11km') and follow the road for 11km to Snagov village. Continue past the village, ignoring the sign 'centru' for a further 2km to the complex (signposted 'Baza Turistică Snagov').

Admission to the complex costs €5 Monday to Friday for nonguests, and €1.50 on Saturday and Sunday.

Complex Turistic Snagov Parc (☎ 794 0236; sites per sq metre €0.50, d with shared shower €20; ☼ May-Sep) This place on the northern lakeshore is

another large complex, with sites and double rooms There are paddle boats to hire (€5 per hour) and a clean beach to lounge on.

Vila 23 (☎ 312 0448; r €38, incl breakfast) A true blast from the past, filled with men in dark glasses. It's an ageing hotel near Ceauşescu's pad on the southern side of the lake. The grandiose reception hall is a visual treat.

Getting There & Away

The best way to get here is to grab a maxitaxi, which go hourly from the Piaţa Universităţii via Piaţa Romană, and the Press House in Bucharest (€1 each way).

Otherwise, there are five local trains that run between May and September to and from Gară de Nord and Snagov Plajă – a stop in the middle of oak forest – which is 10 minutes' walk from Complex Astoria.

Both Elvis Villa (p68) and Youth Hostel Villa Helga (p68) arrange informal guided tours to Snagov, and both charge €10 per person.

CĂLDĂRUȘANI MONASTERY

This idyllic **monastery** lies 6km southeast of Snagov. Be amazed at its incredible collection of icons painted by 16-year-old Nicolae Grigorescu in 1854 at the monastery's distinguished painting school. Eight exquisite icons line the walls of the former monks' dining hall, along with robes saturated in gold thread from the 19th century.

It was built in 1638 under the guidance of Wallachian prince Matei Basarab (r 1632– 54), and was forced into the international spotlight when Swedish tennis champion Björn Borg married Romanian player Mariana Simionescu here.

In 1945 a fire destroyed the building and it took eight years to rebuild between 1950 and 1958. Today, 25 monks live in the beautiful white complex, which is open to visitors day or night. They also take in people who ask for hospitality, offering bed and board for a donation.

Getting There & Away

A state bus, No 452, leaves from the Press House in Bucharest at 7.30am and 5.30pm, returning to the city at 8.50am and 6.50pm. The journey takes one hour each way (€0.75) and goes straight to the monastery gates. Or you can take bus No 448, which leaves every hour, and get off at Urziceni, at the signpost 'Monastirei Căldărușani' to the left; it's a 3km hike from here. To get back, walk to the junction and there's a bus every hour to Bucharest.

By car, take the E60 highway north to Ploiești for 16km, turn right onto the 101C road to Fierbinți. Go for another 16km and do a left at the sign for the monastery.

Some Bucharest-Galați trains, departing from Gară de Nord, stop at Greci (50 minutes, five daily), where you alight for Căldărușani. The monastery is a 2km walk north from the train station.

MOGOȘOAIA PALACE

One of Romania's most remarkable **palaces** (☎ 312 8894; Str Valea Parcului; admission with/without guide €2/1; ☼ 10am-6pm Tue-Sun) lies 14km northwest of Bucharest in Mogoșoaia (literally, Mogoș' wife). Mogoșoaia Palace was built by Wallachian prince Constantin Brâncoveanu between 1698 and 1702 as a summer residence for his family and an inheritance for his son Ștefan. It is considered to be among the country's finest examples of Brâncoveanu architecture. Built within a large court and surrounded by a lake and oak forests, the palace's main feature is a traditional balcony that winds around the front façade.

Following the death of Ștefan at the hands of the Turks in Istanbul in 1714, the palace was turned into an inn. It was then plundered and made into a warehouse by occupying Russian forces in 1853. At the end of the 19th century the estate was handed down to the Bibescu family, descendants of the Brâncoveanus through the female line. A large guesthouse was built and, in 1912, Prince George Valentin Bibescu (1880–1941) relinquished Mogoșoaia Palace to his wife, Martha (1886–1973). Under her guidance, Italian architect Domenico Rupolo restored the estate. The guesthouse was rebuilt, taking the fish market in Venice as its model. State-owned since 1956, the palace served as a museum until the 1970s, when Ceaușescu closed it and took the furniture for his own use.

Prince George Valentin Bibescu is buried in the small, white church (1688) on the estate. A path from the main entrance to the palace leads to the **Bibescu family tomb**, where Elizabeth Asquith (1898–1945), the daughter of former British prime minister Henry Herbert Asquith, lies. She married Prince Antoine Bibescu in London in 1919.

The **grave of 'Lenin'** is also located at Mogoșoaia Palace. Following the 1989 downfall of Romanian communism, the statue of Lenin that stood outside Bucharest's Press House was removed from its pedestal and dumped on wasteground behind the palace kitchens on the Mogoșoaia estate. The head of Lenin's 5m-tall bronze body lies peacefully against that of **Petru Groza**, the Communist prime minister at the head of the 1945 government that forced King Michael to abdicate in 1947.

Getting There & Away

A daily bus (€0.75) runs from Filaret bus station in Bucharest. Alternatively, take tram

No 20 from Gară de Nord to the last stop on the line (in the Laromet district), from where bus No 460 trundles to/from Mogoşoaia.

By car, take national road DN 1A.

ŞTIRBEI PALACE

Just 18km north of Bucharest Ştirbei Palace (Palat Ştirbei; Str Ştirbei Vodă 36) was a Communist Party hotel until 1989. Built by Wallachian prince Barbu Ştirbei between 1855 and 1864, it was here that the Romanian government signed a preliminary WWI peace treaty with Germany on 5 March 1918. After WWII the palace – also known as Buftea Castle – was turned into a guesthouse for important state guests.

Today, the pretty castle, enclosed in lush parkland, is a three-star **hotel** (☎ 313 1500; s & d from €38) and restaurant oozing old-style grandeur. Anyone can stay here. As well as rooms in the main building, there are excellent-value rooms in **Vila Parc** (r from €10), a small villa in the wooded grounds.

Getting There & Away

From Bucharest's Gară de Nord, there are numerous local trains to Ploieşti daily, some of which stop at Buftea, the stop closest to Stirbei Palace (34 minutes). Bus No 460 links Laromet and Buftea (see Getting There & Away under Mogoşoaia Palace on p80).

Entering Buftea by car from the south, bear north along the Bucharest-Ploieşti road (the main road through the village), pass the post office and immediately turn left onto Str Otului. At the end of Str Otului, turn right.

CERNICA

The breathtaking monastery-complex of Cernica (Sfânta Mănăstire Cernica) boasts some of the loveliest interior paintings in Romania. This undiscovered gem is nestled on a small island in the middle of Cernica Lake 14km east of Bucharest. Two **churches**, some chapels, a cemetery, seminary and a small **museum** are contained within the intensely beautiful fortified complex, founded on the site of a former 17th-century church in 1781.

An earthquake in 1842 destroyed much of the complex, but it's now impossible to tell what damage was caused as it was restored successfully in the 1990s. A smaller

church, **St Nicolae's Church** (Biserica Sfântul Nicolae din Ostrov) was built in 1815, but it was not until the mid-1800s, under the guidance of St Calinic of Cernica, that the monastery really flourished.

Between 1831 and 1838 **St Gheorghe's Church** (Biserica Sfântul Gheorghe) was built, a library and seminary were opened and a school for religious painting set up. After WWII the monastery was closed, not reopening until 1995. Some 50 monks live on the island complex – joined by a causeway to the mainland. The graves of Romanian painter Ion Ţuculescu, and writer and priest Gala Galaction, are in the cemetery on the lakes shore, in front of St Gheorghe's Church.

Getting There & Away

From Bucharest, take tram No 14 or 46 to the end of the line in Pantelimon. From there, swap to bus No 410 or 459, which both stop directly outside the monastery gates. Tickets cost €0.20 and the trip takes 20 minutes.

By car, take Road 3 to Pantelimon, and turn right towards Budeşti.

SLOBOZIA
☎ 21 / pop 57,000

Slobozia's main draw is modelled on TV's *Dallas* from the 1980s, though even JR wouldn't recognise his faux home now. Originally built by a Ewing fanatic in the style of their Dallas ranch, the **Samson Holiday Park** (Parcul de Vancaţă Samson; ☎ 243 236 152), 1km west of Slobozia, is a shadow of its former self. The new owner has taken out the kitsch (except for a bizarrely misplaced Eiffel Tower) – and frankly there's no reason now to go except as a pleasant stopover on the route between Bucharest and Constanţa. It's on the E60, 125km east of Bucharest by car.

Hotel Dallas (☎ 0243-236 150; s/d €20/25) This hotel sits in landscaped gardens and has a sheriff as a security guard. At the time of writing, the hotel was undergoing massive renovations in the hopes of resurrecting its successful past as an exotic tourist attraction; a large pool, tennis courts and a huge restaurant will be added.

Several maxitaxis leave daily from Piaţa Bucur Obor in Bucharest to Constanţa, stopping at Slobozia on the way, or you can take the twice-daily Constanţa train from Bucharest.

Transylvania

TRANSYLVANIA

CONTENTS

Transylvania – the word alone conjures up images of haunted castles, werewolves and vampires. There's Gothic galore here to keep visitors happy even if they're likely to leave without bite marks on their necks. The 14th-century castles at Râşnov and Bran, for example, could be straight out of a Count Dracula movie. Yet its connection to a literary myth is but a small part of what makes Transylvania an enchanting – not to mention romantic and exciting – destination for travellers of all persuasions. Spectacular mountain ranges, whose sheer rock faces appear like gigantic walls, offer some of Romania's best hiking and skiing, not to mention pure eye candy that in Europe is matched only by Switzerland's mountain ranges.

The area is culturally vibrant thanks in part to Saxon and Hungarian communities living in towns their ancestors founded centuries ago. For medieval art and history buffs, Transylvania offers an unparalleled chance to experience an overlooked corner of the old Austro-Hungarian empire; it's a glimpse of what pre-Industrial Europe was like.

Transylvania forms the central region of Romania, bordered to the east, south and west by the Carpathian Mountains. Southeastern Transylvania is dominated by the Prahova Valley with Romania's leading ski resorts. The Făgăraş Mountains and a string of medieval Saxon cities are within easy reach. Just north and east of here is Romania's Hungarian enclave, known as Székely Land, the cradle of Magyar culture. The southwest of the region is home to a string of Dacian and Roman citadels, including the fantastic remains of the Roman capital Sarmizegetusa.

TOP FIVE

- Pet wild wolves in the Carpathians near **Piatra Craiului** (p101)
- Travel back in time while strolling through the medieval streets of **Braşov** (p86), **Sighişoara** (p124) and **Sibiu** (p115)
- Learn that some royal families do have good taste in furniture at Peleş Castle in **Sinaia** (p109)
- Go hiking, horseback riding and salt mining before plunging into **Cluj-Napoca's** wild nightlife (p144)
- Measure the thickness of the walls of the **Saxon fortified churches** (p149) near Sighişoara

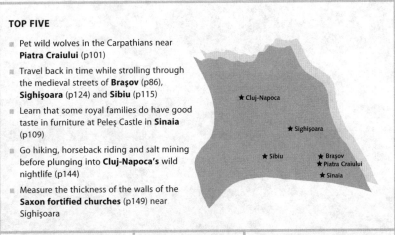

- POPULATION: 4.47 MILLION
- AREA: 57,056 SQ KM
- AVERAGE MONTHLY WAGE: €55

TRANSYLVANIA

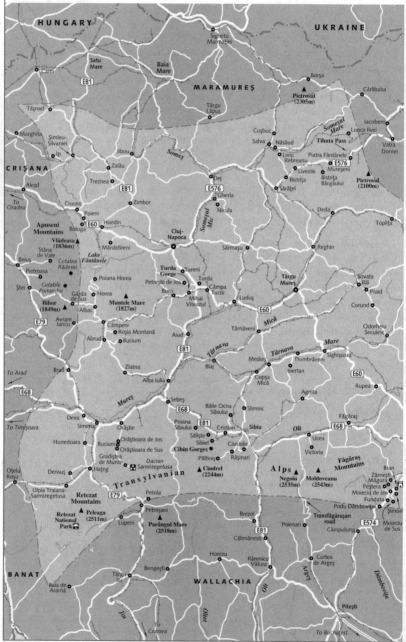

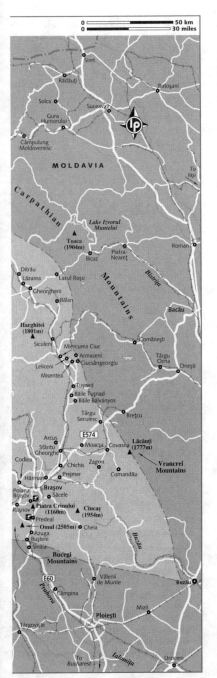

TRANSYLVANIA

HISTORY

For a thousand years, up to WWI, Transylvania was associated with Hungary. In the 10th century a Magyar (Hungarian) tribe, the Székelys, settled in what it called Erdély ('beyond the forest' – the literal meaning of Transylvania). In the 12th century Saxon merchants arrived to help defend the eastern frontiers of Hungary. The seven towns that they founded – Bistriţa (Bistritz), Braşov (Kronstadt), Cluj-Napoca (Klausenburg), Mediaş (Mediasch), Sebeş (Mühlbach), Sibiu (Hermannstadt) and Sighişoara (Schässburg) – gave Transylvania its German name, Siebenbürgen (both the origin and meaning of the term are disputed, but it roughly means 'seven boroughs').

Medieval Transylvania was an autonomous unit ruled by a prince responsible to the Hungarian crown. The indigenous Romanians were serfs. After the 1526 Turkish defeat of Hungary the region became semi-independent, recognising Turkish suzerainty.

In 1683 Turkish power was broken and Transylvania came under Habsburg rule fours years later. The Catholic Habsburg governors sought to control the territory by favouring first the Protestant Hungarians and Saxons and then the Orthodox Romanians. In 1848, when the Hungarians launched a revolution against the Habsburgs, Romania sided with the Austrians. After 1867 Transylvania was fully absorbed into Hungary. In 1918 Romanians gathered at Alba Iulia to demand Transylvania's union with Romania.

This unification has never been fully accepted by Hungary and from 1940 to 1944 it set about re-annexing much of the region. After the war, Romanian communists moved to quash Hungarian nationalist sentiments. Currently, however, feelings of resentment have subsided somewhat and Romania's relations with its western neighbour continue to strengthen. Still, one feels an extant mistrust between the communities, and the Hungarians publish maps of the region with only Hungarian place names (even street names), as if they were not located in Romania, making things confusing for non-Hungarian tourists.

SAXON LAND & THE PRAHOVA VALLEY

The area colonised by Saxons from the 12th century onwards lies north of the Prahova valley, which leads to the Carpathians. Attacks by Tartars and Turks prompted them to fortify their churches and towns with sturdy walls, providing tourists today with an opportunity to visit some of the most imposing religious structures in Europe. Though an estimated 150,000 Germans left Romania in the 1990s, their influence is still felt in what they still refer to as Siebenbürgen. Their legacy of fortified churches, defensive towers and medieval dwelling houses is especially resplendent in Sibiu, Sighişoara and Braşov.

The Prahova Valley snakes its way north along the Prahova River from Sinaia to Predeal, just to the south of Braşov. Romania's kings, queens and dictators had summer residences along this 48km stretch, renowned today for skiing and hiking. To the west are the stunning Bucegi Mountains, whose 326.63 sq km of hiker's paradise are protected as the Bucegi Natural Park. Straddling them is the Făgăraş chain, which dominates the region between Braşov and Sibiu.

BRAŞOV

☎ 268 / pop 308,600

After Bucharest, which most tourists visit by default, Braşov is the most-visited city in Romania. It's already become the Prague of Romania, the Krakow of Transylvania, and attracts a bohemian crowd looking for cheap beer and cool hang-outs in a relaxed Saxon setting, hiking and sports enthusiasts wanting a comfy urban base for terrific nature excursions, and architecture and history buffs. They collide mainly in the compact old town, a blend of centuries-old Saxon houses and trendy chill-out bars, a time-defying space where cobblestone meets chrome in a heady mix.

Established on an ancient Dacian site at the beginning of the 13th century by Teutonic Knights, today's Braşov is a shining testimony of Saxon architectural splendour and a favoured base of tourists who appreciate its proximity to mountains and castles. Many, however, find that Braşov has become too tourist-savvy and after a few days head to less 'discovered' places.

Braşov started as a German mercantile colony named Kronstadt (Brassó in Hungarian). Located at the junction of three principalities, it became a major medieval trading centre. The Saxons built ornate churches and town houses, protected by a massive wall that still remains. The Romanians lived at Schei, just outside the walls to the southwest.

One of the first public oppositions to the Ceauşescu government flared here in 1987. Thousands of disgruntled workers took to the streets demanding basic foodstuffs. Ceauşescu called in the troops and three people were killed in the supression.

Piaţa Sfatului, the central square, is the finest in the country, lined with baroque facades and outdoor cafés. It's the shining face of modern Braşov, which since the revolution has reinvented itself as Romania's trump card.

Orientation

Str Republicii, Braşov's pedestrian-only promenade, is crowded with shops and cafés. At its northern end is B-dul Eroilor, with museums and hotels; the boulevard also links two other main thoroughfares, Str Mureşenilor to its west and Str Nicolae Bălcescu to its east. The train station is 3km northeast of the town centre.

Mt Tâmpa looms over the town to the southeast.

MAPS & PUBLICATIONS

Though not up to its usual standards, Amco's *Braşov City Plan* (€1.90) is what you'll have to settle with. It includes maps of Poiana Braşov and Predeal. The fold-up

---

FROM BRAŞOV WITH LOVE

Between 1950 and 1960, when Romania still considered itself Moscow's buddy, Braşov was named 'Oraşul Stalin', with the Russian dictator's name emblazoned into the side of Mt Tâmpa thanks to artistic deforestation. At the time, the name was sadly apt, as ruthless, forced industrialisation yanked thousands of rural workers from the countryside and plunked them into the city in an attempt to crank the totalitarian motor of industry.

Braşov Ghid Turistic şi Comercial (€1.25) has great maps of surrounding towns and villages such as Râsnov and Cristian.

The multilingual *What, Where, When Braşov* city guide is published every two months and is available free from most hotels. The free, biweekly Romanian magazine *Zile şi Nopţi* (Days and Nights; www .zilesinopti.ro, in Romanian), found in bars and cafés, is worth picking up for the most up-to-date listings.

Information

A good start to your trip to Braşov is a look at www.brasov.ro.

BOOKSHOPS

These all have a selection of maps, souvenir photo books and some English-language texts. They are generally open from 9am to 6pm Monday to Friday and from 10am to 5pm on Saturday.

Librărie Aldus (☎ 452 556; Str Apollonia Hirscher 4)
Librărie George Coşbuc (☎ 444 395; Str Republicii 29)
Librărie Universitas (☎ 442 306; Piaţa Sfatului 5)

CULTURAL CENTRES

Alliance Française (☎ 419 338; B-dul Eroilor 25; ✆ 9am-5pm Mon, Wed & Fri, 1-8pm Tue & Thu)
British Council (☎ 474 214; B-dul Eroilor 33; ✆ 9am-8pm Mon-Fri)
German Democratic Forum (☎ 511 614; Str Gheorghe Băiulescu 2; ✆ 2-5pm Mon-Tue, 10am-noon Wed-Thu)

EMERGENCY

Salvamont (☎ 471 517; Str Varga 23) Call them to verify mountain weather conditions or in case of an emergency on the mountains; they'll come to the rescue at any time of the day.

INTERNET ACCESS

Blue Net Club (☎ 0740-839 449; Str Amata Romanas 26; per hr €0.40; ✆ 24hr)
Internet Club (☎ 0722-657 005; Sfântu Ioan 28; per hr €0.30; ✆ 9am-11pm)

MEDICAL SERVICES

Aurofarm (☎ 443 560; Str Republicii 27; ✆ 24hr)
EuroFarmacie (☎ 411 248; Str Republicii 19; ✆ 7.30am-9pm Mon-Fri, 8am-2pm Sat) This is one of the best-stocked in town.

MONEY

There is a 24-hour exchange office inside the train station, and many others (along with numerous ATMs) along B-dul Eroilor, along Str Republicii and throughout the centre. **Banca Comercială Română** (Piaţa Sfatului 14; ✆ 8.30am-5pm Mon-Fri, 8.30am-noon Sat) changes travellers cheques and gives cash advances on Visa/MasterCard.

POST & TELEPHONE

The **central post office** (☎ 411 609; Str Iorga Nicolae 1; ✆ 7am-8pm Mon-Fri, 8am-1pm Sat) is opposite the Heroes' Cemetery. The main **telephone centre** (B-dul Eroilor; ✆ 7am-7pm) is between the Capitol and Aro Palace Hotels.

TOURIST INFORMATION

There are no tourist offices in Braşov so you have to rely on travel agencies and tour operators, but luckily there are several good ones in town.

Aventours (☎ 0722-746 262; www.discoveromania .ro) and **Roving România** (☎ 0744-212 065; www .roving-romania.co.uk) These two share an office at Str Paul Richter 1 (☎ 472 718; ✆ no set office hours) and can provide indispensable information. Their speciality is small-group, tailor-made tours to off-the-beaten-track parts of Romania, led by English-speaking experts. Famous for their 4x4 jeep tours of remote mountainous regions and bucolic villages, they can also set you up on a day tour in the vicinity of Braşov.

Aro-Palace (☎ 478 800; www.aro-palace.ro; Str Mureşenilor 12; ✆ 8am-5pm Mon-Fri, 9am-2pm Sat) In the hotel of the same name, this company organises similar tours, but its service costs more and is less personal.

Coroana (☎ 444 630; Str Republicii 62; ✆ 9am-6pm Mon-Sat, 9am-2pm Sat) Adjoining the hotel of the same name, the office may seem a tad ramshackle, but the staff are a super-friendly, nonpushy bunch who can help with accommodation and set up tours to Bran and Râsnov (€30), and up the fabulous Transfăgărăşan road (see p114), including hiking and a cable-car trip (€90).

Sights

PIAŢA SFATULUI

This sprawling square is the heart of medieval Braşov. In the centre stands the **council house** (Casa Sfatului), from 1420, topped by a **Trumpeter's Tower**, in which town councillors, known as centurions, would meet. This old city hall today houses the **Braşov Historical Museum** (☎ 472 363; adult/child €0.50/0.25;

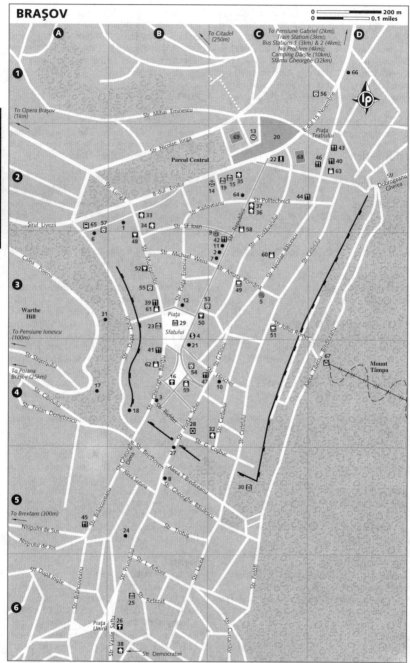

BRAŞOV

To Citadel
(250m)

To Pensiune Gabriel (2km);
Train Station (3km);
Bus Stations 1 (3km) & 2 (4km);
No Problem (4km);
Camping Dârste (10km);
Sfântu Gheorghe (32km)

To Opera Braşov
(1km)

Str Mihai Eminescu

Str Nicolae Iorga

Parcul Central

Piaţa
Teatrului

Str Dobrogeanu
Gherea

B-dul Eroilor

Str Lungă

Str Sadoveanu

Str Politechnicii

Şirul Livezii

Str Sf Ioan

Calea Poienii

Str Muresenilor

Str Michael Weiss

Str Amata Română

Warthe
Hill

Piaţa
Enescu

To Pensiune Ionescu
(100m)

Piaţa
Sfatului

Str Nicolae Bălcescu

Str Castelului

To Poiana
Braşov (25km)

Str Stejerisului

Str Dupa Ziduri

Str Gheorghe Bariţiu

Str Cerbului

Str Julius Römer

Str Cibiului

Str Traian Demetrescu

Aleea Tiberiu Brediceanu

Mount
Tâmpa

Str Castelului

Hirscher

Str G Dima

Str Richter

Str Poarta Scheii

Str G Coşbuc

Str Gheorghe
Dima

Str Beethoven

Aleea T Brediceanu

Aleea Saturn

Str Gheorghe Bălulescu

To Brextans (300m)

Str Brâncoveanu

Nisipului de Sus

Nisipului de Jos

Str Trotuş

Str Vasile Saftu

Str După Iniste

Str Brâncoveanu

Str Prundului

Str I Arbore

Str Lacea

Str Petofi

Str Ciocrlanilor

Retezat

Piaţa
Unirii

Str Democraţiei

0   200 m
0   0.1 miles

TRANSYLVANIA

(✆ 10am-6pm Tue-Sun), in which the history of the Saxon guilds is recounted.

Opposite is the Renaissance **Hirscher House** (built 1539–45), also known as the 'Merchants House'. It was thoughtfully built by Apollonia Hirscher, the widow of Braşov mayor Lucas Hirscher, so that merchants could do business without getting rained on. Today it shelters the Cerbul Carpaţin restaurant (p92). On the square's western side stands the charming **Mureşenilor House Memorial Museum** (Muzeul Memorial Casa Mureşenilor; ☎ 477 864; admission €0.15; ✆ 9am-3pm Mon-Fri), which honours the family of Jacob Mureşan, the first editor of the *Gazeta Transylvania*, a political newspaper published in the 19th century. There's a touching collection of personal letters and objects.

Braşov's main landmark is the **Black Church** (Biserica Neagră; adult/child €1/0.50; ✆ 10am-5pm Mon-Sat, mass 10am Sun), the largest Gothic church between Vienna and Istanbul and still used by German Lutherans today. Built between 1383 and 1477, it looms forebodingly just south of the square. Its name comes from its appearance after a fire in 1689. The original statues on the exterior of the apse are now inside and some 120 fabulous Turkish rugs (gifts from merchants who returned from shopping sprees in the southern Ottoman lands) hang from the balconies. Considering it's a Lutheran church, it is

incredibly picturesque. Worshippers drop coins through the wooden grates in the floor and hope for the best.

The church's organ, built by Buchholz of Berlin in 1839, has 4000 pipes and is believed to be the only Buchholz preserved in its original form. Since 1891, organ recitals have been held in the church throughout July and August, at 6pm on Tuesday, Thursday and Saturday (€1.50). Equally impressive is the church's bell; weighing in at seven tonnes, it's the largest in Romania.

OLD TOWN
Northeast of the square, the pedestrianised Str Republicii provides respite from the traffic that detracts from the charm of the rest of the Old Town. Along and around this street you'll find boutiques, restaurants, bakeries and the occasional gem, such as the **Kron Art Gallery** (see p93), an enchanting space hosting changing exhibits. At the promenade's northern end is a **memorial wooden cross** commemorating victims of the December 1989 revolution. In the **Heroes' Cemetery** opposite, a memorial slab lists those who died.

Head west to B-dul Eroilor, where the **Art Museum** (☎ 444 384; B-dul Eroilor 21; adult/child €0.40/0.20; ✆ 10am-6pm Tue-Sun) and the **Ethnographic Museum** (☎ 443 990; B-dul Eroilor 21; adult/child €0.40/0.20; ✆ 10am-6pm Tue-Sun) adjoin each other.

The former has a permanent pottery and decorative arts exhibition, a national art gallery of Romanian paintings from the 18th century to contemporary times, and temporary exhibitions. Silver crafted in Braşov during the 16th century, fur and sheepskin coats, Saxon cloth costumes and Romanian girdles are among the exhibits in the ethnographic museum, which also has an excellent selection of souvenirs and crafts for sale.

ALONG THE DEFENSIVE WALL

The western section of the defensive wall begins south of B-dul Eroilor along Str După Ziduri. Built in the 15th century as protection against the Turks, it was 12m high and 3km long. Part of this medieval wall remains, though most was taken down in the 19th century to allow for the city's expansion. Seven bastions were also raised around the city at the most exposed points, each one defended by a guild whose members, pending danger, tolled their bastion bell. The **Blacksmiths' Bastion** (Bastionul Fierarilor) is at the southern end of Str După Ziduri. To the west of the wall lie the **Black Tower** (Turnul Neagru) and the **White Tower** (Turnul Alba).

Follow the city wall southeast, past **Catherine's Gate** (Poarta Ecaterinei), built in 1559 (the only original medieval city gate to survive intact), and the **Schei Gate** (Poatra Schei), built in 1828, to the 16th-century **Weavers' Bastion** (Bastionul Țesătorilor; Str Castelui). Visit the **Weavers' Bastion Museum** (Muzeul Bastionul Țesătorilor; ☎ 472 368; adult/child €0.40/0.20; ☯ 10am-4pm Tue-Sun), with a fascinating scale model of 17th-century Braşov created in 1896.

Above the Weavers' Bastion is a pleasant promenade through the forest overlooking Braşov. Halfway along is the **Tâmpa cable car** (Telecabina Tâmpa; ☎ 443 732; adult/child return €0.80/0.40; ☯ 10am-6pm Tue-Fri, 10am-7pm Sat-Sun), offering stunning views from the top of Mt Tâmpa.

Braşov's original defensive fortress was built on this mount, but when Vlad Țepeş attacked Braşov (1458–60), the citadel was dismantled and 40 merchants were impaled on top of Mt Tâmpa. You can hike to the top following zigzag trails from the cable-car station (one hour, red triangles) or from Aleea Brediceanu opposite Le Bastion café

(yellow triangles). It's worth the extra beads of sweat for the view, and remember, those poor merchants had a much tougher time on the mountain!

In 1524 a new wooden **citadel** (Cetate; ☎ 417 614; admission free; ☯ 11am-midnight) was built in Braşov, on top of Citadel Hill, though the stone wall ruins you now see are from the 16th and 17th centuries. Today the citadel houses two good beer patios, a so-so disco and an expensive restaurant. Steps lead up to it from Str Nicolae Iorga, on the north side of Heroes' Cemetery. It's also accessible by car.

SCHEI DISTRICT

In Saxon Braşov, Romanians were not allowed to enter the walled city but were banished to the Schei quarter in the southwest. Entry to this quarter from the walled city was marked by the **Schei Gate** (Str Porta Schei). Passing through it, the sober rows of Teutonic houses change to the small, simpler houses of the Romanian settlement. Almost immediately to the east you come to **Str Storii**, the narrowest street in Braşov. Further south along Str Prundului is the first **Romanian lyceum**, which opened in Braşov in 1850 and was where the first Romanian opera, *Crai Nou* (New Moon), written by Ciprian Porumbescu (1853–83), was performed in 1882.

Continue south to Piața Unirii and the black-spired Orthodox **St Nicholas' Cathedral** (St Nicolae din Scheii; ☯ 6am-9pm), first built in wood in 1392 and replaced with a stone church in 1495 by the Wallachian prince Neagoe Basarab (r. 1512–21), who supported the Romanian community in Saxon-dominated Transylvania. In 1739 the church was enlarged and its interior heavily embellished. Beside the church is the first **Romanian School Museum** (1495; ☎ 443 879; adult/child €0.40/0.20; ☯ 9am-5pm Tue-Sun), which is more interesting than it sounds. This was for centuries one of the few centres of learning for the Romanian people; a printing press that opened here in 1556 produced some of the first books written in Romanian.

Activities

Hire a helicopter for an aerial twirl of Braşov. Call **Brextrans** (☎ 443 666; Str Dealul Spirii 52). The downside? It's €400 an hour for up to eight people.

BACHELOR PARTY – ROMANIAN STYLE

The first Sunday in May is a swinging time to be in Braşov, especially for single men...for purely sociological reasons, of course. Those without dirty minds read on...

A centuries-old tradition, the **Juni Pageant** (Sărbătoarea junilor), still colourfully unfolds through the streets of Schei. Groups of single young men don traditional Schei armour and, sword in hand, ride from Piaţa Unirii, through the Schei Gate, to Piaţa Sfatului, followed by the married men. The parade ends up on Mt Tâmpa for several hours of energetic folk dancing. During Saxon domination, this was the one day of the year Romanians were allowed to enter the walled city. The costumes worn by the young men are incredibly detailed, ornate and elaborate, some over a century old and weighing several kilograms from the beads and silver jewellery sewn into them. The tradition was not meant to ensure that the single men found potential brides, but one can imagine how many trial runs were enacted as the party wound down.

Braşov is a good base for biking, trekking, skiing and climbing in the Carpathians. See the Activities chapter (p39) for excellent Braşov-based organisations and guides.

Festivals & Events

Beyond the fantastic Juni Pageant (see the boxed text above), Braşov proudly hosts other events, including the International Chamber Music Festival, which is usually held the first week in July in various venues around town, with a final concert at Bran Castle.

In August an International Photographic Art Exhibition is hosted at the Art Museum, and in early October Piaţa Sfatului gets raucous and sudsy during a one-week International Beer Festival – another goodie.

December welcomes the beautiful De la Colind la Stea (From the Carol to the Star) music festival. Choirs and theatre groups from various countries perform traditional Christmas carols and nativities. The four-day festival is usually held in the Sică Alexandrescu Drama Theatre.

Sleeping

BUDGET

Maria and Grig Bolea (☎ 311 962) This pair is hard to miss at the train station, even if you try; they meet almost every train. Maria is an institution unto herself in Braşov and she now has an international reputation. She's so famous that she even has impersonators, fake Marias running after tourists trying to take them into their homes. Half of our reader's letters praise her helpfulness and say she made their stay marvellous. The other half complain about her pushy, domineering ways and warn to steer clear.

She places tourists in private homes (€10 per person), some of which can be winners, others not so great. You takes your risks!

Kismet Dao Villa (☎ 514 296; www.elvisvilla.com /brasov; Str Democraţiei 2B; bed €10-11, d €26) This is one of the country's finest hostels: well organised, spotless, modern and well located (behind Piaţa Unirii). Staff have a good sense of humour and know how to keep spirits high (all guests get a free beer). Dorm rooms have from five to nine beds. Take Bus No 4 from the train station to the last stop.

Pensiune Ionescu (☎ 473 091; annabrasov@yahoo .com; Str Stejerişului 16; s/d €13/19) You feel like you're in the country here, in a lovely spot overlooking the city, though it's just a steep 10-minute walk up cobblestoned Str Cibinului from the Old Town. Each visitor gets a separate cabin in the sprawling garden, so you never feel like you're living in someone else's home. Breakfast is not included. An excellent choice.

Pensiune Gabriel (☎ 0744-844 223; Str Toamnei 4, B11 Sc et1 ap1; per person €13) This comes recommended by a number of our readers. A 10-minute walk northeast of the centre, the place is clean and friendly and the owner super-helpful, often driving guests to Bran and other places.

Hotel Aro Sport (☎ 442 840; Str Sfântu Ioan 3; s/d €9/12) Don't listen to what locals say about this hotel. It has a nasty reputation but is surprisingly pleasant for a bare-bones budget hotel. The shared washrooms are spotless and spacious, and rooms are tiny but quite decent.

Hotel Postăvarul (☎ 477 448; fax 418 469; Str Republicii 62; s/d/t with shared bathroom €13/18/27) This one-star behemoth is not a bad option if you want to be in the centre of town.

AUTHOR'S CHOICE

Beke Guesthouse (☎ 511 997; Str Cerbului 32; per person €10) This is a true winner, run by Hungarian-speaking Magda and Alexandru Beke. There's a Mediterranean air to the liveliness of their courtyard, though the clean, inviting singles/doubles with shared bathroom are very peaceful. Each has a different feel to it, so check them out before making a choice. Some have separate entrances and their own (nearly antique) stoves. The Bekes are so lovely and genuinely sweet, you may feel compelled to give them a hug; if you do, you won't have been the first. Breakfast is not included.

Situated in a 1910 building with old-world granduer, the rooms on offer are unmemorable and the lower floors can be subject to noise from the casino below.

Camping Dârste (☎ 259 080; Calea Bucureşti 285; tent space/hut €4/7) Just what you'd want in a camping ground: a location right on a busy, polluted road. This place, 10km southeast of the centre, is not particularly recommended.

MID-RANGE

Hotel Coroana (☎ 477 448; fax 418 469; Str Republicii 62; s/d/t with private bathroom €38/53/72) Located in the same building as the Postăvarul, the two-star Coroana has rooms with private bathroom that seem a bit expensive for what's on offer.

Hotel Capitol (☎ 418 920; fax 472 999; B-dul Eroilor 19; s/d €56/72; 🕸) How does a a three-star high-rise relic from the 1960s get away with high prices when it offers little to justify them? A central location perhaps?

TOP END

Hotel Aro Palace (☎ 478 800; www.aro-palace.ro; Str Mureşenilor 12; s/d/ste €83/107/117; 🕸) This is impressive mainly for its Art Deco facade facing Parcul Central. Plush rooms feature nice touches such as cable TV, phone and fridge; credit cards are accepted.

Eating

RESTAURANTS

La Republique (☎ 0744-351 668; Str Republicii 33; mains €0.50-3; 🕑 9am-midnight) Being one of the most pleasant places on the pedestrian strip makes it worth a visit. That it is a creperie

already makes it unique (both meat-filled and dessert crepes are delicious); the friendly service and fresh coffee complete the picture nicely.

Pizza Roma (☎ 411 835; Str Apollonia Hirscher 2; pizzas €1.75-3; 🕑 11am-1am) Just off the main square, this place only serves pizzas, but they're the best in town, thin-crust and delicious. For dessert there are many icecream and *gelato* dishes.

Ischia Tour (☎ 478 693; Str George Bariţu 2; mains €2.50-4; 🕑 10am-midnight) Decorated to give the impression of being in an Italian village, this charming place has some Romanian dishes on its extensive menu, but you'd best go with its specialties such as lasagna and fish dishes. It's the kind of place you feel like lounging about in for hours.

Pepper Jack's (☎ 417 614; Str Brâncoveanu 38; mains €3-6) This is a rather pricey Mexican-Romanian restaurant just south of the centre. The Transylvanian section in its cellar has some tasty (and cheaper) options, and the burritos hit the spot.

Cerbul Carpaţin (Carpathian Stag; ☎ 443 981; Piaţa Sfatului 12; mains €3-6; 🕑 10am-midnight) Braşov's most famous restaurant is located in the Hirscher House (1545). Romanian dishes are the highlight here, though the restaurant's interiors (a marble staircase, elegant wine cellar) get more raves than the food. Some nights there's live folk music.

Cetate Braşov (☎ 417 614; mains €3-6; Dealul Cetăţii) The bird's-eye view of Braşov might aid digestion of the so-so food on offer. It's housed within the walls of the old fortress, and its labyrinthine interior is an experience in itself. Chamber-music recitals and folk dances are regularly held in the medieval saloon for unenthusiastic crowds of German tourists.

QUICK EATS

Cofetăria Modern (Str Mureşenilor 1) While not as modern as the name would suggest, this cafeteria sells items running the full range from cakes and pastries to potato chips and chocolate bars.

Old Centre Bistro (☎ 419 100; Str Nicolas Bălcescu 67; meals €2-3; 🕑 10am-midnight) This is a decent option for a quick bite; its specialities are cold platters and standard fast food.

Poiana Soarelui (🕑 7am-10pm Mon-Fri, 8am-9pm Sat, 8am-2pm Sun) This is your best bet for divine pastries, cakes and croissants. If you can resist the smell here, you just aren't human.

SELF-CATERING

The fruit and vegetable market is at the northern end of Str Nicolae Bălcescu. Next to the market is the handy **Luca Supermarket** (☉ 24hr).

Drinking

CAFES

Kron Art Café (☎ 474 157; Str Postăvarului 18; ☉ 9am-9pm) It serves only speciality coffees and teas, but what better place for an espresso than surrounded by antiques, sculptures, paintings and other works of art in what is primarily an art gallery. It's worth inquiring about the occasional concert evenings it hosts.

Rex Café (☎ 473 591; Str Castelului 58) Just off the main drag, this is a good place for an iced cappuccino and some light snacks.

PUBS & BARS

Festival 39 (☎ 478 664; Str Mureşenilor 23; ☉ 10-1am) By far, this is the best bar in town for a relaxed drink. It manages to pull off both a lively and subdued atmosphere at the same time: the clientele seem surreally happy and the staff are gregarious, but the brick walls, soft music, dozens of candles and antiques have a soothing effect that makes you feel like moving in for a while. Speciality cocktails cost €1.50 to €3.

Saloon (☎ 477 317; Str Mureşenilor; ☉ 11-2am) While its attempt to outdo the Wild West (can you say 'more Catholic than the Pope'?) is mildly amusing, this is a great place to pull off your cowboy boots and relax. Rock and blues (and sometimes country) fills the air.

Opium (☎ 0788-331 415; Str Republicii 2) Swanky and sexy, this is the city's premier lounge bar, with its deep-red velvet decor, couches, dim lights, emphasis on cocktails and a spacey mix of acid jazz and deep house.

Entertainment

CINEMAS

Braşov has several cinemas, the most central of which is the **Royal** (☎ 419 965; Str Mureşenilor 7).

CLUBS

Most discos charge varying entry fees, usually from €1 to €2, and mainly on weekends. Clubs are busier outside of summer when students are back in town and in need of action.

No Problem (☎ 311 934; B-dul Saturn 32) As the city's premier pick-up joint, its name is no doubt the appropriate answer to one of the frequent propositions heard here. Hugely popular, this disco is northeast of the centre. Take a taxi there (€1.50).

Aquarium (☎ 418 850; Piaţa Teatrului 1) This is another popular disco, located within the Sică Alexandrescu Drama Theatre (see the following section). It's a three-floor emporium, comprising a restaurant with decent international cuisine, a shaded terrace for lounging and, of course, the sweaty dance floor on the third floor.

Student Culture House (Casa de Cultură Studenteasca; ☎ 443 900; B-dul Eroilor 29) Next to the Transylvania University, this hosts everything from discos to drama. Performances by the Student English Theatre Club (Clubul de Teatru în Engleză) are occasionally held here.

Grădina de Vară is an open-air disco sometimes held on summer weekends up on the hill in the citadel. It's popular with both teens and tourists.

OPERA & BALLET

The **Gheorghe Dima State Philharmonic** (☎ 441 378; Str Apollonia Hirscher 10) has a good reputation and performs mainly between September and May, as does the **Opera Braşov** (☎ 415 990; Bisericii Române 51), which stages mainly classics. Tickets for theatrical, classical music and ballet performances can be purchased at the **Agenţie de Teatrală** (☎ 471 889; Str Republicii 4), just off Piaţa Sfatului.

THEATRE

Sică Alexandrescu Drama Theatre (☎ 418 850; Piaţa Teatrului 1) has plays, recitals, and opera year-round, while the **Puppet Theatre** (Teatrul de Păpuşi Arlechino; ☎ 442 873; Str Apollonia Hirscher 10) stages creative shows for kids.

Shopping

One of the best selections of souvenirs can be found at the Ethnographic Museum (see p89).

Galerie de Artă (Str Mureşenlior 1) It sells modern art as well as ceramics and glass works.

Artizana (Str Republicii 48) Offerings here include traditional folk costumes, rugs and sculptures.

TRANSYLVANIA

Ascent (☎ 477 855; www.ascent.ro in Romanian; Piaţa Sfatului 17) This is a superb sports store and has water bottles, whistles, boots, maps and anything else you might need for hiking. It can hook you up with personal mountain guides too.

Sport Virus (☎ 418 115; Str Gheorghe Bariţiu 24) There is a smaller selection of sportswear and gear here, but it's quality stuff.

Star (☉ 9am-8.30pm Mon-Fri, 9am-7pm Sat) This is the central department store of Braşov.

Doua Roti (☎ 470 207; Str Nicolae Bălcescu 55; ☉ 8am-4.30pm Mon-Fri) It sells used bikes and parts, and does repairs.

Getting There & Away
TRAIN
Advance tickets are sold at the **Agenţie de Voiaj CFR office** (☎ 470 696; Str Republicii 53; ☉ 8am-6pm Mon-Fri, 9am-1pm Sat). International tickets can also be purchased in advance from **Wasteels** (☎ 424 313; www.wasteelstravel.ro), in the main hall of the **train station** (☎ 410 233).

Braşov is well connected to Mangalia/Constanţa (four per day), Sighişoara (€5, four per day), Cluj-Napoca (€8, four per day) and Oradea (one per day) by fast trains. Local trains to/from Sinaia run frequently. There are 10 trains to Sibiu (€5.50, 2½–3¾ hours), all stopping at Fagaraş (one hour), with one extra personal train to Fagaraş taking 1½ hours. There are 18 trains to/from Bucharest (three to four hours), including the Pannonia Expres and the Ister, which go to Prague (10½ hours) and Budapest (11 hours), respectively, and the Dacia, which runs to Vienna (15 hours).

The left-luggage office (open 24 hours) is located in the underpass that leads out from the tracks.

BUS
It's not hard to get anywhere from Braşov, especially by maxitaxi (minibus). The hard part, as usual, is finding the schedules; Braşov is a particular case in point (see p348).

Most maxitaxis leave from **Autogară 1** (☎ 426 882), next to the train station. There are maxitaxis to Bucharest every half-hour from 6am to 7.30pm, plus hourly maxitaxis on a Târgu Mureş–Sighişoara–Braşov–Buşteni–Bucharest route. Two maxitaxis a day head to Bistriţa via Târgu Mureş, and two head to Constanţa via Slobozia. There

are at least five maxitaxis to Fagaraş en route to Sibiu, and three per day to Galaţi and Braila. Regular bus services include one per day to Iaşi, Gheorgheni, Miercurea Ciuc, Piatra Neamţ, Târgu Neamţ, Târgu Mureş and Sfântu Gheorghe; and two to Târgovişte and Bacău.

Autogară 2 (☎ 426 332; Str Avram Iancu 114), west of the train station, has buses to Râşnov, Bran and Moieciu, marked 'Moieciu-Bran', every half-hour. Other major daily buses include one daily to Făgăraş Câmpulung and Curtea de Argeş, two to Piteşti, and eleven to Zărneşti.

Few buses use **Autogară 3** (☎ 333 173; Str Hărmanului 47A) in the east of the town.

The main bus stop in town is the 'Livada Poştei', at the western end of B-dul Eroilor in front of the County Library (Biblioteca Judeţeană). From here catch bus No 20 to Poiana Braşov (€0.50, every half-hour). Buy your ticket from the kiosk opposite the Student Culture House before boarding. Bus No 25 leaves every half-hour for Cristian.

There are no international bus routes handled by Romanian companies. All European routes are handled by **Eurolines** (☎ 424 313; ☉ 8am-9pm), which has an office inside the train station and sells tickets for buses to Germany, Italy, Hungary and other European destinations.

Getting Around
Bus No 4 runs from the train station and Autogară 1 into town, stopping at Piaţa Unirii in the centre. From Autogară 2, take bus No 12 or 22 from the 'Stadion Tineretului' stop on nearby Str Stadionului (turn right out of the station, walk to the end of the street) into the centre.

Avis (☎ 413 775) has an office inside Hotel Aro Palace. **Hertz** (☎ 471 485; B-dul 15 Noiembrie 56) is another option. Rental companies based in Bucharest will deliver cars to Braşov and other destinations for a fee.

You shouldn't have too much trouble finding honest taxis in Braşov, but it's best to call a reputable company like **Ro Taxi** (☎ 949 or 319 999) or **CCB** (☎ 414 141).

AROUND BRAŞOV
☎ 268
There are plenty of things to see and do around Braşov. As well as the Saxon fortresses of Prejmer, Hărman and Râşnov,

you can easily visit the mountain resort of Poiana Braşov or the over-touted Bran Castle in a day.

Prejmer & Hărman

Prejmer (Tartlau) is an unspoiled Saxon town, first settled in 1240, with a picturesque 15th-century **citadel** (admission free; ☼ 11am-5pm Tue-Fri, 9am-3pm Sat, 11am-5pm Sun) surrounding the 13th-century **Gothic Evangelical church** in its centre. The fortress was the most powerful peasant fortress in Transylvania. Its 272 small cells on four levels lining the inner citadel wall were intended to house the local population during sieges. Its outer defensive wall – 4.5m thick – is the thickest of all the remaining Saxon churches. These fortified churches are listed collectively as Unesco World Heritage sites.

Hărman (Honigburg – literally 'honey castle'), 7km from Prejmer, is a small Saxon village, also with a 16th-century peasant **citadel** at its centre. Inside the thick walls is a 52m weathered **clock tower** and a 15th-century **church** (admission by donation; ☼ 9am-noon & 1-5pm Tue-Sun). Ask for the key from the Burghüter (warden), a German-speaker who you can also hire to be your guide. Ring the bell on the left of the main door (look for the Bitte Läuten! sign). The colourful houses facing the main square are typical of the Saxon era, with large rounded doors and few windows. Like Prejmer, rural Hărman hasn't changed much since the 19th century.

GETTING THERE & AWAY

You'll save much time by taking a taxi to either Prejmer or Hărman from central Braşov (about €3).

There are 17 daily trains from Braşov to Hărman (€0.40, 15 minutes) and Ilieni (the station closest to Prejmer Citadel; €0.50, 22 minutes), destined for Târgu Mureş, Deva and Întorsura Buzăului.

As you arrive at Ilieni look for the tall tower of the citadel church, south of the railway line. Walk south on Str Nouă for about 500m, then left on Str Alexandru Ioan Cuza. Turn left at the end to reach Str Şcolii on the right. The citadel is straight ahead. From Hărman's station, either grab a cab to the centre or walk 200m northeast, turn right, cross the highway and continue straight for 2km to the centre of town.

From Braşov there are four daily buses to Premjer (€0.25, 25 minutes), with two extra services Saturday and Sunday.

Râşnov

Many who poke around the castle ruins of Râşnov's 13th-century hilltop **fortress** (Cetatea Râşnov; ☎ 230 255; adult/child €1.20/0.80, parking €0.25; ☼ 8am-5pm Tue-Sun) feel they are more dramatic and less touristy than Bran's castle. Râşnov is certainly a memorable experience, and gives a good feel of what life inside castle walls must have been like. The stunning panoramic views of the surrounding plains towards the Piatra Craiului mountains are alone worth the trip.

The fortress was built by the Teutonic Knights as protection against Tartar, and later Turkish, invasions. Indeed, almost immediately after its completion, the fortress suffered its first Tartar attack in 1335. The fortress remained functional until 1850, when it was abandoned for ruin.

AROUND BRAŞOV

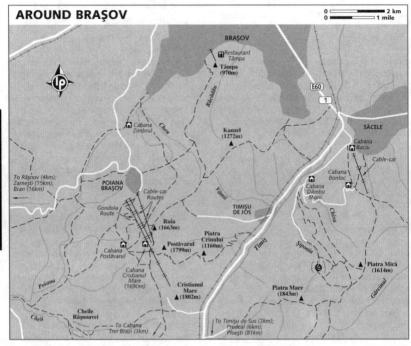

Visitors can wander around the grounds, church, chapel, weapons tower and jail and peer down the 146m-deep well, dug by two Turkish prisoners who were promised freedom once it was completed (it took them 17 years!). Peeking into alleyways, peering around corners and freely wandering around the ruins are the main pleasures here – kids of all ages will love exploring. There are rooms with exhibits and places to grab a snack, and many of the buildings are in the midst of a long restoration process.

The town itself is worth a gander. While undeniably run-down, it exudes old-world charm with its small houses sitting on dirt roads (no concrete apartment blocks around). It has preserved its look and feel of a century ago.

SLEEPING & EATING

A number of houses near the central square have *cazare* (rooms for rent) signs in their windows. The one hotel of note in town doesn't warrant much noting.

Hotel Cetate (☎ 230 266; d with private bathroom €18) Located below the castle on the road to Poiana Braşov and about 2km from the bus stop to/from Braşov, this dreary hotel is open year-round and has a restaurant.

Camping Valea Cetăţii (☎ 230 266; cabins €5.25) Adjoining the Hotel Cetate, this camping ground is open from June to August.

GETTING THERE & AWAY

Buses marked 'Bran-Moieciu' leave every half-hour from Braşov's Autogară 2 for both Râşnov (40 minutes) and Bran (one hour).

From the bus stop in Râşnov, walk 100m east towards the mountains, turn right at Piaţa Unirii and watch for the hillside stairs in the courtyard of the unmarked Casa de Cultură (on your left). The castle is a 15-minute walk uphill. A second entry route leads from a road between the camping ground and Hotel Cetate.

POIANA BRAŞOV

☎ 268

Poiana Braşov (1030m), on the slopes of Postăvarul Massif in the southern Carpathians, is Romania's premier ski resort. Unlike its sister resort of Sinaia, 'Braşov's Clearing' offers few challenges for advanced skiers. But the beauty of this intermediate resort lies in its sheltered, forested location which guarantees good skiing between early December and mid-March. Some years, you can ski here as late as May. In summer take the cable car to the top of Mt Postăvarul (1802m) for a panoramic view of Braşov and the surrounding Carpathians.

The newly built **St Ivan Butezatorul church** (Str Valea Dragă) in the centre is done in the Maramureş style (presumably for ski tourists who won't make it that far), made entirely of wood and with a tall spire, looking particularly striking against its mountain backdrop.

Orientation

The main road that runs through town from Braşov is called Str Poiana Soarelui, at the southern end of which is the cablecar station (Staţie Telecabină). At the very centre of town is the unmistakable Capra Neagră restaurant and casino. Just north of here Str Poiana Ursului (the so-called 'old road' to Braşov) branches off to the northeast, heading towards the Complex Favorit (a commercial centre that has all but fallen to ruins but is slated for major renovations) and the main car park, where the central bus stop is located. The first bus stop from Braşov lets people off on Str Poiana Soarelui just north of Str Poiana Ursului; this is a more convenient starting point.

Information

The local **Salvamont** (☎ 286 176; Cabana Cristianul Mare) will come to the rescue any time of the day in case of emergency. There is no tourist information office in Pioana Braşov, but hotels compete in terms of the information and services they offer, so it pays to shop around. The best ski school in town is run by the **Ana Group** (☎ 407 330), which owns the Sport, Bradul and Poiana hotels.

Sleeping

Most travel agencies in Braşov take bookings for hotels in Poiana Braşov. Except for a couple of weeks over Christmas and New Year, you can always find a room at the resort. Note that many hotels raise their prices considerably between December and mid-March, some almost doubling them. Prices listed here are for the off

season. Generally, the lower-end hotels (with doubles under €30) do not raise their prices at all.

To get to the cheap end of the resort, follow Str Poiana Ursului away from the centre. It's worth wandering around there for a while and checking places out yourself.

BUDGET

Cabana Cristianul Mare (☎ 486 545; beds €5) At 1690m is this large wooden chalet with an attached restaurant overlooking the slopes. It's open throughout the year except for a few weeks in November.

Cabana Postăvarul (☎ 312 448; beds €5) At 1585m (15 minutes downhill), this one gets fewer tourists and so is a bit more relaxed.

Poiana Ursului (☎ 262 216; Str Poiana Ursului; d with shared bathroom €15) Just opposite the main car park/bus stop, this is a cheap, though shabby, option. On site is a very small, very sad 'zoo'.

Perched on the hill above town, off the road to Braşov, are numerous low- and high-end options. Following the turn-off to Râsnov and Bran then veering left onto Str Poiana Doamnei brings you to several good places.

Hotel Caraiman (☎ 262 208; Str Poiana Doamnei; s/d €17/22) This is a good mid-sized option, with 66 decent rooms. Mountain bikes are rented out here.

MID-RANGE

Hotel Alpin (☎ 262 380; www.hotelalpin.ro; Str Poiana Doamnei; s €37-46, d €49-75, ste €115; ☒ ☒) It's hard not to notice this hotel towering over its little hill, peeking through the trees at the lower town. The good news is that the hotel is a full-service centre, has a large pool and decent rooms, offers free ski rental, does not raise prices in the wintertime and is open to bargaining on prices (for multiplenight stays, for example). The less good news is that this is a large hotel (125 rooms) and has a sterile, impersonal feel to it.

Vila Diana (☎ 262 040; Str Poiana Ruia; s/d/ste €45/55/65; ☒) Somehow this large, rusticlooking bungalow manages to be thoroughly modern, classy and cosy. Beds are large enough for a game of softball and most rooms have private balconies. There's an on-site sauna, and the hotel offers ski rental for guests. It's on the east side of Str Poiana Soarelui at the turn-off to Bran.

TRANSYLVANIA

Casa Viorel (☎ 262 431; Str Poiana lui Stechil; d €35-45, ste €55) This is among the resorts' nicest places to stay, hidden amid forest at the northeastern end of the resort (turn right after Hotel Poiana Ursului). It's run by the same enterprising couple who run Coliba Haiducilor (see below).

The luxurious Sport, Bradul and Poiana Hotels at the eastern end of the resort are owned by the Ana group (☎ 407 330; office@ anahotels.ro) – the **Poiana** has very comfy single/ double rooms for €56/75. The **Bradul**, hidden among trees, has equally cosy singles/ doubles for €61/85. **Hotel Sport**, wedged between the Poiana and Bradul, is the most exclusive of the three, with doubles/suites for €93/141 (€174/190 in ski season). Bikes can be rented here. The on-site nightclub Top Disco attracts an older crowd.

Eating
Coliba Haiducilor (Outlaws' Hut; ☎ 262 137; Str Drumul Sulinarului; mains €2-5) This unbeatable place is at the southern end of the resort near the cable-car station. It is beautifully decorated in traditional rustic style, and a fire burns in the hearth in wintertime while live folk bands play. There's even a mini 'museum' in which traditional weaving looms are displayed. The food is plentiful and wholesome.

Stâna (☎ 475 948; mains €2-4) It's a bit of a trek to get to, but worth every step and stumble along the way. A rustic restaurant housed on a sheep farm 1.3km along a dirt

track off the main road leading to Poiana Braşov (signposted 200m before entering town), it serves home-made cheese and other delectable products.

Capra Neagră (☎ 262 191; Str Poiana Soarelui; mains €1-3) Consider this as a last resort. It's a tacky restaurant-bar-casino-disco smack in the middle of town.

Getting There & Away
From Braşov, bus No 20 (€0.50, every 30 minutes) runs from the Livada Poştei bus stop, opposite the County Library at the western end of B-dul Eroilor, to Poiana Braşov.

BRAN
For many travellers, Bran, 30km south of Braşov, is their first or only glimpse of rural Romania. This gives a skewed vision of reality; not every village in the country shakes with the rumble of tourist buses and the rattle of Dracula key chains. Bran was the first part of Romania to be developed as a tourist hub in the 1960s. Many properties were never nationalised and cash was poured into the little village to make it the gold mine it is today. With its luxury villas kitted out with hot water and indoor plumbing, and tourist buses with German, French and Italian license plates clogging the streets, the town is far from representative.

Bran is nestled in a mountain pass between the Bucegi and Piatra Craiului

---

SKIING AT POIANA BRAŞOV

Poiana Braşov has only two black slopes (though each is over 2km in length) but guarantees good intermediate skiing (maximum drop 755m) from December to mid-March. This resort is popular with snowboarders, and has the best-developed boarding and downhill-ski school in the country. There is little off-piste skiing here. The longest run is almost 4km long, easy but very scenic. Overall there are 12 runs, and the resort boasts three cable cars, one chairlift and eight drag lifts. Check out www.poiana-brasov.net for regular reports from skiers.

A gondola, stationed near Hotel Teleferic, takes you up to Cristianul Mare (1802m). Cable cars – one departing from next to the gondola station and the other from near Hotel Bradul – drop you off near Cabana Cristianul Mare (1690m; €3 return). Two of the more popular ski lifts are beyond the Hotel Poiana and are favoured by snowboarders for the slalom in the area.

A number of the hotels run ski schools, but the largest is run by the **Ana Group** (☎ 407 330). A six-day ski school, consisting of four hours' group tuition a day, costs €50/36 per adult/child (four-day course €24/17, five-day course €40/30). Private lessons are €12/20 for one/two adults an hour, and €8/14 for children. A three-day snowboarding course costs €24. Ski instructors speak English, German and French. Skis, poles, boots and snowboards can be hired through the ski school or at some hotels for about €10 a day.

HIKING AROUND POIANA BRAŞOV

The Postăvaru Massif nestles between the Cheii Valley, Timişului Valley and Poiana Braşov, and bristles with great hiking opportunities. There are dozens of trails of varying levels of difficulty to choose from.

From Poiana Braşov you can hike to Cristianul Mare (1802m, three hours, marked with red crosses), the massif's highest peak. From the top the trail leads down to the road which links Timişu de Jos (on the Sinaia–Braşov rail line) with Timişu de Sus (2½ hours, red triangles). Turn left for Jos, right for Sus.

You can also hike directly down to Timişu de Jos from Cabana Cristianul Mare in three to four hours. The trail is marked from the cabana with blue stripes, then blue crosses. Instead of following the blue-cross trail where the path diverges, you can continue following the blue-stripe trail which eventually takes you over the top of Mt Tâmpa to **Braşov**. This trail (1½ hours) follows the old Braşov road.

From Poiana Braşov you can also easily hike to **Râşnov** (two to three hours, blue stripes) or tackle the more strenuous hike to Predeal (five to seven hours, yellow stripes).

---

ranges, and during the 15th and 16th centuries was an important frontier town on the main road leading from Transylvania into Wallachia. Today tourists come for only one thing: to see the so-called Dracula's Castle and to stock up on Dracula T-shirts, mugs and ashtrays. Bran is also the end point of several daring hiking trails across the Bucegi mountains.

Orientation & Information
The centre of Bran lies either side of the main north–south Braşov–Piteşti road (Str Principală). The entrance to Bran Castle, signposted 'Muzeul Bran', is on the left as you enter the town from Braşov. The main cluster of shops, cafés and currency exchanges is centred on this junction.

The bus stop is just south of the junction on Str Principală, next to the park, on the other side of which is Str Aurel Stoian. The central post and telephone office is south of Bran centre, past the Vama Bran museum on the road to Moieciu. There's a 24-hour **Internet club** (Str Principală 504; per hr €0.26) right next to the sprawling souvenir market at the castle entrance.

A good organisation based here is **Centrul Agroturistic Bran** (☎ 238 308; www.turism-bran.ro; Str Principală 504). It mainly organises tours (taking in Râşnov and Braşov) but can suggest individual routes too.

Bran Castle
Despite popular myth, **Bran Castle** (adult/child €1.60/0.50; ☷ 9am-5.30pm Tue-Sun), most commonly known as 'Dracula's Castle', was not built

by Vlad Ţepeş, the 15th-century Wallachian prince upon whom the novelist Bram Stoker is (incorrectly) supposed to have based his vampire, Count Dracula. The castle, perched atop a 60m peak in the centre of Bran village, was in fact built by Saxons from Braşov in 1382 to defend the Bran pass against Turks. The closest the place comes to anything remotely connected with Dracula is that Vlad *might* have sought refuge here for a few nights on his flight from the Turks in 1462, following their attack on the Poienari fortress in the Argeş Valley (see p186). For real Dracula country, head north to Bistriţa (see p159).

From 1920 the castle was inhabited by Queen Marie and it remained a summer royal residence until the forced abdication of King Michael in 1947.

Bran Castle, with its fairytale turrets and Mediterranean whitewashed walls, is far from menacing. Many rooms have gone through a modern redecoration and look as if they are inhabited by rich eccentrics. Much of the original, fabulous furniture imported from Western Europe by Queen Marie is still inside the castle; indeed, these wonderful pieces are the highlight of any visit here. To appreciate the castle's nooks and crannies, arrive as early as possible, before the groups start parading through. A fountain in the courtyard conceals a labyrinth of secret underground passages.

Free guided tours of Bran Castle are available in English, French, Romanian and Italian. Your ticket for the castle includes entrance to the small open-air **ethnographic**

museum at the foot of the castle and the **Vama Bran Museum** (see the following section).

Around Bran Castle

From the castle, walk south along Str Principală past the centre of the village to the **Vama Bran Museum** (entry incl with Bran Castle admission; 9am-5.30pm Tue-Sun), housed in the former customs house. Various archaeological treasures as well as many photographs of the castle are displayed.

Opposite the former customs house are some remains of the old **defensive wall** which divided Transylvania from Wallachia (best viewed from the soldiers' watchtower in the castle). On the southern side of the wall is an endearingly petite stone **chapel**, built in 1940 in memory of Queen Marie. The church, now boarded up, is a copy of a church in the queen's palace grounds in Balcic, Bulgaria (formerly southern Dobrogea). A **memorial tomb** where the queen's heart lies has been carved in the mountain, on the north side of the wall.

Festivals & Events

September is the month of the Sâmbra Oilor, a pastoral festival celebrated with great gusto in Bran and its surrounding villages. To hang out and get ghoulish with US Peace Corps volunteers, arrive here at Halloween.

Sleeping

There is no shortage of places to stay in Bran – which also means that privacy and quiet are at a premium. Wandering around town, you'll see dozens of *cazare* signs in private homes, and there are at least 30 two- and three-star *pensiunes* (whole houses given over to tourists) plus a few hotels to choose from. See www.ruraltourism.ro for detailed descriptions of several *pensiunes* in Bran.

Antrec (236 884; Str Aureli Stoian 340; 9am-8pm) This outfit arranges accommodation in private homes in and around Bran. It's best to call in advance as the office is often closed, regardless of the stated office hours.

Cabana Bran Castel (236 404; dm €5) Just 600m from the castle, this place serves meals and is open year-round. From the bus stop, turn right along Str Principală then right along Str Aureli Stoian (or cut across the park instead); continue for 50m

and then turn left onto a narrow path by the side of the yellow-painted hospital. Cross the bridge over the stream and bear left up to the cabana.

Hanul Bran (236 556; Str Principală; d/tr €13/20) You get a private shower and toilet (hot water not guaranteed) but in ratty surroundings whose grungy corridors even Count Dracula would not have darkened. It's just two blocks north of the castle.

Vila Bran (236 866; vilabran@xnet.ro; Str Principală 238; s/d €15/23) Sublimely located in a picturesque orchard, where you can lounge and swing in hammocks, this two-building complex also has a billiard room and tennis court. Rooms are bright, comfy, snug and decorated with pine furniture. Farm animals complete the picture.

Popasul Reginei (236 834; Str Aureli Stoian 398; d €27) Rooms in this villa-style hotel are very comfortable. The restaurant is decidedly ho-hum but has the most varied menu in the village and is probably your best bet. There's an outdoor pool.

Eating

Aside from the Popasul Reginei (see above), there are a few pizzerias near the Vama Bran Museum, and several convenience stores on the main drag. However, nothing can beat the home-made cheese, jam, țuică (fruit brandy) and other culinary delights you will be treated to if you stay in a private home.

Getting There & Away

Buses marked 'Bran-Moeciu' (€0.50, one hour) depart every half-hour from Braşov's Autogară 2. Return buses to Braşov leave Bran every half-hour between 5.30am and 7.30pm Monday to Friday and between 6.40am and 5.40pm Saturday and Sunday. All buses to Braşov stop at Râşnov and Cristian.

From Bran there are also 11 buses daily to Zărneşti (€0.30, 40 minutes), and two to Piteşti originating from Braşov.

AROUND BRAN

Bran's surrounding villages are enchanting in their rural attractiveness. Modern luxury villas abound but the wild landscape remains untouched. Traditional occupations such as sheep farming, wool weaving and cheese making are vital to the villagers' daily survival. Agro-tourism is well developed and finding a bed is no problem.

Some 3km southeast along a dirt track from Bran is the village of **Şimon**, from where hiking trails lead into the Bucegi Mountains. **Moieciu de Jos**, 4km southwest of Bran on the road to Câmpulung, is known for its pine-aroma cheese, still religiously made by many families in the village. It celebrates a **summer festival** at the end of June. From Moieciu de Jos, a dirt track leads northwest to **Peştera**, named after the village's 160m-long cave said to be full of bats. From Peştera, it's an easy 6km ride/hike north through **Măgura** to **Zărneşti**.

A few kilometres southeast of Moieciu de Jos is **Cheia**, home to one of the region's few intact 19th-century painted churches. Wool has been manufactured in this village since the Middle Ages. Continuing south along the upper course of the Moieciu River, you reach **Moieciu de Sus**, with another pretty village church. Hiking trails into the **Bucegi Mountains** are marked from here.

Staggering views of the mountains unfold along the road signposted to Câmpulung, proffering a breathtaking panorama at 1290m before reaching the minuscule **Fundata**, 25km south of Bran, where you can cross-country ski or hire a mountain bike. On the last Sunday of August this village holds the highly worthwhile, fascinating **Mountain Festival** (Nedeia Muntelui), bringing together local artisans and tradespeople.

Continuing south along the same road, you come to **Podu Dâmboviţei**, home to the Peştera Dâmbovicioarei. This 870m-deep cave is not particularly noteworthy but the drive to it is. Sheer rock faces line either side of the road, as do villagers who stand on the roadside selling their home-made cheese (*caşcaval de casă*), sausages, smoked and dried meats, and fresh milk. *Coajă*, another unique cheese wrapped in bark, is sold in several villages in this area.

Antrec (see p100) provides English- and French-speaking guides and arranges hikes, fishing trips, bear-watching and cheese-tasting tours in the area.

Zărneşti

While the town itself has a creepy, *Twilight Zone* edge to it (it couldn't be due to the fact that one of Romania's largest arms manufacturers is based here, could it?), it's an excellent springboard to the incredible richness of the Piatra Craiului National Park and the base for one of the country's most interesting ecological projects.

The miniscule village of Sinca Noua, 27km north of Zărneşti along the 73A road to Sercaia, is slowly developing into Romania's first ecological village. Over the next few years, all agriculture will be organic, the surrounding forests will be certified by the Forest Stewardship Council, and an ecotourism infrastructure developed. Contact **Christoph Promberger** (☎ 0744-532 798; christoph@clcp.ro) for possibilities of exploring and staying in this area; he runs a guesthouse and equestrian centre, Equus Silvania, there.

PIATRA CRAIULUI NATIONAL PARK
Headquartered in Zărneşti, this newly formed **park** (☎ 223 008; www.pcrai.ro; Str Raului 27) covers 14,800 hectares of formidable landscape. Its office can provide all the information you need about hiking, climbing, skiing or even driving around the Piatra Craiului mountain range. As there is a range of trails to choose from, each varying quite a bit in its level of difficulty, your trip could benefit greatly from the office's sage advice.

LARGE CARNIVORE CENTRE
The **Large Carnivore Centre** (☎ 0744-532 798; christoph@clcp.ro) is an outgrowth of the former Carpathian Large Carnivore Project, which from 1993 worked towards the survival of Romania's large wolf, brown bear and lynx populations, and is involved in government lobbying, research, public-consciousness raising and ecotourism. The centre, to be officially inaugurated in early 2005, is an interpretative centre about the relationship between large carnivores and humans. It will consist of an exhibition hall and adjacent large enclosures (two to three hectares each) for the seven large mammal species of Romania (wolf, bear, lynx, red deer, roe deer, wild boar, chamois). Hand-raised wolves, which happily mingle with tour groups, serve as vital educational tools.

To visit a unique bear hide from which you can safely observe bears in their natural habitat, or for other wildlife-related tours of the region and any visit to the centre, contact **Carpathian Nature Tours** (☎ 0745-512 096; cnt@rdslink.ro) in Zărneşti. Prices are reasonable and include transport, and you can also rent bicycles. Even before the centre's inauguration, it will be possible to arrange excellent hands-on visits and tours.

Sleeping

There are numerous *pensiune* options in Moieciu de Jos and Moieciu de Sus as well as in Zărneşti (particularly along Str Carpaţi). Check out www.ruraltourism.ro for detailed descriptions of options in both Moieciu de Jos and Moieciu de Sus.

Crăiasa Munţilor (☎ 476 763; d €15) Smack in the centre of Moieciu de Sus at No 73, this place has several doubles with pottery stoves, wooden furnishings and shared bathrooms.

Casa Orleanu (☎ 0745-978 023; orleanu@yahoo.com; s/d €20/40) Also in Moieciu de Sus at No 125, this place has six rooms for two or four people, decked out in rustic style. The price includes breakfast and supper. Mihai and Nathalie, who run the place, also run the adjoining Centrul de Ecologie Montană, a mountain and ecology centre which organises guided hikes and botanical/nature trails and rents mountain bikes. To get here from

the end of the village opposite the trout basin, bear left where the road forks.

Pensiune Mosorel (☎ 236 307; Str Dr I Şenchea 162; per person €25) Located in Zărneşti, this *pensiune* has rustic, simple rooms and is the closest you'll get to a hotel in town. The staff are helpful and can give hiking advice; even better, they rent bikes.

Getting There & Away

From Zărneşti, there are two daily buses to Şimon, nine to Moieciu de Jos (via Bran), and eleven to Braşov's Autogară 2. Five daily trains link Braşov with Zărneşti (€0.80, 50 minutes), stopping at Cristian and Râşnov on the way.

PREDEAL
pop 6420

It might well be Romania's highest skiing spot (1033m), but it's definitely not Romania's hottest. Unlike its sister resorts, Predeal, 25km south of Braşov, has just a couple of slopes, which generally attract hordes of local kids on school camps. The resort has six runs overall, served by two chairlifts and two drag lifts. Just south of the town is where Transylvania officially begins. There isn't much to attract the

---

PRINCELY HIKING

Climbers, hikers and lovers of grandiose scenery rave about Piatra Craiului and its twin-peaked 'Stone of the Prince' – Piatra Mică (1816m), marked by a large stone cross, and La Om (2238m) – which offers climbers one of Romania's greatest challenges. The 25km-long range stretches from Zărneşti down to Podu Dâmboviţei and rises from the ground in near-vertical limestone towers which never fail to make onlookers' jaws drop in awe.

If you're hiking from Bran, the quickest route is along the dirt road to Predulut, through the village of Tohaniţa to **Zărneşti**, where the mountains are more easily accessed via several well-indicated trails. A good starting point is from the **Cabana Gura Raului**, at the southwestern end of Zărneşti. This is the main entrance to the Piatra Craiului National Park, with information panels and an on-site restaurant. Three trails begin directly behind it. From the northwestern end of Zărneşti other trails end up at **Cabana Curmătura** (1250m). Another route follows the road signposted 'spre Cabana Plaiu Foii 12km'. Some 2km along this road, a diverging trail takes you to the **Colţul Chiliilor** peak (1125m, two hours, marked with blue stripes).

Alternatively, you can drive along the appallingly bombed-out dirt road (if you've got a spare set of shocks with you) 12km to **Cabana Plaiu Foii** (849m), where a trail also leads through Fantăna lui Botorog to Cabana Curmătura (three hours, 6km, yellow triangles).

The most challenging route from Cabana Plaiu Foii is through the Cheile Zărneştiului to the Regugiul Grind and up to **Vârful Omu** (2502m, three to four hours, red circles). This route is not possible in winter and is recommended only for experienced climbers; ropes are needed in places.

In May/June and September, Piatra Craiului receives heavy rainfall. Summer storms are frequent and in winter much of the mountain cannot be accessed. Avalanches are common.

visitor here, though if you're interested in unchallenging ski runs, this resort tends to be less crowded than the others.

Orientation & Information

In case of emergency, **Salvamont** (☎ 456 269) is the place to call. The **Tourist Information Centre** (☎ 455 330; www.predeal.ro in Romanian; Str Intrarea Gării 1; ☑ 10am-6pm), in a modern building with huge glass windows in front of the train station, is a good first stop. B-dul Mihai Săulescu is the main street in town, running north–south, parallel to the train tracks. It's right outside the train station. The **post office** and **telephone office** (both ☑ 8am-7pm Mon-Fri, 9am-2pm Sat) are just opposite the **Complex Commercial** (B-dul Mihai Săulescu 62a), a shopping centre where you'll find sports stores, exchange offices, ATMs and fast-food joints. Just north of here is the **Policlinică Farmacie** (☑ 9am-6pm Mon-Fri, 9am-3pm Sat-Sun).

The best map is included in Amco Press' *Braşov City Plan*.

Predeal's chair *(telescaun)* and drag *(teleski)* lifts, run by the **Clăbucet Zona de Agrement** (☎ 456 451), depart from the eastern end of Str Telefericului, which is on the eastern side of the train tracks, best accessed by an underpass approximately 350m south of the train station along B-dul Mihai Săulescu.

Activities

The **Fulg de Nea** (Snow Flake; ☎ 456 089; Str Telefericului 1), close to the ski lift, is Predeal's central ski school, a ski club with fitness centre, sauna and an **ice skating** rink in winter (€2 including skate hire). Horse-drawn **sleigh rides** can also be arranged. Outside there are three **tennis** courts (€2 per hour). A six-day ski school comprising four hours' tuition per day costs €30. A day's rental of ski equipment is €5. Most of the hotels also arrange ski school and rental; however, they go through the ski school and add a small commission.

Sleeping

If you can make it through the swarm of babushkas at the train station offering you rooms to stay, there's an **accomodation office** (dispecerat cazare; ☎ 455 042; Str Panduri 6; ☑ 9am-8pm) which can help find rooms in private homes, usually for around €10 per person including breakfast. Booking through the

Tourist Information Centre can get you discounts on some hotels.

Predeal boasts villas galore, many very luxurious and privately owned. A handful of these upmarket properties – including one which belonged to Ceauşescu (see Eating, below) – are owned by the government but can be rented out by the **Predeal Protocol Service** (☎ 455 222; Str Nicolae Bălcescu 39). They cost between €40 and €150 a night for the entire villa. The **Fulg de Nea** ski school (see Activities, above) operates a 16-bed villa (per bed €6) behind the ski centre. Book in advance as it is often filled with groups of school children. Breakfast isn't included.

BUDGET

Cabana Sosire (☎ 455 431; d/tr €14/20) Practically located at the foot of the ski lift, this cabana has slightly above-average rooms. There's also a disco for apres-ski unwinding. Bookings are made through next-door Hotel Premier (see below).

Chalet Vânătorul (☎ 455 285; Str Trei Brazi 3; d €18) Some 3km west of the resort on the road to Trei Brazi, this is a lovely place, and meat-lovers will find their paradise in the restaurant.

Hotel Carmen-Ana (☎ 456 656; Str Mihai Săulescu 121; s/d €13/20) Opposite the train station, this is reasonably priced, reasonably cheerful, and all the rooms have private bathrooms.

MID-RANGE

Hotel Orizont (☎ 455 150; orizont@com.pcnet.ro; Str Trei Brazi 6; s/d €22/27) This is Predeal's top hotel. It has all the mod cons, including a health club, swimming pool, tennis court, sauna and massage parlour. The hotel's Romanian restaurant and flashy cocktail bar overlook the pool.

Hotel Premier (☎ 457 140; hotelpremier@xnet.ro; Str Teleferic; s/d €29/41) This is another modern, first-class hotel, boasting a fitness centre, billiard room and sauna.

Eating

Most hotels have a restaurant of sorts, and there are plenty of fast-food options along Str Mihai Săulescu.

Casa Ţărănească (Str Libertăţii 63; mains €2-6; ☑ 10am-11pm) Housed inside what was Ceauşescu's private holiday villa in the northeast of the village, this is highly recommended. The luxury villa, with its large,

TRANSLYVANIA

lamp-lit terrace surrounded by fir trees, is now a folklore restaurant. It serves traditional Romanian dishes to the sound of serenading violinists.

Getting There & Away

The **Agenţie de Voiaj CFR** (☎ 456 203) is inside the **train station** (☎ 456 330; Str Intrarea Gării 1).

Predeal is on the main Cluj-Napoca–Braşov–Bucharest line, with most local and express trains serving this route stopping here. Between here and Braşov (35 to 45 minutes) there are some 35 trains daily. The Dacia, Pannonia and Ister Expres trains to Vienna, Prague and Budapest, respectively, call at Predeal exactly 30 minutes before/after calling at Braşov.

All maxitaxis heading to/from Braşov stop at Predeal's train station on the way, making it a quick and convenient way to get to Braşov and points south, such as Bucharest.

BUŞTENI

☎ 244 / pop 11,300

Ten kilometres south of Predeal, along the main road running through the Prahova Valley between Braşov and Sinaia, is Buşteni (885m), hovering beneath the mighty Caraiman (2384m) and Coştila (2490m) peaks to the west and Mt Zamora (1519m) to the east. Between the Caraiman and Coştila peaks lie the highest conglomerate cliffs in Europe.

Buşteni, coupled with Sinaia, is the main starting point for hikes into the Bucegi Mountains. Many fine trails are readily accessed from the top of the cable car. Rock climbers find their heaven here too.

While its surroundings are spectacular, the town itself is characterless and highly unpleasant, mainly due to the incessant traffic that barrels down its main street, B-dul Libertăţii. Whereas truck and commercial traffic is forced to go around Sinaia, it has no choice but to charge through Buşteni, making the centre noisy and smelly any time of the day or night.

Orientation

The train station backs onto the main street, B-dul Libertăţii, easily identifiable by the large WWI memorial in front of it. The cable car, Hotel Caraiman, post office and commercial complex are at the southern end of town (turn left from the train station). To get to the cable car, continue south down B-dul Libertăţii 200m past Hotel Caraiman then turn right onto Str Telecabinei.

MAPS & PUBLICATIONS

There is a large-scale town map on B-dul Libertăţii in front of the post office on which all the hotels, the cable-car station and walking trails are marked. Otherwise, Amco Press' *Ploieşti* map (€1.90) has a helpful and detailed map of Buşteni.

The best hiking map by far is the Hungarian Dimap's fold-out *Five Mountains from the Carpathian's Bend* (covering the Piatra Craiului, Bucegi, Postăvarul, Piatra Mare and Ciucaş ranges, plus a Braşov city map; €2), with English text. Another helpful map with English trail descriptions is the free *Tourist Prahova Map* published by the Association of Turism Montan. Otherwise, several Romanian-language maps (the best published by Bel Alpin, €2) can also be found in sports stores and some travel agencies. Older, dowdier maps are sold at the cable-car stations in Sinaia and Buşteni.

Information

In case of emergency on the mountain, **Salvamont** (☎ 320 048; Primărie, B-dul Libertăţii 91) will come running any time of the year. Access the Internet at **Galaxy Club** (Str Libertăţii 53; per hr €0.50; ☽ 24hr). There are several exchange bureaus in the centre, among them **Exchange House** (B-dul Libertăţii 142; ☽ 9am-6pm Mon-Fri, 9am-2pm Sat). The **post** and **telephone office** (☎ 321 646; B-dul Libertăţii 93; ☽ 7am-9pm Mon-Fri, 8am-2pm Sat) is 50m south of the train station.

The choice of travel agencies is better in Sinaia (p107), but if you're stuck, try **Agenţi de Turism de Buşteni** (☎ 323 180; B-dul Libertăţii 200; ☽ 9am-7pm Mon-Fri), who can answer some questions when they're actually in the office. More helpful is **Asociaţia de Turism Ecologică şi Socială** (☎ 320 772; Str Caraiman 7; ☽ 9am-6pm Mon-Fri). The English- and French-speaking staff will happily assist lost travellers and can organise bookings for the region's cabanas.

CEZAR PETRESCU MEMORIAL MUSEUM

Between the wars, Buşteni was home to Romanian novelist Cezar Petrescu (1892–1961), whose realist works attempted to reflect a 'psychology of failure' in modern Romanian life. His house at the northern end of the town is now a **memorial museum** (☎ 321 080; Str Tudor Vladimirescu 2; admission €0.20; ⏱ 9am-5pm Tue-Sun). Turn right out of the train station; Str Tudor Vladimirescu is the fourth street on the left (about 500m).

Activities

HIKING & SKIING

Peripatetic tourists are drawn here for one reason: the magnificent Bucegi Mountains, which offer numerous hiking and ski trails, accessible from the top of Buşteni's 25-person **cable car** (☎ 320 306; adult/child one way €2.40/1.35; ⏱ 8am-3.45pm Tue-Sun), a trip in which is major experience in and of itself. From Buşteni, it's also possible to hike 8km south to Sinaia or 10km north to Predeal (see p106). Hotel Silva (see Sleeping, p106) rents skis for €5.50 a day.

MOUNTAIN BIKING

The plateau of the Bucegi Mountains is relatively flat, making mountain biking – on level with the clouds – a real thrill. Bikes are best rented in Sinaia.

Sleeping

BUDGET

See the Sinaia section (p110) for other cabanas in the Bucegi Mountains.

You'll find dozens of rooms to rent up Str Caraiman and south along Str Unirii. These are quiet streets, near the cable car, with several good options to choose from.

TRANSYLVANIA

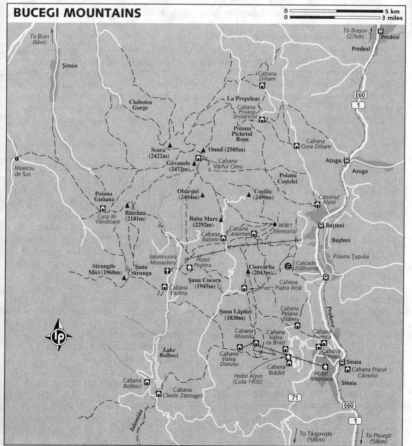

BUCEGI MOUNTAINS

0 — 5 km
0 — 3 miles

To Bran (6km)

Şimon

Ciubotea Gorge

La Prepeleac

Cabana Diham

Poiana Izvoarelor

Poiana Pichetul Roşu

To Braşov (27km)

Predeal

E60 1

Cabana Gura Diham

Azuga

Azuga

Scara (2422m)

Omul (2505m)

Gǎvanele (2472m)

Cabana Vârful Omu

Poiana Costelei

Moieciu de Sus

Obârşiei (2404m)

Costila (2490m)

Cǎminul Alpin

Poiana Guǎana

Bǎtrâna (2181m)

Baba Mare (2292m)

WW1 Memorial

Buşteni

Casa de Vânǎtoare

Cabana Babele

Cabana Caraiman

Buşteni

Ialomicioara Monastery

Hotel Peştera

Ciorcârlia (2043m)

Cascada Urlǎtoarea

Poiana Ţapului

Strungile Mici (1968m)

Şaua Strunga

Şaua Cocora (1945m)

Cabana Piatra Arsǎ

Cabana Padina

Şaua Lǎptici (1830m)

Cabana Poiana Stânei

Lake Bolboci

Cabana Miorila

Cabana Valea cu Brazi

Cabana Furnica

Cabana Schiori

Cabana Valea Dorului

Hotel Alpin (Cota 1400)

Cabana Brǎdet

Hotel Montana

Sinaia

Cabana Piscul Câinelui

Sinaia

Cabana Bolboci

Cabana Cheile Zǎnoagei

71

To Târgovişte (58km)

To Ploieşti (58km)

E60 1

Prahova

Ialomita

BUCEGI MOUNTAINS

The Bucegi Mountains are Romania's best-kept secret, rivalling Slovakia's Tatra Mountains and even the Alps when it comes to trekking. Getting lost is difficult, thanks to a network of marked trails, while most cabanas are open year-round to shelter hikers and cross-country skiers. The only danger is the weather: winter is severe and summer thunderstorms are common.

From **Buşteni** take the cable car up to **Cabana Babele** (2206m). From Babele a trail leads to the giant WWI memorial cross at 2284m (one hour, marked with red crosses). From here a path (red crosses) leads to the top of Caraiman Peak (2384m). On the peak the path becomes wider, turning into a trail that continues towards Omu Peak across Bucegi Plateau. It gets close to the Coştila Peak (2490m) on top of which is a rocket-like TV transmitter (out of bounds to the public). Alternatively a trail (three to four hours, blue crosses) leads from the lower cable-car station to **Cabana Caraiman** (2025m), where you can pick up the trail to the WWI cross (30 to 45 minutes, red circles).

From Cabana Babele you can hike south following a yellow-stripe trail to **Cabana Piatra Arsă** (1950m). From here you can pick up a blue trail that descends to **Sinaia** via **Poiana Stânii** (three hours). An even more interesting destination is the **Ialomiciora Monastery**, accessible by trail (1½ hours, blue crosses) or via a second cable car from Babele, where you'll find a small hermitage built partially inside the Ialomiţa cave. Visitors are welcome to spend the night there; there is also the Hotel Peştera nearby.

A more ambitious expedition involves taking the cable car from Buşteni to either of the two cable-car stations and hiking northwest across the mountains to **Bran Castle**, where there are buses to Braşov. You can do this in one strenuous day if you get an early start from Babele, but it's preferable to take two days and free camp or spend a night at **Cabana Vârful Omu**. From the TV transmitter, there is a trail (two hours, yellow-marked) leading to Cabana Vârful Omu on the summit. North of Babele the scenery becomes dramatic, with dizzying drops into valleys on either side. From Omu to Bran Castle is tough but spectacular – a 2000m drop through the tree line into thick forest, then onto a logging road leading to the castle (six hours, yellow triangles). Don't even think of climbing up from Bran to Omu.

Oti-Dor (☎ 321 820; Str Caraiman 20; per person €10) This is a comfortable place, with a country-home feel and welcoming hosts. It also has a dining room which seats 60.

Cabana Babele (☎ 315 304; beds €3-7) Peched high at 2206m, this has provided refuge to hikers since 1937. Today it offers beds in double rooms and mattresses on dorm floors; the price is according to season and level of comfort.

Other cabanas in the area include **Cabana Caraiman** (2025m; beds €3), which has 40 places in shared rooms, and **Cabana Vârful Omu** (beds €3), a very simple place with 35 mattresses in dorms. It is open from May to September only.

MID-RANGE

Hotel Alexandros (☎ 320 138; B-dul Libertăţii 153; s €38-62, d €52-78, ste €192; 🕸 ⊠) This stately complex north of the train station is the most luxurious option around. The two-star (cheaper) rooms are good value. There's an on-site tennis court (€10 per hour).

Hotel Silva (☎ 321 412; www.hotelsilva.ro in Romanian; Str Telecabinei 24; d €16-25, ste €20-32) This mammoth building lords over a hill right in front of the cable car and as such is surrounded by swarms of hikers and skiers at nearly all hours of the day. The back-facing rooms have great mountain views, but the interiors are drab and a tad depressing; despite the impressive exterior, this a two-star affair.

Eating

You can stock up on supplies in the commercial complex at the southern end of B-dul Libertăţii or at the cluster of shops at the foot of the cable-car station.

Restaurant Autoservice (mains €1.50; 🕑 noon-9pm Tue-Sat, noon-5pm Sun) Adjoining the Hotel Caraiman, this is a cafeteria-style setup slopping up the cheapest eats in town.

Prama The King (☎ 324 120; B-dul Libertăţii; mains €2-4; 🕑 10am-midnight) By far the best bet in town. A lightly medieval-themed pub/restaurant, it has a relaxed ambience and decent, if standard, meals.

Getting There & Away

Buşteni has no Agenţie de Voiaj CFR. Buy tickets at the train station on B-dul Libertăţii. As with Predeal, Buşteni is on the main Bucharest–Cluj-Napoca line, with all local trains between Braşov and Bucharest stopping at Buşteni.

From Buşteni, buses to Azuga and Sinaia depart every half-hour between 6am and 10pm from the main bus stop on B-dul Libertăţii. All maxitaxis heading to and from Braşov can be flagged down anywhere on the main street.

During the summer, maxitaxis marked 'Gura Diham' depart for Cabana Gura Diham. They leave on the hour, between 7am and 10pm, from outside the train station. Return buses leave Gura Diham hourly between 7.30am and 10.30pm.

SINAIA

☎ 244 / pop 14,240

It's not dubbed the Pearl of the Carpathians for nothing. Sinaia boasts not only Romania's hottest skiing, but also the country's most fabulous palace. Despite being Romania's most popular ski resort, it has retained an earthy elegance, a refusal to turn into commercial kitsch. Yet it would be hard to mess up such gorgeous surroundings: at once floating at an altitude of 800–930m in the narrow Prahova Valley and lying at the foot of the fir-clad Bucegi Mountains, Sinaia seems to have sprouted naturally from its wooded nest.

The resort is alleged to have gained its name from Romanian nobleman Mihai Cantacuzino who, following a pilgrimage he made to the biblical Mt Sinai in Israel in 1695, founded the Sinaia Monastery. It later developed into a major resort after King Carol I selected the area for his summer residence in 1870 and built what is today Romania's most beautiful palace.

Until 1920, the Hungarian-Romanian border ran along Predeal Pass, just north of Sinaia.

For readers' convenience, this area has been included in Transylvania in this book, even though is is administratively part of Wallachia.

Orientation

The train station is directly below the centre of town. From the station climb up the stairway across the street to busy B-dul Carol I. Hotel Montana and the cable car are to the left; the monastery and palace are uphill to the right. Also to the right is the 1911 Edwardian-style casino, modelled after the famous one in Monte Carlo.

MAPS & PUBLICATIONS

For hiking maps see p104. Amco's fold-out *Ploieşti* (€1.90) includes a so-so city map. There is also a city map at the top of the stairs from the train station, plus a map of hiking trails on the corner of B-dul Carol I and Str Cuza Vodă. Other, older and faded maps are sold at the cable-car station. Check out the streetpaper *Zile şi Nopţi* and its website www.zilesinopti.ro for club and entertainment listings.

Information

INTERNET ACCESS

Club Green Point (☎ 312 973; B-dul Carol I, 41; per hr €0.50; ⏰ 9am-2am)

Internet Room (per hr €0.50; ⏰ 10am-10pm) This is located in the Hotel International lobby.

EMERGENCY

If you run into problems in the mountains or need to check weather conditions, contact **Salvamont** (☎ 313 131; Primărie, B-dul Carol I; also at Cota 2000 at top of chairlift).

MONEY

The currency exchange inside the Luxor Agenţie de Turism offers good rates; it's open 8am to 8pm daily. The **Banca Comercială Română** (B-dul Carol I; ⏰ 8am-5.30pm Mon-Fri, 8.30am-12.30pm Sat), next to the town hall, cashes travellers cheques, gives cash advances on Visa/MasterCard and has an ATM.

POST & TELEPHONE

The central **post office** (☎ 311 591; ⏰ 7am-8pm Mon-Fri, 8am-noon Sat) and **telephone office** (⏰ 10am-6pm Mon-Fri, 10am-2pm Sat) are both at B-dul Carol I 33.

TOURIST INFORMATION

Dracula's Land (☎ 311 441; B-dul Carol I, 14; ⏰ 9am-6pm) Despite its tacky name, make this your first stop in town. It's one of the country's most active, enthusiastic travel agencies and doubles as a tourist information bureau, happy to help with any kind of question even if unrelated to its own services,

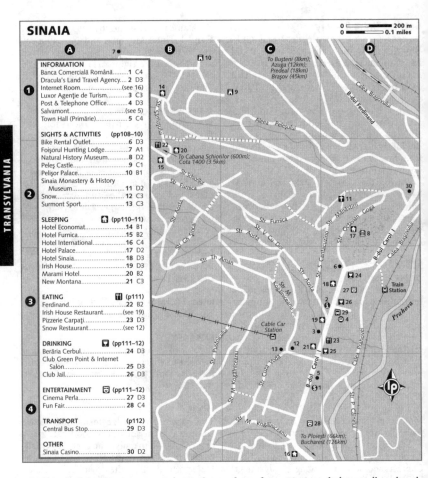

SINAIA

0 — 200 m
0 — 0.1 miles

INFORMATION
Banca Comercială Română........1 C4
Dracula's Land Travel Agency.... 2 D3
Internet Room.............................(see 16)
Luxor Agenţie de Turism..............3 C3
Post & Telephone Office...............4 D3
Salvamont...................................(see 5)
Town Hall (Primărie)....................5 C4

SIGHTS & ACTIVITIES   (pp108–10)
Bike Rental Outlet.........................6 D3
Foişorul Hunting Lodge.................7 A1
Natural History Museum................8 D2
Peleş Castle.................................9 C1
Pelişor Palace............................10 B1
Sinaia Monastery & History
   Museum...................................11 D2
Snow..12 C3
Surmont Sport............................13 C3

SLEEPING   (pp110–11)
Hotel Economat..........................14 B1
Hotel Furnica..............................15 B2
Hotel International........................16 C4
Hotel Palace...............................17 D2
Hotel Sinaia...............................18 D3
Irish House.................................19 D3
Marami Hotel..............................20 B2
New Montana..............................21 C3

EATING   (p111)
Ferdinand...................................22 B2
Irish House Restaurant.............(see 19)
Pizzerie Carpaţi..........................23 D3
Snow Restaurant.....................(see 12)

DRINKING   (pp111–12)
Berăria Cerbul............................24 D3
Club Green Point & Internet
   Salon......................................25 D3
Club Jail....................................26 D3

ENTERTAINMENT   (pp111–12)
Cinema Perla..............................27 D3
Fun Fair.....................................28 C4

TRANSPORT   (p112)
Central Bus Stop.........................29 D3

OTHER
Sinaia Casino.............................30 D2

To Buşteni (8km);
Azuga (12km);
Predeal (18km);
Braşov (45km)

To Cabana Schiorilor (600m);
Cota 1400 (3.5km)

Cable Car
Station

Train
Station

To Ploieşti (66km);
Bucharest (126km)

which include booking accommodation (at a 25–40% discount) and arranging a wide array of hiking and ski tours.

Luxor Agenţie de Turism (☎ 314 124; fax 314 251; B-dul Carol I, 22; ☻ 9am-5pm Mon-Sat) This outfit usually runs three or four excursions (€5 to €10 per day) in and around Sinaia per day; they are posted in the front window. It can also arrange a hiking guide for €25 to €50 per day, depending on the number of people in the group.

Sights
SINAIA MONASTERY
Some 20 monks call the **Sinaia Monastery** (Str Mănăstirii; admission by donation; ☻ 8am-5pm) home. The large Orthodox church (Biserica Mare)

dates from 1846, and the smaller church (Biserica Veche) from 1695. Monks retreated into the Bucegi Mountains from the 14th century but it was not until the late 17th century that they built a monastery.

Tache Ionescu (1859–1918), a leading liberal statesman who led the Romanian delegation at the Paris Peace Conference (1918–20) and briefly headed one of the first postwar governments in Romania, is buried here. Born in Ploieşti, Ionescu contracted cholera as a child and was sent to Sinaia Monastery to convalesce. Following his death, his second wife built a vast mausoleum at the monastery in his memory. Quotations from his speeches are carved in stone on the mausoleum's interior walls.

KEEPING ACTIVE IN SINAIA

For dazzling, dizzying skiing, you have come to the right place. For endless hiking trails with dramatic, panoramic views, this is where it all begins. For kamikaze mountain-bike rides, prepare your helmets. The key to getting the most out of the trails is having a good map (see p86).

Sinaia offers 40km of wild skiing around Mt Furnica; its slopes are considered Romania's most challenging. Its exposed position often sees cable cars grinding to a halt as the wind blows up, but skiing is, on average, guaranteed four days out of seven. If they aren't moving here, ask around or call the stations in nearby Buşteni or Azuga; weather conditions can change even over a few kilometres. The 2.5km Carp trail, which descends from Vf Furnica to Cota 1400, is the most challenging. There are several intermediate and easy trails too. Located on top of the Bucegi plateau above the Sinaia resort is an 8km cross-country track.

Many hotels arrange ski schools and hire, but it's cheaper and more fun to go direct to the central ski shop and school, **Snow** (☎ 311 198; ana_bogdan@yahoo.com; Str Cuza Voda 2a). Private lessons cost €10 an hour; group tuition is €7 per person an hour. There are more than 400 skis and snowboards for rent (about €10 a day). Hanging on the walls are a 50-year-old sleigh, archaic snowshoes and wooden skis from the 1930s (used in the 1948 Olympics), all of which can be rented by those in search of esoteric thrills on the slopes. Nearby is **Surmont Club** (☎ 311 810; www.surmont.ro in Romanian; Str Cuza Voda 2), which sells sports gear, rents skis and can inform you on sporting competitions in the area.

The Montana 30-person **cable-car station** (☎ 311 674; to Cota 1400 one way/two way €1.30/2.40, to Vf Furnica one way/two way €2.70/4.70, children half-price; ☒ 8am-4pm Tue-Sun) is behind Hotel New Montana. The downside to skiing here is that there are often long lines for the single cable car, and the chairlifts could benefit from a face-lift.

The wealth of hiking trails accessible from here are connected with ones from Buşteni (p106). It's therefore possible to hike from here all the way to Bran or Râsnov in a very long (14 to 16 hours) day, or preferably two. A particularly nice route (seven to 10 hours, yellow and blue stripes) starts at either the lower cable car station or higher up from the cable car at Cabana Mioriţa, to the Cabana Piatra Arsă, down to the Ialomiciora Monastery and then up to the Omul peak (where there's also a cabana). Many of these trails become magnets for adrenalin-seeking mountain bikers come summer.

Beside the new church is a small **History Museum** (Muzeul de Istorie; adult/child €0.80/0.40; ☒ 8am-5pm) in which some of the monastery's treasures are displayed, including the first translation of the Bible into Romanian (in the Cyrillic alphabet), dating from 1668.

PELEŞ CASTLE

Most visitors are led through here with their jaws scraping the floor in amazement. This magnificent **royal palace** (☎ 310 918; compulsory tours adult/child €2.50/€1.25; ☒ 11am-5pm Wed, 9am-5pm Thu-Sun), with its fairy-tale turrets rising above acres of green meadows, is one of Romania's must-sees. The effect of wandering through the stunning halls and rooms listening to the guide rattling off an endless list of exotic materials used to furnish them (alabaster, gilded linden wood, mother of pearl, Turkish silk etc) is dizzying.

Intended as a summer residence by Romania's longest-serving monarch, King Carol I (outside there is a statue of him looking mighty proud of himself), it was the first castle in Europe to have central heating and electricity. Construction started on the 3500-sq-metre edifice, built in a predominantly German-Renaissance style, in 1875. Some 39 years, more than 400 weary craftsmen and thousands of labourers later, it was completed, just months before the king died in 1914. King Carol I's wife Elisabeta was largely responsible for the interior decoration.

During Ceauşescu's era, the castle's 160 rooms were used as a private retreat for leading communists and statesmen from around the globe. US presidents Richard Nixon and Gerald Ford, Libyan leader Moamar Gaddafi and PLO leader Yasser Arafat were all entertained by the Romanian dictator in Peleş' fanciful rooms, each of which is furnished to reflect a different country.

Rembrandt reproductions line the walls of the king's office, while a row of books in the library conceals a secret escape passage leading to the 2nd floor. There is a gallery of mirrors and the dining room has a leather-clad ceiling. Scenes from age-old Romanian fairytales adorn the stained-glass windows in the poetry room. In the Council Room, panels made from 14 kinds of wood bore witness to the signing of Romania's neutrality for the last two years of WWI. Peleş Castle was off limits to the public from 1947 to 1975, when it was reborn briefly as a museum. Extensive renovation was completed in 1990.

Tickets are sold either at the ticket counter at the nearby Pelişor Palace (see next section) or under the arches in the centre of the building where a door is signposted 'foreign tourists'.

PELIŞOR PALACE & FOIŞORUL HUNTING LODGE

Marie, wife of King Carol's nephew Ferdinand (1865–1927), did not get on with her uncle-in-law and loathed Peleş Castle. So, in fine royal fashion, King Carol built Ferdinand and Marie a castle of their own, just a few hundred metres uphill from Peleş, completed in 1892.

Built in a mock German-medieval style, **Pelişor Palace** (☎ 312 184; compulsory tours adult/child €2/0.65; ❨ 11am-5pm Wed, 9am-5pm Thu-Sun) was furnished according to Marie's own designs – pretty pastel decorations in a simple Art Nouveau style which westerners tend to relate to more than the florid splendour of Peleş. Most of the furniture was imported from Vienna. Marie used four apartments while Ferdinand had just one. The bed in which Romania's second king died at the age of 62 from cancer can still be seen today. Marie died nine years later in the golden room, the walls of which are entirely covered in heavy gold leaves.

At the western end of the Peleş estate is the Swiss-chalet-style **Foişorul Hunting Lodge**, built as a temporary residence by King Carol I before Peleş Castle was completed. Here Marie and Ferdinand spent their first summer together in Romania. Their son, the future King Carol II, briefly lived here with his mistress Elena Lupescu. During the communist era, Ceauşescu used it as his private hunting lodge. The building is now in state hands and is closed to visitors.

BUCEGI NATURE RESERVE MUSEUM

Behind the Hotel Palace in the central park, this small **natural history museum** (Muzeul Rezervaţiei Bucegi; ☎ 311 750; admission €0.40; ❨ 9am-7pm Tue-Sun, 9am-5pm Mon) features some of the natural wonders of the Bucegi Nature Reserve, which encompasses the 300-sq-km Bucegi mountain range. Two rooms in the cellar exhibit stuffed animals, flowers and birds, including the edelweiss, the delicate flower so abundant in the region. There are also temporary art exhibitions.

Activities

Mountain bikes can be rented at the **rental outlet** (☎ 314 906; Str Octavia Goga 1; per hr/day €1.60/13; ❨ 9am-8pm), which can also help you find villas and chalets for rent outside of Sinaia. See the boxed text on p109 for ski-rental locations.

Sleeping
BUDGET

For details of other cabanas within hiking reach of Sinaia, see p105.

Hotel Furnica (☎ 311 851; Str Furnica 50; s/d €15/24) The building is so impressive from the outside with its faux-Jacobian flourishes and grand courtyard, you can send a snapshot back home and everyone will think you came into fast money for having stayed here. The inside shows another, grungier side, but for the price and surroundings, it's not a bad place.

Cabana Schiorilor (☎ 313 655; Str Drumul Cotei 7; d €22, 5-bed r €20) Pretty fancy as far as cabanas go, it has an on-site, elegant restaurant. It's easily walkable from the centre.

Cabana Brădet (☎ 315 491; bed €5) At 1300m, this has 28 beds in shared rooms. It is accessible via the Cota 1400 cable-car station.

Cabana Valea cu Brazi (☎ 313 605; bed €6) Situated above the cable car at 1510m, this has room for 48 persons. It's a ten-minute walk along a path from the Cota 1400.

Hotel Piatra Arsă (☎ 311 911; s/d €18/25) and the 50-bed **Cabana Piatra Arsă** (☎ 311 911; bed €3-8) are both at 1950m. The latter is a large, modern chalet. There is a restaurant, tennis court, running track, sauna and pool here; numerous sports teams from across Romania come here to train.

MID-RANGE

Hotel Economat (☎ 311 151; fax 311 150; Aleea Peleşului 2; s/d €20/24) This has the same impressive Jacobian exteriors as the Hotel Furnica that make you feel like you're living it up, only with better interiors. Just a few minutes' walk from the Peleş Castle, the hotel also runs a series of other one- to three-star villas in the area and so can offer a wide range of accommodation starting from €10 per person. Though it's quite a hike up from the centre, it's one of the best bets in town.

Irish House (☎ 310 060; www.irishhouse.ro; B-dul Carol I, 80; s/d €27/40) Another good option, the 12 modern rooms are as large as apartments and furnished accordingly. From the rooms, you won't have to go too far for good food (see Eating, below), but are far enough not to hear noise from the bar.

Marami Hotel (☎ 315 560; www.marami.ro; Str Furnica 52; s/d/ste €50/60/65; 🔀 🖳) If you aren't fussy about odd colour combos accented with pinksand blues (there must have been a sale on pastel paints the day the rooms were decorated), this is one of the best hotels in Sinaia. This modern hotel sits on a quiet stretch of road, within walking distance to the Peleş Castle, and has jazzy pluses such as a fitness room and Internet access.

Hotel Sinaia (☎ 311 551; fax 310 625; B-dul Carol I, 8; 2-star s/d €20/32, 3-star s/d €27/48) This looms forebodingly in all its concrete weightiness over the centre of town. In the 1960s this 242-room giant might have impressed; today it intimidates. Use of the fitness centre and pool cost extra. Rooms are standard and comfortable.

Hotel Palace (☎ 310 625; Str Octavian Goga 4; 2-star s/d €37/54, 4-star s/d/ste €48/70/110; 🔀) For those who love lugubrious, endless corridors and an air of faded glory (the building dates to 1911), this is your place. The four-star doubles, however, are very impressive; yes, that is a bidet. The on-site nightclub attracts an older crowd.

Hotel International (☎ 313 851; fax 313 855; Str Avram Iancu 1; 3-star s/d €40/56, 4-star s/d €54/72; 🔀) There's luxury in the air at this grand place at the southern end of town which boasts full services. The rooms are decent, but not as regal as the main entrance would lead you to believe.

TOP END

New Montana (☎ 312 751; www.newmontana.ro; B-dul Carol I, 24; s/d/ste €77/95/107; 🔀) Despite being a high-rise, this has a pleasant, airy feel to it and spacious, tastefully decorated rooms. It's wheelchair accessible.

Eating

There are numerous kebab and fast-food stands along B-dul Carol I and inside the Perla Bucegi shopping complex.

Pizzerie Carpaţi (☎ 310 680; B-dul Carol I, 39; mains €2-3; 🕑 9am-11pm) Rely on this place for decent pizzas and traditional dishes.

Irish House (☎ 310 060; www.irishhouse.ro; B-dul Carol I, 80; mains €2-4; 🕑 10am-midnight) About the only thing remotely Irish in the place is the green ceiling; the menu is basically Romanian, but the food is good and the dining hall roomy and comfy.

Ferdinand (☎ 0722-526 110; Str Furnica 63; mains €2.50-4; 🕑 11am-midnight) One of the best bets in town, this has a high, arched ceiling topping a rustic dining room. Far enough from the busy centre to offer a relaxing setting for a few beers, it's also a good choice for a top-notch meal; chicken in raspberry wine sauce is the house speciality.

Entertainment

For a resort town, Sinaia is suspiciously placid come nightfall. Films are shown in English with Romanian subtitles at **Cinema Perla**, on B-dul Carol I opposite Hotel Sinaia. During summer, there is a **fun fair** for kids at the southern end of B-dul Carol I.

TRANSYLVANIA

The **Berǎria Cerbul** (☎ 314 724; B-dul Carol I at Str Octavian Goga), one of the most popular places in town, is a traditional-style bar serving Romanian beer, barbecued *şaşlik (shaslik)* hot dogs and grilled meats in its summer garden.

Club Green Point (☎ 312 973; B-dul Carol I, 41; 🕑 9-2am) is often the most crowded place in town, with an Internet salon, a large billiard hall and disco that pumps it out until the last client has staggered away. It attracts a mixed clientele.

Otherwise, try **Club Jail** (☎ 310 131; 🕑 9pm-3am), a block north. It's a flashy disco with goonish bouncers and female dancers who seem to have forgotten most of their clothes somewhere.

Alternatively, try the crowded **Disco Diana** (admission €1.50; 🕑 9pm-3am) inside the Hotel Sinaia.

Getting There & Away

Sinaia is on the Bucharest–Braşov rail line – 126km from the former and 45km from the latter. All express trains stop here, and local trains to Buşteni (8km), Predeal (19km) and Braşov are frequent. Approaching Sinaia from the south, don't get off at Halta Sinaia Sud – a small stop 2km south of Sinaia centre.

Buses run every 45 minutes between 6.20am and 10.45pm from the central bus stop on B-dul Carol I to Azuga and Buşteni. From here you can catch all maxitaxis linking Braşov with points south, such as Bucharest, Brǎila and Constanţa.

FǍGǍRAŞ MOUNTAINS

☎ 268

The dramatic peaks of the Fǎgǎraş Mountains cut a serrated line south of the main Braşov–Sibiu road and shelter dozens of glacial lakes. The famed Transfǎgǎrǎşan road (p114) cuts through the range from north to south.

Fǎgǎraş & Victoria

Despite its name, Fǎgǎraş town (population 43,900) is not the prime access point to the Fǎgǎraş Massif. Most hikers pass straight through en route to neighbouring Victoria (population 10,800), the main access point to hike south into the mountains. Fǎgǎraş' only attraction is its 13th-century fortress which houses the **Fǎgǎraş County Museum**

HIKING FROM VICTORIA

One of the best stations to get off at is Ucea (59km from Sibiu), from where you can catch one of seven daily buses to **Victoria**. From Victoria you can hike to **Cabana Turnuri** (1520m) in about six hours. The scenery is stunning once you start the ascent. The next morning head for **Cabana Podragu** (2136m), four hours south.

Cabana Podragu is a good base if you want to climb **Mt Moldoveanu** (2543m), Romania's highest peak. It's a tough uphill climb, but the views from the summit are unbeatable. Otherwise, hike eight hours east, passing by Mt Moldoveanu, to **Cabana Valea Sambetei** (1407m). From Cabana Valea Sambetei you can descend to the railway in Ucea, via Victoria, in a day.

(Muzeul Ţǎrii Fǎgǎraş; 🕑 9am-3.30pm Tue-Fri, 9am-2pm Sat & Sun).

SLEEPING

Cabanas in the Fǎgǎraş Mountains include **Cabana Turnuri** (1520m; 20 beds; bed €6), a six-hour hike from Victoria, and **Cabana Podragu** (2136m; 68 beds; beds €6), four hours further to the south.

Hotel Progresul (☎ 211 634; Str Republicii 14; s/d €5/7) This grim slab of concrete sitting on the main square in the centre of Fǎgǎraş is only for those stuck in town with no cash. Shared washrooms in dour corridors lined with shabby rooms are its main draws.

Hotel Montana (☎ 212 327; Str Negoiu 98; s/d/tr €18/22/24) For Fǎgǎraş, this is a great option, and just 100m from the bus station. It's clean, modern and friendly, and the multilingual staff are happy to provide travel information to wayward travellers; they also organise excursions. The owners have plans to build a touristic complex in Sâmbǎta de Sus. It's worth dropping in!

Hotel Victoria (☎ 241 916; Piaţa Libertǎţii; d €5-8) On offer here are drab rooms with or without shower and toilet, though it matters little as none has hot water. It sits as if dumped onto the main, lifeless square.

Palermo Pensiune (☎ 242 973; Str 1 Decembrie 1918, 3; d €14) Victoria's best option is next to the post office and 150m from Hotel Victoria. This comfortable place has an on-site restaurant, a backyard terrace and decent rooms. You can also change money and exchange traveller's cheques there.

GETTING THERE & AWAY

Făgăraș' bus and train stations are next to each other on Str Negoiu. The bus station is all but completely closed. Five daily maxi-taxis head to Brașov, there are regular maxi-taxis to Victoria, and occasional services to Mediaș and Sighișoara. The train station is a major meeting point for hikers and back-packers. Trains from Făgăraș to Brașov (six daily) and Sibiu (seven daily) stop at Ucea. Four daily trains go to/from Bucharest.

Victoria's bus station is on Str Tinere-tului. The nearest train station is 7km north of Victoria at Ucea. All local trains from Brașov, Făgăraș and Sibiu stop here. Buses from Victoria to Ucea depart throughout the day from the main town square.

Sâmbăta

Ten kilometres southeast of Victoria lies the Sâmbăta complex, home to one of Roman-ia's wealthiest monasteries and a key access

point to the Făgăraș Mountains. Nicolae Ceaușescu rightly deemed the place suffi-ciently idyllic to build a private luxury villa for himself and Elena in the grounds of the monastery.

The lavish 1696 **Brâncoveanu Monastery** (admission free; ☺ 9am-6pm) derives its name from its original founder, Wallachian prince Constantin Brâncoveanu (r. 1688–1714), who built the Orthodox monastery on the family estate. Seen by the Habsburgs as the last bastion of Orthodoxy in the Făgăraș region, the monastery was practically des-troyed. Now 35 monks live here.

In 1926 restoration work started on Sâmbăta's ruins and was completed in 1946. Despite not being an original, the monastery remains a fitting testament to the great art renaissance inspired by the 17th-century Wallachian prince. Its fame today is derived from its workshops of glass icons, run by the monastery's monks, residents since the early 1990s. There is a **glass icon museum** (☎ 241 237; admission €1) in the complex with lovely ex-amples of 17th- and 18th-century glass icons from Nicula, as well as other relics.

TRANSYLVANIA

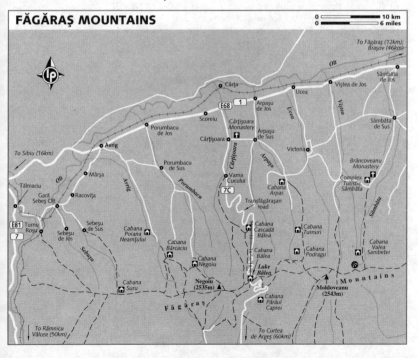

FĂGĂRAȘ MOUNTAINS

0 — 10 km
0 — 6 miles

To Făgăraș (12km);
Brașov (46km)

Sâmbăta
de Jos

Cârța

Ucea

Viștea de Jos

E68 1

Arpașu
de Jos

Scoreiu

Cârțișoara
Monastery

Arpașu
de Sus

Sâmbăta
de Sus

Porumbacu
de Jos

Cârțișoara

To Sibiu (16km)

Avrig

Victoria

Brâncoveanu
Monastery

Porumbacu
de Sus

Complex
Turistic
Sâmbăta

Mârșa

Vama
Cucului

Tălmaciu

7C

Cabana
Arpaș

Racovița

Transfăgărașan
road

Cabana
Cascadă
Bâlea

Cabana
Turnuri

E81 7

Turnu
Roșu

Sebeșu
de Sus

Cabana
Poiana
Neamțului

Cabana
Valea
Sâmbetei

Sebeșu
de Jos

Cabana
Bârcaciu

Cabana
Bâlea

Cabana
Podragu

Cabana
Negoiu

Cabana
Suru

Negoiu
(2535m)

Lake
Bâlea

Moldoveanu
(2543m)

Mountains

Fă g ă r a ș

Cabana
Pârâul
Caprei

To Râmnicu
Vâlcea (50km)

To Curtea
de Argeș (60km)

THE LONG & WINDING ROAD

Built out of Ceaucescu's fanatic zeal to conquer nature, the Transfăgărăşan road (the 7C), Romania's highest asphalted road, provides an unforgettable experience behind the wheel. Boldly charging up and down one of Romania's highest mountains, this two-lane road sometimes has the narrowest of shoulders separating it from the edge of a cliff. Driving its length is an adventure in itself, with breathtaking scenery around every one of the dozens of twists and turns.

Running from Piteşti via Curtea de Arges in the south to Highway 1 in the north (which links Braşov with Sibiu), the Transfăgărăşan is most commonly accessed from the north, where a 35km drive will take you up to the haunting glacial Lake Bâlea (2034m), where even in midsummer there is snow.

Starting from Highway 1 in the north, the drive starts innocuously enough, passing by a rundown village or two and a turn-off to the Cârtişoara monastery, known for its glass icons. Suddenly at Km12 the road starts to sharply incline and begins a series of jagged turns through the lush forest. For a change, here you must beware of deer, not cows and horse-drawn carts.

As you keep climbing, the trees start to shrink and thin out, their lifting veil replaced by unfolding views of sheer rock face. By Km20 your ears are popping. At Km22 you arrive at the Cascada (waterfalls). Pull over to collect your thoughts and breath. The 360-degree panoramic views here are stunning; walls of mountains surround the area, and the distant waterfalls' slash of white appears like a lightning bolt in a grey sky. There are souvenir stands here, a restaurant and the **Cabana Bâlea Cascada** (☎ 269-524 255; s/d/ste €12/16/42), as well as a **cable car** (one way €2.50; ☿ 8am-5pm) which whisks you up to Lake Bâlea. Alternatively, follow the scenic blue-cross trail (2½ hours).

The remaining 13km up to Lake Bâlea are a maze of razor-sharp zigzags hanging over precipices framing breathtaking views. Every kilometre up the mountain brings with it amazement at the sheer feat building the road was, and a shiver or two for the workers who undoubtedly suffered during its construction.

The climax is Lake Bâlea, hovering like a mirror among the rocks, sometimes shrouded by clouds which come billowing over the peak above it. **Cabana Bâlea** (☎ 269-524 277; s/d/ste €20/27/46) is here, standing proudly after a full restoration; it's one of the pricier cabanas in Romania, but one of the nicest as well. There's a decent restaurant and a few souvenir stands. The temperature here is easily near zero, even if it's steaming hot at the foot of the mountain, and the vegetation is minimal and miniature.

No public transport follows this route, which is closed in winter and whenever the weather gets too rough, in which case the waterfalls are the highest you can reach by car. Some bikers and hikers walk up the road, but it's a maniacal venture, not to mention hazardous for the cars who must already drive at a snail's pace.

After an 887m-long tunnel through rock under the Palţinu ridge, the road descends the south side along the Arges Valley. As is usually the case with southern slopes of mountains, it is less impressive than its northern side, but there are lovely spots along the way. After re-entering forest, just when you think the fun is over, the road suddenly hugs the shores of the picturesque Lake Vidraru and crosses a 165m-high arched dam (1968). Beyond the lake, just off the road, is the Poienari Castle, the real Dracula's castle (where Vlad Tepeş ruled; see p186).

The road was built in the 1970s over the course of 4½ short years (short as main stretches of it could only be worked on in the summer months). While the scheme fits well within Ceauşescu's overall megalomania, he also had more practical reasons for building it. Though other routes east and west of here cut an easier north–south route, he thought it wise to secure the Carpathian crossing at the traditional border between Wallachia and Transylvania. The Soviets had recently invaded Czechoslovakia (in 1968), and he did everything to ensure that his territory would be protected were anything like that to happen to him.

And so the decree was ordered, and monumental work began: on the northern side alone, six million kilograms of dynamite were used to blast out 3.8 million cubic metres of rock. Some 40 overworked soldiers are known to have died in accidents during its hasty construction. It was opened with great fanfare on September 20 1974.

Of all of the dictator's schemes, this is perhaps the most used and best appreciated. (For more description of the highway's southern side, see p187).

SLEEPING

It's possible to stay the night at the monastery; call the museum or just show up. It has rooms with one to four beds in them (from €5 per person).

Complex Turistic Sâmbăta (☎ 241 239; per person from €6) Close to the main entrance of the monastery, this complex has wooden chalets for two to four people. Bathrooms are shared and there is a small bar and restaurant.

Cabana Sâmbăta Popas (810m; tent space/dm free/€3) This is signposted 1km north from the monastery complex.

Cabana Valea Sâmbetei (1407m; dm €2-4) With 100 beds, this is a large chalet, and it's embraced by spectacular mountain scenery. It's a lovely, three-hour hike (red triangles) via a trail from the monastery. From here, further trails go to the Moldoveanu and Negoiu peaks.

Villa Andra (☎ 219 198; d €13) This is one of the several guesthouses near the monastery, 350m away. It has a quiet garden and rustic rooms.

SIBIU

☎ 269 / pop 167,380

You might just start to believe Romanians' claim to an Italian heritage in this lively 12th-century Saxon city. People seem to smile more here than in other parts of the country, in what is arguably Romania's prettiest and most pleasant city. The main pedestrian drag channels an almost Mediterranean flow of life at all hours, as partygoers, window shoppers and café culturists intersect; even Braşov seems cool and reticent in comparison. Anyone who appreciates Saxon old towns will find heaven here as medieval charm perseveres. Though there are more buildings awaiting repair here than in Braşov or Sighişoara, the meandering, narrow, cobblestone streets twisting out of view, the picturesque courtyards, even the crumbling stone staircases provide an ephemerally romantic ambience.

Founded on the site of the former Roman village of Cibinium, Sibiu (Hermannstadt to the Saxons, Nagyszében to Hungarians) has always been one of the leading cities of Transylvania. During the peak of Saxon influence, Sibiu had 19 guilds, each representing a different craft, within the sturdy city walls protected by 39 towers and four bastions. Under the Habsburgs from 1703

to 1791 and again fr[...] served as the seat of t[...] of Transylvania. In 2[...] the German Democra[...] mayor and has rema[...] ever since, placing the [...] German leadership.

Sibiu's remaining 5500 German-speaking Saxons celebrate Maifest on 1 May, when they flock to Dumbrava forest for pagan frolicking and beer drinking. The town also hosts an International Astra Film Festival (www.astrafilm.ro) every second May and an excellent International Theatre Festival (www.sibfest.ro) in early June.

This is one of the most wheelchair-friendly cities in Romania, with most pavements, staircases and hotels having ramps.

Orientation

The heart of historic Sibiu is the three interlocking squares, Piaţas Mare, Huet and Mică. The pedestrianised Str Nicolae Băulcescu is the main artery running northeast into Piaţa Mare. The lower Old Town lies to the north of the main squares.

MAPS & PUBLICATIONS

There are several fold-out city maps available at hotels and bookshops, the most detailed of which is Amco's *Sibiu City Plan* (€1.85). The free biweekly *Şapte Seri* (www.sapteseri.ro) is a helpful Romanian listings booklet.

Information
BOOKSHOPS

Librăria Humanitas (☎ 211 434; Str Nicolae Bălcescu 16; ☿ 10am-7pm Mon-Fri, 11am-6pm Sat) Your best bet in town, with a great selection of maps, local-interest books and Romanian CDs and CD-ROMs.

Librăria Schiller (☎ 0722-196 932; Piaţa Mare 7; ☿ 9am-5pm Mon-Fri, 10am-1pm Sat) Sharing space with the tourist information centre, this is another good source for (mainly German) maps, guides and history books about the city and environs.

EMERGENCY

Salvamont (☎ 216 477, 0745-140 144; Str Nicolae Bălcescu 9; ☿ 8am-4pm Mon-Fri) Provides a 24-hour emergency rescue service for hikers and skiiers in trouble.

INTERNET ACCESS

Click (☎ 212 468; Str Ocnei 11; per hr €0.40; ☿ 9-2am Mon-Sat, 2pm-2am Sun)

.a (☎ 0745-161 455; Str Dr I Lupaş 21; per hr
. ⊗ 24hr)

LIBRARIES & CULTURAL CENTRES

American Centre & Library (☎ 216 062, extension 121; B-dul Victoriei 10) and **German Cultural Centre & Library** (☎ 216 062, extension 123) These two are located in the same building just across from the British Council.

British Council Centre & Library (☎ 211 056; bc .sibiu@sibiu.rdsnet.ro; B-dul Victoriei 5-7; ⊗ 1-9pm Mon & Thu, 9am-3pm Tue, Wed & Fri) This centre organises events and has a reading room.

French Cultural Centre (☎ 218 287; Str Mitropoliei 3) Inside the Student Culture House (Casa de Cultură Studenţească).

MEDICAL SERVICES

Farmasib (Str Nicolae Bălcescu 53; ⊗ 7am-11pm Mon-Fri, 8am-10pm Sat-Sun)
Nippur-Pharmacie (Str Nicolae Bălcescu 5; ⊗ 9am-7pm Mon-Fri, 9am-2pm Sat)

MONEY

ATMs are located all over the centre as well as in most hotels. The **Banca Comercială Română** (Str Nicolae Bălcescu 11; ⊗ 8.30am-5.30pm Mon-Fri, 8.30am-12.30pm Sat) changes travellers cheques and gives cash advances.

POST & TELEPHONE

Central post office (Str Mitropoliei 14; ⊗ 7am-8pm Mon-Fri, 8am-noon Sat)
Telephone office (Str Nicolae Bălcescu 13; ⊗ 7am-7.30pm Mon-Fri, noon-7.30pm Sat)

TOURIST INFORMATION

For questions related to sporting activities in and around Păltiniş, contact SC Păltiniş (p112).

Bulevard Travel Agency (☎ 218 125; Piaţa Unirii 10; ⊗ 9am-6pm Mon-Fri) Inside the Hotel Bulevard, it offers some pricey local tours and tours to Maramureş but specialises in sending locals abroad.

Tourist Information Centre (☎ 211 110; www.sibiu .ro; Piaţa Mare 7; ⊗ 9am-5pm Mon-Sat, 10am-1pm Sun) A great first stop. One of the few official tourist offices in the country, it has an ace, can-do staff who can help with anything, including puzzling out Byzantine bus schedules. There are photo books of regional hotels and guesthouses to make choosing a place to stay easier.

Sights & Activities

PIAŢA MARE & AROUND

The expansive Piaţa Mare was the centre of the old walled city. A good start for exploring the city is to climb to the top of the former **Council Tower**, built in 1588, which links Piaţa Mare with its smaller sister square, Piaţa Mică. The view of the Făgăraş Mountains beckoning to the south is superb.

Other buildings of note include the baroque **Roman Catholic Cathedral**, built between 1726 and 1733 by a Jesuit order. In front of this is a large **memorial statue** to the people who fought in the 1848 peasant uprisings. The **Brukenthal Museum** (☎ 217 691; Piaţa Mare 4-5; adult/child €1/0.50; ⊗ 9am-5pm Tue-Sun) is the oldest and likely finest art gallery in Romania. Founded in 1817, the museum is in the baroque palace (1785) of Baron Samuel Brukenthal (1721–1803), a former Austrian governor. Apart from paintings, there are excellent archaeological, folk-art and silverware collections. Brukenthal's original library is intact.

Perhaps the square's most impressive building, however, is the **Banca Agricola** at Piaţa Mare 2. Just west of here is the lovely **Primăriă Municipiului** from 1470, now the **City History Museum** (☎ 218 143; Str Mitropoliei 2; adult/child €0.80/0.40; ⊗ 10am-5pm Tue-Sun), which contains further exhibits from Brukenthal's palace.

Nearby, on Piaţa Huet, is the Gothic **Evangelical Church** (built 1300–1520; ⊗ 11am-3pm Mon-Sat, services Sun), its great five-pointed tower visible from afar. Don't miss the four magnificent baroque funerary monuments in the upper nave, and the 1772 organ with 6002 pipes (it's Romania's largest). The tomb of Mihnea Vodă cel Rău (Prince Mihnea the Bad), son of Vlad Ţepeş, is in the closed-off section behind the organ. This prince, who ruled Wallachia from 1507 to 1510, was murdered on the square in front of the church after attending a service. A fresco of the Crucifixion (1445) is up in the sanctuary.

Other standouts here include the 13th-century **staircase passage** on the square's west side, and the 18th-century **Staircase Tower** (Turnul Scărilor) on the north side.

Piaţa Mică is small and quaint, its buildings a muted rainbow of pretty pastel colours. The wonky stairway at its eastern end leads down to Piaţa Aurarilor and maze of picturesque, narrow, cobblestone streets. The **Pharmaceutical Museum** (☎ 218 191; Piaţa Mică 26; adult/child €0.60/0.30; ⊗ 10am-6pm Tue-Sun) has a small collection of antique drug jars and creepy medical tools. The **Franz Binder Museum of World Ethnology** (☎ 218 195; Piaţa Mică 11; adult/child €0.80/0.40; ☺ 10am-6pm Tue-Sun) has a permanent display called 'Culture and Art of the Peoples of the World', which includes an Egyptian mummy.

Heading northeast from Piaţa Mare along Str Avram Iancu, you come to the **Ursuline Church**. Founded by Dominican monks in the 15th century, it was later transformed into a school, then turned over to Ursuline nuns in 1728.

LOWER TOWN

To reach the Lower Town from Piaţa Mică, you can walk along the road that goes under the **Iron Bridge** (1859). The bridge's nickname is 'Liar's Bridge' after the tricky merchants who met here to trade and the young lovers who declared their 'undying' love on it. Yeah, right! The staircase next to the bridge leads to the Lower Town, as does the staircase passage off Piaţa Huet, which offers a picturesque slice of the old town wall and several arches to walk under.

While the Lower Town has fewer sights per se, it makes for a great strolling area. Here you can see many houses sporting eyeball-looking windows popping out of red-tiled rooftops, a style particular to Sibiu. Enchanting courtyards and decorated garage doors and gates are also plentiful here. This is a less touristy area where you can observe 'real life'; second-hand stores and repair shops stand next to patisseries, and flowerpots stand carefully placed on crumbling window panes.

STR MITROPOLIEI & OLD CITY WALLS

Str Mitropoliei extends southwestwards from Piaţa Huet. The street's standout is the 1906 **Orthodox Cathedral** (Str Mitropoliei 35), a miniature copy of Istanbul's Hagia Sofia, with all the Byzantine bells and whistles you could shake a minaret at. The street is lined with memorial plaques to Romanian notables who stayed there however briefly. The plaque at No 19 honours Transylvania's Memorandumists of 1892, the leaders of the Romanian National Party who addressed a memorandum to the emperor Franz Joseph in Vienna calling for an end to discrimination against Romanians. In apt response, 29 of their members were convicted of agitating against the state and imprisoned.

The influential **Transylvanian Association for Romanian Literature & Culture**, known as Astra, was founded in 1861 at Str Mitropoliei 20, in protest at the intense Magyarisation of Transylvania in the mid-19th century. Astra's nationalist calls for Romanians to stand up for their liberty and identity were voiced in *Tribuna*, Transylvania's first Romanian newspaper, written and printed in Sibiu from 1884. The group is memorialised by Parcul Astra, the quiet park near the end of the street.

Southeast of here, Str Cetăţii lines a section of the **old city walls**, constructed during the 16th century. As in Braşov, different guilds protected each of the 39 towers – there's the Linenmakers' Tower, the Potters' Tower and the Barbers' Tower. Walk northeast up Str Cetăţii, past the **Thick Tower**, which once housed Sibiu's first theatre. The **Natural History Museum** (☎ 218 191; Str Cetăţii 1; adult/child €0.80/0.40; ☺ 10am-5pm Tue-Sat) dates from 1849 and has an average collection of stuffed beasties.

The **Haller Bastion** stands at the northeasternmost end of Piaţa Onofreiu, the continuation of Str Cetăţii. The bastion is named after the 16th-century city mayor Petrus Haller, who had the red-brick tower built with double walls in 1551. When Sibiu was hit by the plague, holes were drilled through the walls to enable corpses to be evacuated more quickly from the city. The bastion was consequently dubbed the 'gate of corpses'.

OUTSIDE THE CENTRE

South of the centre, close to the university, is the **Museum of Hunting Arms & Trophies** (Muzeul de Arme şi Trofee de Vânătoare; ☎ 217 873; Str Şcoala de Înot 4; adult/child €0.60/0.30; ☺ 9am-5pm Tue-Sun), which has a large collection of stuffed deer heads and other remnants of animals sure to make vegetarians feel faint. For fans only. At the southern end of Şcoala de Înot is the 21-hectare **Sub Arini Park**, filled with tree-lined avenues and beautifully laid-out flowerbeds. The **Complex Nataţie Olimpia** is also here, complete with swimming pool, canoeing and rowing facilities, and tennis courts. There is also a **Municipal Stadium**, where Sibiu's football team plays.

Highly recommended is a trip to the **Museum of Traditional Folk Civilization** (Muzeul Civilizaţiei Populare Tradiţionale Astra; ☎ 242 599; Calea

TRANSYLVANIA

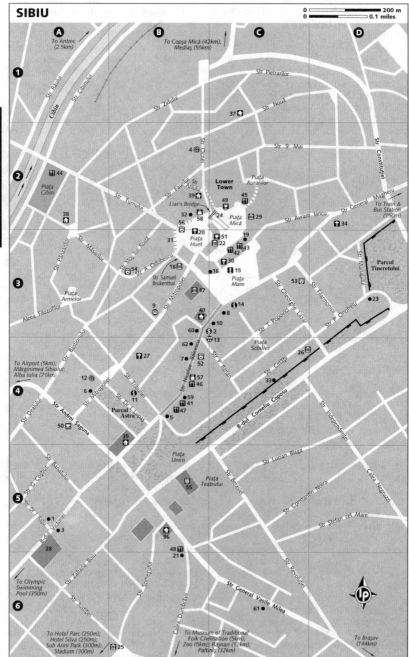

TRANSYLVANIA

Răşinarilor 14; adult/child €1.25/0.75; 10am-6pm Tue-Sun Jun-Sep, 9am-4pm Tue-Sun Oct-May), 5km southwest of the centre. Trolleybus No 1 from the train station goes there (get off at the last stop and keep walking less than 1km), though it's an easy and pleasant bike ride there. Devoted to preserving all aspects of Romanian folk heritage, from musical and literary traditions to traditional house-building, the Astra society was instrumental in constructing what is one of Romania's best sites for seeing the past in action. A great many authentic rural buildings and houses have been reassembled in the park to create an open-air ethnographic museum. At the adjacent **zoo** (Calea Răşinarilor; adult/child €0.75/0.40; 10am-6pm Tue-Sun Jun-Sep, 9am-4pm Tue-Sun Oct-May) you can hire a boat and row yourself around the lake. If you'd rather stay on dry land, **Explorer Sport** (216 641; Calea Dumbrăvii 14; 9am-6pm Mon-Sat) rents mountain bikes for €5 a day, and also does repairs.

Sleeping
BUDGET
If you hang out at the bus or train station long enough, you're bound to get an offer of a private room.

Hotel Halemadero (212 509; Str Măsarilor 10; d/tr €13/20) West of the centre, this friendly, family-run hotel overlooks a pleasant garden and patio.

SC Tourism & Hospitality (0788-233 188; nicolae.lalu@xnet.ro; apt €16-22) They can fix you up

with a two- or three-star apartment in the centre, near Hotel Continental. The building is grotty but the apartments are spacious and clean; considering the price and the privacy, this is the best deal in town. You must call or write in advance.

Hotel Parc (424 455; Str Şcoala de Înot 1-3; s/d/ste €16/20/36) Head here if you care more about your wallet than comfort. A musty eight-storey concrete blob some 2km southwest of the centre, it has grim rooms, but you can comfort yourself with the stale bread for breakfast.

Antrec (220 179; sibiu@antrec.ro; Str D Bagdazar 6) They arrange rooms in private houses in villages surrounding Sibiu for around €10 a night, including breakfast. They're in an inconvenient location in northern Sibiu (call or write first).

Popas Turistic (214 022; tent space/cabins €4/10) Not highly recommended is this run-down affair 4km southwest of the town centre (take trolleybus No 1 from the train station directly to the site).

MID-RANGE
Hotel Bulevard (216 060; Piaţa Unirii 10; s/d/ste €24/27/45) This behemoth is well located in the centre, but dates from 1876 and for better or worse feels like it. There's a stalwart old-world grandeur to its exteriors and lobby, but in the stodgy rooms you feel boxed into the 1960s. It's wheelchair accessible.

Hotel Silva (☎ 442 141; fax 216 304; Aleea Eminescu 1; s/d €26/35) This chalet-style hotel overlooks the tennis courts in the tranquil, tree-filled Sub Arini Park. Located near Hotel Parc, it's an easy walk from the centre.

Hotel Împăratul Romanilor (☎ 216 500; www .aurelius.compace.ro; Str Nicolae Bălcescu 2-4; s/d/ste €44/58/85; 🔌 ⊠) Founded in 1555 as a restaurant, this grand hotel is Sibiu's most luxurious. You could be forgiven for thinking you had wandered into an oversized antique shop in the lobby, with decorative pieces from just about every known style since the 16th century placed willy-nilly. The rooms are simple and elegant, but the real draw is the huge restaurant with sliding glass ceiling and equally over-the-top furnishings.

Hotel Continental (☎ 218 100; www.continental hotels.ro; Calea Dumbrăvii 2-4; s/d/ste €45/60/86; ⊠ 🔌) For a high-rise block of 182 rooms, this is a welcoming place, though mainly geared to business travellers. It's fully wheelchair accessible.

Eating

Dori's (Piaţa Mică 14; 🕑 7am-5pm Mon-Fri, 8am-2pm Sat) Look no further in Sibiu for a cheap (ie a bit greasy but delicious) fill. The tiny patisserie serves freshly baked sesame-seed bread, meat rolls and yoghurt. It's generally packed.

AUTHOR'S CHOICE

Hotel Ela (☎ 215 197; www.hotel-ela.as.ro; Str Nouă 43; s/d/t €16/19/22) One of Sibiu's best bets, this Lower Town guesthouse has just nine rooms, all clean and comfy – some even have bunk beds for the kids. Situated in a quiet area outside the main tourist drag, there's also a courtyard for morning coffee, and a kitchen and laundry room available. Fun-loving, feisty owners complete the rosy picture.

Hotel Podul Minciunilor (☎ 217 259; Str Azilului 1; d €16) Located on an ambient Lower Town street where cats and flower-pots vie for space on window ledges, this small guesthouse has old fashioned bedspreads your great aunt might have made for your house-warming party and boasts nice views onto tiled rooftops. It's renovated, if a tad stuffy.

AUTHOR'S CHOICE

Pizzerie (☎ 0744-210 769; Piaţa Mică 23; mains €3-5; 🕑 noon-11pm Mon-Sat) Despite the bland name, this is one of the city's top dining spots, with creative fish and pork dishes and the best Italian food in the city. Even the sickly baby-blue and hospital-green decor doesn't spoil the appeal of the mouthwatering food. Just sit facing the window, keep your eyes on the Old Town rooftops and enjoy the meal.

Sinuba Pizzeria (☎ 216 005; Calea Dumbrăvii 12; mains €1-3; 🕑 8am-11pm) Great fast food you can point to, including lasagna, *mamaliguţa* (p43) and the proverbial pizza, are served in a clean and always-packed hall which doubles as a friendly, boisterous hang-out.

Restaurant Bufniţa (☎ 214 133; Str Nicolae Bălcescu 4; mains €2-4; 🕑 10am-11pm) Serving standard fare on nice wooden tables isn't quite enough to cover up a stodgy formality that reigns supreme here. It'll do in a pinch, though.

La Turn (☎ 213 985; Piaţa Mare; mains €2-5; 🕑 11am-midnight) Its terrace right on the main square is always packed. The gruff service is made up for by an eye-catching menu including schnitzel stuffed with brains and numerous vegetarian choices. The relaxed decor is British pub meets American tavern. If you're with kids, its roominess makes it the most convenient place to bring them to.

Prima (Str Nicolae Bălcescu 23; 🕑 7.30am-9pm Mon-Fri, 7.30am-7pm Sat, 9am-3pm Sun) This is a convenient grocery store.

Dobrun (Str Nicolae Bălcescu 39; 🕑 6am-9pm Mon-Fri, 7am-3pm Sat, 8am-2pm Sun) This is the place towards which all heads turn; it's a small pastry and bread shop which entices by aroma alone. Find heaven here!

Stock up on vegetables and fruits at the market on Piaţa Cibin, northeast of Str Măsarilor near Hotel Halemadero.

Drinking

Crama National Domn'titi (☎ 218 238; Piaţa Mică 18; 🕑 7pm-1am) This is the city's main student hang-out: see the well-thumbed and beer-stained books of literature in front of undergrads enthusiastically discussing Dostoevsky and Eminescu. The spacious

---

AUTHOR'S CHOICE

Spielplatz (Piaţa Huet 13; ☯ 10am-1am) Off the main drag in several respects, this is where locals let it all hang out. The decor might be described as grunge *ancienne* with a stylish touch, the music is a refreshing blend of funk and hip hop, the drinks are inexpensive; in short, it's the perfect place to unwind.

---

brick cellar bar boasts 10 kinds of beer, and plastic pizza slices for just €0.15!

Art Café (☎ 0722-265 992; Str Filarmonicii 2; ☯ 11am-midnight) A bohemian delight, this is located in a cosy cellar inside the state philharmonic building. Its walls are covered with graffiti and adorned with musical instruments, and there are regular exhibits of local art.

Fashion Café (☎ 214 250; Str Andrei Saguna 15; ☯ 24hr) Not as trendy as its name implies, this large hall with billiard tables (€1.30 per hour) makes a decent hang-out, despite the metal grid garden chairs. Light meals are served.

Chill Out (☎ 0788-314 800; www.chilloutsibiu.ro; Piaţa Mică 23; ☯ 10am-2am) Something different goes on every night in this cellar club that attracts a slightly trendy if alternative crowd. Enjoy DJs, house parties or theme nights, or just kick back and get elegantly wasted.

Entertainment
CINEMAS
Cinema Tineretului (☎ 211 420; Str Alexandru Odobescu 4) The auditorium-cum-disco is filled with sofas and coffee tables, inviting you to sit back in comfort and relax over a beer while watching your favourite Hollywood hero in action. A real treat!

Studionul Astra (☎ 218 195, extension 26; Piaţa Huet 12) This screens alternative art films; it also hosts the annual International Astra Film Festival in May.

THEATRE & CLASSICAL MUSIC
Agenţie de Teatrală (☎ 217 575; Str Nicolae Bălcescu 17; ☯ 8am-8pm Mon-Fri, 9am-3pm Sat) Tickets for major events are sold here; check out the posters in the office.

Philharmonic (☎ 210 264; Str Filarmonicii 2) Founded in 1949, this has played a key role in maintaining Sibiu's prestige as a main cultural centre of Transylvania.

Radu Stancu State Theatre (☎ 413 114; B-dul Spitelor 2-4) Plays are usually in Romanian, with occasional productions in German. It hosts the International Theatre Festival in June.

Puppet Theatre (Teatrul de Păpuşi; ☎ 211 420; Str Alexandru Odobescu 4) Kids are entertained only between October and July.

Shopping
Antik (☎ 211 604; Str Nicolae Bălcescu 23; ☯ 10am-6pm Mon-Fri, 10am-2pm Sat) The best place to pick through old German knick-knacks.

Art Antik (☎ 211 115; Piaţa Huet 1; ☯ 10am-6pm Mon-Fri, 9am-2pm Sat) You can find antique items here plus souvenir glass icons.

Getting There & Away
AIR
Tarom (☎ 211 157; Str Nicolae Bălcescu 10; ☯ 8am-6pm Mon-Fri) no longer operates flights to Bucharest, but you can hop on a Munich-bound plane five times weekly for as low as €255 for a return flight. **Carpatair** (☎ 229 161; www.carpatair.ro), which has an office at the airport, has six weekly flights to Munich and three weekly to Stuttgart, via Timişoara.

TRAIN
You can buy advance tickets at the **Agenţie de Voiaj CFR office** (☎ 216 441; Str Nicolae Bălcescu 6; ☯ 7.30am-7.30pm Mon-Fri). The train station is at the eastern end of Str General Magheru, on Piaţa 1 Decembrie.

Sibiu lies at an awkward rail junction; getting here and away is best by bus and maxitaxi. For Sighişoara, you have to change at Copşa Mică or Mediaş. For Alba Iulia, you have to change at Vinţu de Jos. Cluj-Napoca is the most irksome to get to: there is one direct train a day (€5, four hours) leaving in the middle of the night; otherwise, you need to change at Copşa Mică or Vinţu de Jos.

BUS
The **bus station** (☎ 217 757) is opposite the train station and is the usual muddle of private companies with no centralised timetable in sight. If your Romanian is good, call for info; otherwise get the tourist information centre to do it for you. **Transmixt** (☎ 217 757) serves the majority of routes. **Eurolines**

TRANSYLVANIA

(☎ 213 536; sibiu@eurolines.ro; Str General Vasile Milea 13; ⏲ 9am-5pm Mon-Fri) sells tickets to many European destinations.

Daily bus and maxitaxi services include at least seven to Cluj-Napoca (€3.20, three hours), five to Târgu Mureş (€3, three hours), as well as to Timişoara, Bucharest, Alba Julia, Braşov, Deva, Mangalia and Sighişoara.

Maxitaxis to Râsnari and Păltiniş (€1.15, 1¼ hours, three a day) leave from the roundabout in front of the train station, and buses to Cisnădie leave every half-hour from platform No 9.

Getting Around

Trolleybus No 1 connects the train station with the centre.

TO/FROM THE AIRPORT

Sibiu airport (☎ 229 235) is 5km west of the centre. Tarom (p344) runs a shuttle bus, departing from its office one hour before flights depart. Trolleybus No 8 runs between the airport and the train station.

TAXI

To call a taxi dial ☎ 444 444 or ☎ 212 121.

CAR RENTAL

Advantage (☎ 216 949; Str Nicolae Bălcescu 37) has Dacias for as low as €29 per day. Other makes run from €40 to €70 a day.

AROUND SIBIU

☎ 269

Cisnădie, Răşinari & Păltiniş

Eight kilometres south of Sibiu, on the road to Păltiniş, is the Saxon fortified church of Cisnădie (Heltau in German, Nagydisznód in Hungarian). Work started on defensive walls around the church in 1430 but they were destroyed by a Turkish attack on the town in 1493. Ask in the village for the key to the bell tower, which offers eye-pleasing views of this red-roofed town. Three main streets run through Cisnădie; the church is south of the middle street.

The charming shepherd village of Răşinari, famed for its local carpentry and sheep farming, is 4km south of Cisnădie and is one of the wealthiest villages in the region. There are two small rivers running through it, three churches and a monastery in the slow process of being built. Ethnographic

exhibits – featuring the long wooden ladels *(tâlv)* used for sampling the plum brandy *(ţuică)* stored in large wooden kegs – are displayed in the village museum. This is also the birthplace of Romanian poet and politician Octavian Goga (1881–1939).

The main road through Răşinari starts a steep climb before climaxing at Păltiniş (1470m), one of the prettiest and most convenient stepping stones to excellent hiking trails in Romania (see the boxed text on p123). Romania's first mountain resort (founded in 1894), it's nestled at the foot of the Cindrel Mountains (also known as the Cibin Mountains) and is readily accessible by transport from Sibiu (see p121). Services are above average and the surroundings are staggeringly beautiful. The last remnants of its golden past as a fashionable resort were wiped out in 1992 when its wooden nine-pin bowling alley was moved to the open-air museum in Sibiu.

Păltiniş' **Reception Centre** (☎ 574 040) is run by an enthusiastic ex-Peace Corps volunteer who stayed on and single-handedly made this resort one of the best-managed in the country. It can book accommodation (see Sleeping, below), hook you up to the Internet (€1 per hour), alert you to weather conditions on the mountains, plus rent mountain bikes (€1 per hour), skis and snowboards (€10 per day). It hosts a Snow Festival (Sarbatori Zapezii) during the second week in April, replete with soapbox derbies and build-your-own-sleigh competitions, and the Mountain Jazz Festival (Jazz ca Munte) on the first weekend in August. Păltiniş also rumbles in the second week of August when part of the national off-road car rally rolls through.

SLEEPING

For places to stay in Păltiniş, contact either the **Reception Centre** (☎ 574 040), available 24 hours, or, in Sibiu, the extremely efficient **SC Păltinis** (☎ 223 860; www.scpaltinis.ro in Romanian; Str Tribunei 3; ⏲ 9am-5pm Mon-Fri). Either can find accommodation to suit any budget, from dorm beds for €5 to three-star doubles for €35; there's a great range to choose from.

Cabana Mai (☎ 557 269; www.pensiunea-mai.ro; s/d/ste €25/40/60) Some 5km beyond Răşinari towards Sibiu, this is the best place between Sibiu and Păltiniş. Rooms are huge and most have splendid views of the velvety

CINDREL MOUNTAINS

The Cindrel (or Cibin) Mountains' highest peaks – Mt Cindrel (2244m) and Mt Frumoasa (2170m) – shelter two large glacial lakes.

From **Păltiniş**, you can enjoy what experts say are the country's best-marked hiking trails. Better still, almost all of the trails are perfect for mountain biking too.

From Păltiniş' Reception Centre, where you can pick up a map of the region and trails, there's a 4km trail to **Şanta**, where there is a small refuge for campers to spend the night. The most popular route (3.5km, red circles) descends to the **Cibin Gorges** (Cheile Cibinului). From here the trail continues northeast, past **Lake Cibin** to **Cabana Fântânele**. The next day continue in the same direction to **Sibiel** village (three to 3½ hours, blue crosses). Alternatively, follow another blue-cross trail to the neighbouring village of **Fântânele**.

Heading back south from Cabana Fântânele, a trail (red crosses and blue circles) cuts down a valley to **Şaua Şerbănei**, where you pick a separate trail leading to the **Cânaia refuge** (7½ to eight hours for the whole trip, blue circles).

More adventurous alpinists should follow the trail from **Cabana Păltiniş** south, past the Cânaia refuge (5½ to 6½ hours, red stripes) to the summit of **Mt Cindrel**. Heading northwards, red stripes also indicate the way to **Răşinari** village (six to seven hours), with its Cabana Mai.

From Păltiniş it is an easy day's hike to most of the villages in Mărginimea Sibiului (see below).

green valley. The restaurant serves scrumptious meals from 8am to 11pm, including fish you can catch yourself in the stream behind the cabana. There are several hiking trails nearby.

GETTING THERE & AWAY

An alternative way to get to Răşinari is by taking trolleybus No 1 from the Sibiu train station to the last stop. Then take the tram (same side of road as Dumbrava Park; every half-hour) to Răşinari.

See p121 for more information.

Mărginimea Sibiului

The villages in the so-called Mărginimea Sibiului ('borders of Sibiu') represent the heart and soul of traditional rural (ie Romanian) Transylvania. Scattered throughout the region west of Sibiu, they have preserved an old way of life: here you see not only the ubiquitous horse and plough, but also artisans engaged in woodwork, carving and weaving. Painting icons on glass and colouring eggs are pastimes here as much as surfing the Web is in Bucharest, and the local cuisine, including shepherd's polenta (with loads of fresh cream and milk), is enough to keep you purring for days. The region is best explored by bike.

Lying 15km west of Sibiu is the delightful **Cristian** (Grossau in German, Kereszténysziget in Hungarian). This village was settled by Saxons in the 14th century and is therefore not part of Mărginimea Sibiului, but it makes for a picture-postcard stop along the way. Red-roofed houses and vibrant washed walls are overshadowed by a grandiose fortified church in the centre of the village. Visitors can climb the tower of the church for an aerial view. Ask for the key at the green-painted house, down the road behind the eastern fortress wall. Local history is covered in the petite **village museum** (Muzeul Sătesco; ☾ noon-5pm Tue-Sun), next to the local prefecture in the centre of the village.

Orlat, founded in the early 14th century, is today home to one of the largest village orphanages in Romania. Just 4km away is **Gura Râului**, a charming, sleepy town with a massive dam several kilometres out of town. In **Sibiel**, 5km west of Orlat, the **Zosim Oancea Icons Museum** (☎ 553 818), one of Romania's best, is well worth visiting. The museum, in a blue-painted building next to the village church (1765), houses a collection of more than 700 icons richly painted on glass, as well as furniture and ceramics.

From Sibiel, head 6km north to **Sălişte**, another quaint village rich in local folklore. In **Galeş**, 2km west of Sălişte, is a small ethnographic and art museum. It is at the southern end of the village, across the bridge opposite a salami factory. A dirt track leads from Galeş to **Poiana Sibiului**,

TRANSYLVANIA

famed for its fantastic coloured eggs decorated with bright, geometric motifs.

SLEEPING & EATING

Be sure to check out Rural Tourism (www.ruraltourism.ro), a web-based service which provides details (and photos) of many guesthouses in the area. Also, dozens of homes in each village have *cazare* signs hanging in their windows; finding a place to stay is rarely a problem. In Sibiel, for example, an agro-tourism scheme involves some 20 families who open their homes to tourists, feeding you with fresh eggs and milk for breakfast and laying on a small feast of home-grown produce at dinner time. This successful business is run by **Dorina Petra** (☎ 554 198). A night's accommodation including all meals costs €15 to €20 per person.

Hotel Spack (☎ 579 262; Str II 9; s/d €14/25) Staying here is comparable to a cosy night at home. The small, family-run *pensiune* is on the edge of Cristian on the road to Orlat.

Câmpean (☎ 572 364; Gura Râului 833; per person €7) This is a dreamy place to stay in Gura Râului. A small guesthouse on the site of a small farm (there are buffaloes!), it's run by friendly French-speaking owners who can entertain kids, both the child and adult varieties, with fun horse-drawn cart and sleigh rides. Meals are about €2 extra.

GETTING THERE & AWAY

Local trains from Sibiu to Sebeş stop at Cristian (€0.40, 15 minutes), Sibiel (€0.70, 25 minutes), Sălişte (€1, 35 minutes) and Miercurea Sibiului (€2, 1¼ hours). There are five trains daily between Sibiu and Sebeş. The only buses serving the area go from Sibiu to Orlat (€0.70, eight per day).

Around Mediaş & Copşa Mică

If Transylvania's pristine landscape has left you with a hankering for pollution, you may consider a visit to Mediaş (population 61,740), a thriving industrial town 55km north of Sibiu, or its notorious twin, Copşa Mică, 13km to its southwest. It was in Mediaş (Mediasch in German, Medgyes in Hungarian) that Saxon church leaders met in 1544 to mark the first Lutheran synod in Transylvania. The fortified **Evangelical Church of St Margaret** dominates the old town, just north of Piaţa Regele Ferdinand (a few

minutes' walk north of the train station). A church was built on the site in the 13th century but it was not until 1447 that the present edifice was constructed. A 74m-tall tower (struck by lightning four times) was added in 1482, while the church's altar, dating from 1485, is considered one of Transylvania's most precious pieces of medieval Saxon art. For details about other fortified churches closer to Sighişoara, see p129.

Copşa Mică, traditionally Romania's black pit, is a major junction for connecting trains between Sibiu and Sighişoara. Until the early 1990s, the factory producing black carbon (used in tyres) and a metalworks plant spewed out filth that left the surrounding area covered in soot all year long; sheep were black from it, laundry could not be hung outside, and the health effects were apalling – two thirds of children showed some signs of mental illness. Since the fall of the communist regime, the town has made a dramatic turnaround, with Euro-standard filters on the metalworks plant, and the closing of the carbon factory. White snow was seen for the first time in decades. Still, the belching smokestacks visible from afar are a shocking sight in contrast to the beauty of the rest of the region.

Getting There & Away

Mediaş is on the Cluj-Napoca–Bucharest line. To get to Sighişoara from Sibiu you have to change trains at Copşa Mică or Mediaş. All international trains between Bucharest and Budapest stop at Mediaş. Buses and maxitaxis link Mediaş with Copşa Mică, Târgu Mureş and Sibiu.

SIGHIŞOARA
☎ 265 / pop 36,180

Of all the dreamy spots throughout Transylvania that make you feel like you're floating through another time and space, Sighişoara's citadel wins the time-travel cake by a long shot. Sighişoara (Schässburg in German, Segesvár in Hungarian) has an enchantingly preserved medieval citadel as its core, and is surrounded by beautiful hilly countryside. It tends to seduce visitors' hearts more than any other city in Transylvania.

Nine towers remain along its intact city walls, which encircle sloping cobbled streets lined with 16th-century burgher

SPACED OUT

Walking the charming cobblestone alleys of Sighişoara, the idea of space exploration might seem somewhat out of place. Yet it wasn't for one of Sighişoara's most beloved residents. Though he was born in Sibiu, Hermann Oberth (1894–1989), considered one of the fathers of modern astronautics and rocketry, is revered as a local boy (don't remind anyone that he spent only a few years here as a child). A square is named after him, and a corner of the History Museum (p127) is dedicated to him.

Inspired by Jules Verne as a sky-gazing tyke, Oberth started to design space rockets at the age of 14. Later, studying medicine and physics in Munich, he wrote prolifically about the possibility and mechanics of space travel. Most of his dissertations were dismissed by the scientific community but in 1929 he had what ended up being his big break: his designs were used to build model spaceships for the kitschy Fritz Lang film *Woman on the Moon*. That year, the German army launched a rocket research program. Hmm...

During WWII, Oberth codeveloped the V2 rocket for the Germans, then continued research in the US before retiring and publishing books on alternative energy sources and space exploration.

There is a Hermann Oberth Space Museum in Germany, near Nuremberg.

houses and untouched churches. There are a thousand corners to discover here. Yet as easy as it is to get lost in fantasy land, there are enough kicking clubs, interesting places to visit and ace accommodation to keep you focused on more earthly pleasures. One could easily spend several days in and around Sighişoara.

Settled by the Romans, the town was first documented as Castrum Sex. Saxon colonists settled here from the 12th century and built it into a thriving crafts and trading town; today, there are fewer than 500 Germans in the city. Sighişoara was also the birthplace of Vlad Ţepeş (you can fill your tummy in his natal home; see p129) and therefore attracts hordes of Dracula tourists.

Sighişoara is in the midst of rejuvenation; only in recent years has a sudden influx of (German) investment started pouring into town, resulting in painted houses and new hotels and pavement cafés. Locals are already decrying that the citadel is not as 'local' as it was. No matter how full of tourists the citadel gets, however, it somehow never loses its unhurried natural charm.

It is worth visiting the market on Wednesday and Saturday, when Roma and villagers from outlying regions come into town on their horse-drawn wagons to sell their wares. The week-long Medieval Festival of the Arts in late July is more of a wild drinking party than anything cultural, but the colourful costumes are pretty to look at, especially through beer suds.

Orientation

Follow Str Gării south from the train station to the unmistakably Soviet war memorial, where you turn left to the St Treime Orthodox church. Cross the Târnava Mare River on the footbridge here and take Str Morii to the left, then keep going all the way up to Piaţa Hermann Oberth and the old town. Many of the facilities you'll want are found along a short stretch of Str 1 Decembrie 1918.

MAPS

Cartographia publishes the highly detailed, excellent *Sighişoara* fold-out map (€2), covering the city and environs.

Information
CULTURAL CENTRES

Thanks to major funding by aircraft manufacturers Messerschmidt, the **Stag House** (Casa Cu Cerb; ☎ 776 425; Str Şcolii 1) is in a slow process of turning into a German Cultural Centre; call to see if it has officially opened.

INTERNET ACCESS

There is Internet access in the basements of the **Burg Hostel** (see Sleeping; per hr €0.40; ☼ 7am-1am) and the **Café International & Family Centre** (see Eating; per hr €0.40; ☼ 10am-6pm Mon-Sat). Otherwise, there's **Internet Café** (☎ 771 269; Str Libertăţii 44; per hr €0.60; ☼ 9am-11pm), directly south from the train station.

MONEY

There are numerous exchange offices lining the city's main street, Str 1 Decembrie 1918.

TRANSYLVANIA

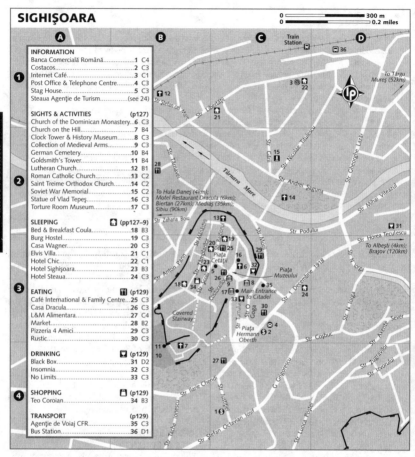

SIGHIŞOARA

0 _____ 300 m
0 _____ 0.2 miles

INFORMATION
Banca Comercială Română...............1 C4
Costacos...2 C3
Internet Café....................................3 C1
Post Office & Telephone Centre.........4 C3
Stag House.......................................5 C3
Steaua Agenţie de Turism.............(see 24)

SIGHTS & ACTIVITIES (p127)
Church of the Dominican Monastery...6 C3
Church on the Hill.............................7 B4
Clock Tower & History Museum.........8 C3
Collection of Medieval Arms..............9 C3
German Cemetery..............................10 B4
Goldsmith's Tower............................11 B4
Lutheran Church................................12 B1
Roman Catholic Church......................13 C2
Saint Treime Orthodox Church...........14 C2
Soviet War Memorial.........................15 C2
Statue of Vlad Tepeş.........................16 C3
Torture Room Museum.......................17 C3

SLEEPING (pp127–9)
Bed & Breakfast Coula......................18 B3
Burg Hostel......................................19 C3
Casa Wagner....................................20 C3
Elvis Villa..21 C1
Hotel Chic.......................................22 C1
Hotel Sighişoara...............................23 B3
Hotel Steaua....................................24 C3

EATING (p129)
Café International & Family Centre...25 C3
Casa Dracula...................................26 C3
L&M Alimentara...............................27 C4
Market...28 B2
Pizzeria 4 Amici...............................29 C3
Rustic...30 C3

DRINKING (p129)
Black Box..31 D2
Insomnia...32 C3
No Limits...33 C3

SHOPPING (p129)
Teo Coroian.....................................34 B3

TRANSPORT (p129)
Agenţie de Voiaj CFR........................35 C3
Bus Station......................................36 D1

Train Station

To Târgu
Mureş (52km)

Târnava Mare

To Hula Daneş (4km);
Motel Restaurant Dracula (6km);
Biertan (27km); Mediaş (35km);
Sibiu (90km)

To Albeşti (4km);
Braşov (120km)

Piaţa
Cetaţii

Piaţa
Muzeului

Main Entrance
to Citadel

Covered
Stairway

Piaţa
Hermann
Oberth

Banca Comercială Română (Str Justiţiei 12;
🕑 8.30am-4pm Mon-Fri)
Costacos (Piaţa Hermann Oberth 21; 🕑 9am-5pm
Mon-Fri, 9am-1pm Sat) Gives cash advances.

POST & TELEPHONE
The **post office** (☎ 771 055; Str 1 Decembrie 1918,
17; 🕑 7am-8pm Mon-Fri) and **telephone centre**
(🕑 7am-9pm Mon-Fri, 8am-8pm Sat) share the same
building.

TOURIST INFORMATION
Sighişoara has a dearth of reliable travel
agencies and no official tourist information
office, reflecting a nascent, inept tourism
infrastructure – suprising in a city that's an
obvious tourist magnet.

Café International & Family Centre (☎ 777 844;
Piaţa Cetatii 8; 🕑 10am-6pm Mon-Sat) This is a multi-
functional, nonprofit agency (see also p129), founded by
Nazarenes from Massachussets, whose staff can effectively
double as a tourist office; they know more about the city
than most official agencies! They also organise the city's
best tours: three times daily Monday through Saturday,
they do 75-minute walking tours (suggested donation
€2) of the Old Town, and twice a week they do a more
adventurous 'off the beaten track' tour, taking in the city's
outskirts and a gypsy neighbourhood. They also sell some
of the best local crafts and souvenirs. All proceeds go to
help local homeless children and the elderly.
Steaua Agenţie de Turism (☎ 772 499; fax 771 932;
Str 1 Decembrie 1918, 12; 🕑 9am-5pm Mon-Fri, 9am-
1pm Sat) Sells city guides and maps, and arranges private
accommodation.

Sights

All Sighişoara's sights are in the old town – the delightful medieval **citadel** – perched on a hillock and fortified with a 14th-century wall, to which 14 towers and five artillery bastions were later added. Today the citadel, which is on the Unesco World Heritage list, retains just nine of its original towers and two of its bastions.

Entering the citadel, you pass under the massive **clock tower** (Turnul cu Ceas). Formerly the main entrance to the fortified city, the tower is 64m tall with sturdy base walls measuring an impenetrable 2.35m. Inside the 1648 clock is a pageant of slowly revolving 80cm-high figurines, carved from linden wood, each representing a character from the Saxon pantheon: Peace bears an olive branch, Justice has a set of scales and Law wields a sword. The executioner is also present and the drum-player strikes the hour. Above stand seven figures, each representing a day of the week.

The figurines can be inspected through glass from the **History Museum** (☎ 771 108; Piaţa Muzeului 1; adult/child €0.80/0.40; ☽ 10am-3pm Mon, 9am-6.30pm Tue-Fri, 9am-3.30pm Sat-Sun) in the 14th-century tower. This highly worthwhile museum has a good collection of Renaissance furniture, medical instruments and a superb view of Sighişoara from the 7th floor. Under the clock tower on the left is the small but memorable **Torture Room Museum** (admission €0.25; ☽ 10am-3pm Mon, 9am-6.30pm Tue-Fri, 9am-3.30pm Sat-Sun), which displays diagrams of torture methods, lovingly detailed in their original German language.

Past the clock tower to the left is a small house containing a **collection of medieval arms** (adult/child €0.40/0.30; ☽ 10am-3pm Mon, 9am-6.30pm Tue-Fri, 9am-3.30pm Sat-Sun).

Immediately inside the citadel, just north of the clock tower, is the 15th-century **Church of the Dominican Monastery** (Biserica Mănăstirii; ☽ 9am-7pm Mon-Sat, 10am-2pm Sun). The Gothic church became the Saxons' main Lutheran church in 1556. Classical, folk and baroque concerts are often held here.

Continuing west towards Piaţa Cetăţii, you come to the house in which Vlad Ţepeş was born in 1431 and reputedly lived until the age of four. The pretty **Casa Dracula**, complete with its original river-stone floor, is now a restaurant (see Eating, p129). For more Vlad worshipping, head to the nearby statue of Vlad Tepeş, hiding itself behind the Church of the Dominican Monastery.

The quiet, minuscule **Piaţa Cetăţii** is the heart of old Sighişoara. It was here that markets, craft fairs, public executions, impalings and witch trials were held. The 17th-century Stag House, overlooking the square on the corner of Str Şcolii, is considered the most representative example of the citadel's architecture.

From the square, turn left up Str Şcolii to the 172 steps of the **covered stairway** (scara acoperită), which has tunnelled its way up the hill since 1642, to the 1345 Gothic **Church on the Hill** (Biserica din Deal, Bergkirche; admission €0.25; ☽ 8am-8pm May-Oct, 9am-4pm Nov-Apr). This Lutheran church, sternly presiding at a height of 429m, is in a perennial state of restoration but worth a visit; the painted altar is lovely, as are the wooden pews (with wafer-thin blankets on them to ease the pain). Right in front is the weedy **German cemetery**, a must for wanderers of cemeteries.

Behind the church are the remains of the **Goldsmiths' Tower**. The goldsmiths, tailors, carpenters and tinsmiths, the only craftsmen to have their guilds and workshops inside the citadel, built eight wells (34m deep) within the city walls to ensure a continuous water supply during times of siege. Guilds existed until 1875.

From the church, head back down the hill, cross Piaţa Cetăţii, then head down Str Bastionul. At its northern end is the **Roman Catholic church** (1896).

Apart from their two churches in the citadel, Sighişoara's Saxon community had a third **Lutheran church**, deliberately sited well outside the city walls. The tin-spired church, sitting inauspiciously at a rail crossing just west of the train station off Str Libertăţii, was used from the 17th century for victims of the plague and infectious diseases.

Sleeping

As elsewhere in Romania, you are likely to encounter people eager to take you home with them at the train station; the prominent operator here is a charming young man named Radu. Readers' letters have been very mixed about him, as the houses he uses, though in the citadel, tend to be in dire need of repairs.

BUDGET

Elvis Villa (☎ 772 546; www.elvisvilla.com/sighisoara; Str Libertăţii 10; bed €10; 🖳) This is practically an institution here. Located just 250m west of the train station, it's sadly not in the citadel, but nothing's far in this small, walkable city. Lots of pluses, such as half a litre of free beer and Internet access, help make this a fun, lively place.

Burg Hostel (☎ 778 489; Str Bastionului 4-6; dm €7, d €24) This is a multistorey, German-run (ie efficient) hostel in the citadel, with a restaurant terrace and a smoky basement lounge bar. Rooms are simple but sterile, and the place has a vibrant, busy feel to its narrow corridors.

Bed & Breakfast Coula (☎ 777 907; Str Tâmplarilor 40; per person €12) Right inside the citadel, this guesthouse is a good choice, with six rooms in a large home where you can share morning tea with grandma in a charming, overgrown garden. Not only does the father make and serve his own wine, the friendly, English-speaking family rent bicycles and organise day trips at very reasonable prices to Biertan and other towns to see some fortified churches.

Hula Daneş (☎ 774 754; tent space €1.30, 2-/4-person hut €5/8) The owners don't mind picking you up from Sighişoara if you call in advance, but it's only 4km out of town on the road to Mediaş; buses to Daneş, Mediaş and Sibiu will stop in front of it, or it's a €2 to €3 taxi ride there. It's not bad as far as Romanian camping grounds go, with a decent restaurant and nearby forest hiking trails. Male visitors are likely to be overtly propositioned by the staff, however.

Hotel Chic (☎ 775 901; Str Libertăţii 44; dm without/with TV €10/13, d without/with private toilet €12/15) Its name may be wishful thinking, but for a place directly opposite the train station, this is very quiet and clean. Dorm rooms are small (two to four persons), toilets clean, and the café downstairs serves decent meals. Local kids outside will ask you for money all the time, but the neighbourhood is safe, if colourful.

Motel Restaurant Dracula (☎ 772 211; dracula .danes@email.ro; d €20, ste €27-36) It's much better than it sounds. Located 6km west of town near Daneş on the main route 14 towards Mediaş, this pleasant, villa-like motel has a lot going on, including an ostrich farm, an adjacent equestrian centre (€7 per hour) and a restaurant noted to be Sighişoara's best (brains reign supreme on the menu but there's more to choose from, and all produce is fresh and locally grown; mains €2 to €5). The rooms are a tad somber and dull, but the surroundings are nice.

Hotel Steaua (☎ 771 594; Str 1 Decembrie 1918, 12; s/d without private toilet €14/19, with private toilet €17/23) The friendliness of the staff is surprising considering that they work is such a grim, musty place. The carpets are seething, the toilets grimy, and the rooms and corridors dark and dank. You might see a vampire or two here. It is, however, cheap and central.

MID-RANGE

Hotel Sighişoara (☎ 771 000; Str Şcolii 4-6; s/d €40/45) This is a great deal; the wooden furniture and slanted ceilings (with windows overlooking citadel rooftops) give a tasteful,

---

AUTHOR'S CHOICE

Casa Wagner (☎ 506 014; www.casa-wagner.com; Piaţa Cetăţii 7; s/d/ste €35/45/70; 🖳 ✗) This is arguably Romania's loveliest hotel. The attention to detail in this subtly elegant place just off the central square shows impeccable taste. The Dutch owner and his Romanian wife have lovingly recreated a Saxon atmosphere with the use of period pieces and antiques: each room is decorated differently but you can find carved wooden bedposts, wrought-iron candle holders, paintings, armoirs, chests and woven carpets on hardwood floors. However, this is not a case of antique overload; simplicity and restraint are key design elements. The apartments (especially room No 3) are large enough to host a ball in and most rooms have off-lit arched or slanted ceilings. The full comforts of modernity (Internet connection, bathrooms with all the frills) have been seemlessly integrated into the old-world design. The equally lovely **restaurant** (mains €2-5; 🕑 9am-midnight) has excellent food at reasonable prices and live violin music after 8pm, plus there's a cosy **wine cellar** (🕑 6pm-1am). Needless to say, the service is impeccable. Anything similar in western Europe would cost two to three times what it does here. Rarely is a hotel this memorable.

comfortable ambience. Corridors under high arched ceilings lend a feel of pleasant roominess. Plus, there's an indoor pool!

Casa Cu Cerb (☎ 777 349; Str Şcolii 1; d €50; ☒) Of interest mainly to royalty fetishists: Prince Charles slept here on a visit in 2003. Otherwise, the rooms are elegant, yes, but cold and starchy, and the overarching atmosphere is unfriendly and elitist.

Eating

Pizzeria 4 Amici (Str Octavian Goga 12; mains €2-4; ⏱ 11am-11pm) The pizzas are very doughy; best to stick to the pasta dishes.

Café International & Family Centre (☎ 777 844; Piaţa Cetatii 8; mains €1-2) Right on the main square, this is a double-whammy oasis: to vegetarians (all the meals here – mainly quiches, soups and salads – are veggie) and homesick Americans (where else in Romania can you find a peanut butter and jam sandwich, brownie, grilled cheese and lemon pie?).

Rustic (☎ 0743-805 355; Str Decembrie 1, 7; mains €2-4; ⏱ 9.30am-12.30am) Very popular with foreigners, this has a very 'man's man' brick-and-wood tavern-style decor, replete with animal pelts on the walls. The price is right, however, the menu is varied, and they serve a mean *sarmalute* (vine or cabbage leaves stuffed with meat).

Casa Dracula (☎ 771 596; Str Cositorarilor 5; mains €2-6; ⏱ 10am-midnight) It has a nasty local reputation as a tourist trap. Considering its name and the fact it's located in the house where little Vlad Tepeş took his first tender steps, at first glance it would appear to be true. However, the Dracula motif isn't jarring, the interiors are comfortable, the menu is varied – of course (bloody) steaks feature prominently, but there are vegetarian dishes too – and the food is good (though not excellent).

The daily market off Str Târnavei has a good selection of fruits, vegetables and cheese. The **L&M Alimentar** (Str Ilarie Chendi 4; ⏱ 24hr) grocery store is well stocked.

Entertainment

Occasional classical concerts are held in the city's churches; check for posted adverts.

No Limits (☎ 518 961; Str Turnului 1; ⏱ 8pm-4am) This slightly upmarket disco is to the right of the arched entry to the citadel, just below the clock tower. It borders on tackiness but gets steamy on weekends.

Insomnia (☎ 0744-172 498; Str Turnului; ⏱ 10-2am) Also to the right of the citadel entrance but up the outdoor staircase, this is Sighişoara's best club, a funky mix of bar, lounge, disco and performance/cinema space. The music is nonpop alternative, the views over the lower city are splendid, and there's a rooftop terrace.

Black Box (☎ 0742-668 385; Str Horea Teculescu 37; ⏱ 10pm-4am Thu-Sat) For a grungier local bar, try this one outside the centre that gets very popular on Friday and Saturday nights.

Shopping

Teo Coroian (☎ 771 677; teo_coroian@email.ro; Str Şcolii 14; ⏱ 9am-9pm) The owner here has a good life: he makes and sells wine as well as plum, pear and apple *palinka* (brandy or schnapps if you will; €5 to €10 per bottle). If the doors are closed, just ring the bell and he'll come downstairs and offer you a taste.

Getting There & Away

The **Agenţie de Voiaj CFR** (☎ 771 820; Str O Goga 6A; ⏱ 8am-4pm Mon-Fri) sells tickets in advance for all trains. Sighişoara is linked by train with Bucharest nine times a day, eight of them going to or from Cluj-Napoca, Satu Mare, Arad, Oradea, Budapest, Prague or Vienna. For trains to Sibiu you have to change at Copşa Mică or Mediaş (three daily).

The **bus station** (☎ 771 260) is next to the train station on Str Libertăţii. Daily bus or maxitaxi services include between three and six daily services to Sibiu and Bistriţa, eight to Târgu Mureş, six to Apold, and hourly services (from 6.15am to 8.15pm) to Bucharest via Braşov. There are regular services to Daneş and Mediaş.

FORTIFIED SAXON CHURCHES

The Târnave plateau, which stretches for some 120km between Braşov and Sighişoara, is traditionally known as Burzen Land (Ţara Bârsei in Romanian). It was to this region that Saxons – mainly from the Franken region in western Germany – were invited by the Hungarian king Geza II in 1123. In the 15th and 16th centuries, following the increased threat of Turkish attacks on their towns, the settlements were strengthened with bulky city walls and fortified churches. Defensive towers in the churches served as observation posts and

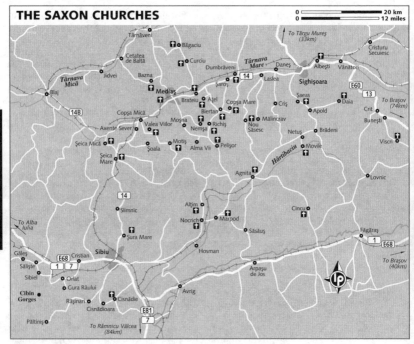

THE SAXON CHURCHES

town entrances were guarded with a port-cullis that could be quickly lowered as the enemy advanced.

Around Mediaş & Copşa Mică

There are a number of fine fortified churches around these two towns. **Bazna** (Baassen in German), a small village first settled in 1302, is northwest of Mediaş (head north towards Târnăveni for 7km then west another 5km). Its late-Gothic St Nicholas' Church was built at the start of the 16th century on the ruins of a 14th-century original. Its highlight is the three pre-Reformation bells (1404) in the church tower. The 6m-tall wall that surrounded the church was partly dismantled in 1870 because the villagers needed bricks to build a wall around the village school. From 1842 onwards the village developed as a small spa resort following the discovery of natural springs which released sulphurous gases.

Băgaciu (Bogeschdorf) is to the north of Mediaş. Follow the main northbound road for 15km, then turn right along a minor road signposted 'Delenii' for 6km. The pre-Reformation, late-Gothic altar in its church, restored in Vienna in 1896, is considered to be the best-preserved Saxon church altar. Heading 4km south along the dirt track from here, you come to **Curciu** (Kirtsch). The decorative stone frieze above the western door, featuring apes and other animals, is unique to this 14th-century village church.

From Copşa Mică, head south along a dirt track to **Valea Viilor** (Wurmloch). The village, dating from 1263, has a quaint fortified church which was raised at the end of the 15th century and surrounded by 1.5m-thick walls. It is on Unesco's list of World Heritage sites.

Şeica Mică (Kleinschelken), first settled in 1316, is 3km west of a turn-off 11km south of Copşa Mică on the road to/from Sibiu. The village was engulfed by fire several times during the 16th century, but remarkably its local church, built in 1414, survived. Its beautiful baptismal font is late-Gothic (1447) and cast from iron. In the church courtyard stands an old well, and the ensemble is surrounded by 15m-tall walls. There's also a small fortified Saxon church in **Şeica Mare**, 4km south of its sister village.

From Mediaş you can also head south towards Agnita. Ten kilometres south along this minor road is **Moşna** (Meschen). Its village church, dating from the 14th century, was completely rebuilt in 1485 in a late-Gothic style. Its centrepiece is the tall bell tower, eight storeys high. **Alma Vii** (Alemen) is just a few kilometres south of Moşna. The four-towered church was built at the start of the 14th century and fortified in the early 16th century. It's seen better days, but has a fairy tale–like quality.

Around Sighişoara

These tiny villages are poorly served by public transport but are within easy hiking distance of one another. Biking is another option, or arrange a day tour with Bed & Breakfast Coula (p128).

Heading west from Sighişoara, you might thinking of filling up your water bottles at the freshwater spring, just off the main road beyond the Motel Restaurant Dracula (p128) in **Daneş**, where there is also a small fortified church. Some 9km south of Daneş is **Criş**. From Laslea, energetic hikers can trek for some 10km south to **Nou Săsesc**; bear right where the road forks or, alternatively, bear left to get to **Mălincrav**. At each of these villages is a small fortified church.

In the industrial town of **Dumbrăveni**, 19km west of Sighişoara, there is a country market on Thursday mornings, where locals sell their cattle, sheep and horses. Beyond, at **Şaroş** a small fortified church is open only on August 15th (St Mary's Day). From there, a road lined with hemp fields (it's used to tie bundles of corn together) heads south 9km to **Biertan** (Birthälm; www.biertan.com in Romanian), the highlight on any fortified church route.

Biertan's fantastic 15th-century **church** (admission €0.50; ⏰ 9am-7pm Tue-Fri & Sun, 9am-4pm Sat, closed 12-1pm) was the site of the Lutheran bishop from 1572 to 1867 and is listed as a Unesco World Heritage site. Its Viennese-style altar (1483–1550) has 28 panels and its three rings of walls stand up to 12m tall. This is the only fortified church in the region which is open and holds regular services; even at that, they're held only once a month, as after Biertan's Saxon priest

moved to Germany in 1995, there is only one priest for four villages.

Near the altar in the church is the sacristy, which once held treasure behind its formidable wooden door with an even more forbidable lock: it has 19 locks in one, and is such a marvel of engineering it won first prize at the paris World Expo in 1900. Inside the grounds are many buildings of interest, including a small bastion which is famous in local lore: couples wanting a divorce were supposedly locked in here together for two weeks as a last attempt to resolve differences. There was only one bed and one set of cutlery. The method was so successful, only one couple decided afterwards to go through with divorce in 400 years!

Aside from the church, Biertan is a pleasure to stroll around, a quiet, friendly town with painted wooden gates and a burgeoning tourist infrastructure which is seeing more and more homes being repainted or opening up to travellers. Six kilometres south of Biertan is the small village of **Richiş**, likewise dominated by a fantastic stone church. From Biertan you can also head east for 2km along a dirt track to **Copşa Mare** (Grosskopisch). The church there dates from the early 14th century and was fortified to fend off Turkish and Tartar invasions in the 16th century, but failed to fend off Székely troops, who attacked the village in 1605 and pillaged the church.

Brateiu, just 6km east of Mediaş, is an almost completely Roma village. Driving through here can be a fascinating or unnerving experience, depending on your taste for adventure. Upon recognising you as a foreigner, one villager after another will descend upon the car, yelling offers to come inside for something to eat, or to buy something. Local Romanians tend to be afraid to enter the town. From Brateiu, continue east along the main road for a further 5km then turn right at the turn-off for **Aţel** (Hetzeldorf). The church, dating from the 14th century, was heavily fortified in 1471. In 1959 the northern tower was levelled to uncover a secret tunnel leading to a neighbouring farmstead.

Viscri is some 45km southeast of Sighişoara. Follow the road towards Braşov and turn right in Buneşti. From here a dirt track leads to the remote village. First mentioned in 1400, the village was heavily damaged by fire in 1638. Its one-room church was built in the 12th century by Székelys and taken over by Saxon colonists in 1185. It is now recognised as a Unesco World Heritage site.

SLEEPING

As there is no system of organised local homestay in the area, your best bet is to look out for *cazare* signs in the windows in these villages.

Casa Otto Wagner (☎ 269 868 249; per person €10) is a lovely oasis, snug up against the old town wall in Biertan, and has clean double and triple rooms. It can also provide meals on request.

SZÉKELY LAND

The eastern realms of the Carpathians, known as Székely Land (Ţara Secuilor in Romanian, Székelyföld in Hungarian), are home to the Székelys, ethnic Hungarians who live and communicate almost exclusively in their Hungarian dialect. Highly organised as a group, they publish their own local booklets and maps (often with place names obstinately written in Hungarian only, making it very frustrating for foreigners to figure out where they are through all those consonants) and have nourished a flourishing cultural life. Yet this is mainly since 1990, as during the Communist regime their population tended to be either roundly ignored or actively suppressed.

A good deal of tension still exists between Romanians and Hungarians, the former resenting the latter's often poor knowledge of Romanian, and the latter carrying lingering resentment of feeling forcibly excluded from society. The question of historical claim to Transylvania is not a settled one, despite 20th-century events which place it squarely in Romanian hands. Some Hungarians and historians feel justified in calling the territory traditionally Hungarian.

The origins of the Székely (pronounced say-kay) people are disputed. Debates rage as to whether they are descendants of the Huns, who arrived in Transylvania in the 5th century and adopted the Hungarian language; or whether they are Magyars who accompanied Attila the Hun on his campaigns in the Carpathian basin and later settled there. Three 'nations' were recognised in medieval Transylvania, the Székelys, the Saxons and the nobles.

During the 18th century the Székelys suffered at the hands of the Habsburgs, who attempted to convert this devout Protestant ethnic group to Catholicism. Thousands of young Székely men were conscripted into the Austrian army. Local resistance throughout Székely Land led to the massacre of Madéfalva in 1764, following which thousands of Székelys fled across the border into Romanian Moldavia.

Following the union of Transylvania with Romania in 1918, some 200,000 Hungarians – a quarter of whom were Székelys – fled to Hungary. It was during this period that the Székelys composed their own national anthem (see the boxed text on p133), in which they beg God for help in the survival of Transylvania. Today many Hungarian tourists flock to the area, especially the 'capitals' of Odorheiu Secuiesc and Miercurea Ciuc, to live out pastoral customs considered 'authentic' and already lost in their motherland.

Maps

Cartographia's *Ţara Secuilor, Székelyföld, Székely Land* map (€3.50) includes a detailed map of the region complete with lengthy historical explanations in Hungarian.

TÂRGU MUREŞ

☎ 265 / pop 163,270

Târgu Mureş is a city with something up its sleeve. It's not much to look at, save for some splendid buildings in the centre, as ugly concrete structures scattered everywhere mar its appeal, and constant traffic gives it an unpleasant edge. However, scratch the surface and you'll find a particularly vibrant city with many funky places to hang out in for a day or two while you learn a few words of Hungarian.

Traditionally a Hungarian stronghold, Târgu Mureş (Marosvásárhely in Hungarian, Neumarkt in German) was first documented as 'Novum Forum Sicolorum' in 1322. It developed as a leading garrison town and later as an important cultural and academic centre. In 1658 it was attacked by

> ### SZÉKELY NATIONAL ANTHEM
>
> Who knows where destiny leads to
> On this rough road and dark night
> Lead your people once again to victory,
> Csaba, Prince Royal, on a heavenly path
> Our ancestors crumble to dust through
> these wars of nations, as cliffs on rough
> seas
> The flood is upon us, oh, overwhelming us
> a hundred fold
> Lord, don't let us lose Transylvania!
>
> As long as we live, Peoples of Hungary, our
> spirit shall not be broken:
> Wherever we are born, whatever corner
> of the earth, whether our fate be good,
> or cruel
> The ravages of Tatars and Turks and the
> Austrian yoke
> Let us inherit our nation, the land of
> the Székely, in a free fatherland, to live in
> happiness.

Turks who captured 3000 inhabitants and transported them back to Istanbul as slave labour.

During the Ceauşescu regime, Târgu Mureş was a 'closed city', with all ethnic groups other than Romanians forbidden to settle here. Large numbers of ethnic Romanians from other parts of Romania were moved into Târgu Mureş to further dilute the Hungarian community.

In 1990 Târgu Mureş was the scene of bloody clashes between Hungarian students, demonstrating for a Hungarian language faculty in their university, and Romanians who raided the local Hungarian political party offices. The Romanian mob attempted to gouge out the eyes of playwright András Sütő, who remains blind in one eye. The violence was apparently stirred up by the nationalist political group Vatra, which paid Romanian peasants from outlying villages to travel to Târgu Mureş, and armed them with pitchforks and axes. Officials later scapegoated local Roma in their investigation of the conflict.

Today Hungarian seems to be undergoing a renaissance in Târgu Mureş with many local songs being in Hungarian only

or in both languages. Oddly, Italian seems to be the favoured foreign language here, perhaps due to several major Italian investments in local businesses.

Carnival comes on the last weekend in June, when the city hosts its Târgu Mureş Days.

Orientation

To make the 15-minute walk into town from the train station, exit the station and head straight to Str Gheorghe Doja, turn left and walk straight up to Piaţas Victoriei, Unirii and Trandafirilor, the main thoroughfare where most hotels and travel agencies are. The citadel is just northeast of Piaţa Trandafirilor.

From the bus station, turn right along Str Gheorghe Doja and follow the street north to Piaţa Victoriei and Piaţa Unirii.

MAPS

There are few good maps of the city, though Grai's *Judeţul Mureş 4 in 1* (€1.50) has a usable city map and a good county map, plus so-so maps of Sighişoara and Reghin.

Information

For maps and books of local interest, try **Librărie Luceafărul** (☎ 250 581; Piaţa Trandafirilor 43; ⏰ 8am-8pm Mon-Fri, 9am-6pm Sat).You can access the Internet at **Electro Orizont** (☎ 219 718; Piaţa Teatrului 12; per hr €1.60; ⏰ 9am-11pm). ATMs are easy to find in the centre, but the **IDM Exchange** (crn Piaţa Trandafirilor & Str Horea; ⏰ 8am-8pm Mon-Fri, 9am-1pm Sat) also gives cash advances on credit cards. The main **post office** (☎ 213 386; Str Revolutei 1; ⏰ 7am-8pm Mon-Fri, 8am-1pm Sat) and **telephone centre** (crn Piaţa Victoriei & B-dul 1 Decembrie 1918; ⏰ 7am-9pm) are at opposite ends of the centre.

Though there's no official tourist office here, **Corbet Transair** (☎ 268 463; www.corbet-trans air.ro; Piaţa Trandafirilor 43; ⏰ 9am-6pm Mon-Fri) more than compensates. The dynamic young team comprise one of the most efficient agencies in Romania and they are recommended even if you are not planning to be in Târgu Mureş; they arrange accommodation and organise a wealth of adventure tours (horseback riding through the Gulgiu mountains, cycling tours, tours to Roma villages) throughout Transylvania. They can also arrange car rental and rural tourism excursions.

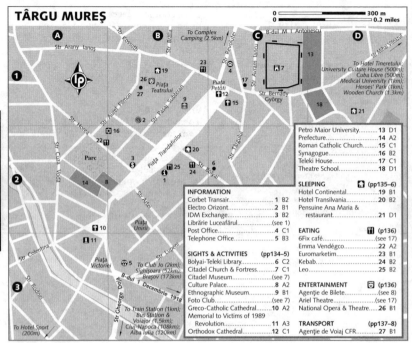

TÂRGU MUREŞ

0 — 300 m
0 — 0.2 miles

Sights

PIAŢA TRANDAFIRILOR

Târgu Mureş' main sights are focused here. At the northern end of the square cross Piaţa Petőfi and head east onto Piaţa Bernády György. Towering above the tiny Piaţa Bernády György is the humble **Citadel Church & Fortress** with its small **museum** (adult/child €0.40/0.20; ⌚ 10am-6pm Tue-Sun). It was founded on the site of the city's original stronghold during the 13th and 14th centuries. The Hungarian Reformed church (1316) it shelters was built by the Dominicans on the site of a former Franciscan monastery. The fortress, comprising six towers, was built around the church between the 15th and 17th centuries. Today the grounds double as a park; it's a quiet respite from the city centre more than an exciting citadel, though the kids might enjoy running along the old wall. A small **Foto Club** (admission free; ⌚ 11am-7pm) on its east side has photo exhibits.

Nestled beneath the citadel walls on Piaţa Bernády György is the yellow-painted, baroque **Teleki House** (built 1797–1803). Joseph Teleki served as governor of Transylvania between 1842 and 1848. It now houses the 6Fix café and Ariel Theatre (p136).

Walk back to Piaţa Trandafirilor, the northern end of which is dominated by the magnificent **Orthodox Cathedral**. The cathedral's interior is one of the most breathtaking of Romania's modern churches. Built between 1933 and 1938, the cathedral partially replaced the tiny wooden church that had served the local Orthodox community since 1773 and is still used for services today.

On the eastern side of Piaţa Trandafirilor, completely overshadowed by the Orthodox Cathedral, is the baroque-style **Roman Catholic church** (Biserica Sfântul Jonos) dating from 1728. In the baroque building (1762) on the western side of the plaza at No 11 is the **Ethnographic Museum** (☎ 215 807; adult/child €0.80/0.40; ⌚ 9am-4pm Tue-Sat, 9am-2pm Sun).

West of Piaţa Trandafirilor, at Str Aurel Filmon 21, is the ornate and well-preserved **synagogue** from 1900. Prior to WWII, some 5500 Jews lived in Târgu Mureş, making up almost a third of the town's population.

A memorial outside pays homage to the holocaust victims.

East of the Piaţa, at Str Bolyai 17, is the **Bolyai-Teleki Library** (☎ 261 857; Str Bolyai 17; admission free; 10am-6pm Tue-Fri, 10am-1pm Sat-Sun). The library, built between 1799 and 1805 in an imposing empire style, houses the private book collection of Samule Teleki, which he donated to the city in 1802. The city is very proud of its collection that now comprises more than 120,000 rare and antique volumes.

The southern end of the square is dominated by Târgu Mureş' most fantastic building, the **Culture Palace** (Palatul Culturii; 10am-4pm Tue-Fri, 9am-1pm Sat-Sun), built in secessionist style between 1911 and 1913. Its glittering steepled roofs, tiled in colourful geometric patterns, shelter a history museum, an art museum and a stained-glass window museum, better known as the **Hall of Mirrors** (Sala Oglinzi). Scenes from traditional Székely fairy tales, ballads and legends are featured in the 12 stained-glass windows which fill the entire length of one wall of the long hall. The concert hall inside has an organ with 4463 pipes. The ground floor houses a contemporary **Art Gallery** featuring some unusual ceramics, paintings and sculptures.

The **Prefecture**, with a tiled roof and bright green spires, is next door to the Culture Palace. In front is a statue of **Lupoaica Romei** (the wolf of Rome), a gift from Rome in 1924. Close by on Piaţa Unirii is the turncoat **Greco-Catholic Cathedral**, a Romanian Orthodox church until its congregation opted to accept the authority of the Vatican.

Behind the church is a **memorial** to the victims of the 1989 revolution.

UNIVERSITY & AROUND

Târgu Mureş enjoys a strong academic tradition and its medical and theatre schools are considered the most distinguished in the country. Eminent scholars include mathematicians Farkas Bólyai (1775–1856) and his son János Bólyai (1802–60) who revolutionised Euclidean geometry.

The university area lies northeast of the citadel. Immediately behind the citadel walls is the private **Petru Maior University**, with the **Theatre School** opposite. During the purges on all non-Romanians during Ceauşescu's regime, the school's flawless reputation suffered: Romanian students were given preferential treatment over Hungarian students. Today 40% of the school's population is Hungarian.

Continue northeast along Str Mihai Viteazul, then turn right onto Str Nicolae Grigorescu. Immediately after the students' **Culture House** (Casa de Cultură), turn left along Str Dr Gheorghe Marinescu. The **Medical University** (Universitatea de Medicină şi Farmacie) is a magnificent 1950s building beyond the hospital. Directly opposite is the **Romanian Heroes' Park** (Parcul Eroilor Români), dominated by a large memorial to those who died during WWII. Further north is a lovely, small, wooden Orthodox church.

Sleeping
BUDGET

Hotel Sport (☎ 131 913; Str Griviţa Roşie 33; s/d/tr €7/13/21) Nothing to write home about, but it's a simple, friendly place, five minutes' walk from the train station. Two rooms share one bathroom.

Hotel Transilvania (☎ 265 616; www.unita-turism.ro in Romanian; Piaţa Trandafirilor 46; s/d without private toilet €10/15, with private toilet €14/17) The cheapest option in the centre, this has very pleasant rooms and clean bathrooms.

Complex Camping (☎ 214 080; Aleea Carpaţi 59; tent space/2-person hut €1.60/8) The same people who run the Hotel Transilvania also run one of the handful of truly excellent camping grounds in the country, located in the northwest end of town on the banks of the river Mureş. Facilities are clean and modern and there's a beach.

MID-RANGE

Pensiune Ana Maria (☎ 264 401; Str A L Papui Ilarian 17; s/d/ste €23/26/29) Forget the lodgings – this place is worthwhile for the breakfast (included) and food alone. Everywhere are jars of herbs and decanters of some of the best home-made ţuica (blueberry and cherry are the best) you'll find anywhere. The owners run a second *pensiune* 3km out of the city (same prices), where they grow all the produce they use in their scrumptious meals. Rooms are simple and comfortable. Reserve and pay for their other *pensiune* here.

Voiajor (☎ 250 750; www.voiajor.ro in Romanian; Str Gheorghe Doja 143; s/d €30/35;) This modern place adds a splash of colour to the city's hotel scene with its brightly painted exterior, cheerful rooms and multilingual, friendly service – this despite the fact that it's connected to the bus station! It even has room service.

Hotel Continental (☎ 250 416; www.continental hotels.ro; Piaţa Teatrului 6; s/d €48/61; ✖ ✖) Though it's considered the top hotel in town, the drab rooms don't justify the price. This is pseudoluxury, with an impersonal feel to it. It's wheelchair accessible.

Hotel Tineretului (☎ 217 441; Str Nicolae Grigorescu 17-19; s/d €25/34) Right inside the university students' Culture House, this is overpriced for the dreary shack it is. Check out the Dr Who–like switchboard at the reception. Rooms with black-and-white only TV are €7 cheaper!

Eating

Euromarketim (Str Călăraşilor 4; ✖ 24hr) Get your late-night necessities in this well-stocked convenience store.

6Fix (☎ 220 428; Str Poştei 2; ✖ 8.30am-11pm) Located inside the Ariel Theatre is a cool, cosy hang-out that serves an array of coffees, teas and light snacks via a hip, insouciant staff to the beat of alternative music.

Kebab (☎ 268 510; Str Bolyai 10; mains €1-3; ✖ 6.30am-10pm Mon-Sat) Despite its bland name, this a gourmet penny-pincher's delight: on one side you have carnivorous treats such as kebabs, on the other a cafeteria-style salad bar and a wide array of excellent hot dishes you can point to. There are also freshly squeezed juices.

Leo (☎ 214 999; Piaţa Trandafirilor 36-38; mains €1-3; ✖ 10am-midnight) This is a popular, lively place that serves food a step above the usual fast food. Romanian dishes, soups and pizzas, ready-made and waiting to be pointed at, are dished out in this two-floor food emporium done up in a pseudocountry theme.

Emma Vendégco (☎ 263 021; Str Horea 6; mains €1-3; ✖ 11am-11pm) This unassuming little restaurant off the main square serves great, mainly Hungarian food. The creative dishes include African soup and fruit soup with wine, though the lamb cutlets and goulash are among the stars of the fail-proof menu.

Pensiune Ana Maria (see Sleeping; mains €2-4) Shame about the amusingly gawdy dining room decor, but the meals here are scrumptuous.

Entertainment

The **National Opera & Theatre** (☎ 264 848; Piaţa Teatrului 1) hosts a colourful array of plays and operettas in Romanian. The lovely **Culture Palace** (☎ 267 629; crn Piaţa Trandafirilor & Str Enescu; p135) houses a children's library (✖ 9am-8pm) whose fanciful decorations and displays would be of interest to kids of all languages. Here too is the **Agenţie de Bilete** (☎ 212 522; ✖ 10am-1pm & 5-7pm Mon-Fri, 10am-1pm Sat-Sun), which sells tickets for a wide variety of theatrical and musical performances, including for the National Opera & Theatre. For alternative theatre pieces (mainly in Hungarian), check out the **Ariel Theatre** (☎ 220 428; Str Poştei 2), where performances geared towards youth are staged between September and May.

Inside the university's Culture House, **Cuba Libre Music Pub** (☎ 216 066; Str Nicolae Grigorescu 17-19; ✖ 10pm-4am Thu-Sat) attracts a vibrant young crowd. Otherwise, for a few drinks head to **Club Jo** (☎ 257 720; Str Livezeni 2; ✖ 10am-midnight Sun-Thu, 10am-4am Fri-Sat), which is packed weekends, quiet other days. It's a huge space with billiards, couches, a terrace, modern art on the walls and a long drink and food menu. It's in the southeastern section of the city, a €2 taxi ride from the centre.

Getting There & Away

The **Agenţie de Voiaj CFR** (☎ 266 203; Piaţa Teatrului 1; ✖ 7.30am-7.30pm Mon-Fri) sells advance tickets. From Târgu Mureş there are two daily trains to Sibiu (5½ hours), and one each to Bucharest (overnight, nine hours), Timişoara (seven hours) and Budapest (eight hours). To get to Cluj-Napoca, you must change at Războieni.

The **bus station** (☎ 221 458) is a five-minute walk south of the train station along Str Gheorghe Doja. Daily bus and maxitaxi services include eight to Sighişoara, seven to Bucharest via Braşov, five to Odorheiu Secuiesc, four to Cluj-Napoca, three to Bistriţa, two to Sibiu, and one to Timişoara and Iaşi. There are also three daily buses to Budapest (€14). Tickets for buses to other European destinations can be purchased through Corbet Transair (p351).

Getting Around

Târgu Mureş is small enough to cover by foot. Bus Nos 2, 16 and 17 go to the train and bus stations.

ODORHEIU SECUIESC

☎ 266 / pop 38,830

The industrious inhabitants of little Odorheiu Secuiesc (Székelyudvarhely in Hungarian), 97% of whom are ethnic Hungarians, have worked hard to make their lovely town a thriving bastion of Magyar culture. Well organised and efficient, they have made theirs a relatively prosperous town and it shows: streets and parks are meticulous, houses well maintained. There's not much to do here, but a climb up the surrounding hills and casual strolls through the unhurried streets make for a pleasant visit.

Settled on an ancient Roman military camp, Odorheiu Secuiesc developed as a small craft town during the reigns of the Hungarian Árpád kings between the 11th and 13th centuries. In 1485 King Matthias Corvinus (r. 1458–90) granted Odorheiu Secuiesc 'free royal town' status, enabling its different craft guilds to host commercial fairs. The Craftmen's Market, held every June, carries on the tradition by displaying the artwork of local artisans.

Orientation

The train and bus stations are a 10-minute walk from the centre. Exit the stations and head south down Str Bethlen Gábor until you come to Piaţa Márton Áron. From here bear right to Piaţa Primeriei, where most of the sights are.

The citadel is northeast of Piaţa Primeriei along Str Cetăţii.

MAPS

Odorheiu Secuiesc published by Geocart (€1.50) can be bought at the **Corvina bookshop** (Piaţa Primeriei 23; ☉ 9am-6pm Mon-Fri, 9am-1pm Sat).

Information

The Tea Pub (see Eating, p138) has Internet access (per hour €0.60), as does the hotel **Korona Panzió** (see Sleeping, p138; per hour €0.60; ☉ 10am-11pm). Hotels and banks along Str Kossuth Lajos have ATMs. The **post office** (☎ 212 046; Str Kossuth Lajos 35; ☉ 7am-8pm Mon-Fri) is on the main street. The **telephone office** (Piaţa Primeriei; ☉ 7am-9pm Mon-Fri) is near Hotel Târnava-Küküllő.

TOURIST INFORMATION

Bartha Edit (☎ 211 629; barthadici@yahoo.com) For a personal and unique city or rural tour, contact this enthuasistic, knowledgeable Székely guide. Her English is excellent and her knowledge of history and the Székely area formidable.

Eurotour (☎ 210 269; eurotour@easynet.ro; Str Kossuth Lajos 15; ☉ 9am-5pm) This friendly bunch can also help arrange accommodation and tour bookings.

Tourinfo (☎ 217 427; www.tourinfo.ro; Piaţa Primeriei 1; ☉ 9am-6pm Mon-Fri) This is the town's official tourist office, but staff speak only Hungarian and Romanian. In principle, they can help with all kinds of bookings; in practise you might just end up admiring the exhibits in their small art gallery.

Sights

Odorheiu Secuiesc's medieval **citadel** *(vár)*, built between 1492 and 1516, is almost fully intact today, and houses an agricultural college. Visitors can freely stroll the grounds around its inner walls.

Odorheiu Secuiesc has no fewer than two Greco-Catholic, two Orthodox, three Hungarian Reformed, and four Roman Catholic churches. At the western end of the main square, Piaţa Primeriei, stands the **Franciscan Monastery & Church** (Szent Ferencrendi Templom és Kolostor; ☎ 213 016; Piaţa Primeriei 15; admission free; ☉ 10am-6pm Tue-Sun), built from 1712 to 1779. Walk east past the impressive **city hall** (1895–96) to the 18th-century baroque **Hungarian Reformed Church** (Református Templom). Bearing right onto Piaţa Márton, follow the pedestrian pathway to one of the town's first **Roman Catholic churches** (Római Katolikus Plébániatemplom; built 1787–91).

The town's best church lies 2km north of the centre on Str Bethlen Gábor. The **Chapel of Jesus** (Jézus kápolna) is one of the oldest architectural monuments in Transylvania, built during the 13th century. The chapel gained its name from the war cries of Székely warriors who, during a Tartar invasion, cried to Jesus for help. They got it and built a chapel to commemorate their victory.

Odorheiu Secuiesc's colourful history is explained – in Hungarian – in the **Haáz Rezsó Museum** (☎ 218 375; Str Kossuth Lajos 29; adult/child €0.80/0.40; ☉ 9am-5pm Tue-Sun). The museum was founded from a collection of folk objects belonging to local art teacher Haáz Rezsó that date from 1900 onwards.

Sleeping

Tourinfo (see above) can set you up in one of many guesthouses in and out of town for €10 to €20 per person.

TRANSYLVANIA

TRANSYLVANIA

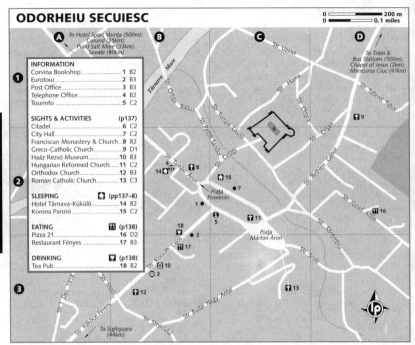

ODORHEIU SECUIESC

0 — 200 m
0 — 0.1 miles

To Hotel Sport Voința (500m);
Corund (25km);
Praid Salt Mine (33km);
Sovate (40km)

To Train &
Bus Stations (500m);
Chapel of Jesus (2km);
Miercurea Ciuc (47km)

INFORMATION
Corvina Bookshop.........................1 B2
Eurotour...2 B3
Post Office.....................................3 B3
Telephone Office...........................4 B2
Tourinfo..5 C2

SIGHTS & ACTIVITIES (p137)
Citadel...6 C2
City Hall...7 C2
Franciscan Monastery & Church..8 B2
Greco-Catholic Church.................9 D1
Haáz Rezső Museum...................10 B3
Hungarian Reformed Church......11 C2
Orthodox Church.........................12 B3
Roman Catholic Church..............13 C3

SLEEPING (pp137–8)
Hotel Târnava-Kükülö.................14 B2
Korona Panzió.............................15 C2

EATING (p138)
Pizza 21.......................................16 D2
Restaurant Fényes......................17 B3

DRINKING (p138)
Tea Pub.......................................18 B2

Hotel Sport Voința (☎ 211 377; Str Bányai János 26; dm €3) Very run down, this is not the cheeriest of places, but it'll do for a night or two if you have a few drinks before retiring.

Korona Panzió (☎ 218 061; Piața Primeriei 12/2; s/d €20/30; 🖳) No doubt this is the best deal in town. The simple rustic style fits the country villa theme. The in-house restaurant serves up good dishes, and the bar is a popular hang-out for locals. There's free Internet access in the morning only for guests.

Hotel Târnava-Kükülö (☎ 213 963; www.kukullo .ro; Piața Primeriei 16; s/d/ste €45/55/65; 🗙) This is considered the top of the line. Some guests may think they are paying for more than they are getting, but it does have full services, comfortable rooms and a fitness centre.

Eating & Drinking

There are some fast-food joints along Str Bethlen Gábor north of Piața Márton Áron.

Tea Pub (☎ 218 027; Str Kossuth Lajos 20; 🕑 8am-11pm) This makes an excellent hang-out, serving only tea and alcohol. There's Internet access, and on Tuesday evenings there's

an English conversation workshop you can join in on.

Restaurant Fényes (Str Kossuth Lajos 19; mains €2-4; 🕑 9am-10pm) This is your typical large, socialist-inspired restaurant, serving decent meals.

Pizza 21 (☎ 0723-212 121; Str Jószef Attila 21; mains €2-3; 🕑 10am-midnight Mon-Fri, noon-midnight Sat-Sun) This is where local pizza-lovers go. It dishes up delicious pizzas and doubles as a great place to grab a beer and chill.

Getting There & Away

The **Agenție de Voiaj CFR** (☎ 213 653; Str Bethlen Gábor 63) is at the train station. Odorheiu Secuiesc is awkward to get to by train, with only personal train (p351) services three times daily to Sighișoara (1½ hours), from where transfers are available to Brașov and other destinations. From the **bus station** (☎ 217 979; Str Târgului 10), 100m south of the train station, there is one bus daily to both Brașov and Gheorgheni, three to Sovata (all leaving before 9am!), five to Târgu Mureș, and seven to Miercurea Ciuc. There are up to three daily buses to Budapest and additional services to Debrecen, Szeged and Pécs (all in Hungary) operated by **Csavargó** (☎ 218 077), **Scorpion Trans** (☎ 218 495) and **Trans Tur** (☎ 217 979).

AROUND ODORHEIU SECUIESC
Corund, Praid & Sovata

Just 25km north of Odorheiu Secuiesc is the small village of **Corund** (Korond), renowned throughout Romania for its green, brown and cobalt-blue pottery. Local potters sell their wares from open-air stalls set up in the centre of the village. Many simply lay out their colourful crafts on the grass.

Some 8km further north along the road to Sovata is **Praid**, known for its **salt mine** (☎ 240 200; www.salinapraid.ro; Str Állomás 44; admission €2; ☉ 8am-8pm), which sees nearly 250,000 visitors each summer alone. Many undertake extended treatments for bronchitis and other respiratory illness at the base 120m below surface. Others just take a refreshing tour (on one of the small buses), visiting the chapel and museum inside. It's a memorable place. Near the entrance is a delightful saltwater outdoor **pool** (☉ 10am-7pm).

Sovata, 7km further north, has been a resort since the early 19th century. Five lovely lakes surround the town, all with reputed curative waters. The most popular is the saltwater Lacu Ursu (Bear Lake) for its supposed ability to cure infertility, and both Lacu Aluniş (Hazelnut Lake) and Lacu Negru (Black Lake) are known for their sapropelic mud. Lacu Ursu is impossible to sink in, with 150mg of salt per litre. A 10cm-thick layer of fresh water covers its salty depth and maintains warm temperatures year-round.

Tourinfo (p137) can arrange tours and accommodation in and around Corund, Praid and Sovata.

MIERCUREA CIUC
☎ 266 / pop 45,900

Mention Miercurea Ciuc (Csíkszereda in Hungarian) to any Romanian, and they'll tell you how cold it is there. Sure, it is infamous as the country's coldest city (located in a Carpathian basin, it's annual temperature is 5.9°C), but what better place to produce one of the country's most beloved beers, Ciuc (pronounced 'chook')?

That it's the capital of Székely Land isn't hard to see: most signs are in Hungarian

only, and Romanian is treated as something exotic here, where the population is over 90% Hungarian. It's a friendly city, attractively surrounded by mountains and springs. However, the city itself is none too pretty, with concrete being the construction material of choice.

Founded during the reign of Hungarian king Ladislaus I (r. 1077–95), around a castle which the king built for himself, Miercurea Ciuc quickly developed into a prosperous commercial centre and the hub of Székely cultural activities and culture. Today it is most famous for its Pentecostal Pilgrimage (see p141).

Traditional Székely villages **Leliceni** (4km southeast), **Misentea** and **Ciucsângeorgiu** (another 2km and 4km south), and **Armaseni** (2km north of the latter along a dirt track) lie within easy reach of Miercurea Ciuc.

Orientation

Topo Service's *Miercurea Ciuc Map* (€1.50) is a worthwhile investment.

Information

For cash advances, head to the **Banca Comercială Română** (Kereskedelmi Bank; ☎ 271 766; Str Florilor 19; ☉ 8.30am-5pm Mon-Fri, 8.30am-noon Sat). The **post office** (☎ 224 569; Str Florilor 3; ☉ 7am-8pm Mon-Fri, 8.30am-1pm Sat) is located north of the **central telephone office** (Piaţa Majláth Gusztáv Károly; ☉ 7am-8pm Mon-Fri, 8am-3pm Sat, 2-8pm Sun).

Tourist information can be found at the **Tourist Information Office** (☎ 317 007; http://clmc.topnet.ro/tourinform; Str Florilor 12; ☉ 9am-6pm Mon-Fri, 9am-3pm Sat-Sun), where you can get help with finding accommodation and organising tours. **Delta Travel** (☎ /fax 311 577; Str Stadionului 1; ☉ 9am-5pm Mon-Fri, 10am-2pm Sat) can help mainly with Black Sea vacations, but can arrange extreme sport excursions and skiing holidays, and book accommodation.

Sights
CITY CENTRE

Miercurea Ciuc's centrepiece is its **Mikó Castle**, which today houses the impressive **Székely Museum of Csík** (Csíki Székely Múzeum; ☎ 311 727; adult/child €0.80/0.40; ☉ 9am-5pm Tue-Sun). The castle was built from 1611 to 1621 as a residence for the Hungarian commander-in-chief of the Székely districts, Ference Mikó. Dubbed the 'Golden Bastion' for its

TRANSYLVANIA

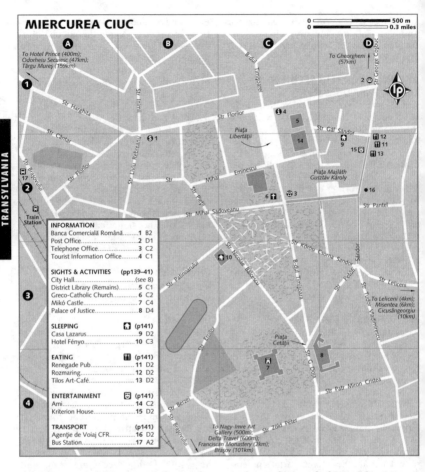

MIERCUREA CIUC

0 ————— 500 m
0 ————— 0.3 miles

To Hotel Prince (400m);
Odorheiu Secuiesc (47km);
Târgu Mureş (159km)

To Gheorgheni
(57km)

Str George Coşbuc

Piaţa
Libertăţii

Piaţa Majláth
Gusztáv Károly

Piaţa
Cetăţii

Train
Station

To Leliceni (4km);
Misentea (6km);
Cicusângeorgiu
(10km)

To Nagy-Imre Art
Gallery (500m);
Delta Travel (600m);
Franciscan Monastery (2km);
Braşov (101km)

INFORMATION
Banca Comercială Română........**1** B2
Post Office..............................**2** D1
Telephone Office.....................**3** C2
Tourist Information Office.........**4** C1

SIGHTS & ACTIVITIES   (pp139–41)
City Hall.............................(see 8)
District Library (Remains)..........**5** C1
Greco-Catholic Church.............**6** C2
Mikó Castle............................**7** C4
Palace of Justice.....................**8** D4

SLEEPING   (p141)
Casa Lazarus...........................**9** D2
Hotel Fényo...........................**10** C3

EATING   (p141)
Renegade Pub.........................**11** D2
Rozmaring.............................**12** D2
Tilos Art-Café.........................**13** D2

ENTERTAINMENT   (p141)
Ami......................................**14** C2
Kriterion House.......................**15** D2

TRANSPORT   (p141)
Agenţie de Voiaj CFR...............**16** D2
Bus Station............................**17** A2

sheer luxury and Renaissance finery, the castle was burnt to the ground by Tartars in 1661, then rebuilt in 1716.

The history of the town is told in the museum, and a library of some 8000 books survives from Miercurea Ciuc's 17th-century Franciscan monastery. There are also many archaeological exhibits, an ethnographic section featuring the traditional, brightly coloured woven fabrics, and an outdoor section which recreates 18th- and 19th-century Székely pastoral life. The **Palace of Justice**, built in 1904, and the baroque **city hall** (1884–98), both built in an eclectic style, are on the opposite side of Piaţa Cetăţii.

From Piaţa Cetăţii walk back north up B-dul Timişoara into the modern centre.

At the northern end of Piaţa Libertăţii turn right onto Str Florilor, then take the first right. This leads you to the heart of the city's **Civic Centre**, created in the late 1980s as part of Ceauşescu's systemisation plans. While most of the older buildings in this area were bulldozed to make way for concrete blocks, a canary-yellow, regal building from 1903 which housed the **National Bank of Romania** managed to survive – just. In 1984 the entire building was uprooted from its foundations and moved 128m east on rollers to make way for the **district library**, which has since been demolished.

The **Nagy-Imre Art Gallery** (☎ 313 963; Str Nagy Imre 175; admission €0.40; ❧ 9am-5pm Tue-Sun), displays various works by the revered Székely artist whose body rests in the walls of the whitewashed church.

FRANCISCAN MONASTERY
Two kilometres south of the centre in the Şumuleu district (Csíksomlyó in Hungarian) is a fine Franciscan monastery, built in 1442 by Iancu de Hunedoara (János Hunyadi), governor of Hungary from 1446 to 1452, to commemorate his great victory against the Turks at Marosszentimre.

The monastery today is the site of Miercurea Ciuc's main tourist draw, the Pentacostal Pilgrimage, when about 300,000 Székelys flock here on Whit Sunday (end of May) to celebrate their brotherhood. The pilgrimage dates from 1567 when, in an attempt to convert the Székely peoples to Catholicism, Hungarian troops attacked the monastery. On Whit Sunday a bloody battle was fought on a field close to the monastery, from which the Székely side emerged triumphant.

From the bus station, take bus No 11, 21, 40, 41 or 42, or enjoy a pleasant walk. There are hiking trails into the forested hills from the monastery.

Sleeping
Casa Lazarus (☎ 0722-953 531; Str Gál Sándor 9; dm €6) The cheapest place in town. Rooms with four or five beds have their own shower and toilet.

Hotel Prince (☎ 316 908; www.topnet.ro/prince; Str Harghita 74; s/d €18/24) Located on a quiet, central street, its size (only 20 rooms) makes this a cosy option. Rooms are simple but comfortable; the overall atmosphere is as familial as staying at a friend's house. There are two restaurants on site. Walk along Str Harghita and cross the bridge over the tracks.

Hotel Fényo (☎ 530 132; Str N Bălcescu 11; s/d €40/50; ✕ 🖵) Sitting near the citadel, this is a lovely place with comfortable rooms and pluses like internet connection and services such as car rental. Some rooms are equipped for wheelchair-bound guests.

Eating
Tilos Art-Café (Cafeneaus Tilos; ☎ 316 814; Str Pétoffi 7; mains €1-3; ✆ 10am-midnight) This super-stylish place, decked out like an old-fashioned bookshop inside, has tables on the street outside in summer. The town's young

bohemians hang out here and there are regular artistic 'happenings' hosted here.

Rozmaring (☎ 215 841; cnr Str Gál Sándor & Str Pétoffi; mains €2-4; ✆ 10am-11pm) This traditional Hungarian restaurant serves delicious meals in a folk-styled dining room.

Renegade Pub (☎ 0744-693 821; Str Pétoffi 3; mains €2-3; ✆ 9am-11pm) This is a pizzeria by any other name, serving up decent pizzas and other fare in a relaxed atmosphere. The courtyard terrace is the big draw.

Entertainment
Kriterion Art-Video Film Klub (Str George Coşbuc) Alternative cinema is occasionally screened inside the Kriterion House (Ház Kriterion) above the Pallas Akadémia Bookshop. Look for posters inside Tilos Art-Café.

Ami (basement of the Culture House; ✆ 10pm-3am Fri-Sun) Here a university crowd grooves to nonpop alternative music. Local live bands are featured most weekends, and the atmosphere here is definitely let-it-all-hang-out!

Getting There & Away
The **Agenţie de Voiaj CFR** (☎ 311 924; Str Petőfi Sándor 23; ✆ 7.30am-6pm Mon-Fri) sells advance tickets. From Miercurea Ciuc there are 11 daily trains to Gheorgheni (€2, one hour) and 10 to Braşov (€3, 2-2½ hours) via Sfântu Gheorghe (€2, 1½ hours); two of the Brasov trains continue to Bucharest (€14, five hours), with one continuing to Mangalia (€23, 10 hours).

The **bus station** (☎ 324 334) is 50m north of the train station on Str Braşovului. Two maxitaxis a day go to Târgu Mureş via Sovata and Odorheiu Secuiesc. Buses serve Praid, Piatra Neamţ, Gheorgheni, Târgu Neamţ, Odorheiu Secuiesc and Bucharest. There is a weekly bus to Budapest, though others to Budapest are run daily by **Open World** (☎ 310 171) and thrice weekly by **Itas** (☎ 322 202).

GHEORGHENI
☎ 266 / pop 21,110
The small town of Gheorgheni (pronounced gore-gen; Gyergyószentmiklós in Hungarian), 45km north of Miercurea Ciuc, has few sites of interest and a slight moribund feel to it, but it makes a nice break on the way to or from the Bicaz region to the east. Nestled between the Gurghiu Mountains and the Eastern Carpathians, it's dubbed

the 'cold pole', due to its long winters. Gheorgheni is only 17km from the beautiful Lacu Roșu (p282).

The **Tarisznyás Márton County Museum** (Városi Múzeum Tarisznyás Márton; Str Rácóczi 1; admission €0.40; 9am-5pm Tue-Sat, 9am-1pm Sun), is in an 18th-century building on Piața Petőfi Sándor and well worth a visit to see the intricately carved wooden fence posts and other artefacts of Magyar and Székely culture.

Just 6km north of Gheorgheni on the road to Toplița is the tiny village of Lăzarea (Gyergyószárhegy). Dating from 1235, the predominantly Hungarian village is dominated by its 16th-century **castle** (admission €0.50; 9am-5pm Tue-Sat), surrounded by a pretty sculpture park. It was to Lăzarea Castle that Gábor Bethlen, later to become prince of Transylvania (r. 1613–29), came to seek solace following the death of his son in 1590.

The castle is oddly placed near a 17th-century Franciscan monastery. Signposts from the centre of the village also direct tourists to the village water mill and water-powered sawmill.

Sleeping & Eating

Hotel Mureş (Maros Szálló; ☎ 361 904; B-dul Frăției 5; s/d €19/26) Opposite the Culture House on the same road that leads to the bus and train stations, this is considered Gheorgheni's best hotel. It has a full-service desk, a restaurant, friendly staff and sizable rooms in its four floors.

Pensiune Teke Panzió (☎ 0744-901 218; Str Tuzoltok 51A; s/d €12/15) Combining the look and feel of a guesthouse and mini hotel, this place has snug, modern rooms and a highly recommended dining room.

Motel Restaurant Panzió (☎ 352 736; Str Principala 1087; s/d €13/18) Located in Lăzarea, this place is as comfy as a private home but has all the services of a small hotel. The can-do owners will either leave you to your own devices or help organise a full range of sport and cultural excursions for you. They can even arrange folk-dance evenings.

Getting There & Away

The bus and train stations are 1.5km west of the centre on Str Gării. Gheorgheni is on the rail line linking Braşov with Satu Mare and has the same schedule as Miercurea Ciuc (p141). There are bus and maxitaxi services to and from Cluj-Napoca, Braşov, Lăzarea,

Odorheiu Secuiesc, Miercurea Ciuc, Lacu Roșu, Piatra Neamţ and Târgu Neamţ.

SFÂNTU GHEORGHE
☎ 267 / pop 66,380

Sfântu Gheorghe (Sepsiszentgyörgy), on the banks of the Olt River, 32km northeast of Braşov, is the least interesting of the Transylvanian Hungarian strongholds. There is little to see or do here, and in comparison to other Székely towns, this one feels cold and restrained. The town has its own Hungarian daily newspaper, *Háromszék*, and one of Romania's two Hungarian State Theatres, while many street signs and shop boards are in Hungarian only.

First documented in 1332, the town developed as a cultural centre for the Székelys from the 15th century onwards when it became a free town. It was left devastated by Turkish attacks between 1658 and 1671, and a plague in 1717. Today it's a town whose pulse is hard to notice, of interest primarily to those investigating Székely culture.

Orientation

The bus and train stations are a 10-minute walk east of the centre along Str 1 Decembrie 1918, which begins at the stations and ends in the town centre and Central Park at Piața Libertății. From there, Str Libertății begins southward, turning into Str Kós Károly after 300m. Str Jozef Bem intersects Str 1 Decembrie 1918 some 400m east of Str Libertății.

Information

CULTURAL CENTRES
The Democratic Alliance of Hungarians in Romania (Romániai Magyar Demokrata Szövetség; ☎ 316 152; Str Gábor Áron 14). It has a small library with material in English as well as Hungarian.

MONEY
Banca Comercială Română (7.30am-3pm Mon-Fri) Opposite IT&T on Str Jozef Bem.

TOURIST INFORMATION
International Tourism & Trade (IT&T; ☎ 316 375; Str Jozef Bem 2; it&t@honoris.ro; 9am-5pm Mon-Fri) The top travel agency in town. Its English-speaking staff sell local maps, and arrange car rental, guided tours, and accommodation at Ceaușescu's former hunting lodge, Arcus Castle, 3km south of town.

Tourist Information Bureau (☎ 316 474; Str 1 Decembrie 1918, 2; sepsinfo@sepsi.ro; ☺ 7.30am-3.30pm Mon-Wed, 7.30am-5pm Thu, 7.30am-2pm Fri) Has a few local maps for sale and can provide general information about the area. Note that they prefer to list their address with the Hungarian street name Str Petőfi Sándor.

Sights

The **Székely National Museum** (Székely Nemzeti Múzeum; ☎ 312 442; Str Kós Károly; adult/child €0.40/ 0.20; ☺ 9am-5pm Tue-Sun) is housed in a building which is itself a masterpiece, designed by leading Hungarian architect Kós Károly between 1911 and 1913. The museum, founded in 1879, has an extremely comprehensive display of Székely culture, including an open-air exhibit of traditional porches, gates and wooden houses. The main building has a large exhibit on the 1848 revolution. It is 200m south of Central Park.

North of the centre, following Str Kossuth Lajos and crossing a bridge over the Debren River, you'll come to the **Fortificată Reformată church**, in whose cemetery you can see some lovely examples of traditional Székely wooden crosses and grave posts.

Sleeping & Eating

There are several drab concrete hotels in the centre, and numerous cafés and fast-food joints to choose from.

Pensiunea Szentgyörgy (☎ 327 116; Str Kós Károly 39; s/d €8/16) This B&B is a better option than the hotels. Though it's 1.5km south of town, it's near the banks of the sweet little Simeria River, and has a comfortable interior.

Kolcza (☎ 351 436; Str Spitalului 30; mains €2-4; ☺ 8.30am-1am) This is an exceptionally good restaurant, in a quiet corner of town. It serves up delicious goulash, impossibly tasty chicken soup, and other Hungarian dishes. Wash it down with some plum țiuca. If coming from the centre, walk south along Str Libertății and turn right at the end of Central Park, go under the underpass and keep going straight for about 500m.

Getting There & Away

Buy tickets at the **Agenţie de Voiaj CFR** (☎ 311 680; Str Mikó Imre 3; ☺ 9am-4pm Mon-Fri). From Sfântu Gheorghe three trains daily go to Covasna (€0.90, one hour), and 13 to Braşov (€1 to €2, 30 to 45 minutes). The bus station

TRANSYLVANIA

THE DECLINE OF THE INCLINE

For many generations Romania's oldest forestry railway snaked its way up mountainous terrain from the spa town of Covasna, northeast of Braşov, to Comandău village (1012m). What was so unique in its appeal was its inclined plane.

The forestry railway, completed in 1892, was the first of its kind in the country to use iron rails and steam locomotives. Its purpose was to transport wood down the valley from Comandău, a primitive logging settlement. To see photos of the original Kraus steam locomotive in action, see www.frank-engel.de/ro_cov_e.htm.

Every weekday two steam trains transporting trimmed wood lumbered up the valley to Siclău (1232m). Here the wood was loaded onto open wagons to make the final part of its journey down the inclined plane to Covasna. Horses were used to manoeuvre the loaded wagons into position then, with the careful use of brakes, the wood was slowly lowered down the mountain. Its weight was ingeniously counterbalanced against empty wagons at the bottom of the line. For an explanation of this inventive system, see www.steam.demon.co.uk/trains/roman4.htm.

In October 1999 operations came to a grinding halt. Due to financial strains, the railway line and sawmill closed, leaving the Comandău community, at the top of the line, without income. But leave it to enterprising Germans to save the day – a group of German investors have bought the railroad and, at the time of writing, plan to reopen the line for 12-minute tourist rides in an original steam locomotive.

With the closure of this line, the forest railway of Vişeu de Sus, in the Vaser Valley in Maramureş (p262), remains the last commercially used steam narrow-gauge railway in Romania. However, today most of the lumber from the forest is hauled by diesel locomotives.

The site is 5km southwest of the centre of Covasna. Follow signs for Cardiologie and pass the ratty camping ground. Comandău Days, with games, concerts and general merry-making, are celebrated in the first days of August. For the latest developments on the functioning of the train for tourists, visit www.kisvasut.hu/comandau/english/index_uk.html.

is 50m north of the train station. There are services to Covasna, Miercurea Ciuc, Piatra Neamţ, Târgu Neamţ and Braşov.

AROUND SFÂNTU GHEORGHE
Covasna
The spa town of Covasna (Kovászna in Hungarian), 28km east of Sfântu Gheorghe in the 'Fairy Queen Valley' (Valea Zânelor), has long been dubbed the 'valley of a thousand springs' for its popular curative mineral water. The black mud that bubbles from the resort's 'Devil's Pond' (Baia Dracului) is more menacing.

The main appeal of this typical spa resort is its unique inclined plane, the starting point of Romania's oldest narrow-gauge forestry railway which snakes 10km up the western flanks of Mt Vrancei (1777m) to Comandău village (see the boxed text on p143). This is a highly recommended visit. Other than this, the town has a heavily medicinal air to it, as do the hobbling tourists who frequent it.

GETTING THERE & AWAY
From Covasna, there are two daily buses to Sfântu Gheorghe (€0.80, 50 minutes). Daily train services include three trains to Sfântu Gheorghe (€0.90, one hour) and Târgu Secuiesc (€0.55, 30 minutes), and two to Breţcu (€1.40, 2½ hours). For Braşov, you must go to Sfântu Gheorghe and get a train or bus.

NORTHERN TRANSYLVANIA

During WWII, northern Transylvania fell under pro-Nazi Hungarian rule. Under the Diktat of Vienna of 30 August 1940, the Axis powers, Germany and Italy, forced Romania to cede 43,493 sq km and a population of 2.6 million to Hungary. During the four years of occupation, thousands of Romanians were imprisoned and tortured while entire villages were massacred. Northern Transylvania was not recovered until 25 October 1944 when, following the liberation of Satu Mare, the territory fell back into Romanian hands.

CLUJ-NAPOCA
☎ 264 / pop 331,990
There's a sassy, savvy feel to Cluj-Napoca and its residents. Everyone here seems to

walk with a strut, decked out in fashionable styles that may not have even made it to Bucharest. People are living in a hip, happening city, and they know it. While not as photogenic as other Transylvanian cities, there are trendy bars galore and cool places with cool people throughout the extended centre. Prices may be slightly higher than in the rest of Romania, but at least every café knows what a long espresso is! This stylishness is partially due to the large university population (60,000); you know you're in a university town when there is a street named after Emile Zola and a lingerie store named Marioana (pronounced like the city's favourite weed).

Cluj-Napoca also makes a perfect urban base from which to explore the Huedin region (p156) and surrounding Apuseni mountain chains Trascăului, Mare and Gilălui, as well as the nearby Turda Gorge and salt mine (p156).

Cut in two by the Someşul Mic River, Cluj-Napoca is as Hungarian as it is Romanian. Its location has long made it a crossroads, which explains its present role as an educational and industrial centre. Known as Klausenburg to the Germans and Kolozsvár to the Hungarians, Cluj in the mid-1970s became known as Cluj-Napoca, adding the name of the old Roman settlement in this area to emphasise its Daco-Roman origin. This move of Ceauşescu's was only partially successful; almost everyone simply refers to the city as 'Cluj'.

The history of Cluj-Napoca goes back to Dacian times. In AD 124, during the reign of Emperor Hadrian, Napoca attained municipal status and Emperor Marcus Aurelius elevated it to a colony between AD 161 and 180. Documented references to the medieval town, known as 'Castrum Clus', date back to 1183. German merchants arrived in the 12th century and, after the Tartar invasion of 1241, the medieval earthen walls of 'Castrenses de Clus' were rebuilt in stone. From 1791 to 1848 and after the union with Hungary in 1867, Cluj-Napoca served as the capital of Transylvania. It still has one of the most vibrant economies in Romania.

Since 1992, Cluj-Napoca has made the headlines thanks to ultra-nationalist mayor George Funar, who has made his feelings toward Hungarians clear in a series of much-ridiculed steps, including painting

THE GREAT CLUJ ROBBERY

Visitors to Cluj-Napoca often remark on how (relatively) prosperous it looks. Perhaps more than it should. Sure, its proximity to western markets and its highly educated (and cheap) workforce have ensured foreign investment. Yet there's another unexpected reason for its affluence: it was the site of one of Eastern Europe's most successful pyramid schemes in the early 1990s, and its consequences are still felt today.

In a truly bizarre series of events hard to imagine even today, one Ion Stoica set up Caritas Bank in early 1992 and promised a population wholly unused to terminology like interest rates, loans and capital redistribution an eight-fold return on their investment in three months. Within a year the company had some three million people invest an estimated US$1.5 billion and had to move out of its offices and take over the municipal sports centre! People – together with their life savings – from rural outlying areas (and eventually from Hungary, Moldova, Ukraine and Germany) were crowding trains and buses en route to Cluj-Napoca. Stoica's ads were broadcast on TV and the government seemed to turn a blind eye to the blatantly illegal scheme in operation.

For a while, the gold rush yielded high returns, and thousands made tons of money to spend on luxury items or to invest in businesses. New shops opened. The crime rate increased, especially robberies and break-ins. At a time when the inflation rate was in triple digits, Romania got a heady dose of capitalism injected into its veins via Cluj-Napoca, but it was already starting to get the shakes.

Doomed to collapse at some point, the fall came in early 1994; Stoica went to Bucharest to get new investments, disappeared when things got tight, and briefly ended up in jail (on a minor charge of taking money from the local council), where he wrote a best-selling book. Hundreds of thousands of ordinary Romanians lost their life savings in these final months. In two short years, Stoica's scheme had managed to ingrain a two-tiered have/have-not system in Cluj-Napoca that is still not evident in other parts of Romania.

The scheme was vastly profitable for Stoica, his pals and government officials all the way up to President Iliescu, who let it continue. It also created an artificial boost to the economy and yielded billions of lei in taxes. It was so successful from the government's point of view, other pyramid schemes were unofficially sanctioned after Stoica's, all of which collapsed, and none was as thriving as that which put some polish on Cluj-Napoca and gave an extra lilt to the steps of its residents.

everything from rubbish bins to parking posts in the colours of the Romanian flag (is dumping garbage in flag lookalikes an act of national pride?), forbidding the display of Hungarian signs, removing the word *Hungariae* from the statue of Hungarian king Matthias Corvinus and dozens of other acts designed to provoke or subjugate the Hungarian population. He has the support of the lower classes but is considered an embarrassment and was widely expected at the time of writing to be booted out of office once and for all in local elections sometime in 2004.

Orientation
MAPS & PUBLICATIONS
The excellent Cartographia publishes the detailed *Cluj-Napoca* (€2). *What Where When Cluj-Napoca* (www.bucurestiwww.ro) is a free quarterly English and Romanian magazine with good news and events articles as

well as handy listings. It's available in bookstores, hotels and cafés.

Information
BOOKSHOPS
Gaudeamus (Map p148; ☎ 439 281; Str Iuliu Maniu 3; ⊗ 10am-7pm Mon-Fri, 10am-2pm Sat) You'll find some maps, lots of art books and mainly Hungarian titles.
Librăria Humanitas (Map p148; ☎ 439 475; Str Napoca 7; ⊗ 9am-7pm Mon-Fri, 9am-5pm Sat) The largest selection in town.

CULTURAL CENTRES & LIBRARIES
American Cultural Center & Library (Map p148; Str Iuliu Maniu 22; ⊗ 8am-5pm Mon-Fri, 8am-3pm Sat) The library has some 7200 titles.
British Council (Map p146; ☎ 593 290; www.british council.ro; Str Arany Janos 11; ⊗ centre 9am-5pm Mon-Fri; library 1-7pm Mon & Wed, 9am-3pm Tue, Thu & Fri) An excellent stock of books, magazines and videos, and a good resource centre.

TRANSYLVANIA

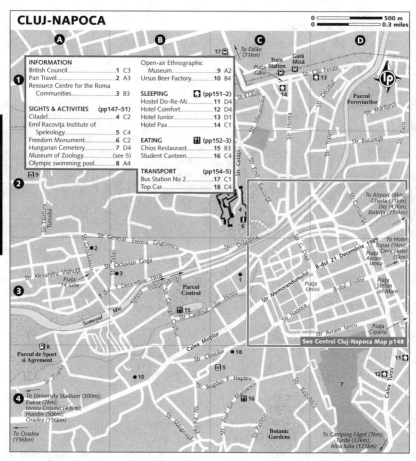

CLUJ-NAPOCA

INFORMATION
British Council.....................1 C3
Pan Travel.........................2 A3
Resource Centre for the Roma
  Communities......................3 B3

SIGHTS & ACTIVITIES   (pp147–51)
Citadel............................4 C2
Emil Racoviţa Institute of
  Speleology........................5 C4
Freedom Monument..................6 C2
Hungarian Cemetery................7 D4
Museum of Zoology............(see 5)
Olympic swimming pool.............8 A4

Open-air Ethnographic
  Museum...........................9 A2
Ursus Beer Factory...............10 B4

SLEEPING   (pp151–2)
Hostel Do-Re-Mi...................11 D4
Hotel Comfort.....................12 D4
Hotel Junior......................13 D1
Hotel Pax.........................14 C1

EATING   (pp152–3)
Chios Restaurant..................15 B3
Student Canteen...................16 C4

TRANSPORT   (pp154–5)
Bus Station No 2..................17 C1
Top Car...........................18 C4

French Cultural Centre (Map p148; Centre Culturel
Français; ☎ 598 551; Str Ion Brătianu 22; ☽ 2-7pm Mon,
10am-7pm Tue-Fri, 10am-1pm Sat Sep-Jul) The centre
arranges contemporary art exhibitions, music festivals, jazz
nights and film screenings. Its mediatheque is well stocked.

German Cultural Centre (Map p148; Deutsches
Kulturzentrum; ☎ 597 936; Str Universităţii 7-9;
☽ 6-7.30pm Mon & Thu, 4-7pm Tue & Wed, 4-6pm Fri)
This location hosts cultural events and film evenings, and
has a library.

Resource Centre for the Roma Communities
(Map p146; ☎ 420 480; Str Tebei 21; ☽ 10am-7.30pm
Mon-Thu, 10am-2pm Sat) This centre is an outgrowth of
the Soros Open Foundation and provides information on
minorities in Romania, especially the Roma.

United States Embassy (Map p148; ☎ 594 315) Has
a small information office on the same floor as the German

Cultural Centre, which gives out travel advisories and
displays Iraq's Most Wanted posters.

INTERNET ACCESS
Internet Café (Map p148; Str 21 Decembrie, 20; per hr
€0.35; ☽ 8am-2am)

Supernet (Map p148; ☎ 430 425; Str Iuliu Maniu 1; per
hr €0.40; ☽ 24hr) Supposedly open around the clock but
often closes when staff feel like it.

MEDICAL SERVICES
For a well-stocked and central pharmacy,
try **Clematis** (Map p148; Piaţa Unirii 11; ☽ 8am-10pm).

MONEY
Those sour-faced goons that you see hanging around the western side of Piaţa Unirii

are, well, goons in the outdated business of black-market moneychanging. Hence this area of the city centre is duly known by locals as 'Wall Street'. Steer clear of these leather-clad toughies. The city is full of ATMs and legitimate exchange offices. The **Banca Comercială Română** (Map p148; ☎ 591 227; Str Gheorghe Barițiu 10-12; ☺ 8am-3pm Mon-Fri) gives cash advances and changes travellers cheques.

POST & TELEPHONE

The **central post office** (Map p148; Str Regele Ferdinand 33; ☺ 7am-8pm Mon-Fri, 8am-2pm Sat) and the main **telephone centre** (☺ 7.30am-8pm Mon-Fri, 8am-1pm Sat) share the same building.

TOURIST INFORMATION

See www.cjnet.ro for general information on the city. See p150 for other associations which could help you get the most out of your stay. Retro Hostel (p152) organises some of the most enjoyable trips to outlying areas.

Pan Travel (Map p146; ☎ 420 516; www.pantravel.ro; Str Grozăvescu 13) A top-notch outfit which can book accommodation, and car and mobile-phone rental, provide you with English- or French-speaking guides or prepare an à-la-carte tour circuit.

Transylvania Ecological Club (Map p148; Clubul Ecologic Transilvania; ☎ 431 626; www.greenagenda.org; Str Sindicatelor 3, Apt 6; ☺ 11am-5pm Mon-Fri) One of the most active grass-roots environmental groups in the country tries its best to sensitise a largely uninterested population in the methods of environmental preservation in the Huedin region and the Apuseni mountains. It can provide a wealth of advice about activities in the region, suggest guides and even organise trips. It often works in collaboration with Green Mountain Holidays (p150).

Youth Hostels România (Map p148; YHR; ☎ 586 616; www.hihostels-romania.ro; Piața Lucian Blaga; ☺ 9am-5pm Mon-Fri) Ideally located inside the imposing Student's Culture House (Casa de Culture a Studentilor), which lords over Piața Lucian Blaga, this office can make bookings for youth hostels throughout Romania.

Sights

PIAȚA UNIRII   Map p148

The vast 14th-century **St Michael's Church** dominates Piața Unirii. The neo-Gothic tower (1859) topping the Gothic hall church creates a great landmark. The church is considered to be one of the finest examples of Gothic architecture in Romania and was built in four stages. The three naves and

vestry were the last to be completed at the end of the 16th century. The choir vaults, built in the 14th century, were rebuilt in the 18th century following a fire. Daily services are held in Hungarian and Romanian, and organ concerts often take place in the evening.

Flanking the church to the south is the bulky 1902 **equestrian statue of Matthias Corvinus** (Mátyás Corvinus) – the famous Hungarian king, the son of Iancu de Hunedoara (János Hunyadi) and ruler of Hungary between 1458 and 1490. The statue has been the stick in notoriously anti-Hungarian mayor Gheorghe Funar's craw since he took office. After erasing the word *Hungariae* from it, he gave the go-ahead for an archaeological dig to take place in front of the statue in the hopes of finding an excuse to remove it. That failed (though the square is still marred by the dig), so in a snit he decided not to illuminate it, as Ivram Iancu's statue is one block over.

On the eastern side of the square is the excellent **National Art Museum** (☎ 496 952; Piața Unirii 30; adult/child €0.80/0.40; ☺ noon-7pm Wed-Sun), housed inside the baroque Banffy Palace from 1791. Its 22 rooms are filled with paintings and artefacts including a 16th-century church altar. The inner courtyard makes a lovely place for a tea break. A **Pharmaceutical Museum** (☎ 597 567; Str Regele Ferdinand 1; adult/child €0.40/0.20; ☺ 10am-4pm Mon-Sat) is diagonally across the street, on the site of Cluj-Napoca's first apothecary (1573).

The **Ethnographic Museum** (Muzeul Etnografic al Transilvaniei; ☎ 592 344; Str Memorandumului 21; adult/child €0.80/0.40; ☺ 9am-5pm Tue-Sun) has a fine collection of folk costumes and beautiful woven carpets. This is only the indoor section, however, and true ethnographic fiends should head to the **open-air section** (Map p146; adult/child €1/0.50) northwest of the centre in the Hoia forest (take Bus No 27 from the train station). Traditional sawmills, wells, wine and oil presses, roadside crosses, fruit dryers, potters' workshops, sheepfolds and much more are all here in this marvellous outdoor display of folk architecture.

PIAȚA MUZEULUI & AROUND

This charming neighbourhood is pleasant to explore on foot, dipping into courtyards for a peek at local life. A sense of history is thick here, partially thanks to the remnants

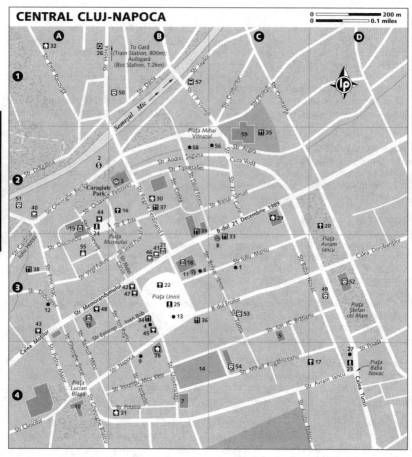

CENTRAL CLUJ-NAPOCA

of archaeological digs that have been going on here since 1991 in the southern and northeastern sections of the square. On the eastern side of the square is a beautifully decorated 15th-century **Franciscan church** (Map p148; Biserica Franciscanilor; admission free), one of the city's oldest structures. The Music High School next to it used to contain a monastery; if you ask nicely inside the school they'll let you see the impressive Gothic dining hall.

The **National History Museum of Transylvania** (Map p148; ☎ 495 677; Str Constantin Daicoviciu 1; adult/child €0.50/0.25; ☺ 10am-4pm Tue-Sun) has been open since 1859. All the captions are in Romanian but there are English- and French-speaking guides. This museum presents

one of the most comprehensive accounts of Transylvanian history, with more than 400,000 objects in its collection. Kids will love the mammoth tusks and ghoulish ancient human remains on the 1st floor.

Northwest of the square, on the banks of the river you'll see the **Hungarian State Theatre & Opera** (see Entertainment, p154), one of only two in Romania today. By crossing the footbridge west of the theatre, or the bridge across Str Regele Ferdinand to the east, you can climb Citadel Hill (a number of footpaths wind up towards the eyesore that is Hotel Transylvania, towering pathetically on top of it). There is an **obelisk freedom monument** (Map p146) in memory of those who died during WWI. Some ruins of

INFORMATION			Pharmaceutical Museum	21 B3	Diesel Bar	42 B3

TRANSYLVANIA

the 15th-century **citadel** (Map p146), enlarged in 1715, still remain but you'd have to be an archaeologist or detective to find them. The most impressive thing about this area is the commanding view over the city.

Head back down the hill then bear north along Str Horea. At No 21 is the **Synagogue of the Deportees**. The grand Moorish-style building is just one of three remaining synagogues in Cluj-Napoca. This was built in 1987 in memory of the 16,700 Jews deported to Auschwitz from Cluj-Napoca in 1944. In the early 1990s an institute for Jewish and Hebrew studies was established at Cluj-Napoca's Babeş-Bolyai University.

SOUTH OF PIAŢA UNIRII

On Str Mihail Kogălniceanu is a **Hungarian Reformed Church** (Map p148; Str Mihail Kogălniceanu 16) built by the king of Hungary, Matthias Corvinus, in 1486. The statue of St George slaying the dragon in front of the church is a replica of the 14th-century original, carved by the Hungarian Kolozsvári brothers, which is now displayed in Prague. Organ concerts are regularly held in the church.

Further east is the sprawling Piaţa Ştefan cel Mare. South of this is the smaller Piaţa Baba Novac on which there's a **statue** of its namesake in front of the **Tailors' Bastion** (Bastion Croitorilor). The bastion, dating from the 1550s, is the only one that remains from the medieval fortified city. The square on which it stands is named

after one of Mihai Viteazul's generals, who was executed by Hungarian nobles here in the 17th century.

Cluj-Napoca's fragrant **Botanic Gardens** (Map p146; ☎ 597 604; Str Gheorghe Bilaşcu 42; adult/child €0.40/0.15; ☯ 9am-8pm), from 1930, lie south of the university ghetto. Covering 15 hectares, the green lawns embrace greenhouses, a Japanese garden and a rose garden with some 600 different varieties. In summer allow several hours to explore it. The Japanese garden and six greenhouses are especially enchanting.

Just east of here is an immense, highly memorable **Hungarian cemetery** (Házsongárdi temető), where dozens of revered Hungarian notables are buried. There are many lovely 18th- and 19th-century tombstones. You can purchase an excellent map (Térke Press; €2) of the cemetery at Gaudeamus bookshop (p145).

UNIVERSITY & AROUND

The **Babeş-Bolyai University** (Map p148; ☎ 405 300; www.ubbcluj.ro; Str Mihai Kogălniceanu 1B), home to some 17,500 students, is the largest university in Romania after Bucharest. Founded in 1872, Hungarian was the predominant language there until 1918. Internationally, it's famed for being home to the world's only university institute of speleology (the study of caves). The student ghetto is inside the triangle formed by Calea Moţilor, Str Mărginaşă and Str Pasteur, and is full of small cafés, bistros, Internet salons and

---

BRAVE NEW WORLD

Emil Racoviţă (1868–1947) was Romania's most heroic scientist. He created a new branch of science through which the great mysteries of the underground world came to be unravelled.

The son of an Iaşi nobleman and a Sorbonne graduate, Emil Racoviţă's first pioneering move was in 1897 aboard the wooden whaler *Belgica* for a polar expedition led by Norwegian explorer Roald Amundsen (the first man to reach the South Pole, in 1911). In March 1898 the *Belgica* became trapped in Antarctic ice. It remained stuck until March 1899, having drifted 3500km. The expedition provided the first meteorological data recorded hourly over a one-year period, as well as a collection of 1600 botanical and zoological specimens.

Emil Racoviţă's adventures whirled him around the globe. In 1904 he discovered a new species of cave crustacean in Majorca. In 1905 he pioneered the use of photographic slides and in 1907 gave birth to biospeleology as an independent science. During his lifetime he explored some 1200 caves in Europe (many of which were in Romania) and Africa.

In 1920 the **Emil Racoviţă Institute of Speleology** opened in Cluj-Napoca, where Racoviţă remained until 1940 when, following the Hungarian occupation of northern Transylvania, his institute sought refuge in Timişoara. He returned in 1944, only to be struck down by pneumonia. Even on his deathbed, Emil Racoviţă remained loyal to his homeland: while famine raged through the country, the heroic professor gracefully declined a dish of chicken and sour cream offered to him, explaining he would eat the same as his famine-struck countrymen – dry *mămăligă* (corn meal).

---

local hang-outs; it has a completely different look and feel from the city centre.

Though the main university building is south of Piaţa Unirii, many faculties of note are located in this 'ghetto'. A small **Museum of Zoology** (Map p146; ☎ 596 116; Str Clinicilor 5; admission €0.80; ☼ 9am-3pm Mon-Sat) is worth a visit, as is the fascinating **Emil Racoviţă Institute of Speleology** (☎ 595 954), housed on the 2nd floor of the same building. The institute was set up in 1920 by internationally renowned Romanian biologist Emil Racoviţă (1868–1947) and a small **museum** (admission €0.40; ☼ 9am-5pm Mon-Fri) inside the institute has a fascinating collection of his work. It includes extraordinarily detailed drawings of whales, and lots of information about the spectacular caves in Romania and some of the discoveries that have been made in them.

WEST OF THE CENTRE

In the much-loved **Central Park** (Parcul Central), you can hire boats to row on the small lake, or enjoy a drink and meal at the lakeside restaurant Chios (see Eating, p153). Southwest of the park is the **Ursus Beer Factory** (Calea Mănăştur 2-4), where Ursus beer has been brewed since 1878.

The **university stadium**, further west, is home to FC Universitatea, who have matches here regularly. The stadium is close to the Olympic-sized **swimming pool** (Map p146; ☎ 588 777; adult/student €1.30/1) in the **Sport & Leisure Park** (Parcul de Sport şi Agrement, sometimes still referred to as Parcul Central). Here you will also find outside tennis courts, a **fitness club** (Sala Sport; ☎ 586 915), running tracks, an athletes' pavilion and FC Universitatea's clubhouse.

Activities

Cluj-Napoca is a major centre for mountain biking and caving enthusiasts, with the Apuseni Mountains to the southwest offering a wealth of caves and trails (p151)

Clubul de Cicloturism Napoca (Map p148; ☎ 450 013; office@ccn.ro; Str Sindicatelor 3, Apt 8) These outdoors-lovers can help with all your two-wheeler questions. They usually organise one major two-week bike trip in the summer but also help find cycling guides, and suggest great cycling routes and places to rent bikes throughout the region.

Green Mountain Holidays (☎ 257 142; www.green mountainholidays.ro; Str Pincipală 305) Located in the village of Izvoru Crişului, 43km west of Cluj-Napoca on the road to Huedin, this is a terrific ecotourist organisation, highly recommended for an environmentally friendly, activity-filled week or two in the Apuseni Mountains. The website offers extremely detailed information about the accommodation available (from €150 per week) and the

APUSENI MOUNTAINS

Southwest of Cluj-Napoca, the Western Carpathians harbour the Apuseni Mountains. The central part is dominated by the peaks of Mt Bihor (1849m) and Mt Vlădeasa (1836m). Most travellers head straight for the **Padiş Plateau**, where numerous caves and subterranean rivers hide beneath the earth's surface. An officially protected area, the plateau's highest peaks are Mt Măgura Vânătă (1642m) and Mt Cârligatele (1694m).

You can access Padiş by road from the east in **Poiana Horea** or from the west in **Pietroasa**. Both roads are difficult to navigate in bad weather but eventually lead to **Cabana Padiş** (1280m; 45 beds), from where numerous hiking trails begin. Bookings for the cabana can be made through the **Tourism Agency Romanta** (☎ /fax 064-255 064) in Bologa (see p157).

From **Gârda de Sus**, 10km west of Albac, a trail leads to Cabana Padiş (five to six hours, blue stripes). Few hikers access Padiş from **Stâna de Vale** in the northwest although it is possible (5½ to six hours, red stripes).

From Cabana Padiş the most popular circuit leads southwest along the polluted Ponorului River to the fantastic **Cetăţile Ponorului** (Cetatea Ponorului; six hours, blue circles). The citadel is one of the plateau's greatest natural wonders, leading underground to a damp chamber in which the Ponorului River sinks its way through the chamber's numerous holes; some are as deep as 150m.

Another trail, marked first by red stripes then by red circles, leads from the cabana north along a track to **Poiana Vărăşoaia**. From here, red circles bear east to the **Rădesei Citadel** (Cetăţile Rădesei), another underground chamber with impressive rock formations. The route then circles **Someşul Cald**, a natural storage lake, before heading back south to the cabana. If you continue to follow the red stripes north through the Stâna de Vale ski resort you'll arrive at **Cârligatele Peak** (1694m).

The Apuseni region's caves, including the Bear Cave, Scărişoara Ice Cave and Meziad Cave, are discussed in the Crişana & Banat chapter (p226).

hiking, caving, rock-climbing, horseback riding treks. Activities take place in the Huedin microregion (p156).

Daksa (☎ 0740-053 550; soteria@soteria.ro) Some of the best horseback riding excursions are offered by this experienced, friendly group, located just outside Cluj-Napoca. Excursions last from three to seven days and take in small villages and chats with shepherds. Prices range from €40 to €80 per person per day, including lodging, equipment and three daily meals. For kids, they have donkey rides. You don't have to be a kid to enjoy riding in a horse-drawn carriage.

Festivals & Events

The Transylvania International Film Festival is held at the end of May. Early October sees the three-day American Music Festival with free concerts at the University's concert hall. In mid-August there is the excellent International Folk Music and Dance Festival of Ethnic Minorities in Europe. In early September there's the Cluj-Napoca Music Festival, which mainly features classical performances.

Sleeping

Unless you're staying at a hostel, accommodation will most likely be your main expense here; Cluj-Napoca's places to stay are more expensive than in other cities and it's hard to find a bargain. Both the Transylvania Ecological Club and Pan Travel (p147) can help you find amazing places to stay in the Apuseni Mountains and rural areas of northwestern Transylvania for about €10 a night.

BUDGET

Hotel Pax (Map p146; ☎ 432 927; Piaţa Gării 1-3; s/d with shared toilet €16/18, d with private toilet €23) Being opposite the train station makes it noisy, but at least it's clean.

Hotel Junior (Map p146; ☎ 432 028; Str Cări Ferate 12; s/d without private toilet €16/24, d with private toilet €32) It's on a busy, dusty street near the train station, but its rooms are simple and comfortable.

Hotel Vlădeasa (Map p148; ☎ 594 429; Str Regele Ferdinand 20; s/d/tr without private toilet €14/21/27, with private toilet €17/24/32) OK, so it smells a tad musty, but the place is tidy and comfy, the rooms have grand, high ceilings and the

TRANSYLVANIA

TRANSYLVANIA

AUTHOR'S CHOICE

Retro Hostel (Map p148; ☎ 450 452; www.retro.ro; Str Potaissa 13; dm €10-13; 🖳) Not only is this the very definition of what a hostel should be, it's a kind of traveller's one-stop shopping centre: here you can buy maps and CD-ROMs, join fun tours of the surrounding areas, order a therapeutic massage and follow it with a bottle of *țiuca* from the front desk. Its tours are the least expensive and among the most comprehensive on offer in the city. Small but spotless rooms hold from three to eight people, and the atmosphere's always lively and super-friendly. There's free Internet and ISIC card-holders get a 5% discount.

---

motel-like entrance via a courtyard balcony is an exotic touch.

Hostel Do-Re-Mi (Map p148; ☎ 586 616; yhr@ mail.dntcj.ro; Str Braşov 2-4; dm €7) This place is located in the university dormitory occupied by music students from September through May; consequently rooms are available only in the summer. The staff really try hard, but their enthusiasm can't cover up the gloominess that enfolds the place. Repairs are foreseen, but so far the bathroom and showers are a tad skanky. It's doubtful the place inspires many melodious compositions! From the train station take trolleybus No 3 three stops to Piaţa Cipariu, walk south along Str Andrei Mureşanu, then take the first right along Str Zrínyi Miklóos to the end.

Camping Făget (☎ 596 234; tent space/2-person hut free/€2 per person) You get what you pay for at this shabby camping ground 7km south of Cluj-Napoca. There's an on-site restaurant. Take bus No 35 from Piaţa Mihai Viteazul south down Calea Turzii to the end of the line. From here it is a marked 2km hike.

MID-RANGE

Vila Casa Albă (Map p148; ☎ 534 556; Str Emil Racoviţă 22; d €53-64, ste €77; 🛦 🗶) Surrounded by gardens near the base of Citadel Hill, this is a good choice for something more upmarket. Small (18 rooms) and quiet (it's on a leafy residential street), it boasts large, tastefully decorated rooms and bathrooms larger than some Manhattan apartments. But heaven is in the details here, with luxurious pluses such as bidets and cotton bathrobes.

Hotel Comfort (Map p146; ☎ 598 410; Calea Turzii 48; s/d/ste €24/37/48; 🖳) This is a modern, clean and friendly place. Beds are low, ceilings are high and soft pastels envelop you everywhere.

Hotel Victoria (Map p148; ☎ 597 963; B-dul 21 Decembrie 1989, 54-56; s/d/ste €35/43/51) This is a

good deal with its elegant, old-world exteriors, ultra-stylish, modern interiors and reliable service desk. There's also a pleasant terrace café.

Hotel Topaz (☎ 414 021; Str Septimiu Albini 10; s/d/ ste €40/50/65) With bright colours splashed all over the place, this is a very pleasant hotel, with compact, nicely renovated, modern rooms.

Continental Hotel (Map p148; ☎ 591 441; www .continentalhotels.ro; Str Napoca 1; s/d without private toilet €17/28, with private toilet €48/62, ste with private toilet €72-86) It may be stately on the outside, but it's disappointing on the inside. Nonetheless, the rooms with shared shower and toilet are the cheapest in central Cluj-Napoca. More expensive rooms are nice but overpriced for what they offer. There are 15% discounts for weekend stays and IYH members get a 10% discount on the cheap rooms (be warned: they can be noisy).

Onix Hotel (☎ 414 076; Str Septimiu Albini 12; s €25-48, d €29-55, ste €45-92; 🖳) It has two-, three- and four-star rooms, but while some suites have spa baths, the rooms here are unmemorable and the atmosphere sterile. An adjoining nightclub features nightly erotic dancing and the hotel seems very proud of this.

Eating
RESTAURANTS

Pizza Y (Map p148; ☎ 0722-218 210; Piaţa Unirii 1; mains €1-3; 🕒 9am-midnight) This has been a fixture on the pizza scene for years. In a courtyard just off the southern end of the square, it serves an amazing 34 types of pizza, and pastas and fresh salads.

Restaurant Privighetoarea (Map p148; ☎ 593 480; Str Regele Ferdinand 16; mains €1-3; 🕒 9am-7pm) This serves up hearty portions of meat, potatoes and more traditional soups, spicy meatballs and hot breaded cheese. The attached fast-food outlet to the left serves a variety of pizzas, salads and light snacks.

Roata (Map p148; ☎ 592 011; Str Alexandru Ciura 6A; mains €2-3.50; ☿ noon-midnight Tue-Sat, 1pm-midnight Sun-Mon) This is one of the city's highlights – period. The traditional Romanian dishes taste as good as home cooking here, and served as they are on a small terrace with moss-covered stones and potted plants vying for space, you're likely to start feeling at home very quickly. They don't overdo folkiness here, though nice touches such as clay plates are appreciated. There are European dishes too, for those who are squeamish about trying things they can't pronounce, but stick to the specials, such as the succulent Varza de la Cluj (cabbage, meat, onions) or delicious soups.

Chios Restaurant (Map p146; ☎ 596 395; mains €2-5; ☿ noon-1am) Right by the lakeside in Central Park on the site of the former casino, this is popular more for its location and the adjoining terrace bar than for the food, which is decent but standard.

Hubertus (Map p148; ☎ 596 743; B-dul 21 Decembrie 1989, 22; mains €7-13; ☿ 10am-midnight) Animal-lovers will want to boycott this place; if the deer head on their business card isn't enough, the small courtyard decorated with hunting motifs will do it. Even the walls' pretty pastel colours don't soften the fact that the city's most expensive restaurant is for *real* men who can pay big bucks to eat them (venison, along with bear, features on the menu).

QUICK EATS

There are a number of fast-food joints (including the popular Sora) inside the Shopping Mall at B-dul 21 Decembrie 1989, 5. There are also several places for a hot pastry, fast Romanian food or pizza slice lining Str Regele Ferdinand, north of Piața Unirii. The strip for kebabs is Str Napoca, between Piața Unirii and Piața Lucian Blaga.

Student canteen (Map p146; Str Professor Ion Marinescu; mains €0.50-2; ☿ 9am-6pm) Don't all student canteens have nasty reputations? This one lives up to expectation, but for dirt-cheap 'meals' and the chance to see how students live, this is the place to go.

Hungry Bunny (Map p148; Piața Unirii 12; mains €0.50-1.50; ☿ 10am-midnight) It serves up cheap Western-style doughnuts and burgers.

SELF-CATERING

For fresh produce, stroll through the packed **central market** (Map p146), behind the Complex Commercial Mihai Viteazul shopping centre located on Piața Mihai Viteazul. The **Sora supermarket & shopping mall** (Map p148; ☿ 24hr) is located at B-dul 21 Decembrie 1989, 5.

Drinking

Cofetăria Jazz (Map p148; ☎ 593 467; Str Emil Isac 23; ☿ 8am-10pm Mon-Fri, 10am-10pm Sat-Sun) The walls are decked out with black-and-white photos of jazz legends and the space caressed by the jazz piped through the speakers. The real stars here are the fattening pastries and eclectic assortment of coffees and juice cocktails.

Crema (Map p148; ☎ 0723-161 002; Piața Unirii 25; ☿ 9am-1am) Cluj-Napoca's most style-concious café/bar looks to London and Paris for inspiration (and prices!). Done up in faux-Renaissance and Gothic decor with attractive, mannequin-like staff, it's a place where the trendy come for their martini or espresso and listen to lounge and trance music.

Flowers (Map p148; Piața Unirii 23; ☿ 8am-10pm Mon-Fri, 10am-10pm Sat-Sun) Right next door to Crema but worlds away in look, feel and clientele. It's more stylish than Crema because it doesn't try to be. Modest and cosy enough for a down-to-earth conversation, it has a wide selection of teas and coffees, served to the beat of underground house and classical music.

BARS & CLUBS

The nightlife in Cluj-Napoca, primarily Friday and Saturday nights, is nothing less than sizzling, with each of its dozen main clubs packed to the rafters with fun-seekers of all backgrounds, ages and sexualities, all jostling shoulders with a minimum of complexes. Piața Unirii is the site of many watering holes, but clubs and bars are spread out throughout the centre, and in Cluj-Napoca, it pays to go exploring.

Diesel Bar (Map p148; ☎ 598 441; Piața Unirii 17; ☿ 9am-3am) It tends to be the most happening

TRANSYLVANIA

disco come the weekend. It spins mainly pop-dance and retro hits in its cavernous space.

Flash Bar (Map p148; ☎ 599 020; Piaţa Unirii 10) It may not be as popular as Diesel Bar, but attracts a more stylish crowd who pose on the couches and by the beautifully lit bar.

Harley Davidson Club (Map p148; ☎ 590 552; Piaţa Unirii 15-16; ☯ 9am-3am) Shirking trendiness, this has a more down-to-earth feel to it. Two or three Saturdays a month it hosts gay discos (www.gaycluj.go.ro), frequented by lots of young hustler types.

Basement (Map p148; B-dul 21 Decembrie 1989, 8) It may be awkwardly lodged in the bowels of the Sora shopping centre (the harsh lighting in the halls as everyone exits, trashed, at 3am is none too flattering!), but there is a fever-pitch energy with its mainly younger crowd.

Latino Club (Map p148; ☎ 0722-750 611; Str Memorandumului 23; ☯ 8pm-4am) The ingredients here: salsa music, fancy cocktails and waitresses dressed up in something resembling 'exotic'.

Euphoria (Map p148; ☎ 0745-393 333; Str Muzeiu 4; ☯ 11am-2am) In daytime there's a quiet terrace under the stern gaze of Constantin Daicoviciu's statue; by night the dark cellar inside becomes a friendly and relatively low-key alternative bar/disco.

Entertainment

Şapte Seri (www.sapteseri.ro) is a free biweekly booklet listing all the latest goings-on (Romanian only). It's available in cafés, hotels and entertainment venues.

CINEMAS

Cinema Favorit (Map p148; ☎ 530 757; Str Horea 6) is one of several cinemas in the centre.

THEATRE & CLASSICAL MUSIC

Organ recitals are held two or three times a week in St Michael's Church (see p147).

National Theatre Lucian Blaga (Map p148; ☎ 591 799; Piaţa Ştefan cel Mare 24) was designed by the famous Viennese architects Fellner and Hellmer and a performance here is well attended. The **opera** (☎ 597 175) is in the same building. Tickets can be bought in advance from the **Agenţie de Teatrală** (Map p148; ☎ 595 363; Piaţa Ştefan cel Mare 14; ☯ 11am-5pm Tue-Fri). Tickets for classical concerts hosted by the **State Philharmonic** (Map p148; Filarmonica de Stat; ☎ 430 063; Str Mihail Kogălniceanu) are also sold here. Look out for performances at the **Puck Puppet Theatre** (Map p148; Teatrul de Păpuşi Puck; B-dul Eroilor 8), sometimes held in a courtyard.

Hungarian State Theatre & Opera (Map p148; ☎ 593 469; Str Emil Isac 26-28), close to the river, stages Hungarian-language plays and operas. Tickets are sold in advance at the box office inside the theatre.

Shopping

Galeriile de Artă Populară Româneasca (Map p148; ☎ 0722-339 263; www.popart.ro; Str Georges Clemenceau 2; ☯ 10am-6pm Mon-Fri, 10am-2pm Sat) has the city's best collection of handicrafts and souvenirs, some of which are true works of art, not the usual touristy junk. Ceramics, woodcarvings, textiles and costumes are nicely displayed in the cosy shop.

Getting There & Away

AIR

Tarom has at least two daily direct flights to Bucharest (one way/return €99/110). It also has thrice weekly direct flights to Frankfurt and Vienna, and six weekly to Munich. Tickets can be bought at the airport one hour before departure or from the **Tarom city office** (Map p148; ☎ 432 524; Piaţa Mihai Viteazul 11; ☯ 8am-7pm Mon-Fri, 9am-1pm Sat). **Carpatair** (☎ 416 016; cluj-napoca@carpatair.ro; airport office) runs flights to Italy.

TRAIN

Tickets for international trains have to be bought in advance at the **Agenţie de Voiaj CFR** (Map p148; ☎ 432 001; Piaţa Mihai Viteazul 20; ☯ 7am-7pm Mon-Fri).

Services include one daily to Iaşi (nine hours), Târgu Mureş (2¼ hours) and Sibiu (four hours), two daily to Mangalia (13 hours), three daily to Timişoara (seven hours), six daily to Bucharest (7½ hours), nine daily to Huedin (45 to 75 minutes) and ten daily to Oradea (2¼-4½ hours). Two daily trains go to Budapest (five hours). The smaller Găra Mică, 100m east of the central train station, is for short-distance trains only.

BUS

As confused as the bus situation is everywhere in Romania, your detective skills will especially come in handy here as buses leave from several destinations throughout the city. It's best to go to these places yourself and either check posted times or (better still) ask for the latest information.

From Autogară 2 (there is no No 1) one daily bus or maxitaxi goes to Braşov, two to Abrud, three to Zalău, four each to Dej, Piatra Neamţ and Târgu Mureş, five to Baie Mare, and eight to Bistriţa. Ten weekly buses to Budapest and three weekly to Chişinau also leave from here. Other daily buses to Budapest leave from a parking lot 100m west of the train station.

From a parking lot on the corner of Str Iaşilor and Str IP Voineşti, two companies run seven daily buses to Turda, five of which end up at Târgu Mureş and two of which continue to Aiud and Alba Iulia. Also from here, the reliable **Dacos** (www.dacos.com.ro in Romanian) runs daily buses to Bucharest and four daily to Sibiu. **Atlassib's** (☎ 535 446) buses to Germany and Italy also depart from here.

Getting Around
TO/FROM THE AIRPORT

Cluj-Napoca airport (☎ 416 702) is 8km east of the town centre in the Someşeni district. Bus No 8 runs from Piaţa Mihai Viteazul to the airport.

TRAM, TROLLEYBUS & BUS

Trolleybus No 9 runs from the train station into town. Bus No 27 takes you to within a 10-minute walk of the open-air ethnographic museum northwest of the centre in Horea forest.

CAR

Some of the travel agencies listed previously (p147) can help with car rental.

Top Car (Map p146; ☎ 450 500; Str Clinicilor 33) has Dacias from €30 per day and foreign

makes from €50, with discounts after the third rental day.

TURDA

☎ 264 / pop 60,400

Turda, 27km southeast of Cluj-Napoca, was an important salt-mining town in the 13th century. In the mid-16th century it was the seat of the Transylvanian Diet and hence one of the richest towns in the region. Today this small market town preserves a number of stately baroque and Magyar facades. Your reason for coming here will, however, most likely be strictly practical – to hike or catch a bus to Turda Gorge (Cheile Turzii), or breathe in the salty fumes at its huge salt mine.

Orientation & Information

Turda's handful of shops is centred on the main street, Str Republicii, including the **central post and telephone office** (Str Republicii 31; ☎ 7am-8pm).

You can change money at the **Banca Post** (Str Republicii 24; ⊗ 8.30am-12.30pm Mon-Fri). The bank also has an ATM.

Salt Mines

Salt was first mined at the Turda **salt mines** (☎ 311 690; Str Salinelor 54; adult/child €1/0.50; ⊗ 9am-5pm) in 1271. Following their closure in 1932, the abandoned 45-sq-km mines were used as a cheese deposit. Today part of the site serves as a day centre for sufferers of lung and bronchial diseases, and the temperature remains at a constant 10° to 12°C.

Some of the deeper mines, including Ghezala (80m deep), partially filled with a lake, are no longer safe. But visitors are free to wander around, or even play table tennis at the very bottom of the largest cave. It's a memorable experience, especially for the kids. Though it's fairly well lit, it's a good idea to bring your own torch (flashlight). Oh, that odd smell you're sure to notice – no, it's not salt, it's the lingering odour of decomposing horses which were unfortunate enough to die inside after being used to haul carts of salt and debris in and out of the mine decades ago.

To get to the mine, turn left at the first fork in the village (approaching from the north) onto Str Basarabiei. Go straight across the crossroads to the end of Str

Tunel, then turn left onto Str Salinelor. It's a €1 taxi ride from the town centre.

Turda Gorge

Turda Gorge (Cheile Turzii) is a short but stunning break in the mountains southwest of Turda. You can hike the gorge's length in under an hour, so plan on camping a night or two in order to explore the surrounding network of marked trails – see the map outside Cabana Cheile Turzii or ask the cabana staff for a free photocopied map of the *Cheile Turzii şi Împrejurimi Trasee Turistice*.

Most people access the gorge from **Cabana Cheile Turzii** (450m), at the southern foot of Turda Gorge. From Turda a trail (three to four hours, 13km, blue crosses) leads hikers through Mihai Viteazul village to the cabana. There is also a shorter and more pleasant cross-country route from Turda (two hours, red crosses). By vehicle, the turn-off marked Cheile Turzii is 2km west of Mihai Viteazul on the main Turda–Abrud road.

A good two-hour trek is the red-cross trail through the gorge, followed by the red-circle trail up and over the peak before returning to Cabana Cheile Turzii.

It is also possible to approach the gorge at its more dramatic northern end, from **Petreştii de Jos**. Upon entering the village, bear left at the first fork; from here, a trail is marked with red crosses. You can also hike from Turda Gorge to Cluj-Napoca, via Deleni and Camping Făget (10 to 12 hours, 29km, red stripes).

Maps of the gorge are sold at the entrance, where there is a €0.70 entrance fee.

Băile Turda

Only 2km east of Turda lies the small spa resort of Băile Turda, allegedly built on the site of an old Roman salt mine. The resort's outdoor swimming pool and mini aqua park get packed in summer. There are a couple of tennis courts and a small, dilapidated and sad **zoo** (parcul zoologic; adult/child €0.50/0.25; 10am-6pm Tue-Sun). People muck about in the supposedly curative mud that is all around the area.

Sleeping & Eating

Hunter Prince Castle (315241; www.huntercastle.ro; Str Sulutiu 4-6; s/d €50/60) This regal hotel boasts creatively furnished, beautiful rooms which incorporate a lot of stone walls and antique furniture. Pacifists might take offence to the animal heads and pelts liberally strewn on the walls in unexpected places, but otherwise this is classy place. There's a full bar and restaurant too.

Hotel Arieşul (316 844; Str Ceanului; s/d €13/18) Though Băile Turda is a depressing place to stay the night, if you're stuck, this offers medicinal baths, saunas and massages.

At Turda Gorge's northern end, you can free camp in the grassy valley. Otherwise, try the noisy **Cabana Cheile Turzii** (tent space/s/d €1.50/7/9) at the southern foot of the gorge. An on-site **restaurant** serves simple meals. To get there, buses to Corneşti or Câmpeni stop 2km west of Mihai Viteazul village, next to the signposted turn-off for Cheile Turzii (the gorge). From here it is a 5km hike along a gravel road north to the cabana. If you are driving, do not attempt this steep road after heavy rains.

Getting There & Around

From Cluj-Napoca's Piaţa Mihai Viteazul there are seven daily buses for Turda (€1, 40 minutes). From Turda there are buses to Corneşti and less frequent ones to Câmpeni, going via the Turda Gorge turn-off. Both depart from Piaţa Republicii in the centre of the town. From the centre of Turda, city bus No 15 runs from Str Republicii to Băile Turda and bus No 20 runs to Câmpia Turzii.

HUEDIN MICROREGION

264

Boasting a bucolic paradise seemingly lost in time, similar to Maramureş' landscape, this small region west of Cluj-Napoca offers pristine countryside, a dreamer's and hiker's paradise. The microregion is comprised of the main town Huedin and 12 surrounding communities, taking up 155,700 hectares in which only 39,000 people live, mostly in rural, mountainous settlements. There are waterfalls, caves, mountains, rolling fields, wooden churches and villages where crafts are performed to visit in this area where both Romanian and Hungarian tradition survives.

Huedin (Bánffyhunyad in Hungarian) itself, 52km west of Cluj-Napoca, is an unexciting place (save for its 16th-century

Protestant church famed for its oddly painted wood-panel ceiling), and is used as a stepping stone to the surrounding villages. It lies at the heart of a predominantly Hungarian enclave known as Kalotaszeg, much beloved by Hungarian folklorists as a stronghold of pastoral Transylvanian Magyar culture. In Budapest's Ethnography Museum, there is a huge, seven-room exhibit devoted entirely to Kalotaszeg.

Your best contacts for organising stays and activities in the area are Green Mountain Holidays (p150) and the Transylvania Ecological Club (p147), which produces several maps of the region. The Retro Hostel (p152) also organises trips to the region.

Mănăstireni

Mănăstireni (Magyargyerömonostor in Hungarian) is 16km southeast of Huedin, south from the main Cluj-Napoca–Huedin road. To get there from Huedin, you pass **Izvorul Crişului**, known as Körösfő to Hungarians. Towering on a hilltop above the village is a small church (1764) considered to be among the most representative of the Protestant churches in this region.

Mănăstireni is noted for its 13th-century **church**. It was built by the Gyeröffy family, with a Gothic apse added in the 15th century. Many original woodcarvings are visible inside the church, which also boasts a fine wood-panelled ceiling. Its pews, gallery and ceiling are all painted. During the 1848 revolution, 200 Hungarians died at the battle of Mănăstireni; they were buried in a mass grave which today rests beneath lake waters in the village.

Poieni, Bologa & Săcuieu

Twelve kilometres west of Huedin is the small village of Poieni, 2.8km from Bologa. The ruins of a 13th-century **medieval fortress** tower above it. Some 81m of the original wall remains, as do remnants of the citadel's bastions. You can hike up the hill to the ruins from the centre of the village.

Equally interesting is the old **water mill** (*moară de apă*), still in use today. Clothes continue to be washed in the whirlpool close to the mill. The entrance to the mill is 3km from the main road on the left in the centre of the village. The citadel can clearly be seen opposite.

In Săcuieu, 10km south of Bologa, on top of Dealul Domnului (literally 'God's Hill'; 950m) is one of Romania's few sequoia trees, of which the predominantly Hungarian residents are extremely proud.

Ciucea

Ciucea village, 22km west of Huedin, is a place of pilgrimage for Romanians and Hungarians alike, having been home to Romanian poet and politician Octavian Goga (1881–1939) and to Hungary's most controversial 20th-century poet, Endre Ady (1877–1919).

The house in which Goga lived, at the eastern end of the village next to the silver-spired church, is today a memorial **museum** (Muzeul Octavian Goga; admission €0.40; ⊙ 10am-5pm Tue-Sun). Goga was born in a small village close to Sibiu but lived in a mansion in Ciucea between 1915 and 1917, prior to his move into politics, which led to his disastrous 44-day reign as prime minister in 1937.

Goga, who campaigned fervently for the rights of Romanians in the face of Hungarian domination, bought this country mansion from the afore-mentioned Endre Ady. The poet, who slammed Hungary as a cultural backwater, spent several years living in Ciucea towards the end of his life. He also had a **wooden church**, dating from 1575, transported here from the Cluj-Napoca region in order to preserve it. It is today cared for by a group of nuns.

On Saturday in the village of Negreni, located 5km west of Ciucea, there's a large flea market where you can find everything from old gramophones to handmade Roma costumes.

Sleeping

Pension Romanta (☎ 255 064; d €10) This is a delightful guesthouse next to the Bologa turn-off on the main Huedin–Poieni road. It can also arrange rural homestays throughout the area.

Hotel Montana (☎ 253 090; s/d €14/17) There should be little reason to stay overnight in Huedin itself, but if you must, this hotel, 2km from the centre of Huedin on the road to Cluj-Napoca, isn't bad. There's a 24-hour restaurant with a large outdoor dining area.

Bianca and **Radu** (☎ 432 242; s/d €12/15) are two adjoining hotels in Beliş, a lovely village

16km to the south of Huedin. They are on the banks of a picturesque lake, as is the **Popas Turistic Bradet** (☎ 547 206; dm €5), a clean, no-frills youth hostel. You can also camp wild in the area.

Getting There & Around

From Huedin, several daily buses make trips to the surrounding villages. But travelling by bus here is unpredictable and may force you to sit in dusty stations waiting a long time for the next bus. Private transport, bike or hitchhiking are better options, even with a tour group. There are three daily buses from Huedin to Beliş. Two daily buses from Cluj-Napoca to Oradea stop at Huedin.

Nine daily trains from Cluj-Napoca go to both Huedin (50 to 80 minutes) and Ciucea (70 to 110 minutes), some on their way to Oradea.

ZALĂU

☎ 260 / pop 70,000

Zalău, 86km northwest of Cluj-Napoca, is an uninspiring modern provincial town with many concrete blocks of flats, in the foothills of the Meşes Mountains. The steep decline into town from Cluj-Napoca along hairpin turns is about the most exciting part of the place. The first town to be chronicled in Transylvania, it was here that the Roman-Dacians built what is today believed to have been the most important military and cultural stronghold in the Roman-Dacian empire.

Orientation & Information

The bus station is 1km north of the centre at Str Mihai Viteazul 54. Bus No 1 runs from the centre to the train station, which is 6km north of the centre in the village of Crişeni.

You can change money, cash travellers cheques and get cash advances on credit cards at **Banca Comercială Română** (Piaţa Iuliu Maniu 2; 8am-2pm Mon-Fri). The **Silvania Comtur travel agency** (☎ 611 862; Piaţa Unirii 1; 9am-5pm Mon-Fri), inside Hotel Porolossim, can help get you to the Roman ruins and arrange other tours.

ROMAN POROLISSUM

The Roman settlement of Porolissum in AD 106 stood on the ultimate northern boundary of Roman Dacia. The settlement was rapidly fortified, following which it developed as a leading administrative, economic and civilian centre. By the end of the 2nd century, it had been granted the status of a municipality.

The 'Municipium Septimium Porolissensis', which some historians believe could even have briefly served as the capital of Dacia, was built within the walls of a giant castle. The 20,000 inhabitants who lived behind the walls were defended by some 7000 soldiers.

Many of the walls have today been rebuilt on the original site of the Porolissum above Zalău town. The main entrance to the castle, the stadium and the amphitheatre have all been partially reconstructed, enabling visitors to appreciate the magnitude of an original Roman stronghold; it's officially open from 9am to 6pm daily. A lone shepherd, who tends the site, guides visitors around for €0.20 per person. If he is not at the main entrance to the complex, try the house marked 'casă' on the small dirt track leading up to the castle.

To get to the Porolissum (9km out of town), take bus No 8 from the central bus stop on Str Mihai Viteazul to the village of Moigrad. From here it is a good 20-minute hike uphill to the fortress.

The history of the Roman fortress is explained in the **Zalău History Museum** (☎ 612 223; Str Unirii 9; adult/child €0.60/0.30; 10am-6pm Tue-Sat) in Zalău's centre. Various Roman-Dacian statues unearthed in the Porolissum are displayed here.

Sleeping

Hotel Mereşul (☎ 661 050; Str Unirii 5; s/d €22/26) One of the more modern options around, its rooms are clean and moderately stylish.

Hotel Porolissum (☎ 613 301; Piaţa Unirii 1; s/d €29/55) Overpriced for what you get, but the rooms are comfortable and the front-desk staff helpful. The restaurant is considered one of the best in town, and the bar attracts locals as well as tourists.

Getting There & Away

The **Agenţie de Voiaj CFR** (☎ 612 885; Str Tudor Vladimirescu 2) sells advance tickets. Zalău is on a small branch line between Carei and Jibou. To get to Dej, Braşov, and Baia Mare, change at Jibou. From Zalău there are three daily trains to Carei (two hours), eight to Jibou (40 minutes), and one express service to Bucharest (12½ hours)

The **bus station** (☎ Str Mihai Viteazul 54) is 1km north of the centre. Daily bus services from Zalău include one to Târgu Lapuş and Ciucea, two to Baia Mare and Huedin, three to Bucium and Oradea, and three to Cluj-Napoca.

CLUJ-NAPOCA TO BISTRIŢA

☎ 264 / pop 24,000

There are a few places worth stopping at on the main road northeast from Cluj-Napoca to Bistriţa, some of which are pleasant, while one is chilling.

Gherla

Once a predominantly Armenian settlement called Armenopolis in the 17th century, the small market town of Gherla is 45km north of Cluj-Napoca. It has a pretty Renaissance-style castle and a baroque Armenian church (1784–1804), one of the largest in Europe. It is also the only town in Romania whose original city planning utilised a grid system.

The town is best known, however, for its prison. **Gherla prison** (Str Andrei Mureşan 2), still functioning today, gained notoriety in the 1950s for its so-called 're-education program'. Using severe psychological pressure and physical torture, hundreds of dissident students were tormented until they ratted on their former friends and allies and were then made to torture them in turn. This scheme was also used in Black Sea coast prisons and worker camps. In 1951 the re-education program was halted but conditions inside the prison remained harsh. In 1970, during floods, 600 prisoners drowned in their cells after the prison director ordered the inmates to be locked in before fleeing the building himself.

In the cemetery close to the prison is a **memorial** to those who died there, erected in 1993.

The prison is on the left as you enter Gherla at its southern end. As you face the prison from the main road, the cemetery is to the right on Str Dejului.

Gherla has a small **History Museum** (☎ 241 947; Str Mihai Viteazul 6; admission €0.40; 🕑 9am-4pm Mon-Fri), which conveniently fails to mention the existence of any prison.

SLEEPING

Your best bet in Gherla is to stay at a *pensiune*; the central hotels are pretty dismal.

Pensiunea Acasă (☎ 206 309; auto_extaz@yahoo.com; Str Dejului 51C; s/d €13/17) Reasonably priced, if unmemorable, this place has a large dining room with decent cuisine.

Nicula

The small village of Nicula, located 9km east of Gherla, is famed for its 16th-century monastery and exquisite icons painted on glass.

The age-old folk art of painting on glass was practised in Nicula as early as the 11th and 12th centuries. Icons of the saints were painted and put in peasants' houses to keep evil spirits at bay. Nicula became famed for its glass icons only in the 18th century after, according to legend, an icon of the Virgin Mary in the wooden church of the village monastery miraculously shed tears for 26 days in 1699. Henceforth, icons painted on glass in Nicula became much sought-after items, as it is believed that an icon of the Virgin Mary contains healing powers. Peasants wash the icon with water from the epiphany then give this water to people consumed by an evil spirit. Some 300,000 believers make a pilgrimage here every 15 August, St Mary's Day.

BISTRIŢA

☎ 263 / pop 86,200

This small and unassuming market town is at the heart of 'Dracula land', lying as it does at the southwestern end of the Bârgău Valley and Tihuţa mountain pass which leads from Transylvania into Moldavia. The dramatic countryside west and east of town has more bite than anything you'll find at Bran. It was here that *Dracula* author Bram Stoker made his leading character, Jonathan Harker, stay the night on the eve of St George's Day before continuing his journey east to Dracula's castle. While local businesses understandably try to capitalise on this, there's no stench of crass commercialisation here.

First chronicled in 1264, Bistriţa (Bistritz in German) was one of the seven original towns founded by the Saxons, whose presence can still be seen and felt in the old town's quaint 15th- and 16th-century merchants' houses. Witch

TRANSYLVANIA

BISTRIŢA

INFORMATION
Banca Comercială Română.......1 D1
Coroana Tourist Company.......2 C1
Librăria Casa Carta.................3 B2
Librăria Radu Petrescu.............4 D1
Post & Telephone Office.........5 C1
Sală Internet.......................6 C2
Tourist Information Centre......7 D2
Transylvanian Society of
   Dracula.........................(see 2)

SIGHTS & ACTIVITIES   (p161)
Codrişor Swimming Pool...........8 D3
Coopers' Tower....................9 C3
County Museum...................10 D1
Evangelical Church...............11 C2
Galeriile de Arta................(see 14)

Orthodox Church.................12 D1
Roman Catholic Church...13 B2
Şugălete........................14 C2

SLEEPING   (p161)
Coroana de Aur..................15 C1
Hotel Bistriţa...................16 D1
Hotel Codrişor.................17 D3
Hotel Cora......................18 D3

EATING   (pp161–3)
24-hour Supermarket......19 D1
Corrida........................(see 20)
Crama Veche..................20 D3
Pizzeria Raymond...........21 D1
Restaurant Coronita.......22 C1
Restaurant Excellent.......23 C2

DRINKING   (pp161–3)
Just Fine Club.................(see 14)

TRANSPORT   (p163)
Agenţie de Voiaj CFR.......24 C1
Bus Station....................25 A2

OTHER
Flora Complex.................(see 19)
House of Culture...............(see 7)

---

trials were common events in Bistriţa during medieval times.

Today lovely little Bistriţa is far from prosperous; wooden houses in the centre of town seem to warp. Yet it has a friendly village-trapped-in-a-town feel. Local pride is palpable here and is evidenced by the many ornate flowerbeds and gardens snuck into every available corner, and by the cleanliness of the streets. Life continues here at an unhurried pace. You'll see linen hanging in courtyards, people leaning out of their windows on the main street, and you'll hear the sounds of chickens blend with traffic in the centre. Street life is colourful, particularly in the evenings around the tiny Piaţa Mică.

In August the city hosts the international folk, dance and traditions festival Nunata Zamfirei.

MAPS & PUBLICATIONS

The Tourist Information Centre publishes the *Bistriţa-Năsăud County* map (€0.65), including a city map, available at its offices and in bookstores.

Information

BOOKSHOPS

Librăria Casa Cartu (☎ 233 379; Str Mihai Eminescu 4-5; ☀ 9am-7pm Mon-Fri, 10am-2pm Sat) This has the best selection of maps.
Librăria Radu Petrescu (☎ 212 306; Str Petru Rareş 1; ☀ 8.30am-7pm Mon-Fri, 10am-2pm Sat)

INTERNET

Sală Internet (Piaţa Mică 14; per hr €0.40; ☀ 10am-2am)

MONEY

Banca Comercială Română (Piaţa Petru Rareş; ☀ 8am-6pm Mon-Fri, 8am-12.30pm Sat) Will cash travellers cheques and has an ATM.

POST & TELEPHONE

The **post office** (Piaţa Petru Rareş; ☀ 8.30am-4.30pm Mon-Fri, 8.30am-noon Sat) shares a building with the **telephone office** (☀ 7.30am-8pm Mon-Fri, 8am-2pm Sat).

TOURIST INFORMATION

Coroana Tourist Company (☎ 212 056; www.draculatra nsylvania.ro; Piaţa Petru Rareş 7a; ☀ 8am-6pm Mon-Fri) As well as being Antrec's representative for the region, the company arranges day trips to Dracula's castle on the Tihuţa pass, and is in cahoots with the fun-loving **Transylvanian Society of Dracula** (☎ 231 803), which adjoins the office. Together, they can tell you the secret procedures to become a bloodthirsty member of the vampire legend–addicted group.

Tourist Information Centre (☎ 219 919; cit@ bistrita.astral.ro; Str Albert Berger 10; ☺ 9am-6pm Mon-Fri) Located inside the House of Culture, this small office is run by one of the most active and innovative travel agencies in the country, **Caliman Club Holidays** (☎ 0744-600 140). A small outfit that still packs a whallop, it offers a range of mountain-biking, hiking, rafting, kayaking, windsurfing, skiing and snowboarding excursions in the nearby mountains and lakes for small groups or individuals. Of course, it can also provide lots of free information too and help with accommodation booking in the region.

Sights

The towering **evangelical church** (Biserica Evanghelică; ☺ 3-6pm Mon-Fri, 10am-2pm Sat-Sun) dominates Piaţa Centrală. Built by the Saxons in the 14th century, and today in a state of perpetual renovation, the Gothic-style church dominates its surroundings with its 76.5m-tall steeple and still serves Bistriţa's small Saxon community.

Facing the church on the north side of the square is the fine **Şugălete** row of terraced buildings, which in medieval times was bustling with trading activities. Built between 1480 and 1550, the 13 houses were bound together with stone arches and in the 16th century a portico was added. Here too is the **Galeriile de Arta** (☎ 0788-304 165; Piaţa Centrala 24; ☺ 10am-7pm Tue-Sun), with changing exhibits.

An **Orthodox church**, built between 1270 and 1280, is the centrepiece of Piaţa Unirii. Nearby, the **County Museum** (Muzeul Judetean; ☎ 230 046; B-dul General Grigore Bălan 19; admission €0.20; ☺ 10am-6pm Tue-Sun) has crafts from Saxon guilds.

Remains of the city's 13th-century walls lie south of the town along the **municipal park**'s northwest side. Bistriţa suffered many attacks by the Turks and Tartars during the 16th and 17th centuries and the citadel and most of the bastions intersecting the city wall were destroyed. In 1530 Wallachian prince Petru Rareş (r. 1541–46) besieged

Bistriţa, forcing its Saxon inhabitants to finally surrender. The **Coopers' Tower** remains at the western end of the park, close to the bridge across the Bistriţa River.

Activities

To cool off or lounge about, there's the **Codrişor swimming pool** (adult/child €0.40/0.15), an outdoor pool on the south side of the river. The municipal park is a pleasant and safe strolling ground both day and night.

Sleeping

Coroana de Aur (☎ 232 667; www.coroanadeaur.bn.ro; Piaţa Petru Rareş 4; s/d/ste €17/23/27) Bram Stoker's character Jonathan Harker stayed here and so do most foreigners. There was no such hotel at the time *Dracula* was published, but one was later built to make history right and keep the tourist buses coming. The 'Golden Crown' exploits its fictitious links with its Salon Jonathan Harker, a hall decked out with antlers and Gothic trinkets, which might be fun for a Dracula-themed cocktail. Otherwise, the hotel is nothing special. There's wheelchair access.

Hotel Bistriţa (☎ 231 056; www.hotel-bistrita.ro; s €14-18, d €22-25) Modest yet stylish, this villa-style hotel is a good option. It's popular with tour groups and deals with overflow when the Coroana de Aur across the street is booked out.

Hotel Codrişor (☎ 227 352; Str Codrişor 29; s/d €17/23) Most rooms in the town's nicest hotel overlook the slow-flowing Bistriţa River, just south of the centre. Rooms are small but well furnished and the terrace restaurant draws many locals.

Hotel Cora (☎ 221 231; Str Codrişor 23; s/d €16/23) Just behind the Codrişor is this somewhat less exciting but decent option.

Eating & Drinking

Inside the **Flora Complex** (Piaţa Mori 54) is a 24-hour supermarket.

Restaurant Coroniţa (Piaţa Petru Rareş 4; mains €2-4; ☺ 10am-11pm) The atmosphere's stuffy and tacky, but if you're craving breaded brains and Golden Mediaş wine try this place, adjoining the Coroana de Aur hotel.

Restaurant Excellent (☎ 0723-396 622; Piaţa Mică 7; mains under €2; ☺ 8am-midnight) When you walk in, you may look at the uninspiring surroundings and wonder, 'where's the excellence?' However, a cheap fill-up with

TRANSYLVANIA

THE DRACULA MYTH

Fifteenth-century Wallachian prince Vlad Ţepeş is all too often credited with being Dracula, the vampire-count featured in the classic Gothic horror story *Dracula* (1897) written by Anglo-Irish novelist Bram Stoker.

This madcap association of these two diabolical figures – one historical, the other fictitious – is nothing more than a product of the popular imagination. But while Romanians increasingly reap the tourist reward of this confusion, many are concerned that the identity of a significant figure in their history has been overshadowed by that of an immortal literary vampire.

The 'real' Dracula, Vlad Ţepeş, was born in 1431 in Sighişoara, and ruled Wallachia in 1448, 1456–62 and 1476. He was outrageously bloodthirsty, but he was not a vampire. His princely father, Vlad III, was called Vlad Dracul (from the Latin *draco*, meaning 'dragon') after the chivalric Order of the Dragon accredited to him by Sigismund of Luxembourg in 1431. The Romanian name Drăculea – literally 'son of Dracul' – was bestowed on Vlad Ţepeş by his father, and was used as a term of honour. Another meaning of *draco*, however, was 'devil' and this was the meaning that Stoker's novel popularised.

While Vlad Ţepeş was undoubtedly a strong ruler and is seen by some Romanians as a national hero and brave defender of his principality, his practices were ruthless and cruel. Notorious for his brutal punishment methods, ranging from decapitation to boiling and burying alive, he gained the name 'Ţepeş' ('impaler') after his favourite form of punishing his enemies – impaling. A wooden stake was carefully driven through the victim's anus, to emerge from the body just below the shoulder in such a way as to not pierce any vital organs. This ensured at least 48 hours of unimaginable suffering before death. Ţepeş had a habit of eating a full meal (rare, one presumes) outside, watching his Turkish and Greek prisoners writhing on a stake in front of him.

Though this arouses (hopefully!) disgust in the modern reader, Vlad was truly a man of his time; this torture was not unusual in medieval Europe. Ţepeş' first cousin, Ştefan cel Mare, is said to have 'impaled by the navel, diagonally, one on top of each other' 2300 Turkish prisoners in 1473. That Vlad was likely raped repeatedly as a boy and teen in his captive years in a Turkish prison adds another dimension to his favoured method of torture.

Bram Stoker's literary Dracula, in contrast, was a bloodsucking vampire – an undead corpse reliant on the blood of the living to sustain his own immortality. Until 1824 in Stoker's adopted England a wooden stake was commonly driven through the heart of suicide victims to ensure the ill-fated corpse did not turn in its grave into a vampire. In Romania vampires form an integral part of traditional folklore. The seventh-born child is particularly susceptible to this evil affliction, identifiable by a hoof as a foot or a tail at the end of its spine.

Stoker set *Dracula* in Transylvania, a region the novelist never set foot in. The novel, originally set in Austria, was first entitled *The Undead*. But following critics' comments that it was too close a pastiche of Sheridan le Fanu's *Camilla* (1820) – a vampire novel set in southern France – Stoker switched titles and geographical settings. Count Dracula's fictitious castle on the Borga pass was inspired by Cruden Bay castle in Aberdeenshire, where Stoker drafted much of the novel. The historical facts were uncovered at the British Museum in London.

While Vlad Ţepeş died in 1476, and Stoker in 1912, Count Dracula lives on, sustaining an extraordinary subculture of fiction and film. The novel itself has never been out of print (it was first translated into Romanian in 1990), while movie-makers have remade the film countless times, kicking off with Murnau's silent *Nosferatu* in 1922 and multiplying into dozens of spin-offs. Tom Cruise, for example, would never have added fangs to his repertoire if it weren't for Stoker's original hero having started a lineage leading to Anne Rice's Lestat.

Dracula fan clubs have been set up around the globe. The New York club alone attracts more than 5000 hungry members, many of whom meet up with fellow fans at the annual Dracula World Congress. Closer to 'home', the Transylvanian Society of Dracula continues the tradition and offers Dracula theme tours (p161).

AUTHOR'S CHOICE

Crama Veche (☎ 218 047; Str Albert Berger 10; mains €2-5; ⏰ noon-midnight) It's impossible to go wrong here and at its adjoining **Corrida** terrace restaurant/bar, inside and next to the House of Culture. Inside is a cosy cellar dining room serving delicious regional Romanian and Hungarian specialities, but the sprawling terrace is the real winner, the most popular place in town for light meals or sampling local wines and beers.

delicious home-made food is guaranteed here.

Pizzeria Raymond (Piaţa Petru Rareş 6; mains €2-3; ⏰ 9am-midnight) This is another popular local hang-out.

Just Fine Club (Piaţa Centrala 21; ⏰ 10am-1am) This is the town's premier chill-out club, in a cavelike cellar with dim lighting, couches and lounge music.

Getting There & Away

BUS

Fourteen daily buses go to Mureşeni Bârgăului (€1), 12km beyond Bistriţa Bârgăului, with reduced services on weekends. Two daily buses creak their way up to Vatra Dornei (€1.60), but you'd be better off with the two maxitaxis that run to Suceava and Botoşani via Vatra Dornei. Maxitaxis also head north twice a day to Romuli (€1.20), Satu Mare (€5) and Baie Mare (€4). Three a day go to Sibiu (€5) and Sighişoara (€3.20), while four a day go to and from Cluj-Napoca (€2.75) as well as Braşov (€6) via Târgu Mureş (€2.10).

TRAIN

The **Agenţie de Voiaj CFR** (Piaţa Petru Rareş; ⏰ 8am-5pm Mon-Fri) is next door to the Coroana Tourist Company. There's an overnight train service to Bucharest (€16, 10 hours). There are four daily trains to Cluj-Napoca (€5 to €8, three to four hours), two to Deda (€3, two hours), and one to Dej (€3, two hours) and Vatra Dormei (€5, four hours).

BÂRGĂU VALLEY

From Bistriţa the road runs east up the Bârgău Valley and across the Tihuţa mountain pass, to Vatra Dornei in Moldavia. This is a land seemingly suspended in time.

Bram Stoker wrote floridly about the area, and though he himself never visited, his descriptions are quite accurate. While the landscape is not as rugged and foreboding as he described, the area is unforgettably atmospheric. The snaky, narrow main road winds its way slowly upwards, past subdued villages and farms, past both steep and gentle hills, springs, creeks, and sheep grazing in the conifer-sweetened air.

The village of **Livezile**, 8km east of Bistriţa along the valley road, is home to a small folk museum. Some 15km beyond, the village of **Bistriţa Bârgăului** stretches south along a side road. There are several camp sites here. Another 15km further south along this sideroad is the lovely **Lake Colibiţa**, a great place for a private swim and picnic or wild camping. Caliman Club Holidays (p161) is building a youth hostel by the lake, to be opened by 2005.

After **Mureşeni** the road starts to climb steeply on its approach to the **Tihuţa Pass**, which peaks at 1200m. A hiking trail (red circles) leads from here to **Piatra Fântânele** at the top of the pass.

The main reason most people break their journey at Piatra Fântânele is not so much for the fine hiking that it offers but rather for the **Hotel Castel Dracula**, a complete commercial con that somehow manages to persuade guests otherwise, despite its theme-park tackiness. The castle-hotel, better known as Dracula's Castle, towers 1116m high on the spot where Stoker sited his fictitious Dracula's castle (see how life imitates art?). The views of the pass are great from here. The architect who designed the jagged-edged building clearly studied Dracula movies. Rooms are kitted out thematically, the highlight being 'Dracula's vault', where visitors are given a short, candlelit tour around his 'coffin'. A 'surprise' occurs near the end of the tour, designed to give visitors a little jolt (it's not much of one, but a Canadian visitor had a heart attack on the spot here in the mid-1990s).

In the small village of **Lunca Ilvei**, 20km north of Piatra Fântânele, is the excellent **Ştefan cel Mare Equestrian Centre** (☎ 263-378 470; www.riding-holidays.ro). The centre offers the unique opportunity to explore the surrounding mountains, valleys and the Borgo Pass by horseback or horse-drawn carriage (a fun ride is from Lunca Ilvei to Dracula's

Castle). They'll also take you to meet with mountain shepherds.

Sleeping

The Ştefan Mare Equestrian Centre (see previous) can arrange guesthouse accommodation in Lunca Ilvei to suit any budget, and can also organise basic accommodation at a sheepfold – finally you'll be able to tell friends that you've slept with shepherds!

Hotel Castel Dracula (☎ 263-266 841; fax 263-266 119; s/d/t €40/53/59). The hotel accepts credit cards and has a sauna, restaurant and bar. Nonguests can visit Dracula's vault for €1.

Vila din Carpaţi (☎ 230-374 312; per person €15) Some 6km south of Poiana Stampei and 26km west of Vatra Dornei, this modern place has five doubles with a bathroom shared between two rooms. It also has wooden cabanas to rent.

Getting There & Away

Two buses and two maxitaxis run between Bistriţa and Vatra Dornei daily (€1.60 to €3).

SOUTHWEST TRANSYLVANIA

Traces of ancient civilisation are more evident in this region south of Cluj-Napoca than anywhere else in Romania. The cradle of the early Dacian kingdom was in the southwestern realms of these parts. The kingdom managed to withstand attacks by its powerful Roman neighbour until AD 106, when the Dacian stronghold was finally conquered. The Roman emperor Trajan created a new capital north of the Retezat Mountains. Remains of the great gold, copper and salt mines are still evident.

The union of Transylvania with Romania in 1599 and again on 1 December 1918 was proclaimed in Alba Iulia, the largest city in this region. Every 1 December hundreds of people descend upon the city to celebrate Romania's national day.

During the 18th and 19th centuries this region served as a stronghold of resistance against Habsburg domination, giving birth to the first great uprising by Romanian peasants in 1784 and remaining the only region not be conquered by Habsburg forces during the 1848–49 revolution.

ABRUD

Abrud is a dull and dusty town, appealing only as a base to explore the Roşia Montană gold mine. Ten kilometres east of Abrud are the staggering basaltic twin peaks of the **Detunatele** (1169m). The main access point for these magnificent peaks – known as Detunata Goală (Hollow) and Detunata Flocoasă (Flocky) – is in **Bucium** village. From Abrud, head east along the main Abrud–Alba Iulia road for 1km. Turn left at the turning signposted for Mogoş and continue for 9km until you reach Bucium. The trail leading to the top of the Detunatele (red stripes) begins at the bottom of a narrow dirt track beside the white church in the village centre. From the Detunatele a trail leads to Roşia Montană (2½ hours, blue circles and red triangles).

Getting There & Away

From Abrud bus station there are 10 daily buses to Câmpeni (15 minutes), two to Deva (1¼ hours), two to Cluj-Napoca (2½ to three hours), and four to Alba Iulia (three hours) and Brad (45 minutes). There is also one bus on to Avram Iancu (45 minutes, weekends only). No trains reach this area.

ROŞIA MONTANĂ

Roşia Montană is 7km northeast of Abrud. From the Abrud–Câmpeni road, turn east 4km north of Abrud at the signpost for Roşia Montană (literally 'Red Mountain').

Gold has been mined in this village since Dacian times. The Romans exploited this gold mine, which enjoyed its most lucrative period during their rule. Enough gold was allegedly mined to build a road of gold from Roşia Montană to Rome. Between WWI and WWII, Romania was ranked second in Europe in gold extraction, mainly thanks to this lucrative gold mine.

Long after the gold reserves were believed to have dried up, a Canadian mining company, Gabriel Resources, uncovered a gold deposit believed to be the largest in Europe and began setting up the continent's largest opencast mine. As such a project would involve the resettlement of 2000 people and would indelibly pollute the environment, it has been at the centre of major protests by the local population, among Romania's first main ecological protests. At the time of writing, with the

Romanian government wavering before granting Gabriel Resources final licences in the face of local opposition, with EU environmentalist disapproval and with production costs skyrocketing, it is unclear if the project will go ahead.

For tourists, the projected mine has meant the closing of a 400m-long stretch of the **old Roman galleries**, which used to provide a look inside the old mine. Just outside the mine entrance, a small **mining museum** (admission €0.50; ☉ 7am-3pm) remains open, with reproductions of water-powered wooden stamps used to crush the ore in the 18th century. During the 19th century there were 700 such stamps positioned on the shores of Roşia Montană's surrounding lakes. Each winter, when the lakes froze, work at the mine would grind to a halt.

Roşia Montană celebrates Varvara, the patron saint of the mine, on 6 October.

Getting There & Away

Roşia Montană is difficult to visit without private transport. There are occasional bus services from Abrud, from where a taxi might be the best idea.

ALBA IULIA
☎ 258 / pop 71,530

Alba Iulia (Karlsburg and Weissenburg to Germans, Gyula Fehérvár to Hungarians) holds a special place in the Romanian national consciousness, as it was here in 1599 and again on 1 December 1918 that the union of Transylvania with Romania was proclaimed. However, aside from an important past and an interesting citadel, most agree that today's Alba Iulia is of very limited interest – a modern, concrete-dominated city that leaves little impression on the visitor.

Alba Iulia was known by the Dacians as Apulum, serving both as the capital of Upper Dacia and later, during Roman times, as the largest centre in the Dacian province of the Roman empire. From 1542 to 1690 Alba Iulia was the capital of the principality of Transylvania. Romania's national day (1 December) is a time of major celebrations in Alba Iulia today, where countless bottles of a well-known brand of local sparkling wine such as Margaritar or Romantine Brut are poured.

Orientation

The city is divided into three parts. The citadel – the pedestrianised 'upper town' – houses all the historic sights, museums and university buildings. The new town is west of the citadel, while the lower town area resembles a building site – most of the town's older buildings were bulldozed under Ceauşescu to make way for a civic centre that never happened.

A peculiarity to Alba Iulia is a stubborn attachment to old street names, bound to cause confusion for visitors: different maps have a mixture of old and new street names, and residents often use a creative blend of the two. Most maps, booklets and brochures use the old names; our map uses the new ones which, eventually, will come into greater usage. Some you may need to know about: Str Dr Ioan Ratiu used to be Str Avantului; Str Rubin Patiţa used to be Str Primăverii; Str Frederic Mistral used to be Str Parcului.

The adjacent bus and train stations are some 2km south of the citadel.

MAPS

Incredibly, there are few reliable maps of Alba Iulia; some travel agencies use Lonely Planet's!

Information

For books of local interest, try **Librăria Humanitas** (☎ 826 007; B-dul 1 Decembrie 1918; ☉ 10am-6pm Mon-Fri, 10am-2pm Sat). For Internet access try **Club 76** (☎ 819 540; Str Avram Iancu 3; per hr €0.40; ☉ 9am-11pm) or **Internet Domino** (☎ 834 981; Str Dr Ioan Ratiu 2; per hr €0.40; ☉ 24hr). The **Banca Comercială Română** (B-dul Regele Carol I, 35; ☉ 8.30am-2pm Mon-Fri) cashes travellers cheques and gives cash advances. The main **post office** (☎ 812 852; B-dul Brătianu 1; ☉ 7am-8pm Mon-Fri) and **telephone office** (☉ 10am-6pm Mon-Fri) adjoin each other.

For a city of such national importance, it's suprising that Alba Iulia has no official tourist office or effective tourist infrastructure. The staff at the Hotel Transylvania are used to answering tourists' questions.

Albena Tours (☎ 812 140; albenatours@rdslink.ro; Str Fredric Mistral 2; ☉ 10am-6pm Mon-Fri) arranges wine-tasting tours of the region, books accommodation in Alba Iulia and Blaj, and can also put you on a group tour of any region in Romania.

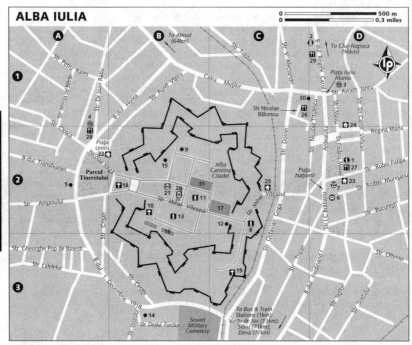

ALBA IULIA

0 — 500 m
0 — 0.3 miles

Sights

ALBA CAROLINA CITADEL

The imposing Alba Carolina Citadel, richly carved with sculptures and reliefs in a baroque style, is the dominant sight of the city of Alba Iulia. It was originally constructed in the 13th century, although the fortress you see today was built between 1714 and 1738 to a design of Italian architect Giovanni Morandi Visconti. There are English and French information panels placed throughout the citadel, making it quite easy to delve into its history without a guide.

Str Mihai Viteazul runs up from the lower town to the **first gate** of the fortress, adorned with sculptures inspired by Greek mythology. From here, a stone road leads to the **third gate** of the fortress, dominated by an equestrian statue of Carol VI of Austria. Above the gate is **Horea's death cell** (Celula lui Horia), now housing a small museum to commemorate the leader of the great 1784 peasant uprising.

A footpath leads from the gate to an **Orthodox church** (Biserica Memorială Sfânta Treime), outside the southeastern corner of the inner fortress walls. The wooden church, brought to Alba Iulia in 1990 from Maramureş, stands on the site of a former Metropolitan cathedral built by Mihai Viteazul in 1597 and destroyed by the Habsburgs in 1713.

Today the Romanian army occupies the **Princely Court**, former residence of the princes of Transylvania, which was built in several stages from the 16th century onwards. In front of it, on Str Mihai Viteazul, stands a large **equestrian statue** of Mihai Viteazul (Michael the Brave), ruler of Romania from 1593 to 1601. On 1 November 1599 he visited Alba Iulia to celebrate the unification of Wallachia, Moldavia and Transylvania – a union that crumbled after his assassination a year later.

The statue faces **Unification Hall** (Sala Unirii; 1900), built as a military casino. In this hall the act of unification between Romania and Transylvania was signed during the Great Assembly of 1 December 1918.

In the park on the eastern side of Unification Hall is the 22.5m **Costozza monument**, which commemorates the soldiers and officers of the 50th infantry regiment of Alba Iulia who were killed while fighting in the Habsburg army against Italy in the battle of Costozza in 1866. Erected in 1937, the obelisk sports a strikingly Soviet look.

Inside the former Babylon building (1851) just west of Unification Hall is the impressive **Unification Museum** (Muzeul Unirii; adult/child €0.50/0.25; ᗺ 10am-5pm Tue-Sun). The museum vividly recounts the history of Romania from the Paleolithic and Neolithic periods through to 1944 and is considered one of the top museums in the country on the history of Transylvania. One corner of the Unification Museum is devoted to the peasant revolutionaries Cloşca, Crişan and Horea. The highlight is a replica of the wheel used to crush Cloşca and Horea to death in 1785 (Crişan sensibly killed himself in prison before he could be tortured to death). A plaque on the wall recounts the orders issued by the judge who determined their ghastly death:

...they are to be taken to the torture place and there killed by being tied to a wheel and squashed – first Cloşca, then Horea. After being killed their bodies are to be cut into four parts and the head and body impaled on the edge of different roads for everyone to see them. The internal organs – their hearts and intestines – will be buried in the place of torture...

Beyond the equestrian statue is an austere 18th-century **Catholic Cathedral**, built on the site of a Romanesque church destroyed during the Tartar invasion of 1241. Many famous Transylvanian princes are buried here.

The highly impressive **Orthodox Cathedral** (originally known as the 'Church of the Coronation') was built on the old site of the citadel guardhouse in 1921–22 for the coronation of King Ferdinand I and Queen Marie in 1922. Their frescoed portraits remain intact on the rear wall of the church. Designed in the shape of a Greek circumscribed cross, the cathedral is surrounded by a wall of decorative colonnades which form a rectangular enclosure with peaceful gardens within. A 58m-tall bell tower marks the main entrance to the complex. This is easily the most aesthetically beautiful part of the citadel.

The 1780 **Batthyaneum Library**, inside a former baroque church, is in the northern area of the citadel, as is the former **military hospital**.

FORK'S HILL

Just south of the citadel is Fork's Hill (Dealul Furcilor), the spot where peasant revolutionaries Horea and Cloşca died. It is marked with a small **obelisk monument**. A year after their grisly deaths on 22 August 1785, Emperor Joseph II abolished serfdom among Romanian peasants in Transylvania.

Sleeping

Victoria (☎ 816 354; Str Mihai Viteazul 6; s/d without private toilet €16/24, with private toilet €22/43) Situated next to the eastern entrance of the citadel, this no-frills guesthouse has a good location, though its nonstop bar ensures a constant serenade for its guests. There's an on-site restaurant.

Hotel Transilvania (☎ 812 052; www.unita-turism .ro in Romanian; Piaţa Iuliu Maniu 22; s/d €20/27) Despite the bloodcurdling script used on this 1960s-era hotel's front sign, this is no kitsch Dracula-themed place. Run-down but perfectly fine, this is a friendly and reasonably priced option.

Hotel Cetate (☎ 811 780; Piaţa Unirii 3; s €21-28, d €29-45, ste €70) Overlooking the citadel, there are both two- and three-star rooms in what is Alba Iulia's most comfortable, pleasant hotel.

Hotel Parc (☎ 811 723; Str Rubin Patiţia 4; s/d/ste €35/43/65) It's considered the top place in town, but it's pretty much a joyless affair, though the pool and spa bath are nice.

Eating & Drinking

There is a small market selling fresh fruit and vegetables as well as dried and tinned products behind the Agenţie de Voiaj CFR office, off Calea Moţilor on Str Nicolae Bălcescu. Along Calea Moţilor, next to the market, there are several outdoor terrace bars, pizzerias and good places for meals. For light snacks, there are several cafés lining Str Frederic Mistral. There's also a 24-hour **pizzeria** on the first floor of Internet Domino (p165).

Prometeu (Str Rubin Patiţia 4) This fast-food joint serves the bare minimum, with hot dogs and hamburgers the high point of its menu.

Ristorante Roberta (☎ 819 980; B-dul Regele Carol I; mains €1.50-3; ❍ 9am-midnight) This is your best bet in town. It may have a dowdy interior, but the the food – mainly Italian – is excellent, and the daily specials are very good deals.

Pub Amicii Mei (☎ 834 069; Str Dr Ioan Ratiu 1; ❍ 24hr) Though the male clientele look like they share a common past as boxers, this is one of the best options for a pub/bar in town. The cellar bar is ultra cosy. Be warned that there's a strip club upstairs, so the bar attracts a certain 'element'.

Getting There & Away

The **Agenţie de Voiaj CFR** (☎ 813 689; Calea Moţilor 1; ❍ 8am-6pm Mon-Fri) sells advance tickets. International tickets can only be purchased here. There are four daily trains to Cluj-Napoca (€3, two hours), three to Timişoara (€6, 4½ hours), Sibiu (€2, 3¾ hours) and Bucharest (€5, nine hours), two to Iaşi (€8, 11½ hours) and one daily to Prague (€14, 16 hours) and Vienna (€12, nine hours). Direct bus and maxitaxi services from Alba Iulia's **bus station** (☎ 812 967) include 11 daily to Cluj-Napoca, four to Sibiu, three to Aiud, two to Oradea, and one to Târgu Mureş and Abrud. Local Bus No 18 runs from the stations to the centre.

DEVA

☎ 0254 / pop 75,000

Dinky Deva is a pleasant mining town with its own crumbling citadel, southwest

from Alba Iulia. Despite being blown to smithereens in 1849 after its gunpowder deposits exploded, the historic citadel is a popular haunt with visitors and bored teenagers alike.

Deva's real claim to fame is that it's home to Romania's top gymnastics club, Cetate Liceul de Educaţie Fizica şi Sport Deva, the training ground for the country's elite Olympic gymnastics team. So keep your eyes peeled for sweaty, muscly types (of both sexes).

Orientation

The train and bus stations are five minutes' walk north of the centre at Piaţa Garii. From the train station, walk straight up B-dul Iuliu Maniu until it meets B-dul 1 Decembrie. From the crossroads, B-dul 1 Decembrie leads into Str Mareşal Averescu and B-dul 22 Decembrie to the east. The main hotels, the telephone office and Cinema Patria are dotted here. Citadel Hill is at the western end of B-dul 1 Decembrie. Many of Deva's streets have been renamed recently so prepare for mismatching maps!

Information

There's a 24-hour **pharmacy** (☎ 224 488; Str Împăratul Traian) named Remedia near Piaţa Victorei.

You will find a currency exchange at the reception of Hotel Deva. The **Banca Comercială Română** (Str G Coşbuc; ❍ 8.30am-6pm Mon-Fri, 8.30am-12.30pm Sat) has two ATMs outside, and can change travellers cheques, transfer money and give cash advances on Visa/MasterCard. The RomTelecom telephone centre also has an ATM.

The **post office** (B-dul Decebal; ❍ 8am-8pm Mon-Fri, 8am-2pm Sat) and the Romtelecom **telephone centre** (cnr B-dul Iuliu Maniu & B-dul 1 Decembrie; ❍ 8am-8pm Mon-Fri, 8am-2pm Sat) are both centrally located.

The friendly, English-speaking **Agenţie de Turism Sarmis** (☎ 213 173; sarmis.deva@unita -turism.ro; Mareşal Averescu 7; ❍ 8am-6pm Mon-Thu, 8am-2pm Fri) is at the back of landmark Hotel Sarmis.

Sights

Stretch your legs with a climb up 300m to the 14th-century **Citadel**, which crowns the small mining town below. Work started

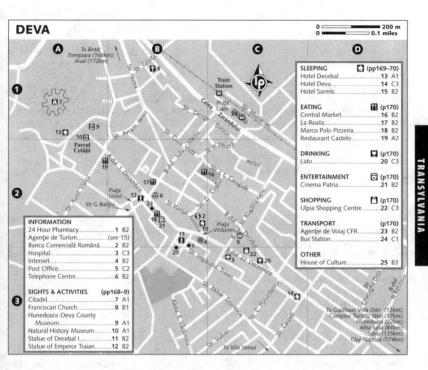

DEVA

0 — 200 m
0 — 0.1 miles

To Brad;
Timişoara (168km);
Arad (172km)

Train
Station

Parcul
Cetăţii

Piaţa
Unirii

Str G Bariţiu

Piaţa
Victoriei

To Gasthaus Villa Dörr (12km);
Complex Turistic Strei (17km);
Hunedoara (2km);
Alba Iulia (84km);
Sibiu (135km);
Cluj-Napoca (174km)

To Vila Venus

TRANSYLVANIA

on the stone fortress in 1385 under the Habsburg Ardeal kings. Legend says that the wife of the mason was buried alive in the fortress walls to ensure its safekeeping.

Religious activist Dávid Ferenc (1510–79), advocator of the Unitarian faith, was imprisoned in Deva's citadel, where he died. In 1784, during the peasant uprising led by Horea, Crişan and Cloşca, the fortress served as a refuge for terrified nobles fearful of being killed by militant peasants. In 1849 Hungarian nationalists attacked Austrian generals sheltering in the fortress. The four-week siege ended with the mighty explosion of the castle's gunpowder deposits, which left the castle in ruins.

A brief history of Deva and its sister citadels, as well as extensive archaeological findings from the various sites amid the Orăştie Mountains, are exhibited in the small but excellent **Hunedoara-Deva County Museum** (Muzeul Judeţean Hunedoara-Deva; admission €0.25; ☺ 10am-5pm Tue-Sun), housed in the former Magna Curia Palace. This palace was built by Prince Gábor Bethlen in 1621.

It is at the foot of Citadel Hill adjoining a small park.

Housed in a separate building next to the County Museum is the **Natural History Museum** (Muzeul Stiinţe ale Naturi; admission €0.50; ☺ 10am-5pm Tue-Sun), which is a musty paradise for children.

Sleeping

Budget options are limited: there's nothing on offer below €25 a night for a double.

Hotel Sarmis (☎ 214 730/731; Piaţa Victoriei 3; s/d €25/40) A white vision of ugliness, the Sarmis however has reasonable, clean rooms and is dead central.

Hotel Deva (☎ 211 290; B-dul 22 Decembrie 110; s/d €25/40) The sister hotel to Sarmis is another case of concrete carnage with large everything, spacious rooms, enormous restaurant and usual bizarre Soviet atmosphere. Thoroughly missable.

Hotel Decebal (☎ 212 413; B-dul 1 Decembrie; s/d €25/29) Close to the foot of the citadel, this place has faded glamour by the bucket-load with its dark spacious interior and clean, once-impressive rooms.

Vila Venus (☎ 212 243; Str Mihai Eminescu 16; d €84) Proper luxury – Deva's finest hotel, which lacks only a restaurant.

Gasthaus Villa Dörr (☎ 261 316, 0723-741 108; Str Biscaria 90; doerr@smart.ro; s/d €25/30). Ten kilometres east of Deva, in Simeria village, is this hotel, run by a German- and Romanian-speaking couple. It is the only budget option near Deva and has large rooms, some with balcony, and a popular restaurant. Reach it by taking the eastbound road from Deva, turn left after 8km, following signs to the hotel, which is a further 2km on the village road.

Eating & Drinking

La Roata (Str Bejan 61; meal €5-10) A set menu is available with soup, bread, meat, potatoes and salad. Classic peasant dishes can be enjoyed on a pleasant terrace shaded by pine trees.

Restaurant Castelo (Cnr B-dul 1 Decembrie & Str 1 Avram Iancu; meal €5) Pizza fans will rejoice at yet another Romanian pizza joint. In a nice spot at the foot of Citadel Hill on a leafy road.

Marco Polo Pizzeria (B-dul 1 Decembrie Block A; pizzas from €1) is a popular meeting place, while beer-seekers can try the excellent **Lido** (☎ 227 536; cnr B-dul 22 Decembrie & B-dul Decebal) terrace bar close to Hotel Deva.

Shopping

Ulpia Shopping Centre (B-dul 22 Decembrie) Contemporary mall with a supermarket, terrace bar and western designer shops to keep shopaholics amused.

Getting There & Away

Buy tickets in advance at **Agenţie de Voiaj CFR** (☎ 218 887; B-dul 1 Decembrie, Block A; ☼ 8am-8pm Mon-Fri).

Deva has excellent national and international train links. Express services to/ from Deva daily include four to Arad (€5), four to Bucharest (€15), five to Timişoara, one to Cluj-Napoca, one to Prague and one to Vienna.

The **bus station** (Piaţa Garii) is next to the train station. State buses from here to Arad, Brad, Câmpina, Oradea, Bucharest, Sibiu and Timişoara. However, there's usually only one service daily and none at weekends.

Better are the maxitaxis which run every half-hour to Hunedoara. They also scoot

to and from Arad, Alba Iulia, Petroşani and Lupeni.

The No 6 maxitaxis also do a circuit of Deva, running when full, costing €0.10 per journey.

HUNEDOARA

Nowhere in Romania is the contrast between past and present so stark as in Hunedoara, south of Deva. The giant skeletons of the steel mills stand as a rusting frame to eastern Europe's loveliest castle. The intact 14th-century Gothic **Corvin Castle** (☼ 9am-5pm Tue-Sun; adult/student €1/0.50) is considered to be one of Transylvania's greatest architectural gems – and it certainly deserves this title.

The fantastical monument stands as a symbol of Hungarian rule (both János Hunyadi and his son Matthias Corvinus, two famous Hungarian kings, made notable improvements), which made it pretty unpopular with Ceauşescu.

The fairy-tale castle, which is believed to be built on old Roman fortifications, is a stunning sight with three pointed towers, a drawbridge and high battlements. Five marble columns with delicate ribbed vaults support two halls, the Diet Hall above and Knight's Hall below, both from 1453. The castle wall was hewn out of 30m of solid rock by Turkish prisoners.

The fortress was extensively restored by Iancu de Hunedoara (János Hunyadi in Hungarian) from 1452 onwards. The castle, most recently restored in 1952, today houses a **feudal art museum**.

Corvin Castle can be reached from the adjacent bus station, by heading south along B-dul Republicii, then turning right onto B-dul Libertăţii. It is signposted from the bridge.

Sleeping

Hunedoara has one hotel, **Hotel Rusca** (☎ /fax 0254-712 002, B-dul Dacia 25; r €20), but try to avoid staying in this dingy fleapit, a five-minute walk from the train station.

Getting There & Away

The bus and train stations are at B-dul Republicii 3. There are maxitaxis every half-hour running between Deva and Hunedoara (22km).

From Bucharest, Braşov, Sibiu and Arad, take a train to Simeria then change onto a local train to Hunedoara. Alternatively, take a train as far as Deva then get a bus.

THE DACIAN & ROMAN CITADELS

The area immediately south of Hunedoara is an archaeologist's delight, being home to the capital of Dacia (Sarmizegetusa) and a church built from a Roman soldier's mausoleum, as well as the capital of Roman-conquered Dacia (Ulpia Traiana-Sarmizegetusa). The fortresses are recognised as Unesco World Heritage sites.

Archaeologists at the **National History Museum of Transylvania** (☎ 264-191 718, 264-195 677) in Cluj-Napoca arrange frequent digs and summer camps. Contact the museum in advance to arrange some volunteer work on site.

Sarmizegetusa

Dacians settled in what is today Romania from the 3rd century BC onwards. The Dacians built up a magnificent kingdom, centred in Sarmizegetusa (the capital) and surrounded by a defensive circle of fortifications in the Orăştie Mountains.

Sarmizegetusa remained unconquered by the Romans until AD 106, when Roman forces led by Trajan forced the Dacians to retreat north. The Dacian city was divided into three parts – two civilian areas and the middle sacred zone which contains the places of worship. Visitors are allowed to walk around the ruins.

Dacian Sarmizegetusa is a good 30km south of Orăştie along a dirt road, past the villages of Orăştioara de Jos, Bucium and Orăştioara de Sus. The ruins are actually 8km from the village of Grădiştea de Munte, at the end of the dirt track.

Costeşti

Sarmizegetusa was defended in the northwest by a fortress at Costeşti on the banks of the Oraşului River, the ruins of which remain. From Sarmizegetusa follow the road back north towards Orăştie and bear right at the turn-off for Costeşti.

The fortress at Costeşti, conquered by the Romans in AD 102, was 45m by 45m square and was defended by several surrounding walls. The entire northern stretch from here along the banks of the Oraşului to Orăştie was protected by lookout towers and bastions. Remains of a Roman camp

once fortified with ramparts and ditches still remain between the villages of Bucium and Orăştioara de Jos.

Densuş

The church in Densuş is on Romania's top-10 list of fabulous historic treasures. The stone church, built between the 11th and 12th centuries, stands on the ancient site of an edifice dating from the 4th century, which archaeologists believe to have been the mausoleum of a Roman soldier. The church was constructed from stones taken from the Roman city of Ulpia Traiana-Sarmizegetusa.

Archaeologists conclude that the church, believed to have been built as a court chapel, was built by a Romanian noble family, only falling under Hungarian rule from the 14th century onwards. There are fragments of a 15th-century fresco inside the church.

Densuş is east of Sarmizegetusa. From Orăştie bear 18km west to Simeria then continue south for 33km to Haţeg. From here, follow the Caransebeş road 7km southwest to Toteştii. In Toteştii, turn left. Densuş is at the end of this dirt track.

Ulpia Traiana-Sarmizegetusa

Following the Romans' defeat of Decebal's forces in AD 106, they built up a spectacular array of towns for themselves, setting their capital of conquered Dacia in Ulpia Traiana, some 15km south of Densuş on the main Caransebeş road. Just to confuse things, the name of the former Dacian capital was added to the Roman city's name. It was now known as Ulpia Traiana-Sarmizegetusa.

Archaeologists have unearthed only a fraction of the great city, which was believed to have covered an area of 60 hectares. During the early 14th century, the stones of the Sarmizegetusa ruins were used by local villagers to build churches and it was not until the 1800s that the dismantled ruins fell under the protection of the Deva Archaeological Society and later the National Museum of Transylvania. Remains of the Roman Forum, complete with 10m-tall marble columns, have already been uncovered, as have numerous temples devoted to the Roman deities, the amphitheatre, the palace of Augustales, a mausoleum and two suburban villas on the northern side of the

TRANSYLVANIA

town. Many tools, ceramics, ivory combs and other Roman treasures yielded from Sarmizegetusa are exhibited in the Deva history museum.

Every summer, between 21 July and the end of August, archaeologists from Cluj-Napoca descend upon Ulpia Traiana-Sarmizegetusa to continue their long task. There is a permanent **archaeological base** (☎ 054-762 170) close to the site which welcomes visitors year-round.

Places to Stay

Opération Villages Roumains (☎ 054-646 194; Str Principală 63a) in Beriu, 8km south of Orăştie on the road to Dacian Sarmizegetusa, arranges accommodation in private homes throughout the region from €12 a night, including breakfast. It can also supply tourists with an English- or French-speaking guide for €10 to €20 for a half/full day.

There is a small **camping ground** (camping/bungalows free/€5; ⏾ May-Sep) next to the archaeological site in Sarmizegetusa. Staff at the archaeological base can also help with accommodation and can often point you in the direction of rooms in private homes.

In Haţeg, try **Hotel Belvedere** (☎ 054-777 604; s/d €5/10), 2km from the centre on the road to Petroşani. There is also a swimming pool and in summer an open-air disco.

Three kilometres southeast of Haţeg at Sântămaria Orlea is the **Hanul Sântămaria Orlea** (☎ 054-777 768; d/tr €25/38).

RETEZAT MOUNTAINS

The mountains, comprising two peaks, gain their name (meaning 'cut off') from the flat-topped pyramid shape of these peaks. Most of the stunning territory is covered by the **Retezat National Park** (www.retezat.ro in Romanian), Romania's oldest (established in 1935). Covering 38,047 hectares of pristine mixed forest and glacial plateaus (including some 80 glacial lakes), the area is considered a Unesco Biosphere Reservation. Carnivores large and small (especially the cute marmot) roam the region wildly. The region is among Europe's last remaining largely untouched stretches of wilderness and provides unforgettable

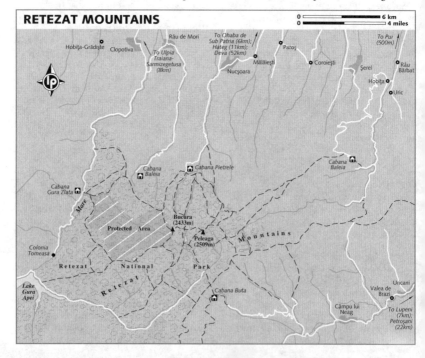

RETEZAT MOUNTAINS

hiking experiences among its valleys, peaks, rivers and gorges.

East of the Retezat Mountains lies the Jiu Valley, Romania's largest mining region, centred on the towns of Petroşani, Petrila and Câmpii lui Neag in the northern end of the valley. Petroşani makes a useful base for hiking expeditions into the Retezat Mountains.

From Petroşani you can head 57km south down the Jiu Valley to Târgu Jiu (p188). The southbound road running parallel to this road to the east is said to be the highest road in Romania, peaking at 2142m. It is only possible to cross the mountains along this road by 4WD vehicles.

From Târgu Jiu there are seven trains daily to Petroşani (1¼ to 1¾ hours). From Hunedoara and Deva, change at Simeria.

Activities

Hiking is excellent here. The main access point is Ulpia Traiana-Sarmizegetusa, northwest of the mountains, from where a trail (6½ hours, 19.5km, red crosses) leads to Cabana Gura Zlata. This trail follows a dirt track which, in dry weather, is suitable for vehicles too. Continuing 12km south you come to Lacu Gura Apei.

Another northerly access point is Nucşoara. Hikers can catch a local train from Simeria (36km), Petroşani (44km) or Târgu Jiu (94km) to Ohaba de Sub Patria, then follow the trail south, through Nucşoara, to Cabana Peitrele (six to seven hours, blue stripes). This and the Gura Zlata are the two most popular cabanas in the Retezat Mountains, with numerous hiking trails marked from each.

From Ohaba de Sub Patria (9km) take a local train to Pui train station, from where you can hike 3km south along a paved road to Hobiţa. From Hobiţa a trail leads to Cabana Baleia (4½ hours, blue triangles).

The main starting point from the east is Petroşani, at the northern end of the Jiu Valley. Daily buses run to Câmpu lui Neag, 28km west of Petroşani. There is a cabana in Câmpu lui Neag where you can take a breather before picking up one of a number of mountain trails. From here a 3½- to four-hour trail leads to Cabana Buta in the southeastern Retezats.

TRANSYLVANIA

Wallachia

CONTENTS

WALLACHIA

Wallachia (Ţara Românească) has sat in the shadows of the soaring Carpathian Mountains, the rural idyll of Maramureş and the elegant Hapsburgs cities of Crişana and Banat – until now.

This flat region has a tranquil charm all of its own which is waiting to be discovered. Some of Romania's most beautiful and peaceful monasteries lie on its northern edges, snuggled into the mountain seams. And some of the country's quirkiest, off-the-beaten-track attractions, such as Câmpina's spooky Haşdeu Castle or Târgu Jiu's open-air museum of sculptor Brâncuşi's work, should lure you here. It is the heart of Roma culture – you'll see horses and carts tearing through villages and unusual Roma houses. And the spectacular Transfăgărăşan road – said to be one of the highest roads in Europe – cuts dramatically across the Făgăraş Mountains, passing Romania's real 'Dracula's castle' from its start point at Curtea de Argeş.

The Danube River flows along the southern edge of Wallachia and is best seen between Moldova Veche and Drobeta-Turnu Severin in the west, where it breaks through the Carpathians at the legendary Iron Gates (Porţile de Fier), a gorge on the Romanian–Yugoslav border.

Wallachia has many treasures and few tourists. Discover this region before everyone else does.

TOP FIVE

- Hiking up 1480 steps to the 'real' Dracula's castle at **Poienari** (p186)
- Visiting the region's monasteries – the peaceful **Horezu** (p188), the exquisite **Curtea de Argeş** (p185) and the awe-inspiring **Bistriţa** (p187)
- Drinking Ţuica (fruit brandy) around a campfire, dancing to traditional music and feasting on Romanian dishes in the rural village of **Arefu** (p186)
- Travelling along the **Transfăgărăşan road** (p187), stopping en route at the spectacular **Lake Vidraru** (p187)
- Letting Brâncuşi's Endless Column connect your spiritual and physical worlds in **Târgu Jiu** (p190)

Lake Vidraru
Bistriţa
Horezu
Poienari
Târgu Jiu
Curtea de Argeş
Transfăgărăşan road
Arefu

POPULATION: 5.24 MILLION	AREA: 58,732 SQ KM	AVERAGE MONTHLY WAGE: €58

WALLACHIA

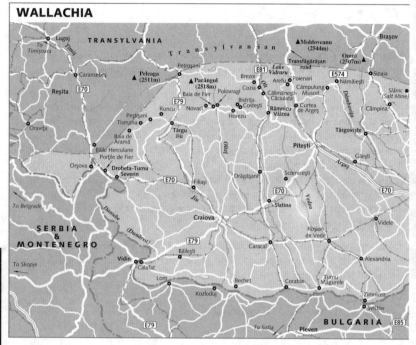

HISTORY

Before the formation of Romania in the 19th century, the Romanians were known as Vlachs, hence Wallachia. Romanians call Wallachia 'Țara Românească' (Land of the Romanians).

Founded by Radu Negru in 1290, this principality was subject to Hungarian rule until 1330 when Basarab I (r 1310–52) defeated the Hungarian king Charles I and declared Wallachia independent, the first of the Romanian lands to achieve independence. The Wallachian princes *(voievozi)* built their first capital cities – Câmpulung Muscel, Curtea de Argeș and Târgoviște – close to the protective mountains, but in the 15th century Bucharest gained ascendancy.

After the fall of Bulgaria to the Turks in 1396 Wallachia faced a new threat, and in 1415 Mircea cel Bătrân (Mircea the Old; r 1386–1418) was forced to acknowledge Turkish suzerainty. Other Wallachian princes such as Vlad Țepeș (r 1448, 1456–62, 1476) and Mihai Viteazul (r 1593–1601) became national heroes by defying the Turks and refusing to pay tribute. In 1859 Wallachia

was united with Moldavia, paving the way for the modern Romanian state.

PLOIEȘTI

☎ 244 / pop 250,000

Ploiești, the main city in the Prahova region, ranks as Romania's second-most important industrial city. Dubbed the city of 'black gold', oil has been refined here since 1857, and is a source of enormous pride to its inhabitants.

Glamorous it may not be, but Ploiești has a nice little centre and several interesting museums.

Orientation

Ploiești has four train stations, but most travellers will only use the southern station (Gară Sud) and the western station (Gară Vest). If you are arriving from Moldavia you'll stop at the southern train station, a 15-minute walk from the centre. Exit the station and head north up B-dul Independenței to Piața Victoriei. All the hotels, museums and restaurants are centred on this square.

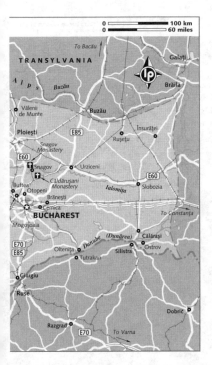

From Transylvania, you will arrive at the western train station. From here, take bus No 1 or 2 to Piaţa Victoriei in the centre. If you are coming from Bucharest or Târgovişte you could arrive at either station; get off at the southern station, as it's closer to the centre.

Information
MONEY
Eurom Bank (☎ 540 351; Piaţa Victoriei 6) offers cash transfers, cashes travellers cheques and has an exchange.

There is an ATM and exchange office next to McDonalds on Piaţa Victoriei.

POST
The central **post and telephone office** (Piaţa Victoriei 10; ☼ 7am-8pm Mon-Fri, 8am-noon Sat) is south of Piaţa Victoriei on B-dul Republicii.

TOURIST INFORMATION
Agenţia de Turism Passion (☎ 514 507, 515 118; Piaţa Victoriei 3; ☼ 9.30am-5pm Mon-Fri) is the best choice in Ploieşti as there's no official tourist information office. Friendly staff offer maps, information and hotel bookings, hunt-

ing and fishing trips and wine tours of the Prahova Valley.

There's an **Agentia de Turism** (☼ 8.30am-6pm Mon-Fri, 9am-12.30pm Sat) inside Hotel Central (below).

Sights
The **Museum of Oil** (Muzeul Naţional al Petrolului; ☎ 523 564; Dr Bagdazar 8; ☼ 10am-5pm Tue-Sun; admission €0.50) charts Ploieşti's place as Romania's *Dallas*.

Nearby is the **History & Archaeology Museum** (Muzeul de Istorie şi Arheologie; ☎ 514 437; Str Toma Caragiu 10; ☼ 9am-5pm Tue-Sun; admission €0.30), housed in a former girls' school dating to 1865.

One of the treasures of the **Clock Museum** (Muzeul Ceasului; ☎ 542 861; Str Nicolae Simachei 1; ☼ 9am-5pm Tue-Sun; admission €0.30) is an 18th-century rococo Austrian clock that belonged to the Wallachian prince Alexandru Ioan Cuza.

In the centre of the park on Piaţa Victoriei, there is a **memorial** to the victims of the 1989 revolution, as well as a **Liberty Statue**. The **Culture Palace** (Palatul Culturii), at the northern end of the square, is home to the **Biology Museum** (Muzeul de Biologie Umană; ☼ 9am-5pm Mon-Fri, 9am-1pm Sat & Sun; admission €1) and the **Museum of Popular Art** (Muzeul de Artă Populară).

Opposite the **Culture Palace** (Palatul Culturii) is the impressive **St John's Cathedral**, dating from 1810. To its east lies the **Central Market**, housed in two large, domed buildings.

The main **Art Museum** (Muzeul de Artă; ☎ 511 375; B-dul Independenţei 1; ☼ 9am-4.30pm Mon-Fri) displays the work of Romanian painters and is worth a look around. It is housed in a large white building.

Sleeping
Hotel Prahova Plazza (☎ 526 850; Str Dobrogeanu Gherea 11; s/d €20/30) A Soviet architect's delight, with large, clean rooms.

Hotel Central (☎ 526 641; B-dul Republicii 9; s/d €52/72) At the time of writing it was undergoing a giant face-lift after the last earthquake destroyed it. The old facade is strangely adrift from the new structure.

Eating
The hotel restaurants are your best bet for a simple, filling meal.

Braserie (Piaţa Victoriei; ☼ 9am-11pm; mains €3) This place is above Cinema Patria and it

WALLACHIA

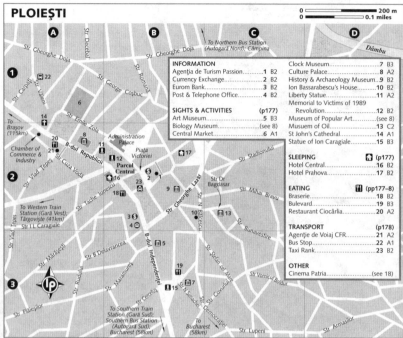

PLOIEŞTI

0 — 200 m
0 — 0.1 miles

INFORMATION	
Agenţia de Turism Passion..............1 B2	
Currency Exchange..........................2 B2	
Eurom Bank....................................3 B2	
Post & Telephone Office..................4 B2	

SIGHTS & ACTIVITIES	(p177)
Art Museum...................................5 B3	
Biology Museum.........................(see 8)	
Central Market...............................6 A1	

Clock Museum................................7 B3	
Culture Palace.................................8 A2	
History & Archaeology Museum......9 B2	
Ion Bassarabescu's House.............10 B2	
Liberty Statue..............................11 A2	
Memorial to Victims of 1989	
Revolution.................................12 B2	
Museum of Popular Art............(see 8)	
Musuem of Oil..............................13 C2	
St John's Cathedral.......................14 A1	
Statue of Ion Caragiale................15 B3	

SLEEPING	(p177)
Hotel Central...............................16 B2	
Hotel Prahova...............................17 B2	

EATING	(pp177–8)
Braserie.......................................18 B2	
Bulevard......................................19 B3	
Restaurant Ciocârlia.....................20 A2	

TRANSPORT	(p178)
Agenţie de Voiaj CFR...................21 A2	
Bus Stop.....................................22 A1	
Taxi Rank...................................23 B2	

OTHER	
Cinema Patria...........................(see 18)	

overlooks Piaţa Victoriei. There is a small menu of Romanian staples such as meat soups, salads and meat dishes. Good for refuelling rather than savouring.

Restaurant Ciocârlia (☎ 526 348; B-dul Republicii 65; mains €3) Enjoy nice views of the cathedral while you eat simple pizzas or light snacks.

Bulevard (☎ 521 500; Str Goleşti 25; mains €3-5) Enjoy the simple Romanian dishes at this eatery with the best summer garden in town.

Get your fresh vegies and fish from the monster-sized **central market** (B-dul Unirii).

Getting There & Away
BUS

There are two bus stations: long-distance buses arrive at and depart from the **northern bus station** (Autogară Nord; Str Griviţei 25), and buses to nearby villages use the **southern bus station** (Autogară Sud; Str Depoului), a two-minute walk from the southern train station.

The southern bus station has services to Bucharest (€1.50, 59km, one daily), Câmpina (€0.75, 32km, eight daily) and Târgovişte (€1, 52km, two daily).

TRAIN

You can purchase train tickets in advance from the **Agenţie de Voiaj CFR** (☎ 542 080; B-dul Republicii 17; 7am-8pm Mon-Fri).

Fast trains to/from Bucharest, Constanţa, Timişoara, Craiova and Moldavia use the **southern train station** (Gară Sud; Piaţa 1 Decembrie 1918), the closest train station to the town centre. Local trains only use the western train station (Gară Vest).

From the southern train station, services include those to Bucharest (€3, 12 daily), Braşov (€5, six daily), Cluj-Napoca (€14, two daily), Baia Mare (€15, two daily) and, in summer, Constanţa (two daily).

Trains to Budapest from Bucharest stop at the southern train station, as does the daily Warsaw train.

Getting Around

Bus Nos 1 and 2 travel from the southern train station to Piaţa Victoriei in the city centre and then on to the western train station. From here, bus No 2 continues to the university.

CÂMPINA & AROUND

☎ 244

Travelling out of Ploieşti is a surreal experience. Romania's Texas has miles of flat, bleak landscape pitted by constantly moving oil drills.

Heading 32km north of Ploieşti into the Prahova Valley you come to Câmpina. Approaching this small town, you pass a memorial to pioneering pilot Aurel Vlaicu, who met his death in 1913 after his plane crashed as he attempted to cross the Carpathians.

Câmpina has Romania's strangest monument, eerie Haşdeu Castle, and a museum dedicated to artist Nicolae Grigorescu.

Sights

HAŞDEU CASTLE

Get spooked in this creepy tribute to fatherly love. The **castle** (☎ 335 599; B-dul Carol I 197; ⏱ 9am-5pm Sep-Apr, 10am-6pm May-Aug; adult/student €1/0.50) was built by history professor Bogdan Petriceicu Haşdeu in memory of his academically brilliant daughter, Iulia, who died of tuberculosis at the age of 19 – just before she was to become the first woman to enter the Sorbonne in Paris.

Although Iulia was buried in the Belu Cemetery in Bucharest it was here that her father held seances to communicate with her – and composed the eerie funeral music said to be communicated from daughter to father via the spirit world.

NICOLAE GRIGORESCU MUSEUM

Romania's signature **museum** (Muzeul Nicolae Grigorescu; ☎ 333 598; B-dul Carol I 166; adult/student €0.50/0.25), dedicated to its most famous artist, is the pride of Câmpina. It charts the life and works of Nicolae Grigorescu (1838–1907) who started his career painting icons to support his family. He studied in Paris, doing a short stint at the studio of Sebastion Cornu where he studied with Pierre Auguste Renoir. His works attracted the attention of the Barbizon group and of Napoleon III, who bought two of his paintings in 1867.

SLANIC

This **salt mine** (admission €1) lies 40km west of Ploieşti in the Prahova region. Inside the salt mountain, excavated between 1912 and 1970, is a famous centre of health and treatment with a salt pool. Visitors descend 220m down via the original mine elevator to the heart of the mountain, a surreal white womb with statues carved in salt and spectacular walls. There's a small hotel mostly used by Romanian health tourists.

From Ploieşti's southern train station, maxitaxis (minibuses) run to Slanic every 45 minutes (or when full), and a daily local train leaves from Ploieşti's western train station.

Sleeping

Hotel Muntenia (☎ 333 091; B-dul Carol I 61; s/d €25/31) The only choice in the area is OK for a one-night stopover.

Getting There & Away

From Ploieşti's southern bus station there are several daily buses to Câmpina (32km). There are also five daily trains from Ploieşti's western station to Câmpina.

Maxitaxi services run between Sinai and Câmpina.

TÂRGOVIŞTE

☎ 245 / pop 100,000

All eyes were on Târgovişte, 49km northwest of Bucharest, following the dramatic arrest here of communist president Nicolae Ceauşescu and his wife Elena on 22 December 1989.

The Ceauşescus hijacked a car in Titu, 44km northwest of Târgovişte, where they were spotted by two soldiers who finally caught up with them in the town. Four days later, the first bloody images of the hastily arranged court session and execution by firing squad inside the military garrison flashed across the world's TV screens, 'proving' the hated pair was dead.

Aside from its spotlight in history, Târgovişte is a charming market town dating from 1396. It was the capital of Wallachia from 1418 to 1659, after when the capital was moved to Bucharest. During the 15th century, Vlad Ţepeş, the notorious impaler with whom the fictitious Dracula is associated, held princely court here.

Orientation

The town centre is a 20-minute walk east of the train station. Exit the station and head east, past the military barracks (p180), up B-dul Castanilor, then turn right into B-dul Mircea cel Bătrân (previously Str Victoriei). All eastbound buses along this street stop in

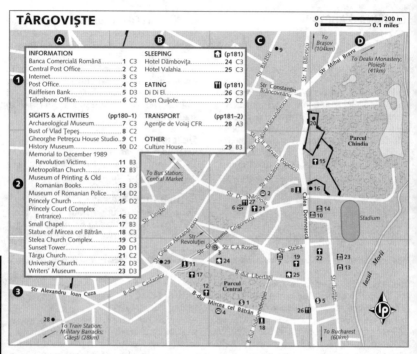

TÂRGOVIŞTE

0 ____ 200 m
0 ____ 0.1 miles

INFORMATION
Banca Comercială Română............1 C3
Central Post Office......................2 C2
Internet..................................3 C3
Post Office.............................4 C3
Raiffeisen Bank.........................5 D3
Telephone Office.......................6 C2

SIGHTS & ACTIVITIES (pp180–1)
Archaeological Museum...............7 C3
Bust of Vlad Ţepeş....................8 C2
Gheorghe Petrescu House Studio..9 C1
History Museum........................10 D2
Memorial to December 1989
  Revolution Victims..................11 B3
Metropolitan Church...................12 B3
Museum of Printing & Old
  Romanian Books......................13 D3
Museum of Romanian Police........14 D2
Princely Church.......................15 D2
Princely Court (Complex
  Entrance)............................16 D2
Small Chapel..........................17 B3
Statue of Mircea cel Bătrân.........18 C3
Stelea Church Complex...............19 C3
Sunset Tower..........................20 D1
Târgu Church..........................21 C2
University Church.....................22 D3
Writers' Museum.......................23 D3

SLEEPING (p181)
Hotel Dâmboviţa......................24 C3
Hotel Valahia.........................25 C3

EATING (p181)
Di Di El..............................26 C3
Don Quijote..........................27 C2

TRANSPORT (pp181–2)
Agenţie de Voiaj CFR.................28 A3

OTHER
Culture House........................29 B3

To Braşov (104km)
To Dealu Monastery; Ploieşti (41km)
Str N Bălcescu
Str Mihai Bravu
Str Constantin Brâncoveanu
Str Gheorghe Alexandrescu
Str Pârvan Popescu
Parcul Chindia
To Bus Station; Central Market
Str Dr Marinoiu
Str Linişei
Str Gheorghe Ieremia Grigorescu
Str Revoluţiei
Str Gheorghe Alexandrescu
Str C A Rosetti
Str Stelea
Calea Domnească
Stadium
Str Justiţiei
Iazul Morii
Str Alexandru Ioan Cuza
B-dul Castanilor
B-dul Libertăţii
B-dul Mircea cel Bătrân
Parcul Central
B-dul Independenţei
To Bucharest (60km)
To Train Station; Military Barracks; Găeşti (28km)

---

the centre. The bus station and central market are 3km northwest of town; turn right as you leave the bus station, then cross the large roundabout and take any eastbound bus down Calea Câmpulung.

The main shops, banks and hotels are in the modern centre clustered around Central Park (Parcul Central; p181), which is straddled by B-dul Libertăţii to the north and B-dul Mircea cel Bătrân to the south. The Princely Court and key museums are in the older part of town, along Calea Domnească.

Information

MONEY

At **Banca Comercială Română** (B-dul Independenţiei; 8am-12.30pm Mon-Fri) you can cash travellers cheques, get cash advances on Visa/MasterCard or use the two ATMs. Hotel Dâmboviţa (p181) also offers a currency exchange service.

POST & TELEPHONE

The **central post office** (Str Dr Marinoiu; 7.30am-8pm Mon-Fri, 8am-1pm Sat) dates from 1906. To its north is the **telephone office** (Str Ion Rădulescu; 7am-8.30pm).

TOURIST INFORMATION

Surprise! There's no tourist office! Instead head straight for the Princely Court (below) where you can buy tourist brochures in English or French (€0.75) covering all the main sights.

Sights

The **military barracks**, where the Ceauşescus were executed, are immediately on the right as you leave the train station. At the hasty trial the pair faced joint charges of being accomplices to the murder of some 60,000 people, of genocide, and of attempting to flee Romania with state money, totalling US$1 billion, stashed away in foreign bank accounts. None of the charges were proven. It's forbidden to enter or to take photographs of the garrison at the western end of B-dul Castanilor.

Princely Court (Curtea Domnească; Calea Domnească 181; 9am-9pm Tue-Sun; admission €0.75). During the 15th century, the bloodthirsty prince

Vlad Ţepeş resided here. The court was built in the 14th century for Mircea cel Bătrân (Mircea the Old) and remained a residence for Wallachia's princes until the reign of Constantin Brâncoveanu (r 1688–1714). Mircea cel Bătrân fortified his court with defensive towers and from the 27m-high **Sunset Tower** (Turnul Chindiei), guards would announce the closing of the city gates as the sun went down. It houses an exhibition recounting – in Romanian – the stories of Vlad Ţepeş' life: one display describes how he made sure impaled Turkish soldiers had their eyes cut out so they couldn't see the heavenly maidens they believed awaited them after death.

The local **History Museum** (Muzeul de Istorie Dâmboviţa; cnr Calea Domnească & Str Justiţei; 9am-5pm Tue-Sun; admission €0.30) is near the **Museum of Romanian Police** (Muzeul Poliţiei Române; 9am-5pm Tue-Sun; admission €1.50).

The **Museum of Printing & Old Romanian Books** (Muzeul Tiparului şi al Cărţii Româneşti Vechi; 612 877; Str Justiţei 3-5) is housed in a 17th-century palace built by Constantin Brâncoveanu for his daughter Safta. A small **Writers' Museum** (Muzeul Scriitorilor Dâmboviţeni) adjoins the book museum.

Opposite is the **University Church** (Biserica Universităţii), dating from the 19th century. In front of it are busts of local academic Ienăchiţă Văcărescu (1740–97) and Radu de la Afumaţi, ruler of Wallachia from 1522 to 1529.

The **Stelea Church Complex** (Complexul Biserica Stelea) was founded as a monastery by Moldavian prince Vasile Lupu (r 1634–53) in 1645 as a peace offering to Wallachian ruler Matei Basarab.

In **Central Park** a marble cross stands outside a **small chapel** dedicated to the victims of the December 1989 revolution. Also in the park is the 18th-century **Metropolitan Church**. At its monks' quarters, the 16th-century **Dealu Monastery** on a hill 3km northeast of the centre, the head of the great Wallachian prince Mihai Viteazul (Michael the Brave) is buried. Beheaded on the orders of the Habsburg general George Basta on 3 August 1601, Viteazul is still hailed as the crusader of Romanian nationalism. It was at this monastery that he swore his allegiance to the Hungarian emperor Rudolph II in 1598.

A few blocks north of the park is the partially frescoed **Târgu Church** (Biserica Târgului;

Str Ion Rădulescu). The 1654 church was painted during the 17th and 18th centuries but destroyed during an earthquake in 1940. Extensive renovations followed in 1941 and again in the 1970s. Inside is a **memorial plaque** to local priest and teacher Professor Georgescu, who was among the thousands to die while toiling under communist forced labour to build the Danube–Black Sea Canal in Dobrogea (p214).

Gheorghe Petreşcu House Studio (Casa Atelier Gheorghe Petreşcu; Str Bărătiei; admission free) was where the Romanian painter (1872–1949) spent the last 20 years of his life. He captured most of the town's major sights on canvas.

Sleeping

Hotel Valahia (634 491; B-dul Libertăţii 7; s/d €19/25) The Valahia has a strange, slightly spooky air due to the contrast of being quite grand but a bit dark and dingy. It has a strange air about it but reasonable, spacious rooms.

Hotel Dâmboviţa (613 961; office@hoteldambovita.ro; B-dul Libertăţii 1; s/d €26/36) This central hotel has some rooms with balconies overlooking the park.

Eating

Di Di El (212 916; Calea Domenască, Block A; mains €3) Excellent pizzas (17 types!) and authentic Italian spaghetti are served on the pavement terrace here.

Don Quijote (Str Dr Marinoiu 9; mains €5) A popular, cosy and inviting place with a small outside terrace and stone fireplace. Large portions of good Romanian fodder are served.

Getting There & Away

BUS

Major services from Târgovişte include those to Bucharest (€1.50, 78km, 10 daily), Câmpulung Muscel (€1.50, 73km, four daily), Ploieşti (€1, 52km, two daily) and Braşov (€2, 90km, two daily).

TRAIN

The **Agenţie de Voiaj CFR** (611 554; B-dul Castanilor 2; 7am-7pm Mon-Fri), just north of the train station, sells advance tickets.

From Târgovişte there are local trains to Ploieşti's western train station (1¾ hours, five daily). To get to Târgovişte from other cities, you have to change trains at Ploieşti.

PITEŞTI
☎ 248 / pop 180,000

Piteşti holds an important place in Bucharest's industrial heritage. The infamous, sturdy and altogether Romanian Dacia cars have been produced here since 1966. Dacias may be the butt of endless jokes but they've kept Romania on the move in the face of bad roads and enormous potholes. In mid-1999, French car manufacturer Renault paid US$50 million for a majority stake in Dacia and promised US$220 million of investment.

Piteşti boasts one of the country's few stretches of pristine motorway, linking it to Bucharest (114km east), and has a lovely pedestrianised centre lined with trendy new bars.

Orientation

Piteşti has two bus stations and two train stations, although the southern stations are the most useful for travellers. Buses to/from Bucharest and other major cities in Romania use the southern bus station (Autogară Sud), off B-dul Brătianu on Str Abatorului Târgul din Vale. All Bucharest and Curtea de Argeş trains stop at the southern train station (officially Piteşti Sud but known as Piteşti) on B-dul Republicii. It's here you'll also find gleaming maxitaxis. Bus Nos 2, 4 and 8 run between the train station and the town centre.

B-dul Republicii leads north from the train station towards the town centre. The main pedestrianised street, Str Victoriei, is lined with most of the town's hotels and restaurants.

Information
MONEY

The **Banca Comercială Română** (B-dul Republicii 83; ⏱ 8.30am-5pm Mon-Fri) cashes travellers cheques,

---

FROM VICTIM TO TORTURER

From 1949 to 1952 a unique and experimental 'student re-education program' was introduced in Piteşti, Gherla and Aiud prisons as a means of torturing political prisoners. The program was implemented by Eugen Ţurcanu, an inmate at Piteşti prison, acting on the orders of the Securitate. Ţurcanu rounded up a core team of torturers from among his fellow inmates.

'Re-education' induced tortured prisoners to become torturers themselves. The first stage of this grotesque process involved the prisoner confessing all his crimes and 'anti-state' thoughts that he'd failed to earlier reveal to Securitate interrogators. He then signed a declaration in which he consented to his re-education. Scrubbing floors with a rag between the teeth, eating soup hoglike with both hands tied behind the back, licking toilets clean and being beaten to unconsciousness were just some of the persuasive methods used.

Religiously inclined prisoners, dubbed 'Catholics', were baptised each morning with a bucket of urine. Others were forced to don a white sheet in imitation of Christ and wear a penis carved from soap around their necks. Fellow prisoners kissed the soap pendant and the prisoner was flogged by other inmates in imitation of Christ's ordeal on the road to Golgotha.

Next, the victim was forced to disclose the names of fellow inmates who'd shown him kindness or sympathy. He then had to renounce his own family, 'reviling them in such foul and hideous terms that it would be next to impossible ever to return to natural feelings towards them', according to former political prisoner Dimitru Bacu in his novel The Anti-Humans.

In the final stage of the program, victims had to prove their successful 'regeneration' – by inflicting the same mental and physical abuse on new prison recruits. If they refused they were driven through the program again. Those who slackened in their new role as re-educator spent time in the prison's incarceration cell, black room, or isolation cell.

The incarceration cells were 1.8m-tall upright coffins with a small hole for ventilation. One or two prisoners had to stand in these cells for eight to 15 days. The black room was 2.7 sq metres and windowless. Up to 30 prisoners were detained here for a maximum of three weeks without water. Isolation cells were reserved for sentences of three months or more, and many prisoners kept in these cells died of tuberculosis.

In 1954 Eugen Ţurcanu and 21 other prisoners were secretly tried and sentenced to death for the murder of 30 prisoners and the abuse of 780. The Securitate denied all knowledge of the program.

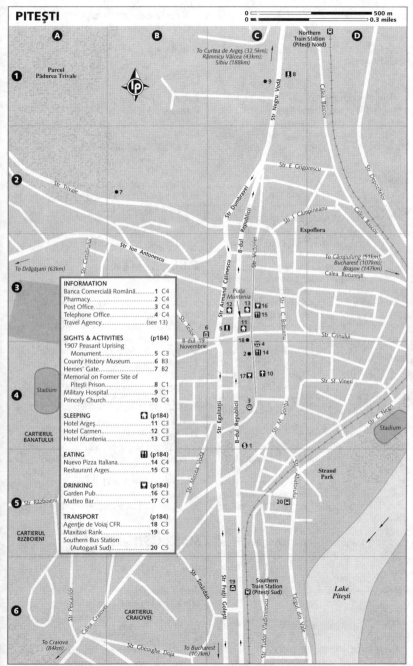

PITEŞTI

0 — 500 m
0 — 0.3 miles

INFORMATION
Banca Comercială Română........................1 C4
Pharmacy...2 C4
Post Office..3 C4
Telephone Office..4 C4
Travel Agency.....................................(see 13)

SIGHTS & ACTIVITIES   (p184)
1907 Peasant Uprising
Monument..5 C3
County History Museum.............................6 B3
Heroes' Gate..7 B2
Memorial on Former Site of
Piteşti Prison..8 C1
Military Hospital..9 C1
Princely Church..10 C4

SLEEPING   🛏 (p184)
Hotel Argeş..11 C3
Hotel Carmen...12 C3
Hotel Muntenia..13 C3

EATING   🍴 (p184)
Nuevo Pizza Italiana.................................14 C4
Restaurant Argeş.....................................15 C3

DRINKING   🍷 (p184)
Garden Pub..16 C3
Matteo Bar..17 C4

TRANSPORT   (p184)
Agenţie de Voiaj CFR................................18 C3
Maxitaxi Rank..19 C6
Southern Bus Station
(Autogară Sud)....................................20 C5

Parcul
Pădurea Trivale

To Curtea de Argeş (32.5km);
Râmnicu Vâlcea (43km);
Sibiu (188km)

Northern
Train Station
(Piteşti Nord)

Str Trivale

Str Ion Antonescu

To Drăgăşani (63km)

Str E Grigorescu

Str I Câmpineanu

Expoflora

To Câmpulung (51km);
Bucharest (107km);
Braşov (147km)
Calea Bucureşti

Str Dumbravei

B-dul Republicii

Str Victoriei

Str Armand Călinescu

Piaţa
Muntenia

Str C Brătianu

Str Crinului

Str Sf Vineri

Str Teior

B-dul 19
Novembrie

Str Egalităţii

B-dul Republicii

Str M Scriu

Str C Negri

Stadium

Strand
Park

CARTIERUL
BANATULUI

Stadium

CARTIERUL
RĂZBOIENI

Str Războieni

Str Mircea Vodă

Str Abatorului

Str Pescarilor

Calea Craiovei

CARTIERUL
CRAIOVEI

Str Smârdan

Str Fraţii Goleşti

Southern
Train Station
(Piteşti Sud)

Str Tudor Vladimirescu

Târgul din Vale

Lake
Piteşti

To Craiova
(84km)

Str Gheorghe Doja

To Bucharest
(107km)

Str Negru Vodă

Calea Bascov

Str Depozitelor

Calea Bascov

WALLACHIA

gives cash advances on Visa/MasterCard and has an ATM.

POST
Central Post Office (Str Victoriei; ✉ 9am-7pm Mon-Fri, 9am-noon Sat)

TOURIST INFORMATION
The **Hotel Muntenia Travel Agency** (☎ 625 450; entrance on Str Victoriei; ✉ 8am-8pm Mon-Fri) can arrange excursions to Curtea de Argeş, sells outdated maps of Piteşti and organises car rental.

Sights
After WWII **Piteşti prison** (Str Negru Vodă), just north of the city centre, was a site of the Communist government's 'Student Re-education Centre' because of its high security and isolation. Operational since 1900, it was not until 1949, following the arrest of some anti-Communist students in 1948, that psychiatric abuse became a major feature of the already harsh prison regime. More than 30 prisoners died and hundreds were tortured during the four years of the experiment (see the boxed text, p182).

Today a tall, mosaic-tiled column in memory of those who died marks the spot where the prison stood. The **memorial** stands between the first two of three apartment blocks built on the site. A **military hospital** (Spitalul Militar; 1881) still stands opposite.

The existence of the prison and the atrocities committed are completely ignored in the **County History Museum** (Muzeul Judeţean de Istorie; Str Armand Călinescu 4; ✉ 10am-6pm Tue-Sun; admission €0.30). Crossing the park nearby you pass the **monument** in memorial to those who died in the 1907 peasant uprising.

On Str Victoriei, the unusual St George's Church (Biserica Sfântul Gheorghe), more commonly known as the **Princely Church** (Biserica Domnească), was built by Prince Constantin Şerban and his wife Princess Bălasa between 1654 and 1658.

Sleeping
Piteşti's central hotels huddle around Piaţa Muntenia.

Hotel Argeş (☎ 625 450; s/d €15/24) It's the town's cheapest option; clean but noisy.

Hotel Carmen (☎ 222 407; B-dul Republicii 84; s/d €23/26) This small, friendly place with contemporary decor offers excellent value.

Hotel Muntenia (☎ B-dul Republicii; s/d from €26/36) Monstrously ugly, fantastically old-fashioned but it's dead centre.

Eating & Drinking
Hotel Carmen (mains €5-10) This hotel restaurant is the best in town, with an international menu in stylish surroundings.

Nuova Pizza Italiana (Str Victoriei 8; ✉ 9am-11pm; mains €3) This eatery serves all the usual Italian favourites.

Matteo Bar (Str Victoriei 2; ✉ 9am-11pm) Take in the buzz here with trendy Piteşti people enjoying bar snacks and beer.

Garden Pub (☎ 0723-201 254; Str Victoriei 20; ✉ 10am-11pm) Relax on the lovely terrace's wooden tables here with large jugs of beer.

Getting There & Away
BUS
Maxitaxis depart from outside the southern train station, and go to Constanţa (€8), Craiova and Bucharest (€2, every 15 minutes).

All state buses use the southern bus station (Autogară Sud). Services include buses to Râmnicu Vâlcea (€1.25, 75km, two daily), Braşov (€1.50, 136km, two daily), Bucharest (€2, 108km, three daily), Craiova (€1.50, 142km, one daily) and Târgu Jiu (174km, one daily).

TRAIN
The **Agenţie de Voiaj CFR** (☎ 630 565; Str Domniţa Bălaşa 13) sells advance tickets.

Trains to/from the **southern train station** (Piteşti Sud; ☎ 627 908; B-dul Republicii) include swanky Inter-City (IC) services to/from Bucharest (€4, three daily), and Craiova (three daily), as well as *rapid* trains to Constanţa (€9, one daily).

SCORNICEŞTI
Infamous in Romania, Scorniceşti was not only the birthplace of Nicolae Ceauşescu but also one of the first villages to be bulldozed and rebuilt as characterless Soviet blocks under his Collectivisation scheme.

Ceauşescu spent the first 11 years of his life in the small rural village, 38km southwest of Piteşti, which also hit the headlines in 1976 when the remains of Europe's first *Homo sapiens* were allegedly found here.

In 1988 the centre of the village was razed and rebuilt along with a gigantic football stadium – a present from Ceauşescu to his home town. The ornate street lamps and grandiose flowerbeds which run the length of the central street somehow failed to make their way into other systemised villages.

Ceauşescu's **childhood home** was spared. Prior to 1989, the small cottage housed a museum dedicated to him, but following the revolution the museum was closed. The house, at the northernmost end of the village, is tended by Ceauşescu's sister who lives in a small house opposite but is not officially open to visitors. A photograph of Ceauşescu at his mother's funeral in 1977 and another of him and Elena admiring corn in a field are displayed on the chimney breast in the hallway. In the bedroom there is a painting of his parents and above the bed a tapestry portrait of Ceauşescu.

Ceauşescu's mother, Alexandra (1889–1977), and father, Andruţa (1890–1972), are buried in the family grave in the village cemetery further north along the main road.

CURTEA DE ARGEŞ
☎ 248

Curtea de Argeş was a princely seat in the 14th century after the capital of Wallachia was moved here from Câmpulung Muscel. The town's church is considered to be the oldest monument preserved in its original form in Wallachia, while the monastery (or Episcopal cathedral), sculpted from white stone is unique for its chocolate-box architecture and the royal tombs it hides.

The historic town is a gateway to the Făgăraş Mountains.

Orientation

The train station, a 19th-century architectural monument, is 100m north of the bus station on Str Albeşti. The centre is a 10-minute walk along Str Albeşti then up the cobbled Str Castanilor and along Str Negru Vodă. Continue on until you reach a statue of Basarab I, from where all the major sights, camping ground and hotels (signposted) are a short walk.

Information

There is a **tourist office** (☎ 722 530; B-dul Basarabilor 27-29; ☼ 8am-4pm Mon-Fri, 10am-12.30pm Sat) within Hotel Posada.

The **post office** (B-dul Basarabilor 121; ☼ 7am-8pm Mon-Fri) and the telephone office are in the same building.

Located next to Hotel Posada is **Raiffeisen Bank** (B-dul Basarabilor; ☼ 8.30am-6.30pm Mon-Fri), where you can change money, cash travellers cheques or use the ATM.

Sights
PRINCELY COURT

The ruins of the **Princely Court** (Curtea Domnească; ☼ 9am-5pm; admission €1), which originally comprised a church and palace, is in the city centre. The church was built in the 14th century by Basarab I, whose statue stands in the square outside the entrance to the court.

Basarab died in Târgovişte in 1352. His burial place near the altar in the princely church at Curtea de Argeş was discovered in 1939. The princely court was rebuilt by Basarab's son, Nicolae Alexandru Basarab (r 1352–68), and completed by Vlaicu Vodă (r 1361–77). While little remains of the palace today, the 14th-century church (built on the ruins of a 13th-century church) is almost perfectly intact. The church is lovingly tended by a dedicated, French-speaking caretaker.

HISTORIC CENTRE

The **County Museum** (Muzeul Orăşenesc; ☎ 711 446; Str Negru Vodă 2; ☼ 9am-4pm Tue-Sun) charts the history of the region. Rising on a hill are the ruins of the 14th-century **Sân Nicoară Church** (Biserica Sân Nicoară).

CURTEA DE ARGEŞ MONASTERY

This fantastical **Episcopal cathedral** (Mănăstirea Curtea de Argeş) was built between 1514 and 1526 by Neagoe Basarab (r 1512–21) with marble and mosaic tiles from Constantinople (now Istanbul). Legend has it that the wife of the master stonemason, Manole, was embedded in the stone walls of the church, in accordance with a local custom which obliged the mason to bury a loved one alive within the church to ensure the success of his work. The story goes that Manole told his workers that the first wife to bring their food the next day would be the one entombed alive. The workers duly went home and warned their women – it was hence Manole's wife who made the fateful visit.

The current edifice dates from 1875 when French architect André Lecomte du Nouy was brought in to save the monastery, which was in near ruins, from demolition.

The white marble tombstones of Carol I (1839–1914) and his poet wife Elizabeth (1853–1916) lie on the right in the monastery's *pronaos* (entrance hall). On the left of the entrance are the tombstones of King Ferdinand I (1865–1927) and the British-born Queen Marie (1875–1938) whose heart, upon her request, was put in a gold casket and buried in her favourite palace in Balcic in southern Dobrogea. Following the ceding of southern Dobrogea to Bulgaria in 1940, however, her heart was moved to a marble tomb in Bran. Neagoe Basarab and his wife Stâna are also buried in the *pronaos*.

In the park opposite lies the legendary **Manole's Well** (Fântâna lui Manole). Legend has it that Manole tried – and failed – to fly from the monastery roof when his master, Neagoe, removed the scaffolding to prevent him building a more beautiful structure for anyone else. The natural spring marks his supposed landing pad.

Sleeping

Hotel Posada (☎ 721 451; posada@cyber.ro; B-dul Basarabilor 27-29; s €21-25, d €22-30) Try to get a front-facing room here to watch the sunset over the mountains. It offers both renovated and unrenovated rooms.

Hotel Confarg (☎ 728 020; Str Negru Vodă 5; s/d €21/33) A super-sleek and affordable option.

Sân Nicoară (☎ 722 126; Str Plopis 34; d chalets €9, 6-bed apt €20) Located behind Sân Nicoară church, Sân Nicoară has six-bed apartments and wooden chalets with double beds. Turn right at the Basarab I statue along Str Sân Nicoară. The site is 100m up the hill on the right and has a terrace bar and small grocery kiosk.

Eating & Drinking

Montana Pizzerie (B-dul Basarabilor; pizza €2) This place serves up fresh pizzas and beer. Most nights there is live music.

Restaurant Capra Neagră (☎ 721 619; Str Alexandru Lahovary; mains €3) Sit on the terrace here and enjoy its Romanian dishes.

Disco Ti Amo (B-dul Basarabilor; ⏱ to 5am; admission €0.75) Pumps out big beats to red fairy lights until late/early.

Getting There & Away

There are six daily local trains running to/from Pitești; change at Pitești for all train routes.

State buses run from the **bus station** (Str Albeşti) to/from Arefu, Câmpulung Muscel, Braşov and Bucharest (two daily). Check the station boards, as some buses travel only on weekdays and some only on weekends.

A daily maxitaxi to Bucharest via Pitești leaves at 8am from outside Hotel Posada. Other maxitaxis go to/from Arefu and Pitești from an unofficial **maxitaxi stop** (cnr Str Mai 1 & Str Lascăr Catargiu).

POIENARI & AREFU

☎ 248

From Curtea de Argeş, Dracula fiends head north up the spectacular Argeş Valley to **Poienari Citadel** (Cetatea Poienari). In 1459, Turks captured by Vlad Ţepeş in revenge for killing his father and brother marched along this route. At the end of the march, the Turks built the defensive fortress for the bloodthirsty prince. The result: a castle strategically positioned to guard the entrance from Transylvania into the Argeş Valley. It's considered by Dracula buffs to be Romania's 'real' Dracula's castle.

Some 1480 steps lead up from the side of a hydroelectric power plant to the ruins. A substantial amount of the castle, which towers on a crag above the village, fell down the side of the mountain in 1888. Tickets (€1) to the castle are sold by the castle-keeper at the top of the steps.

Six kilometres south of Poienari Citadel is **Arefu**, a tiny village inhabited solely by descendants of the minions who served Vlad Ţepeş – allegedly! The village has a well-established agrotourism scheme, so visitors can sit around camp fires, sing folk songs and listen to tales told by villagers whose forebears mingled with the notorious impaler.

Legend has it that in 1462, when the Turks besieged Poienari Citadel, the Arefians helped Vlad Ţepeş to escape into the mountains. His wife, convinced they would not escape from the surrounded castle, had already flung herself from the turret. As an expression of gratitude, Ţepeş gave the Arefians their pasture lands. A document signed by Mircea Ciobanul (r 1545–52) in 1540 attests to the people of Arefu being granted 16 mountains and 14 sheepfolds by Ţepeş.

Just 1km north of the fortress lies the artificial **Lake Vidraru**, which was dammed between 1961 and 1966 to feed the hydro-electric power plant. From here the towering **Transfăgărăşan road**, a mountain pass which peaks at 2034m, crosses the Carpathians into Transylvania. The tunnel cutting between the Negoiu and Moldoveanu peaks is 845m long. The pass, allegedly built by the army as a training exercise, is only open for about three months of the year. A sign at the side of the road south of Poienari Citadel shows whether the pass is open or shut.

Sleeping

Villagers in Arefu open their homes to travellers. Ask at the little *biblioteca* (library) for agrotourism members, or knock on the following doors.

The **Tomescu family** (☎ 730 102; per person €25) at house No 229 has three clean rooms and hosts Romanian feasts and *ţuica*-fuelled sing-alongs around the campfire. Rooms are also available at house Nos 53a, 330, 348 and 384.

Pensiunea Dracula (☎ 0740-757 400; s/d €10/18) This *pensiune* is 1km south of Poienari in Căpăţânenii village.

Valea Cu Peşti (☎ 721 451; posada@cyber.ro; d €25) This chalet-style hotel lies on the eastern side of Lake Vidraru.

Cabana Cumpăna (☎ 0788-361 022; s/d €21/27) This place is situated on the western side of Lake Vidraru. Advance bookings can also be made through Hotel Posada (p186) in Curtea de Argeş.

NĂMĂIEŞTI

Some 11km north of Câmpulung Muscel (itself 50km north of Piteşti) is one of Romania's most unusual sights: a monastery built into a mountain cave, above the Târg River Valley. Legend has it that **Nămăieşti Monastery** (Nămăieşti Mănăstire) dating from 1547, was founded by a shepherd who had a dream of a great church inside the rock face. It is claimed that a 16th-century icon shows the only 'real' face of the Virgin Mary and it apparently works miracles. Unfortunately this place is accessible only by public transport.

WEST TO TÂRGU JIU

☎ 250

The main road leads west from Curtea de Argeş to the industrialised town of **Râmnicu Vâlcea**. For accommodation, **Antrec** (☎ 749 706) has an office here and **Hotel Alutus** (☎ 736 601; Str General Praporgescu 10; r €30) is in the town centre.

From Râmnicu Vâlcea head north up the Olt Valley to **Călimăneşti-Căciulata**, a twin-spa resort with 1200m-deep hot and cold mineral springs. It was awarded a gold medal for its mineral waters at Vienna in 1873 and was a favourite haunt of Napoleon III who had waters brought from them to treat his kidney stones. The old Roman town comes to life during the first week of August, when it hosts a large **folk music and crafts festival**. Accommodation can be arranged through **Călimăneşti-Căciulata SR** (☎ 750 270; Calea lui Traian 413).

Just 2km north are the **Cozia** and **Turnul Monasteries**. The monastery at Cozia was built by Mircea cel Bătrân in the late 14th century and today shelters the Wallachian prince's tomb. The original fountain dates from 1517, to which another was added by Constantin Brâncoveanu in 1711.

Costeşti

Fifty-one weeks of the year, the mountain village of Costeşti in the southern Carpathians, 2km north along a dirt track signposted off the main Râmnicu Vâlcea–Târgu Jiu road, is a sleepy village. During the first week of September, it buzzes with flamboyant dancing, music-making, horse-trading and copper-pot-selling, as Romania's Roma community flocks here by horse and cart or Mercedes for the **Roma Festival**.

Thousands of Roma attend, lucrative business deals are struck and marriages arranged. The festival is also attended by the two rival figureheads of the Roma community – the self-proclaimed emperor of Roma worldwide, Iulian Rădulescu, and the Romanian Roma king, Florin Cioabă.

Costeşti is 82km east of **Cem Romengo**, a symbolic 'Roma State' declared in an outlying district of Târgu Jiu by emperor Iulian Rădulescu in March 1997. The Cem Romengo, which has no official frontiers, was proclaimed after 40 Roma were arrested for building houses on state-owned agricultural land.

Bistriţa & Arnota Monasteries

Bistriţa Monastery (Mănăstirea Bistriţa) is 8km to the north of Costeşti. The current

WALLACHIA

Brâncoveanu-style building (1856) was built on the site of a former 15th-century monastery. The first book printed in Wallachia (1508) is preserved in the monastery. Until 1982 the monastery sheltered one of the country's largest schools for handicapped children, now housed in a separate building at the entrance to the estate. Some 800m from the main monastery building is the **Peştera Sfântul Gheorghe**, a hillside chapel hidden in the 'St George' cave in the hill face and previously used to keep the monastery's treasures safe.

From Bistriţa, a forest road leads 4km north to the smaller **Arnota Monastery** (Mănăstirea Arnota). Ancient crosses are carved in the sheer rock face lining the southern end of this road. Wallachian prince Matei Basarab, who started building the monastery in 1636 (it was completed in 1706), is buried here.

Horezu Monastery

One of Romania's treasures, splendid **Horezu** in its idyllic mountain setting, is a Unesco World Heritage site, 7km further west along the Târgu Jiu road. Built during the reign of Constantin Brâncoveanu, it is considered one of Romania's finest examples of the unique synthesis of Western and Oriental architectural styles for which he became famed. The church has an unusually large *pronaos* and open porch supported by ornate stone-carved columns. During the 17th and 18th centuries Horezu housed the country's most prestigious fresco-painting school. Ask the nuns to show you the Princely Chapel – it's a treasure trove of religious artefacts.

SLEEPING
Horezu Monastery (r €20) The complex boasts 20 modern, clean rooms in possibly Romania's loveliest setting. There's no food available, however, and it's not possible to ring ahead. The monastery is signposted off the main road 3km east of Horezu village.

Antrec arranges rooms in private homes for €10 a night; in Horezu village contact the **Dragiţu family** (☎ 860 183) or the **Figura family** (☎ 860 113).

Polovragi & the Women's Cave

From Horezu a dirt road heads west to the 18th-century **Polovragi Monastery** (Mănăstirea Polovragi), founded by Radu the Handsome (r 1474–75) in 1470. Every year in June the monastery hosts a **folk craft fair**.

The **Women's Cave** (Peştera Muierilor; ☽ 9am-7pm May-Sep; adult/child €1/0.50), at the gateway to the Galbenul Gorges, 3km from Baia de Fier, contains the bones of women who used to retreat into the cave for safety during invasions in the Middle Ages. Guided tours (in Romanian) of the 4-million-year-old cave are given every hour. Wear a jumper, as it's 10°C year-round.

TÂRGU JIU
☎ 253 / pop 98,200

Târgu Jiu is home to the internationally famed modernist sculptures of Constantin Brâncuşi (1876–1957). It also lies in the heart of the Jiu Valley mining region. Frequent strikes in this region from the 1980s onwards paralysed industrial activity, forcing the Communists to give in to the miners' militant demands. The miners' mass descent upon Bucharest in 1990 ended in bloodshed and their 1991 rampage led to the fall of Petre Roman's first post-Revolution government.

In early 1999, 10,000 striking miners smashed their way through police barricades as they marched towards Bucharest in protest against layoffs and low wages. After a 17-day strike, a deal was struck with the government for pay rises and the reopening of pits closed in 1998. But when the government reneged on the deal six days later, more violent protests and riots were sparked.

Protest leader Miron Cozma was sentenced to 18 years in prison over the 1991 protests. This harsh sentence was intended to show the International Monetary Fund (IMF) that the government was determined to forge ahead with plans to close hundreds of coal mines and loss-making factories, and pay off Romania's staggering US$3 billion foreign debt.

During WWII Târgu Jiu prison was home to communist party leader Gheorghe Gheorghiu-Dej; Nicolae Ceauşescu, the then secretary-general of the Union of the Communist Youth; and Ion Iliescu, who replaced Ceauşescu as president in 1990.

Orientation
Târgu Jiu centre, east of the Jiu River, is a 15-minute walk from the bus and train

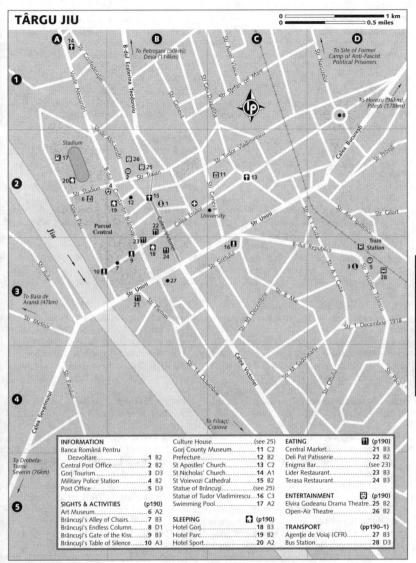

TÂRGU JIU

INFORMATION		
Banca Română Pentru		
Dezvoltare..........................**1**	B2
Central Post Office............**2**	B2
Gorj Tourism......................**3**	D3
Military Police Station.........**4**	B2
Post Office.........................**5**	D3

SIGHTS & ACTIVITIES	(p190)	
Art Museum.......................**6**	A2
Brâncuşi's Alley of Chairs.....**7**	B3
Brâncuşi's Endless Column....**8**	D1
Brâncuşi's Gate of the Kiss...**9**	B3
Brâncuşi's Table of Silence..**10**	A3

Culture House....................(see 25)	
Gorj County Museum.........**11**	C2
Prefecture........................**12**	B2
St Apostles' Church............**13**	C2
St Nicholas' Church............**14**	A1
St Voievozi Cathedral.........**15**	B2
Statue of Brâncuşi..............(see 25)	
Statue of Tudor Vladimirescu.**16**	C3
Swimming Pool.................**17**	A2

SLEEPING		(p190)	
Hotel Gorj........................**18**	B3
Hotel Parc........................**19**	B2
Hotel Sport.......................**20**	A2

EATING		(p190)	
Central Market...................**21**	B3
Deli Pat Patisserie..............**22**	B2
Enigma Bar........................(see 23)	
Lider Restaurant.................**23**	B3
Terasa Restaurant...............**24**	B3

ENTERTAINMENT		(p190)	
Elvira Godeanu Drama Theatre..**25**	B2
Open-Air Theatre................**26**	B2

TRANSPORT		(pp190–1)	
Agenţie de Voiaj (CFR).......**27**	B3
Bus Station.......................**28**	D3

WALLACHIA

stations. Exit the station and turn right along Str Nicolae Titulescu, which becomes B-dul Republicii, until you reach Str Unirii, the main thoroughfare. Head 500m west along Str Unirii then turn right onto Calea Victoriei. The main hotels, shops and restaurants are dotted along the pedestrianised area.

Information
MONEY
There's a currency exchange inside the Gorj Tourism office (p190).

Banca Română Pentru Dezvoltare (8am-4.30pm Mon-Fri), in the centre on Calea Victoriei, cashes travellers cheques, gives cash advances on Visa/MasterCard and has an ATM.

POST & TELEPHONE

The **central post office** (Str Vasile Alecsandri; ☷ 7am-7pm Mon-Fri) is near Str Traian, not far from the **central telephone office** (Str Traian 1; ☷ 7.30am-9pm Mon-Fri).

TOURIST INFORMATION

Gorj Tourism (☎ 224 320; gorjtourism@xnet.ro; ☷ 8am-6pm Mon-Fri, 8am-1pm Sat) is an Antrec agent and sells regional maps (€3).

Sights

Târgu Jiu's Brâncuşi tour starts in **Central Park** (Brâncuşi Park; ☷ 6am-10pm May-Dec, 7am-8pm Jan-Apr), at the western end of Calea Eroilor, with three of the four sculptures (1937–38) that Brâncuşi built in memory of those who died during WWI. The entrance to the park is marked by his **Gate of the Kiss** (Poarta Sărutului), an archway reminiscent of Bucharest's Triumphal Arch constructed the year before. It is also in commemoration of the reunification of Romania. The stone archway bears folk art motifs from Brâncuşi's native Oltenia. Flip a coin on top of the archway for good luck!

Continue along the park's central mall to the **Alley of Chairs** (Aleea Scaunelor). The dwarf-sized stone stools are grouped in trios either side of the avenue.

The alley leads to the third sculpture, the riverside **Table of Silence** (Masa Tăcerii). Each of the 12 stools around the large, round, stone table represents a month of the year. The sculptures were undergoing renovation at the time of writing.

The small **Art Museum** (Muzeul de Artă; ☎ 214 156; Str Stadion; ☷ 10am-5pm Tue-Sun; admission €0.50) has a photographic exhibition on the life and works of Brâncuşi.

Brâncuşi's most famed sculpture, the **Endless Column** (Coloana Fără Sfârşit), endowed to the town in 1937, sits at the eastern end of Calea Eroilor. The 29.35m-tall structure, threaded with 15 steel beads, is considered as much a triumph of engineering as of modern art. According to New York–based World Monuments Fund it ranks as one of the planet's top 100 works. Standing right underneath it is where his synthesis of heaven and physicality meet, with the column seemingly rising ad infinitum. The column was restored in 2000 at a cost of €4 million.

In front of the Elvira Godeanu Drama Theatre (below) stands a **statue** of Brâncuşi, armed with his sculpting chisel.

The **Gorj County Museum** (Muzeul Judeţean Gorj; ☎ 212 044; Str Geneva 8; ☷ 10am-5pm Tue-Sun; admission €0.25), which gained its name in 1996 after the city of Geneva presented Târgu Jiu with the **trio of clocks** that stand in front of the **statue** of Tudor Vladimirescu.

Sleeping

Gorj Tourism books rooms (about €10) in private homes.

Hotel Sport (☎ 214 402; s/d €15/18) This is the town's cheapest option. It's behind the stadium, off B-dul Constantin Brâncuşi.

Hotel Parc (☎ 215 981; B-dul Constantin Brâncuşi 10; r €35, t €46) After a renovation this place now sparkles with Romanian grandeur.

Hotel Gorj (☎ 214 814; Calea Eroilor 6; s/d €22/30) Only stay in the renovated rooms here, as the unrenovated rooms are substandard and have little running water.

Eating

Choice is limited in Târgu Jiu and often hotels are the best bet for a hearty meal. Hotel Parc has the cleanest and nicest dining.

Lider Restaurant (☎ 219 002; Calea Eroilor 11; mains €5) This place serves perennially popular pizza. The **Enigma** bar downstairs is packed at weekends.

Deli Pat Patisserie (Calea Eroilor) Next door to Lider, this place is handy for a quick cup of coffee and a creamy cake.

Terasa Restaurant (Calea Victoriei) This spot, behind Hotel Gorj, is famed for its *mititei* (spicy meatballs). Wash them down with local beer served on tap.

Stock up on fresh fruit and vegetables at the **central market** (Str Unirii), at the southern end of Central Park.

Entertainment

Open-air concerts and theatrical performances are held in summer at the **open-air theatre** (Str Vasile Alecsandri 53). Close by is the **Elvira Godeanu Drama Theatre** (Teatrul Dramatic Elvira Godeanu; ☎ 216 494; cnr Str Stadion & Str Confederaţiei).

Getting There & Away
BUS

The **bus station** (☎ 243 339; Str N Titulescu 5) is 100m south of the train station. A major service runs from here to Bucharest (257km, one daily) via Piteşti (174km) and Petroşani (57km).

Maxitaxi services run from the bus station to Timişoara (€7, four daily), Cluj-Napoca (€5, one daily), Alba Iulia (€4, one daily), Baia Mare (two daily), Drobeta-Turnu Severin (two daily) and Orşova (two daily).

TRAIN

The **Agenţie de Voiaj CFR** (☎ 211 924; Str Unirii, Block 2; ☺ 7am-7pm Mon-Fri) sells advance tickets.

From Târgu Jiu there are fast trains to Craiova (€3, three hours, four daily), Bucharest (€5.50, five hours, four daily) and Timişoara (€5.50, four daily). Northbound to Petroşani (1¼ to 1¾ hours), there are three local trains and one *accelerat* daily.

WEST FROM TÂRGU JIU

The village of **Runcu**, 16km west of Târgu Jiu, is the site of the large **folk art and crafts fair** (Simpozion Satul Românesc Traditional) held every year during the last weekend in August. Continuing west, turn left 1km before Peştişani and follow the dirt track for a couple of kilometres until you reach **Hobiţa**, the birthplace of Constantin Brâncuşi. The sculptor lived in the village until the age of 10 and the tiny cottage in which he spent his childhood years now houses a small museum dedicated to the artist.

Some 20km further west is **Tismana Monastery** (Mănăstirea Tismana; 1375), one of Romania's oldest monasteries and an important centre for Slavonic writing. The original monastery was founded by monk and calligrapher Nicodim in a small stone church, later to be grandly rebuilt in 1508 by Wallachian prince Radu cel Mare. The region west beyond Tismana is a major karst area in the southwestern Carpathians, providing intrepid explorers with countless caves. In **Padeş**, there is a stone pyramid monument constructed in 1921 to mark the spot where Craiovan-born revolutionary Tudor Vladimirescu (1780–1821) issued his 'Proclamation of Padeş' on 4 February 1821. In his proclamation, Vladimirescu, who later died at the hands of the Turks, called for the 'evil ones' ruining the country to be disposed of, leading to a series of uprisings against Ottoman rule in 1821.

Some 10km southwest of Padeş is the **Ponoâre Nature Reservation**, a protected lilac forest stretching for some 8 hectares. Each spring, a **folk festival** is held to mark the blossoming of the trees.

DROBETA-TURNU SEVERIN

☎ 252 / pop 115,000

Drobeta-Turnu Severin is on the bank of the Danube (Dunărea) River bordering Yugoslavia. Though of ancient origin, the present town was laid out in the 19th century when its port was built. It's best known for the Iron Gates Museum's incredible scale model of the old Roman bridge that spanned the Danube to Yugoslavia.

Orientation

From the train station, walk up to B-dul Republicii (B-dul Carol I). Follow this road east for 600m or so to Hotel Continental Parc, at the intersection of Str Bibiescu. The town centre lies one block north of here. The bus station is at the eastern end of Str Brâncoveanu.

Information

Banca Comercială Română (cnr Str Coştescu & Str Aurelian; ☺ 8.30am-5.30pm Mon-Fri, 8.30am-12.30pm Sat) has an ATM, currency exchange and facilities for money transfers and travellers cheques.

The **post office** (Str Decebal 41; ☺ 7am-8pm Mon-Fri, 8am-1pm Sat) is adjacent to the **telephone office** (☺ 8am-8pm Mon-Fri, 8am-2pm Sat).

Sights

The **Iron Gates Museum** (Muzeul Porţilor de Fier; ☎ 325 922; B-dul Republicii; ☺ 9am-5pm Tue-Sun; adult/child/student €0.50/0.25/0.25) is housed in the former Trajan school for girls, dating from 1922. The museum was opened the day before the 1972 unveiling of the mammoth Porţile de Fier hydroelectric power station, 10km to the west. It contains a fine exhibition on the natural history of the Danube.

Other sections of the museum cover history, ethnography, astrology, popular art, the evolution of man, and archaeology. Particularly impressive is the scale model of the Roman bridge constructed across the Danube in AD 103 by the Syrian architect Apollodor of Damascus, on the orders of the Roman emperor Trajan. The **Trajan Bridge** stood just below the site of the present museum, and the ruins (*ruinele podului lui Traian*) of two of its pillars can

WALLACHIA

still be seen towering beside the Danube. Northeast of the bridge ruins lie the remnants of **Castrul Drobeta**, a 2nd- to 6th-century Roman fort built to protect the bridge.

West of the castle ruins, also in the museum grounds, are the ruins of the 16th-century medieval **Severin Church** (Biserica Mitropoliei Severinului), including the remains of the crypt that lies protected beneath glass.

In the basement of the Iron Gates Museum is a dingy **aquarium** displaying various fish species prevalent in the Danube, including the giant Somnul fish.

At the southern end of the town's main square, check out the huge metal **fountain**. It has 'arms' that spray water as they rotate and draws the crowds each night.

Eleven kilometres north of Drobeta is **Topolniţa Cave** (Peştera Topolniţa), which ranks among the largest caves in the world (more than 10,000m long on four levels).

Sleeping & Eating

Hotel Continental Parc (☎ 312 851/52; B-dul Republicii 2; s/d €35/50) This place has the monopoly on clean, comfy rooms but it's largely deserted. The restaurant offers a cheap, tasty menu with fish, meat and vegetable dishes and has a shady terrace overlooking the park. Drobeta-Turnu Severin's social life revolves around the hotel, and there's an outside bar and café which is packed in summer.

Aurora (Str Bibiescu) is a café/bar with a covered pavement terrace; there's a small delicatessen adjacent. The opening times vary according to how the owners feel on the day!

For fresh fruit and vegetables, head to the **Hala Radu-Negru indoor market** (Str Coştescu), near Str Unirii.

Getting There & Away

BUS

From Drobeta-Turnu Severin there is a service to Porţile de Fier (25 minutes, daily at 1.30pm).

Maxitaxis depart from the bus station. There's a service running to and from Craiova and Băile Herculane which stops at Drobeta-Turnu Severin (daily at 3.45pm except Sunday).

A private bus (€8, pay the driver) departs daily from outside the Drobeta-Turnu Severin train station to Negotin and Pojarevat in Yugoslavia. Theoretically the bus is sched-uled to leave at midnight. In reality, it leaves when full. Return buses from Negotin and Pojarevat also depart for Drobeta-Turnu Severin when they are full.

TRAIN

Book tickets at the **Agenţie de Voiaj CFR** (☎ 313 117; Str Decebal 43; ☉ 7am-7.30pm Mon-Fri).

Most fast trains between Bucharest and Timişoara stop here. Services include those to Bucharest (€9, five hours, 10 daily), Craiova (€5, 1½ to 2½ hours, 10 daily), Timişoara (€9, 3½ hours, nine daily), Băile Herculane (€3, one hour, nine daily) and Orşova (25 minutes, four daily). In summer there are trains to Constanţa (€15, six hours, two daily).

IRON GATES, ORŞOVA & THE CAZAN GORGES

The infamous **Iron Gates** (Portile de Fier) at Gura Văii tower above the Danube 10km west of Drobeta-Turnu Severin. This monstrous, concrete hydroelectric power station was a Romanian-Hungarian joint venture, conceived in 1960 and completed 12 years later. On top of the dam wall runs the road linking Romania to Yugoslavia (see p191).

An area of 115,000 hectares around the power station has been conserved as the **Iron Gates National Park** to protect the flora and fauna of the region. A similar venture, the **Djerdap National Park**, was created across the river in Yugoslavia.

The Porţile de Fier at Gura Văii stand on the site of **Old Orşova** (Orşova Veche), one of 13 settlements to be swallowed up by the artificial lake, created to curb this treacherous stretch of the Danube.

New Orşova (Orşova Nouă) lies 15km upstream of Gura Văii. Between Gura Văii and **Comarnic**, a village 2km north of New Orşova, the railway is said to cross 56 viaducts and bridges and go through nine tunnels. A further 15km upstream are the spectacular **Cazan Gorges** (Cazanele Mici and Cazanele Mari).

Sleeping

Motel Continental (☎ 252-329 235) About 12km east of Drobeta-Turnu Severin on the E752 to Băile Herculane, is this convenient stopping point for motorists heading to/from Yugoslavia.

Getting There & Away

BUS

There is a service to Porțile de Fier from Drobeta-Turnu Severin (25 minutes, daily at 1.30pm). The daily maxitaxi to/from Băile Herculane and Drobeta-Turnu Severin stops in Orşova.

TRAIN

Fast trains to/from Drobeta-Turnu Severin stop at Orşova (four daily).

CRAIOVA

☎ 251 / pop 315,000

The university town of Craiova, founded on the site of the Dacian stronghold of Pelendava, prides itself on its strong academic tradition and the wealth of prominent characters who have passed through on their journey to stardom: Wallachian prince Mihai Viteazul was born here, the world-famous sculptor Constantin Brâncuşi carved his first sculptures from scrap wooden crates in the town, and the first cartridge fountain pen was invented by Craiovan-born Petrache Poenaru (1799–1875). Today, Craiova is better known as the source of Craiova beer!

Prior to the war in Yugoslavia, IAR93 subsonic jet fighter-bombers were manufactured in Craiova for the Romanian and Yugoslav airforces. Production ground to a halt in 1992, however, after the UN imposed trade sanctions against Yugoslavia. Workers at the plant blocked the Craiova–Piteşti highway with a military plane in mid-1997 in a desperate bid to get their jobs guaranteed.

Following the outbreak of the conflict in Kosovo in 1999, UN sanctions against Yugoslavia were widened. With the conflict's end and the change of Yugoslav government, trade sanctions were finally lifted in late 2000.

Orientation

The northern bus station (Autogară Nord), from which buses to/from most other towns arrive/depart, is next to the train station, 1km northeast of the centre on B-dul Carol I (B-dul Republicii). Bus No 1 runs from the train station to the centre and the northern bus station. There are no buses to the southern bus station (Autogară Sud); a taxi from the centre should cost no more than €1.50.

Information

MONEY

Banca Comercială Română (cnr Calea Unirii & Str Alexandru Ioan Cuza; 🕒 8.30am-5.30pm Mon-Fri) Cashes travellers cheques, gives cash advances and has an ATM.

TTC currency exchange (Str Olteț 1; 🕒 9am-8pm Mon-Sat)

POST & TELEPHONE

Central Post Office (cnr B-dul Stirbei Vodă & Calea Unirii; 🕒 7.30am-7pm Mon-Fri, 8am-1pm Sat) **Telephone Office** (Calea Unirii 69; 🕒 7.30am-7pm)

TOURIST INFORMATION

Mapamond Agenție de Turism (☎ 415 071/73; travel@mapamond.ro; Str Olteț 2-4; 🕒 8am-8pm Mon-Fri, 9am-2pm Sat, to 7pm Oct-May) Friendly, English-speaking staff hand out maps and guides and are agents for Antrec.

Sights

ART MUSEUM

The **museum** (Muzeul de Artă; ☎ 412 342; Calea Unirii; 🕒 10am-5pm Tue-Sun; admission €0.30) is the town's treasure, with an incredible collection of Brâncuşi's finest works, including *The Kiss*, *The Thigh* and *Miss Pogany*. The museum is housed in the Dinu Mihail Palace, built from 1900 to 1907 by the wealthy Romanian nobleman Constantin Dinu Mihail and was home to former Polish president Ignacy Moscicki in 1939 and later to Ceauşescu. The room of mirrors is worth the trip to Craiova alone.

HISTORIC CENTRE

Overlooking Calea Unirii, in the central square, is a **statue** of Mihai Viteazul who was born in Craiova. To its eastern side is the **prefecture**, bearing a memorial plaque to Craiova's victims of the 1989 revolution.

The **Natural History Museum** (☎ 419 435; Str Popa Şapcă 4; 🕒 10am-5pm Tue-Sun; admission €0.30) has a tiny display of natural oddities. In the park opposite is the red-brick **Holy Trinity Church** (Biserica Sfânta Treime). Behind the church is the city's **Opera & Operetta Theatre** (Str Ion Marinescu), a former school which was a revolutionary hide-out during June 1848.

Craiova's old town lies east of Calea Unirii around Piața Veche (Old Square). An excellent **Ethnographic Museum** (Muzeul Olteniei Secția de Etnografie; 🕒 10am-5pm Tue-Sun; admission €0.25), housed in a former governor's house dating from 1699, stands on Str Hala at

WALLACHIA

WALLACHIA

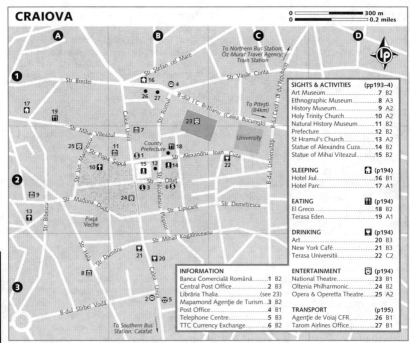

CRAIOVA

SIGHTS & ACTIVITIES	(pp193–4)
Art Museum	7 B2
Ethnographic Museum	8 A3
History Museum	9 A2
Holy Trinity Church	10 A2
Natural History Museum	11 B2
Prefecture	12 B2
St Hramul's Church	13 A2
Statue of Alexandra Cuza	14 B2
Statue of Mihai Viteazul	15 B2

SLEEPING	(p194)
Hotel Jiul	16 B1
Hotel Parc	17 A1

EATING	(p194)
El Greco	18 B2
Terasa Eden	19 A1

DRINKING	(p194)
Art	20 B3
New York Café	21 B3
Terasa Universitii	22 C2

ENTERTAINMENT	(p194)
National Theatre	23 B1
Oltenia Philharmonic	24 B2
Opera & Operetta Theatre	25 A2

TRANSPORT	(p195)
Agenţie de Voiaj CFR	26 B1
Tarom Airlines Office	27 B1

INFORMATION	
Banca Comercială Română	1 B2
Central Post Office	2 B3
Librăria Thalia	(see 23)
Mapamond Agenţie de Turism	3 B2
Post Office	4 B1
Telephone Centre	5 B3
TTC Currency Exchange	6 B2

the end of Str Dimitru. Displayed inside **St Hramul's Church** (1928) is the Madona Dudu icon said to perform miracles for those who pray in front of it.

Sleeping

Mapamond (p193) arranges rooms for €10 a night in private homes in surrounding villages.

Hotel Parc (☎ 417 257; Str Bibescu 16; s/d €26/30) Clean pleasant rooms set in lavish, abundant gardens.

Hotel Jiul (☎ 414 166; www.jiul.ro; Calea Bucureşti 1-2; s/d €25/35) This place is larger than Hotel Parc and popular with business travellers.

Eating

Cultural Craiova is not a culinary hot spot – try these or rely on your hotel restaurant for sustenance.

El Greco (☎ 416 549; Str Al Cuza 9; ☺ 9am-1am; mains €3-5) Proper pizza served with creamy milkshakes and excellent spaghetti dishes.

Terasa Eden (Calea Unirii; mains €3) Shady outdoor bar serving meat dishes, Romanian staples and passable pizzas.

Entertainment

BARS

Terasa Universitatii (Str Al Cuza) Opposite the University, this bar is packed night and day with students and is a noisy and fun hang-out.

New York Café (☎ 419 198; Calea Unirii) Sink back in one of the many comfortable black lounges and enjoy your favourite drink.

Art (Calea Unirii) Not far away from New York Café is this popular cellar bar.

THEATRE & CLASSICAL MUSIC

Highly recommended are performances at the impressive **National Theatre** (Teatrul Naţional; Calea Bucureşti) and the **Opera & Operetta Theatre** (Teatrul de Operă şi Operată; Str Ion Marinescu 12). Tickets for both are sold at the **Agenţia Teatrală** (☎ 413 755; ☺ 10am-12.30pm & 4-6.30pm), adjoining the main National Theatre building.

Classical concerts are performed by the **Oltenia Philharmonic** (Filarmonica Oltenia; Calea Unirii). The **ticket office** (☎ 411 284; ☺ 10am-1pm & 4-7pm) is inside the main Philharmonic building.

Getting There & Away

AIR

Craiova Airport (☎ 411 112; E70, Craiova–Bucureşti km 3)

Tarom (☎ 411 049; Piaţa Unirii, Complex Unirea)

BUS

The **northern bus station** (Autogară Nord; ☎ 411 187; Str Argeş 13), next to the train station, is where the main daily services depart. Maxi-taxis leave from here to Bucharest (€5, every 30 minutes), Piteşti (€2, two daily) and Calafat (€2, two daily). State buses run scant services to Râmnicu Vâlcea and Târgu Jiu.

Murat travel agency (☎ 414 434), outside the northern bus station, runs a bus to Istanbul via Bucharest, departing at 10.30am daily except Saturday (€75 return).

The **southern bus station** (Autogară Sud; ☎ 428 065; Str N Romanescu), 5km south of town, runs rural routes around Craiova.

TRAIN

Book tickets at the **Agenţie de Voiaj CFR** (☎ 411 634; Complex Unirea; 🕒 7am-7.30pm Mon-Fri).

All fast trains between Bucharest and Timişoara stop at Craiova's **train station** (B-dul Carol I/B-dul Republicii). Services include trains to Bucharest (€9, three hours, 12 daily), Timişoara (€10, five hours, seven daily), Calafat (2½ hours, five daily), Budapest (€40, two daily) and Belgrade (€33, one daily).

CALAFAT

☎ 251

The small town of Calafat, on the Danube opposite Vidin in Bulgaria, makes a convenient entry/exit point to/from Bulgaria. Car ferries cross the river hourly and there are frequent local trains to/from Craiova, from where you can catch a fast train on to Bucharest or Timişoara.

For cashing cheques and money withdrawals, there's a **Banca Commercială Română** (☎ 230 661; Str 1 Decembrie 3).

If you have some spare time, visit the **Art Museum** (Muzeul de Artă; Str 22 Decembrie) and the **monument** to the 1877–78 War of Independence against the Turks.

The ferry landing is in the centre of Calafat, about four blocks from the train station.

There are local trains to/from Craiova (107km, 2½ hours, five daily). If you're continuing on to Bucharest or elsewhere, buy a ticket for your final destination and, as soon as you reach Craiova, go into the train station and purchase a compulsory seat reservation for your onward express train.

The car ferry to Bulgaria crosses the Danube here (€13 plus an additional €2 per person in cash only, 30 minutes, hourly). Cars can spend several hours waiting to cross but pedestrians can avoid the queues and walk on in both directions.

In March 2000, after almost a decade of negotiations, the Romanian and Bulgarian governments agreed on the construction of a new bridge here over the Danube River (although Romania wanted the bridge to be built further east). The €155 million bridge, funded by the Bulgarian government and the European Union, will connect Calafat with the Bulgarian city of Vidin.

GIURGIU

☎ 246

A typical dusty border town, Giurgiu is the main route from Bucharest to Bulgaria. Trains rumble across the 4km-long bridge that spans the Danube River, while motorists cross via the ferries into Ruse.

Orientation & Information

Giurgiu's train and bus stations are five minutes' walk from the centre. Exit the station and walk up Str Gării to the main street. Giurgiu's northern train station (Giurgiu Nord) is 5km out of town; local trains run between the two train stations. Most trains heading for Bulgaria depart from the northern station.

The post office and central market are on Str Constantin Brâncoveanu. Turn right at the bridge crossing, then right onto Str Constantin Brâncoveanu. To get to the centre from here, turn left onto the main street.

Sleeping & Eating

Hotel Steaua Dunării (☎ 217 270; Str Mihai Viteazul 1; s/d €12/16) Without being rude, Giurgiu's only (semi)functional hotel is dated, expensive and desolate. But if you're desperate, it's next to the main (Ro-Ro boat) ferry terminal.

La Perla & Terasa Ana (mains €5) Helping to while away those hours waiting for a ferry is this decent, clean restaurant with a nice terrace overlooking the Danube. It's next to the smaller ferry port.

Getting There & Away

BOAT

The main ferry terminal for Ro-Ro boat arrivals and departures is next to Hotel Steaua Dunării (€5 per car plus a €1 tax as it's a private road). The crossing from Giurgiu to Ruse takes 20 minutes; boats leave when full so there's no timetable and it runs 24 hours.

Cheaper and quicker, with smaller queues, is the *bac* (ferry) which departs from the main port/harbour; follow the signs to the port from the centre of town (€5 per car plus an additional €1 for every passenger). The crossing takes 10 minutes and the ferry operates 24 hours, departing when full.

CAR & MOTORCYCLE

The main E70 highway from Bucharest to Giurgiu leads directly to the bridge crossing, signposted 'Punctul de frontieră Giurgiu'. Toll tickets are sold at the two white kiosks in the centre of the road to the bridge as you approach the customs control zone. It's €7 per car and €2 per motorbike or bicycle. A compulsory €10 ecological tax is levied by the Bulgarian authorities.

TRAIN

Most Giurgiu–Ruse trains (4km, every 15 minutes) depart from the northern train station.

The daily *Bosfor* train to Istanbul from Bucharest passes through the northern train station at 3.32pm, and leaves in the other direction on its way to Bucharest at 3.30pm. The daily *Bulgaria Expres* from Bucharest stops at Giurgiu at 9.33pm, and leaves on its way to Bucharest at 4.50am. The daily *Transbalkan* train from Bucharest stops at the northern train station at 1.35pm, and leaves for Bucharest at 5.56pm.

CĂLĂRAŞI, OSTROV & AROUND

Industrial Călăraşi offers yet another exit point. A ferry crosses the Danube to Ostrov (still in Romania) from where you can cross into Silistra in Bulgaria.

For travellers on foot this is the only place to cross – you're not permitted to cross at Giurgiu without transport. The crossing is 8km south of Călăraşi, and is served by a maxitaxi (€0.50).

The ferry takes cars (€4), motorbikes (€1.50) and foot passengers (€0.30); tickets are sold at the small green hut. It takes 30 minutes and the ferry generally operates between 6am and 7pm daily, but sometimes goes 24 hours, departing when full. In summer services can be disrupted if the level of the Danube is low.

Once in Ostrov you can continue east to the Black Sea coast, or cross the border into Silistra. As you come off the ferry a one-way street leads you directly to the customs control point. Continuing past the border control, the eastbound road to Dobrogea follows the Romanian/Bulgarian border for a further 200m.

Ostrov village proper is 5km east of the ferry terminal and border crossing. From here, for some 15km, the eastbound road follows the twists and turns of the magnificent Danube River, making it one of the most scenic drives in Romania. This majestic riverside stretch peaks at the **Derveni Monastery** (Mănăstirea Derveni), which overlooks Lake Bugeaculi, south of the Danube. The road continues east into northern Dobrogea.

Northern Dobrogea

CONTENTS

Northern Dobrogea is a kingdom unto itself within Romania. Lacking what have become Romanian icons (mountains, wooden churches, Draculas), the land between the Danube River (Râul Dunărea) and the Black Sea (Marea Neagră) is enveloped in its own sweet mysteries. The 193.5km sea border provides a *litoral* (coast) that's a magnet for beach bums, sun-worshippers and party animals. Yet those seeking waterfront seclusion, archaeological digs and swarms of exotic birds won't be disappointed, either.

Many Romanians consider this region of the country the least typically 'Romanian'. Odd, as it is mainly here where Romania's much-vaunted ties with ancient Rome can be felt, thanks to a wealth of ancient treasure. Statues, busts, sarcophagi and other archaeological finds are so numerous, you'll see them casually lying around in parks and squares, particularly in Constanța and Mangalia. The region is likely considered to be 'other' partially as it's the country's most ethnically diverse. Sizeable Turkish, Tatar, Bulgarian, Ukrainian and Lippovani/Old Believer settlements add to the mix, giving the area a refreshing burst of multiculturalism.

Despite history and culture, marine life rules supreme here. For a 65km stretch south of Mamaia, that life takes the form of beach resort towns which erupt in an orgy of sun-lovers, nudists, curative mud feasts and blaring discos. It's one big outdoor party. The Danube Delta to the north is another world entirely, attracting bird-lovers and seekers of peace and solitude. Here a fantastic, tangled web of ever-eroding canals, riverbeds and wetlands in Europe's second-largest delta boasts remote fishing villages, stretches of deserted beach and pelicans galore.

TOP FIVE

- Learn the ins and outs of beach bumming anywhere around **Mamaia** (p207)

- Find out why stinky, sulphurous mud in **Eforie Nord** (p209) is good to slap onto your naked body

- Relive ancient Rome in **Histria** (p215) or **Adamclisi** (p214)

- Hear yourself scream: 'Look! Pelicans!' in the canals and lakes of the **Danube Delta** (p215)

- Visit a traditional fishing village such as **Sfântu Gheorghe** (p222) or **Jurilovca** (p223) in the delta

POPULATION: 1.01 MILLION   AREA: 15,570 SQ KM   AVERAGE MONTHLY WAGE: €58

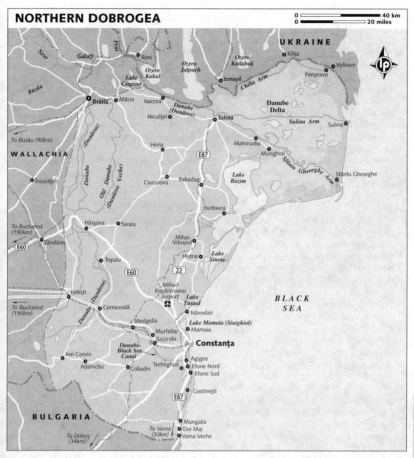

NORTHERN DOBROGEA

NORTHERN DOBROGEA

History
In 1878 Northern Dobrogea became part of Romania when a combined Russo-Romanian army defeated the Turks in Bulgaria. Southern Dobrogea was ceded to Bulgaria.

In antiquity the Dobrogea region was colonised first by the Greeks and then by the Romans, both of whom left behind much for visitors to admire. Histria, 70km north of Constanța, is the oldest Greek settlement in Romania, founded in 657 BC. From AD 46, Dobrogea was the Roman province of Moesia Inferior. At Adamclisi (Tropaeum Traiani) the Romans scored a decisive victory over the Geto-Dacian tribes, making possible their expansion into regions north of the Danube. Dobrogea later fell under Byzantine control, and in 1418 was conquered by the Turks.

Once Romanian flags flew over Dobrogea, much was done to integrate it to the 'mainland' as soon as possible, and with the completion of the formidable bridge over the Danube at Cernavodă (1895), a vital rail link was established between Constanța and the capital. At this time, the coast started to develop as a summer leisure destination; to this day, summer tourism is the backbone of the region's economy.

Ecology
LITORAL BEACHES
There are no Blue Flag beaches here, though this is more a matter of bureaucracy and

finance than cleanliness. Four are currently in assessment for receiving the rating and many others meet the 27 criteria. Beaches in northern Mamaia are judged to be quite clean and the ones closer to the Bulgarian border benefit from good water circulation. The beaches in southern Mamaia are among the least clean of the *litoral* – they are overcrowded and several big hotels discharge used pool water here. Beaches at Eforie Nord and Costineşti still have no wastewater management system, though they will soon be in place thanks to EU funding.

Fifteen first-aid points were set up along the coast in 2003, staffed by volunteers, ensuring greater beach safety. Some 50 lifeguards are on duty in Mamaia alone.

Generally, swimming in the Black Sea is pleasant: there are no undercurrents to worry about, the sands are fine and golden, and water salinity is a decent 17%.

Mare Nostrum (☎ 241-831 099; mare-nostrum@cier.ro; B-dul Mamaia 296) is a nongovernmental organisation (NGO) dedicated to promoting ecotourism and a greater awareness of environmental issues in the area, including actively working to keep the beaches and waters clean.

GESS (☎ 241-756 422; gess@dial.kappa.ro) is an ecological group headquartered in Mangalia whose mandate is to study ecology, marine biology and cave biology, as well as to promote awareness of ecological issues. It's an excellent source of information about these matters; diving options along the coast; and the Movile cave, in which GESS was directly involved in the discoveries made there (p213).

DANUBE DELTA

The delta's ecosystems have been much maligned by humans, starting with the shortening of the Sulina canal at the end of the 19th century. In the decades following, dozens of small canals were dug throughout the region in an attempt to increase fish stocks and to facilitate transport. Large-scale frenzied reed cutting during the communist period disturbed the natural filtering process that reeds have for the river as well as unbalancing the habitat for birds, fish and insects. In addition to this, dams were built, which destroyed bird nesting grounds; sections of the delta were drained for agriculture; and exotic birds were hunted. Human

meddling has changed the delta forever. Whereas in the early 1900s there were 10 to 15 million birds in the region, there are now under half a million.

Many strides have been made in the last decade. Pollution has been reduced and reed cutting has been vastly curbed. Ecotourism is continuing to develop as tourist options become more eco-friendly.

The headquarters of the **Danube Delta Biosphere Reserve** (DDBR; ☎ 240-518 945; arbdd@ddbra.ro; Str Portului 34A) is in Tulcea. The **Danube Delta Research Institute** (☎ 240-524 550; www.indd.tim.ro; Str Babadag 165), also in Tulcea, is a good source of information.

CONSTANŢA

☎ 241 / pop 337,200

If all port cities have an air of mystery, Constanţa's comes in blustery gusts. Romania's largest port and third-largest city evokes romantic notions of ancient seafarers, the Roman poet Ovid and even the classic legend of Jason and the Argonauts (they fled here from King Aietes). Constanţa's original name Tomis means 'cut to pieces', in reference to Jason's beloved Medea, who cut up her brother Apsyrtus and threw the pieces into the sea near the present-day city.

Emperor Constantine fortified and developed the city and later renamed it after his sister. By the 8th century the city had been destroyed by invading Slavs and Avars. After Constanţa was taken by Romania in 1877, the town grew in importance, with a railway line being built to it from Bucharest. By the early 1900s it was a fashionable seaside resort frequented by European royalty.

The city beaches are less popular (and more polluted) than those in the resorts to the north and south, and the city itself can seem devoid of people even in mid-summer, as party-goers head to where the action is. However, the city offers a bit of everything: beaches, a picturesque Old Town, archeological treasures and a peaceful Mediterranean air with the charm of dilapidated Venice back alleys. Its few excellent museums can be seen in an afternoon.

Constanţa hosts the annual **National Romanian Folk Festival** at the beginning of August. **Constanţa Days** are held on or around May 21; these city days see concerts and general merry-making taking over the city.

Orientation

Constanţa's train station and main southern bus station (Autogară Sud) are 1.5km west of the old town. The northern bus station (Autogară Nord), serving destinations north towards the delta, is 3km north of the centre, on Str Soveja.

Most facilities are on the main artery, B-dul Tomis, which runs from the new town in the north to the old town and towards the port in the south. The semipedestrianised Str Ştefan cel Mare is another main thoroughfare, the main focus of which is the large Tomis Department Store.

MAPS & PUBLICATIONS

There are few good maps of the city. The best of the lot, published by Amco Press, includes a city map, maps of all the resorts, and shows public transport routes. It costs €1.90 and is available in bookstores, major hotels and travel agencies.

The free English and German magazine *What Where When Constanţa* (www.bucurestiwww.ro) contains helpful listings and news articles and can be found at most hotels, as can both *Best of Constanţa*, a free monthly listings booklet, and the weekly Romanian-language *Seara de Seara* (www.searadeseara.ro), which is the most comprehensive listings booklet for all the hot spots between Mamaia and Vama Veche.

Info Litoral (see Tourist Information on p203) publishes the excellent *Cultural Tourist Guide Dobrogea* (€2.65). This is a highly worthwhile guide in English and German that is chock-full of history, practical listings, suggested itineraries and resort maps.

Information

BOOKSHOPS

Librăria Mihai Eminescu (Map p202; ☎ 614 658; Str Ştefan cel Mare 47) Has a decent selection of maps and dictionaries.

Librăria Sophia (Map p202; ☎ 616 365; Dragoş Vodă 13) The best bookshop for English- and French-language books.

CONSULATES

Russian Consulate (Map p202; ☎ 615 168; Str Mihai Viteazul 5)

Turkish Consulate (Map p201; ☎ 611 135; B-dul Ferdinand 82)

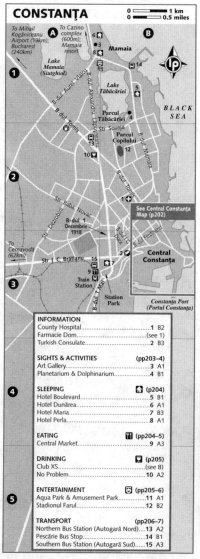

CONSTANŢA

Chinese Consulate (☎ 617 833; B-dul Carpaţi 7)

CULTURAL CENTRES & LIBRARIES

The **British Council** (Map p202; ☎ 618 365; Str Mircea cel Bătrân 104A; ⏰ 2-8pm Mon, Wed & Fri, 9am-3pm Tue & Thu) runs a small library located inside the Biblioteca Judeţeană Constanţa (district library).

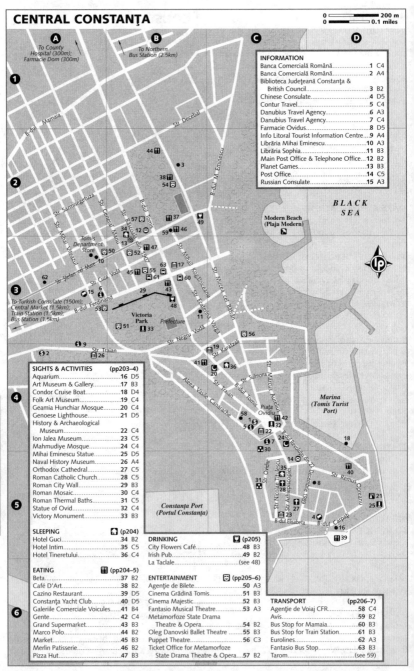

CENTRAL CONSTANŢA

0 — 200 m
0 — 0.1 miles

INFORMATION
Banca Comercială Română..............1 C4
Banca Comercială Română..............2 A4
Biblioteca Judeţeană Constanţa &
  British Council..........................3 B2
Chinese Consulate.......................4 D5
Contur Travel............................5 C4
Danubius Travel Agency..................6 A3
Danubius Travel Agency..................7 C4
Farmacie Ovidus.........................8 D5
Info Litoral Tourist Information Centre...9 A4
Librăria Mihai Eminescu.................10 A3
Librăria Sophia.........................11 B3
Main Post Office & Telephone Office.....12 B2
Planet Games...........................13 B3
Post Office............................14 C5
Russian Consulate......................15 A3

BLACK
SEA

Modern Beach
(Plaja Modern)

Marina
(Tomis Turist
Port)

Constanţa Port
(Portul Constanţa)

To County
Hospital (300m);
Farmacie Dom (300m)

To Northern
Bus Station (2.5km)

To Turkish Consulate (150m);
Central Market (1.5km);
Train Station (1.5km);
Bus Station (1.5km)

Tomis
Department
Store

Victoria
Park

Prefecture

Str. Traian

Piaţa
Ovidiu

B-dul Elisabeta

INTERNET ACCESS

You can access the Internet at **Planet Games** (Map p202; ☎ 552 377; cnr Str Ştefan cel Mare & Str Răscoala din 1907; per hour €0.50; ☺ 24hr).

MEDICAL SERVICES

County Hospital (Map p201; Spitalul Judetean; ☎ 662 222; B-dul Tomis 145)

Farmacie Dom (Map p201; ☎ 519 800; B-dul Tomis 146; ☺ 24hr)

Farmacie Ovidus (Map p202; ☎ 614 576 B-dul Revoluţiei 22; ☺ 8am-7.30pm Mon-Fri, 8am-1pm Sat) This is just off Str Remus Opreanu.

MONEY

Most hotels and travel agencies have exchange outlets, and there are numerous exchange offices, several of which are open around the clock, lining B-dul Tomis south of B-dul Ferdinand.

Banca Comercială Română (Map p202; ☎ 638 200; Str Traian 1; ☺ 8.30am-5.30pm Mon-Fri & 8.30am-12.30pm Sat) changes travellers cheques (1% commission), gives unlimited cash advances on Visa and MasterCard and has an ATM. There's another **branch** (Map p202; Str Traian 68), which has the same opening hours.

POST & TELEPHONE

The main **post office** (Map p202; ☎ 552 222; B-dul Tomis 79-81; ☺ 8.30am-8pm Mon-Fri, 8.30am-1pm Sat) and **telephone office** (Map p202; B-dul Tomis 79-81; ☺ 8.30am-10pm) share the same building.

TOURIST INFORMATION

Info Litoral Tourist Information Centre (Map p202; ☎ 555 000; www.infolitoral.ro; Str Traian 36, Scara C, Apt 31; ☺ 9am-5pm Mon-Fri) This is a highly recommended first stop – the friendly, well-informed staff will help answer any kind of questions; enter from behind the building. It also sells maps and booklets.

Contur Travel (Map p202; ☎ 619 777; www.contur.ro; Piaţa Ovidiu 14 Block B; ☺ 9am-5pm Mon-Fri) A truly helpful, multilingual bunch, Contur's speciality is developing tailor-made tourist circuits around the coast, the delta and elsewhere. It can also get you discounts in some hotels.

Danubius (Map p202; ☎ 615 836; excursion@danubius .ro; B-dul Ferdinand 36; ☺ 9am-7pm Mon-Fri, 9am-2pm Sat) Though it mainly deals with groups, it can also handle individual bookings. In a group, a day-trip to Histria will cost about €65; otherwise, a half-day trip to Histria for up to three people will cost €100. Its second office (Map p202; ☎ 619 039; Piaţa Ovidiu 11) has the same opening hours but only sells airline tickets.

Sights

Constanţa's most renowned attraction is the **History & Archaeological Museum** (Map p202; ☎ 618 763; Piaţa Ovidiu 12; admission adult/child €0.50/0.25; ☺ 9am-8pm Jun-Sep, 10am-6pm Tue-Sun Oct-May). There's something here for everyone. The kids will like the bones of a 2nd-century woman and the mammoth tusks; otherwise there are many 2nd-century Roman statues (discovered under the old train station in 1962) and 4th century Roman coins. The centrepiece is the fantastic 2nd-century serpent Glykon, which is carved from a single block of marble. Most displays have English and/or French explanation panels.

Roman archaeological fragments spill over onto the surrounding square. Behind the museum is the 3rd-century **Roman mosaic** (Edificiul Roman cu Mozaic; Map p202; admission adult/child €0.50/0.25; ☺ 9am-8pm Jun-Sep, 10am-6pm Tue-Sun Oct-May), discovered in 1959 and believed to have housed a commercial building. A staircase led from the museum's lower terrace to the Roman public **thermal baths** (Map p202), at the southern end of the cliff. Parts of its foundation remains today and are best viewed from Aleea Vasile Canarache.

The **statue of Ovid** (1887; Map p202; Piaţa Ovidiu) commemorates the outlaw-poet who was exiled to Constanţa in the 8th century by Emperor Augustus. He looks lost in deep thought but he may simply be depressed; he reputedly disliked Tomis intensely and wrote some of his most self-pitying verses here. His grave is believed to lie below the statue.

South of the square is the imposing **Mahmudiye Mosque** (1910; Map p202; Str Arhiepiscopiei), which has a 140-step minaret that you can climb when the gate is unlocked. This is Romania's main mosque, where the Mufti (the Muslim spiritual head) is located. The other mosque in the city is the **Geamia Hunchiar Mosque** (1868; Map p202; B-dul Tomis). Two blocks further south is the **Orthodox cathedral** (1885; Map p202; Decembrie 1989). A small **archaeological site** lies south of it, displaying walls of houses dating from the 4th to 6th centuries. Constanţa's **Roman Catholic church** (Biserica Romano-Catolica Sfântul Anton; Map p202; Str Nicolae Titulescu 11) is one street west of the Orthodox cathedral.

Continue south to the small **Ion Jalea Museum** (Map p202; ☎ 618 602; Str Arhiepiscopiei 13; admission adult/child €0.28/0.14; ☺ 10am-6pm Wed-Sun), which houses many of the local sculptor's works in a fabulous Moorish-style house.

A peaceful promenade meanders along the waterfront, offering sweeping views of the Black Sea. Have a beer or coffee on the terrace of the bulky, French-style Art Nouveau **Cazino Restaurant** (see Restaurants p205). Opposite is a dismal **aquarium** (Map p202; ☎ 611 277; admission adult/child under 5 €0.50/ free; ⏰ 9am-8pm Jun–mid-Sep, 10am-6pm Tue-Sun mid-Sep–May). Further along the promenade is the 8m-high **Genoese Lighthouse** (1860; Map p202; off Str Remus Opreanu) and a **pier**, which has a fine view of old Constanţa. Behind the lighthouse, a tragically poised **statue of Mihai Eminescu** (1934; Map p202; off Str Remus Opreanu) looks out to the sea.

Some museums in town worth checking out include the **Folk Art Museum** (Muzeul de Artă Populară; Map p202; ☎ 616 133; B-dul Tomis 32; admission adult/child €0.40/0.20; ⏰ 9am-8pm Jul-Aug, 10am-6pm Tue-Sun Sep-Jun), which has handicrafts and costumes. Further north along the boulevard is the **Art Museum & Gallery** (Map p202; ☎ 617 012; B-dul Tomis 84; admission adult/child €0.50/ 0.25; ⏰ 10am-6pm Tue-Sun), with mostly still-life and landscape paintings and sculptures. Contemporary exhibits are held in an adjoining art gallery. The **Naval History Museum** (Map p202; Muzeul Marinei Române; ☎ 619 035; Str Traian 53; admission adult/child €0.80/0.40; ⏰ 10am-6pm Tue-Sun Jun-Sep & 9am-5pm Tue-Sun Oct-May) is housed in the old Navy high school. The captions are in Romanian.

Near the city's main intersection, B-dul Ferdinand and B-dul Tomis, is **Victoria Park** (Map p202), which has remains of the 3rd-century **Roman city wall** and the 6th-century Butchers' tower, loads of Roman sculptures and the modern **Victory Monument** (1968).

Heading north towards Mamaia, you pass Constanţa's **Planetarium & Dolphinarium** (Map p201; ☎ 831 553; B-dul Mamaia; admission adult/ child €0.80/0.40; ⏰ 8am-9pm Jun–mid-Sep & 8am-4pm mid-Sep–May), on the southeastern shores of Lake Tăbăcăriei.

Activities

You can sail aboard the **Condor** (☎ 0744-689 228; €4 per person per hour for a group of 14; ⏰ around 9am May-Sep), moored at the marina known as the Tomis Turist Port (Portul Turistic Tomis), at the eastern end of Str Remus Opreanu, opposite the Yacht Club.

Delphi (☎ 0722-336 686) provides a flexible range of scuba-diving opportunities in the area to suit all budgets. Call for details.

Sleeping

Hotel Tineretului (Map p202; ☎ 613 590; fax 611 290; B-dul Tomis 24; s/d €20/23) This five-storey, two-star hotel has neat, clean rooms, some with a classic view onto the sea with garbage dumps in the foreground, others onto a mosque and kebab stands.

Hotel Maria (Map p201; ☎ /fax 616 852; B-dul 1 Decembrie 1918; s/d €36/45; 🐕) This more modern option, situated across from the park that faces the train station, has lots of glass, chrome and deep blue to soothe your sunshattered nerves. There's only 12 rooms, so it's cosy and quiet.

Hotel Guci (Map p202; ☎ /fax 695 500; Str Răscoala din 1907, 23; s/d/ste €60/67/85; 🐕 ✖) This modern, moderately luxurious three-star hotel offers full services, including Jacuzzi, laundry, massage and gym. It's behind the central post office.

Eating
RESTAURANTS

Gente (Map p202; ☎ 709 383; Piaţa Ovidiu 7; mains €2-4; ⏰ 10am-11pm) This place is hard to miss – its bright pastels are the only splashes of colour on the square – and it would be a shame if you did. While technically a pizzeria, Gente's menu also has Romanian cuisine and a variety of salads. Its mussels in pesto sauce (€2.30) is a popular dish.

Beta (Map p202; ☎ 673 663; Str Ştefan cel Mare 6A; mains €2-4; ⏰ 8am-1am) This modern food emporium with a sprawling terrace is sure to satisfy all with its 100 different meals, from club sandwiches (€1.60) and Thai chicken

---

AUTHOR'S CHOICE

Hotel Intim (Map p202; ☎ 617 814; Str Nicolae Titulescu 9; s/d/ste €23/29/35) Situated on a quiet side street in the old town, and once (in 1882) briefly home to the Romanian poet Mihai Eminescu, this hotel has a faded elegance – with bed covers and lampshades that would make granny smile – perfectly in keeping with the city. The bathrooms are spotless, the ceilings high, and rooms are decked out with TV, fridge and stereo. A great deal!

(€3.40) to breakfast omelets and special vegetarian and children's meals.

Cazino Restaurant (Map p202; ☎ 617 416; B-dul Elisabeta 2; mains €2-6; ☼ 11am-midnight) Despite the decent (but no better) food and rather stuffy service, this may still be worth a splurge for its large outdoor terrace overlooking the sea.

CAFÉS & QUICK EATS

Constanţa Yacht Club (Map p202; Str Remus Opreanu; dishes €1-3) It may serve light snacks, copious amounts of beer and seafood dishes, but people come here not for the food but for the sea view from its two terraces.

Café D'Art (Map p202; ☎ 612 133; B-dul Tomis 97; mains €1-3; ☼ 9am-1am) This is an intimate place snuggled up to the Drama Theatre. Especially popular as an evening drinking hole (cocktails €2), it's also packed during the day by those seeking a good place to people-watch while enjoying a light meal.

Fast-food outlets serving kebabs, burgers and hot dogs are dotted all over town. There are some inside the modern **Galeriile Comerciale Voicules** (Map p202; off B-dul Tomis), and 24-hour joints can be found in the colourfully seedy section of B-dul Tomis south of Str Traian. **Pizza Hut** (Map p202; ☎ 518 430; Str Răscoala din 1907, 10) does deliveries.

SELF-CATERING

Stock up on fruit, cheese and vegetables at the **central market** (Map p201; ☼ 7am-4pm) between the train station and southern bus station. There is another **market** (Map p202; off Str Răscoala din 1907) in the centre. The **Grand Supermarket** (Map p202; B-dul Tomis 57; ☼ 24hr) has a good choice of cakes, biscuits and staple foods. Freshly baked breads and pastries are sold at the **Merlin Patisserie** (Map p202; Str Ştefan cel Mare), opposite Beta.

Drinking

City Flowers Café (Map p202; ☎ 555 855; B-dul Tomis 55; ☼ 8am-2am) This has everything a trendy chill-out bar should have: a glass-covered bar, sofas and couches, tropical plants, pricey cocktails (around €3 a pop), black lights, trip-hop music – and attitude.

Irish Pub (Map p202; ☎ 550 400; Str Ştefan cel Mare 1; ☼ 9am-1am) You can always count on the tried and true. It's pretty much what you'd expect from a Romanian Irish Pub, and has an attractive, orderly wood interior and popular terrace that almost overlooks the sea. There's a full menu of decent and standard-priced meals.

Nightlife in Constanţa is mainly limited to bars, as the city couldn't possibly compete with the disco fanfare in nearby Mamaia. However, **No Problem** (Map p201; ☎ 513 377; B-dul Tomis 253; ☼ 10pm-5am Thu-Sat) sees some heat.

Entertainment

New foreign films are presented at **Cinema Majestic** (Map p202; ☎ 664 411; Str Ştefan cel Mare 33). In summer, films are also screened at **Cinema Grădină Tomis** (Map p202; B-dul Ferdinand), an outside cinema in Victoria Park.

Colourful cabarets, pantomimes and musicals are performed at the **Fantasio Musical Theatre** (Map p202; Teatrul de Revistă Fantasio; ☎ 618 843; B-dul Ferdinand 11). The **Puppet Theatre** (Map p202; Teatrul de Păpuşi; ☎ 618 992; Str Karatzali 16) can be fun for the kids, even if performances are in Romanian.

NORTHERN DOBROGEA

The more literary should head to the **Metamorfoze State Drama Theatre & Opera** (Map p202; ☎ 615 268; Str Mircea cel Bătrân 97) in the central park. You can get tickets at the **ticket office** (Map p202; B-dul Tomis 97; ☉ 9am-6pm Mon-Fri, 9am-noon Sat, 5-6.50pm Sun). The theatre is also home to the Black Sea Philharmonic (Filarmonica Marea Neagră).

Ballets are performed at the **Oleg Danovski Ballet Theatre** (Map p202; ☎ 519 045; Str Răscoala din 1907, 5), in a building that used to house a Turkish *hamam* (bathhouse). Tickets for all performances are sold at the **Agenţie de Bilete** (Map p202; ☎ 664 076; Str Ştefan cel Mare 34; ☉ 10am-5pm).

FC Farul Constanţa, the city's cherished football team (they are six-time national champions), has its home ground at the 5000-seat **Stadionul Farul** (Map p201; ☎ 616 142; Str Primăverii 2) in Parcul Copilului (Children's Park).

Getting There & Away
AIR
In summer there are international flights from Athens and sometimes Istanbul to Constanţa's **Mihail Kogălniceanu airport** (☎ 255 100), 25km from the centre.

As road and train connections with the capital are so good, **Tarom** (Map p202; ☎ 662 632; Str Ştefan cel Mare 15; ☉ 8am-6pm Mon-Fri, 8.30am-12.30pm Sat) has only a once-weekly flight to Bucharest (one-way adult/student €50/26).

BUS
Constanţa has two bus stations. From the **southern bus station** (Autogară Sud; Map p201; ☎ 665 289; B-dul Ferdinand), buses to Istanbul (€25, 17½ hours) depart daily. Tickets are sold in advance from **Özlem Tur** (☎ 514 053), just outside the bus station. There are three maxitaxis daily to Brăila (€4) and 10 daily to Galaţi (€4.80), each of which stop at Constanţa's **northern bus station** (Autogară Nord; Map p201; ☎ 641 379; Str Soveja 35) on the way. Maxitaxi No 23 to Mamaia also departs from here.

From the northern bus station services also include at least one daily maxitaxi to Chişinău (€9, 9 hours) and Iaşi (€8, 7 hours), and four to Histria (€1.25, 1½ hours). Maxitaxis leave for Tulcea (€2.65, 2½ hours) every 30 minutes from 6am to 7.30pm.

If you're travelling south along the Black Sea coast, buses are infinitely more con-venient than trains. Exit Constanţa's train station, turn right and walk 50m to the long queue of maxitaxis, buses and private cars destined for Mangalia (€1), stopping at Eforie Nord, Eforie Sud, Neptun-Olimp, Venus and Saturn.

Eurolines (Map p202; ☎ 662 704; Str Ştefan cel Mare 71), as well as selling bus tickets to European destinations, can arrange car rentals and sell last-minute plane tickets to Germany.

TRAIN
Constanţa's **train station** (Map p201; B-dul Ferdinand) is near the southern bus station, 1.5km from the centre. The 24-hour left-luggage office is downstairs.

The **Agenţie de Voiaj CFR** (Map p202; ☎ 617 930; Aleea Vasile Canarache 4; ☉ 7.30am-8.30pm Mon-Fri & 8am-1pm Sat) sells long-distance tickets only; for the local train service (down the coast), buy your tickets at the train station. Student discount tickets are sold at the last window on the left.

There are 11 to 15 daily trains to Bucha-rest (€6.25, 2½ to 4½ hours), though some terminate at Bucureşti Obor. The fastest is the intercity 'Marea Neagră'. There are daily services to Suceava, Cluj-Napoca, Satu Mare, Galaţi, Timişoara and other destinations. As many as 19 trains a day head from Constanţa to Mangalia (€0.95, one to 1¼ hours), stopping at Eforie Nord, Eforie Sud, Costineşti and Neptun.

There are one to two daily trains to Chişi-nău in Moldova (€10, 12 hours). The Ovid-ius train to Budapest also runs overnight (€16, 17 hours) via Bucharest and Arad.

In winter there are reduced services.

Getting Around
TO/FROM THE AIRPORT
Mihail Kogălniceanu airport (☎ 255 100) is 25km northwest of the centre on the road to Hârşova. **Tarom** (Map p202; ☎ 662 632; Str Ştefan cel Mare 15; ☉ 8am-6pm Mon-Fri, 8.30am-12.30pm Sat) runs a shuttle bus from its office 1½ hours before flight departures. All public buses to Hârşova (from the northern bus station) stop at the airport.

BUS & TROLLEYBUS
Public transport runs from 5am to 11.30pm. A ticket costs €0.40, good for two rides. Trol-leybus No 100 links the train station and the southern bus station with the northern bus

station. Trolleybus Nos 40, 41 and 43 go from the southern bus station to the centre. No 43 continues to the Stadionul Farul south of Lake Tăbăcăriei, and the No 41 goes to Mamaia. No 40 goes to the Pescărie bus stop at the southern edge of Mamaia.

Buses No 42 (from the Fantasio bus stop on B-dul Ferdinand) and No 43 go to the northern bus station.

CAR & MOTORCYCLE

Avis (Map p202; ☎ 616 733; Str Ştefan cel Mare 15; 🕙 8am-6pm Mon-Fri, 9am-1pm Sat) shares an office with Tarom. Travel agencies can also help in renting a car.

MAMAIA

☎ 241

Mamaia is Romania's party central. It's a mere 8km strip of beach between the freshwater Lake Mamaia (also known as Lake Siutghiol) and the Black Sea, but it's Romania's most popular resort. It gloats over golden sands, an aqua park, restaurants, nightclubs and a raucous atmosphere. There are over 60 hotels and tourist complexes squeezed together in a 100m strip along the shore. Consider yourself forewarned!

According to legend, the resort gained its name from the desperate cries of a fair maiden, who, during the time of the Ottoman Empire, was kidnapped by a Turk and taken out to sea in a boat. As the wind howled, her frantic cries for her mother – 'Mamaia! Mamaia!' – could be heard for miles around. Today, cries of joy are heard from holiday-makers who come from around Romania to soak up the sun.

Mamaia hosts an annual **National Pop Music festival** (🕙 early Sep) which brings together bands from across Romania in catchy pop unity.

Information

The **Gibraltar Travel Agency** (☎ 634 466; gibraltartravel@fx.ro; B-dul Mamaia 135-137; 🕙 9am-6pm), inside the Millennium Business Centre, can help with car rental, accommodation and excursion bookings.

Every hotel has a currency exchange, and ATMs are easy to find. To change travellers cheques you have to go to Constanţa.

The **telephone & post office** (🕙 8am-8pm Mon-Fri) is 200m south of the Cazino complex on the promenade.

> **CLAMMY**
>
> There is a species of soft-shell white clams from Chesapeake Bay, Massachusetts, which live off the coast in Mamaia. Brought over by accident on a boat in the 1960s, they are now thriving here and have taken over local species. They're served as a delicacy in local restaurants as either *mia alba* or *scoica alba*.

Salvamar operates medical huts staffed with lifeguards on the beach between 15 June and 15 September.

Sights

Mamaia's number-one attraction is its wide, golden **beach**, which stretches the entire length of the resort. The further north you go, the less crowded it becomes, though the facilities become sparser, too.

In summer, **boats** (☎ 252 494; €3 return; every 30min 9am-midnight) ferry tourists across Lake Mamaia to **Ovidiu Island** (Insula Ovidiu, where the poet's tomb is located) from the Tic-Tic wharf opposite the Staţia Cazino bus stop. On the island, you can arrange boat tours and jet-ski rides.

A tall-spired **wooden church** from Maramureş has been brought to the area in an attempt to Romanianise the otherwise 'you-could-be-anywhere' surroundings and it now sits awkwardly on the eastern bank of Lake Mamaia.

Near Hotel Perla is an **art gallery** (Map p201; ☎ 547 389; B-dul Aurel Vlaicu). Head here to give your hedonistic, sun-drenched vacation a cultural edge.

The modern, huge **Aqua Park** (opp Hotel Perla; 🕙 8am-10pm mid-May–mid-Sep; admission adult/child under 12/child under 3 €8/4/free) keeps the crowds moistened. Adjacent is an **amusement park**.

Just north of Hotel Bucureşti, by the banks of Lake Mamaia, there are opportunities for waterski, yacht, windsurf board and rowboat rental.

Sleeping

Centrul de Cazare Cazino (🕙 831 200, 555 555; 🕙 10am-9pm mid-Jun–mid-Sep) On the 1st floor of the Cazino complex, this place has lists of available accommodation. Booking hotel rooms through travel agencies (see

NORTHERN DOBROGEA

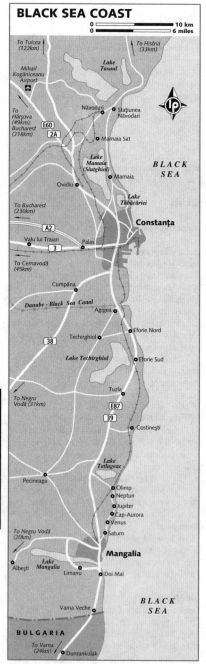

BLACK SEA COAST

NORTHERN DOBROGEA

Information p203) can save you as much as 15% on the rack rate.

Popas Hanul Piraţilor (☎ 831 454; tent site/ 2-room huts €3/8) A campground 3km north of Mamaia's northern limit, this has shabby huts, but an on-site café and stretches of fine sand nearby. As there is no longer any camping allowed on the beach in Mamaia proper, this is a good option.

Bus No 23 and maxitaxi 23E stop in front of it.

Hotel Perla (Map p201; ☎ 831 995; perlam@ rdslink.ro; s/d/ste €45/48/69; ⚒ 🖳) Lording over the resort's main entrance, this huge hotel is both a landmark and reliable service centre. It's a busy, efficiently run place, and fully wheelchair accessible. The mini palm trees outside stay healthy throughout the year thanks to special hormone injections!

Hotel Dunărea (Map p201; ☎ 831 894; s/d €24/32) Nearby, with its soft-orange pastel décor, this is one of the resort's smaller hotels.

Hotel Boulevard (Map p201; ☎ 831 533; fax 831 606; B-dul Mamaia 294; s/d €61/69) This is a good choice among Mamaia's four- and five-star options. Modern, and offering full services, it's also slightly out of the main drag (located just south of Mamaia proper) while just a 10- to 15-minute walk to the beach.

Eating

Almost every hotel has an adjoining restaurant and there are numerous fast-food stands and restaurants lining the boardwalk.

Orange Plazza (☎ 0722 500 577; mains €2-5; ⏰ 10-6am) Located in the northern part of the resort, this is a good bet. It changes its menu every three months and has an eclectic international menu. There's also an on-site pub and disco.

Insula Ovidiu (☎ 252 494; mains €2-5; ⏰ 24hr) This famous restaurant on Ovidiu Island is worth a visit. Seafood is the speciality of the house.

Drinking

Some of the hottest discos on the strip are **Club XS** (Map p201; ☎ 831 212), next to Hotel Perla; **Club XXI** (100m sth of the casino); and next door the gigantic, slightly tacky **Cleopatra** (☎ 831 237).

Getting There & Away

Tickets for trains departing from Constanţa (see p206) can be bought in advance at the

Agenţie de Voiaj CFR (☎ 617 930), which adjoins the post and telephone office on the promenade.

The simplest and quickest way to travel between Constanţa and Mamaia is by maxitaxi. Maxitaxi Nos 23, 23E and 301 depart regularly from Constanţa's train station and go north along Mamaia's 8km strip, stopping at major hotels. Maxitaxi No 23 stops near Constanţa's northern bus station as well. Buses No 41 and 47 also take you from Constanţa to the northern end of Mamaia.

In summer a shuttle runs up and down Mamaia's 5km boardwalk.

The northbound bus No 23 goes to the neighbouring resort of Năvodari and the camp ground.

If arriving in a non-Constanţa-registered vehicle, you are required to pay a €0.50 road tax at the roadblocked entrance to Mamaia.

EFORIE NORD & LAKE TECHIRGHIOL
☎ 241

Eforie Nord, 14km south of Constanţa, is the first large resort south of the city. Beaches are below 10m to 20m cliffs and are as crowded as in Mamaia. Tiny **Lake Belona**, behind the southern end of the beach, is another bathing spot.

Within walking distance to the town centre is **Lake Techirghiol**, famous for its black sapropel mud, effective against rheumatism. Its waters are five times saltier than the sea (with 80g of mineral salt per litre; *Tekir* is the Turkish word for 'salt'). The small town gets uncomfortably crowded throughout the summer, packed with restaurants, discos and thousands of revellers. However, the choice of accommodation is more varied than in Mamaia.

Eforie Sud, 4km south of Eforie Nord, is a more run-down version of its northern sister, but both have been privy to a 10-billion lei rejuvenation project, which will see building and beautifying projects continuing through to 2011.

Orientation & Information
The train station is a few minutes' walk from the centre. Exit the train station and turn right. Turn left at the roundabout then left onto B-dul Republicii, the main drag. Buses from Mangalia and Constanţa stop on B-dul Republicii near the post office.

Most hotels and restaurants are on Str Tudor Vladimirescu, which runs parallel to B-dul Republicii along the beach.

There is a currency exchange in practically every hotel. The **telephone office** (B-dul Republicii 11; ☎ 7am-9pm Mon-Fri, 11am-7pm Sat & Sun) is inside the **central post office** (B-dul Republicii 11; 8am-8pm Mon-Fri, 8am-6pm Sat).

Mud Baths
Wallow in black mud – and smell like... rotten eggs! From the train station, cross the tracks and head south (left) for about 300m. To your right is the entrance to the **public mud baths** (admission €1.05; 8am-8pm) of Lake Techirghiol. Single-sex changing rooms lead to separate beaches where people with aching whatnots stand around nude, slather on the green-black glop and bask in the sun until it cracks. On-site massages cost €2.65.

Most of the major hotels offer mud baths at much higher prices.

Sleeping
Camping Meduza (☎ 742 385; tent site/d/2-bed hut €1.75/5.50/6.70) This cramped space is behind the Prahova Hotel at the northern end of town. Walk north along Str Tudor Vladimirescu and turn left after Club Maxim. The doubles are in a drab concrete building. The place is always noisy but it's close to the action and offers laundry service.

Terasa Efes Pilsen (☎ 743 042; Str Tudor Vladimirescu 1; d €10) Humbly sitting atop a fast-food joint, this is one of the most economical options in town. Though it's on a busy intersection, the rooms aren't overly noisy, and are comfortably equipped. Bathrooms and showers are shared but there are only four rooms. Breakfast isn't included but the food stand downstairs has lots of goodies.

Hotel Decebal (☎ 742 977; adjoining the train station; s/d €20/27) This is a very pleasant, quiet hotel with a nice stone terrace – only it's right next to the train station, meaning a 15-minute walk to the beaches.

Hotel Britannia (☎ 704 100; fax 704 171; Str Tudor Vladimirescu 39-43; s/d €72/96;) This is one of the most luxurious places in town, near the northern end of the beach. It boasts indoor and outdoor pools, and is wheelchair accessible.

AUTHOR'S CHOICE

Villa Horiana (☎ 741 388; Str Alexandru Cuza 13; s/d €35/55; 🔀) No doubt the best place to lay your party-weary head in Eforie Nord is here, in this converted bungalow. There are only four rooms, but they're fully furnished and big enough for four persons. Some have their own balcony. The sumptuous home cooking by the super-friendly owners is almost reason enough to stay here.

Eating

The main market is 200m north of the bus stop, opposite the white orthodox church.

Cofetăria Pescăruş, (B-dul Republicii; mains €1-3; 🕒 11am-1am) Opposite the post office, this cafeteria-style joint is handy because you can point to the type of grease you want. It's good for a cheap fill-up and has live music from 9pm.

Nunta Zamfirei (☎ 741 651; Str Republicii; mains €2-6; 🕒 6pm-1am) This Romanian restaurant is famed for its folk song-and-dance shows. Walk north along B-dul Republicii and turn left onto the small track opposite the public thermal baths.

Union (☎ 741 177; Str Tudor Vladimirescu 26; mains €2-4; 🕒 24hr) If you have an aversion to folk costumes, this is the place for you. The menu varies every 10 days, and the place becomes a disco late at night.

333 (☎ 0723 173 333; Str Andrei Mureşanu 1; meals €1-3; 🕒 8am-1am) Totally relaxed, this pub, café and bistro on the corner of Str Republicii doubles as a cool hangout. It's the place to come and pose.

Getting There & Away

The **Agenţie de Voiaj CFR** (B-dul Republicii 11; ☎ 617 930) is inside the post office building.

All trains between Constanţa and Mangalia stop at Eforie Nord, but you're better off on a maxitaxi (€0.50; see p203).

FROM COSTINEŞTI TO SATURN

☎ 241

This stretch of the *litoral* extends the party mood from north to south at the resorts of Costineşti, Olimp, Neptun, Jupiter, Cap Aurora, Venus and Saturn. Costineşti, the only resort without a cliff backing, is synonymous with 'youth' to most Romanians; it's a rare sight to see anyone over 30 here.

The double resort of Neptun-Olimp was until 1989 the exclusive resort of Romania's Communist Party. Ceauşescu had his own luxury villa here. Today, there's still a moneyed, elite air to these attractive resorts that cater to a slightly older clientele. Two artificial lakes (Neptun I & II) separate the resorts from the sea.

Jupiter is not a very scenic youth hangout, Cap Aurora has some nice spots and benefits from being the coast's smallest resort, while Venus and Saturn have the least-expensive hotels on the coast, mainly in high-rise concrete blocks. The latter has made a name for itself as a treatment centre for locomotor and gynaecological problems. Delightful. These four resorts are moribund compared to their northern neighbours.

Information

The Info Litoral Tourist Information Centre in Constanţa (see p203) can provide you with detailed information about these resorts, and it (or any travel agency in Constanţa) can help with hotel booking.

Changing money is not a problem at the resorts, with most hotels providing the service and numerous kiosks set up near the beaches. ATMs can be found as well.

Activities

Jet skis and boards for **wind surfing** can be hired from the northern end of Neptun's beach or from the jetty in Costineşti. There is also a **yacht club** (☎ 752 395) on the beach in Neptun. Both resorts have a **bowling alley**.

The **Mangalia Stud Farm** (Herghelia Mangalia; ☎ 753 215) is at the southern end of Venus, 3km from Mangalia. It has a small racecourse and you can ride for an hour for about €6.

Festivals & Events

Costineşti hosts a **national film festival** in August and a **jazz festival** in early September. Contact the Info Litoral Tourist Information Centre for details.

Sleeping
BUDGET

In Costineşti, **Sim Val Car** (☎ 586 736) can help find you a room in someone's house for about €10 per person if you call first. In Neptun, try booking via the **accommodation**

office (☎ 701 300; ☼ 24hr Jun-Sep), inside the Levent Market on the main street. You'll also find many signs outside private homes advertising *cazare* (rooms) in each resort.

There are numerous options along the strip, including finding a forest clearing and pitching a tent for free. In Costineşti, there's a camp ground at the resort's northern end. There are also camp grounds at the southern end of Lake Neptun II, at the northern end of Olimp, and at the northern end of Saturn.

MID-RANGE

Vila La Răscruce (☎ 0745-685 714; Str Schitului 61; s/d €21/24) This brings some welcome visual relief to the surroundings, as the exteriors are done up in a pseudo-folk, wooden rustic style. Rooms are standard and unexciting, but clean.

Hotel Albert (☎ 731 514; hotelalbert@idilis.ro; d/ste €35/50) One of the best bets along the coast, this is located smack in between Neptun and Olimp. It's slightly secluded from the bustle and tastefully mixes modernity with rustic décor.

Hotel Opal (☎ 731 372; fax 731 854; s/d from €22/26-28; ste €35) This place in Cap Aurora is good for seekers of the kitsch and the exotic. It's a concrete giant built in the shape of a pyramid. It offers full services but no-one would call it upmarket.

Most of the hotels in Olimp look out to sea. Try also the **Hotel Panoramic** (☎ 701 033; fax 701 133; s/d €30/38).

Getting There & Away

By train, the Halta Neptun station is within walking distance of the Neptun-Olimp hotels, midway between the two resorts. The other resorts are best reached by the shuttle buses and maxitaxis that drive along the coast from Mangalia, through Saturn, Venus and Jupiter–Cap Aurora, to Neptun-Olimp and Eforie Nord. The small maxitaxis stop in the centre of Saturn, Venus and Jupiter–Cap Aurora.

MANGALIA

☎ 241 / pop 44,300

Ancient Greek Callatis is today a little town that, compared to the fanfare of its northern-resort cousins, has a pulse that's difficult to detect. It's better known for its several minor archaeological sites and health centres for elderly European tour groups who are bent on various cures. Mangalia is Romania's second-most important harbour, though mainly for military purposes and ship repairing.

Mangalia hosts an annual **Young Actors Festival** in the last days of August.

Orientation

Mangalia's train station is 1km north of the centre. Turn right as you exit the station and follow Şoseaua Constanţei (the main road) south. At the roundabout, turn left for Hotel Mangalia and the beach, continue straight for the pedestrianised section of Şoseaua Constanţei, where most facilities are located, and then at the second roundabout make a right onto Ştefan cel Mare for the post office and central bus stop.

Information

There is a small tourist **information kiosk** (☼ 8.30am-4pm) outside the train station that gives out leaflets and can help with booking accommodation.

The multilingual reception of Hotel President can be helpful. The hotel's tourist office organises day trips to the Danube Delta and Murfatlar vineyards.

Most hotels have currency exchanges. One of the numerous **currency exchange offices** (Str Ştefan cel Mare 16; ☼ 7.30am-10pm) is opposite the post office. You can cash travellers cheques or get cash advances on Visa and MasterCard at the **Banca Comercială Română**, (Şoseaua Constanţei 25; ☼ 8am-4pm Mon-Fri).

The **telephone office** (☼ 7am-10pm) and **post office** (☼ 7am-9pm Mon-Fri, 8am-4pm Sat, 11am-7pm Sun) is at Str Ştefan cel Mare 14-15.

La Maxim (per hour €0.65; ☼ 24hr) is an internet shack right on the beach, in front of Hotel Zenit. **Graphity** (☎ 758 284; Str Ştefan cel Mare 16; per hour €0.50; ☼ 24hr) is another option.

Sights

Mangalia's sights can be seen in two to three hours. The **Callatis Archaeological Museum** (☎ 753 580; Str Şoseaua Constanţei 26; ☼ 8am- 8pm) has a good collection of Roman sculptures. Just past the high-rise building next to the museum are some remnants of a 4th-century **Roman-Byzantine necropolis**.

At the south side of Hotel Mangalia, along Str Izvor, are the ruins of a 6th-century **Palaeo-Christian basilica** and a **fountain**

(Izvorul Hercules) dispensing sulphurous mineral water that, despite the smell, some people drink.

Cultural events take place in the **Casă de Cultură**, near Hotel President, which has a large socialist mural on the façade. One block east of the post office is the Turkish **Sultan Esmahan Mosque** (Moscheea Esmahan Sultan; Str Oituz; admission €0.40; ☼ 9am-8pm). Built in 1525, it's surrounded by a lovely garden and well-kept cemetery. It serves the 800 Muslim families living in Mangalia.

From here, head east down Str Oituz to the beachfront where, in the basement of Hotel President, remains of the walls of the Callatis citadel dating from the 1st to 7th centuries are open for all to see in the so-called **Callatiana Archaeological Reservation** (Muzeul Poarta Callatiana; ☼ 24hr). There's an adjoining **art gallery**.

Sleeping
BUDGET
Antrec (☎ 759 473; Str George Murnu 13, Block D, Apt 21; ☼ 24hrs, calls only) It arranges rooms in private homes in Mangalia and other coastal resorts from €13 a night.

The nearest camping grounds are in Saturn and Jupiter-Cap Aurora. To get to Camping Saturn from Mangalia, follow Şoseaua Constanţei 1km north from Mangalia's train station to the Art-Deco Saturn sculpture, turn right, walk 50m then turn left.

MID-RANGE
Hotel Mangalia (☎ 752 052; www.mangalia-turism.radiotel.ro; Str Rozelor 35; s/d €26/40) A 1960s holdout, this is a popular choice. It's one of the few hotels on the coast with full wheelchair access; there are ramps onto the beach. There's a charge for 'extras' such as television and fridge (about €1.50).

Hotel President (☎ 755 861; www.hpresident.com; Str Treilor 6; s/d/ste from €44/69/117) This is the top place to stay south of Constanţa – a four-star luxury hotel with a fully-fledged business centre. The lobby is breezy and dynamically decorated but the rooms are a tad drab.

Hotel Zenit (☎ 751 645; Str Treilor 7), **Hotel Astra** (☎ 751 673; Str Treilor 9) and **Hotel Orion** (☎ 751 156; Str Teilor 11) are surprisingly pleasant three-star options on the promenade. All have singles/doubles with private bath for €26/31.

Eating
Cafe del Mar (☎ 0723 356 610; Str Treilor 4; mains €2-4; ☼ 24hr) You can't go wrong here. There's a great double-decker terrace, stylish interiors and one of the most varied, fanciful menus around – it's the only place on the coast you can get US-style buffalo wings (€1.85) and potato skins (€1.70)!

Stock up on packed-lunch delights at the **food market** (Piaţa Agroalimentară; Str Vasile Alecsandri) behind Hotel Zenit.

For fast food, salads and soups try the self-service **Fast Food outlet** (below Terasa President) on the beach in front of Hotel President.

Getting There & Away
BUS
Maxitaxis from Constanţa stop at Mangalia's train station and also in front of the post office, where all maxitaxis running up the coast to Olimp (every 20 minutes) and down the coast to Vama Veche stop. Maxitaxis to Constanţa (€1) run regularly from 5am to 11pm, to Doi Mai (€0.30) every 15 minutes from 6am to 10pm, and to Vama Veche (€0.35) every hour from 6am to 7pm.

TRAIN
The **Agenţie de Voiaj CFR** (☎ 752 818; Str Ştefan cel Mare 14-15; ☼ 7.30am-8.30pm Mon-Sat, 8.30am-1.30pm Sun) adjoins the central post office.

Mangalia is the end of the line from Constanţa. From Constanţa there are 19 trains daily in summer to Mangalia (€0.95, one to 1¼ hours), five of which are direct to/from Bucharest's Gară Obor (€7, 4½ hours). In summer there are also express trains to/from Iaşi, Sibiu, Suceava, Cluj-Napoca and Timişoara.

DOI MAI & VAMA VECHE
☎ 241
This remote stretch of the coast near the Bulgarian border holds a special place in the Romanian consciousness, conjuring up images of a bohemian paradise with desolate stretches of windswept beaches, where nudists and nonconformists of all creeds come together. During the Communist regime, Vama Veche (literally 'old customs point') was reserved for staff of the Cluj-Napoca university and developed its reputation as a haven for hippies, artists and intellectuals.

CAVE DWELLERS

In 1986 the Romanian speleologist Cristian Lascu made the fantastic discovery of the **Movile Cave** (Peştera Movile). The cave, 3.5km from Limanu, contained 32 new species of flora and fauna and two new genuses dating from the Upper Miocene period five-million years ago. Invertabrates there energise themselves via chemosynthesis, feeding on a thick layer of sulphur-consuming bacteria formed on top of the water in the vacuumed cave. Though the same process has been found in other world caves, Movile was the first to be discovered. This attracted the attention of NASA, always interested in alternate life forms, and they worked with GESS (see Ecology on p199) for a while on this project.

That was then. Vama Veche's parking lot is now crammed with expensive cars from Bucharest, free camping is a thing of the past, there are loud beachside bars for every musical taste, and nudists are the exception rather than the rule. A visible construction boom foretells big plans for the future.

Doi Mai has also been built up in the last few years but not as obviously as Vama Veche, its beach is smaller and offers views onto a shipyard. It has retained a small village charm and can make a pleasant base. Both towns are good alternatives to the more standard, noisier resorts to the north.

While the noise level is on the increase in Vama Veche, things rarely get wilder than on August 10th of every year, when the village hosts **House Parade**, a festival of international DJs right on the beach.

Activities

In Doi Mai, **Patrician Activ** (☎ 0722 846 876; www.patrician.as.ro) can hook you up with diving gear (€22 for a 90-minute dip). Also in Doi Mai, Casa Oana (see Sleeping below) rents bicycles for €1.50 an hour. **Jet Skis** can be rented on the northern end of the beach in Vama Veche for €18 an hour.

Sleeping

Casa Oana (☎ 743 900; Str Gheorghe Bunoiu 152; d €20) This is a bonafide B&B in Doi Mai – a lovely house with eight fully furnished, cozy rooms. Copious breakfasts are served in the garden.

Dispencerat Cazare (☎ 0722 889 087; www.vama vecheholidays.ro) Just around the corner from popular Bar Bibi in Vama Veche, this office can hook you up with a room in town for about €10 (that is, if they happen to be open or feel like answering the phone).

Hotel-Restaurant Lyana (☎ 0744 671 213; d €19) This is right on the beach in Vama Veche. Its decent rooms promise a sea view – as well as the noise from all the beach discos. Its restaurant is the most elegant in the village.

There's free **camping** at the southern end of Vama Veche's beach, and not on the beach itself, only on the grasslands. The area is packed and uncomfortable. There are cold/hot showers (€0.40/0.65) near the centre of the beach.

Eating

Bar Bibi (☎ 0722 241 216; mains €2-4; ☘ 10am-2am) This is one of the most popular hangouts and eateries in Vama Veche, on the main drag 50m from the beach. The meals are excellent and the 1st-floor pub is one of the saner places to be in the evening.

Dobrogean (☎ 743 689; cnr Str Kogalniceanu & Str Dobrogeanu; mains €2-4; ☘ 8am-1am; 💻) This is your best bet in Doi Mai, though there are lots of cafés on Str Kogalniceanu, the main road. The décor is country-rustic, the menu is varied and there's Internet access on-site.

AUTHOR'S CHOICE

Hellios Inn (☎ 732 929; Str Gheorghe Bunoiu; www.hellios-inn.ro; s/d €10/20) One of the most pleasant options on the whole coast, this place is located in Doi Mai. Tastefully done up like a two-storey villa, with all 50 rooms facing an inner courtyard full of flowers, its rooms are small but cozy, with wood, stone or brick walls. The windows in some rooms are merely holes in stone. There's a huge bar and restaurant with open roof, a wine cellar and a large swimming pool. It's the last house on the street.

Getting There & Away

Maxitaxis serve Doi Mai and Vama Veche regularly from Mangalia (see p212).

TO BULGARIA

From the south end of Vama Veche you can walk or drive across the border into Bulgaria. The crossing is open 24 hours. If you cross on foot, be prepared for a 6km hike to Durankulak, the first settlement inside Bulgaria.

Motorists can also cross into Bulgaria at Negru Vodă, 15km west of Mangalia on the main Constanţa–Dobriø highway (E38). Kardam, the first village inside Bulgaria, is 5km from the border crossing.

THE DANUBE–BLACK SEA CANAL

The Danube Canal runs for 64km from Cernavodă (the site of Romania's nuclear reactor; a total of five reactors are planned for the area) in the west to Agigea on the eastern coast. The canal, which opened in 1984, shortens the sea trip from Constanţa to Cernavodă by 400km.

Murfatlar

As they approach Constanţa, the canal and railway pass through the Murfatlar area, where Romania's best-known dessert wines are produced. The profitable Murfatlar vineyards are northwest of the small town of Basarabi, some 14km west of Constanţa. Wine-tasting and guided tours of the factory are possible – but only for groups of 20 or more. Most travel agencies arrange group wine-tasting tours to Murfatlar.

ADAMCLISI

In the southwestern part of Adamclisi, 64km to the southwest of Constanţa, are the remains of the Roman city Tropaeum Traiani. The city was destroyed during Goth attacks in the 3rd century and rebuilt during the reign of Constantine I (r AD 306–37). Following the domination of Dobrogea by the Turks in 1418, the settlement was renamed Adamclisi (meaning 'man's church').

The highlight of the region is a 30m-high marble triumphal monument. The original **Tropaeum Traiani Monument** was built from 106 to 109 to honour the Traian victory over the Dacians in Adamclisi. Today's monument is a replica of the original, rebuilt in the 1970s with noticeable socialist aplomb. The sides of the base are decorated with pictorial scenes of that decisive battle, identical to parts of the famous Traian Monument in Rome. This is an important monument for Romanians, linked with their Roman heritage as it is – even though it glorifies defeat of the Romanian people's earlier ancestors, the Dacians.

Pillars, friezes and other fragments of the original monument are displayed in the **Tropaeum Traiani Museum** (☎ 618 763; ☿ 9am-6pm Tue-Sun). To get to the museum head west from the monument into Adamclisi and follow the signs for 'Muzeul Adamclisi'.

Adamclisi is difficult to reach by public transport. Buses departing daily from Constanţa's northern bus station to Daeni via Ostrov pass through Adamclisi. From

---

THE DEATH CANAL

The Danube–Black Sea canal took 30,000 people around nine years to construct. Some 300 million cu metres of land were manually excavated and 4.2 million cu metres of reinforced concrete shifted by workers. This canal was only part of a centuries-old dream to build an inland waterway linking the North and Black Seas, which was finally realised in 1992 when a 171km canal between the Main and Danube Rivers in Germany was opened.

Thousands of lives were lost during the Communists' first attempt at building the canal – or 'death canal' (canalul morţii) as it was known – between 1949 and 1953. During the Communist purges of this period some 180,000 political prisoners were interned in forced-labour camps in Romania; 40,000 of them were worked to death on the project.

The project was abandoned in 1953 and resumed again in 1975 when a more suitable route was followed.

Together with the House of the People in Bucharest, the canal has gone down in history as one of the Communists' most costly follies – and not just financially.

BLEATING ON THE ROAD AGAIN

Another facet of Romania's 'lost-in-time' nature is transhumance. For those of you who don't use this word on a weekly basis, it means the movement of livestock over large distances. In Romania, shepherds still move their sheep (and occasionally goat) flocks over hundreds of kilometres each autumn and spring in search of better grazing lands. Each autumn, the bleating of thousands of sheep, and the tender pitter-pat of their little hooves can be heard descending from high up in the Carpathian Mountains down to more fertile plains around Timişoara and especially across the Dobrogea and Danube Delta plains regions. There are even some villages near Lake Razim where places and families bear typically Transylvanian names from shepherds who fell in love with local women and settled here. In the spring, they make their way back to Transylvania.

Though little documentation of this practice exists, it's estimated that only 10% to 15% of Romania's shepherds (not all of them male, by the way) still go through with these long marches. Yet their numbers are on the decrease. Private farmers complain vociferously about strange flocks crossing and munching on their territory, and this ancient tradition is slowly losing its place in the modern world.

Romania is among the last places in Europe where this practice is still engaged as a matter of livelihood; in other places, a minor version of it is sometimes staged for the benefit of tourists. It has an important place in Romanian folklore (songs and proverbs, for example) – plus it results in better-fed (and thus better tasting) sheep.

Constanţa's southern bus station, the one daily bus to Băneasa stops at Adamclisi.

HISTRIA

Histria, settled in 657 BC by Greek traders, is Romania's oldest town. It rapidly became a key commercial port, superseding Constanţa. But subsequent Goth attacks coupled with the gradual sandlocking of the harbour led to its equally rapid decline, and by the 7th century AD the town was abandoned. Its ruins were discovered in 1914.

Citadel

If you've seen the lost city of Pompeii, Histria Citadel (Cetatea Histria) may disappoint. If you haven't, you will find the walls, baths and paved roads left at the **Histria Archaeological Complex** (☎ 618 763; admission €1; ☺ 9am to 8pm) to be quite superb. Visitors are free to walk around the original streets of the ancient fortified city. Wild camping on the grounds is also permitted.

Archaeological relics uncovered at the site are displayed in the **Histria Museum** (☎ 618 763; free admission; ☺ 9am to 8pm) at the entrance to the site. From the entrance, paths lead visitors through the ancient city's remains, and pass by the big tower into the western sector where most of the public buildings, thermal baths and the civil

basilica stood. Close by is the Christian basilica, built with stones from the old theatre in the 6th century AD.

On the cliffs in the eastern sector is the 'sacred zone' (zona sacră) where archaeologists have uncovered remains of a Greek temple believed to be built at the end of the 6th century BC.

The complex is 4km south of Histria village. From Constanţa, turn east off the main road at the signpost for 'Cetatea Histria'. The complex is a further 7km along this road.

Getting There & Away

Getting to Histria is tough without private transport. Four buses depart from Constanţa's northern bus station, but the 4km hike from the stop puts many off. Taxis are hard to find here.

DANUBE DELTA

You need time and patience to explore the Danube Delta (Delta Dunarii). A marvellous world where water, fish and birds call the shots, its greatest treasures are not laid out for all to see easily. Yet hitching a ride with fishermen or hiring a small boat to explore the smaller waterways and float

NORTHERN DOBROGEA

DELTA PERMITS

In principle, visitors need travel permits to travel in the delta. If on a group excursion of any kind, these are automatically handled by the operator. If you hire a local fisherman, ask to see his valid permit. The only time you'll need to buy one (€1) is if you go boating or foraging independently. The Information and Ecological Education Centre in Tulcea (see Tourist Information p218) can issue these for you. If inspectors (and there are many of them) find you without one, you can be liable for a fine of up to €200. You need separate permits to fish or hunt.

among the exotic wildlife is one of the area's greatest pleasures.

At the end of its long journey across Europe the mighty Danube River spills into the Black Sea just south of the Ukrainian border. Here the Danube splits into three channels – the Chilia, Sulina and Sfântu Gheorghe arms, creating a 4152-sq-km wetland (3446 sq km of which are in Romania) that provides sanctuary for some 300 species of birds and 150 species of fish. Reed marshes cover 1563 sq km, constituting one of the largest expanses of reed beds in the world. Almost thirty different types of ecosystems have been counted.

This is Europe's youngest and least stable land, the river's average discharge of 6300 cubic metres per second ensuring that the landscape is forever evolving. The Sfântu Gheorghe lighthouse built by the sea in 1865 now stands 3km from open waters.

The Danube Delta is protected under the DDBR (see Ecology on p200), set up in response to the ecological disaster that befell it during Ceauşescu's attempt to transform it, incredibly, into an agricultural region. There are 18 protected areas – 506 sq km (8.7% of the total area) including a 500-year-old forest and Europe's largest pelican colony. The delta is included in Unesco's World Heritage list.

Wherever you intend to go in the delta, stock up on supplies and mosquito repellent. Remember that the Danube is polluted water; although locals may use it to make tea and soup, do not drink it! (p354 for what to do if you experience tummy trouble). Still, sampling some Danubian cuisine (p44) is part of the experience of visiting the area. While fresh fish served in restaurants is generally fine to eat, some visitors report upset stomachs after eating fish in private homes that has not been cooked enough.

The delta's population incorporates large Ukrainian (24%) and Lipovan (13%) communities. Lipovanis form a majority in Mila 23, Jurilovca, Mahmudia, Periprava and a trio of remote villages north of Sulina: Sfiştofca, CA Rosetti and Letea. For religious reasons, they may be the only group of non-smokers in Romania! Predominantly Ukrainian villages include Murighiol, Sfântu Gheorghe and Caraorman.

Climate
This is the most humid region in Romania, particularly during summer (July average 24°C). In spring up to 70% of the region is flooded. Winters are mild and it is extremely rare for the channels to ice over.

Bird-watching
Halfway between the North Pole and the equator, the Danube Delta is a major migration hub for thousands of birds to/from Mongolia, Siberia, India, Africa and China. Prime times are mid-April to mid-May and late October, when half the world's population of red-breasted geese winter here. Long-tailed ducks, whooper swans, black-throated divers and clouds of white storks are equally abundant at this time.

Europe's largest white pelican and Dalmatian pelican colonies are also here, along with 60% of the world's population of pygmy cormorants.

Protected species typically found in the delta include the roller, white-tailed eagle, great white egret, mute swan, falcon and bee-eater.

Protected zones shield the largest bird colonies. Large green signs in most villages, most in Romanian, show visitors where these zones are and what birds can be found there. There are 65 observation towers dotted throughout the delta. Bird-watchers usually congregate around Lake Furtuna,

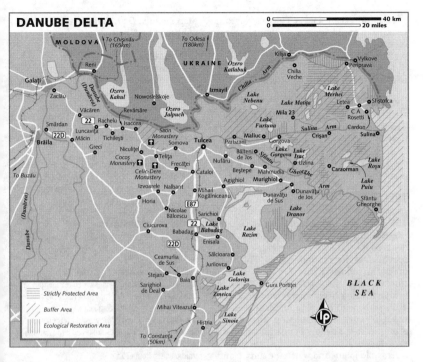

DANUBE DELTA

0 — 40 km
0 — 20 miles

Map showing Danube Delta region with Strictly Protected Area, Buffer Area, and Ecological Restoration Area.

Murighiol, the brackish areas around Lake Razim and Lake Babadag, and Histria.

Ibis Tours (see Tourist Information on p218) in Tulcea arranges bird-watching trips, as do specialist travel agencies abroad (p347).

Getting Around

In the delta proper it's easy to hire rowing boats from fishermen. This is the only way to penetrate the delta's exotic backwaters.

NAVROM FERRIES

Navrom (☎ 511 553) operates passenger ferries year-round to towns and villages in the delta. It also runs its own tours on weekends. On Saturday, tours head to Sulina, leaving at 8am and returning at 8pm (€4.80); on Sunday at the same hours tours sail to Sfântu Gheorghe (€4.80). You get to see the landscape but there is little time for true exploring.

A regularly scheduled ferry for Sulina departs from Tulcea at 1.30pm Monday to Friday (€4, four hours), while the return departs Sulina at 7am Tuesday to Friday and

Sunday. It makes stops at Partizani, Maliuc, Gorgova and Crişan (€2.65) on the way. To get to Mila 23 and Caraorman, disembark at Crişan and catch a local boat.

The Sfântu Gheorghe ferry departs from Tulcea at 1.30pm Monday, Wednesday, Thursday and Friday (€4, 5½ hours), returning at 6am Tuesday, Thursday, Friday and Sunday. These boats stop at Bălteni de Jos, Mahmudia and Murighiol.

Ferries to Periprava from Tulcea depart at 1.30pm Monday, Tuesday, Wednesday and Friday (€5, four hours), stopping at Chilia Veche. Return ferries leave Periprava at 5am on Tuesday, Wednesday, Thursday and Sunday.

FLAPPING BY

Words you might (hopefully) hear on your Delta excursions: *barbiţă* (pelican); *vâtlan* (cormoran); *raţă mare* (great duck); *nagât* (lapwing); *lopătar* (spoon bill); *vultur codalb* (white-tail eagle); *ştiucă* (pike); *crap* (carp); and *nisetru* (Black Sea sturgeon).

NORTHERN DOBROGEA

Ferry tickets are sold at Tulcea's Navrom terminal from 11.30am to 1.30pm. In summer the queues are long, so get in the correct line early (each window sells tickets to a different destination). There are also ticket counters on the ferries themselves.

HYDROFOILS

Hydrofoils to Sulina (1½ hours, €5.25) depart from Tulcea's AFDJ Galaţia terminal, next to the floating ambulance, every day at 2pm. They stop in Maliuc (€1.80) and Crişan (€2.65) on the way. The return trip is at 7pm. Purchase tickets on board.

TULCEA

☎ 240 / pop 94,750

Tulcea (pronounced tool-*cha*) is usually passed through quickly en route to the delta, so most tourists miss its unassuming appeal. Despite reminders that Tulcea is mainly an industrial town (eg the billowing smoke from the brick factory outside town), it has a lively energy and an allure of its own, with hopping nightclubs and a sizeable Turkish population that lends a multiethnic flavour. For strolling, there is a broad riverfront promenade where lovers hold hands and watch the sunset, and delightful – if slightly run-down – side-streets (try the area behind the Natural History Museum, and up the hill along Str Gloriei).

Tulcea was settled by Dacians and Romans from the 7th to 1st centuries BC, when it was called Aegyssus.

Orientation

The Tulcea arm (braţul Tulcea) of the Danube loops through Tulcea, cutting off the northern part of town (a sparsely populated area known as Tudor Vladimirescu, where the city's **beach** is located) from the main part of Tulcea where all the facilities are located.

MAPS & PUBLICATIONS

The only city map you're likely to find is included in the *Tulcea Guide*, sold for €1 in the museums. There are numerous detailed maps of the delta available at hotels and bookstores, including Amco's *The Danube Delta* (€1.90), which has many photos and detailed information about local marine life. The best delta map is Eco Touristic Map *Danube Delta Biosphere Reserve* (€2), published by Olimp.

Information

A floating **ambulance station** (staţia de ambulanţă; ☯ 24hr) is moored in front of Culture House on the riverfront. Some of its crew speak English.

To connect to the Internet, head to **Spatial Net** (Str Păcii 66; per hour €0.40; ☯ 24hr). At the **Anason Pharmacy** (☎ 513 352; Str Babadag 8), there's an all-night dispenser.

All the hotels have currency exchanges. The **post office** (☎ 512 869; Str Babadag 5; ☯ 7am-8pm Mon-Fri, 8am-noon Sat) and **telephone centre** (☯ 7am-8pm) share the same building.

TOURIST INFORMATION

Atbad (☎ 514 114; www.atbad.ro; Str Babadag 11) Offers full-board excursions. See under Sleeping p219 for details.

Danubius Travel Agency (☎ /fax 517 836; Hotel Europolis; ☯ 8.30am-6.30pm Mon-Fri & 9am-1pm Sat) It arranges a variety of day-trips from Tulcea, usually for under €20 per person including lunch.

Ibis Tours (☎ /fax 512 787; www.ibistours.net; Str Babadag 6, Ap14) Arranges wildlife and bird-watching tours in Dobrogea and the delta, led by professional ornithologists, from €30 a day.

Information and Ecological Education Centre (☎ 519 214; www.deltaturism.ro; Str Portului 34A; ☯ 8am-6pm) This should be your first stop. Located inside the building opposite the AFDJ hydrofoil terminal, this office is a representative of Antrec and is run by the DDBR. It can book a range of accommodation and also provide helpful advice and assist in making tours. It can also help you get fishing, hunting and travel permits. Booklets and maps are available here.

Nouvelles Frontières/Simpa Turism (☎ /fax 515 753; office@simpaturism.ro; Hotel Delta) It organises numerous river tours (usually a few euro more expensive than other travel agencies). Its boats hold around 80 to 100 people.

Sights

In front of the **St Nicholas Cathedral** (Str Progresului 37) there's a **memorial** to local victims of the 1989 revolution. Nearby is a fabulous **Greek Orthodox church** (Str G Doja). Northeast you'll find the **Azizie Mosque** (1863; Str Independenţei), which the charismatic, elderly gatekeeper will open upon request. As you stroll along the river, note the **Independence Monument** (1904) perched regally on Citadel Hill, at the far eastern end of town. You can reach it by following Str Gloriei to its end.

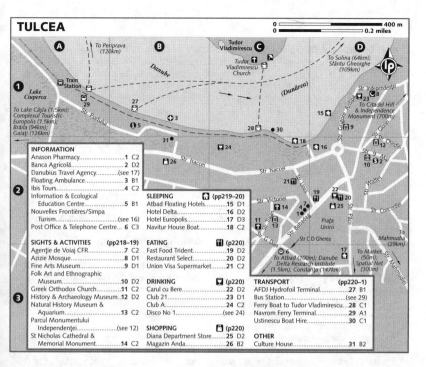

TULCEA

0 — 400 m
0 — 0.2 miles

INFORMATION

Anason Pharmacy	**1** C2
Banca Agricolă	**2** D2
Danubius Travel Agency	(see 17)
Floating Ambulance	**3** B1
Ibis Tours	**4** C2
Information & Ecological Education Centre	**5** B1
Nouvelles Frontières/Simpa Turism	(see 16)
Post Office & Telephone Centre	**6** C3

SIGHTS & ACTIVITIES	**(pp218–19)**
Agenţie de Voiaj CFR	**7** C2
Azizie Mosque	**8** D1
Fine Arts Museum	**9** D1
Folk Art and Ethnographic Museum	**10** D2
Greek Orthodox Church	**11** C2
History & Archaeology Museum	**12** D2
Natural History Museum & Aquarium	**13** C2
Parcul Monumentului Independenţei	(see 12)
St Nicholas Cathedral & Memorial Monument	**14** C2

SLEEPING	🛏 **(pp219–20)**
Atbad Floating Hotels	**15** D1
Hotel Delta	**16** D2
Hotel Europolis	**17** D3
Navitur House Boat	**18** C2

EATING	🍴 **(p220)**
Fast Food Trident	**19** D2
Restaurant Select	**20** D2
Union Visa Supermarket	**21** C2

DRINKING	🍸 **(p220)**
Carul cu Bere	**22** D2
Club 21	**23** D1
Club A	**24** C2
Disco No 1	(see 24)

SHOPPING	🛍 **(p220)**
Diana Department Store	**25** D2
Magazin Anda	**26** B2

TRANSPORT	**(pp220–1)**
AFDJ Hydrofoil Terminal	**27** B1
Bus Station	(see 29)
Ferry Boat to Tudor Vladimirescu	**28** C1
Navrom Ferry Terminal	**29** A1
Ustinescu Boat Hire	**30** C1

OTHER	
Culture House	**31** B2

All of Tulcea's museums are open Tuesday to Sunday from 9am to 6pm May to August and 8am to 4pm September to April. They charge €0.40 admission.

Some ruins of the old citadel can be seen in the archaeological site known as the **Parcul Monumentului Independenţei**, next to the **History & Archaeology Museum** (☎ 513 626; cnr Str Gloriei & Str Chindiei). The **Folk Art and Ethnographic Museum** (☎ 516 204; Str 9 Mai, 4) has Turkish and Romanian traditional costumes, fishing nets, rugs and carpets among its exhibits.

The **Natural History Museum & Aquarium** (☎ 515 866; Str Progresului 32) highlights the delta's fauna with lots of stuffed birds and a basement aquarium. The **Fine Arts Museum** (☎ 513 249; Str Grigore Antipa 2) has over 700 wood and glass icons and a large collection of Romanian paintings and sculptures, including some Surrealist and avant-garde works.

Festivals & Events

Tulcea hosts the annual **International Folk Festival of Danubian Countries** (🌣 Aug), where local songs, games and traditional activities are played out to a Danubian backdrop. Tulcea is also the site of a **Winter Carnival** (🌣 Dec), where you can partake in Delta wintertime customs while nursing cups of hot mulled wine.

Sleeping

Hotel Delta (☎ 514 720; www.deltahotelro.com; Str Isaccei 2; s/d €35/47; 🕃) A city landmark, it boasts the most luxurious rooms around, some according a nice view of the river. There's a restaurant and bar.

Navitur House Boat (☎ 518 894; fax 518 953; d €10) The boat is not the cleanest and staff speak little English, but the tiny double cabins with shared bath (no hot water) are among the cheapest places to stay in town. It's moored opposite Hotel Delta.

Atbad (☎ 514 114; www.atbad.ro; Str Babadag 11) The boatels Delta 2 and Delta 3 (three- and four-star, respectively), run by Atbad, are worth considering. They dock about 100m north of Hotel Delta. The boatels go out on one-, two- and three-day excursions (about €50 per person, per day), including to some

NORTHERN DOBROGEA

AUTHOR'S CHOICE

Hotel Europolis (☎ 512 443; www.europolis.ro; Str Păcii 20; s/d €19/24; 🖳) Rejoice over the spacious rooms with huge bathrooms. The staff can help arrange all kinds of tours. For the same prices, you can stay at its Complexul Touristic Europolis, a resort-like hotel by Lake Câşla, 2km outside of Tulcea's city limits. Though favoured by groups, the site is lovely, in the thick of nature. Water-bikes and small boats can be rented and there are walking trails.

---

isolated areas. Meals are available on board. It's a convenient, hassle-free way of exploring the delta. Contact Atbad in advance for times of departure and destinations; they change regularly.

No camping is allowed within Tulcea's city limits. However, there are many areas where wild camping is permitted on the banks of the canal within a few kilometres of the city – ask at the Information and Ecological Education Centre for details.

Eating & Drinking

Restaurant Select (☎ 510 301; Str Păcii 6; mains €2-4; ⏲ 9am-midnight) Treat yourself to a top-notch meal here; the cuisine is excellent and prices extremely reasonable. From its varied menu, choose from fish, frog legs, pizza and the local speciality, *tochitura Dobrogeana* (p43). The menu is in six languages. The dining room is archly formal, but sit on the terrace.

Fast Food Trident (Str Babadag; mains €1-3; ⏲ 11am-midnight) This is an excellent spot for cheesy pizzas and pasta. It's opposite the Diana Department Store.

Carul cu Bere (Str Păcii 6; mains €1-3; ⏲ 9am-midnight) This adjoins Restaurant Select and has a fun terrace that's great to enjoy a beer and to people-watch. A lively crowd usually heads here to pull back a few, and light meals are served too.

There's a string of cafés, kebab and fast-food joints along Str Unirii.

Stock up on picnic supplies and fresh fruits at the **produce market** (Str Păcii) or the **Union Visa supermarket** (Str Unirii).

Two side-by-side clubs on the waterfront form Tulcea's disco central. **Disco No 1** (Str Isaccei) has seen better days, while **Club A** (Str Isaccei) , just around the corner, is much more popular, and has two dance floors and a modern, flashy interior. Club A attracts a mixed-age crowd and plays pop and dance hits. **Club 21** (Str Grigore Antipa 10; ⏲ 7pm-4am; terrace ⏲ 8am-11pm) is a cozier variant, with

couches and low lighting and true club house music.

Shopping

Magazin Anda (Str Isaccei 23; ⏲ 9am-6pm) has camping gear and supplies.

Diana Department Store (☎ 0722-703 632; Piaţa Unirii 1; ⏲ 9am-7pm Mon-Fri, 9am-5pm Sat-Sun)

Getting There & Away

The **Agenţie de Voiaj CFR** (☎ 511 360; Str Unirii 4; ⏲ 9am-4pm Mon-Fri) is on the corner of Str Babadag. From the **train station** (☎ 513 706; Str Portului) there are only two, slow trains to Constanţa daily (€3.65, five hours). There is one daily train to Bucharest (€7, six hours).

The **bus station** (☎ 513 304) adjoins the **Navrom ferry terminal** (Str Portului). As many as 15 buses and maxitaxis head to Bucharest (€7), at least nine to Galaţi (€2.25), five to Brăila (€2.25), nine to Murighiol (via Mahmudia; €1.20) and one a day to Iaşi (€9) and Piatra Neamţ (€9.75). There are two daily buses to Jurilovca (€1.75). Maxitaxis to Constanţa (€4) leave every half-hour from 5.30am to 8pm.

One bus a day heads to Istanbul (€34).

Getting Around

Bus No 4 departs from the bus and train stations, runs along Str Isaccei and heads down Str Păcii. A small motorboat continuously links the southern and northern sections of Tulcea (tickets €0.05).

Private motorboats lined up at the harbour cost upwards of €20 an hour for up to 10 people. **Ustinescu Boat Hire** (☎ 526 042) has a boat moored near the Tudor Vladimirescu ferry.

TULCEA TO PERIPRAVA

The 120km Chilia channel (braţul Chilia), the longest and largest channel, snakes along Romania's border with Ukraine before fanning out into some 40 tiny rivers forming a mini-delta of its own. It's the least touristed of the delta's main arms.

Navrom ferries only call at **Chilia Veche** and **Periprava**, which is 30km from the sea. Immediately west of Periprava are the two islands of **Babina** and **Cernovca**, which were diked by Ceauşescu in the late 1980s as part of his drive to turn the region into agricultural land.

South of Periprava lies the impressive **Letea forest** (Pădurea Letea), which covers 2.8 sq km. A national park since 1938, it is today protected by the DDBR. Tourists can visit Letea village nearby and spend a few days touring the surrounding waterways. Expect to pay local fishermen at least €50 a day.

For information on ferries to/from Chilia Veche and Periprava, see p217.

TULCEA TO SULINA

The Sulina arm, the shortest channel of the Danube, stretches 63.7km from Tulcea to Sulina. The Navrom's ferry's first stop is at **Partizani**, from where you can find a fisherman to row you to the three lakes to the north: Tataru, Lung and Meşter. Next stop is **Maliuc**, where there is a hotel, and camp ground with space for 80 people. North of Maliuc is **Lake Furtuna**, a snare for bird-watchers.

The ferry's next stop is the junction with Old Danube, 1km upstream from **Crişan**. There are several *pensiunes* (whole houses given over to tourists) in the village, all charging about €10 per person. Try **Pensiune Gheorghe Silviu** (☎ 511 279) or **Pensiune Pocora** (☎ 511 279). There is also the DDBR's **Crişan Centre for Ecological Information & Education** (☎ 519 214; office@deltaturism.ro; 🕑 8am-4pm Tue-Sun), which features wildlife displays, a library and a video room. At the main Crişan ferry dock, ask about side trips to **Mila 23** and **Caraorman**.

SULINA

☎ 240 / pop 5000

There's a faded romance to Sulina, and its position, dangling off the edge of Europe, gives it a poetic allure that's lived up to by its quiet **beach**, a **lighthouse** (1870) and a 19th-century British **cemetery**. First written about in AD950, this is the delta's largest village, with some 50% of the population living here.

A canal dug between 1880 and 1902 shortened the length of the Tulcea–Sulina channel by 20km, ensuring Sulina's future as the delta's main commercial port. After WWI Sulina was declared a 'free port' and trade boomed. Greek merchants dominated business here until their expulsion in 1951. The village has been in a slow process of economic decay ever since.

At the time of writing, there were plans to start a maxitaxi service from Sulina to Sfântu Gheorghe along a dike, which would increase mobility options greatly.

Orientation & Information

The ferry dock is located in the centre of town, with a few shops and bars to the west. There are no banks. The **DDBR office** (🕑 10am-6pm Tue-Sun, May-Oct) is at house No 1 near the dock.

Sleeping

You can camp on the beach. As you get off the ferry, watch for people offering private rooms (around €10 per person).

A few hundred metres west along the riverfront from the Sulina Cinema is a small sign pointing to the friendly **Pensiune Astir** (☎ 543 379; s/d €10/20). The **Pensiune Delta Sulina** (☎ 0722-275 554; s/d €18/25) is a comfortable, three-star option.

Getting There & Away

For information on ferries and hydrofoils see p218

TULCEA TO SFÂNTU GHEORGHE

☎ 240

The Sfântu Gheorghe arm (braţul Sfântu Gheorghe) stretches 109km southeast from Tulcea to the fishing commune of Sfântu Gheorghe. A road runs along more than half of the Sfântu Gheorghe arm, making it more accessible to travellers.

From Tulcea, a potholed road – horrid even by Romanian standards – leads 13km southeast to **Nufăru**, a village boasting archaeological finds from the 12th and 13th centuries. The Navrom ferry's first stop is at **Bălteni de Jos**.

The ferry's second stop is at **Mahmudia**, 28km from Tulcea, developed on the site of the ancient Roman walled city of Salsovia (sun city). Emperor Constantine had his co-ruler and rival Licinus killed here.

Ferries stop at **Murighiol** (Violet Lake), 45km from Tulcea, which was a Roman military camp in the 2nd century BC. It's a 3km walk to the river from the maxitaxi stop: keep walking in the same direction that the maxitaxi was travelling and turn left after the last house. The stacks of reeds you see piled up by the dock are headed to Germany; Germans big on folk-chic are the biggest importers of Delta reeds, used to make thatched roofs for their upscale country homes.

The most popular day trip from Murighiol is northeast to **Uzlina**, once reserved as an exclusive hunting ground for Ceauşescu. Just beyond is a trio of lakes – Uzlina, Isac and Isăcel – that are popular for spotting pelicans, egrets and grey herons.

From Murighiol, the road continues 5km south to **Dunavăţu de Sus**.

Sleeping

In Mahmudia, there are numerous *cazares* and *pensiunes* to stay at, as well as one bonafide hotel, **Leo** (☎ 545 550; s/d €24/31), a large and modern full-service centre on the riverfront.

Murighiol has more options, the best of which is **Pensiune Riviera** (☎ 545 910; d €15 including three meals a day). Headquarted just 50m down the road where the maxitaxi lets you off (further in the same direction), this B&B (the large sign is impossible to miss) can easily arrange boat trips into the canals for about €15 an hour. Otherwise, **Camping & Hotel Pelican** (☎ 514 341; d/hut/tent site €26/12/2.50), 3km from the maxitaxi stop, and 1.5km from the Navrom ferry port, has the advantage of being near the river but is otherwise a lonely, drab place. Some people camp wild by the riverbanks here.

Nouvelles Frontières/Simpa Turism (see Tourist Information on p218) will take bookings for rooms aboard the gleaming **Cormoran Hotel Complex** (☎ 0744 656 372, 515 753; s €30-75, d €36-87), a luxurious oasis smack in the middle of the delta at Uzlina. It has various types of accommodation in the area and prices vary accordingly. There is a restaurant, bar, disco and sunbathing terrace. Guests can waterski, windsurf, and hire small rowing boats or motorboats to explore the delta (at higher prices than elsewhere).

Getting There & Away

For ferry schedules to the area, see p217. There are nine daily maxitaxis from Tulcea to Murighiol (via Mahmudia; €1.20).

SFÂNTU GHEORGHE
☎ 240 / pop 1000

The ferry continues downstream from Murighiol, past Ivancea – one of the delta's largest geese-nesting areas – to the fishing village **Sfântu Gheorghe** (pronounced sfant-u gore-gay). First recorded in the mid-14th century by Visconti, a traveller from Genoa, this is one of the best villages to sample traditional cooking; but the black caviar for which the village is famed (it is the only place in the delta where sturgeon are caught) is a delicacy reserved for religious feasts.

There are no tourist sights here, and that is precisely the point of taking the trouble to visit. Highlights include spying on life in a traditional fishing village, listening to the frogs compete in the ponds, and the 40-minute hike to the beach, where the Danube majestically enters the Black Sea. There are no beach services and few people – just deserted stretches of fine sand. From the dock, walk past the main square, then head right, eastward.

Also of note is the architecture of the well-tended homes here, most of which have Byzantine-influenced porches under ornamental arches.

The only note of disharmony here is rung by the monstrous eyesore defacing the seascape to the north of Sfântu Gheorghe's beach. This was another Ceauşescu brainchild: believe it or not, it's a gigantic metal aeolian windmill. Meant to be among the planet's largest, it instead worked for two months before starting its main function: rusting.

Sleeping

Pensiune Mareea (☎ 0744-30639; www.mareea.go.ro; s/d €19/24) The best place around is a 250m walk straight from the dock. Aside from the comfortable lodgings and scrumptious home-cooked meals, the owners offer a full range of boat excursions, from €8 per person to €120 for a four-person, full-day trip into varied landscapes. From here, boats take in both sea and lake/canal ecosystems.

There are several *cazares* and *pensiunes* here: you can accept an offer from those who greet the boat, or ask around. Wild camping is possible on the beach, but it gets very windy and it's a long 2km hike in the dark.

Getting There & Away
Only ferries make it to Sfântu Gheorghe (see p217). There are plans to start a maxitaxi service over the dike to Sulina by 2004.

AROUND LAKE RAZIM
Lake Razim, which flows into Lake Goloviţa at its southern end, is the largest permanent water expanse in the delta.

From Tulcea, a dirt road leads south to **Agighiol** and **Sarichioi**, on the northwestern tip of Lake Razim. Houses in all of the villages along this route are crowned with thatched-reed roofs, typical to the delta.

Babadag is on the southwestern edge of Lake Babadag. Some 5000 Turkish families live in the area, and have built stylish new houses on the town's fringes, providing a fresh architectural contrast to the faceless concrete buildings in the centre.

The **Mosque Ali Gazi Pasha** (Str Mihai Viteazul; admission €0.40; 8am-9pm), opposite the bus station, is Romania's oldest architectural Muslim monument, built in 1522. It's surrounded by a pleasant garden with apricot trees. Services are held on Friday at 1.15pm. From here head north to the moribund **Hotel Dumbrava** (561 302; Str Republicii), which has musty doubles for €7.

From Enisala the road continues to **Jurilovca** (also reachable via a turn-off the E87, 13km south of Babadag). This fishing village, untouched by the tourist industry, is much loved for its attractive location. From here, it's possible to hire a boat to take you across to **Gura Portiţei** (1½ hours), on the eastern shores of Lake Goloviţa. Recently, this remote section of sand and reed banks has taken a commercial turn with the opening of the **Complex Turistic Gura Portiţei** (0740 534 140, 0724 214 224; campsite/d/ste €1.50/8/35), which boasts a restaurant, disco, long stretches of beach and which offers boat excursions into the delta.

Getting There & Away
Few buses from Tulcea head this far south, which makes this part of the delta almost impossible to explore without private transport, including a bicycle.

UPRIVER FROM TULCEA
Celic-Dere, Saon & Cocoş Monasteries
Though this region is host to numerous monasteries, three are particularly well known. Together roughly forming a triangle, these were built in areas where archeological digs had previously uncovered significant finds. Some locals believe that the area within the triangle has special energy.

From Tulcea, head west along the main Tulcea–Smârdan road (E87) for 29km, then turn left for 8km to the **Celic-Dere Monastery** and its **religious ethnographic museum** (admission €0.40). The interior frescoes (by Gheorghe Eftimiu) are colourful. Return to the main road and continue 3km until the turn-off (on your right) for the **Saon Monastery**. Built as a hermitage in 1846, it became a monastery in 1881.

Cocoş Monastery is another 8km along the E87, then another 4km off a side road to your left (south). It houses a **medieval book and icon museum** (admission €0.40; 10am-4pm Tue-Sun). Though founded in 1833, the current buildings were all reconstructed after 1910.

It is possible to stay overnight (males only) at these monasteries. They do not take reservations – just show up and speak to the monks.

Niculiţel
The ruins of a 4th-century **paleo-Christian basilica** (Basilica Martirică Niculiţel; 10am-7pm) are in Niculiţel, 31km west of Tulcea. It was only uncovered in 1971 following heavy storms that exposed part of the martyrs' crypt, which contained bones of four martyrs.

A modern building shields the remains where archaeologists work today. Parts of the church walls have been reconstructed, and the centre of the church is still being excavated. Nearby is the sweet, small **Sfântu Anastase church**.

North of Niculiţel, **swamps** stretch for some 10km to the Danube. Bargain with a local fisherman to take you exploring in a kayak.

INTO MOLDAVIA
From the Danube Delta, the cities of Galaţi and Brăila, administratively part of Moldavia, are the gateways to further travel

NORTHERN DOBROGEA

EUROPE'S ONLY LEPER COLONY

Not exactly a source of national pride, but Romania is home to Europe's only known remaining leper colony, based in the village of Tichileşti, 44km west of Tulcea. The existence of the leprosarium was wholly denied during the Ceauşescu regime and even today few delta residents know of, or admit to, its chilling presence.

The colony was founded in 1929 when 180 lepers were banished from northern Bucovina (present-day Ukraine). Orthodox monks from the Tichileşti Monastery gave them shelter and in 1931 a hospital was established in the small village. Queen Marie financed the building of two pavilions.

Between 1952 and 1957 there were over 280 leprous exiles in Tichileşti. Today it's home to 29 patients, the last one admitted in 2000. Patients require continual treatment and lead a semi-independent life in small cottages in the 'village'.

Following auctions of Ceauşescu's personal belongings in 1998 and 1999, some clothes were donated to the leper colony – a perfect irony.

The colony is closed to all except friends and relatives of patients.

to Bucharest, Transylvania (via Braşov) or Suceava and Iaşi. Exiting the Danube Delta region involves a short ferry across the Danube River; this is included in bus and maxitaxi (p350) prices.

Galaţi & Brăila

Galaţi (pronounced ga-*lahts*) and Brăila are neighbouring cities near the confluence of the Danube, Siret and Prut Rivers. Perched in an unattractive backwater of Romania, at the jagged borders of Moldova and Ukraine, these two industrial cities 21km apart are merely used as transit points between Tulcea and Transylvania or Moldavia. The cities offer better connections eastwards than further north into Moldavia.

Galaţi (population 325,050), home to Romania's largest steel mill, has shabby shipyards scattered for kilometres along the riverside. Massive housing complexes fill the centre and cover entire hillsides. Brăila (population 230,687) is more pleasant, though still has a run-down, slightly aggressive air. Both were once important, flourishing ports. Romania's naval fleet is paraded in Galaţi in all its glory every year on Navy Day, the second weekend in August.

GETTING THERE & AWAY

In both cities, the bus and train stations are adjacent to each other. The most efficient mode of transport to and from here is via maxitaxis. There are no longer any ferries or hydrofoils to and from Tulcea.

From Brăila, there are 20 buses or maxitaxis to Galaţi (€1), 10 to Bucharest (€6), seven to Constanţa (€6), five to Tulcea (€2.25), three to Suceava (€8) and Braşov (€5.30) and two to Sibiu (€7). Maxitaxis to Braşov, Constanţa and Galaţi leave from platform No 1 across the street from the main bus station. Most of these buses and maxitaxis originate in Galaţi, from where there's also a thrice-daily bus service to Iaşi.

From both cities, there are five daily trains to Bucharest (€11, four to six hours), two to Constanţa (€9, six hours) and one to Braşov (€7, five hours) and Oradea (€20, 17½ hours) via Suceava (€10, seven hours), and Vatra Dornei (€13, 10 hours).

Crişana & Banat

These regions are the natural jewel in Romania's crown. Some of the country's best-kept secrets are here: the soaring Apuşeni Mountains, deep caves, gorges, waterfalls and thermal waters alongside the exquisite, crumbling architecture of the Hapsburg empire. The areas of Crişana (north of the Mureş River) and Banat (to the south) have a spirited independence found nowhere else in Romania and a sense of regional identity, ethnic diversity and European influence. It was in Timişoara that the seeds of the 1989 revolution were sown, a fact of which these charming, tenacious people are mightily proud.

Crişana and Banat once merged imperceptibly into Yugoslavia's Vojvodina and Hungary's Great Plain. Until 1918 all three regions were governed jointly, and although Subotica (Yugoslavia), Szeged (Hungary) and Timişoara now belong to three different countries, all three cities bear the unmistakable imprint of the Habsburgs.

Oradea, Arad and Timişoara, which were once large military fortresses intended to defend Austria–Hungary's southeastern flank, were handed to Romania following WWI, despite their predominantly Hungarian populations. The region has benefited from greater links to the West, via Hungarian and Yugoslav TV, and the resulting exposure to the political changes in the former East Germany.

This is the door to Romania from the west – go through it and explore the caves, the spa resorts and ski runs surrounded by thick, ancient forests.

TOP FIVE

- Sinking into the soothing thermal waters of Băile Herculane's **Roman baths** (p243)

- Seeing the ancient stalactites and stalagmites in the magnificent **Bear Cave** (p232) and the surreal **Scărişoara Ice Cave** (p232)

- Lingering in Timişoara's beautiful **Metropolitan Cathedral** (p239) during a candle-lit service

- Skiing, hiking, cycling or gazing at the western **Apuşeni Mountains** (p231)

- Spending a sunny afternoon swimming in one of Timişoara's **outdoor pools** (p239), an evening at the **opera** (p242) and a nightcap in a **Piaţa Victoriei** (p241) bar

Bear & Ice Caves
Western Apuşeni Ranges
★ Timişoara
Băile Herculane

★ TELEPHONE CODE: 03 | ★ POPULATION: 4.7 MILLION | ★ AREA: 227,420 SQ KM

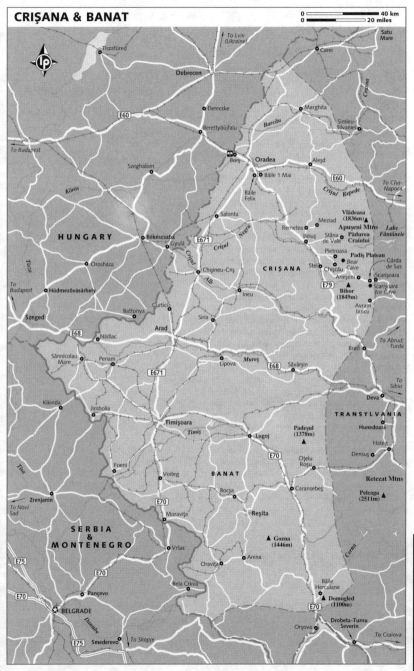

CRIŞANA & BANAT

0 — 40 km
0 — 20 miles

To Lviv (Ukraine)

Satu Mare

Tiszafüred

Carei

Debrecen

Derecske

Marghita

Simleu-Silvaniei

E60

Berettyóújfalu

Barcău

Crasna

To Budapest

Szeghalom

Borş

Oradea

Aleşd

E60

To Cluj-Napoca

Băile 1 Mai

Crişul Repede

Lake Fântânele

Băile Felix

Vlădeasa (1836m)

Körös

HUNGARY

Békéscsaba

Salonta

Meziad

Apuseni Mtns

Remetea

Stâna de Vale

Pădurea Craiului

Gyula

E671

Crişul

Negru

Beiuş

Pietroasa

Padiş Plateau

Gârda de Sus

Orosháza

Crişul

Chişineu-Criş

CRIŞANA

Stei

Bear Cave

Chişcău

Scărişoara

To Budapest

Hódmezővásárhely

Alb

Ineu

E79

Arieşeni

Scărişoara Ice Cave

Tisza

Szeged

Curtici

Siria

Bihor (1849m)

Avram Iancu

Battonya

E68

Nădlac

Arad

To Abrud; Turda

Sânnicolau Mare

Periam

E671

Lipova

Mureş

Săvârşin

Brad

E68

To Sibiu

Kikinda

Jimbolia

Deva

TRANSYLVANIA

Timişoara

Timiş

Lugoj

Padeşul (1378m)

Hunedoara

E70

Haţeg

Foeni

Oţelu Roşu

Densuş

BANAT

Bocşa

Caransebeş

Retezat Mtns

Zrenjanin

Voiteg

Reşita

Peleaga (2511m)

To Novi Sad

Moraviţa

SERBIA & MONTENEGRO

E70

Gozna (1446m)

Vršac

Anina

Cerna

E75

Oraviţa

E70

Bela Crkva

Băile Herculane

Domogled (1100m)

Pančevo

BELGRADE

E70

Danube

Orşova

Drobeta-Turnu Severin

E75

Smederevo

To Skopje

To Craiova

HISTORY

Historical Banat is today divided between western Romania, eastern Hungary and northern Yugoslavia. First settled in the 6th century BC, by AD106 the region was part of the Roman province of Dacia. From the end of the 9th century until the Ottoman conquest of Banat in 1552, the region was under Hungarian rule.

In 1699 the Turks relinquished Hungary to Austria but held Banat until their defeat by Habsburg prince Eugene of Savoy in 1716. In 1718 Banat became part of the Austro-Hungarian empire.

The Treaty of Trianon in 1920 split the territory among Romania, Hungary and Yugoslavia, setting Banat's current borders.

ORADEA
☎ 259 / pop 223,700

Elegant Oradea lies a few kilometres east of the Hungarian border, in the centre of the Crișana region, at the edge of the Carpathian Mountains.

Of all the cities of the Austro-Hungarian empire, Oradea has best retained its 19th-century romantic style. It was ceded to Romania in 1920 and has since taken on an air of faded grandeur, but it is a lovely place to stop, whatever direction you're heading in.

Orientation

The train station is a couple of kilometres north of the centre; tram Nos 1 and 4 run south from Piața București (outside the train station) to Piața Unirii, Oradea's main square. Tram No 4 also stops at the northern end of Calea Republicii – a five-minute walk south to the centre.

The main square north of the river is Piața Republicii (also called Piața Regele Ferdinand I).

Information

INTERNET ACCESS
Game Star Internet Café (Str Mihai Eminescu 4; ♥ 24 hr; per hr €0.50)

MEDICAL SERVICES
24-Hour Pharmacy (☎ 418 242; Str Libertății junction with Piața Ferdinand)

MONEY
Cash transfers, ATMs and currency exchange facilities can be found at:

Eurom Bank (☎ 210 023; Piața Independenței 35; ♥ 9am-4pm Mon-Fri)
HVB Bank (☎ 406 700; Piața Unirii 24; ♥ 9am-4pm Mon-Fri)

POST & TELEPHONE
Post Office (☎ 136 420; Str Roman Ciorogariu 12; ♥ 7am-7.30pm Mon-Fri)
Telephone Office (Calea Republicii 5; ♥ 8am-8pm daily)

TOURIST INFORMATION
There is no official tourist information centre. Instead try **Panda Tours** (☎ 477 222; Str Iosif Vulcan 6; ♥ 9am-7pm Mon-Fri, 9am-1pm Sat), which has English-speaking staff.

Sights

Oradea's most imposing sights are on its two central squares, Piața Unirii and Piața Republicii. The **Orthodox Moon Church** (Biserica cu Lună; 1784; Piața Unirii) has an unusual lunar mechanism on its tower that changes position in accordance with the moon's movement.

In the centre of Piața Unirii stands an equestrian **statue of Mihai Viteazul**, the prince of Wallachia (r 1593–1601), who is said to have rested in Oradea in 1600. East of the statue, overlooking the Crișul Repede River, is the magnificent **Vulturul Negru** ('Black Vulture'; 1908) hotel and shopping centre. The mall, with its fantastic stained-glass ceiling, links Piața Unirii with Str Independenței and Str Vasile Alecsandri. A **statue of Mihai Eminescu**, the 19th-century poet, overlooks the river on its southern bank.

Heading east along the river, turn right on to Piața Decembrie 1. In Central Park is the **Culture House** in front of which is a large **monument** to soldiers who fought for Romanian independence during WWI.

Across the bridge from Piața Unirii the magnificent neoclassical **State Theatre** (Teatrul de Stat), designed by Viennese architects Fellner and Hellmer in 1900, dominates Piața Republicii. Nearby, in the centre of Traian Park, stands a small **museum** dedicated to the Hungarian poet Endre Ady (1877–1919), who lived for four years in Oradea before his undignified death from syphilis.

The **Roman Catholic cathedral** (Str Stadionului), built between 1752 and 1780, is the largest in Romania. Organ concerts are occasionally held here.

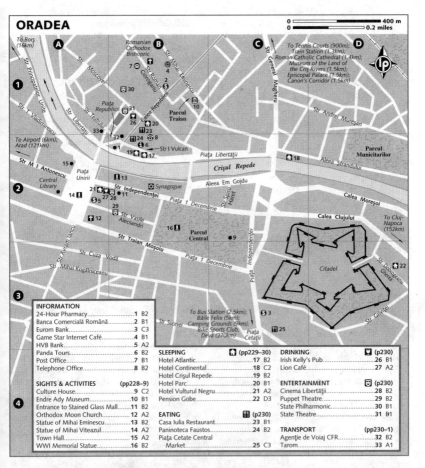

ORADEA

0 — 400 m
0 — 0.2 miles

The adjacent **Episcopal Palace** (Episcopia Ortodoxă Română; 1770) boasts 100 fresco-adorned rooms and 365 windows, and houses the **Museum of the Land of the Criş Rivers** (Muzeul Ţării Crişului; ☎ 412 725; B-dul Dacia 1-3; ☻ 10am-5pm Tue-Sun; admission €1), with history and art exhibits relevant to the region. Immediately outside the museum entrance, busts of Romania's leading statesmen and kings stand on parade. To the right are busts of Wallachia's princes.

Note **Canon's Corridor** nearby, a series of archways along Str Stadionului that dates back to the 18th century.

The **citadel**, south of the river, was built in the 13th century but has since been converted into government offices.

Sleeping
BUDGET

Pension Gobe (☎ 414 845; Str Dobrogeanu Gherea 26; dm €12) A member of Youth Hostels România, it is the city's cheapest option and has three- to four-bed rooms, small restaurant, and a bar.

Hotel Vulturul Negru (Black Vulture; ☎ 449 259; Str Independenţei 1; s/d/tr €5/10/22) Dark and slightly strange, this backpackers' institution is housed within a 1908 Art Nouveau building.

Hotel Crişul Repede (☎ 232 509; Str Libertăţii 8; s/d/tr €10/17/20) This ageing hotel, overlooking the river, has cleanish, large rooms.

Hotel Parc (☎ 418 410; Calea Republicii 5-7; s/d €20/25) Ignore the crumbling façade – inside it's clean and gleaming white. It's the best of the budget bunch.

Strandul cu Voluti (cabins/tent sites per person €6/2; ☒ May–mid-Sep only), in Băile 1 Mai, 9km southeast of Oradea.

Camping Venus (☎ 318 266; tents & 2-3 bed bungalows per person €10) This camping ground is only 500m from Strandul cu Voluti. Take a southbound tram No 4 (black number) from the train station or an eastbound tram No 4 (red number) from Piața Unirii to the end of the line, then catch bus No 15 to the last stop.

MID-RANGE

Hotel Atlantic (☎ 414 953; Str Iosif Vulcan 9; s/d €40/47) Rejoice! Classy, contemporary rooms with marble bathroom, spa and your own private bar.

Hotel Continental (☎ 418 655; Aleea Ștrandului 1; s/d €56/70) A nine-storey business hotel with thermal pool, nightclub and – dare we say it – horrendously outdated blue interiors à la motorway service station.

Eating

Calea Republicii is lined with cheap and cheerful eateries and cafés. Oradeans enjoy a spot of evening strolling, and this is the street to do it in. Alternatively, stop for a coffee or ice-cream yourself and keep the people-watching tradition alive.

Paninoteca Faustos (Calea Republicii 3; mains €2) Watch the world go by while munching pizzas, salads and tiramisu.

Casa Iulia Restaurant (☎ 413 438; Calea Republicii 5; mains €3-4) Smart, minimalist joint with a trendy bar, and a massive outdoor terrace with live music on Thursday evening. It serves the usual soups, salads and grilled dishes.

Hotel Atlantic Restaurant (above; ☎ 414 953; meal €20) This elegant restaurant offers the best menu in town, with hearty goulash, Mexican chicken, and speciality steak dishes. Sadly, there is little choice for vegetarians.

Entertainment

CINEMAS

The highly atmospheric **Cinema Libertății** (☎ 434 097; Str Independenței 1), in the Vulturul Negru building, shows films in their original language with Romanian subtitles.

BARS

Most of Oradea's terrace cafés and restaurants double as bars in the evening.

Lion Café (Str Independenței 1; ☒ 7am-1am) Trendy by day, packed by night.

Irish Kelly's Pub (☎ 413 419; Calea Republicii 2) Hosts a rowdy crowd on its outside terrace.

THEATRE & CLASSICAL MUSIC

Tickets for performances at the **State Philharmonic** (Filarmonica de Stat; ☎ 430 853; Str Moscovei 5) can be purchased from its **ticket office** (☒ 10am-6pm Mon-Fri) inside the **State Theatre** (Teatrul de Stat; ☎ 130 885; Piața Republicii 4-6; ☒ 10am-11am, 5-7pm; tickets €3-12).

Kids big and little will enjoy the shows at Oradea's **Puppet Theatre** (Teatrul de Păpuși; ☎ 433 398; Str Vasile Alecsandri 8).

Getting There & Away

AIR

Tarom (☎ 131 918; Piața Republicii 2; ☒ 6.30am-8pm Mon-Fri, 10am-1pm Sat) operates three flights a week to Baia Mare, daily flights to Bucharest and two weekly flights to Satu Mare from Oradea **airport** (☎ 416 082; Calea Aradului km6). Fares are US$75/112 one-way/return, plus taxes (Tarom does not accept euros).

TRAIN

The **Agenție de Voiaj CFR** (☎ 130 578; Calea Republicii 2; ☒ 7am-7pm Mon-Fri) sells advance tickets for internal and international train trips.

Daily fast trains from Oradea include three to Budapest (€28), two to Bucharest (€16), five to Băile Felix, three to Cluj-Napoca (€8), one to Brașov and three to Timișoara (€5).

BUS

From Oradea **bus station** (autogară; ☎ 418 998; Str Războieni 81), south of the centre, there are daily services to Beiuș, Deva and Satu Mare. More than 20 maxitaxis (minibuses) run daily to/from Băile Felix.

There are daily bus services to Budapest leaving from outside the train station: a state bus (€12, 10 hours; purchase your ticket from the driver before departure) and maxitaxis (€16 one way).

CAR & MOTORCYCLE

The border crossing into Hungary for motorists at Borș, 16km west of Oradea, is open 24 hours.

Getting Around

Oradea **airport** (☎ 413 985/51) is 6km west of the centre on the Oradea–Arad road. Tarom runs a shuttle bus to/from the airport, which leaves from its office one hour before flights are scheduled to arrive or depart.

BĂILE FELIX

☎ 259

Băile Felix, 5km southeast of Oradea, is a famous year-round spa resort where city dwellers flock to splash in thermal pools. In summer you can barely move for inflatable balls, lilos and children. It has a rowdy package-holiday feel so forget napping in the sun. There's a large open-air thermal swimming pool here and several smaller pools covered by the rare *Nymphea lotus thermalis*, a giant white water lily.

The most popular public pools are **Strand Apollo** and **Strand Felix** (both ☼ 8am-7pm, closed Nov-Apr; admission €1), by the Staţia Băile Felix bus stop.

Sleeping

Pensiunea Veronica (☎ 318 481; Str Băile Felix 9; s & d €20) The 10 double rooms at this gorgeous pink family-run chalet, off the main drag, are the best in the resort.

Hotel International (☎ 318 445; s/d €34/42) On the eastern side of the resort, this large, family-friendly hotel offers a sauna and body treatments, and currency exchange at reception.

Hotel Muncel (☎ 318 460; s/d €15), not far from Hotel International, has a pool and treatment centre, as well as a travel agency, **Turism Felix** (☎ 318 321).

The nearest official **camping grounds** are 3km away at Băile 1 Mai (see p230), but many camp in the resort's main car park.

Getting There & Away

Maxitaxis run every 15 minutes or whenever full between Oradea and Băile Felix (€1.50 one way). Local trains also run daily from Oradea, stopping first at Staţia Băile Felix, then at the major hotels.

BEIUŞ & MEZIAD CAVE

Sixty-three kilometres southeast of Oradea, approaching the western fringe of the Apuşeni Mountains, is the small market town of **Beiuş**, from where you can visit the **Meziad Cave** (Peştera Meziad; ☼ 9-11am & 2-4pm; adult/child €0.75/0.25), discovered in 1859. The cave features an enormous opening and entrance tunnel, which has equally enormous stalactites with a curved shape. A good torch is recommended as there is no electric light in the cave.

From Beiuş's town centre, follow the signpost for 'Peştera Meziad' for 11km. When you get to the village of Remetea, bear right at the fork next to the Cămin Cultural building and continue for 9km until you reach Meziad. Turn left at the first fork, then cross the small white bridge to a gravel road. The main office for the cave is 4km along this road. The entrance to the cave is a further 1.5km, which is not accessible by car.

Sleeping

Wild camping is permitted around the cave. Alternatively, you could hike on from the cave for three hours (path not accessible by car) to 'Coada Lacului' (Tale of the Lake) where camping is permitted by the lake.

One kilometre from Beiuş is **Motel Desira** (☎ 259 322 420; d €30), which has five clean rooms and offers currency exchange.

Getting There & Away

Beiuş's train and bus stations adjoin each other on the southern edge of town. Its scant train services include daily local trains to Ploieşti (€6), Arad (€2), Cluj-Napoca (€3) and Bucharest (€6), and to Oradea (€1.50, three a day).

From Oradea there are two daily buses to Stâna de Vale via Beiuş. Services are greatly reduced on weekends.

STÂNA DE VALE

Scenic Stâna de Vale is a small alpine resort (1300m) in the Pădurea Craiului Mountains in the Bihor Massif. It lies at the end of a forest road 27km east of Beiuş. Between December and February it is transformed into a bustling ski centre. In summer it is a delightfully quiet hiking resort. It's worth a night's stay to breathe in the pine-scented air and amble through wooded glades.

The **ski lift** is next to the camping ground. It is possible to hire skis and have lessons. A couple of **hiking trails** lead into the Apuşeni Mountains. One of the trails (5½ to six hours; marked with red stripes) takes you to **Cabana Padiş** in the heavily karstic Padiş Plateau. Another more challenging trail (six hours; marked with blue triangles) leads to the **Meziad Cave** (above). Don't attempt it in bad weather or in winter.

Sleeping

In summer, it is best to bring your own tent and pitch it in the **camping ground** (cabins per person €12) at the western end of the resort.

The resort's main hotel is **Hotel Iadolina** (☎ 0744 599 334; d 2-star €27, 3-star €32). **Cerbul Vila & Restaurant**, opposite Hotel Iadolina, is open in winter only. The **ICCR Beiuş Restaurant** (mains €2) has a simple menu but good, fresh food.

Getting There & Away

The dusty train and bus stations are huddled together at the southern end of the resort. There are two daily buses between Oradea and Stâna de Vale via Beiuş (€1). Otherwise, hitch or hike. Local trains link Băile Felix to Beiuş, from where you can get to Stâna de Vale and surrounding villages.

BEAR CAVE

The **Bear Cave** (Peştera Urşilor; ⏰ around 10am-5pm; adult/child €1.50/1) – named after skeletons of the extinct cave bear (*Ursus spelaeus*) found by quarry workers in 1975 – is one of Romania's finest caves. It's well worth a day trip from Oradea, 82km northwest.

The magnificent galleries of the Bear Cave (482m) extend over 1000m on two levels. Stupendous stalactites and stalagmites loom from every angle, creating uncanny shapes in the half-darkness. The stalactites, many of which are believed to be 22,000 to 55,000 years old, grow 1cm every 20 years.

Compulsory guided tours allow you to spend an hour or so exploring the cold (a constant 10°C) stalactite-filled chambers of the cave. Note that the formations are delicate and must not be touched, and no rubbish should be dropped.

Sleeping

Pensiunea Daniadis (☎ 0722 699 847; d €10) At the foot of the Bear Cave, this wooden chalet has seven rooms, each with shared bathroom, and a charming restaurant.

La Fluturi (☎ 259 329 085; cabins €6) This idyllic camping ground, in the town of Chişcău, sits near a bubbling stream and has six wooden cabins.

Getting There & Away

Without private transport the region around the cave is tricky to navigate. There's one daily bus running between Beiuş, Chişcău and Stei. From Oradea by car, head south through Beiuş, follow Hwy E79 for a further 8km along the Crişul Negru River, then turn left at the turn-off for Pietroasa and Chişcău. Continue 4km along this road; the cave is signposted on the right.

Hotel Muncel (p231) in Băile Felix runs day tours to the Bear Cave.

SCĂRIŞOARA ICE CAVE

Cave buffs should head straight to this fantastic **ice cave** (Peştera Gheţarul de la Scărişoara; ⏰ 10am-4pm Tue-Sun; adult/child €1.50/1).

The cave was first documented in 1863 by Austrian geographer Arnold Schmidt, who wrote up his findings, accompanied by detailed maps. This documentation enabled the Romanian scientist and speleologist Emil Racoviţa (1868–1947) to pursue further explorations between 1921 and 1923. Believed to be one of only 10 of this kind in Europe, the cave is filled with 7500 cubic metres of ice. The ice, at an altitude of 1150m, dates to the Ice Age when the Apuseni Mountains were covered in glaciers.

The maximum temperature inside the cave in summer is 1°C; in winter it drops to -7°C. Safety precautions inside the cave are not up to Western standards, and lighting is nonexistent. Bring your own torch (flashlight) or ask the keeper for an oil/carbon lamp (*lampă cu carbid*).

Getting There & Away

From Beiuş, head south to Ştei. Two kilometres further south, turn left, following the signs for Arieşeni and Gârda de Sus. From Gârda de Sus, a rough gravel track leads to the ice cave. The track is impassable by car after 6km, so you must hike the remaining 13km in the Arieş Valley. It is impossible to access the cave from Scărişoara village.

GÂRDA DE SUS & AROUND

The village of **Gârda de Sus** lies in the Arieş River valley in the Apuseni Mountains. Until 1932 it was classified as part of Scărişoara village. Traditional folk costumes, resembling those worn by early Dacian tribes, are still worn in the village for festivals.

Arieşeni, about 8km away, is a village renowned for its traditional folk customs and wooden church. Two kilometres west of Arieşeni, on the border of the Bihor and Alba Counties, is a 753m-long **ski slope** (⏰ 9am-6pm Dec-May), signposted 'Teleschi Vârtop'.

About 20km south of Gârda de Sus is the village of **Avram Iancu**, formerly known as Vidra de Sus.

The nearby **Roşia Montană Eurogold mine** (☎ 254 233 680), the biggest gold reserve in Europe (a Canadian joint venture), has attracted fierce criticism from scientists, geologists and environmental campaigners for polluting the local water sources with chemicals and deposits. On the other hand, people in nearby Gârda de Sus rely on the mine for employment and are just as fiercely opposed to shutting down the site.

Sleeping

The Belgian charity Opération Villages Roumains has helped Gârda de Sus establish its own agrotourism scheme whereby tourists can stay in their homes. The local representative in Gârda de Sus is **Ioan Stefanuţ** (☎ 258 778 065, 0744 700 871; 🕙 9am-5pm) at house No 31. In Arieşeni, ask for **Marta Maghiar** (☎ 0744 278 219) at house No 13. If a house has a sign reading 'Retea Turistica' in the window it means they have rooms to rent.

Mama Uţa (☎ 258 778 008; cabins €6, tent sites €1) This popular summer spot, at the western end of Gârda de Sus, has 14 wooden cabins and a noisy bar and grill.

Hotel Apuşeni (☎ 258 779 023; hotelApuşeni@ gmx.net; Bubeşti 87A; d €20) This friendly hotel, about 15km east along the road to Arieşeni, has fantastic views, gorgeous rooms and a sun terrace with hill views.

Cabana Vârtop (☎ 0744 560 427, 0745 776 541; d €20) Amid rolling hills in Arieşeni, this chalet has amazing views and its own ski run.

Casa Noastrâ (☎ 258 779 122, 0744 322 215; r €30) This luxury chalet has a trout farm and swimming pool.

Getting There & Away

From Gârda de Sus, hikers can head north to the Padiş Plateau. A trail marked by blue stripes (five to six hours) leads from the village to **Cabana Padiş** (p231).

ARAD

☎ 257 / pop 187,000

The gateway to Hungary, Arad is situated in lush wine-making country on the banks of the Mureş River, which loops around the city's 18th-century citadel then flows west to Szeged in Hungary. Arad developed as a major trading centre during Turkish occupation of the city between 1551 and 1687. It boasts elegant late-19th-century architecture, the charming legacy of the Austro-Hungarian empire.

Orientation

The train station is a few kilometres north of the centre, with the bus station two blocks west on B-dul Revoluţiei. To reach town, take tram No 1, 2 or 3 south down B-dul Revoluţiei (known simply as 'the boulevard').

Information

INTERNET ACCESS

Club Pro Net (☎ 270 533; pronet@pro-net.ro; B-dul Revoluţiei 67; per hr €0.75)
Internet Café (Str Tribunal Dobra 8; 🕙 9.30am-1.30am; per hr €0.75)

MONEY

Currency exchange offices line B-dul Revoluţiei. For ATM, currency exchange and cash transfer facilities go to **Banca Ţiriac** (Piaţa Avram Iancu 11; 🕙 9am-3.30pm Mon-Fri, 9am-12.30pm Sat) and **Banca Commercială Română** (☎ 254 460; B-dul Revoluţiei 72; 🕙 9am-4pm Mon-Fri).

There is also an ATM outside Supermarket Ziridava (p235).

POST & TELEPHONE

The **post office** (☎ 232 222; B-dul Revoluţiei 46-48; 🕙 7am-7pm Mon-Fri) adjoins the **telephone office** (B-dul Revoluţiei 44; 🕙 8am-8pm daily).

TOURIST INFORMATION

Arad's new official tourist information office, **Info Tour Arad** (☎ 270 277; infotourarad1@ yahoo.com; B-dul Revoluţiei 84-86; 🕙 9am-5pm Mon-Fri), has free city maps, plenty of info about the region and contacts with agrotourism homestay organisation Antrec.

Sights

Arad's large, star-shaped **citadel** was built under the orders of the Habsburg empress Maria Theresa between 1763 and 1783. The Austrian architect and general Filip Ferdinand Harsch was commissioned to design the Vauban-style, six-pointed star. It stands on the site of an old fortress built in 1551 by the Turks. Today, the citadel houses a military barracks and is closed to the public.

After crushing the liberal revolution of 1848, the Habsburgs hanged 13 Hungarian generals outside the citadel. A **monument** to

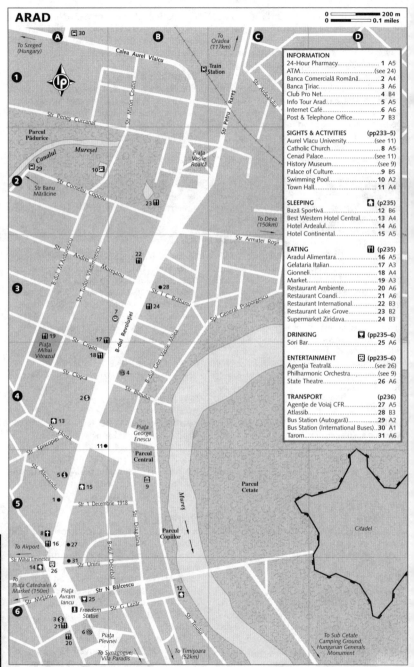

ARAD

these men stands outside the southern walls of the citadel.

The U-shaped, neoclassical **town hall** (B-dul Revoluţiei) is Arad's most impressive building. The clock ticking on the tower atop the 1876 building was purchased in Switzerland in 1878. Framing the town hall is the steepled **Cenad Palace** (Palatul Cenad), constructed by the Arad Cenad Railway Company at the end of the 19th century, and the **Aurel Vlaicu University** building, decorated in Viennese rococo motifs and built to house the local administration's treasury.

Near the town hall, in front of Central Park, is the local **History Museum** (Muzeul de Istorie; ☎ 280 114; Piaţa George Enescu 1; ⏲ 10am-4pm Tue-Sun; admission €1), which has some interesting photos and artefacts. It is based inside the **Palace of Culture** (built between 1911 and 1913), also home to Arad's **Philharmonic Orchestra** (p236). Busts outside the building pay homage to leading literary figures, including Romanian poet George Coşbuc (1866–1918) and post-romantic historian Alexandru Xenopol (1847–1920).

To the east of the museum, along the Mureş River, lies **Youth Park** (Parcul Copiilor). At the southern end of B-dul Revoluţiei is the 1874 neoclassical **State Theatre** (p236).

South of the theatre is the Jewish community's **synagogue** (Str Dobra 10). It was built between 1827 and 1834 in typically Moorish style. Enter via Str Cozia.

Sleeping
PRIVATE ROOMS

Antrec arranges rooms in private homes in and around Arad for about €15 to €20, including breakfast. Bookings can be made in advance through the friendly, English-speaking bods at Info Tour Arad (p233).

HOTELS

Arad has a good selection of hotels, all reasonably affordable.

Bază Sportivă (☎ 251 059; Str Teiului 1; r €5.50) These rooms above the sports club are cheap-as-chips and basic but clean.

Hotel Ardealul (☎ 280 840, 280 925; B-dul Revoluţiei 98; s/d unrenovated €16/23, renovated €22/30) This converted concert hall, dating from 1841, has a music room where Brahms, Liszt and Strauss once gave concerts.

Vila Paradis (☎ 287 377; Str Molidului 5; s/d €22) Five kilometres south of the centre, this is

a good choice with simple, clean and comfy rooms. Breakfast costs extra.

Best Western Hotel Central (☎ 256 636, 256 543; central@inext.ro; Str Horea 8; s & d €53) This five-storey hotel has all mod-cons and a lovely terrace café overlooking its summer garden.

Hotel Continental (☎ 281 700; fax 281 832; conti@inext.ro; B-dul Revoluţiei 79-81; s & d €94) Splurge on some well-deserved luxury at Arad's up-market choice, with its international standards of accommodation and service.

Eating
RESTAURANTS

Restaurant Ambiente (Piaţa Avram Iancu 9; ⏲ 10am-midnight; meal €25) This swanky wood-lined eatery has caviar and steak on the menu, and a bar covered with banknotes!

Restaurant Coandi (☎ 284 688; Piaţa Avram Iancu 11; meal €20) Coandi is a popular joint with large tables, so expect to be sat with people of all nationalities for a noisy, fun feed. The portions of Romanian classics are huge.

Restaurant Internaţional (☎ 257 145; B-dul Revoluţiei 26-38; meal €10) Once glittering, now a bit drab, this brasserie and restaurant has soups, salads and meat/fish dishes galore.

Restaurant Lake Grove (Pădurice Park, northern end of B-dul Revoluţiei; ⏲ 10am-3am; meal €20) A nice spot on the lake with leafy, decked gardens. It's popular with tour groups as the menu has everything from pasta to pudding.

CAFÉS

B-dul Revoluţiei is lined with cafés and bars. Try **Gionneli** (cnr B-dul Revoluţiei & Str Crişan' ⏲ 24 hr) for a caffeine fix or **Gelateria Italian** (B-dul Revoluţiei), a few doors further north, for *bella* Italian ice-cream. It has 20 different flavours, including bubble-gum and cola, and is always packed.

SELF-CATERING

Arad has two open-air **markets**, one on Piaţa Mihai Viteazul and another on Piaţa Catedralei, at the western end of Str Meţanu. For groceries, go to the large Western-style **Supermarket Ziridava** (B-dul Revoluţiei; ⏲ 8am-8pm Mon-Sat) or the well-stocked **Aradul Alimentara** (⏲ 24 hr), at the southern end of B-dul Revoluţiei.

Entertainment
BARS

Piaţa Avram Iancu is the place to head for terrace café-bars. One of these is the bikers' joint **Wings** at the southern end of the square.

Sori Bar (☎ 281 478; Str Nicolae Bălescu 2) This is a popular drinking spot, with a small, smart terrace and some café-style meals (€15).

THEATRE & CLASSICAL MUSIC

The **Philharmonic Orchestra** (tickets from €2), inside the Palace of Culture (p235), holds concerts on weeknights at 7pm. Check the schedule of events at the palace or ask at Info Tour Arad. Tickets are sold at the **box office** (☎ 280 519) two hours before performances begin. Arad's **Agenţia Teatrală** (☺ 11am-1pm Tue-Sun), which sells tickets to local theatre performances, is at the back of the **State Theatre** (Teatrul de Stat; ☎ 280 018; B-dul Revoluţiei 103).

Getting There & Away

AIR

Tarom (☎ 211 777; www.tarom.ro; Str Unirii 1; ☺ 7am-7pm Mon-Fri, 9am-2pm Sat) has three flights a week to Bucharest (US$75/107 one-way/return, plus taxes; note that Tarom does not accept euros). There are also three flights a week to Verona (Italy) from Arad.

BUS

Arad has two bus stations, one for **international buses** (Str 6 Vânători 2) and the domestic **autogară** (☎ 273 323; Str Banu Mărăcine), two blocks west of the train station.

Daily internal buses from Arad's *autogară* include two to Timişoara (€2), one to Bucharest (€9) and one to Craiova. State buses also run to Szeged (€10) and Budapest (€15) from here.

Private companies selling tickets for international buses to (for example) Hungary, France and Spain line B-dul Revoluţiei. These buses are considerably more comfortable than the state buses, with air con, clean seats and free tea and coffee; prices are obviously higher. Try **Atlassib** (☎ 270 562; B-dul Revoluţiei 35), which has express coaches running twice-weekly to Germany and Austria.

CAR & MOTORCYCLE

The border crossing into Hungary is 52km west of Arad, in Nădlac. This is the major road crossing from Romania into Hungary, so it can get congested. It is open 24 hours a day.

TRAIN

Tickets for trains to Hungary and Austria have to be bought in advance from the **Agenţie de Voiaj CFR** (☎ 280 713; B-dul Revolutiei; ☺ 8am-8pm Mon-Fri).

Arad train station (☎ 230 633; Piaţa Gării 8-9) is a major railway junction. Daily fast services include five to Budapest (€30), five to Vienna (€67), five to Bucharest (€16), five to Timişoara (€3), one to Constanţa and one to Cluj-Napoca.

To get to Hunedoara from Arad, you have to get a train to Deva and then take a bus from there to Hunedoara.

Getting Around

Tarom operates a free shuttle bus from its office to Arad **airport** (☎ 254 440). It departs one hour before flights are scheduled to take off.

TIMIŞOARA

☎ 256 / pop 332,277

Tenacious Timişoara (ti-mi-*shwa*-ra) stunned the world as the birthplace of the 1989 revolution. Romania's fourth largest city is known by residents as 'Primul Oraş Liber' (First Free Town), for it was here that the Romanians' rebellious spirit flourished with the first anti-Ceauşescu protests which prompted his fall from power. With its charming Mediterranean air, regal Hapsburg buildings and a thriving cultural and sporting scene, it's a city that's loved by residents and tourists alike.

Timişoara, dubbed the 'city of flowers' after the ring of pretty parks that surrounds it, is one of the country's most developed cities. Timiş County, of which Timişoara is the administrative centre, is the richest agricultural area in Romania.

Orientation

Confusingly, the northern train station (Timişoara-Nord) is west of the city centre. From here, walk east along B-dul Republicii to the Opera House and Piaţa Victoriei. To the north is Piaţa Libertăţii; Piaţa Unirii, the old town square, is two blocks further north. Timişoara's bus station is beside the Idsefin Market, three blocks from the northern train station. Take B-dul General Drăgălina south from the train station to the canal, cross the bridge and head west to the next bridge.

MAPS

Hotfoot it around Timişoara with Amco Press's *City Plan* (1:10,000; €2), sold in most bookshops. There is a tourist map in the bilingual city guide *What? When? Where? Timişoara*, available free all over the city. Be aware that although many street names have changed, many maps and locals still use old names.

Information

BOOKSHOPS

Humanitas (Map p240; ☎ 433 180; Str F Mercy 1; ⊙ 9am-7pm Mon-Fri) Sells some English-language books about Romania.

Librăria Mihai Eminescu (Map p240; ☎ 494 123; Piaţa Victoriei 2; ⊙ 9am-7pm Mon-Fri, 9am-1pm Sat) Stocks a less exhaustive range than Humanitas.

CULTURAL CENTRES

British Council (Map p240; ☎ 497 678; Str Paris 1; ⊙ 1-7pm Mon, Tue & Thu, 9am-3pm Wed & Fri)

French Cultural Centre (Map p240; Centrul Cultural Francez; ☎ 490 544; 201 453; B-dul CD Loga 46)

INTERNET ACCESS

Internet Java (Map p240; ☎ 432 495; Str Pacha 6; ⊙ 24 hr) Surfing costs €0.75 per hr inside the Java Coffee House (p241)

Internet Café (Map p240; ⊙ 9am-1am Mon-Fri, 9am-3pm Sat; per hr €1) It's located inside Cinema Timiş (p241)

MEDICAL SERVICES

Farmacie Remedia (Map p240; B-dul Revoluţiei 1989; ⊙ 7am-8pm Mon-Fri, 8am-3pm Sat)

Sensi Blu Pharmacy (Map p240; ☎ 406 153; Piaţa Victoriei 7; ⊙ 8am-8pm Mon-Fri, 9am-8pm Sat & Sun)

MONEY

Cash travellers cheques, arrange transfers or access your decreasing funds at:

Volksbank (Map p240; ☎ 406 101; Str Piatra Craiului 2)

HVB Bank (Map p240; ☎ 306 800; Piaţa Victoriei 2; ⊙ 9am-4pm Mon-Fri)

There's a **currency exchange** (⊙ 8am-6pm Mon-Fri, 8am-1pm Sat) inside Hotel Continental (p241). Cardinal Tourist Agency has an ATM and currency exchange.

POST & TELEPHONE

The **central post office** (Map p240; ☎ 491 999; B-dul Revoluţiei 2; ⊙ 8am-7pm Mon-Fri, 8am-noon Sat) can get busy, so if it is, there's a **branch** (Map p240; Str Macieşilor; ⊙ 8am-7pm Mon-Fri) near B-dul Revoluţiei.

The central **telephone office** (Map p240; B-dul Mihai Eminescu; ⊙ 7am-9pm) has fax facilities.

TOURIST INFORMATION

Cardinal Tourist Agency (Map p240; ☎ 491 911; B-dul Republicii 6; ⊙ 8am-6pm Mon-Fri, 9am-1pm Sat) Offers group tours, and there are friendly, French-speaking staff.

Information Centre (Map p240; ☎ 437 973; Str Proclamatia de la Timişoara 1; ⊙ 10am-8pm Tue-Sat, 10am-2pm Sun). This is a brand-spanking new official information centre, where you can book canoe trips, wildlife tours or just hotels.

Qual Tours (Map p240; ☎ 294 411; Str Nicolaus Lenau 10; office@qualtours.ro; ⊙ 9am-6pm Mon-Fri) Staff speak excellent English and French, and can organise car hire, tours of the region, and guides.

Sights

PIAŢA UNIRII   Map p240

Gorgeous Piaţa Unirii, in the heart of the old town, is Timişoara's most picturesque square – so-called 'Union Square' because of the imposing sight of the Catholic and Serbian churches facing each other. The eastern side of the square is dominated by the baroque **Roman Catholic Cathedral** (Catedrală Episcopală Romano-Catolică; ☎ 430 671; Piaţa Unirii 12), built in 1754. The main altar painting was completed by Michael Angelo Unterberger, director of the Fine Art Academy in Vienna. On the opposite side is the **Serbian Orthodox Church** (Biserica Ortodoxă Sârbă), built the same year as its Catholic counterpart; local Banat artist Constantin Daniel painted the interior.

The **Trinity Column**, in the square's centre, was erected by the people of Timişoara at the end of the 18th century in thanks to God for allowing them to survive the plague that hit the town between 1738 and 1739. Overlooking the square is the baroque **Old Prefecture Palace** (Palatul Vechii Prefecturi; 1754), which houses an **Art Museum** (Muzeul de Artă; ⊙ 10am-4pm Tue-Sun; admission €0.75).

From Piaţa Unirii, walk east along Str Palanca to the **Banat Ethnographic Museum** (☎ 434 967; Str Popa Sapca 1; ⊙ 10am-4pm Tue-Sun; admission €0.50), housed in the oldest building in Timişoara, within the city's remaining 18th-century bastion. Allow an hour to drift through the exhibits of traditional costume and craft. In October a **national beer festival** is held here. Nearby is a landmark **fountain**, which has all the points of the compass round its circular design.

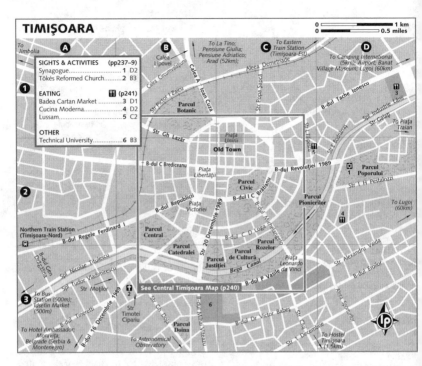

TIMIŞOARA

SIGHTS & ACTIVITIES (pp237-9)	
Synagogue	1 D2
Tökés Reformed Church	2 B3

EATING 🍴 (p241)	
Badea Cartan Market	3 D1
Cucina Moderna	4 D2
Lussam	5 C2

OTHER	
Technical University	6 B3

The **Great Synagogue** (Str Mărăşeşti 6) was built in 1865 and is an important keynote in Jewish history. Jews in the Austro-Hungarian empire were fully emancipated in 1864 (they could finally own land and have a profession), the year when permission was given to build the synagogue. The synagogue once hosted concerts by the Philharmonic Orchestra, which refused to play music by Nazi-sympathiser Richard Wagner.

PIAŢA LIBERTĂŢII TO PIAŢA VICTORIEI   Map p240

Walk south from Piaţa Unirii past the **town hall** (1734), built on the site of 17th-century Turkish baths, to **Piaţa Libertăţii**. It was here that the leader of the 1514 peasant revolt, Gheorghe Doja, was tortured before being executed. Doja's peasant army, after an initial victory, was quickly quashed, captured and killed. Legend has it that upon Doja's public execution, his followers were forced to eat parts of his body as an appetiser before their own executions. Look for the canon ball embedded in the wall of a building on Str Ungareanu, close to Piaţa Libertăţii.

The central **statue of Saint Nepomuk and the Virgin Mary** was made in 1756 in Vienna and brought to Romania on the Danube in memory of plague victims. Mary holds a lily, the symbol of purity, and her gold star-studded halo was added during the statue's restoration in 2000.

Continue along Str Lucian Blage to the 14th-century **Huniades Palace**. Built between 1307 and 1315 by the Hungarian king Carol Robert, Prince of Anjou, it was redesigned under the Habsburgs in the late 18th century. It houses the **Banat History Museum** (Muzeul Banatului; ☎ 491 339; Piaţa Huniades 1; 🕙 10am-5pm; admission €1), which is worth visiting . Note the column topped with the figures of **Romulus and Remus**, a gift from the city of Rome.

Head west to the marble 18th-century **National Theatre & Opera House** (p242). It was directly in front of the Opera House on this square that thousands of demonstrators gathered on 16 December 1989, following the siege on Lászlo Tökés's house (see p25). On 17 December tanks rolled into Opera Square and fired into the crowd. By 20

December the 100,000-strong crowd had taken over some tanks, and the army retreated. The bloodshed then spilled over to Bucharest. A memorial plaque on the front of the Opera House now reads: 'So you, who pass by this building, will dedicate a thought for free Romania.'

At the southern end of Piaţa Victoriei, there is a stunning sculpture and several large wooden crosses – **memorials** to those who died during the revolution. Behind the memorial cross is the exotic Romanian Orthodox **Metropolitan Cathedral**, built between 1936 and 1946. Unique to the church are its electrical bells cast from iron imported from Indonesia. A collection of 16th- to 19th-century icons is displayed in the basement.

SOUTH OF THE CENTRE

The 1989 revolution began at the **Tökés Reformed Church** (Biserica Reformată Tökés; Map p238; ☎ 492 992; Str Timotei Cipariu 1), where Father László Tökés spoke out against the dictator. Following attempts by the Securitate to remove Tökés and his wife from their home above the church, several thousand ethnic Hungarians and Romanians formed a human chain around the building. But Securitate troops broke through the human barrage and arrested the pair. Today, Tökés's own small apartment is privately inhabited.

On the southern bank of the Bega Canal is the **University of West Timişoara** (UWT; Map p240; ☎ 490 009; B-dul Vasile Pârvan 4), established in 1944.

Two kilometres south of the centre, on Calea Martirilor, is Timişoara's **Astronomical Observatory** (Observatorul Astronomic), where hundreds gathered on 11 August 1999 to witness the total eclipse of the sun. To get to the observatory, take tram No 8 from the northern train station.

The **Banat Village Museum** (Muzeul Satului Bănăţean; ☎ 225 588; Str Al. CFR 1; ⏱ 1-8pm Tue-Sun Jun-Sep, 10am-4pm Nov-Feb), 6km northeast of the centre, exhibits more than 30 traditional peasant houses dating from the 19th century. The open-air display was created in 1917. Take tram No 1 (black number) from the northern train station.

Activities

SWIMMING

Take a dip at one of Timişoara's outdoor pools – perfect for lazy summer days.

> ### TIMIŞOARA TRIVIA
>
> - Timişoara was built on a swamp – the Metropolitan Cathedral has 5000 oak supports underneath it!
> - Legend has it that Beethoven's girlfriend haunts the mint green building in the northwestern corner of Piaţa Unirii.
> - Hated dictator Ceauşescu never stayed a single night in Timişoara.
> - Hollywood's original Tarzan, Jonny Weissmuller, was born in a Timişoara suburb.
> - Frenchman Gustave Eiffel, who engineered Paris's Eiffel Tower, built a bridge over the city's Bega canal.
> - Timişoara was the first European city to introduce horse-drawn trams (in 1869) and the first to sport electric street lighting (in 1889).
> - The world record for drawing 'speed cartoons' is held by Timişoara artist Ştefan Popa (he can draw 131 cartoons in one minute).
> - Every October Timişoara hosts Romania's week-long national beer festival.

Terasa Eminescu Complex (Map p240; ☎ 229 212; ⏱ 10am-7pm; admission €1) Loud pumping music and hordes of students make this a social rather than sporty day-out.

Strand Complex (Map p240; ☎ 203 663; ⏱ 24hr; admission €1) This place is just as popular.

CANOEING

Book trips on Bega Canal (which flows through the city) and on Mureş River at the tourist information centre (p237), or contact adventure company **Pepetour** (☎ 354 924; peptour@equillon.ro). Extreme-sports lovers can get their thrills thanks to the tour agency **Latura Extremă** (contact@latura.ro), which organises adventure trips, paintballing and rafting.

Sleeping

BUDGET

Hostel Timişoara (☎ 491 170; Str Arieş 19; dm €9) Take tram no 8 from the northern train station to this large, super-modern hostel, 2km from the centre.

Pensiune Adriatico (☎ 280 398; Str II de la Brad 1C; s/d €20/34) A charmingly eccentric pension with clean, comfy rooms and a pizzeria.

CENTRAL TIMIŞOARA

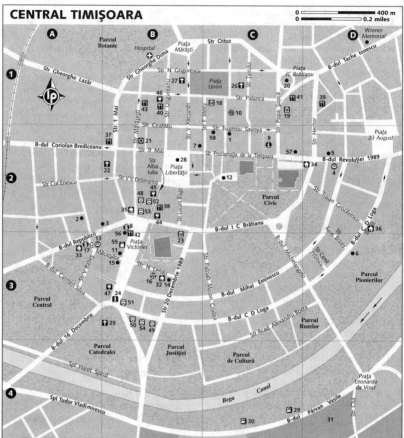

Camping International (☎ 208 925; campingint ernational@yahoo.com; Aleea Pădurea Verde 6; tent sites €2.50, 4-bed chalets with central heating €54) This excellent camping ground is nestled in the Green Wood forest on the opposite side of town from the northern train station. The main entrance is on Calea Dorobanţilor. From the station catch trolleybus No 11 to the end of the line. The bus stops less than 50m from the camping ground. There is a restaurant here, too.

MID-RANGE
Pensiune Giulia (☎ 709 640; Str Etolia 3; s/d €24/30) A gorgeous pension with contemporary art on the walls and all mod-cons.

Hotel Cina Banatul (Map p240; ☎ 491 903; B-dul Republicii 3-5; s/d €25/30) The best-value pad in Timişoara, with clean, ultramodern rooms and a good restaurant.

Hotel Central (Map p240; ☎ 490 091; Str Lenau 6; d €30) Undergoing extensive renovation at the time of writing.

Hotel Timişoara (Map p240; ☎ 498 852, 295 278; Str 1 Mai 2; s/d 2-star €38/42, 3-star €42/52) Inside this soaring Soviet delight is a fabulously dated interior, grand comfort and sauna, gym and so on.

Hotel Continental (Map p240; ☎ 494 144; secret ariat@hotelcontinental.ro; B-dul Revoluţiei 3; s/d €49/56) Hiding in this Soviet eyesore are clean, large rooms.

Villa International (Map p238; ☎ 499 339; B-dul CD Loga 48; s & d €60) Once used for the political elite, this relic of the Ceauşescu era now has faded glory and a remarkable history.

TOP END
Hotel Ambassador (☎ 306 880/81/82; contact@ambass ador.ro; Str Mangalia 3; s/d €79/94) The Ambassador is a plush haven for an indulgent stay, with a sauna, gym, outdoor terrace and almost over-the-top luxury.

Eating
CAFÉS & QUICK-EATS
Chicago 'B' (Map p240; ☎ Alba Iulia 1; ☼ 10am-11pm) This Austrian-style café serves dreamy, creamy coffees, lattes and cappuccinos.

Lussam (Map p238; ☎ 496 872; B-dul Tache Ionescu 55; ☼ 24 hr) An infamous all-night pizza joint – go there for a feed when the clubs close.

Java Coffee House (Map p240; ☎ 432 495; Str Pacha 6; ☼ 24hr) Go online or just chill out with a frothy caffeine hit.

Horse Pizzeria (Map p240; ☎ 229 666; Str Popa Şapc; meal €5) Slabs of mouth-watering pizza starting at €1 – bargain!

There are plenty of lovely terrace cafés lining Piaţ Unirii and Piaţa Victoriei where you can while away the time.

RESTAURANTS
Lloyd Restaurant (Map p240; ☎ 294 949; Piaţa Victoriei 2; mains €12-15) Dine here on exquisite international/Romanian dishes of shark, smoked salmon and a spit-roast joint.

La Tino (☎ 226 455; Calea Aradului 14; mains €5) Classy Italian food and a wide choice of delicious pizzas are offered here.

Crama Bastion (Map p240; ☎ 221 199; Str Hector 1; mains €8) Classic Romanian dishes vie with the wine list for attention at this traditional restaurant in this 18th-century fortification.

Cucina Moderna (Map p238; ☎ 202 405; Str Soc rates 12B; mains €8-10) Cucina Moderna serves international-style dishes with a Spanish twist using Romanian ingredients.

Grizzly (Map p240; Str Ungureanu 7; mains €2-3) This cosy dark-wood bar with funky-pink walls offers good choice for vegetarians, such as spinach crepes, cauliflower soup and Serbian hotpot.

SELF-CATERING
Timişoara has a colourful central produce **market** (Map p240; Str Brediceanu Coriolan) near Str 1 Mai. There is also the well-stocked **Stil Supermarket** (Map p240; Str Mărăşeşti 10; ☼ 24 hr).

Entertainment
CINEMAS
Timişoaraians are devoted film-lovers and there are plenty of screens in town. Films are shown in their original language at these cinemas (tickets cost €1 to €3): **Cinema Timiş** (Map p240; ☎ 491 290; Piaţa Victoriei 7); **Cinema Capitol** (Map p240; ☎ 493 396; B-dul CD Loga 2); and the brilliant outdoor **Cinema de Vară** (Map p240; B-dul CD Loga 2), which is far more fun!

BARS & NIGHTCLUBS
Hang out with sociable locals at night in the terrace café-bars on Piaţa Victoriei, downing bottles of the local Timişoreana Pils beer for around €1 a bottle. **Violeta Bar**, at the southern end of the square, is particularly popular. Otherwise, be seen in these funky haunts:

Lemon (Map p240; Str Alba Iulia 2; ☼ from 10pm) This club in the cellar of a piano bar has hip-hop and house DJs.

Club 30 (Map p240; ☎ 201 115; inside Cinema Timiş; ⏱ 6pm-3am Fri & Sat) Cruise to the blues in this cool jazz joint.

Revolution (Map p240; Str Ungureanu 9) So trendy it hurts, this eclectic bar has techno/house DJs on weekends.

Discoland (Map p240; ☎ 490 008; Piaţa Iancu Huniade 1; ⏱ 11pm-5am) Stagger in here and shake your stuff in a happy, disco-tastic kind of way. It also has salsa nights.

THEATRE & CLASSICAL MUSIC

The **National Theatre & Opera House** (Teatrul Naţional şi Opera Română; Map p240; ☎ 201 284; Str Mărăşeşti 2) is highly regarded. Buy tickets in the nearby **Agenţia Teatrală** (☎ 499 908; ⏱ 10am-1pm & 5-7pm Tue-Sun; tickets from €1).

Close by is the **German State Theatre** (Teatrul German de Stat; Map p240; ☎ 201 291; Str Mărăşeşti 2). Get tickets at its **box office** (⏱ 10am-7pm Tue-Sun, closed Mon), at the Str Alba Iulia entrance.

Classical concerts are held most evenings at the **State Philharmonic Theatre** (Filharmonia de Stat Banatul; Map p240; ☎ 492 521; B-dul CD Loga 2). Tickets (from €1) can be bought at the box office inside the Philharmonic Theatre or from the Agenţia Teatrală.

Event details are generally advertised in the local press and on posters around town.

Shopping

Galeria Helios (Piaţa Victoriei 7; ⏱ noon-6pm Mon-Fri, 1-3pm Sat) A good place for artwork and ceramics.

Banat Ethnographic Museum (p237) Offers hand-made crafts, costumes and carvings.

Getting There & Away

AIR

Tarom (Map p240; ☎ 490 150, 200 003; B-dul Revoluţiei 3-5; ⏱ 7am-7pm Mon-Fri, 7am-1pm Sat) has four daily flights to Bucharest (US$75 plus tax US$5; please note that Tarom does not accept euros) from Timişoara. It has international flights weekly to New York and European cities, and a daily flight to Milan.

Angel Airlines (Map p240; ticketing@angelairlines .ro; Str Eugeniu de Savoya 7) has three flights per week to Bucharest. At the same address is **Yugoslav Airlines** (JAT; Map p240; ☎ 495 747), which runs daily international flights to Europe, Turkey and Ukraine.

TRAIN

All major train services depart from the **northern train station** (Gară Timişoara-Nord; Map

p238; ☎ 491 696; Str Gării 2). You can purchase tickets in advance from the **Agenţie de Voiaj CFR** (Map p240; ☎ 491 889; Piaţa Victoriei 2; ⏱ 8am-8pm Mon-Fri, 9am-7pm Mon-Fri for international tickets). The station's **left-luggage office** (⏱ 24 hr) is in the underground passageway to the tracks.

Daily fast trains include eight to Bucharest (€16), one to Cluj-Napoca (€8), five to Băile Herculane (€6), one to Baia Mare via Arad (€9), three to Budapest (€38) and one to Belgrade (€14), which leaves from Timişoara at 5.08am.

BUS

The small, shabby **bus station** (autogară; ☎ 493 471; B-dul Maniu Iuliu 54; ⏱ 6am-8pm Mon-Fri) has six platforms from where slow state buses run daily to Campeni, Arad, Sibiu and Rimincu Valcea, and one daily at 2pm to Budapest (€10). A weekly bus runs to Szeged in Hungary leaves at 3pm from platform 1 (linea 1). Inside the station is **Murat** (☎ 497 868) for bus tickets to Istanbul.

Maxitaxis run daily to Oradea, Arad Brad, Deva and Campeni.

Getting Around

TO/FROM THE AIRPORT

Timişoara **airport** (☎ 491 637; Calea Lugojului) is 12.5km northeast of the centre. Tarom (above) runs a free shuttle bus from its office on B-dul Revoluţiei. Bus No 26, which stops outside Hotel Continental, also goes to the airport.

TRAM, TROLLEYBUS & BUS

All public transport runs between 4.45am and 11.15pm. Tickets (€0.15) are sold at kiosks next to tram and bus stops. Tram No 1 runs from the northern train station (Gară Timişoara-Nord) to Piaţa Libertăţii, Hotel Continental and the eastern train station (Gară Timişoara-Est). Tram No 4 runs from Hotel Continental to Piaţa Traian (Piaţa Romanilor). Trolleybuses Nos 11 and 14 travel from the northern train station east down B-dul Regele Ferdinand I, then turn north on Str 1 Mai.

CAR

Avis (☎ 203 234) has an office at Timişoara airport. Cars can also be hired at Qual Tours (p237).

BĂILE HERCULANE

☎ 255

Treat yourself – take your weary body to this delicious spa resort for some serious pampering and fresh mountain air. Legend has it that Hercules himself bathed in the natural springs that still flow today in Băile Herculane – so you'll be in good company! The first baths were built by Roman legions following their invasion of Dacia. Inspired by the incredible healing powers of the springs, they named the resort Ad Aquas Herculi Sacras, meaning the 'Holy Water of Hercules'.

During the early 19th century, Băile Herculane developed as a fashionable resort, attracting royal visitors such as Habsburg emperor Franz Josef. Sadly, most of the grand hotels and baths now stand empty and neglected, although renovation work was underway at the time of writing.

Mt Domogled (1100m) towers over Băile Herculane to the west, dominating the Cerna Valley in which the resort lies. The extensive forest reservation surrounding the resort, which has been protected since 1932, includes rare trees, turtles and butterflies. It truly is a small piece of heaven.

Orientation

Băile Herculane lies either side of a road that follows the Cerna River. The train station is at the junction of the main Drobeta-Turnu Severin–Timişoara highway and the Băile Herculane turn-off.

The resort is split into three parts: the residential area is at the western end of the resort on Str Trandafirilor; the concrete blocks of the newer satellite resort are 2km east of the residential area; and the historic centre is at the resort's easternmost end (8km from the train station).

Information

There's no tourist office in Băile Herculane. Try the **Agenţia de Turism** (☎ 560 454) inside Hotel Hercules, where some of the staff speak English.

You can cash travellers cheques, use the ATM or exchange currency at the **Banca Comercială Română** (Piaţa Hercules 4; ☯ 8.30am-5pm Mon-Fri). There's also a **currency exchange office** (☯ 10am-7pm Mon-Fri) on the 3rd floor of Hotel Roman (p244).

The central post office is next to the **CFR office** (Piaţa Hercules 1; ☯ both 7am-8pm Mon-Fri).

Sights

All sights lie in the historic centre. Many Roman baths were destroyed during the Turkish and Austrian-Hungarian occupations, but some ancient Roman baths stand well preserved in the **Roman Bath Museum** (Terma Română; inside Hotel Roman, Str Română 1; admission €0.25). Feel the heat from the natural 54°C water running under the hotel. One of the exhibits is a 2500-year-old carving of Hercules. People have broken off parts and chewed them (his genitals are notably missing sections as men have chewed these chunks for sexual potency!) The 2000-year-old baths are still used – the water is cooled down to 37°C and masseurs line the small marble baths.

Natural springs from which drinking water flows – believed to be good for stomach problems – are dotted throughout the historic centre. To the side of the hotel flows the **Hercules II spring** (Izvorul Hercules).

The resort's **central pavilion** (Str Cernei 14) was built during the 1800s by the Habsburgs as a casino and restaurant. Today, it houses a few small shops and a small **History Museum** (Muzeul de Istorie; ☯ 10am-4pm Tue-Sun; admission €0.25). Beside the steps leading up to the museum entrance stands a 200-year-old **Wellingtonia Gigantea tree**, famed for its enormous size. On the opposite side of the river stand the derelict **Austrian baths**.

Activities

PAMPERING

Wallowing in a thermal pool or being pummelled into oblivion by a masseur is all part and parcel of a stay in Băile Herculane.

Hotel Roman (p244) has a thermal swimming pool (€2) which is open to nonguests. Hotel Cerna (p244) also has a thermal pool (adult/child €0.50/0.25) and treatment centre.

The Seven Springs (Izvoare 7) thermal pool and camping ground are 4km north of Hotel Roman, from where you catch a maxitaxi (€0.25). Seven Springs becomes crowded and noisy in summer.

DAY TRIPS

Day trips to **Hobiţa** (p191), to see Brâncuşi's memorial house, **Tismana Monastery** (p191) and other sites leave from Hotel Cerna (p244) at 9am on Sunday (returning at 6pm). The trips cost €8 per person; ask at reception for information.

HIKING & CLIMBING

Directly behind Hotel Roman stands **Brigands' Cave** (Peştera Haiducilor), named after the thieves who would hide in the cave, waiting for their prey to roll by. A path leads up to the cave from the hotel. A second path (2.5km; marked with blue stripes) leads to the **Grota cu Aburi Cave**. A trail (3km; marked with red stripes) starting from the centre of Băile Herculane at the **Brasseria Central** (Str Izvorului 1) leads to the **Munk natural spring** (Izvorul Munk), east of the Grota cu Aburi Cave.

Southeast of the resort, the **White Cross** (Crucea Albă) is a popular hiking trail (marked with yellow stripes). It starts from Str 1 Mai next to Hotel Cerna.

The rock face behind Hotel Roman is a favourite for climbers in summer.

Sleeping

Most hotels in Băile Herculane have costly, short-stay rates (one to three days) and cheaper, long-stay rates (three to 21 days). All prices listed are short-stay rates. If you plan to stay longer – negotiate! Top hotels fill up in July and August, and the resort is very quiet from mid-September to mid-May.

BUDGET

Hotel Cerna (☎ 560 436; Str 1 Mai 1; s/d from €10/13) This yellow ornate building has old-fashioned but reasonable rooms.

Located between the old and new resorts, the **Popas Flora camping ground** (☎ 560 929; Str Castanilor 25; bungalows per person €4; ☉ May-Oct) has two- and four-bed bungalows overlooking the Cerna River. There are communal showers and toilets.

MID-RANGE

Hotel Hercules (☎ 560 880; Str Izvorului 7; s/d €28/41) Average, clean rooms await you at this dated complex with sauna.

Hotel Roman (☎ 560 390; Str Română 1; s/d €35/49) Built into the side of the mountain on the site of a natural spring, this concrete vision offers massage and sauna, the ancient baths and a reasonable restaurant.

Hotel Ferdinand (☎ 561 131, 561 121; office@hotel-ferdinand.ro; Piaţa Hercules; s/d € 42/65) This is the resort's newest and best hotel – classy luxury, good prices and the most charming mountain-side wooden terraces, which are candle-lit at night.

Do not be tempted to stay at Hotel Apollo opposite – there is a smell of sulphur from the cellar baths, although the hiking map inside the lobby is worth a look.

Hotel Afrodite (☎ 560 730; Str Complexelor 2; s/d €30/42) In the newer part of Băile Herculane, this hotel has 218 reasonable rooms.

Hotel Diana (☎ 560 495; Str Complexelor 1) There is little difference between the this and the Afrodite. Watch out for two-tiered prices for locals and foreigners (who pay substantially more than locals) as they're illegal.

Eating

Băile Herculane has few restaurants beyond those inside its hotels. The inhouse restaurants of Hotel Ferdinand and Hotel Roman serve the best food – €10 and €2–3 resepctively for a main course.

Entertainment

Next door to the minimarket is the popular **Bar Cezar**, but the hottest nightspot in town is **Club 69** (Str Izorului).

Youngsters also hang out at the *discotecă* in the basement of the old **Central Pavilion** (Str Cernei 14).

Getting There & Away

TRAIN

The train station is 5km southwest of the satellite resort. The **Agenţie de Voiaj CFR** (☎ 560 538; Piaţa Hercules 1) is in the historic centre.

Băile Herculane is on the main Timişoara–Bucharest line and has many daily fast services, including seven to Bucharest, seven to Timişoara, one to Budapest (3.33am), one to Constanţa and two local trains to Orşova.

BUS

Maxitaxis run daily, except Sunday, between Craiova, Băile Herculane and Drobeta-Turnu Severin from outside the post office in Piaţa Hercules. The timetable is posted to a tree. The Drobeta-Turnu Severin service leaves daily at 2.30pm sharp (€1).

Getting Around

Maxitaxis run all day to/from the train station, along the 8km length of Băile Herculane to the historic centre, stopping on the way at the residential area and satellite resort (€0.20 one way).

Maramureş

Travel no further. You've found what you were looking for. A place where rural medieval life remains intact. Where peasants live off the land as their parents did, and generations before them. Where tiny villages, steeped in local customs and history, sit among rolling hills and dreamy landscapes. Imagine going back 100 years – welcome to Maramureş.

Idyllic, charming, harbouring memories of a forgotten time – there's simply too much to say about this world treasure. The last peasant culture in Europe is thriving here, with hand-built ancient wooden churches, traditional music, colourful costumes and ancient festivals. Discovering this part of the world is a time-travel adventure. The region was effectively cut off from Transylvania by a fortress of mountains and has remained untouched by the 20th century. It escaped the collectivisation of the 1940s, systemisation of the '80s and the Westernisation of the '90s – and as such is living history.

Medieval Maramureş exists in the Mara and Izei Valleys. Eight of its churches – in the villages of Bârsana, Budeşti, Deseşti, Ieud, Plopis, Poienile Izei, Rogoz and Surdeşti – are on Unesco's list of World Heritage Sites (1999).

TOP FIVE

- Tremble at the fiery visions of hell lavished on **Poienile Izei church** (p261)
- Marvel at the famed wooden churches of **Budeşti** (p259), **Surdeşti** (p254) and **Ieud** (p262)
- Enjoy the joke of the beautifully painted wooden crosses in **Săpânţa's Merry Cemetery** (p260)
- Experience Romanian rural life in the **Izei** (p260) and **Mara Valleys** (p258) by staying with a family and learning medieval ways
- Ride up through the Vaser Valley on a narrow-gauge railway from **Vişeu de Sus** (p262)

| POPULATION: 920,000 | AREA: 10,722 SQ KM |

History

Maramureş, with Baia Mare as its capital, was first documented in 1199. Hungary gradually exerted its rule over the region from the 13th century onwards. Tartar invasions of the Hungarian-dominated region continued well into the 17th and 18th centuries, the last documented battle being on the Prislop Pass in 1717. Numerous churches sprang up in Maramureş around this time to mark the Tartars' final withdrawal from the region.

Maramureş was annexed by Transylvania in the mid-16th century, then ceded to the Austrian empire in 1699. It was not until 1918 that Maramureş was returned to Romania.

Between 1940 and 1944 the Maramureş region – along with northern Transylvania – fell under pro-Nazi Hungarian rule.

SATU MARE

☎ 261 / pop 130,000

Satu Mare (Big Village) has a large ethnic Hungarian population. Many people still refer to the town by its former Hungarian name, Szatmar. It's also arguably the ugliest town in all Romania – a grand, communist architectural experiment which

---

MARAMUREŞ CULTURE

It is often said that Maramureş contains Romania's soul. Here is a land of traditions, customs and ancient superstitions, unchanged for hundreds of years.

The region has a long history of using wood to build houses and churches. Homes were built with logs, then thick beams with incredible joins. Traditionally the homes of the Mara, Cosău and Izei Valleys used oak, while in Bârsana pine was traditionally used, and this is still the case. Roofs are tall and steep, the oldest covered in thatch.

Immense carved wooden gates now illustrate the social status and wealth of inhabitants, yet originally they were only built by royal landowners to guard against evil. The gates were the symbolic barrier between the safe interior and the unknown outside world, and people placed money, incense and holy water under them for further protection against dark forces. Carvings include the Tree of Life, the snake (guardian against evil), birds (symbols of the human soul) and a face (to protect from spirits). Sacalas Gheorghe (1860–1934) was one of the region's most gifted carvers.

Maramureş is particularly famed for its wooden churches, many of which are Unesco World Heritage Sites. The Orthodox churches are divided into the ante nave, nave and altar. Gothic-style towers rise up to 50m above the churches, and it is a testament to the builders' technical expertise that they survive the harsh winters of the region.

Wood is still the main raw material used for a variety of purposes such as wooden gourds at weddings, carved religious seals and painted icons. Wooden crosses also dot the landscape; the wooden crucifix in the village of Berbeşti (p258) is of great historical importance as it is the oldest of its kind in the region.

Another feature of Maramureş is its unique folk music. One place to experience it is at **Hora de la Prislop**, the major Maramureş festival (p264), held annually on the second Sunday in August. The festival's *hora* dancers stamp their feet, swing their upper body, and clap vigorously to the rhythm of a *ţâpurituri*, a chanted rhyme drummed out by three musicians on a traditional *zongora* (a type of viola), a *cetera* (shrill violin) and a *doba* (bongo made from fir or maple wood, covered with goat or sheep hide).

Family life is the source of many customs and rites of passage. Birth is seen as the passing of the soul from the unknown world to the known, or 'white', world. A *botejunea* (party) is held to celebrate each birth. Marriage ceremonies mix ancient and Christian rituals. The ceremonies begin at the homes of both parties, and they make their way to the church separately. It is not until the couple are bound that the revelling begins – and the party doesn't end until dawn.

Death is bound in as many rituals. When someone dies their body is washed, dressed in traditional clothing, then laid out in their home for three days. The burial service takes place on the fourth day and is accompanied by a poetic verse recounting the person's personality and deeds. If an unmarried boy or girl dies they are given a symbolic wedding at the burial to assure they lived a full life.

There are several regional myths, including those about Marţolea, a mythical woman who punishes other women if they work on Tuesday evenings, and Vârcolac, a man who turns into a werewolf at full moon and attacks people

MARAMUREŞ

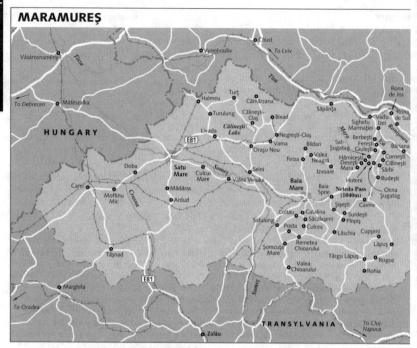

went horribly wrong. None-the-less it has a certain charm because of its dubious looks, but you won't be buying postcards!

Orientation

The train and bus stations are adjacent at the northern end of Str Griviţei, to the east of the centre. South of the centre the Someş River crosses the town from east to west.

Information

CULTURAL CENTRES

Centre Socio Cultural Franco Romanian (☎ 0766-784 080) Has a film club and French library.

INTERNET ACCESS

Free Internet access is available at the **History Museum** (B-dul Lucaciu 21; admission €0.75; ☒ 10am-5pm Tue-Sun).

MONEY

The **Banca Română** (Str 25 Octombrie; ☒ 8.30am-4.30pm Mon-Fri) cashes travellers cheques, gives cash advances on Visa/MasterCard and has an ATMs, as does the nearby **Banca Comer-cială Română** (☒ 9am-5pm Mon-Fri).

POST & TELEPHONE

Central post and telephone office (Str Octombrie; ☒ 7am-7pm Mon-Fri)
Branch post office (Piaţa Păcii; ☒ 7.30am-7.30pm)

TOURIST INFORMATION & TRAVEL AGENCIES

Accord Travel agency (☎ 737 915; www.accord-travel .ro; B-dul IC Brătianu 7) Sells maps of the region, arranges tours of Maramureş and rents cars.
Agenţia de Turism Dacia (inside Hotel Dacia; ☒ 8am-3pm Mon, Wed & Fri, 8am-4pm Tue & Thu, 10am-1pm Sat) Sells tickets for international buses from Bucharest.

Sights

Satu Mare's sights are centred on or around Piaţa Libertăţii.

The town's **art museum** (cnr Str Cuza Vodă & Piaţa Libertăţii; admission €0.30; ☒ 10am-5pm Tue-Sun) is large enough to spend some time checking out local works.

On the northern side of the square is the former **city hall and royal court**, which now houses Hotel Dacia. Continuing north down the alleyway next to the hotel, you come to a small courtyard, in the centre of

which stands a 45m-tall **fire tower** (Turnul Pompierilor; 1904).

A **Roman Catholic cathedral** lies on the eastern side of Piaţa Libertăţii. Building began on the cathedral in 1786; its two towers were added in 1837. Badly damaged during WWII, it remained closed until 1961 when restoration was completed.

On Piaţa Păcii, immediately north, is the town's large **Hungarian Reformed Church**. In front of the church is a statue of Ferenc Kölcsey who founded the Hungarian school next door. Satu Mare's Orthodox community worships at the **Orthodox church** at the eastern end of Str 1 Decembrie 1918.

Prior to WWII about 13,000 Jews lived in Satu Mare, which then boasted eight synagogues and a school. Most Jews were deported to death camps in 1944 and most of their synagogues destroyed, although the **Great Synagogue** (1920) is still in use today.

Sleeping

Hotel Dacia (☎ 714 276/7; Piaţa Libertăţii 8; s/d €33/43) Grand dame of the lush, leafy square, with stately rooms.

Hotel Villa Bodi (☎ 710 861; villa_bodi@datec.ro; Piaţa Libertăţii 5; s/d €45/80) This plush 'villa' is dressed in an elegant 19th-century European style. It also has a sauna and Jacuzzi.

Accord Travel (☎ 737 915; www.accord-travel.ro; B-dul IC Brătianu 7) This is the official agent for Antrec and arranges private accommodation in rural homes for €15 to €20 per night.

Eating & Drinking

Aside from Hotel Dacia's enormous showpiece restaurant there are a couple of other reasonable options.

Restaurant Corso (☎ 714 726; Piaţa Libertăţii; mains €5) This restaurant, next to the State Philarmonic, has an outside terrace during the warmer months and draws a trendy local crowd. It buzzes in summer.

Restaurant Miorita (Str Mihai Viteazul 5; mains €5) Local cuisine is served in a sunny, green environment. Live bands play most nights.

Teatrul de Nord (☎ 715 876; Str Horea 5) This theatre has a popular outside bar during summer.

Entertainment

Posters advertising what is on where in the city – including underground dance parties – line walls and bollards.

THEATRE & CLASSICAL MUSIC

The **State Philharmonic** (☎ 712 666/616; Piaţa Libertăţii 8) is tucked in an alleyway beside Hotel Dacia. Plays in Romanian are performed at the **Teatrul de Nord** (☎ 715 876; Str Horea 5). Tickets for both venues are sold at **Agenţia Teatrală** (☎ 712 106; Str Horea 6; ✆ 10am-4pm Mon-Fri), opposite the Teatrul de Nord.

Getting There & Away

AIR

Satu Mare airport (☎ 768 640) is situated 9km south of the city on the main Oradea–Satu Mare road.

There's a flight between Satu Mare and Bucharest (single/return US$75/124 plus about €4 tax each way) daily except Sunday.

BUS

The **bus station** (autogară; ☎ 768 439) is a 10-minute walk east of the centre. Local daily services include 10 buses to Baia Mare (59km); and one each to Negreşti-Oaş (50km), Oradea (133km) and Turţ (35km).

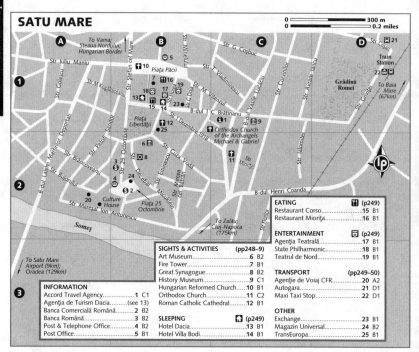

SATU MARE

0 — 300 m
0 — 0.2 miles

INFORMATION	
Accord Travel Agency	1 C1
Agenţia de Turism Dacia	(see 13)
Banca Comercială Română	2 B2
Banca Română	3 B2
Post & Telephone Office	4 B2
Post Office	5 B1

SIGHTS & ACTIVITIES	(pp248–9)
Art Museum	6 B2
Fire Tower	7 B1
Great Synagogue	8 B2
History Museum	9 C1
Hungarian Reformed Church	10 B1
Orthodox Church	11 C2
Roman Catholic Cathedral	12 B1

SLEEPING	(p249)
Hotel Dacia	13 B1
Hotel Villa Bodi	14 B1

EATING	(p249)
Restaurant Corso	15 B1
Restaurant Mioriţa	16 B1

ENTERTAINMENT	(p249)
Agenţia Teatrală	17 B1
State Philharmonic	18 B1
Teatrul de Nord	19 B1

TRANSPORT	(pp249–50)
Agenţie de Voiaj CFR	20 A2
Autogara	21 D1
Maxi Taxi Stop	22 D1

OTHER	
Exchange	23 B1
Magazin Universal	24 B2
TransEuropa	25 B1

A daily maxitaxi (minibus) leaves from outside the train station (Gara) for Budapest (€13).

TRAIN

Agenţie de Voiaj CFR (☎ 721 202; Str Bujurdui; ⏲ 7am-7pm Mon-Fri) sells all train tickets.

There is one daily train to Budapest departing at 1.57am. There are 10 daily trains to Baia Mare; one to Timişoara via Oradea (€9); three to Bucharest via Oradea or Baia Mare (€15); one to Cluj-Napoca (€11); and one daily to Constanţa (summer only).

A taxi from the station to Piaţa Libertăţii costs €0.50.

ŢARA OAŞULUI

☎ 261

Ţara Oaşului, literally 'Land of Oaş', refers to the geographical depression in the eastern part of Satu Mare district. The origin of the name is unclear although some say that Oaş is derived from the Hungarian word *vos* (iron), named after the supposed brutish, ironlike nature of the region's inhabitants. It certainly has a Wild West feel.

Turţ

The northern village of Turţ, 27km northeast of Satu Mare, is a colourful small town with houses painted chocolate-box pastels. Its centrepiece is a magnificent, new **Orthodox church** built and paid for by the town's 2300 families. Seven domes grace it and the interiors are painted with stunning scenes from the Old and New Testaments. It took five years to build and was finished in 2001.

Turţ once boasted Romania's finest **pălincă factory**, producing the fiery plum brandy almost identical to traditional Romanian *ţuică* except that it was distilled more than three times. The now-deserted factory is opposite strawberry fields, at the southern end of the village. Turţ also hosts a **folk music festival**, one of Romania's finest.

The remainders of the town's mining history lie in the southeastern part of Turţ. From Satu Mare, follow the northbound Budapest road to Turulung village. Turţ is signposted on the right just after the village. There's no hotel or restaurant here.

Negreşti-Oaş & Around

Heading southeast from Turţ, through the lakeside **Călineşti-Oaş**, you come to **Negreşti-Oaş**. The main reason for stopping in this small village is to visit the **Open-air Museum** (Muzeul Satului Oşenesc; admission €0.30; ☺ 10am-5pm Tue-Sun). Its small collection includes a traditional farm and pig sty from Moişeni, a wine press from nearby Oraşu Nou, and a washing whirlpool and felting mill, methods still used by villagers to wash clothes and rugs. There's also a small **Oaş History Museum** (Muzeul Ţării Oaşului; Str Victoriei) in the village.

Four kilometres south of Negreşti-Oaş is **Vama**, traditionally a ceramics and pottery centre of which little evidence remains today. **Valea Măriei**, 2.5km west, is a small alpine resort.

Four kilometers northwest of Negreşti-Oaş (off the Călineşti road) is **Bixad**, a 200-year-old hilltop monastery. It has great views and a beautiful church, but at the time of writing it was being renovated.

Sleeping & Eating

Popas Turistic Lacu Albastru (☎ 839 047; cabins €10) Located 1km southwest of Călineşti-Oaş, opposite Albastru Lake, it has nine four-bed cabins, communal showers and a small bar/grill. You can camp at Popas Turistic or on the field opposite for €3.

Cabana Pintar (☎ 853 535; r €18-25) As well as providing accommodation, this cabana, in Valea Măriei, also has a restaurant.

To reach the more attractive **Cabana Teilor** (☎ 851 329; s/d €20/28) and **Cabana Valea Măriei** (☎ 850 750; s/d €20/28), turn right along the forest track, immediately opposite Cabana Pintar. Cabana Teilor, at the end of the left fork, has a tennis court and an excellent restaurant. Accord Travel in Satu Mare (p248) takes bookings for both cabanas.

Getting There & Away

There are buses daily except Sunday from Satu Mare to Negreşti-Oaş (1½ hours), from where they continue to Turţ. This area is difficult to reach without private transport, so you may have to flag down a lift or jump on a horse and cart.

BAIA MARE

☎ 262 / pop 149,000

Baia Mare (Big Mine), at the foot of the Gutâi Mountains, is the seat of Maramureş County. The town was first documented in 1329 and developed as a gold-mining town in the 14th and 15th centuries. In 1446 the town became the property of the Iancu de Hunedoara family. In 1469, under the rule of Hungarian king Matthias Corvinus (Iancu de Hunedoara's son), the town was fortified.

Baia Mare gained notoriety during Ceauşescu's regime as home to the Romplumb and Phoenix metallurgic plants which released more than 5 billion cu metres of residual gases into the atmosphere each year, smothering the town with a permanent sulphur-dioxide/metal powder smog. In the early 1990s, a new smoke stack was built in an attempt to alleviate air pollution.

The town was again thrown into the environmental hot seat in early 2000, when a poisonous spill from the Aurul gold mine caused one of Europe's worst environmental disasters. On 30 January a tailings dam burst, causing cyanide-contaminated water to leak from the gold mine – part-owned by Australian Esmeralda Enterprises – contaminating the Someş and Tisa Rivers before spilling into the Danube and finally the Black Sea.

With six neighbouring countries affected, the water supply of 2.5 million people contaminated, fish stocks decimated and the rivers' ecosystems devastated, the full impact of the spill may not be known for another two decades. Drinking water remains unpotable and fish stocks polluted.

Orientation

The train and bus stations, west of the centre on Str Gării, are a 15-minute walk from Piaţa Libertăţii, Baia Mare's central square. The Şasar River flows across the north of the town.

Information
INTERNET ACCESS
Internet Checker (Piaţa Revoluţiei; ☺ 24hr; per hr €0.25)

MONEY
Banks that cash travellers cheques and offer cash transfers, ATM facilities and currency exchange include:
Banca Commerciala Romana (B-dul Unirii 15; ☺ 8.30am-1pm Mon-Fri)
Banca Post (☎ 220 350; B-dul Traian 1B; ☺ 8.30am-5pm Mon-Fri, 8.30am-noon Sat)

West Bank (☎ 224 586; B-dul Unirii 7; ⊗ 8.30am-4.30pm Mon-Fri)

POST

Central post office (B-dul Traian 1B; ⊗ 7am-8pm Mon-Fri) Has fax and cash transfer facilities.

TOURIST INFORMATION

Mara Holidays (☎ 226 656; office@hotelmara.ro; inside Hotel Mara, B-dul Unirii 11; ⊗ 9am-5pm Mon-Fri) Helpful, English-speaking staff arrange car hire and walking, trekking and horse-riding tours, provide maps, and can book accommodation through Antrec.

Sights

Transylvanian prince Iancu de Hunedoara (János Hunyadi in Hungarian), royal gov-ernor of Hungary between 1446 and 1453, lived in the now-crumbling, 15th-century house **Casa Iancu de Hunedoara** (Piaţa Libertăţii 18). In 1456 he successfully hammered the Turks on the banks of the Danube close to Belgrade. Hunedoara died of the plague in Belgrade that same year. Today, his house has temporary exhibitions arranged by the local history museum.

Hunedoara's life story and that of Baia Mare is told in the local **History Museum** (Muzeul de Istorie; ☎ 211 927; Str Monetăriei 1; admission €0.50; ⊗ 8am-4pm Tue-Fri, 10am-2pm Sat & Sun).

Looming above Piaţa Libertăţii is **Stephen's Tower** (Turnul Ştefan). The 14th-century Gothic-style tower was initially topped with a bell but this was replaced by a mechanical

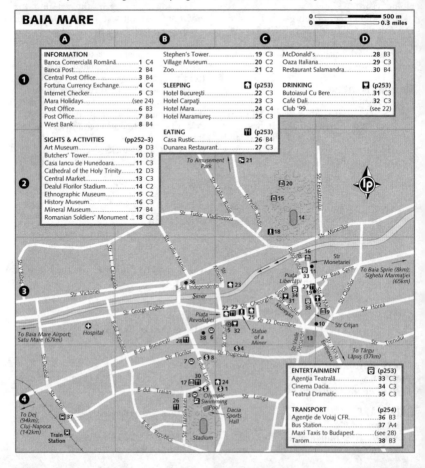

BAIA MARE

0 —————— 500 m
0 —————— 0.3 miles

INFORMATION	
Banca Comercială Română	1 C4
Banca Post	2 B4
Central Post Office	3 B4
Fortuna Currency Exchange	4 C4
Internet Checker	5 C3
Mara Holidays	(see 24)
Post Office	6 B3
Post Office	7 B4
West Bank	8 B4

SIGHTS & ACTIVITIES (pp252-3)	
Art Museum	9 D3
Butchers' Tower	10 D3
Casa Iancu de Hunedoara	11 C3
Cathedral of the Holy Trinity	12 D3
Central Market	13 C3
Dealul Florilor Stadium	14 C2
Ethnographic Museum	15 C2
History Museum	16 C3
Mineral Museum	17 B4
Romanian Soldiers' Monument	18 C2

Stephen's Tower	19 C3
Village Museum	20 C2
Zoo	21 C2

SLEEPING ⌂ (p253)	
Hotel Bucureşti	22 C3
Hotel Carpaţi	23 C3
Hotel Mara	24 C4
Hotel Maramureş	25 C3

EATING ⑪ (p253)	
Casa Rustic	26 B4
Dunarea Restaurant	27 C3

McDonald's	28 B3
Oaza Italiana	29 C3
Restaurant Salamandra	30 B4

DRINKING ⑦ (p253)	
Butoiasul Cu Bere	31 C3
Café Dali	32 C3
Club '99	(see 22)

ENTERTAINMENT ⑧ (p253)	
Agenţia Teatrală	33 C3
Cinema Dacia	34 C3
Teatrul Dramatic	35 C3

TRANSPORT (p254)	
Agenţie de Voiaj CFR	36 B3
Bus Station	37 A4
Maxi Taxis to Budapest	(see 28)
Tarom	38 B3

clock in 1628. Behind the tower is the **Cathedral of the Holy Trinity** (Catedrala Sfânta Treime; Str 1 Mai), close to the local **Art Museum** (Muzeul de Artă; ☎ 213 964; Str 1 Mai 8; ☺ 10am-4pm Tue-Sun).

The **central market** (cnr Str 22 Decembrie & Vasile Alecsandri) is surrounded by the only remaining part of the 15th-century city walls – and near the **Butchers' Tower** where famous brigand Grigore Pintea Viteazul was shot in 1703.

Heading north from the market across the footbridge over the Şasar River, the **Dealul Florilor Stadium** (Stadionul Dealul Florilor) is home to the Baia Mare football club. Open-air Masses are often held on Sunday next to the WWI **Romanian Soldiers Monument** (Monumentul Ostaşilor Români) in the park to the west of the football stadium.

Northwest of the football stadium is the **Ethnographic Museum** (Muzeul Etnografic; ☎ 212 845) in which all the traditional trades of the Maramureş region are represented.

The **Village Museum** (Muzeul Satului; admission €1; ☺ 10am-5pm Tue-Sun, closed 16 Oct–14 May), behind the Ethnographic Museum, displays traditional wooden houses and churches, for which the region is famed.

Baia Mare has a small **zoo** (admission €1; ☺ 10am-5pm Tue-Sun) adjoining an **amusement park** (Str Petőfi Sándor 28).

The **Mineral Museum** (Muzeul de Mineralogie; B-dul Traian 8) is close to the Jewish Cemetery. There is a monument to the Jews deported from Baia Mare to Auschwitz during WWII. Until 1848, Jews were not allowed to live in the city because of a 17th-century law forbidding them from settling in Hungarian mining towns.

Sleeping

Baia Mare has no budget options except for homestays which must be booked in advance. The hotels in the centre are not cheap.

Mara Holidays (☎ 226 656; office@hotelmara.ro; inside Hotel Mara at B-dul Unirii 11; ☺ 9am-5pm Mon-Fri) This is an agent for Antrec and arranges rooms in private homes in the region for around €15 to €20 per night, including a gut-busting, home-cooked breakfast.

Hotel Bucureşti (☎ 217 290; Str Culturii 4; s/d/q from €16/18/35) Overlooking Piaţa Revoluţiei, this landmark monstrosity has cheap, clean rooms and buzzing nightlife.

Hotel Mara (☎ 226 660; office@hotelmara.ro; B-dul Unirii 11; s/d €36/47) Weary travellers can treat themselves to power showers and comfortable beds here.

Hotel Maramureş (☎ 216 555; hotelmm@multinet .ro; Str Gheorghe Şincai 37; s/d €45/55) Grand three-star hotel with faded charm but comfortable rooms.

Hotel Carpaţi (☎ 214 812; office@hotelcarpati.ro; Str Minerva 16; s/d €55/70) A three-star tower with all mod-cons.

Eating

Casa Rustic (Calea Unirii 14a; mains €5) Fabulous, cheap restaurant, with fish, soups and salads and whole roasted piglet or chicken on the menu.

Oaza Italiana (☎ 214 913; Str Culturii 4; mains €2-3) Large pizzas, pumping music and drinks make this place on Piaţa Revoluţiei, behind Hotel Bucureşti, a noisy winner.

Restaurant Dunarea (cnr Piaţa Libertăţii & Str 1 Mai; mains €2-3) Tiled mosaic walls and gingham tablecloths add a rustic touch to this restaurant serving cutlets, schnitzel and salads.

Restaurant Salamandra (☎ 237 600; B-dul Traian; meals €5-10) Traditional Maramureş dishes are served here.

The **central market** (cnr Str 22 Decembrie & Str Vasile Alecsandri) is beneath the Butchers' Tower.

Entertainment

CINEMA
See English-language films with Romanian subtitles at **Cinema Dacia** (☎ 214 265; Piaţa Revoluţiei 7; tickets €1).

BARS & DISCOS
Café Dali (Piaţa Revoluţiei) Get yourself a Dirty Bitch (Baileys and vodka) for €1 at this cocktail heaven.

Butoiasul Cu Bere (Str Gheorghe Şincai 13) Beer cellar–style bar in this revamped, cobbled part of the old town.

Club '99 (Str Culturii 3; ☺ 6pm-4am) For die-hard disco fans only!

THEATRE
Plays are performed in Romanian at the **Teatrul Dramatic** (☎ 211 124; Str Crişan 4). Tickets can be bought in advance at the **Agenţia Teatrală** (cnr Piaţa Libertăţii & Str Podul Viilor; ☺ 10am-noon & 4pm-6pm Tue-Sun).

Getting There & Away

AIR

Tarom (☎ 221 624; B-dul Bucureşti 5; ☼ 8am-6pm Tue-Fri) operates five flights weekly between Baia Mare and Bucharest (one-way US$75, return US$124, business class US$143, all plus tax). It is worth noting that Tarom doesn't accept euros.

BUS

Infrequent services run from the **bus station** (☎ 431 921; Str Gării 2) to outlying villages. There are two daily buses to Satu Mare (€1.50), two to Cluj-Napoca (€3), and four to Sighetu Marmaţiei via Baia Sprie (€1.50). The No 8 bus, which stops outside Hotel Mara, goes to Baia Sprie.

Maxitaxis run twice daily (except Sunday) to Satu Mare (€1.30) and once daily to Bistriţa (€4). There's a daily maxitaxi to Budapest, leaving from outside McDonalds, on Str Dragoş Vodă, at 10pm (€16, six hours).

TRAIN

Advance tickets are sold at **Agenţie de Voiaj CFR** (☎ 219 113; Str Victoriei 5-7).

From Baia Mare **train station** (☎ 220 950; Str Gării 4) there is one daily train to Budapest (€28, eight hours) at noon; 10 daily to Satu Mare; one to Bucharest via Cluj-Napoca and Braşov; and one to Timişoara (€9).

Getting Around

The **airport** (☎ 223 394) is 9km west of the centre at Tăuţi Măgherăuş. Tarom runs a shuttle from its office, leaving town 1½ hours before flight departures. It also meets incoming flights.

AROUND BAIA MARE
Baia Sprie

Baia Sprie, 10km east of Baia Mare, is a small mining town first chronicled in 1329. The mine still operates today, mining approximately 145,000 tonnes of copper, lead and zinc ore annually.

A **roadside cross**, in memory of political prisoners who died in the mine during the communist purges of 1950–56, stands at the foot of the track that leads to the mine. During this period an estimated 180,000 people were interned in hard-labour camps such as those by the Danube–Black Sea canal, or in high-security prisons such as Piteşti, Gherla

and Sighetu Marmaţiei. Between 1947 and 1964, some 200 to 300 political prisoners were committed to forced labour at the Baia Sprie mine, including Corneliu Coposu, secretary to National Peasant Party leader Iuliu Maniu, who was himself imprisoned at Sighetu (see 'Sighet Prison: A Suffering Nation', p256).

The **village church**, bearing a traditional Maramureş tiled roof dating from 1793, is next to a new church in the centre. A **Chestnut Festival** is held in the village each year in September or October.

Şurdeşti & Around

Approaching Şurdeşti from Baia Sprie, you pass through **Şişeşti** village, home to the Vasile Lucaciu Memorial Museum. Vasile Lucaciu (1835–1919), appointed parish priest in 1885, built a church for the village supposedly modelled on St Peter's in Rome. The church was ceremoniously named, and dedicated to, the Union of all Romanians (Unirii Tuturor Românilor).

The towering church at **Şurdeşti**, southwest of Baia Sprie, is one of the most magnificent in the Maramureş region and well worth the hike. Some damage was caused by a botched renovation job but the walls and ceilings remain impressively painted. The tiny church's disproportionately giant church steeple (72m) is considered the tallest wooden structure in Europe – if not the world. The church was built in 1724 as a centre of worship for the Greco-Catholic faithful. Today, it remains a Uniate church. The entire interior of the church is original. The priest and his wife live in the house below the church; the priest's wife will gladly open the church for you. The church is signposted 'Monument' from the centre of the village.

Two kilometres south in **Plopiş** is another fine church with a towering steeple. Ask for the key at the lone house nearby. A further 14km south is the town of **Lăschia**. Its church dates from 1861 and has a bulbous steeple. Note the motifs carved on the outer walls, which are like those traditionally used in carpets.

The last wave of nomadic Tartar tribes from the Eurasian steppe settled in the mining town of **Cavnic**, 8km north of Şurdeşti, as late as 1717. A monument known as the Tartar stone stands in the centre of the small town, first documented in 1445. In 1952 and 1955, political prisoners were sent to the gold and silver mines here.

Heading north from Cavnic along the mountainous **Neteda Pass** (1040m) towards Sighetu Marmaţiei, you pass a small memorial plaque to those who died in the mines under the communist purges.

Baia Mare to Izvoare

North of Baia Mare a dirt road twists and turns through the remote villages of **Firiza**, **Blidari** and **Valea Neagră**, culminating 25km north of Baia Mare at **Izvoare**, where there are natural springs.

Viewing churches is not on the agenda here; wallowing in the mountainous rural countryside dotted with delightful wooden cottages and ramshackle farms is. Izvoare is dominated by pine forests and the rather ugly Statiunea Izvoare complex. The complex is closed between mid-June and mid-September, when it is taken over by local schools as a summer holiday camp. The rest of the year it is open to travellers. In winter a **ski lift** offers stunning aerial views of the fun **sculpture park** spread throughout the grounds of the complex.

This route is not served by public transport, and hitching is difficult as few vehicles pass by. A **hiking trail** (five to six hours, marked with red triangles) leads from Baia Mare to Izvoare; it starts about 3km north of Baia Mare along the Baia Mare–Izvoare road.

Sleeping & Eating

Mogoşa Chalet (☎ 262 260 800; www.mogosa.ro in Romanian; d/tr/q with shared bath €12/16/20) The chalet overlooks Lake Bodi, 731m above sea level. Campers can pitch their tents by the lake. In summer you can hire boats or swim in the lake, and in winter you can skate on the frozen lake or rent skis; there is a nearby chairlift and two **ski lifts** (10am-4pm Tue-Sun). The chalet is located 6km northeast of Baia Sprie. Follow the road to Sighetu Marmaţiei and turn right at the signpost for Mogoşa.

Complex Turistic Şuior (☎ 262 262 080; s/d €21/32) The complex of three brand-new hotels is 1km further along the same road from Mogoşa Chalet. It boasts a new ski lift (opened in winter 2003) and a swanky bar and restaurant in a lovingly created, peaceful setting.

ŢARA CHIOARULUI

The Ţara Chioarului region in the southwestern part of Maramureş takes in the area immediately south of Baia Mare. The numerous villages, most of which boast traditional wooden churches, form a convenient loop – ideal for a two-hour driving tour by private transport.

Sights & Activities

Follow the main road south from Baia Mare to Cluj-Napoca for 14km to Satulung. Three kilometres south of Satulung, take the unmarked turn-off on the left opposite Cabana Stejarul to Finteuşu Mare and continue for 5km until you reach the village of **Posta**. At the top of the hill towers a small wooden church dating from 1675.

Şomcuţa Mare, 24km south of Baia Mare, is home to the annual **Stejarul (Oak Tree) Festival** held in July, which attracts bands and choirs from all over the region. The small **Vălenii Şomcuţei Cave** (Peştera de la Vălenii Şomcuţei), 4km away, is signposted from the centre of the village.

Nine kilometres south of Şomcuţa lies **Valea Chioarului**, the most southern village in Ţara Chioarului. Its delightful, tall church stands next to the bus stop in the centre of the village. Beside the church is a bust of Mihail Viteazul, erected by the village in 1994.

From Şomcuţa Mare a minor road winds its way to **Remetea Chioarului**, 12km northeast. Its tiny church, dating from 1800, is the highlight of Ţara Chioarului. It stands majestically beside the village's extraordinarily ugly, seven-spired, modern church, built in 1996.

Culcea, about 5km northwest of here, has an unremarkable plastered church built in 1720 and extensively renovated in 1939. **Săcălaşeni**, 2km further north, has a small church built in 1442, but sadly a modern church dominates the village.

From **Catalina**, just north again, head west 2km to the predominantly Hungarian village of **Coltău** (Koltó in Hungarian). Hungary's most celebrated poet, Sándor Petőfi (1823–49), lived in the village in 1847, prior to leading the revolution against Habsburg domination of Hungary (1848–49). There's a small memorial house in the centre of Coltău where the poet spent a few months. In the garden stands the giant, 300-year-old cypress tree under which Petőfi sought inspiration.

SIGHETU MARMAŢIEI

☎ 262 / pop 40,000

Sighetu Marmaţiei almost touches the Ukranian border as it's the northernmost town in Romania, lying on the confluence of the Tisa, Iza and Ronişoara Rivers. Its name is derived from the Thracian and Dacian word *seget*, meaning 'fortress'.

Sighet (as it is known locally) is famed for its vibrant **Winter Festival** (27 December), and the colourful peasant costumes worn by locals. Its dusty streets bustle with markets, tucked beneath the domes of churches of all denominations.

Sighetu Marmaţiei's former maximum-security prison is now open as a museum and is a sobering and informative highlight of any visit to northern Romania.

Information

INTERNET ACCESS

Internet Café/Bar (per hr €0.25) Near Millennium.

Millennium (Str Corneliu Coposu; ☾ 10am-10pm Tue-Sat, noon-10pm Sun; per hr €0.20)

MONEY

In addition to the banks listed, there's also an ATM outside Hotel Tisa.

Banca Comercială Română (Str Iuliu Maniu; ☾ 8.30am-2.30pm Mon-Fri)

Banca Română (Calea Ioan Mihaly de Apşa 24; ☾ 9am-5pm Mon-Fri) Has an ATM, cash transfer and exchange facilities.

POST & TELEPHONE

The **post and telephone office** (Str Ioan Mihaly de Apşa 39) is opposite the Maramureş Museum.

TOURIST INFORMATION & TRAVEL AGENCIES

There is no official tourist office. The region's best source of beds, books and information is **Fundaţia OVR Agro-Tur-Art** (☎ 330 171; aramona@gmx.de), in Vadu Izei (6km south), run by a friendly, dynamic team. In Sighet, there's **MM Pangeae Proiect Turism** (☎ 312 228; Piaţa Libertăţii 15; ☾ 9am-4pm Mon-Fri), which offers simple maps and group tours, and a Eurolines agent at Hotel Tisa (p257).

Sights

PIAŢA LIBERTĂŢII & AROUND

Sighet, first documented in 1328, was a strong cultural and political centre, being the birthplace of the Association for the Romanian Peoples' Culture, founded in 1863. On Piaţa Libertăţii stands the **Hungarian Reformed church**, built during the 15th century. Close by is the 16th-century **Roman Catholic church**.

SIGHET PRISON: A SUFFERING NATION

In May 1947 the communist regime embarked on a reign of terror; slaughtering, imprisoning and torturing thousands of Romanians. While many leading prewar figures were sent to hard-labour camps, the regime's most feared intellectual opponents were interned in Sighet's maximum-security prison. Between 1948 and 1952, about 180 members of Romania's academic and government elite were imprisoned here.

Today, four white marble plaques covering the barred windows of the prison list the 51 prisoners who died in the Sighet cells, notably the academic and head of the National Liberal Party (PNL), Constantin Brătianu; historian and leading member of the PNL, Gheorghe Brătianu; governor of the National Bank, Constantin Tătăranu; and Iuliu Maniu, president of the National Peasants' Party (PNŢ). Many simply died of starvation; the prisoners were given 700 calories a day to survive on – the average person needs between 2000 and 2500 – an impossible task in Romania's feared winters.

The prison, housed in the old courthouse, was closed in 1974. In 1989 it re-opened as the **Museum of Arrested Thought** (Muzeu al Gândirii Arestate; ☎ 314 224, 316 848; Str Corneliu Coposu 4; admission free; ☾ 9.30am-6.30pm, 9.30am-4.30pm 15 Oct–15 May). Photographs are displayed in the torture chambers and cells. The memorial plaque outside reads 'In memory of the young, intelligent people at the forefront of Romanian intellectual life who were imprisoned because they did not believe in communism and died, through torture, in this odious prison'.

Possibly the most heart-rending sight is the bronze sculptures in the courtyard, dedicated to those who died. Figures shielding themselves, imploring, covering their mouths in horror, all naked and missing limbs look to the heavens in a frozen symbol of their agony.

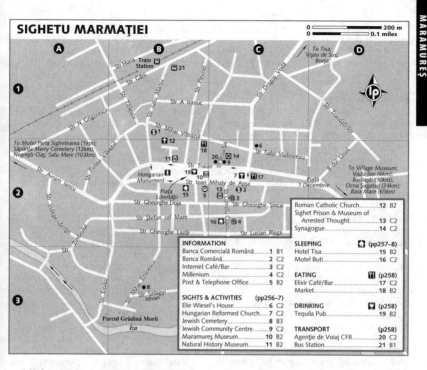

SIGHETU MARMAŢIEI

Off the square is Sighet's only remaining **synagogue** (Str Bessarabia 10). Before WWII there were eight synagogues serving a large Jewish community which made up 40% of the town's population. Jews first settled in Sighet in the 17th century.

Next door is the **Jewish Community Centre** (☎ 311 652; Str Bessarabia 8; ☿ 10am-4pm Tue-Sun), where you can purchase tickets to visit the **Jewish Cemetery** (Str Szilagyi Istvan), a couple of blocks south of the centre (follow Str Eminescu south, then turn left into Str Szilagyi Istvan). The cemetery isn't hard to find – just look for the 6m-high stone wall.

Elie Wiesel, the Jewish writer and 1986 Nobel peace prizewinner, who coined the term 'Holocaust', was born in (and later deported from) Sighet. **Elie Wiesel's house** is on the corner of Str Dragos Vodă & Str Tudor Vladimirescu. His autobiography, *La Nuit* (The Night), was the first account ever published of the horrors of the Nazi concentration camps in WWII. On Str Gheorghe Doja is a **monument** to the victims of the Holocaust.

Maramureş Museum (Piaţa Libertăţii 15; admission €0.50; ☿ 10am-6pm Tue-Sun) displays colourful folk costumes, rugs and carnival masks.

The decrepit but interesting **Natural History Museum** (Muzeul de Istorie si ştiintele Naturii; admission €0.20; ☿ 10am-5pm Tue-Sun) is stuffed with dead animal exhibits. Knock on the door to enter.

VILLAGE MUSEUM

Visit traditional peasant houses from the Maramureş region at the open-air **Village Museum** (Muzeul Satului; ☎ 314 229; Str Dobăieş 40; ☿ 10am-6pm Tue-Sun; adult/child €1/0.50), southeast of Sighet's centre. Allow at least half a day to wander through the incredible constructions. Children love the wooden dwellings, cobbled pathways and 'mini' villages. You can even stay overnight in tiny wooden cabins for €5.50.

Sleeping

Hotel Tisa (☎ 312 645; Piaţa Libertăţii 8; d/tr €24/36) Offers pleasant rooms smack-bang in the centre of Sighet.

Motel Buţi (☎ 311 035; Str Ştefan cel Mare 6; d/tr €25/40) This charming villa has spotlessly clean but small rooms, as well as a bar and pool table downstairs.

Motel Perla Sigheteama (☎ 310613; www.sighetu marmatiei.alphanet.ro; Str Avram Iancu 65; d €25) Just out of town on the road to Săpânţa.

Eating & Drinking

Hotel Tisa has a large, reasonably priced restaurant, which does good breakfasts. The town's **market** (Piaţa Agroalimentara) sells fresh fruit and veg.

Get cosy with the locals at **Elixir Café/Bar** (Str Traian), a busy, smoky joint, serving snacks and beer. Nearby, Tequila Pub is the trendiest place to drink in town.

Getting There & Away

BUS

The **bus station** (Str Gării) is opposite the train station. Several local buses leave daily to Baia Mare (€1.7, 65km), Satu Mare (€2, 122km), Borşa (€0.50), Budeşti (€0.50), Călineşti (€0.50) and Vişeu de Sus (€1.20), and one bus daily to Bârsana, Botiza, Ieud and Mara. A bus leaves for Săpânţa every hour between 8am and 2pm, returning at 4pm and 5pm.

TRAIN

Tickets are sold in advance at the **Agenţie de Voiaj CFR** (☎ 312 666; Piaţa Libertăţii 25; ⏰ 7am-2pm Mon-Fri). There's one daily fast train to each of these towns: Timişoara (€14.50), Bucharest (€14.50, 12 hours), Cluj-Napoca (€9, six hours) and Arad (€13).

MARA VALLEY

The Mara Valley (Valea Mara), with its beautiful rolling hills, is the heart of Maramureş. It takes its name from the Mara River which runs southwest through the valley from Sighetu Marmaţiei to Baia Mare. Villages here are famed for their spectacular churches and carved gateways.

Giuleşti & Around

Heading south from Sighetu Marmaţiei, you reach the tiny village of **Berbeşti**, famed for the 300-year-old *troiţă* (crucifix), a large, Renaissance-style cross carved with solar emblems, which stands by the roadside at the village's northern end. Traditionally, travellers prayed by the cross to ensure a safe journey.

Continuing south is **Giuleşti**, the main village in the Mara Valley and notable for its crumbling wooden cottages with 'pot trees' in their front yards, on which a colourful array of pots and pans are hung to dry. It was here in 1918 that the revolutionary poet Ilie Lazăr summoned delegates from all over Maramureş prior to their signing Transylvania's Union agreement with Romania. Ilie Lazăr's house is preserved and open to tourists as a memorial museum. During the communist crackdown in the early 1950s, Ilie Lazăr was arrested and imprisoned at Sighet prison (see 'Sighet Prison: A Suffering Nation', p256).

The village of **Deseşti** is just a few kilometres southwest of Giuleşti on the road to Baia Mare. Its tiny Orthodox church, built in 1770, was struck by lightning in 1925, destroying much of the outer walls and the steeple. It has since been repaired (and fitted with a lightning conductor). Its interior paintings, by Radu Munteanu, date from 1780 and feature Sodom and Gomorrah.

Close to the church is an oak tree, hundreds of years old and measuring 6m in diameter. It has been preserved as a monument to the extensive oak forest that once covered the area before people felled the trees to build their homes.

Mara, just a couple of kilometres south of Deseşti, is best known for its elaborate wooden fences. These porches are a unique architectural feature of the Maramureş region. In more recent times, the spiritual importance of these outside porches has been overridden by the social status attached to them (see 'Maramureş Culture', p247).

In **Vama**, older porches dating from the 1770s are evident, but plenty of brashly decorated, modern gates have been built in the last 10 years. The tradition of carving the construction date, as well as the sculptor's name, into the gates remains today.

Sat-Şugatag & Around

Seven kilometres south of Giuleşti is **Sat-Şugatag**, home to a church dating from 1642. The church is famed for its fine, ornately carved wooden gate. Sat-Şugatag was first documented in 1360 as the property of Dragoş of Giuleşti.

Mănăstirea is 1km east of Sat-Şugatag. The church here was built by monks in 1633. By 1787 just one monk and four servants remained, and during the reign of Austro-Hungarian king Joseph II the monastery was closed. The original monks' cells are on the northern side of the church. Several 18th-century icons painted on glass and wood have been preserved, as have some of the frescoes on the outside western wall of the church, normally seen on the monasteries of northern Moldova.

Three kilometres south of Mănăstirea is the small spa resort-village of **Ocna Şugatag**, built on a hilltop in 1321. The village is named after its former salt mine, which was exploited until the 1950s (*ocnă* means 'salt mine').

Four kilometres south of Ocna Şugatag is **Hărniceşti**, home to a marvellous Orthodox church dating from 1770. A footpath, signposted 'Spre Monument', leads from the primary school in the centre of the village to the hillside church.

Nine kilometres southeast of Ocna Şugatag is **Hoteni**, known for its Tânjaua de pe Mara folk festival held from 1 May to 14 May to celebrate the first ploughing.

Eastern Mara Valley & Cosău Valley

Heading south from Sighetu, bear left at **Fereşti** along the dirt track leading to Maramureş' least accessible villages. From Baia Mare, you can approach this area through Cavnic, across the Neteda Pass.

Corneşti, the first village along this stretch, has a small 18th-century church with interior paintings by Hodor Toador. **Călineşti**, 7km further south, is where in 1862 archaeologists uncovered a cache of bracelets and ankle chains, believed to date from Roman times. Călineşti has two churches, known as Susani (*sus* meaning 'up') and Josani (*jos* meaning 'low'). The Susani church (1683) is on the left side of the road as you enter the village from the north. But the Josani church, built 20 years earlier, is more spectacular. To get to this church, turn right at the road for Bârsana and continue until you reach house No 385. A small path opposite this house twists and turns its way to the church; follow the upper path when you come to the fork.

From Călineşti a mud track leads to **Sârbi**, inhabited since 1402. Its two churches are built from oak. The Susani church dates from 1667, with interior paintings by Al Ponehachile. Sârbi's Josani church dates from 1665. A traditional 'natural launderette', ingeniously constructed by villagers,

is still used to wash clothes and blankets. Nearby, a wooden thresher, loom and *ţuica* (plum brandy) 'factory' welcomes visitors.

Budeşti, 4km south of Sârbi, is one of the most beautiful villages in Maramureş. Its Josani church, built in 1643, features four small turrets surrounding the main steeple, signifying its role as local law courts. Inside the church is a small collection of icons on glass and wood, dating from 1766. Other exhibits include a glass box containing a real-life miracle – a hunk of wood sliced in half to reveal a perfect blackened cross image. The church's most prized piece, however, is the 18th-century painting of the Last Judgment, preserved in its entirety. The church also houses the undershirt of its most famous 17th-century inhabitant, Grigore Pintea Viteazul (a local Robin Hood), allegedly purchased from the local Romanian community in Budapest for 1000 forint.

Blueberries and 'little angels', or red berries, grow in abundance on the fields surrounding the track.

Sleeping & Eating

Ocna Şugatag is a good base for exploring the Mara Valley. **Fundaţia OVR Agro-Tur-Art** (☎ 262 330 171; aramona@gmx.de), in Vadu Izei, arranges accommodation in private homes in the area for around €15 per night, including breakfast.

Hotel Salina (☎ 262 374 362/034; s & d incl spa treatments €20) The 'health' resort has four salt pools and it's a bargain. It's owned by Sind Romania (Union Romania) and offers cheap holidays to Romanian workers. It also owns the **Camping Complex** (opposite Hotel Salina; tent sites €2, bungalows €10), which has beautifully carved wooden bungalows sleeping up to six people, and **Hotel Craiasca** (☎ 262 374 217; www.craiasca.ro; s/d €15/20), which has two restaurants, a bar and a disco, and offers spa treatments for €3 and three meals per day for an extra €10.

SĂPÂNŢA

☎ 262

Săpânţa village has a unique place in the hearts of Romanians. It boasts the 'Merry Cemetery', the church graveyard famous for the colourfully painted wooden crosses that adorn its tombstones. Shown in art exhibitons across Europe, the crosses attract busloads of visitors who marvel at the gentle humour and human warmth that created them. Villagers seem utterly untouched by the fame that the crosses have created. Life carries on as normal: the old women sit outside their cottages, colourful rugs are hung out on clotheslines and the odd horse and cart trundles past.

The village itself lies 12km northwest of Sighetu Marmației, just 4km south of Ukraine. Locals pop across the border to shop but this crossing is not open to foreigners. Four kilometres from Săpânța, down a gravel road, a new wooden church, which is claimed to be the tallest in Europe at 75m tall, is being built. Critics say the stone base rules out this prize but the jury's still out...

Sleeping & Eating

Villagers rent out their rooms including:

Pensiunea Stan (☎ 372 336; d €10) It's opposite the cemetery entrance, and has five double rooms.

Pensiunea Ileana (☎ 372 137; d €10) This green-tiled house is to the right of Pensiunea Stan.

Camping Poieni (☎ 322 228; tent sites €1.50; cabins per person €3; ⏲ 1 Jun–31 Aug) It is 3km to the south of Săpânța, and has an excellent trout restaurant.

There's a new **bar** and terrace by the cemetery entrance.

Getting There & Away

Buses run every hour (8am to 2pm) from Sighet bus station and return at 4pm and 5pm. The wooden church is down a gravel path off the main Sighet/Negrești-Oaș road. It's a 3km hike from the main road.

IZEI VALLEY

☎ 262 / pop 3000

The lush Izei Valley (Valea Izei) follows the Iza River eastward from Sighetu Marmației to Moisei. The soul of ancient Romania lurks among the valley's tiny rural villages, inside its thatched roofs, tall wooden church steeples, its 'pot trees' and wooden gates outside every home. Traditional crafts are still practised by wood carvers, blanket weavers and glass painters and there's ample opportunity for you to join in.

In mid-July Vadu Izei, together with the neighbouring villages of Botiza and Ieud, hosts the **Maramuzical Festival**, a lively four-day international folk music festival.

Vadu Izei

Vadu Izei is at the confluence of the Iza and Mara Rivers, 6km south of Sighetu Marmației. Its **museum** is in the oldest

---

MERRY CEMETERY

Săpânța's **Merry Cemetery** (Cimitirul Vesel; admission €0.50) was the creation of Ioan Stan Pătraș, a simple wood sculptor who, in 1935, started carving crosses to mark graves in the old church cemetery. He painted each cross in blue – the traditional colour of hope and freedom – and on top of each he inscribed a witty epitaph to the deceased.

Prior to his death in 1977, Pătraș carved and painted his own cross, complete with a portrait of himself and a lengthy epitaph in which he wrote of the 'cross' he bore all his life, working to support his family since his father's death when he was 14 years old. Pătraș' grave is directly opposite the main entrance to the old church.

Every cross tells a different story, and the painted pictures and inscriptions illustrate a wealth of traditional occupations: Shepherds tend their sheep, mothers cook for their families, barbers cut hair, and weavers bend over looms.

Since Pătraș's death, Dumitru Pop, his apprentice, has carried on the tradition. He lives and works in Pătraș' former house and studio, using the same traditional methods. He makes about 10 crosses each year, depending on the mortality rate in the village.

The house where Pop lives and works is also a **museum** (admission by €0.25 donation). In one small room, various pictures carved in wood and painted by Pătraș are displayed. These include portraits of members of the Executive Committee of the Communist Party, and a portrait of Nicolae and Elena Ceaușescu carved in honour of Ceaușescu's visit to Săpânța in 1974. The interior of Săpânța's old church (1886), next to the cemetery, is adorned with painted frescoes.

house in the village (1750). If you visit a private home in this village – and the whole region – you'll quickly realise that little has changed since the 18th century.

Vadu Izei has been supported since the early 1990s by the Belgian charity Opération Villages Roumains, which originally started out as an international pressure group against Ceauşescu's systemisation program. More recently, the village gained financial backing from the European Union's Phare program to develop infrastructure.

The village tourism society, **Fundaţia OVR Agro-Tur-Art** (☎ 330 171; aramona@gmx.de; house No 161), is an unrivalled source of local information. **Nicolae Prisăcaru** (☎ 0721-046 730) or the lovely **Ramona Ardelean** (☎ 0744-827 829) arrange excellent guided tours (in French or English, half/full day €12/20 plus €0.25 per kilometre), as well as picnics, wood-carving or icon-painting workshops, and homestays. They also both sell maps, guides and local crafts in the office at the northern end of the village.

SLEEPING & EATING
Fundaţia OVR Agro-Tur-Art (☎ 330 171; aramona@ gmx.de; house No 161) arranges accommodation (half/full board €14/17) in 20 private homes within the village. Bookings can be made either through the Fundaţia OVR Agro-Tur-Art or directly at the homes involved in the scheme; some of the homes are clearly signposted.

Bârsana
From Vadu Izei continue for 12km through Onceşti to the village of Bârsana (formerly Bîrsana), dating from 1326. In 1720 it built its first church, the interior paintings of which were created by local artists Hodor Toador and Ion Plohod.

The famous and enchanting Orthodox **Bârsana Monastery** (Mănăstirea Bârsana) is a popular pilgrimage spot in Maramureş. It was the last Orthodox monastery built in the region before Serafim Petrovai – head of the Orthodox Church in Maramureş – suddenly converted to Greco-Catholicism in 1711. The 11am service is a magical experience among the rolling hills and wildflowers.

Maria Paşca (☎ 331 165; house No 377; bed/ bed & full board €10/17) has rooms to rent at her home.

Rozavlea
Continue south through Strâmtura to Rozavlea, first documented under the name of Gorzohaza in 1374. Its fine **church**, dedicated to the archangels Michael and Gabriel, was constructed between 1717 and 1720 in another village, then erected in Rozavlea on the site of an ancient church destroyed by the Tartars. The flower-strewn graveyard is a testament to the area's anarchic splendour.

Botiza
From Rozavlea continue south for 3km to Şieu, then take the turn-off right for idyllic Botiza. Botiza's **old church**, built in 1694, is overshadowed by the giant **new church** constructed in 1974 to serve devout Orthodox families.

The Sunday service (9am) is the major event of the week in Botiza. The entire village flocks to the church to partake in the religious activities which continue well into the afternoon.

Opération Villages Roumains runs a local agrotourism scheme, which offers half/full board in local homes for €15/18 per night. Bookings can be made through the local representative, **George Iurca** (☎ 334 110, 0722- 942 140; botizavr@sintec.ro; house No 742; ☻ 8am-10pm), whose house is signposted. George also runs German-, French- and English-speaking tours of Maramureş (€10 to €15 per day, depending on number of participants) and Transylvania, rents out mountain bikes (€5 per day) and organises fishing trips.

Alternatively, ask for Agro-Tur-Art's **Iaon Costinar** (☎ 334 044; house No 790; bed/ bed & full board €10/17), who can also organise accommodation.

Poienile Izei
From Botiza a track leads west to Poienile Izei, home of a church with the most dramatic frescoes of hell you are ever likely to encounter. The church, with its thatched roof, was built in 1604. Its interior frescoes, dating from 1783, have a depiction of hell symbolised by a ferocious bird waiting to swallow up sinners. Australian Aboriginal–style paintings depict the torments inflicted by the devil on sinners who fail to obey the rules represented in the frescoes. To visit, ask for the key at the priest's house – a large wooden house in the centre of the village with an ornately carved terrace.

There are rooms for rent at the homes of **Florentina Petreuş** (☎ 334 204; house No 77; r €17) and **Donita Ilies** (☎ 334 383; house No 135), who speaks French and does excellent home-cooking.

Four kilometres further north along the same dirt track is the village of **Glod**, the birthplace of the popular Maramureş folksinging duo, the Petreuş Brothers.

Ieud

The oldest wooden church in Maramureş is in Ieud, 6km off the road south from Şieu. Century-old customs are still firmly intact in this fervently Orthodox village. Between 1787, when the first marriage was registered, and 1980 there were no divorces in the village.

Ieud was first documented in 1365 but evidence suggests the village was inhabited as early as the 11th century by Balc, Dragoş Vodă's grandson and later prince of Moldavia. In 1364 Ieud's fabulous Orthodox **'Church on the Hill'** (Biserica de Lemn din Deal) was built on castle ruins. It is made from fir-wood and used to house the first document known to be written in Romanian (1391–92), in which the catechism and church laws pertaining to Ieud were coded. The church is generally locked but you can get the key from the porter's house in the centre of the village, distinguishable by its simple, wooden gate.

Ieud's other **church** (Biserica de Lemn din Şes), today Greco-Catholic in denomination, was built in 1717. The church, at the southern end of the village, is unique to the region as it has no porch. It houses one of the largest collections of icons on glass found in Maramureş.

SLEEPING

You can make accommodation bookings through Opération Villages Roumains' representative in Botiza, **George Iurca** (p261), or go straight to **Chindis Dumitru** (☎ 336 100; bed €17), **Liviu Ilea** (☎ 336 039; house No 333) or **Vasile Rişco** (☎ 336 019; house No 705; half/full board €12/15).

Bogdan Vodă

Just to the north, the former village of Cuhea was renamed Bogdan Vodă in 1968 in honour of the Moldavian prince (r 1359–65) from Maramureş, who marched southeast from Cuhea to found the state of Moldavia in 1359. Some of the interior paintings in the village church, built in 1718, draw upon the traditional method of painting on linen, while others are painted directly on wood. The church, dedicated to St Nicholas, is on the left as you enter the village from the north.

Dragomireşti

Four kilometres south of Bogdan Vodă lies the village of Dragomireşti, whose church (1722), in fine Maramureş fashion, was uprooted in 1936 and moved to the Village Museum in Bucharest (p64).

The villagers have since built a new wooden church, on the same site, immediately on the left as you enter the village.

A further 4km east is **Sălistea de Sus**, first documented under the name Keethzeleste in 1365. It has two old churches, dating from 1680 and 1722, along with two new multispired, concrete churches.

VIŞEU & VASER VALLEYS
☎ 262

The wooded mountains rise to dizzying heights around the picturesque Vişeu Valley (Valea Vişeu), which tracks the Vişeu River on its journey south. Breathing in the fresh alpine air here is enough therapy for a lifetime. A railway line links this stretch, from Rona de Jos in the north to Borşa in the south, making it more accessible for travellers without private transport.

The twin villages of **Rona de Jos** and **Rona de Sus**, 19km southeast of Sighetu Marmaţiei, lie just a couple of kilometres apart. Continue south through the unremarkable **Petrova** and **Leordina**, and you eventually come to the spectacular logging village of Vişeu de Sus.

Vişeu de Sus

This gateway to the wonders of the Vaser Valley was first chronicled in 1363, and is growing yearly into a mecca for travellers and nature-lovers. Logging is the town's traditional industry – and it's this tradition which is the catalyst for its newest industry: tourism.

Vişeu de Sus's unique **narrow-gauge railway** winds up and into the Vaser Valley, and is still used to bring wood down from the mountains. The original steam engines now have several diesel locomotive companions, and these days you're likely to see a gaggle of backpackers heading up the hills alongside the lumberjacks (see 'Steamed Up!', below).

Aside from the railway line, the town's main axis is Str 22 Decembrie. The Vaser Valley railway stop is northeast of the centre.

INFORMATION

The **tourist information centre** (☎ 352 285; Str Libertaţii 1; ☺ 9am-6pm Mon-Fri), situated in the library, sells maps of the region, arranges accommodation and books steam train tours (€600 per group). The supply of hiking maps is frustratingly low, but you'll find one good map of the valley's trails here (€1).

SLEEPING

Hotel Brad (☎ 352 999; cnr Str 22 Decembrie & Str Iuliu Maniu; r €27) The 11 simple rooms here must be booked in advance as they fill up quickly during summer.

Hotel Gabriela (☎ 354 526; s/d €13.50/22) Two kilometres from Hotel Brad, on the road to Borşa, is this three-star chalet-style option.

Moisei

Moisei lies 9km southeast of Vişeu de Sus, at the foot of the Rodna Massif. Known for its traditional crafts and customs, Moisei gained fame in 1944 when retreating Hungarian (Horthyst) troops gunned down 31 people before setting fire to the entire village.

Hungarian forces captured the 31 people and detained them in a small camp in Vişeu de Sus without food or water for three weeks. On 14 October 1944, the Hungarian troops brought the prisoners to a house in Moisei, locked them inside, then shot them through the windows. Of the 31, 29 were killed leaving only two survivors. Before abandoning the village, the troops set it on fire, leaving all 125 remaining families homeless.

Only one house in Moisei survived the blaze; the one in which the prisoners were shot. Today, it houses a small museum (Expoziţia Documentar – Istorică Martirii de la Moisei 14 Octombrie 1944), in tribute to those who died in the massacre. Photographs of the 29 who died as well as the two who survived the bloodbath adorn its walls.

STEAMED UP!

Since its construction in 1925, the narrow-gauge railway has been used to carry wood down the mountains. Steam engines were originally used as logging trains on this route. These days, the job's done mostly by diesel engines but there are still four steam engines making the arduous climb.

More than 4000 cu metres of fir wood (brad) is felled each month by the lumberjacks, who are ferried by train each morning 42km up the valley to the logging camp at **Comanu**, close to the Ukrainian border. Once up in the hills they barter cigarettes and vodka for freshly made cheese from the hilltop shepherds.

Tourists can also make the daily journey up past forests filled with elusive wolves and lynx. It's possible to pitch a tent 32km away at the camping grounds of **Făina** or **Valea Babii** (6km further on), but the cabanas are now reserved for workers. From Făina there's a well-marked hiking trail but it should only be undertaken in summer as there are few highly detailed maps of this region. Be wary not to stray near the border as border police are armed.

At **Novaţ** there's an artists' camp where you'll find sculptors in action and hear much frenzied late-night debate under the stars.

The logging train leaves daily at 6am in summer and 7am in winter and begins its homeward journey between 3pm and 4pm. Tickets cost €5 and are bought at the station before boarding the train. There is no strict timetable, however, and the trains depart when the logging company needs them. There is a plan to have a tourist-only train using the route (and departing from a different station), but at the time of writing this hadn't happened.

To get to the wood factory (fabrica de lemn) and **train station** (☎ 262 353 533), turn left opposite Hotel Brad, on the corner of Str 22 Decembrie and Str Iuliu Maniu, continue along Str Carpaţi for 2km and they're on the left. The information office in Vişeu de Sus (above) sells a good map of the Vaser Valley trails (€1).

Just opposite the museum is a circular **monument** to the victims, its 12 upright columns symbolising the sun and light. Ten columns are decorated with a traditional carnival mask and two are decorated with human faces based on the features of the two survivors.

Borşa

Ore has been mined at Borşa, 12km east of Moisei, since the mid-14th century. The area was colonised in 1777 by German miners from Slovakia; eight years later, Bavarian-Austrian miners moved to **Baia Borşa**, 2km northeast of the town, to mine copper, lead and silver.

The **Complex Turistic Borşa**, a small ski resort and tourist complex 10km east of Borşa town proper, is a main entry point to the splendid **Rodna Mountains**, part of which forms the Pietrosul Rodnei Nature Reservation (5900 hectares).

Hiking information is shamefully scarce in this hikers' heaven but there are clearly marked trails leading from the top of the ski lift. Trails include a two-hour hike (in good weather) to the Prislop Pass (p264), and a pleasant one-hour hike signposted 'Cascada Cailor', which leads to the spectacular 40m high 'Horse' waterfall. If you want to stretch your legs before starting on the trails, there's a path leading up underneath the **ski lift** (🕙 7am-6pm; Str Brădet 10).

In winter the Complex Turistic Borşa boasts the largest natural ski run in Europe.

The small, relatively unspoilt resort is fast becoming a haven for more adventurous travellers and skiers who wish to avoid the crowds in the Carpathians.

Staff at the hotels or chalets of the complex are generally helpful. **Hotel Mia** (☎ 342 347; Str Al Cuza 237a) has clean, nice rooms as does **Hotel Perla Maramuresului** (☎ 342 539; Str Victoriei 27) and **Hotel Iezer** (☎ 343 430; Str Decebal 2). **Pensiunea Baluca** (☎ 0740-661 516; Str Moldovei 55) has a **tourist agency** (☎ 0740-661 516).

In winter, you can ski down the 2km-long ski run in the complex.

Nearby Baia Borşa has a less attractive claim to fame – the mining town has suffered appalling contamination, with its lakes and environment destroyed by the mining process.

PRISLOP PASS

Famed for its remoteness, the Prislop Pass is the main route from Maramureş into Moldavia. Hikers can trek east from Borşa across the pass (above). From Moldavia you can head northeast to Câmpulung Moldovenesc and on to the monasteries of southern Bucovina; or south to the natural mineral waters of Vatra Dornei and through to the fantastic Bicaz Lake (p281).

At 1416m a roadside monument marks the site of the last Tartar invasion prior to their final flight from the region in 1717. Nearby is the Hanul Prislop, site of the Hora de la Prislop, the major Maramureş festival (p247).

Moldavia

MOLDAVIA

With its forest-clad hills and tranquil valleys, Moldavia rivals mighty Transylvania when it comes to rich folklore, natural beauty and turbulent history, and even rivals mystical Maramureş as a bucolic paradise of remote villages. The region is famous worldwide for its fantastic medieval painted monasteries, yet Iaşi and Suceava have enough urban pleasures to keep you on your toes or relaxing in chill-out lounges.

In 1359, under Prince Bogdan of Cuhea, Moldavia became the second medieval Romanian principality to secure independence from the Hungarians, providing refuge during the 18th century for thousands who were persecuted in Hungarian-ruled Transylvania. Ştefan cel Mare (Stephen the Great) and his son Petru Rareş erected fortified monasteries and churches throughout Bucovina. Many have miraculously survived centuries of war. After Petru Rareş' defeat by the Turks in 1538, Moldavia regained some of its former glory when it was united with Wallachia by Alexandru Ioan Cuza in 1859. The modern Romanian state was born, with Iaşi as its capital.

Moldavia used to be much larger. Bessarabia, the area east of the Prut River, was annexed by Russia in 1812. Despite being recovered from 1918 to 1940 and again from 1941 to 1944, Bessarabia is now split between Ukraine and the Republic of Moldova. Northern Bucovina is now in southwestern Ukraine.

Confusingly, Romanians refer to Moldavia as Moldova (the Slavic form of Moldavia), a Stalinist legacy; they refer to Moldova as the Republic of Moldova. For information about Galaţi and Brăila in southeastern Moldavia, the gateways to the Danube Delta region, see p224.

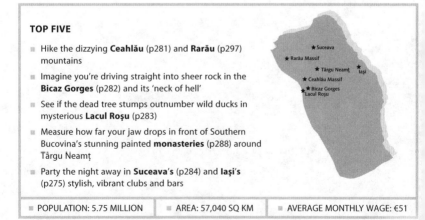

TOP FIVE

- Hike the dizzying **Ceahlău** (p281) and **Rarău** (p297) mountains
- Imagine you're driving straight into sheer rock in the **Bicaz Gorges** (p282) and its 'neck of hell'
- See if the dead tree stumps outnumber wild ducks in mysterious **Lacul Roşu** (p283)
- Measure how far your jaw drops in front of Southern Bucovina's stunning painted **monasteries** (p288) around Târgu Neamţ
- Party the night away in **Suceava's** (p284) and **Iaşi's** (p275) stylish, vibrant clubs and bars

★ Suceava
★ Rarău Massif
★ Târgu Neamţ ★ Iaşi
★ Ceahlău Massif
★ Bicaz Gorges
★ Lacul Roşu

■ POPULATION: 5.75 MILLION   ■ AREA: 57,040 SQ KM   ■ AVERAGE MONTHLY WAGE: €51

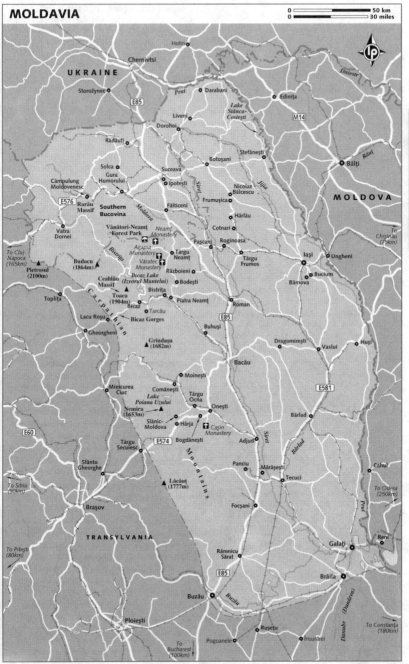

IAŞI

☎ 232 / pop 348,700

Iaşi (pronounced yash) earns its love and respect slowly. It's hard to catch the pulse of this city in which so many contradictory influences produce an uneven, uneasy first impression. Iaşi's past as Moldavia's capital since 1565 has resulted in a city dotted with fabulous buildings, important monasteries and bust-lined streets and parks, yet in between are grey, oppressive concrete blocks. As a university town, there's a fluid, lively energy to the city, yet as the capital of one of Romania's poorest provinces, there's an edgy roughness to it. While thousands of foreign students help lend a cosmopolitan feel to the city, aspects of its blasé service industry – and perhaps the fact that it's 20km from the Moldovan border – make it feel mired in socialist ways.

Founded in the second half of the 14th century, Iaşi has a great cultural tradition; the linden tree under which poet Mihai Eminescu meditated and the memorial houses of the city's most prolific writers remain powerful reminders of this city's literary past. As early as the 17th century, during the so-called flowering of Romanian culture, scholars based themselves here. Romania's first newspaper in Romanian was published here in 1829, and its first university was founded here in 1860. Today, a dozen literary museums are scattered about town.

More importantly, it was here that Moldavian ruler Alexandru Ioan Cuza managed to clinch the unification of Wallachia with Moldavia in 1859, the first major step to forming the country that Romania is today. Iaşi was Romania's capital until Bucharest usurped it in 1862, though it wore the crown again during WWI when the government was briefly moved back here. King Ferdinand and Queen Marie also sought refuge here during the war. During this period Iaşi's notorious history of anti-Semitism took root with the birth of the League of National Christian Defence – the predecessor of the fascist Iron Guard.

Modern Iaşi is the second-largest city in Romania and its streets bustle with student life, restaurants, bars and hot night spots. Each year the university hosts the National Mihai Eminescu Symposium. In October there is the national Festival of Folk Dance and Music.

You will need at least two days to see the main sights.

Orientation

MAPS & PUBLICATIONS

Amco Press' Iaşi city map (€1.85) is handy for its regional map, but for clarity and detail, you can't beat Cartographia's Iaşi (€1.85). Tot o Dată (www.totodata.ro in Romanian) is a free entertainment listings magazine found in shops, cafes and restaurants throughout the city.

Information

For general information and directory assistance, dial ☎ 951 (in Romanian).

BOOKSHOPS

Eurolibris (☎ 210 858; B-dul Carol I, 3-4; 🕑 9am-5pm)
Junimea (☎ 314 664; Piaţa Unirii 4; 🕑 10am-6pm Mon-Fri, 10am-3pm Sat)
Librăria Humanitas (☎ 215 568; Piaţa Unirii 6; 🕑 9am-6pm Mon-Fri, 9am-4pm Sat)

CULTURAL CENTRES

British Council (☎ 316 159; Str Păcurari 4; 🕑 9am-5pm Mon-Fri, library 1-7pm Mon, Tue & Thu, 9am-3pm Wed & Fri) In the same building as the Mihai Eminescu Library.
French Cultural Centre (☎ 237 637; www.ccf.tuiasi.ro in French; B-dul Carol I, 26; 🕑 9am-noon & 1-6pm Mon, Tue & Thu, 9am-noon & 1-9pm Wed, 9am-4pm Fri) Holds film screenings, theatre workshops or concerts and has a well-stocked mediathèque.
Goethe German Cultural Centre (☎ 214 051; B-dul Carol I, 21; 🕑 9am-5pm) Organises cultural events and has an extensive library.

EMERGENCY

Servicii Medicale Mobile (☎ 0722-376 370, 233 300) Offers 24-hour emergency service anywhere in the city.
Sfântu Spiridon University Hospital (☎ 210 690; B-dul Independenţei 1) The city's largest, most central hospital, just behind St Spiridon's Monastery.

INTERNET ACCESS

Discovery (B-dul Ştefan cel Mare şi Sfânt 1; per hour €0.40; 🕑 8am-4am)
Take Net (Şoseaua Arcu 1; per hour €0.40; 🕑 24hr)

MONEY

Banca Comercială Română (B-dul Ştefan cel Mare şi Sfânt 6; 8.30-3pm Mon-Fri) Cashes travellers cheques and gives cash advances.

POST & TELEPHONE

Post office (212 222; Str Cuza Vodă 10; 7am-7pm Mon-Fri, 8am-noon Sat)

Telephone centre (Str Alexandru Lăpuşneanu; 8am-8pm Mon-Fri, 8am-3pm Sat)

TOURIST INFORMATION

Iaşi has no official tourist office.

Icar Tours (216 319; www.icar.ro; B-dul Ştefan cel Mare şi Sfânt 8, basement; 9am-6pm Mon-Fri) The staff are particularly helpful; they mainly deal with Romanians bent on getting away, but can help you rent the least expensive cars in town and book accommodation in and around Iaşi.

Prospect Meridian (211 060; Str Sfântu Lazăr 24; 9am-6pm Mon-Fri) As agents for Antrec, this highly organised bunch arranges rural accommodation, city tours and trips to the Bucovina monasteries as well as other interesting tours.

Sights

PIAŢA UNIRII TO PIAŢA PALATUL CULTURII

Start your city tour on Piaţa Unirii, the main square, with a trip to the 13th floor of **Hotel Unirea** for a bird's-eye view of Iaşi. On a good day you can see the three monasteries across the valley in the Nicolina district to the south. In front of Hotel Unirea stands a bronze **statue of Prince Alexandru Ioan Cuza** (1820–73), who achieved the union of Wallachia and Moldavia.

On the western side of the square is **Hotel Traian** (1882), a neoclassical building designed by Gustave Eiffel – yes *that* Eiffel (of Paris' famous tower fame). The **Union Museum** (Muzeul Unirii; 314 614; Str Alexandru Lăpuşneanu 14) is nearby. Closed for several years for major (and slow) renovation, this large neoclassical building (1812) was Cuza's former residence.

The **Natural History Museum** (B-dul Independenţei 16; adult/child €0.60/0.30; 9am-3pm Tue, Thu & Sat, 9am-4pm Wed, Fri & Sun) has a small collection of stuffed beasties. Alexandru Ioan Cuza was elected prince here in 1859. Opposite is the baroque **Costache Ghica House**, where Romania's first university was founded in 1860.

East at B-dul Independenţei 33 is **St Spiridon's Monastery** (1804). The beheaded body of Grigore Ghica III lies inside a tomb in the church in the monastical complex. His head was sent to the sultan after the Turks killed him in 1777 for opposing them.

The broad, tree-lined B-dul Ştefan cel Mare şi Sfânt leads directly southeast from Piaţa Unirii to the monumental Palace of Culture. Along this way is the giant **Moldavian Metropolitan Cathedral** (built 1833–39). With a cavernous interior painted by Gheorghe Tattarescu, it's Romania's largest Orthodox cathedral. In mid-October thousands of pilgrims flock here to celebrate the day of St Paraschiva, the patron saint of the cathedral and of Moldavia. Inside the cathedral lies a coffin said to contain the bones of St Friday.

Opposite is the central park, lined with bronze busts of eminent literary figures, where local artists sell their masterpieces. At the northeastern end is the **National Theatre** (1894–96). In front of it is a majestic statue of its founder, poet Vasile Alecsandri (1821–90). The theatre was built according to the designs of Viennese architects Helmer and Fellner.

The boulevard's shining pearl is the fabulous **Church of the Three Hierarchs** (Biserica Sfinţilor Trei Ierarhi; 1637–39), unique for its rich exterior, which is embroidered in a wealth of intricate patterns in stone. In its original form, the exterior was covered in gold, silver and lapis. Built by Prince Vasile Lupu to ensure his place in heaven, it was damaged by Tartar attacks in 1650, but its dizzying mix of western Gothic, Renaissance and eastern motifs was later carefully restored.

Inside the church are the marble tombs of Prince Vasile Lupu and his family (to the left), Prince Alexandru Ioan Cuza (to the right), and Moldavian prince Dimitrie Cantemir. Inside the Gothic hall – reconstructed beside the church – is a **museum of 17th-century frescoes** (admission €0.25; 10am-4pm Tue-Sun). In 1994 the church reopened as a monastery. The three saints are celebrated here on 30 January.

At the southern end of B-dul Ştefan cel Mare şi Sfânt stands the giant neo-Gothic **Palace of Culture** (Palatul Culturii; 218 383; adult/child each museum €0.60/0.30, all four museums €2/1; 10am-5pm Tue-Sun), built between 1906 and 1925 and formerly the administrative seat of the town. The palace was built on the ruins of the **old princely court**, founded

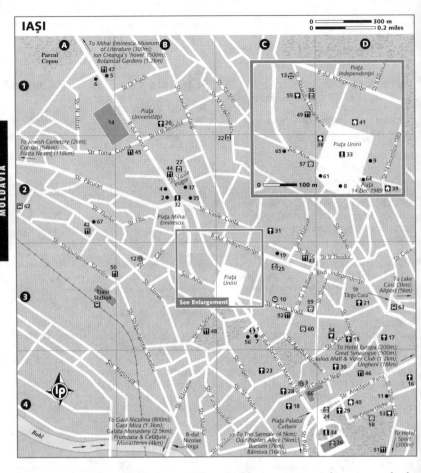

by Prince Alexandru cel Bun (r 1400-32). Some remains of the ruined princely court have been preserved beneath the concrete flooring of what is now the Summer Theatre.

The main attraction of the 365-room building today, however, is the **Gheorghe Asachi Library** and the four first-class museums it houses. The **Ethnographic Museum**, one of the best in the country, has exhibits ranging from agriculture, fishing and hunting to wine making, as well as traditional costumes and rugs from Romania's different regions. The **Art Museum** is split into two galleries – the Galeria de Artă Românească containing over 20 works by Romanian artist Nicolae Grigorescu and others including

Moldavian Petre Achițemie; and the Galeria de Artă Universală, exhibiting foreign works. Highlights of the **History Museum** include portraits of all of Romania's rulers from AD 81. Various mechanical creations and musical instruments are displayed in the less colourful **Science and Technical Museum**. While these museums are worth visiting, a look at the main entrance lobby is itself worth the trip to admire its lavish furnishings and magnificent staircase.

In front of the palace on Piața Palatul Culturii is an **equestrian statue** of Ștefan cel Mare, unveiled in 1883. A **memorial to Iași's** heroes who died in 1989 stands by the entrance to the palace grounds. Opposite is

MOLDAVIA

the **Museum of Old Moldavian Literature** (☎ 261 070; Str Panu Anastasie 54; admission €0.40; ⏰ 10am-5pm Tue-Sun), housed inside the 17th-century Dosoftei House. Dosoftei was the metropolitan of Moldavia between 1670 and 1686 and was responsible for printing the first church liturgy in the Romanian language (1679).

Behind Dosoftei House is **St Nicolas' Royal Church** (Biserica Sfântul Nicolae Domnesc), founded by Ştefan cel Mare in 1492. Little remains of the original church, which was restored and extended by Prince Antonie Roset in 1677, only to be rebuilt by French architect André Lecomte de Noüy in 1884.

MONASTERIES & CHURCHES

Religious architecture makes up an important part of Iaşi's landscape: there are 47 Orthodox churches, seven monasteries, three Catholic cathedrals, one Lippovan church and two synagogues.

In addition to the churches and monastery mentioned in the previous section, the fortified **Golia Monastery** (free admission; Str Cuza Vodă), built in late-Renaissance style and surrounded by rose gardens, is definitely worth a visit. The monastery's walls and the 30m-high tower at the entrance shelter a 17th-century church, noted for its vibrant Byzantine frescoes and intricately carved doorways. The bastions of the surrounding wall were added in 1667. The complex was damaged by fire several times and closed completely between 1900 and 1947. It regained monastery status in 1992 and is still undergoing major reconstruction.

Inside the Golia tower is a Turkish fountain. East of the tower is a **memorial house** to writer Ion Creangă (1837–89), renowned for his short stories based on Moldavian folklore. He lived here between 1866 and 1871.

From Golia Monastery, head south along Str Armeană. On the right at No 22 you pass a small stone-and-brick **Armenian Church** (Biserica Armeană; 1395), considered the oldest church in Iaşi. Extensive renovations have meant that little of the original Armenian architecture remains today. At the southern end of Str Armeană, turn right to **St Sava's Monastery** (Mănăstirea Sfântul Sava; Str Costache Negri 41), a small red-washed church (1625). If instead you turn left along Str Costache Negri you come to the 19th-century **Bărboi Monastery**. The church was built in 1841 on the site of a 17th-century church. Its trompe-l'oeil painted interior is worth a look. A block south is **Barnovschi Monastery** (Grigore Ghica Vodă 26), dating from the reign of Prince Miron Barnovschi-Movilă (r 1626–29). Today, only the main (and impressive) church remains, as the monastery complex was left to ruin throughout Ceauşescu's regime.

JEWISH IAŞI

In the 19th century the city was one of the great centres of Jewish learning in Europe. The world's first professional Jewish theatre opened in laşi in 1876. A statue of its founder, Polish composer and playwright Avram Goldfaden (1840–1908), stands in the central park on B-dul Ştefan cel Mare şi Sfânt. More than one-third of the city's population at this time was Jewish, served by 127 synagogues.

Today only two synagogues remain open. The Great Synagogue (1671) is barely visible amid the concrete apartment blocks surrounding it at Str Elena Doamna 15. There is a small museum inside the synagogue, but contact the **laşi Jewish community** (☎ 214 414) in advance to visit it. In front of the synagogue is a monument to the victims of the 1941 pogrom.

Many of the victims of the Iron Guard's pogroms were buried in four concrete bunkers in the **Jewish Cemetery** (Cimitirul Evreiesc; admission €2.75) on Mountain Hill (Dealul Munteni), east of the centre off Str Păcurari. There's another pogrom monument there, as well as the second, very small synagogue. It's a €2 taxi ride from the centre.

UNIVERSITY & AROUND

The area northwest of the centre, along B-dul Carol I, bristles with student life. Here are the university's main buildings and a host of literary museums.

Behind the **Student Cultural House** on Piaţa Mihai Eminescu (presided over by a large **statue** of the poet), is the Students' House park, the centrepiece of which is the **Voievodes Statuary**. These fantastic, crumbling statues of Moldavia's princes were moved here from the university courtyard in the 1960s. In pairs stand Moldavia's first prince, Dragoş (r 1352–53), and Alexandru cel Bun (r 1400–32); Moldavia's greatest prince, Ştefan cel Mare (r 1457–1504), with Mihai Viteazul (r 1600); Petru Rareş (r 1527–38) and Ion Vodă cel Viteaz (r 1572–74); and Vasile Lupu (r 1634–53) and Dimitrie Cantemir (r 1693).

Just north of here, along the serene Str Vasile Pogor, is the **Pogor House Literary Museum** (Casă Pogor; ☎ 312 830; Str Vasile Pogor 4; admission €0.40; 10am-5pm Tue-Sun), Vasile Pogor's 1850s mansion, where meetings of the literary society were held from 1871. On its lovely grounds stand **rows of busts** of some of the more eminent members of the society, including dramatist Ion Luca Caragiale (1852–1912) and poet Vasile Alecsandri (1821–90).

Another block further north and you get to the heart of laşi's student life. On the east side of the boulevard is Piaţa Universităţii, backed by the **Forty Saints Church**, and on the west is the huge neoclassical **Alexandru Ioan Cuza University** at No 11, where the founder of the fascist Iron Guard, Corneliu Codreanu (1899–1938), once studied.

Further north is **Copou Park**, laid out between 1834 and 1848 during the princely reign of Mihail Sturza. Poet Mihai Eminescu (1850–89) allegedly wrote some of his best works beneath his favourite linden tree in this park. The tree still stands, behind a 13m-high **monument of lions** opposite the main entrance to the park. A bronze bust of Eminescu stands in front of it.

Nearby is the **Mihai Eminescu Museum of Literature** (☎ 344 759; admission €0.20; 10am-5pm Tue-Sun), housed in a rather ugly, white, modern building. The museum recalls the life and loves of Eminescu, Romania's most cherished writer and poet. Though he was married, his great love was Veronica Micle, herself married to a vicar. They outlived their spouses but never married themselves due to Eminescu's deteriorating health – he also considered himself too poor to offer Veronica what she deserved. He dedicated many love poems to her, including: Forehead pale and tresses golden/On my shoulder you incline/And your lips delicious plunder/ Raise up willingly to mine. A bust of Veronica faces the bust of her lover and his favourite linden tree at the end of **Junimea Alley** in the park.

Further to the north are laşi's 0.8 sq km **Botanic Gardens** (Grădină Botanică; admission €0.20; 10am-9pm), on the far side of Parcul Expozitiei, Romania's largest by far. Dating from 1856, they offer 21km of shady lanes to explore, rose and orchid gardens, numerous greenhouses, natural springs and a lake. While the landscaping leaves much to be desired, it's the city's premier strolling grounds.

The attractive residential area of **Ţicău district** rises to the east of B-dul Carol I. The charming *bojdeucă* ('hovel'; ☎ 315 515; Str Simion Bămuţiu 4; admission €0.40; ⏰ 10am-5pm Tue-Sun), built in 1842, where writer Ion Creangă (1837–89) lived with his close friend and mentor Mihai Eminescu, was the first memorial museum established in Romania.

The politician Mihail Kogălniceanu (1817–91) lived for a short time in a 19th-century mansion that is now a **museum** (☎ 258 422; Str Mihail Kogălniceanu 11; admission €0.40; ⏰ 9am-5pm Tue-Sun) devoted to the life of this Moldavian activist. He published numerous papers on the Moldavia National Party during the 1848 revolution and served as Cuza's foreign minister.

SOUTH OF THE CENTRE

Heading out of town along Şoseaua Bucium (DN 224), you pass the **Odd Poplars Alley**, lined with 25 poplar trees and marking another spot where poet Mihai Eminescu sought inspiration.

Southwest of the centre in the Nicolina district are three of Iaşi's most tranquil monasteries, which make for a pleasant day's hike (or take a short ride on Bus No 9 downhill from the Palace of Culture). Perched on top of Miroslavei Hill is the 16th-century fortified **Galata Monastery**, founded in 1582 by Prince Petru Şchiopul, who is buried in the church. The ruins of the monks' living quarters and a Turkish bath are all that remain today. The new church was built in 1847.

East of Galata at the northern end of Str Cetăţuia are the ruins of **Frumoasa Monastery** (1726–33). Built by Prince Grigore Ghica

II, it served as a royal residence in the 18th century. From here, go south along Str Cetăţuia and follow the steep, narrow road to the top of Dealul Cetăţuia to the impressive **Cetăţuia Monastery**. It's quite an uphill hike, but worth the effort. Founded by Prince Gheorghe Duca in 1669, it is preserved in its original form. Between 1682 and 1694 a Greek printing press was housed here.

Activities

There's a decent **swimming pool** (☎ 260 240; Str Anastasie Panu 29-31; admission €1.75; ⏰ 1-5pm & 6-10pm Mon, Wed & Thu, 8.30am-noon, 1-5pm & 6-10pm Fri-Sun) inside the Hotel Moldova. Watersports are possible at Lake Ciric, at the city limits on the road to the airport, but while many head out here for a day's strolling, the water is not very clean for swimming. **Lake Ciurbeşti**, 5km south of the city near the village of Ciurbeşti, is better for a dip.

Sleeping

Iaşi doesn't exactly suffer from an embarrassment of riches when it comes to places to stay; be prepared either to fork out more than you'd planned or accept less-than-exciting options. Prospect Meridian (p269) can set you up in a private home for around €10 per person.

Hotel Sport (☎ 232 800; Str Sfântu Lazăr 76; s/d €16/22) You may need an athlete's fortitude to stomach this grotty, musty but cheap place south of the centre.

Hotel Continental (☎ 211 846; Piaţa 14 Decembrie 1989; d/tr €18/25, s/d with with private toilet €14/24) If you're only staying a night or two, this dark, faceless place will do; at least it's central and the shared bathrooms are clean. Rooms facing the street are noisy.

Hotel Unirea (☎ 240 404; www.hotelunirea.ro; Piaţa Unirii 5; s/d €26/30, unrenovated s/d €22/26) Yes, that eyesore right on Piaţa Unirii is a hotel – a 13-storey concrete blob with rooms that

---

AUTHOR'S CHOICE

Hotel Astoria (☎ 233 888; www.hotelastoria.ro; Str Lăpuşeanu 1; s/d/ste €18/26/35; ✿) You'd think there had to be something wrong: such modern, four-star luxury at two-star prices. This is one of Romania's best deals. Rooms are on the small side (or snug, depending on your level of optimism), but surprisingly plush, welcoming and comfortable. The bathrooms, however, are large enough to hold a small party in. Connected to and run by the Hotel Traian, this is its thoroughly modern cousin.

were probably quite the thing in the 1960s. It has a restaurant and panoramic cafe on the top floor.

Hotel Moldova (☎ 260 240; Str Anastasie Panu 29-31; s/d €43/78) For a grim, 14-storey hotel with yawn-inspiring rooms, the prices here feel inflated. At least it's wheelchair accessible and there's an adjoining indoor swimming pool, sauna and tennis court.

Hotel Traian (☎ 266 666; Piaţa Unirii 1; s/d/ste €49/69/85) The multilingual staff here will make you feel at home in this elegant hotel, designed by Gustave Eiffel. The nice rooms are awash in old-world comfort.

Hotel Europa (☎ 242 000; www.hoteleuropa.ro; Str Anastasie Panu 26; s/d/ste €95/120/200; 🔧 ✕ 🖳) The top choice in Moldavia is this five-star, chrome-and-glass high-rise with all the bells and whistles your credit card will allow for, including a fitness centre and laundry service. Rooms are luxurious but not unforgettable. It's attached to the World Trade Centre.

Eating

If you have got used to the down-to-earth friendliness of most Romanian restaurants, the gruff, Soviet-style of service that prevails in most of Iaşi's eateries might come as a surprise. Just be patient – your waiter or waitress will eventually get around to you...if you flail your arms wildly enough!

RESTAURANTS

Pub Baron (☎ 206 076; Str Sfântu Lazăr 52; mains €2-4; ☽ 24hr) It looks like a pub, with its cosy wooden interiors and beer suds floating in the air, but it's also a great eating option. They are heavy on fresh grills, cooked in brick ovens in the dining room, but there are many salads and fish dishes too.

Ginger Ale (☎ 276 017; Str Săulescu 23; mains €2-5; ☽ 11-1am) Advertised as an Irish-style pub/restaurant, this place feels more like an oversized, old-fashioned cafe with its antique furniture and cosy dining room. A great place for drinks or a full meal, it also offers 20% to 50% discounts daily from noon to 4pm.

Trei Sarmale (☎ 237 255; Str Bucium 52; mains €2-5; ☽ 9-2am) This traditional Romanian restaurant teeters on the edge of kitsch with its folkier-than-thou decor, but the food is mouthwatering. Set inside a 17th-century inn south of town, this could be a fun place for a small group if you get into the mood. Check before you head out there as it is often booked by tour groups. Take a €2 taxi or bus No 30 or 46 from Piaţa Mihai Eminescu and get off at the Bucium stop.

Casa Bolta Rece (☎ 212 255, Str Rece 10; mains €2-6; ☽ 11am-11pm) Set in a spectacular 1786 house, this restaurant's reputation is equally lofty, as it is supposedly Iaşi's top dining experience. However, the socialist-style, gruff service leaves a bad aftertaste. Eat in the wine cellar or on the pleasant terrace and skip the starchy dining room. There is a tacky English menu with plasticised photos to help you choose. For dessert, try the *feteasca neagră* (black pudding served with *mămăligă* and topped with salty sheep's cheese).

CAFES & QUICK EATS

There's fast-food courts inside and across the street from the huge, Western-style Iulius Mall (B-dul Tudor Vladimirescu), 3km southeast of the centre. A big student ghetto nearby means dozens of cheap places to eat. The same goes for a cluster of kebab joints radiating off Piaţa Academiei in the city centre, particularly along Str Sfântu Teodor.

Casa Universitatilor (☎ 340 029 B-dul Carol I, 9; mains €1-2) Meals are dirt cheap here but most

---

AUTHOR'S CHOICE

Casa Pogov (☎ 243 006; Str Vasile Pogov 4; mains €2-4; ☽ 11am-midnight) How to choose where to sit? In the insanely cosy (if damp) basement that used to house the famed Junimea wine cellar, in the elegant main dining hall furnished with antiques or on the multi-tiered terrace looking out over a quiet square? Iaşi's most pleasant restaurant seduces with its great atmosphere and friendly service. While not extraordinary, the food is good and the menu (with some veggie meals) varied.

people come to hang about on the terrace and enjoy a lazy beer while drinking in the scent of the surrounding lime trees.

Family Pizza (☎ 261 647; B-dul Carol I, 26-28; mains €1-2.50; ❤ 24hr) This lively, brightly lit parlour has 25 types of pizza, plus pasta, chicken nuggets (yes, you read correctly) and a week's worth of pastries to choose from. They also deliver.

Metro Pizza (☎ 276 040; Str Străpungerea Silvestru 8; mains €2-3; ❤ 9-1am) This has a deservedly good reputation among students for their great pizzas and their 50% discounts on some meals on weekends.

Zefir (☎ 229 854; Str Cuza Vodă 32-33; mains €1-2.50; ❤ 8am-1pm) This no-frills place has fast-food and restaurant sections, though the menu's the same in both; it's perfect for those who want fast food but like to pretend they're in a restaurant. Mainly meat dishes adorn the simple menu. It's great for a cheap fill-up.

SELF-CATERING

The indoor central **market** (❤ 8am-4pm) is great for fresh fruit and vegetables. It has entrances on Str Costache Negri and Str Anastasie Panu. **Billa** (Str Arcu 29; ❤ 8am-10pm Mon-Sat, 9am-6pm Sun) is a huge, fully stocked supermarket with takeaway food. Other grocery shops are on B-dul Ştefan cel Mare şi Sfânt.

Drinking

Quinta Café (☎ 268 447; Str Sfântu Sava 10; ❤ noon-2am) High ceilings, cushy sofas, antique furniture and wood panelling give this lounge bar a familiar feel; in fact, this is a restored grand house. The music is as subdued as the lighting, which makes people want to curl up with a drink on one of the couches.

Ethos (Piaţa Mihai Eminescu; ❤ 9am-4am) Inside the Student Cultural House, this is a fun pub to hang out in for a beer or a snack. There's usually a live rock band on Thursday night.

City Café (Str Sfântu Lazăr 34; ❤ 11am-1am) Iaşi's beautiful, moneyed people come here for relaxed posing sessions. A high-tech, blue-lit, ultracool bar, it's known for its many cocktails.

Terasa Corsu (☎ 276 143; Str Alexandru Lăpuşneanu 11; ❤ 11-midnight) The concept of a 'bar' is stretched in this huge, amphitheatre-shaped pub with a well-tended garden in the middle. Its spaciousness makes it unique and pleasant.

Entertainment

Vasile Alecsandri National Theatre (☎ 316 778; Str Agatha Bârsescu 18) and the **Opera Română** (☎ 211 144) are in the same impressive neobaroque building. Alternative performances are held in the smaller studio hall (*sală studio*) upstairs, which has its entrance on Str Cuza Vodă. For advance bookings go to the **Agenţia de Opera** (☎ 316 070; B-dul Ştefan cel Mare şi Sfânt 8; ❤ 9am-1pm & 3-5pm Mon-Fri). Tickets cost from €1.50, with 50% student discounts.

Philharmonic (Filarmonica; ☎ 212 509; Str Cuza Vodă 29; box office ❤ 10am-1pm & 5-7pm Mon-Fri) When the much-revered Iaşi State Philharmonic Orchestra is in town its concerts are massively popular; they perform some 200 concerts per season, across Romania and abroad. Concerts of some kind are usually held on Friday nights. Tickets cost from €2 with 50% student discounts.

Luceafărul Theatre (☎ 315 966; Str Grigore Ureche 5) Behind the Hotel Moldova, this theatre puts on very interesting pieces geared to children and young people.

Viper Club (Iulius Mall; ❤ 24hr, disco 11pm-4am) This entertainment emporium features bowling alleys, billiards and video games, and come night-time turns itself into a house-music haven for its young crowd itching to explode across the dancefloor.

Cinema Victoria (☎ 312 502; Piaţa Uniiri 5) See your favourite Hollywood schlockbuster with Romanian subtitles here!

Getting There & Away

AIR

Tarom (☎ 267 768; Str Arcu 3-5; ❤ 8am-6pm Mon-Fri, 8am-noon Sat) has 10 weekly flights to Bucharest (about €90). **Carpatair** (☎ 215 295; www.carpatair.ro; Str Cuza Voda 2; ❤ 9am-5pm Mon-Fri) has a flight Monday to Saturday to Timişoara, from where you can catch connecting flights to Italy and Germany. **Angel Airlines** (☎ 270 457; www.angelairlines.ro), whose office is at the airport, flies seven times weekly to Bucharest (Baneasa airport; about €70) and three times weekly to Suceava (about €20).

BUS

The **central bus station** (☎ 214 720), off Şoseaua Arcu, has got busier in recent years with all the private maxitaxi (minibus) firms opening, so it has started to expand – into chaos. Most buses and maxitaxis leave from somewhere around the bus station, either from the main lot, or on any of the side streets. Others have started using the Billa supermarket (p275) parking lot 600m away. There are four daily maxitaxis each to Târgu Neamţ (€1.60) and Suceava, eight to Bucharest, 18 to Bacău and almost 20 to Piatra Neamţ. In addition, slower buses also head daily to Suceava, Piatra Neamţ, Vatra Dornei, Tulcea and Braşov.

Maxitaxis to Chişinău (€5) leave from outside the Billa supermarket three to four times daily (the only way to find out the times is by showing up and asking around), while up to six daily (slower) buses to Chişinău depart from the bus station. Occasional maxitaxis to Târgu Neamţ depart from Billa. Tickets for the daily bus to Istanbul (€40; 26 hours), which also departs from Billa, are sold at **Ortadoğu Tur** (☎ 257 000; Str Arcu), in a kiosk across the street.

TRAIN

Characters from a Kafka novel must have devised Iaşi's train and bus station system. Nearly all trains arrive and depart from the Gară Centrală (also called Gară Mare and Gară du Nord) on Str Garii. Trains to Chişinău , however, depart from the Gară Niculina (also called Gară International) on B-dul Nicolae Iorga, even though tickets for the trip must be bought from the so-called Gară Mică (the one with the sign saying 'Niculina' on it, go figure), 500m south on Aleea Nicolina. The **Agenţie de Voiaj CFR** (☎ 247 673; Piaţa Unirii 10; ☒ 8am-8pm Mon-Fri) sells advance tickets.

There are five daily trains to Bucharest (€7; seven hours), and one service daily to each of Oradea, Galaţi, Timişoara and Mangalia. Trains throughout the day go to Ungheni, a border town just 21km away.

If you are planning to visit the monasteries in Southern Bucovina, take a train to Suceava then change trains, or take a train bound for Oradea and get off at the Gura Humorului stop. To get to Târgu Neamţ from Iaşi you have to change at Paşcani.

Getting Around
TO/FROM THE AIRPORT
Tarom (p275) operates a free shuttle bus service between its office and the airport

(☎ 271 590). It departs 1½ hours before flight departures.

Bus No 35 runs between Piaţa Eminescu and Copou Park, stopping outside the university en route. Tram No 3 runs between the bus and train stations and the centre.

AROUND IAŞI

Rolling hills, lush vineyards and pretty villages surround Moldavia's 'town of seven hills'. At the **Bucium winery**, 7km south of Iaşi, you can taste a variety of sweet wines as well as Bucium champagne. At weekends, Iaşi residents picnic in **Bârnova Forest**, 16km south of the city and accessible by train.

Cotnari

Cotnari is 54km northwest of Iaşi. Its **vineyards**, dating from 1448, are among the most famed in Romania, producing four to six million bottles of sweet white wine a year. Legend says Ştefan cel Mare described it as 'wine given by God'.

There was a Geto-Dacian stronghold on Cătălina Hill (280m) in Cotnari from the 4th century BC. In 1491 Ştefan cel Mare built a small church in the village and in 1562 a Latin college was founded. During this period French monks arrived bringing grape stocks, which they planted in the village, and by the end of the 19th century Cotnari wine had scooped up prizes at international exhibitions. King Michael I started building a small **royal palace** here in 1947, abandoning it half-complete the same year. It was restored in 1966 and today houses Cotnari Winery's administration.

The winery's most popular wines include white table wines such as *frâncuşa* (dry), *cătălina* (semisweet), and the sweet, golden *grasă* and *tămâioasă* dessert wines.

The **Cotnari Winery** (☎ 232-730 393; fax 730 205; www.cotnari.ro) arranges wine-tasting sessions and tours of its cellars and factory. Every year on 14 September, wine connoisseurs flock to Cotnari to celebrate the harvest.

To get there, continue past the village shop on the road towards Botoşani and Hârlău. The factory is 200m farther on the left.

SLEEPING
Prospect Meridian (☎ 211 060) This company in Iaşi arranges private rooms in Cotnari –

among other places, in the home of the general director of the Cotnari factory, next door to King Michael's palace! There are *cazare* (room) signs in windows throughout the village.

GETTING THERE & AWAY
Three local trains from Iaşi to Hârlău stop at Cotnari daily (€1.50; 1¾ hours).

TÂRGU NEAMŢ
☎ 233 / pop 22,230

The only reasons to come to dull, dusty little Târgu Neamţ (literally, German Market Town) are to visit the ruins of a 14th-century citadel and stock up before heading to the Neamţ, Agapia and Văratec Monasteries.

Considered Moldavia's finest fortress, **Neamţ Citadel** (Cetatea Neamţului; ☎ 0744-702 415; adult/child €0.80/0.40; 🕙 10am-6pm Tue-Sun), perched high above town, is fun to poke around in – kids and natural-born explorers will love it. Built by Petru I Muşat in 1359, it was attacked by Hungarians in 1395, by Turks in 1476 and conquered by Polish forces in 1691, which explains its current state. To get there, follow signs for 'Cetatea Neamţului' along B-dul Ştefan cel Mare. You must park your car at the foot of the citadel and take a heart-quickening but pleasant hike uphill.

Casa Arcaşului (☎ 790 699; Str Cetăţii 40; d/tr €13/16) is a slightly gloomy hotel/restaurant with a quiet, exotic location at the foot of the citadel. Rooms are quite decent.

After exiting Târgu Neamţ's **bus station** (☎ 663 474; Str Cuza Vodă 32), turn right for B-dul Mihai Eminescu and B-dul Ştefan cel Mare and turn left for the train station (1.2km away). There are eight daily buses and minitaxis to Piatra Neamţ, six to Iaşi, two to both Braşov and Suceava, and five weekly to Bucharest (€6.75). To reach the monasteries, there are five daily buses to Agapia (€0.45), four to Văratec (€0.55), three to Neamţ Monastery, and one each to Sihastrea and Gura Humorului. The train station is a lonely place, with only four personal daily trains to Paşcani, where changes to Iaşi and other destinations are possible.

MONASTERIES AROUND TÂRGU NEAMŢ
☎ 233

Târgu Neamţ is ringed by beautiful monasteries noted not for their outstanding artistic treasures but rather as Romania's most active religious centres. Agapia and Văratec are called monasteries even though they house nuns. Locals warn that, while visiting these monasteries, it's best to lock your car, as theft and vandalism are not uncommon. In the villages of Agapia and Văratec, dozens of homes have *cazare* signs in their windows, and guesthouses abound.

Neamţ Monastery
Neamţ Monastery is Moldavia's oldest, and the largest male monastery in Romania. Founded in the 14th century by Petru I Muşat, it doubled as a protective citadel. Ştefan cel Mare built the large church we see today; it remains a classic example of the Moldavian style initiated in his time. The painting in the porch and narthex dates from Muşat's time, while in the altar, the nave and the room in which the tombs are located, the painting dates from 1497. In the fortified compound are a **medieval art museum** and a **memorial house** to novelist Mihail Sadoveanu (1880–1961). The library, with 18,000 rare books, is the largest of any Romanian monastery.

Three daily buses make the 15km journey from Târgu Neamţ, yet you'll probably

---

PINE JUICE, ANYONE?
Summertime in these parts, you'll notice many elderly ladies standing by the road selling plastic bottles filled with a clear liquid. No, it's not Crystal Pepsi, it's…for lack of a better term, pine juice. A syrupy substance best mixed with five parts water, it is distilled from the yellow flowers of male pine trees, boiled in water with generous portions of sugar added. It's supposed to be good for all kinds of bronchial complaints and is used as an expectorant, but forget these medicinal concerns and just enjoy it as a soft drink (mixed with carbonated water, it's quite delicious). It's only made in late spring and early summer when the flowers are young; mature buds and pine needles are toxic.

find it easier to hitchhike along the main road, the No 15B, toward Ceahlău.

Agapia Monastery

The turn-off for **Agapia Monastery** (☎ 244 618; adult/child €0.80/0.50) is 4km south of Târgu Neamţ towards Piatra Neamţ. Within the confines of the monastery walls live 400-plus nuns who toil in the fields, tend vegetable gardens, weave carpets and make embroideries for tourists.

Agapia consists of two monasteries. The larger and flashier **Agapia din Vale** (Monastery in the Valley) is at the end of the village of Agapia itself. Built by Gavril Coci (Vasile Lupu's brother) between 1642 and 1644, its current neoclassical façade dates from reconstructions between 1882 and 1903. Between 1858 and 1861, the young Nicolae Grigorescu (1838–1907) painted the interior of the church with a fantastic mural of eyes that stare at you whichever way you turn. A small **museum** (⏰ 10am-7pm) off to the right contains icons from the 16th and 17th centuries. The main buildings are modern and of little architectural interest, but wandering around the grounds, past the well-tended gardens of the nuns' houses, is a treat.

Agapia din Deal (Agapia on the Hill; admission free), also called Agapia Veche (Old Agapia), is the second monastery, 2.2km from the main monastery complex (follow the road to the right, go through the charming old section of Agapia, full of wooden homes, to the signposted dirt road veering off to the right). It's absolutely worth the hike uphill (only take a powerful car and not after rain, as some sections of the gravel road are extremely steep) to see this quiet, humble monastery. Less ornate than Agapia din Vale, and with only modern frescoes, it nonetheless charms with its peaceful ambience and wooden buildings. It was founded by Lady Elena, wife of Petru Rareş, in 1642–47.

It is occasionally possible for tourists to stay at Agapia din Vale. The turn-off to both monasteries is 4km south from Târgu Neamţ towards Piatra Neamţ.

A dirt road in front of the lower monastery veers to the left towards the small and highly worthwhile **Sihla Hermitage** (Schitu Sihlei; admission free). Some 30 monks live here, on a small plateau in the hills. The cen-tral church is small, wooden and sombre, almost touching in appearance. Though a construction spree is evident on the grounds, indicating imminent enlargement and renovation, this is one of the area's more charming religious sites, mainly due to the nearby cave of Pious Saint Teodora. Teodora supposedly lived in a small cave for 60 years; it's possible to visit her 'home', eerily lit by candles, among the rocks and boulders above the hermitage. Seeing the slab of rock she called a 'bed' certainly gives one pause. Her relics are now in Pecherska Monastery in Kiev.

GETTING THERE & AWAY

All buses between Târgu Neamţ and Piatra Neamţ stop in Săcăluşeşti village, from where it is a 3km hike along a narrow road to the lower monastery; the upper monastery is a further 30-minute walk uphill.

Three daily buses also go from Târgu Neamţ to the lower monastery, listed on bus timetables as 'Complex Turistic Agapia'. From Piatra Neamţ, there are two buses daily.

Văratec Monastery

Six hundred nuns live at **Văratec Monastery** (adult/child €0.50/0.25), 7km south of the Agapia turn-off. Founded in 1785, the complex houses an **icon museum** and a small embroidery school. The **grave of poet Veronica Micle**, Mihai Eminescu's great love, lies within the monastery walls. She committed suicide on 4 August 1889, two months after Eminescu's death. Whitewashed in 1841, the main church incorporates neoclassical elements in its design. Compared to other nearby monasteries, Văratec looks like a modern villa crossed with a small botanic garden.

You can hike to Văratec from Agapia (1½ hours) and to **Secu**, **Sihăstria** and **Schitu Sihlei Monasteries** along clearly marked trails. There are four daily buses to Văratec from Târgu Neamţ.

Vânători-Neamţ Forest Park

The forest and woods surrounding these monasteries and stretching north to the village of Groşi are protected as the **Vânători-Neamţ Forest Park** (☎ 233-206 001; www.vanatoripark.ro). Its headquarters and information centre are in Văratec, on the main road to the monastery. A visit to the **information** centre (8am-4pm Mon-Fri) is highly recommended before any drive or hike through the region; they have detailed maps of hiking trails and can alert you as to whether any sideroads have been closed or blocked. Within the park is the small Dragoș Vodă Bison Reserve, where six bison live in semi-captivity in an enclave open to visitors. There are also small reserves protecting old patches of oak and birch forest.

PIATRA NEAMȚ

☎ 233 / pop 124,000

Piatra Neamț (German Rock), 43km south of Târgu Neamț, is a pleasant, picturesque town, sunk in a valley and embraced by velvety, round hills. Perched above the town to the east is the rocky Pietricica Mountain. To the southwest stands Cernegura Mountain, flanked by an artificial lake, Lake Bâtca Doamnei, at its westernmost foot. Cozla Mountain, which towers over Piatra Neamț to the north, is now a huge park. It has enough going for it to offer a happy day's wandering, and makes a nice base for exploring the surrounding landscape.

The area around Piatra Neamț has been settled since Neolithic times. In the 15th century, Ștefan cel Mare founded a princely court here.

B-dul Republicii leads north from Piața Mareșal Ion Antonescu towards Piața Ștefan cel Mare, where most facilities are located. The old town is located immediately north-west of this square, at the foot of Cozla Mountain.

Information

ATMs can be found, among other places, in hotels and along Piața Ștefan cel Mare; change travellers cheques at **Banca Comercială Română** (B-dul Traian 1; 8am-6pm Mon-Fri, 8am-2pm Sat).

Even if you don't need to post any letters, it's worth popping into the **post office** (☎ 232 222; Str Alexandru cel Bun 21; 7am-8pm Mon-Fri, 10am-1pm Sat) for its old-fashioned wooden interiors; the **telephone office** (☎ 7.30am-8pm Mon-Fri, 7.30am-2pm Sat) is on B-dul Republicii. There are several Internet cafes in town – try **Internet** (Str Ștefan cel Mare 9; per hr €0.40; 8am-midnight) and super-cool

MOLDAVIA

PIATRA NEAMȚ

0 _____ 500 m
0 _____ 0.3 miles

Cozla Park

To Târgu
Neamț
(45km)

To Roman
(47km)

To Lake Bâtca Doamnei (1.5km);
Pensiune Ambiance (3km);
Complexul Touristic Troian (4km);
Bistrița Monastery (11km);
Bicaz (28km)

Str V Ureche

Piața Ștefan
cel Mare

Piața
Libertății

Piața
Petrodava

Piața
Mareșal Ion
Antonescu

Train
Station

To Bacău
(57km)

SIGHTS & ACTIVITIES	(p280)
Art Museum	7 B2
Bell Tower	8 B2
Ethnographic Museum	9 B2
History Museum	10 B2
Natural History Museum	11 C1
Parc Zoologic	12 B1
Petru Rareș School	13 C1
Ruins of Princely Court	(see 13)
St John's Church	14 B1
Statue of Ștefan cel Mare	15 C2

SLEEPING	(p280)
Hotel Bulevard	16 B2
Hotel Ceahlău	17 C2
Hotel Central	18 B2

EATING	(pp280–1)
Cercul Gospodinelor	19 C1
Colibele Haiducilor	20 B1
Diesel	21 C1
Laguna	22 A1
Patisserie Paris & Gelateria Italiana	23 B2

ENTERTAINMENT	(p281)
Tineretului Theatre & Agenție de Teatrală	24 B2

TRANSPORT	(p281)
Agenție de Voiaj CFR	25 C2
Bus Station	26 A2

INFORMATION	
Antrec	1 B1
Banca Comercială Română	2 D3
Internet	3 B1
Post Office	4 B1
Tavernet	5 B2
Telephone Office	6 B2
Top Tours	(see 1)

Tavernet (☎ 220 914; Piaţa Ştefan cel Mare 1; per hr €0.40; ⏱ 9am-midnight).

A good first stop is **Antrec** (☎ 234 204; misu .chiruc@decebal.ro; Str Ştefan cel Mare 17; ⏱ 8am-4pm Mon-Fri), which doubles as the Top Tours travel agency. One of the better organised Antrec branches, they can provide all kinds of helpful information and have photo books of accommodation options in and around the Neamţ region.

Sights

Piaţa Ştefan cel Mare is the city's heart, a pleasant square with a statue of the beloved ruler standing proudly among landscaped flowerbeds. Just west of here is a small pedestrianised square where the remains of Piatra Neamţ's historic heart lie in a series of museums and historical buildings that are grouped into the **Princely Court Museum complex** (Curtea Domnească; ☎ 216 808; www.neamt.ro /cmj in Romanian; each museum €0.40; each museum ⏱ 10am-6pm Tue-Sun), founded in 1497 by Ştefan cel Mare.

Towering over the square is the lovely, somber 1498 **St John's Church** (Biserica Sfântu Ioan) with its 10m-high bell tower. Just opposite are the small **Art Museum** and **Ethnographic Museum**. The art museum has mostly landscapes and still lifes, but the abstract art on the upper floor and modern, fanciful cityscapes in the 1st-floor section are interesting. Ask inside the museums for entrance to the archaeological digs across the street under the **Petru Rareş School** (Liceul Petru Rareş), where ruins of the princely court were found.

The local **History Museum** (☎ 218 108; Str Mihai Eminescu 10; admission €0.40; ⏱ 9am-5pm Mon-Sat) runs through the area's history from the Stone Age onwards. There is also a small **Natural History Museum** (Muzeul de Ştiinţe Naturale; ☎ 224 211; Str Petru Rareş 26; admission €0.40; ⏱ 9am-5pm Mon-Sat).

Cozla Park is a great, sprawling, forested park north of the centre, popular with strollers and city-type hikers. On the way along Str Ştefan cel Mare is the tiny **Parc Zoologic** (admission €0.15; ⏱ 9am-9pm), an outdoor, surprisingly pleasant mini-zoo, with skinny wolves and baboons.

Festivals & Events

Every year at the end of May, Piatra Neamţ hosts a week-long International Theatre Festival, attracting theatre companies from all over Europe.

Sleeping

Antrec (☎ 234 204; Str Ştefan cel Mare 17; ⏱ 8am-4pm Mon-Fri) This agency can recommend some lovely *pensiunes* (guesthouses) outside the city; in general, they are more pleasant than the accommodation you'll find in town.

Complexul Turistic Troian (☎ 241 444; Str Petru Movilă 270; d/tr/ste €16/20/30) Just 4km west of the city, this large, 17-room complex has spacious and rustic-themed rooms and a fun two-floor dining hall. Though on the main road to Bicaz, it's quiet and peaceful inside. All maxitaxis and buses from Piatra Neamţ to Bicaz will stop here for you. Lake Bâtca Doamnei, a good swimming spot, is nearby.

Pensiune Ambiance (☎ 231 431; www.ambiance .ro; Str Petru Movilă 200A; d/4-person rm €20/30) Only 3km west of town, this six-room villa near Lake Bâtca Doamnei is a pleasant option with its glass veranda, rooms with balconies and friendly ambience. One room even has a waterbed. Breakfast is not included.

Hotel Ceahlău (☎ 219 990; Piaţa Ştefan cel Mare 3; s/d/ste €22/40/59; 🕸) Marring the town's skyline is this 11-storey two-star hotel whose dining hall advertises 'cabaret and lap-dancing shows'. While the suites are a good deal, most of the cheaper rooms are mournfully dull. It's fully wheelchair accessible.

Hotel Bulevard (☎ 235 010; B-dul Republicii 38; d €24) Cramped rooms in this mid-sized hotel are uniquely forgettable. The hotel's main plus is its proximity to the stations.

Hotel Central (☎ 216 230; www.hotelcentral.ro; Piaţa Petrodava 1-3; s/d/ste €36/49/70) This huge concrete tower looks less dreary when lit up at night. Rooms are very comfortably furnished, though arguably not worth their pricetags. Skip the post-Communist dining room.

Eating & Drinking

Along Piaţa Ştefan cel Mare are several small cafes and pizzerias.

Patisserie Paris & Gelateria Italiana (☎ 234 330; B-dul Decebal 14; ⏱ 8am-9pm) Choose between superb *gelato* on one side and sumptuous pastries on the other.

Laguna (☎ 232 121; B-dul Decebal 80; ⏱ 24hr) A recommended pizza joint, this modern place decorated in neon red and blues also has a few billiard tables. Evenings it doubles as a popular bar.

Diesel (☎ 222 424; Str Petru Rareş 21; mains €2-3; 9-1am) A slick, pseudo high-tech place adorned in chrome and black leather, Diesel has a wide and varied menu of inexpensive meals and slaps them out to the tune of thumping pop tunes; the thumping gets louder late at night when it doubles as a bar/disco.

Colibele Halucilor (☎ 213 909; Str Ion Creangă; mains €2-3; 10am-11pm) The folk-costumed waitresses look out of place in what's essentially an outdoor pub-restaurant, but the setting among lush forest makes this a pleasant option. The menu is limited to standard Romanian fare.

Cercul Gospodinelor (☎ 223 845; mains €2-5; Str Ion Creangă) Located at the top of the road up to Cozla Park, this is a more modern Romanian option favoured for its panoramic views and tasty food.

Entertainment

Tineretului Theatre (☎ 211 472; Piaţa Ştefan cel Mare 1) Performances are usually held on weekend evenings; get your tickets at the Agenţie Teatrală adjoining the theatre.

Getting There & Away

The **Agenţie de Voiaj CFR** (☎ 211 034; Piaţa Ştefan cel Mare 10; 7am-7.30pm Mon-Fri) sells tickets for the eight daily trains to Bacău, two of which end at Bucharest. There are also five daily trains to Bicaz. The **bus station** (☎ 211 210; Str Bistriţei 1) is near the train station. There are 11 daily maxitaxis to Bacău (€1.60) and Bucharest (€6.70), and 11 buses and maxitaxis to Târgu Neamţ (€1). Two daily buses also go to Agapia and one to Gura Humorului. Other buses head to Suceava, Iaşi, Braşov, Miercurea Ciuc, Vatra Dornei and Gheorgheni.

BICAZ & THE CEAHLĂU MASSIF

☎ 233

This dizzyingly beautiful corner of western Moldavia is a relatively unexplored region offering great hiking opportunities and picturesque mountains and valleys. Together with the Bicaz Gorges and Lacu Roşu (p282), this area offers a varied tableau of Romanian landscapes.

Heading 24km west from Piaţa Neamţ, there's an unassuming turn-off to the relatively well-off village of **Tarcău**, which spreads out for four km along a beautiful

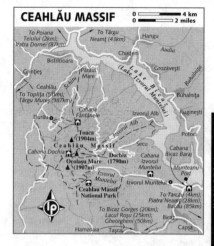

valley nestled between the Măgura Tarcău and Câmpilor mountain peaks. It's a lovely place that feels cut off from time as it stretches lazily along the little Tarcău River. There's a pretty church and not much more here than peace, quiet and bucolic scenery.

Bicaz (pop 9000) 4km further west on the confluence of the Bicaz and Bistriţa Rivers, is a sorry-looking town with little to offer. Locals depend on the nearby giant and scary-looking concrete and (German-owned) asbestos factories west of town for survival, and it feels like a struggling industrial town. However, just north of here, along the road to Vatra Dornei is **Bicaz Lake** (Lacu Izvorul Muntelui, or 'Mountain Spring Lake'), which sprawls northward over 30 sq km. The hydroelectric dam *(baraj)* at the lake's southern end was built in 1950, with several villages being submerged in the process and the villagers relocated.

Near the dam, at the junction 4km north of Bicaz, is a turn-off for the twisting mountain road to Ceahlău (chek-*lau*). A right turn immediately after the bridge will bring you to **Munteanu Port** (☎ 671 350) on the western shores of the lake. There are paddle boats for hire here and nice picnic spots, too. The next village is Izvoru Muntelui, from where hiking trails begin to climb the stunning Ceahlău Massif, Moldavia's most spectacular mountain range. Good trails also snake off from Durău and Ceahlău further along the mountain road, but be warned that this road can be as perilous as it is impressive; horse-drawn carts plod up the narrow, steep and twisting road.

Durău (800m), on the northeastern side of the mountain, is the main stepping stone to hiking trails, and the village has a decent tourist infrastructure. A steep trail (red stripes, one hour) leads to Cabana Fântânele and from there others lead towards Toaca Peak. There is also the small **Durău Monastery** (1830), a complex comprising two churches and quarters for the 35 nuns who inhabit it today. Visitors are welcome. The annual **Ceahlău Folk Festival** also takes place here on the second Sunday in August. Shepherds come down from the mountains while locals don traditional dress.

In **Ceahlău** (550m), 6km north of Durău, are the remains of a princely palace built between 1639 and 1676 and an 18th-century wooden church.

Bypassing the mountain road from Bicaz and continuing north for another 24km, you come to **Grozăveşti**, a village with a wooden church typical of those in Maramureş. The church was built during the 20th century after the old church fell into the lake. Apparently the day the church drowned, the local village priest received a postcard from Maramureş. The postage stamp featured a wooden Maramureş church, thus inspiring him to build his new church in that style.

Sleeping

Durău has the largest choice of accommodation, with hotels and numerous *pensiunes* to choose from.

Antrec (☎ 234 204) This agency in Piatra Neamţ can help set you up within villages throughout the region.

Durău Monastery (☎ 678 383; €5 per person) The nuns still take in the weary and blistered.

Motel Gară (☎ 253 382; Str Republicii 8; d €15) Right beside the train station in Bicaz, this will do for a night – rooms are clean at least. There's an on-site restaurant but their prices don't include breakfast.

Pensiune Igor Ghinculov (☎ 234 20; s/d €10/20) Some 50m beyond the Cabana Paulo, this friendly home have five double rooms with shared bathroom. The owner arranges accommodation in private homes elsewhere in the area.

Hotel Bistriţa (☎ 256 578; s/d €13/18) The smallest and friendliest of the cluster of Durău's hotels is this 20-room place, which also has a decent restaurant. Bathrooms are shared and hot water is limited to a couple of hours in the morning and evening.

Campers can pitch their tents for free outside **Cabana Bicaz Baraj** (430m) at the foot of the dam wall. The cabana has no rooms but serves snacks in its small cafe. **Cabana Izvorul Muntelui** (797m), 12km from Bicaz town on the eastern side of the lake, has a few basic rooms. **Cabana Paulo**, the first cabana you pass on the main road to Durău, has 16 places in a wooden, chalet-style house. Cabanas in the area generally charge under €10 per person.

Getting There & Away

Five daily trains run between Bicaz and Bacău, all of which stop in Piatra Neamţ, and two of which continue to Bucharest. Buses and maxitaxis link Bicaz with Piatra Neamţ throughout the day; buses between Piatra Neamţ and Poiana (six daily), Gheorgheni (once daily) and Braşov (two daily) stop at Bicaz. All of these buses also stop at Tarcău, but it's then a 4km hike through the village.

BICAZ GORGES & LACU ROŞU

Together with Transylvania's Transfăgărăşan road (see Long and Winding Road, p114), the road that slices through the **Bicaz**

AUTHOR'S CHOICE

Pensiunea Frasin (☎ 212 903; soldan@ambra.ro; Tarcău 466; per person €18) This rural paradise practically redefines 'guesthouse'! In the quiet village of Tarcău, this two-storey, four-room modern home surrounded by sprawling gardens is a rural paradise: a running creek and small waterfall provide the soundtrack to a picturesque backdrop of velvety mountains. Guests dine like kings on an outdoor wooden terrace; sumptuously home-made meals are lovingly prepared with fresh local produce. Their *mămăligă* (p43) is no doubt among Romania's best, and the morning milk is still warm from a cow in a neighbouring farm. Completing the picture are warm, friendly hosts who know how to respect guests' privacy. A dream! It's 4km from the main Piatra Neamţ–Bicaz road.

Gorges (Cheile Bicazului) some 20km west of Bicaz is among Romania's most staggering and spectacular. The gorge twists and turns steeply uphill for 5km, cutting through sheer, 300m-high limestone rocks on its journey through the mountains. The narrow mountain road runs directly beneath the overhanging rocks in a section known as the 'neck of hell' (Gâtul Iadului). Dozens of artisans sell locally made crafts from stalls set up beneath the rocks and there are several places to park your car and stagger around, head arched back in wonder. This entire stretch is protected as part of the Hășmaș–Bicaz Gorges National Park (Parcul Național Hășmaș–Cheile Bicazului).

Just a few kilometres west along this road, you cross into Transylvania's Harghita County and immediately hit another splendid site of natural beauty, the resort of **Lacu Roșu** (Red Lake, or Gyilkos tó in Hungarian). The lake (**Lacul Roșu**) is strangely filled with dead tree stumps that jut out of its murky waters at 45 degree angles and is considered one of Romania's weirdest natural wonders. Legend has it that the 'red lake' or 'killer lake' was formed from the flowing blood of a group of picnickers who had the misfortune to be sitting beneath the mountainside when it collapsed, crushing them to death. In fact, a landslide did occur in 1838, eventually flooding the valley and damming the Bicaz River.

This thriving Alpine resort sprang up in the 1970s and is still a magnet for partiers and hikers from both Transylvania and Moldavia. There are dozens of hotels and villas here, as well as 24-hour stores, tourist markets and even a police station and **Salvamont office** (☎ 0745-979 425) for emergency rescues. It's a village without permanent residents. Though the resort is open year round, in summer the area surrounding the lake can get noisy. Lacu Roșu falls administratively under the Székely-dominated Harghita County, and the ever-resourceful Hungarians here have produced several useful, multilingual guides and maps of the surrounding mountains, replete with trails and lots of useful information. These are available at the information kiosk by the side of the lake and can be ordered from **Mark House Publishing** (☎ 266-364 190; www .markhouse.ro). The kiosk also has **boat rental** (2-person rowing boat per hr €1.60). Rare in Romania, there's even a trilingual sign posting the environmentally conscientious dos and don'ts of wild camping.

A flat, scenic trail circles the lake, and other more demanding trails shoot up to the various peaks, all of which offer stunning views. Compared with the oft-travelled hiking trails of Transylvania, hikers and foreign tourists are relatively sparse here.

The main road continues another 26km to Gheorgheni (p141) via the Bucin mountain pass, another twisting snarl of beautiful mountain scenery.

Sleeping

Wild camping is permitted, every other house displays a *cazare* sign and there are plenty of hotels and villas to choose from.

Jasicon Hotel (☎ 266-380 080; iasicon@artelecom .ro; s/d/tr €13/16/24) This 100-bed hotel isn't a bad option, slightly away from the resort's busy centre along the uphill road near the police station. Rooms aren't anything to write home about, but there's a decent restaurant and bar, and hiking trails start directly outside the front door.

Pensiune 18 Borș (☎ 266 570 484; d with/without private toilet €24/18) This little white palace overlooking the southern end of the lake was once Ceaușescu's hunting lodge. Today, this is a top-notch option and visitors can sleep in the dictator's former bedroom – yippee! The villa is signposted on the left almost immediately after you enter Lacu Roșu from the south.

Getting There & Away

In addition to a daily bus from Gheorgheni, the daily Miercurea Ciuc-Piatra Neamț and the twice daily Brașov-Piatra Neamț buses all stop at Lacu Roșu.

SOUTHERN BUCOVINA

Southern Bucovina is a rural paradise as magical and deeply revered as Maramureș. Its painted churches are among the greatest artistic monuments of Europe – in 1993 they were collectively designated World Heritage sites by Unesco. Apart from religious art and fantastic churches, Southern Bucovina is well worth visiting for its folklore,

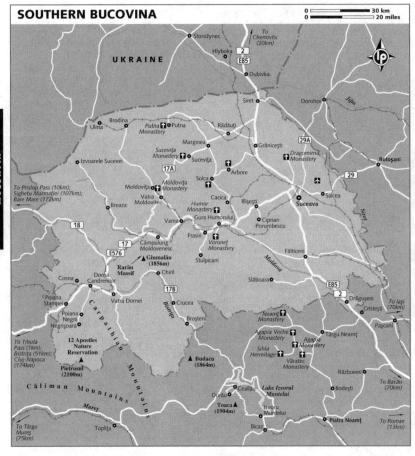

SOUTHERN BUCOVINA

picturesque villages, bucolic scenery and colourful inhabitants.

Southern Bucovina embraces the northwestern region of present-day Moldavia; Northern Bucovina is in Ukraine. In 1775 the region was annexed by the Austro-Hungarian Empire and remained in Habsburg hands until 1918, when Bucovina was returned to Romania. Northern Bucovina was annexed by the Soviet Union in 1940 and incorporated into Ukraine, splitting families apart.

While coordinating transport between the remote villages can be challenging, there are plenty of alternatives to allow you to get the most out of your visit, including hitchhiking, biking, renting a car or arranging a private tour.

SUCEAVA
☎ 230 / pop 117,200

True, Suceava isn't much to look at. At first glance, it appears to be one concrete block connected to another by crumbling concrete promenades. Yet there's a real charm to the city, and not only because of its stunning citadel and beautiful churches. It also harbours some of the country's funkiest, most happening clubs and bars, has great restaurants and a friendly, lively populace.

The capital of Moldavia from 1388 to 1565, Suceava was a thriving commercial centre on the Lviv-Istanbul trading route. By the end of Ştefan cel Mare's reign in 1504, Suceava had some 40 churches. Its decline was initiated when the Turks conquered it in 1675.

During the Ceauşescu regime in the 1980s, Suceava became notorious for its toxic pulp and paper works (still in operation), which used to churn out 20 tonnes of cellulose and fibre waste a day, causing respiratory and nervous disorders known as Suceava Syndrome. Since then, new filters have been installed and pollution has greatly decreased, but the local economy is still dependent on forestry, wood-processing, chemical production and mining for its survival.

Most tourists use Suceava merely as a gateway or urban base to the painted churches of Bucovina, though it can be a fun place to stay a few days.

The colourful **Moldavian Furrier Fair** is held here every year in mid-August.

Orientation
MAPS & PUBLICATIONS
Amco's *Suceava* (€1.40) also features a county map showing the location of the monasteries. There are several booklets and guides to the monasteries, some of which have rudimentary maps. A nicely illustrated and helpful booklet is *Bucovina...The Monastic Archipelago* (€3) published by Tipo and available at local bookshops.

Information
BOOKSHOPS
Librărie Reţeaua (☎ 530 342; Str Mihai Viteazu 23; ◷ 9am-6pm, 10am-4pm Sat)
Casa Cărţii (☎ 530 337; Str Nicolae Bălcescu 8; ◷ 9am-6pm Mon-Fri, 9am-2pm Sat)

INTERNET ACCESS
Assist (☎ 523 044; Piaţa 22 Decembrie; per hr €0.50; ◷ 9am-11pm) Also a fully stocked computer store that can help with any printing needs.
Calculatore (☎ 524 795; Str Curtea Domnească 9; per hr €0.40; ◷ 10am-midnight)

MONEY
There are several ATMs on Piaţa 22 Decembrie and along Str Ştefan cel Mare.
Banca Comercială Română (Str Ştefan cel Mare 31; ◷ 8.30am-2pm Mon-Fri)

POST & TELEPHONE
Post office (☎ 512 222; Str Dimitrie Onciu; ◷ 7am-7pm Mon-Fri, 8am-4pm Sat)

Telephone office (cnr Str Nicolae Bălcescu & Str Onciu; ◷ 7am-9pm Mon-Fri, 8am-4pm Sat)

TOURIST INFORMATION
Central Turism (☎ 523 024; central@suceava.iiruc.ro; Str Nicolae Bălcescu 2; ◷ 8am-4pm Mon-Fri, 8am-1pm Sat) Inside Hotel Suceava, this small office can arrange day-long monastery tours with multilingual guides with just a few hours' notice for about €60, depending on your preferred route.
Ciprian Şlenku (☎ 0744-292 588; monasterytour@ yahoo.com) This highly recommended private tour guide is a specialist in both religion and history and therefore perfect to visit the monasteries with. He's also a can-do kind of guy and arranges tours to suit your schedule.
Icar Tours (☎ 524 894; www.icar.ro; Str Ştefan cel Mare 24; ◷ 9am-6pm Mon-Fri, 9am-1pm Sat) This helpful bunch specialises in monastery tours (€40-70 including car and driver, €15 extra for a guide), which they can set up in a few hours, but they also arrange trips throughout the country, book air tickets and arrange rural homestays in the villages near the monasteries.

Sights
The bulky **House of Culture** (Casa de Cultură) is at the western end of the city's main square, Piaţa 22 Decembrie. North of the bus stop along B-dul Ana Ipătescu lie the foundations of the 15th-century **Princely Palace**. To the west is the impressive **St Dimitru's Church** (1535), built by Petru Rareş in an exciting, clubbed Byzantine style typical of 16th-century Moldavian churches. Traces of the original exterior frescoes can still be seen.

Some 250m northeast is the lovely **Mirăuţi Church** (1375–91), the original Moldavian coronation church, which was rebuilt in the 19th century. This was the original seat of the Moldavian bishop, and it was here that Ştefan cel Mare became Moldavia's ruler. Of particular note is the *Prayer on the Mount of Olives* fresco in the nave. Another outstanding church is on the corner of B-dul Ana Ipătescu and Str Ştefaniţă Vodă. Built by Vasile Lupu in 1643, **Domniţelor Church** (Princesses' Church) is one of the city's loveliest monuments, despite its unfortunate location on a busy street. There is an old well in the small graveyard surrounding it.

West of Piaţa 22 Decembrie is **Hanul Domnesc**, a 16th-century guesthouse that now houses an **Ethnographic Museum** (☎ 214 081; Str Ciprian Porumbescu 5; adult/child €0.80/0.40;

MOLDAVIA

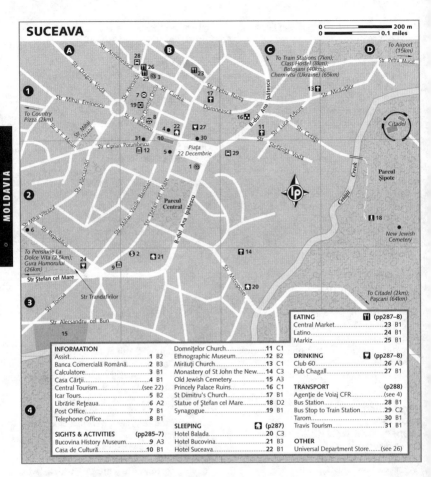

SUCEAVA

9am-5pm Tue-Sun), with a good collection of folk costumes. Next to the post office on Str Dimitrie Onciul is the town's only surviving **synagogue** (1870). Prior to WWII, some 18 synagogues served the local Jewish community.

Following Str Ștefan cel Mare south past **Parcul Central** (Central Park) (Parcul Central) is the worthwhile **Bucovina History Museum** (Muzeul Național al Bucovinei; ☎ 216 439; Str Ștefan cel Mare 33; adult/child €0.80/0.40; 10am-6pm Tue-Sun). The exhibits trace life here from prehistoric times but come to an abrupt end at 1945. Old paintings hang in rooms that formerly glorified the Communist era.

The **Monastery of St John the New** (Mănăstirea Sfântu Ioan cel Nou; 1522) off Str

Mitropoliei, is well worth visiting. The paintings on the outside of the church are badly faded but give you an idea of the church frescoes for which Bucovina is famous.

CITADEL

At the end of the winding Str Mitropoliei, some 3km from the centre, is the 1388 **City of Residence** (Cetatea de Scaun; adult/child €0.25/0.15; 9am-6pm), a citadel fortress that in 1476 held off Mehmed II, conqueror of Constantinople (now Istanbul). It's a vast complex and the highlight of many visitors' trip to Suceava; certainly kids' eyes will light up as they wander around the grounds. Massive stretches of the rectangular structure remain. Near the site a tacky disco and outdoor terrace have been set up.

The original fortress, known as Muşat's Fortress, was built by Petru I Muşat when Suceava was Moldavia's capital. It had eight square towers and was surrounded by defensive trenches. Ştefan cel Mare developed it further, building 4m-thick, 33m-high walls around it so it was impossible to shoot an arrow over. In fact it was never taken, despite many attempts. In 1675 the fortress was finally blown up by the Turks. A century later it was partially dismantled and the stones used to build houses. Restoration work started on the fortress in 1944 and continues to this day, in tandem with archaeological exploration. Today the fortress, which looks as if it has been sliced in half, is slowly sinking into the soft ground below.

The citadel is accessible by car by following Str Mitropoliei to the end or by foot via Str Cetăţii, crossing the bridge and following the footpath that leads to the huge **equestrian statue** (1977) of Ştefan cel Mare. The lavish New Jewish Cemetery is behind the statue.

Sleeping

Hotel Bucovina (☎ 217 048; B-dul Ana Ipătescu 5; s/d €16/21) Favoured among those searching for clues to Romania's Communist past, this 11-storey concrete blob is a 1960s holdout with notable period pieces such as deep-red or dark-brown curtains, box-shaped armchairs, sofa-sized pillows and rain-stained concrete balconies. As bonuses, services include 'a desk for the sale of different goods' and 'hiring of different games'. Have fun!

Hotel Suceava (☎ 521 079; Str Nicolae Bălcescu 2; s €17, d €24-32) This is your best bet in town for the price. Smack in the city centre and

featuring old-fashioned but perfectly comfortable rooms (the more expensive ones having been renovated somewhat), this is a very pleasant place.

Pensiune La Dolce Vita (☎ 526 828; ladolcevita@ warpnet.ro; Calea Obcinilor; d €19; 🗙) The brightly coloured exteriors of this motel-style *pensiune* on the edge of the city on the road to Gura Humorului are more impressive than its cold interiors.

Hotel Balada (☎ 520 408; www.balada.ro; Str Mitropoliei 3; s/d/ste €50/60/95; 🗙) One of the top hotels in the region, this three-storey hotel offers elegance and comfort over pure luxury; rooms have everything you need but are simply furnished. It's on a lovely, quiet street.

Eating & Drinking

Country Pizza (☎ 216 397; B-dul George Enescu 21; mains €1-2; 🕙 10am-11pm) West of the centre, this is a popular place for a cheap, greasy fill-up on ho-hum pizza slices.

Pub Chagall (☎ 0723-961 127; Str Ştefan cel Mare; mains €1-3; 🕙 11-1am) At complete odds with the cold, massive concrete blocks surrounding it is this cosy cellar pub and diner. Though it has a full menu of tasty meals, it's mostly used as a drinking hole. There are three separate rooms, each comfortably set up with wooden tables.

Latino (☎ 523 627; Str Curtea Domnească 9; mains €2-8; 🕙 11am-midnight) This is either the most elegant pizzeria ever or a top-class restaurant that happens to have a full pizza menu – take your pick. The classy, subdued decor is accented by impeccable service and a dazzlingly varied menu that runs the gamut from over 25 kinds of pizza (with real mozzarella!; €1.60 to €3), a dozen first-rate pasta dishes (€2.50) and steaming fresh fish dishes (€3 to €8). Their espresso is sterling as well. Yes, they deliver.

MOLDAVIA

AUTHOR'S CHOICE

Class Hostel (☎ 525 213; www.classhostel.home.ro; Str Aurel Vlaicu 195; per person €13) It may not be centrally located, on the edge of the city, but you feel as if you're in the country in this peaceful, spacious and ultra-modern two-floor house. Monica, the interminably good-natured host, is not only a top-rate tour guide and hostel manager, she's also an excellent cook: breakfasts, made with produce from the garden and local farms, are worth writing a diary entry about! She can arrange monastery tours or show you around the city. It's a super-friendly hostel, one of the country's best, 1km west of Gară de Nord.

MOLDAVIA

AUTHOR'S CHOICE

Markiz (☎ 520 219; Str Vasile Alecsandri 10; mains €1-3; ☯ 8am-11pm) Aside from kebab joints, you can probably count the number of Middle Eastern restaurants in Romania outside Bucharest on one hand; if you did, this one would definitely be the index finger. On offer here are succulent meat and eggplant dishes, hummus, salads and kebabs, all deliciously spiced (spices! imagine!); their pastry shop has sinful desserts. Inside it looks like a fast-food cafe; the terrace is pleasant and favoured as a place to have a few drinks.

Club 60 (☎ 209 440; Str Ştefan cel Mare; ☯ 1pm-1am) Enter here at your own risk: you may never feel like leaving again! Emanating some of the smoothest vibes of any club in the country is this vast, loft-style lounge/bar with wooden floors, antique furnishings, comfy sofas and billiard tables. Soul and hip-hop pour out of the speakers and into the mellowed ears of the young, laid-back crowd. Enter from the back of the Universal Department Store and climb the stairs to the 2nd floor.

There are several fast-food joints on the eastern side of Piaţa 22 Decembrie. The **central market** (cnr Str Petru Rareş & Str Avram Iancuis) is close to the bus station.

Getting There & Away

AIR

Tarom (☎ 214 686; Str Nicolae Bălcescu 2; ☯ 8.30am-5pm Mon-Fri) has four weekly flights to Bucharest (€99 return), and also sells tickets for **Angel Airlines'** (www.angelairlines.ro) three weekly flights to Iaşi and four weekly flights to Bucharest (Baneasa airport).

BUS

The **bus station** (☎ 216 089) is in the centre of town at Str Armenească. Bus and maxitaxi services include 13 daily to Gura Humorului (€1), eight to Botoşani (€1), six to Rădăuţi (€1), five to Iaşi (€3) and Vatra Dornei (€4.50), four to Bucharest (€8) and three daily to Târgu Neamţ (€2). Tickets for international destinations are sold at window No 4. Five daily buses go to Chernivtsi (Cernăuţi) in Ukraine (€4) and three a week to Chişinău in Moldova (€7).

TRAIN

Suceava has two train stations, both some 7km north of the city centre. The **Agenţie de Voiaj CFR** (☎ 214 335; Str Nicolae Bălcescu 8; ☯ 7.30am-8pm Mon-Fri) sells advance tickets. Trains that originate or terminate in Suceava arrive/depart at Gară Nord. Trains that transit Suceava arrive/depart from Gară Sud (Gară Burdujeni).

Train service includes nine to Gura Humorului (get off at the Gură Humorului Oraş stop; 70 mins, €1.50), seven to Vatra Dornei (€5, 3¼ hours), three to Iaşi (€3, 2½ hours) and Timişoara (€13, 13½ hours) and one daily to Bucharest (€11, seven hours). To get to Moldoviţa, change at Vama.

Getting Around

The central bus and trolleybus stop is at the eastern end of Piaţa 22 Decembrie from which all buses and trolleybuses to/from the two train stations arrive/depart. Trolleybus Nos 2 and 3, and bus Nos 20 and 26 run between the centre and Gară Sud. To reach Gară Nord, take trolleybus No 5 or bus No 1, 10, 11 or 28. Maxitaxis are faster; No 1 goes to Gară Nord.

Travis Tourism (☎ 521 603; suceava@travis.ro; Str Ciprian Porumbescu 3) has the best car-rental deals in the city, with Opels from €50 per day.

BUCOVINA MONASTERIES
☎ 230

You needn't be a pilgrim or have a religious bone in your wicked body to appreciate the arresting beauty of Southern Bucovina's monasteries, many – though not all – of which have the distinction of being painted on the outside as well as the inside. While some can be accessed by public transport, and all can be visited on a private tour (see p285), there should be no problem hitching a ride on the main roads. Smoking and wearing shorts and hats (for men) are forbidden and women are required to cover their shoulders. All monasteries have an extra charge for cameras and videocameras (usually €2 for taking photographs).

THE PAINTED BEAUTIES

The painted churches of Southern Bucovina were erected at a time when northern Moldavia was threatened by Turkish invaders. Great popular armies would gather inside the monasteries' strong defensive walls, waiting to do battle. To educate, entertain and arouse the interest of the illiterate soldiers and peasants, who were unable to enter the church or understand the Slavic liturgy, well-known biblical stories were portrayed on the church walls in cartoon-style frescoes.

Most amazing in these vast compositions are the realistic portrayals of human figures against a backdrop not unlike the local landscape (the forested Carpathian foothills). Some frescoes have been damaged by centuries of rain and wind, but more often than not the intense colours have been duly preserved, from the greens of Sucevita to the blues of Voroneţ and the reds of Humor. Natural dyes are used – sulphur for yellow, madder for red, and cobalt or lapis for blue.

All Orthodox monasteries face the east, in keeping with the traditional belief that the light of God shines in the image of the rising sun. An outside porch, likewise tattooed with frescoes, is typical of the Bucovina monasteries. Within, they are divided into three rooms – the first chamber (*pronaos*), the tomb room, and the altar room (*naos*). Women are not allowed to enter the altar, shielded from public view by an iconostasis – a beautifully sculpted, gilded partition in the *naos*. The church domes are a peculiar combination of Byzantine pendentives and Moorish crossed arches with larger-than-life paintings of Christ or the Virgin peering down.

Each monastery is dedicated to a saint, whose patron day is among the most important feast days for the monastery's inhabitants. The nuns or monks are required to fast – no meat, eggs or dairy products – for several days leading up to any religious feast. Wednesday, Friday, Lent, the six weeks after Easter, and the days preceding Christmas are likewise fast days.

Novices are required to serve three to seven years in a monastery before being ordained. Numerous penances have to be observed during this training period; many have to stand motionless in the street for several consecutive days, bearing a plaque indicating that they are waiting for cash donations towards the 'spiritual furthering' of their monastery.

Following the Habsburg occupation of Bucovina in 1785, most monasteries were closed and their inhabitants forced to relinquish their spiritual lives for a civilian one. They were equally persecuted under communism, and it is only since 1990 that the inner activity of these holy sanctuaries has matched the dynamism of their outer façades.

In addition to the accommodation options listed here, **Icar Tours** (☎ 524 894; www.icar.ro) in Suceava and the excellent web site www.ruraltourism.ro are the best places to turn for finding pleasant accommodation in the region.

Dragomirna Monastery

In the village of Mitocul Dragomirna Dragomirna, 12km north of Suceava, is this lovely, small **monastery** (admission €0.40; ☯ 8am-8pm) founded in 1608–09 by the scholar, calligrapher, artist and bishop Anastasie Crimca. The intricate rope lacing around the side of the main church (1627) represents the unity of the Holy Trinity and the short-lived unification of the principalities of Moldavia, Wallachia and Transylvania in 1600. The church tower is 42m high.

Dragomirna's treasure, displayed in the **museum of medieval art** in the monastery grounds, includes a beautifully carved candle made by Bishop Crimca, ornamental carved cedar crosses mounted in silver-gilt filigree, and a large number of missals and religious scripts.

Dragomirna remained inhabited during the Habsburg and later the Communist purges on the Orthodox church. Crimca's dying wish was that a day should not pass without prayers being said in his monastery. Thus seven elderly nuns defied Communist orders and remained alone at the monastery throughout the 1960s and 70s. Today some 60 nuns live here.

It is possible for travellers to stay at the monastery. It's best to hitch or take a taxi from Suceava; there are no buses.

Voroneţ Monastery

The *Last Judgment* fresco, which fills the entire western wall of the **Voroneţ Monastery** (adult/child €1/0.50; ☯ 8am-8pm) is perhaps the most marvellous Bucovine fresco. At the top, angels roll up the signs of the zodiac to indicate the end of time. The middle fresco shows humanity being brought to judgment. On the left, St Paul escorts the believers, while on the right Moses brings forward the nonbelievers. Below is the *Resurrection*.

On the northern wall is *Genesis*, from Adam and Eve to Cain and Abel. The southern wall features another tree of Jesse with the genealogy of biblical personalities. In the vertical fresco to the left is the story of the martyrdom of St John of Suceava (who is buried in the Monastery of St John the New in Suceava, p286). The vibrant, almost satiny blue pigment used throughout the frescoes is known worldwide as 'Voroneţ blue'.

In the narthex lies the tomb of Daniel the Hermit, the first abbot of Voroneţ Monastery (see Putna, p293, for more on Daniel). It was upon the worldly advice of Daniel, who told Ştefan cel Mare not to give up his battle against the Turks, that the Moldavian prince went on to win further victories against the Turks and then to build Voroneţ Monastery out of gratitude to God.

In 1785, occupying Austrians forced Voroneţ's monks to abandon the monastery. Since 1991 the monastery has been inhabited by a small community of nuns.

SLEEPING & EATING

The town of Gura Humorului is a perfect base to visit Voroneţ. Every second house takes in tourists. The usual rate per person per night in a so-called 'vila' is about €13. Only 500m south of the bus station (follow the only path), after crossing the River Moldova there's wild camping possible on the south bank. A few cafes are set up there too and a small tourist complex will be built.

Vila Simeria (☎ 230 746; Str Ana Ipătescu 19; d per person €13) Just 200m from the main post office in Gura Humorului on a quiet side street is this modern, impeccably clean and pleasant two-storey villa. Breakfast is not included.

Vila Ramona (☎ 232 133; Str Oborlui 6; s/d €14/20) A finely furnished home some 300m east of the bus and train station, this place also has a sauna.

Casa Elena (☎ 230 651; www.casaelena.ro; s/d €30/35) A quick 3.5km trip from Gura Humorului

on the northern edge of Voroneţ Monastery, this four-star option has 31 rooms in five different villas, all in a large, luxurious complex. The hotel also has a billiard room, sauna and 24-hour restaurant.

GETTING THERE & AWAY

There are buses on weekdays from Gura Humorului to Voroneţ, departing at 7am, 12.30pm and 2.45pm. A lovely option is to walk the 4km along a narrow village road to Voroneţ. The route is clearly marked and it is impossible to get lost.

Humor Monastery

Of all the Bucovina monasteries, **Humor** (adult/child €0.40/0.20; ☼ 8am-8pm) has the most impressive interior frescoes. It was founded by Chancellor Theodor Bubuiog in 1530 under the guidance of Moldavian prince Petru Rareş. Unlike the other monasteries, Humor has no tower and is surrounded by ramparts made from wood; its traditional Moldavian open porch was the first of its kind to be built in Bucovina.

Its exterior frescoes, dating from 1535, are predominantly red. Paintings on the church's southern exterior wall are devoted to the Holy Virgin, the patron saint of the monastery. There's a badly faded depiction of the 1453 siege of Constantinople, with the parable of the return of the prodigal son beside it to the right. St George is depicted on the northern wall. On the porch is a painting of the Last Judgment: the long bench on which the 12 apostles sit, the patterned towel on the chair of judgment, and the long, horn-like *bucium* (pipe) used to announce the coming of Christ, are all typical Moldavian elements.

Humor shelters five chambers, the middle one (the tomb room) has a lower ceiling than the others. This hides a treasure room *(tainiţa)* where the riches of the monastery were traditionally kept safe. On the right wall as you enter the tomb room is a votive painting depicting the founder, Toader Bubuiog, offering, with the help of the Virgin Mary, a miniature replica of the monastery to Christ. The tomb of Bubuiog, who died in 1539, and of his wife, lie on the left side of the room; a painting of his wife praying to the Virgin Mary is above her grave.

The paintings in the first chamber (*pronaos*) depict various scenes of martyrs. Above the decorative border, which runs around the base of the four walls, is a pictorial representation of the first three months of the Orthodox calendar (*synaxary*). Unlike the other interior paintings, which were restored by Unesco in the early 1970s, the paintings in the altar room have never been restored.

SLEEPING

Dozens of homes here have rooms for rent. However, it is not possible to stay at the monastery. See also p290 for nearby options.

Maison de Bucovine (☎ 0744-373 931; 172 Mănăstirea Humor; s/d €15/22) Only a rosary bead's swing away from the monastery (30m), this unassuming-looking home is a comfortable place to spend the night. The bathrooms, in a separate outbuilding, are clean and modern and the hosts a delight.

GETTING THERE & AWAY

Aside from hitching a ride for the 6km from Gura Humorului, regular maxitaxis depart from next to the towering Best Western Hotel, at the start of the road towards the monastery.

Moldovița Monastery

In the middle of a quaint village **Moldovița Monastery** (adult/child €0.40/0.20; ☺ 10am-6pm) consists of a fortified quadrangular enclosure with towers and brawny gates, with a magnificent painted church at its centre. The monastery has undergone careful restoration in recent years. Its frescoes are predominantly yellow.

The fortifications and surrounding buildings are as impressive as the exterior frescoes. A haunting atmosphere of tranquility reigns here, partly thanks to the lovely tended grounds and beautiful stone buildings. On the church's southern exterior wall is a depiction of the defence of Constantinople in AD 626 against Persians dressed as Turks, while on the porch is a representation of the Last Judgment. Inside the sanctuary, on a wall facing the original carved iconostasis, is a portrait of Prince Petru Rareș, the monastery's founder, offering the church to Christ. All of these works date from 1537.

In the monastery's small museum is Petru Rareș' original throne.

SLEEPING

See www.ruraltourism.ro for some great places to stay in Vama, a small village 14km south of Moldovița on the main Suceava–Vatra Dornei road. Many homes have rooms to rent.

Mărul de Aur (☎ 336 180; d/t per person €7.50) Located between the train station and the monastery, this place offers tired rooms. Downstairs is a smoke-filled restaurant serving basic meals and beer 24 hours. The complex also operates a **camping ground** (camping free, cabins €3.50), 3km out of town on the road to Sucevița.

Casa Alba (☎ 340 404; www.casa-alba.suceava.ro; Vama 5969; s/d/ste €39/46/64) You certainly won't feel a monastic asceticism in this lush, ultra modern and very comfortable villa. Prices are about €10 cheaper from September to June. Follow the one road heading south 5km west of Frasin, which is about 3km east Vama.

GETTING THERE & AWAY

Moldovița Monastery is right above Vatra Moldoviței's train station (be sure to get off at Vatra Moldoviței, not Moldovița). From Suceava nine daily trains go to Vama (1¼ hours), and from Vama three trains leave daily for Vatra Moldoviței (35 minutes).

Sucevița Monastery

The winding, remote mountain road from Moldovița to Sucevița (27km) offers breathtaking views across the surrounding fields and is reason enough to make the trip. It climbs 1100m and passes small Alpine villages. Yet the prize at the end of it is golden too: **Sucevița** (adult/child €0.40/0.20; ☺ 8am-8pm) is perhaps the largest and finest of the Bucovina monasteries.

The church inside the fortified monastic enclosure, built between 1582 and 1601, is almost completely covered with frescoes. Mysteriously, the western wall of the monastery remains bare of any impressive frescoes. Legend has it that the artist fell off the scaffolding while attempting to paint the wall and was killed, leaving artists of the time too scared to follow in his footsteps. The exterior frescoes – predominantly red and green – date from around 1590.

As you enter you first see the *Virtuous Ladder* fresco covering most of the northern exterior wall, depicting the 30 steps from Hell to Paradise. The frescoes inside the arches above the open porch depict the apocalypse and the vision of St John.

On the southern exterior wall is the Jesse tree symbolising the continuity of the Old and New Testaments. The tree grows from the reclining figure of Jesse, who is flanked by a row of ancient philosophers. To the left is the Virgin as a Byzantine princess, with angels holding a red veil over her head.

Inside the church, in the second chamber, the Orthodox calendar is depicted. The tombs of the founders, Moldavian nobles Simion and Ieremia Movilă, lie in the tomb room. The last of the painted monasteries to have been built, this is the only one that wasn't built by Ştefan cel Mare or his family. Ieremia Movilă, who died in 1606, appears with his seven children on the western wall inside the *naos*. Apart from the church, there's a small museum at Suceviţa Monastery in which various treasures and art pieces from the monastery are displayed.

Suceviţa Monastery was first inhabited by monks in 1582. During the Communist era, only nuns over 50 were allowed to stay at Suceviţa. Today, it is a relatively flourishing place.

SLEEPING
It's worth spending a night here and doing a little hiking in the surrounding hills. Wild camping is possible in the field across the stream from the monastery, as well as along the road from Moldoviţa.

Pensiune Agroturistică (☎ 421 306; Suceviţa 478; per person €14) Just 700m from the monastery (signposted) is this delicious guesthouse surrounded by cherry and apple trees. All their food is organically grown on the premises. Rooms are rustic and cosy and the price includes one full meal.

Popas Turistic Bucovina (☎ 417 000; www.popas .ro in Romanian; s/d €24/30, tent space/hut €5/11) Located 3.5km south of Suceviţa on the beautiful road to Vatra Moldoviţei, this complex consists of two charming villas and an excellent Moldavian restaurant. The villas have spacious, excellent rooms, while the cramped wooden huts out back are quite decent. It's open year round and hiking and skiing are possible right from the front door. The owners can also organise any kind of transport you need.

GETTING THERE & AWAY
Suceviţa is the most difficult monastery to reach on public transport. There are only two daily buses from Rădăuţi. Hitching or biking are your best bets. There's a beautiful hiking trail to the Putna Monastery from here (p294).

Solca & Arbore Monasteries
Few tourists make their way to the tiny monasteries of Solca and Arbore; those who do leave disappointed. Arbore has a handful of scarcely visible frescoes on its outside walls while Solca has none at all. Neither monastery is inhabited today and both are often closed; tracking down the person in the village who has the key can prove problematic.

SOLCA MONASTERY
The walled monastery of Solca (also called Tomsa Vodă Monastery), 21km north of Gura Humorului, is today little more than a village church (but one with walls 2.10m thick!) and rarely used. The monastery was built in 1612 as a defence for the village as well as for religious worship. Following the occupation of Bucovina by the Austrians in 1775, it was stripped of its monastic status. The iconostasis inside the church dates from 1895.

A beer factory next door was opened by the monks in the 17th century. In 1810 the Austrian administration opened a larger factory on the same site. This factory – the present-day Solca Beer Factory – still uses the gunpowder cellars of the monastery for storing beer kegs.

ARBORE MONASTERY
Arbore Monastery is 6km east of Solca and 33km north of Suceava. It was built in 1503 by Suceava's chief magistrate, Luca Arbore, who owned the entire village and raised the small church next to his private residence as a family chapel and cemetery. His Gothic-style tomb lies inside the first chamber of the church, beneath a beautiful carved-stone canopy.

Arbore's predominantly green frescoes date from 1541. Bad weather has left most of the walls bare, and it is only the impressive frescoes protected by the protruding walls and overhanging eaves on the western wall that are of interest: scenes from the lives of the saints and Genesis run along the wall in eight registers and faint traces of the *Last Judgment* are evident in the upper right-hand corner.

GETTING THERE & AWAY
Getting to Solca by public transport can be rather tiresome. There are no longer buses from Gura Humorului to Solca but occasional maxitaxis make the trip. From Rădăuţi there is one bus daily to Solca, via Arbore. Hitching is a good idea; Solca is 13km south of Marginea, which is on the well-travelled road between Suceviţa and Rădăuti.

From Gura Humorului there is one bus daily to Arbore. From Rădăuţi to Arbore, there are three daily buses.

Rădăuţi & Marginea
Rădăuţi (rah-*dah*-oots) is a large and boring market town. The only reason to come is to catch a train to Putna or a bus to the monasteries in Arbore, Solca and Suceviţa.

The bus station is on B-dul Ştefan cel Mare, a block north of Rădăuţi's train station on Str Gării. From the bus station, head east along B-dul Ştefan cel Mare until you reach the central square, Piaţa Unirii.

Nine kilometres west of Rădăuţi towards Suceviţa, is **Marginea**, highly worth a brief stop. The tiny village is renowned for its black earthenware and pottery. **Magopăt Ioan** (☎ 566 296; Marginea 1216; ⊙ 9am-7pm) is a darling shop and adjacent exhibit of locally produced pottery, black and otherwise, and other souvenirs. There's a pottery workshop next door that shows how the stuff is made, and you'll often several sweet elderly ladies sitting about knitting colourful folk costumes. This entire area is a pleasure to explore by bike, as each village has its own charm.

GETTING THERE & AWAY
Five daily trains go from Rădăuţi to Putna (1½ hours), two of which require a change at Gura Putnei, and six to Dorneşti (11 minutes) from where there are three trains to Suceava (1¼ hours).

Buses from Rădăuţi include six a day to Suceava, and two to Suceviţa and Guru Humorului. Oddly, there are none to Putna. Double-check the times posted in the bus station with a ticket clerk.

Putna
Legend has it that Ştefan cel Mare, to celebrate his conquest of the fortress of nearby Chilia against the Turks, climbed to the top of a hill overlooking Putna village, 28km northwest of Rădăuţi, and fired his bow and arrow. Where the first arrow landed in the valley below became the site of Putna Monastery's holy well; the second arrow decided the site of the altar; and the third landing was the site of the bell tower. As you approach **Putna Monastery**, you can see the spot where Ştefan cel Mare stood, marked by a large white cross. The monastery, built between 1466 and 1481, is still home to a very active religious community, with groups of monks chanting Mass just before sunset.

In the large building behind the monastery is **Putna Museum**, where a wealth of treasures from the monastery and surrounding regions are displayed, including medieval manuscripts and the Holy Book that Ştefan cel Mare carried when he went to battle. Outside the church are three bells inscribed in Slavic. The largest of the three, dating from 1484, was strictly reserved for heralding royal deaths.

Compared to other Bucovina monasteries Putna is aesthetically underwhelming but dear to the heart of Romanians. The principal reason that tourists make it out here is that Ştefan cel Mare is buried in the tomb room of the church. Below is the grave of his third wife, Maria Voichiţa. On the left is the grave of their two children, Bogdan and Petru. Above the children's grave is that of Ştefan cel Mare's second wife, Maria of Mangop from Greece.

Some 60 monks live at Putna today, practising icon painting, shepherding, wood sculpting and agriculture.

Daniel the Hermit's Cave (Chilia lui Daniil Sihastrul), 2km from the monastery, is another splendid place worth visiting. Inside is a humble wooden table and memorial plaque to the hermit and seer Daniel Dimitru, born in a village near Rădăuţi in the 15th century. He became a monk at the age of 16 and later moved to Chilia where he dug himself a cave in a rock. To get to Chilia from the monastery, turn right off the main road following the sign for Cabana Putna. Bear left at the fork and continue until you reach a second fork in the road. Turn right here, cross the railway

MOLDAVIA

tracks, and continue over a small bridge, following the dirt road until you see the rock, marked by a stone cross on its top, on your left.

SLEEPING

Some people camp in the field opposite Daniel's Cave at Chilia near the train station.

Cabana Putna (per person incl breakfast €5), signposted 50m off the main road through the village leading to the monastery, has three- and four-bed cabins with shared bathrooms, including breakfast.

GETTING THERE & AWAY

Local trains go to Putna from Suceava five times daily (1¼ hours). The large monastic enclosure is at the end of the road, nearly 2km from the station. From Putna there is also one direct train a day to Iaşi (six hours).

You can do as Prince Charles did in May 2003 and hike the 20km from Putna to Suceviţa Monastery in about five hours (though he went the other way). Follow the trail marked with blue crosses in white squares that starts near the hermit's cave. About 4km down the road you turn off to the left.

VATRA DORNEI

☎ 230 / pop 17,650

A fashionable spa resort during Habsburg times, Vatra Dornei, nestled at the confluence of the Dorna and Bistriţa Rivers in the Dornelor depression, today looks and feels as if it's seen better days – and plans to again in the future. Amid the grand but neglected baroque-style buildings there's a vaguely stale medicinal air that speaks of its past as a spa, but a mini-construction boom signals that the town has not thrown in the mud wrap yet. Indeed, it's not only people with aching whatsits who find reason to visit; the hiking trails directly north of town are lovely, and there's good downhill skiing on Dealul Negrii (1300m). Vatra Dornei is home to Romania's largest sparkling mineral water bottling plants, namely Dorna.

Information

EMERGENCY

Pharmacie (Str Mihai Eminescu 26; ☯ 8am-8pm Mon-Fri, 9am-7pm Sat, 9am-3pm Sun)

INTERNET ACCESS

Internet Club (Hotel Parc; per hr €0.50; ☯ 24hr)
Matrix (Str Republicii 5A; per hr €0.50; ☯ 24hr)

MONEY

Banca Agricolă (Str Vladimirescu 10; ☯ 8.30am-2pm Mon-Fri)

POST & TELEPHONE

Post office (Str Mihai Eminescu 8; ☯ 8am-7pm Mon-Fri, 8am-noon Sat)
Telephone office (Str Mihai Eminescu 16; ☯ 7am-10pm Mon-Wed, 8am-noon & 5pm-9pm Thu-Sun)

TOURIST INFORMATION

Bucovina Vacance Tours (BVT; ☎ 373 709; Str Republicii 5; ☯ 8am-1pm & 5-7pm Mon-Fri, 8am-1pm Sat) Located next to Hotel Călimani's main entrance, this group organises monastery tours, Dracula-themed tours and day trips to Maramureş.
Tourist Centre & Salvamont (☎ 372 767; Str Garii; ☯ 9am-6pm Mon-Fri) This is a good first stop; you can pick up free local maps, including one highlighting the local hiking trails (all 30 of them!) and find out about weather conditions in the mountains. Plus, you can book accommodation in hotels or private homes here.

Sights

Vatra Dornei's **park** (Parcul Staţiune) is beautifully laid out with sprawling avenues, well-groomed lawns and neatly arranged flower beds. Bronze busts of national poet Mihai Eminescu and composers George Enescu and Ciprian Porumbescu gaze out from beneath the trees.

You can taste Vatra Dornei's natural spring waters at the **drinking fountain** in the basement of the fairy-tale single-turreted castle in the west of the park. The bicarbonated water is good for curing stomach ills but not recommended for those with high blood pressure or an aversion to sulfurous water. Adjoining the park on Str Republicii is a grandiose, baroque mansion, once home to a bustling casino in Habsburg times but now undergoing capital renovations as it awaits a future rebirth.

The **Natural History Museum** (Muzeul de Ştiinţe Naturale şi Cinegetică; Str Unirii 3; adult/child €0.40/0.20; ☯ 10am-6pm Tue-Sun) displays flora and fauna from the surrounding Căliman and Rarău Mountains. North of the river, opposite the telephone office, is a small **Ethnographic Museum** (Str Mihai Eminescu; adult/child €0.40/0.20; ☯ 10am-6pm Tue-Sun) which seems to open at whim.

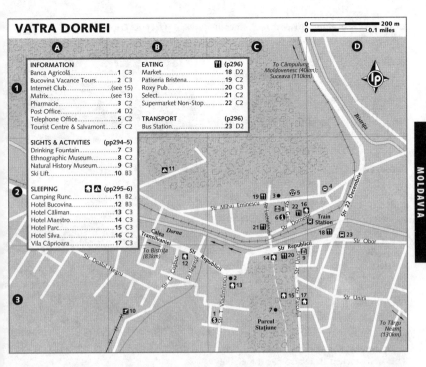

VATRA DORNEI

INFORMATION	
Banca Agricolă	1 C3
Bucovina Vacance Tours	2 C3
Internet Club	(see 15)
Matrix	(see 13)
Pharmacie	3 C3
Post Office	4 D2
Telephone Office	5 C2
Tourist Centre & Salvamont	6 C2

SIGHTS & ACTIVITIES	(pp294–5)
Drinking Fountain	7 C3
Ethnographic Museum	8 C2
Natural History Museum	9 C3
Ski Lift	10 B3

SLEEPING	(pp295–6)
Camping Runc	11 B2
Hotel Bucovina	12 B3
Hotel Căliman	13 C3
Hotel Maestro	14 C3
Hotel Parc	15 C3
Hotel Silva	16 C2
Vila Căprioara	17 C3

EATING	(p296)
Market	18 D2
Patiseria Bristena	19 C3
Roxy Pub	20 C3
Select	21 C2
Supermarket Non-Stop	22 C2

TRANSPORT	(p296)
Bus Station	23 D2

To Câmpulung
Moldovenesc (40km);
Suceava (110km)

Str Mihai Eminescu

Str Dornei

Train
Station

Str 22 Decembrie

Str Obor

Calea Dorna Transilvaniei

To Bistriţa
(83km)

Str Republicii

Str Republicii

Str Unirii

Str Unirii

Str Dealul Negru

Str G Coşbuc

Str Negrii

Str Vladimirescu

Str Parcului

Str Parcului

Parcul
Staţiune

To Târgu
Neamţ
(130km)

MOLDAVIA

There is a **ski lift** (telescaun; return €2; ☉ 10am-5pm Tue-Sun) at the south end of Str George Coşbuc which takes you to the top of Vatra Dornei's main 1300m-high slope on Negrii Hill (Dealul Negrii). It's open year round (but only runs with a minimum of 10 passengers) for those who want to enjoy a summer day's view or the valley's autumn colours.

Sleeping

Vila Căprioara (☎ 372 643; Str Parcului 29; s/d €11/17) The pleasant German-speaking couple who run this villa give it a homy, friendly feel.

Hotel Parc (☎ 0744-964 307; Str Parcului; d €16; 🖳) If you're into true bare-bones places, go with this place set right inside the main park and flanked by a noisy cafe-cum-disco.

Hotel Silva (☎ 371 033; pinaris@assist.ro; Str Dornelor 12; s/d/ste €20/25/37) On the 2nd floor of a commercial complex, this modern (read: lots of chrome and glass and a liberal sprinkling of black) hotel has a fitness centre and a nightclub at your disposal.

Hotel Bucovina (☎ 375 005; Str Republicii 35; s/d/tr €20/27/35) For the price, this is probably the

best deal in town. Though the impressive exteriors that make it look like a massive Swiss chalet are not matched by the interior decor, this is a comfortable place with full services.

Hotel Călimani (☎ 375 314; Str Republicii 5A; s/d/ste €27/35/45) This concrete monster is best used as a landmark than as a place to stay; it's a dour affair. Their apartment suites, however, are surprisingly nice.

Hotel Maestro (☎ 375 288; http://eis.go.ro; Str Republicii; s/d €30/40) If you can afford it, this is a great place to stay. There are only eight (smallish) rooms in this very modern place smack in the centre of town. They run a popular terrace cafe out front, but better still can set you up with ski and snowmobile rentals and accommodation at their lovely Cabana Schiorilor up in the mountains.

Camping Runc (☎ 371 892; tent space/cabin €3/6) This very nice camp ground is on a forest-covered hill overlooking the town from the northeast. It has 43 wooden double cabins with communal showers and toilets. There is a restaurant and bar on the site. To get there, go west along Str Mihai Eminescu until you see a sign on the right.

Eating

There are many eating options along the pedestrianised Str Luceafărului.

Patiseria Bristena (☎ 372 338; Str Mihai Eminescu 28; mains €1-2; ☉ 8am-8pm) In a word: yum. Great cakes and meat-filled pastries, pizza slices and cheap eats create an irresistible aroma in here; the low prices help maintain a wide smile.

Roxy Pub (☎ 0724-587 083; Str Republicii 1; mains €1-3; ☉ 10-2am) The best drinking hole in town is this relaxed hang-out, furnished with wood. Relax here after a day's skiing or hiking. Best of all, there's a Middle Eastern fast-food counter as you enter, serving much more than the usual kebab; their food is superb.

Select (Str Luceafărilui 19; mains €2-4; ☉ 10am-11pm) With an outdoor terrace and decent dinning room serving up standard Romanian dishes, this is one of your best bets in town.

The terrace at Hotel Maestro is also recommended.

Supermarket Non-Stop (Str Dornelor 10; ☉ 24hr) This well-stocked store also has some takeaway meals.

Getting There & Away

The **bus station** (☎ 371 252) is located at the eastern end of town on Str 22 Decembrie. There are eight buses or maxitaxis to Câmpulung Moldovenesc, seven to Gura Humorului, four to Suceava, three to Bistrița, two to both Piatra Neamț and Târgu Neamț and one to both Cluj-Napoca and Rădăuti.

Tickets are sold in advance at the **Agenție de Voiaj CFR** (☎ 371 039) inside the **train station** (☎ 371 197; Str Republicii 1). There are seven daily trains to Suceava (3¼ hours), four of which end up in Iași (5½ hours), three to Timișoara (10½ hours), and one to both Bistrița (five hours) and Oradea (7½ hours.)

AROUND VATRA DORNEI

Vatra Dornei stands in the middle of Romania's most dramatic mountain passes, steeped in legend and famed for their wild beauty and savage landscapes. If you head southwest into Transylvania you cross the

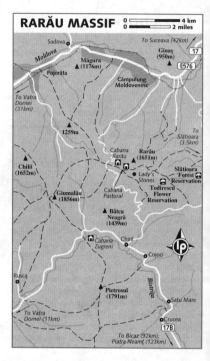

Bârgău Valley and the Tihuta Pass (p163) or, if you've read Bram Stoker's *Dracula*, the Borgo Pass!

In Dorna Candrenilor, 8km west of Vatra Dornei, you can access the **Căliman Mountains**. The highlight of these volcanic mountains is the anthropomorphic rocks, which form a nature reservation called the **12 Apostles Nature Reservation** (Stâncile Doisprezece Apostoli). A trail (marked with blue triangles then red circles) leads from Vatra Dornei to its peak at 1760m. Only tackle this tough climb if you are experienced and have a map and the right gear.

A less challenging route if you have a car is to drive to Dorna Candrenilor, turn left along the road to Poiana Negrii and continue for 14km along road and dirt track until you reach Negrișoara. From here it is a three-hour walk (4km) along a path to the foot of the geological reservation.

Heading north you cross from Moldavia into the Maramureș region via the **Prislop Pass**, which peaks at 1416m (p264).

The road northeast from Vatra Dornei leads via Câmpulung Moldovenesc to Gura

MOLDAVIA

HIKING THE RARĂU MOUNTAINS

The Rarău Mountains, part of the Eastern Carpathians, offer fantastic hiking opportunities. From May to October you can access these mountains and the region's main base for hikers, **Cabana Rarău** (1400m; ☎ 0744-320 496; d €10), from Câmpulung Moldovenesc by car. There's a small restaurant and provisions shop there too. As you enter Câmpulung Moldovenesc from the east, a road on the left is signposted 'Cabana Rarău 14km'. Do not attempt to drive in bad weather unless you have a 4WD, as the road is narrow and extremely pot-holed and rocky in places. Hiking takes three to four hours (follow the red circles).

A second mountain road – slightly less pot-holed – leads up to the cabana from the village of **Pojorâta**, 3km west of Câmpulung Moldovenesc. Hiking takes four to five hours (yellow crosses). This road is not marked on maps. Turn left at the fork after the village post office, cross the railway tracks, then turn immediately left along the dirt road. Note the large stones of Adam and Eve as you enter the village.

Cabana Rarău can also be accessed from the south in the village of **Chiril**, 24km east of Vatra Dornei on the main Vatra Dornei–Durău road. This is the best of the three road options for those determined to drive. Hiking takes three to four hours (blue circles). **Cabana Zugreni** (☎ 230 373 581; d with/without private toilet €13/6), 4km from Chiril on the Vatra Dornei road, is a good option. The adjoining restaurant serves traditional Moldavian meals.

From Cabana Rarău a trail (30 minutes) leads to the foot of Rarău's most prized rocks, the *Lady's Stones* or Princess' Rocks (Pietrele Doamnei). A clutter of crosses crowns the highest (1678m) in memory of the climbers it has claimed. The view from the top is superb.

A trail marked by red stripes and red triangles (five hours) leads from the cabana to the **Slătioara Reservation**. From here another trail (red triangles) leads to the **Todirescu Flower Reservation**.

Humorului from where the trail to Southern Bucovina's monasteries begins.

CÂMPULUNG MOLDOVENESC
☎ 230

This small 14th-century logging and fair town is tucked in the Moldavia Valley at an altitude of 621m. Câmpulung Moldovenesc is a good access point for hiking in the **Rarău Mountains**, 15km to the south. In winter, Câmpulung attracts cross-country skiers. There is also a short 800m ski slope served by a chairlift at the foot of the resort. Between 1786 and 1809 many German miners settled in the region at the invitation of the Habsburg authorities.

A **winter sports festival** takes place in Câmpulung Moldovenesc every year on the last Sunday in January.

Orientation & Information
The main street, Calea Transilvaniei, which runs into Calea Bucovinei, cuts across the town from west to east. The train station is a five-minute walk west of the centre at Str Gării 8. To get to the centre from the main Câmpulung Moldovenesc train station (do not get off at Câmpulung Moldovenesc Est stop), turn left along Str Gării and then right along Str Dimitrie Cantimir until you reach the post office on the corner of Calea Bucovinei. The bus station is at Str Alexander Bogza. From here cut through the market to the left of the station as you exit and you'll see the sign for Hotel Zimbru. Follow that to reach the centre.

The **George Turism travel agency** (☎ 314 567; www.georgeturism.ro in German; Calea Bucovinei 13; 🕑 9am-6pm Mon-Fri) can help you with any of your questions.

Sights
The highlight of Câmpulung Moldovenesc is its bizarre **wooden spoon collection**, displayed in a small house. Love spoons, jewellery made from spoons and a host of other cutlery delights collected by Ioan Ţugui are exhibited in the **museum** (Str Gheorghe Popovici 3; admission €0.25; 🕑 9am-4pm Tue-Sun). Other fun wooden objects are displayed at the **Wood Carving Museum** (Calea Transilvaniei 10; admission €0.25; 🕑 9am-4pm Tue-Sun).

Sleeping

Icar Tours (☎ 524 894; www.icar.ro) in Suceava can help book private rooms here.

Complex Turistic Semenic (☎ 311 714; Str Nicu Dracea 6; d €15) This small, family-run hotel has pleasant, simple rooms, most of which have old ceramic stoves for added warmth in winter. There's also a restaurant serving local dishes, including wild mushrooms from the forest.

Hotel Zimbru (☎ 314 356; rarau-turism@xnet.ro; Calea Bucovinei 1-3; s/d €24/30) This is your typical state-run, 10-storey concrete block that has characterless rooms but friendly service.

Eden Hotel (☎ 314 733; www.hotel-eden.ro; Str Bucovinei 148; s/d/ste €34/46/80) This lovely house has an oasis feel to it and its 12 simple but well-furnished rooms. Service is first-rate, their restaurant excellent and they can also organise folk dance shows and car rental.

Moldova

DAN HERRICK

Moldova

MOLDOVA

Moldova is not exactly what one would call a press darling. If there are any reports at all from this landlocked country, whose location most Europeans don't even know, they highlight intense poverty, illegal organ trading, human trafficking, civil war and communism. Something about wine too.

Such reports about the rarely visited country couldn't possibly conjure up images of sunflower fields, enormous watermelons, bucolic pastoral lands, amazingly friendly people and yes, rivers of delicious wine. They'd also miss the surreal beauty of remote monasteries cut into limestone cliffs, the warmth of villagers who welcome you into their homes and offer fresh peaches, and the sheer vibrancy of urban pleasures in Chişinău, one of Europe's most party-bent capitals.

Moldova's rural countryside is even less developed than Romania's, so the sense of adventure is even more pronounced. Certainly, Moldova lacks the dramatic beauty that has made Romania a tourist draw. There are no mountains here, just gentle rolling plains; no raging rivers, only the tiny Prut and Dniestr. Yet its quieter rhythms unfold with just as much mystery.

Miniature Moldova also has a fascinating ethnic mix, which in the early 1990s erupted into violence when two areas declared their independence: the Turkic Gagauz and the Russian-speaking Transdniestr, where a bloody civil war left over 500 people dead. Today, the areas are calm and visitors get to see what the USSR was like in bizarre Transdniestr.

If coming from Romania, you're likely to notice that prices are generally higher here, despite the poorer economy. Bureaucracy is on the decrease and visitors will find it easy to get anything done the old-fashioned way, by talking to people and figuring it out among yourselves!

MOLDOVA

TOP FIVE

- Stroll **Chişinău's** (p305) tree-studded avenues and experience its kick-ass nightlife
- Take an organised or improvised **wine tour** (p317) at the country's world-famous vineyards, and sip from the fruit of the gods
- See how 13th-century monks lived by visiting fantastic cave monasteries at **Orheiul Vechi** (p320) and **Ţipova** (p321)
- Visit the self-styled republic of Transdniestr and its capital, **Tiraspol** (p327), a surreal, living museum of the Soviet Union
- Hike and canoe during the day and indulge in home-made wine evenings in the **Lower Dniestr National Park** (p322)

Ţipova ★
★ Orheiul Vechi (Trebujeni)
Wine Route
★ ★ Chişinău
★ Tiraspol
Lower Dniestr National Park ★

| POPULATION: 4.43 MILLION | AREA: 33,700 SQ KM | AVERAGE MONTHLY WAGE: $53 |

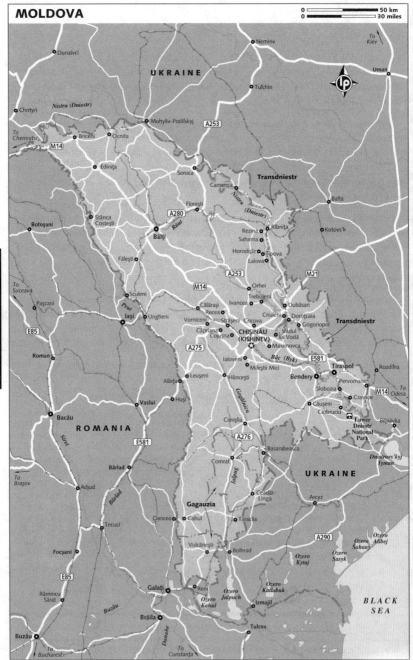

HISTORY
Bessarabia

As with so many Eastern European countries, Moldova has been sliced, diced and tossed from one owner to another in its long history of settlement. Today's Moldova straddles two different historic regions divided by the Dniestr (Nistru) River. Historic Romanian Bessarabia incorporated the region west of the Dniestr, while tsarist Russia governed the territory east of the river (Transdniestr) after defeating the Turks in 1792.

Bessarabia, part of the Romanian principality of Moldavia, was annexed in 1812 by the Russian empire. In 1918, after the October revolution, Bessarabia declared its independence. Two months later it decided to unite with Romania, angering Moscow.

In 1924 the Soviet Union created the Moldavian Autonomous Soviet Socialist Republic (Moldavian ASSR) on the eastern banks of the Dniestr and later moved the capital from Balta (in present-day Ukraine) to Tiraspol.

WWII & Sovietisation

In June 1940 Romanian Bessarabia was occupied by the Soviet army in accordance with the secret protocol attached to the Molotov-Ribbentrop Pact. The Soviet government immediately joined Bessarabia with the southern part of the Moldavian ASSR – namely, Transdniestr. This newly united territory was named the Moldavian Soviet Socialist Republic (Moldavian SSR). The remaining northern part of the Moldavian ASSR was given back to the Ukrainian SSR. Bessarabia experienced terrifying Sovietisation, marked by the deportation of 300,000 Romanians. In June 1941 alone, 5000 families from Bessarabia were deported to Siberia.

In 1941 allied Romanian and German troops attacked the Soviet Union. Bessarabia and Transdniestr fell into Romanian hands. Thousands of Bessarabian Jews were rounded up in labour camps in Transdniestr, from where they were deported to Auschwitz.

In August 1944 the Soviet army reoccupied Transdniestr and Bessarabia and continued where they had left off. In 1949, 25,000 ethnic Moldovans (Romanians) were deported to Siberia and Kazakhstan, followed by some 250,000 from 1950 to 1952. Street names were also changed and Russian-style patronymics were included in people's names. To this day, most Moldovans, though non-Slavic, have names like Andrei, Dimitri and Natasha – rarities in Romania.

Mikhail Gorbachev's policies of *glasnost* (openness) and *perestroika* (restructuring) from 1986 onwards paved the way for the creation of the nationalist Moldovan Popular Front in 1989. In short order, Moldovan written in the Latin alphabet was reintroduced as the official state language and the Moldovan national flag (the Romanian tricolour with the Moldavian coat of arms in its centre) reinstated. Transdniestr stuck to the red banner.

In June 1990 the Moldovan Supreme Soviet passed a declaration of sovereignty. Following the failed coup attempt against Gorbachev in Moscow in August 1991, Moldova declared its full independence.

The Bloody 1990s

Counteracting these nationalist sentiments was an emerging desire for autonomy among ethnic minority groups. In Transdniestr, the Yedinstivo-Unitatea (Unity) movement was formed in 1988 to represent the interests of the Slavic minorities. This was followed in November 1989 by the creation of the Gagauz Halki political party in the south of Moldova, where the Turkic-speaking Gagauz minority was centred. Both ethnic groups' major fear was that an independent Moldova would reunite with Romania.

The Gagauz went on to declare the Gagauz Soviet Socialist Republic in August 1990. A month later the Transdniestrans declared independence, establishing the Dniestr Moldovan Republic. In presidential elections, Igor Smirnov came out as head of Transdniestr, Stepan Topal head of Gagauzia.

Whereas Gaugazia didn't press for more than autonomy within Moldova, Transdniestr settled for nothing less than outright independence. In March 1992 Moldovan president Mircea Snegur declared a state of emergency. Two months later full-scale civil war broke out in Transdniestr when Moldovan police clashed with Transdniestran militia in Bendery (then called Tighina), who were backed by troops from

NOT EXACTLY A NATIONAL SPORT

Did you know that Moldova is world famous for its underwater hockey teams? Well, OK, *infamous* then.

You wouldn't normally associate such a sport as underwater hockey with Moldova (come to think of it, there aren't any countries you'd associate it with, but that's another story...). However, in the 2000 Underwater Hockey Championships held in the world-renowned underwater-hockey metropolis of Hobart, in Tasmania, Australia, the Moldovan men's team puzzled referees and judges by not even knowing how to put their fins and flippers on properly. After being trounced by such stalwarts as Columbia 30-0 and Argentina 23-0, it came out that the entire team had filed for (and eventually received) refugee status with the Australian government.

It's a good thing for Moldovans that Canadians aren't known for their good memories or efficient bureaucracy. Two years later, after much hounding a so-called Moldovan Underwater Hockey Federation based in Tiraspol (in probably the only time Transdniestran officials called themselves 'Moldovan'), the Canadian Embassy in Bucharest granted the women's team visas to participate in the world championships in Calgary.

There was much head-scratching as the Moldovan national anthem was played – and no team came out to play. But how could they? They were in Toronto, filing for refugee status. In this elaborate visa scam, each woman on the team (who no doubt wouldn't know what to do with an underwater puck even if it bit her) had paid organisers some $1200 – not bad for refugee status in Canada.

While this incident sadly spells out an uncertain future for the world of underwater hockey in Moldova, it does speak volumes about the creativity and persistence of Moldovans!

Russia. An estimated 500 to 700 people were killed and thousands wounded in events that shocked the former Soviet Union.

A cease-fire was signed by the Moldovan and Russian presidents, Snegur and Boris Yeltsin, in July 1992. Provisions were made for a Russian-led, tripartite peacekeeping force comprising Russian, Moldovan and Transdniestran troops to be stationed in the region. Troops remain here today, maintaining an uneasy peace.

NATIONAL PARKS & PROTECTED AREAS

Moldova has one nascent national park: the Lower Dniestr National Park (Parcul Naţional Nistrul Inferior), administered by the nonprofit environmental organisation **Biotica** (☎ 22-498 837; www.biotica-moldova.org). Covering over 50,000 hectares of land southeast of Chişinau, it hugs the Dniestr River southward to the border of Ukraine. See p322 for more information.

In addition to this, there are five scientific reserves (totalling 19,378 hectares) and 30 protected natural sites (covering 22,278 hectares). The reserves protect areas of bird migration, old beech and oak forests and important waterways. The Codru Reserve, Moldova's oldest and most frequently vis-

ited, boasts 924 plant species, 138 kinds of birds and 45 mammals. Again, Biotica can provide all information about trips to these sites.

LANGUAGE

In short, a touchy subject. You might find it curious to hear Moldovans avoid mentioning the name of the language they speak, instead referring to it as *limba de stat* (state language) or *limba nostra* (our language). Whether or not there is such a language as Moldovan at all continues to rage among more nationalist circles. The language spoken here is essentially Romanian, but nationalists wishing either to distance themselves from Romanians (who are not overly beloved here) or to snuggle up to Russia insist there is such a language as Moldovan.

Fuel was added to the fire with the 2003 publishing of *Dicţionar Moldovenesc-Românesc*, a Moldovan-Romanian 'dictionary' by Vasile Stati and financed entirely by the Ministry of Culture in yet another politically (ie Communist) motivated move to separate Moldova ever further from Romania. More of a compendium of slang than an actual dictionary, its publication caused a scandal but was unanimously greeted with laughter and dismissal by the general population who know they speak Romanian, no matter what you call it.

The Soviet regime from 1924 onwards attempted to manufacture a 'new' language for its newly created Moldavian ASSR to pave the way for the incorporation of Bessarabia in 1940. Under Soviet 'tutelage', Romanian was written with the Cyrillic alphabet – until 1989! New words were also invented and lists of Romanian words 'polluting Moldovan' drawn up. Some minor differences between Romanian and 'Moldovan' can be heard, and there are varied local expressions. Still, linguists agree that 'Moldovan' is at best a Romanian dialect. The word *mântenesc* is sometimes used for 'thank you' instead of *mulţumesc*.

Recent changes to Romanian have been slow to take root in Moldova; thus you will still see the letter *î* sometimes used even when it is not the first letter in a word. Almost everyone in the republic speaks Russian fluently, and you'll find many flyers, posters and business cards written in Russian only, particularly in Chişinău. In Transdniestr and Gagauzia, Russian is what you'll see on most signs and hear on the street, though Romanian is generally understood.

Traditionally 31 August has been celebrated as **National Language Day**, a national holiday, though since 2001 when Communists got back into power, it has been downplayed considerably.

DANGERS & ANNOYANCES

While you might occasionally run into Soviet-style bureaucracy, it's much less an issue here than in today's Russia; people – even officials! – are generally open and accommodating. While street crime is low (there simply aren't enough foreigners to make this a viable occupation), flashing wealth around is, as in any country, not advisable, especially in places where you might stand out. Be wary of pickpockets on crowded buses and at train stations.

Travelling in the self-declared republic of Transdniestr is safe. Just don't stick your nose into military objects and installations, no matter how pure your intentions; all things military are sensitive topics there.

GETTING THERE & AWAY

Moldova is off the beaten tourist track. Few trains and buses come here from further away than Romania, Ukraine and Hungary, and while there are flights from Western Europe, let's just say it'll be a while before RyanAir flies here. Most flights are eastbound. Most tourists find it easiest to enter via Romania, from where connections are frequent and easy, and then either return to Romania or continue eastward, thereby avoiding the necessity of a double-entry visa. For an up-to-date list of all the open and traversable road borders into Moldova, see www.turism.md/eng/content/69.

If entering Moldova via some parts of the Ukraine, you will pass through Transdniestr, where you might have to purchase a visitor's pass at the border. More often than not, there are no border checks at all from Ukraine into Transdniestr, but then you will probably be stopped when leaving Transdniestr to enter Moldova proper and be made to pay a small fine. For more information on visas, see the Directory chapter (p343).

CHIŞINĂU

☎ 22 / pop 709,900

This may be the capital of one of Europe's poorest countries, but you'd never know it walking its streets. In Chişinău ('kish-i-now' in Moldovan, 'kish-i-nyov' in Russian), Mercedes and Jaguars line up outside one fancy restaurant after another, and fashionably dressed youth strut down boutique-lined avenues. Of course, ask anyone working in those shops – or hanging out at one of the cheaper cafes – how much they earn, and the usual reply would be about $70 a month. The jagged contrast between rich and poor certainly doesn't please the have-nots, but this vibrant, good-natured city is so full of *joie de vivre* that it doesn't get in the way of what's most important here: having a good time.

While photographs of Chişinău tend to show sprawling concrete esplanades smartly bookended by concrete apartment blocks, this is probably the cosiest of all the Soviet-style cities rebuilt after WWII (it was totally destroyed by bombardment and a 1940 earthquake). Just a block away from the main drag you don't feel the concrete at all through the lush foliage that holds the city in its embrace. First chronicled in 1420, Chişinău boasts wide avenues and pleasant parks, and is circled by a ring of parks and lakes.

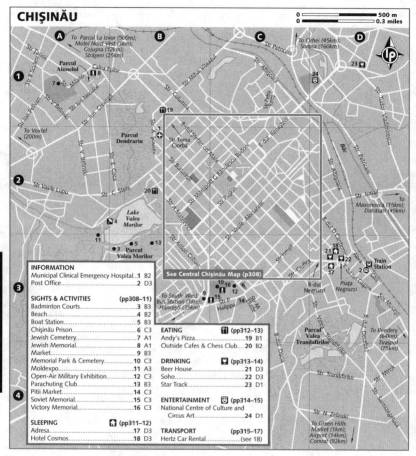

CHIŞINĂU

0 ———— 500 m
0 ———— 0.3 miles

To Parcul La Izvor (500m);
Motel Nord Vest (3km);
Cojuşna (12km);
Străşeni (25km);

To Orhei (45km);
Soroca (160km)

To Voxtel
(200m)

To South-West
Bus Station (1km);
Hânceşti (35km)

See Central Chişinău Map (p308)

To Maximovca (15km);
Dubăsari (45km)

To Bendery
(64km);
Tiraspol
(75km)

To Green Hills
Market (1km);
Airport (14km);
Comrat (92km)

INFORMATION
Municipal Clinical Emergency Hospital..**1**	B2
Post Office...**2**	D3

SIGHTS & ACTIVITIES   (pp308–11)
Badminton Courts......................................**3**	B3
Beach..**4**	B2
Boat Station..**5**	B3
Chişinău Prison...**6**	C3
Jewish Cemetery.......................................**7**	A1
Jewish Memorial.......................................**8**	A1
Market...**9**	B3
Memorial Park & Cemetery.....................**10**	C3
Moldexpo..**11**	A3
Open-Air Military Exhibition....................**12**	C3
Parachuting Club.....................................**13**	B3
Piţii Market...**14**	C3
Soviet Memorial......................................**15**	C3
Victory Memorial.....................................**16**	C3

SLEEPING   (pp311–12)
Adresa..**17**	D3
Hotel Cosmos...**18**	D3

EATING   (pp312–13)
Andy's Pizza..**19**	B1
Outside Cafes & Chess Club....................**20**	B2

DRINKING   (pp313–14)
Beer House...**21**	D3
Soho..**22**	D3
Star Track...**23**	D1

ENTERTAINMENT   (pp314–15)
National Centre of Culture and	
Circus Art...**24**	D1

TRANSPORT   (pp315–17)
Hertz Car Rental...........................(see 18)	

Visitors always marvel at how funky the city is; the Communist government that's been in power since 2001 hasn't put a damper on the nightlife, which swings until the morning hours. One of the positive Soviet legacies the Moldovans inherited is a very Slavic attitude towards partying and enjoying life.

Jews used to comprise 35% of the city's population in 1913; today the figure is about 3%, though recent years have seen a reactivation of the community. In 1903, Chişinău was the scene of a pogrom that resulted in the murder of 49 Jews, 500 injured and 1500 homes and shops vandalised; this was in response to rumours that Jews had ritualistically killed a Christian boy in Dubăsari to make unleavened Passover bread. See www.shtetlinks.jewishgen .org/kishinev for more information about Jewish Chişinău.

More than half of Chişinău's population today is Moldovan; Russians comprise 25% and Ukrainians 13%. As such, Russian is widely used in the city. The city celebrates – and how! – its **City Day** on 14 October, which bleeds into the newly christened **Wine Festival**, which takes place in the first weeks of October. The city's location in the centre of the country makes it an excellent base for day or several-day excursions to other parts of Moldova; it's usually possible to drive anywhere in the small republic and back in a day.

MOLDOVA

Orientation

Chişinău's street layout is a typically Soviet grid system of straight streets.

The train station is on Aleea Gării, a five-minute walk from the centre. Exit the train station, turn right along Aleea Gării to Piaţa Negruzzi, then walk up the hill to Piaţa Libertăţii. From here the main street, B-dul Ştefan cel Mare, crosses the town from southeast to northwest. The city's main sights and parks radiate off this street.

MAPS & PUBLICATIONS

Some city and country maps are still around from the Soviet era, but they're as large as a city block. *Chişinău the Touristic Scheme* ($1.50), published by STRIH, is a good reference.

There are nearly half a dozen decent guides and booklets about the city, the best of which is the hilarious *Chişinău Guide* ($3) published by **Exclusive** (☎ 274 885; mihodo@usa.net). Written with an ironic sense of humour, the booklet describes the country and its people, and has detailed listings of places to see in and around the capital. **Zingan** (☎ 212 087; pavel@zingan.com) has created two stunning CD-ROMs – one about Chişinău, and one about Moldova (with a planned third one about the Wine Route) – virtual guides chock-full of photos, videos, maps and up-to-date listings. They can be found at bookshops, ordered by email or from the homepage of www.allmoldova.com.

Information

For directory assistance, dial ☎ 909 (in Romanian/Moldovan and Russian only).

BOOKSHOPS

Cartea Academica (Map p308; B-dul Ştefan cel Mare 148; 9am-6pm Mon-Sat)

Cartea Universală (Map p308; B-dul Ştefan cel Mare 54; 9.30am-8pm)

Librărie Eminescu (Map p308; ☎ 246 516; B-dul Ştefan cel Mare 180; 9am-6pm Mon-Fri, 10am-5pm Sat)

Oxford University Press (Map p308; ☎ 228 987; Str Mihai Eminescu 64; 9am-6pm Mon-Fri, 10am-5pm Sat)

CULTURAL CENTRES

Alliance Française (Map p308; ☎ 234 510; Str Sfatul Ţării 18; 10am-6.30pm Tue-Sat) They have a well-equipped *mediathèque* and host regular cultural events.

EMERGENCY & MEDICAL SERVICES

Contact the US embassy (p338) for a list of English-speaking doctors.

Felicia (Map p308; ☎ 223 725; B-dul Ştefan cel Mare 62; 24hr) Well-stocked drugstore.

Hotel National (Map p308; ☎ 540 305; B-dul Ştefan cel Mare 4, 4th floor) The emergency suite on the 4th floor provides health care.

Municipal Clinical Emergency Hospital (☎ 248 435; www.ournet.md/~scmu; Str Toma Ciorba 1; 24hr) Provides a variety of emergency services, and a good likelihood of finding English-speaking staff.

Pharmacy inquiries (☎ 725 501; 24hr) Having trouble finding your favourite brand? Call this free phone service to find out in which pharmacy it's stocked.

For emergency assistance dial the following:

Fire ☎ 901
Police ☎ 902
Ambulance ☎ 903

INTERNET ACCESS

Cave Net (Map p308; ☎ 247 467; Str Mitropolit Dosoftei 122; per hr $0.45; 24hr)

Central telephone office (Map p308; B-dul Ştefan cel Mare 65; per hr $0.60; 24hr)

MONEY

There are ATMs all over the centre, in all the hotels and shopping centres. Currency exchanges are concentrated around the bus and train stations and also along B-dul Ştefan cel Mare.

Eximbank (Map p308; ☎ 272 583; B-dul Ştefan cel Mare 6; 9am-5pm Mon-Fri) Can give cash advances in foreign currency.

Victoriabank (Map p308; ☎ 233 065; Str 31 August 1989, 141; 9am-5pm Mon-Fri) American Express' representative in Moldova.

POST & TELEPHONE

Central post office (Map p308; ☎ 227 737; B-dul Ştefan cel Mare 134; 8am-7pm Mon-Sat, 8am-6pm Sun) There is also a post office on Aleea Gării (Map p306 8am-8pm).

Central telephone office (Map p308; B-dul Ştefan cel Mare 65; 24 hr) Book international calls inside the hall marked 'Convorbiri Telefonice Internaţionale'. Faxes and telegrams can also be sent from here. Receive faxes at ☎ 549 155.

TOURIST INFORMATION

There is no Western-style tourist information centre in Moldova, but plenty of agencies can give you information. Most offer discounted rates at some hotels.

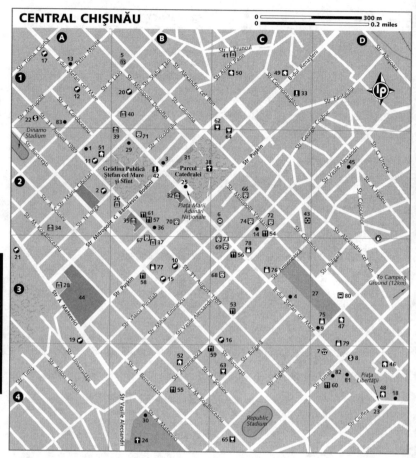

CENTRAL CHIŞINĂU

Moldovar Tur (Map p308; ☎ 270 488; moldovatur@travels.md; B-dul Ştefan cel Mare 4; ◷ 9am-5pm Mon-Fri) This official state tourist agency can arrange tours of the Cricova winery (see Wine Route, p317; slightly more expensive than dealing with Cricova directly, but fewer headaches) and other vineyard tours. They also can find you chauffeured cars.

România Tourism Office (Map p308; ☎ 222 354; B-dul Ştefan cel Mare 151-153; ◷ 9am-5pm Mon-Fri) Get info about Romania and make advance bookings here.

Soleil Tours (Map p308; ☎ 271 312; www.soleil.md; B-dul Negruzzi 5; ◷ 9am-6pm Mon-Fri) A very efficient organisation, they can book accommodation and transport tickets but are known for their multiday excursions into remote Moldova, taking in monasteries and places of interests and incorporating rural homestays.

Voiaj (Map p308; ☎ 546 464; www.voiaj.md; B-dul Negruzzi 7; ◷ 8am-7pm Mon-Fri, 9am-6pm Sat, 9am-5pm Sun) This experienced, customer-friendly agency runs all sorts of tours throughout the country, books plane tickets and can get anything else you need done.

Sights

No one can accuse Chişinău of being over-burdened with tourist sights. Lacking in 'must-sees', it's more a pleasant city to wander about in and discover as you go. Sadly, little remains of its historic heart due to heavy bombing during WWII. There are still some great museums and parks however, and it is fun to see how Communist iconography merges with symbols of Moldovan nationalism.

A good place to begin is smack in the centre, where Chişinău's best-known parks oppose each other diagonally, forming two diamonds at the city's core. The highlights here are the Holy Gates (1841), more commonly known as Chişinău's own **Arc de Triomphe** (Map p308). To its east sprawls **Parcul Catedralei** (Cathedral Park; Map p308), dominated by the city's main **Orthodox Cathedral** (Map p308) with its lovely bell tower from 1836. On the northwestern side of the park is a colourful 24-hour **flower market** (Map p308).

Government House (Map p308; Piaţa Marii Adună), where cabinet meets, is the gargantuan building opposite the Holy Gates. Parliament convenes in **Parliament House** (Map p308; B-dul Ştefan cel Mare 123) further north. Opposite this is the **Presidential Palace** (Map p308).

Grădina Publica Stefan Cel Mare şi Sfint (Ştefan cel Mare Park; Map p308) is the city's main strolling, cruising area. The park entrance is guarded by a 1928 **statue** (Map p308) of Ştefan himself. The medieval prince of Moldavia is the greatest symbol of Moldova's strong, brave past. Every Moldovan will be happy to tell you that during Ştefan's 40-year reign, he lost a mere two battles (out of anywhere from 34 to 47, depending on your source's level of enthusiasm). In the northeast sec-

tion of the park is the large **Cinema Patria** (Map p308; ☎ 232 905; B-dul Ştefan cel Mare 103), built by German prisoners of war in 1947, and still showing films to this day.

The **central market** (Map p308; see Eating) spreads out across a huge area along Str Mitropolit Varlaam, around the bus station. The constant activity of the bustling crowds and tradespeople is reminiscent of Istanbul. Porters scurry around with trolleys to carry goods away, cars honk like crazy as they madly try to squeeze through the bustling crowds, women spit out sunflower seeds and old men huddle in groups haggling for the best bargain.

JEWISH CHIŞINĂU

North of the bus station is a maze of rundown, dusty streets. Many of these streets formed the Chişinău Jewish ghetto. On the street leading east from B-dul Renaşterii to Str Fantalului is a **memorial** (Map p308) to the martyrs and victims of the Chişinău ghetto, inscribed in Hebrew, Moldovan and Russian. At Str Rabbi Ţirilson 4 are the remains of a **yeshiva** (Map p308), Chişinău's Jewish school, which functioned until WWII. Chişinău's only remaining working **synagogue** (Map p308) is close by at Str Habad

Lubavia 8. Before WWII there were over 70 synagogues in Chişinău, each serving a different trade. Glass blowers worshipped at this one.

The city's **Jewish cemetery** (Map p306; Str Milano) is northwest of the centre, next to Parcul Alunelul. Most graves are unkempt and overgrown. Ruins of an old synagogue lie next to the cemetery's surrounding stone wall. In Parcul Alunelul there is a **memorial** (Map p306) to the Jews killed in the 1903 pogrom. The remains of the victims were moved here after the cemetery in which they were buried was bulldozed by the Communists in the 1960s. To get to the park and cemetery take bus No 1 from B-dul Ştefan cel Mare and get off at the Parcul Alunelul stop. Cross the road and walk up the hill and along Str Milano.

MUSEUMS

The **National History Museum** (Map p308; ☎ 242 194; muzeum@mac.md; Str 31 August 1989, 121A; admission $0.25; 9am-6pm Tue-Sat) is the granddaddy of Chişinău's museums, and well worth visiting. It has archaeological artifacts from Orheiul Vechi including Golden Horde coins, Soviet-era weaponry and a huge WWII diorama on the 1st floor where you can speak to a man who spent 12 years as a political prisoner at a worker's camp in desolate Vorkuta in northern Siberia. A statue of Lupoaica Romei (the wolf of Rome) and the abandoned children Romulus and Remus stands in front of the museum. To Moldovans, this is a symbol of their Latin ancestry.

The **Muzeul de Arte Plastice** (National Museum of Fine Arts ; Map p308; ☎ 241 730; Str 31 August 1989, 115; adult/child $0.60/0.30; 10am-6pm Tue-Sun) has an interesting collection of contemporary European (mostly Romanian and Moldovan) art, folk art, icons and medieval knick-knacks. Opposite is the **National Library** (Map p308; ☎ 221 475; Str 31 August 1989, 78a; 9am-5pm Sat-Thu).

The **Archaeology and Ethnography Museum** (Map p308; ☎ 238 307; Str G Bănulescu Bodoni 35; admission $0.15; 10am-6pm Tue-Sat) displays reconstructions of traditional houses from Moldova's different regions and has a colourful exhibition of traditional handwoven rugs, carpets and wall hangings.

National Ethnographic and Nature Museum (Map p308; ☎ 244 002; Str M Kogălniceanu 82; adult/child $1/0.50, English guided tour $5; 10am-6pm Tue-Sun) has some pop art, lots of stuffed animals and exhibits covering the sciences of geology, botany and zoology. The highlight is a life-size reconstruction of a mammal skeleton that was discovered in the Rezina region in 1966.

A few blocks south of here is the state university. Nearby is the **Chişinău History Museum** (Map p308; ☎ 241 584; Str A Mateevici 60A; admission $0.40; 10am-6pm Tue-Sun). It surveys the city's history from its founding with archaeological exhibits and photographs; it's a treat mainly for the old water tower (1892) it's housed in. This is the main meeting place for the Chişinău branch of the notorious **Hash House Harriers** (www.ch3.md). Their bimonthly runs and drink fests to oblivion start here.

Several blocks northeast of the central parks is the **Pushkin Museum** (Map p308; ☎ 292 685; Str Anton Pann 19; admission $0.40; 10am-6pm Tue-Sun), housed in a cottage where Russian poet Alexandr Pushkin (1799–1837) spent an exiled three years between 1820 and 1823. It was here that he wrote *The Prisoner of the Caucacus* and other classics – that is, when he wasn't involved in the amorous intrigues, hard-drinking and occasional violence of his social circles in what was then a rough-around-the-edges distant outpost of the Russian empire.

SOUTH OF THE CENTRE

Bounded by Str A Mateevici and Str Ismail is a **memorial park** (Map p306), dominated by a **victory memorial** to the Soviet army in 1945. An eternal flame burns in the centre in memory of Chişinău's unknown soldiers who died in WWII. Soldiers' graves line the boundaries of the park and there is a small **military cemetery** at its northern end. In the centre of the park is a memorial to those who died during the fight for Moldovan independence in the early nineties. At the far northern end of the park is the **civil cemetery** (Cimitrul Central; Map p308), known locally as the Armenian cemetery, whose main entrance is on the corner of Str A Mateevici and Str Armenească. The blue and silver-domed **All Saints Church** (Map p308) in the centre of the cemetery dates from 1830.

South of the cemeteries, on the corner of Str P Halippa and Str Vasile Alecsandri, is another typically monstrous **Soviet memorial** (Map p306), with a small **market** (Map p306; 7am-4pm) opposite it.

Outside the east border of the park is a small **open-air military exhibition** (Map p308; free admission; 10am-6pm Tue-Sun). It displays Soviet-made tanks, fighter planes and other military toys inherited from Moldova's armed forces. Kids like to swing from the plane wings and tank guns, which point towards the overcrowded **Chişinău Prison** (Map p306), on the opposite corner. Across Str P Halippa is the **Pitii Market** (Map p306; 7am-4pm).

PARKS & LAKES

Chişinău locals' favoured haunt is **Lake Valea Morilor** (Map p306), just west of the centre. Steps lead to the lake and surrounding park from Str A Mateevici (opposite the university). Bus No 29a from the city centre stops outside the university entrance to the park.

The **beach** (Map p306) on the lake's northwestern shores gets packed with sunbathers and swimmers at weekends. You can hire canoes, rowing and paddle boats from the **boat station** (Map p306; per hr $1.50; 10am-9pm Jun-Aug) on the lake's southern shores. There are **badminton courts** (Map p306) close to the university sports school on the southern shore. High-flyers should hike up to the **parachuting club** (Map p306; 223 563; per jump $1; 8am-11pm), just back from the southeastern side of the lake. Get strapped in and plummet 40m on their parachute jump machine – the views are great from the top, where your stomach is likely to remain.

Moldexpo (Map p306; 747 419; Str Ghioceilor 1), also inside Parcul Valea Morilor, is an enormous international exhibition centre constantly hosting major expositions; lots of pouring goes on here during October's Wine Festival. Many tourists come here, however, to see the demoted Communist triumvirate of Lenin, Marx and Engels guarding the entrance. Though they were ignominiously moved here from a prize spot in front of the Parliament building, the pedestals are often overflowing with flowers.

Northwest of the centre on the road to Cojuşna and Ungheni is Chişinău's largest park, **Parcul La Izvor**, on Calea Eşilor. It is dominated by three interconnecting lakes, which you can explore with rented **canoes and rowing boats** (starting at per hour €1). Opposite the park's southern entrance is a **cable-car** station ($0.30 per trip; 7am-noon & 1-7pm Mon-Sat)

that makes a three-minute journey across the valley. To get to the park, take trolleybus No 1, 8 or 23 to the last stop. Maxitaxi (microbus) No 11 runs from Str Studenţilor in the centre to Calea Eşilor.

Sleeping

BUDGET

Hotel Meridian (Map p308; 220 428; meridian@ moldovacc.md; Str Tighina 42; dm with 2-5 beds $5-8 per person, s/d $17/25, d with private shower $30, ste $50) This is for true budget-seekers or lovers of exotic locales; it faces the bus station and has become nearly engulfed by the sprawling central market. Peaceful it's not, but surprisingly it's clean and pleasant, and the staff are very accommodating. They'll even pick you up from the train station ($5) or airport ($10 – three times cheaper than most agencies and hotels charge). All rooms except the dorm rooms have private toilets.

Motel Nord Vest (759 828; Calea Eşilor 30; s/d $20/25) This pleasant 100-bed motel is 3km northwest of the centre on the main Chişinău–Cojuşna highway. The motel has a tennis court, sauna and excellent restaurant and bar. Maxitaxi (minibus) Nos 135 and 136 as well as all buses to Cojuşna stop right in front.

Hotel Turist (Map p308; 220 637; B-dul Renaşterii 13; s $20-26, d $25, ste $40-130) For a cool blast of the Soviet past, try this friendly place: it

---

AUTHOR'S CHOICE

Adresa (Map p306; 544 392; adresa@mdi.net; B-dul Negruzzi 1; apts from $20; 24hr) For short or long-term stays, this reliable agency offers great alternatives to hotels, renting out one- to three-room apartments throughout the city. Though often in large concrete buildings, they are completely private, comfortable and have kitchens. It's also a great way to live as the locals do, using rusty lifts (elevators) or climbing staircases somewhat less than sparkling. Still, they're all safe and clean. Check out the photo album of their options before you agree on one and see where the apartment is on their map. Most aren't right in the centre but are a short taxi ride away. Most importantly, Adresa also handles visa registration.

overlooks a giant Soviet memorial to Communist youth and sports a snazzy socialist mural on its façade. Rooms are comfortable, if slightly kitsch.

Hotel Zarea (Map p308; ☎ 227 625; Str Anton Pann 4; s/d $25/35) This drab high-rise is cheap, but not as cheap as it should be considering the dour rooms. Still, it's decent enough and rooms have private toilets. There's a bar and billiard club.

MID-RANGE

Hotel Naţional (Map p308; ☎ 540 305; mtur@dnt .md; B-dul Ştefan cel Mare 4; s/d $36/48; ⚒) This 17-floor giant and its 319 ho-hum rooms is run by Moldova Tur. There are good services here like a small post office, a medical care room, shops, bar and restaurant.

Hotel Cosmos (Map p306; ☎ 542 757; cosmos@ moldova.net; Piaţa Negruzzi 2; d $49, ste $89-189; ⚒) There's no good reason to stay in this concrete tower with dull, plasticised, over-priced rooms save for access to the shopping centre downstairs, their full service desk and central location.

TOP END

Mesogios (Map p308; ☎ 278 498; Str Armenească 23; apts $75-130; ⚒ 💻) Each of their beautiful, ultra-modern apartments is slightly different, some split level, some with restored furniture, and all of them fully equipped and with kitchenettes. The building, peeking through some trees on a quiet stretch of road, is a lovely example of Art Nouveau.

Jolly Alon (Map p308; ☎ 232 233; www.jollyalon .com; Str Maria Cibotari 37; s/d $120/140, ste $145-195) The enticing sofas at reception are enough to make you want to check in immediately. Though the rooms aren't quite as luxurious, they are very spacious. Be sure to ask for one with a view over the park.

Flowers (Map p308; ☎ 277 262; hotelflowers@hotbox .ru; Str Anestiade 7; s/d/ste $120/140/160; ⚒ ✉ 💻) If your credit limit's in good standing, this is the place. Enormous rooms with high ceilings are exquisitely decorated with tasteful restraint, incorporating paintings by local artists and, of course, a jungle's worth of plants and flowers. Prices include breakfast and supper.

Eating

The assortment of great places to eat in Chişinău deserves a separate chapter; these are some of the best, but we encourage you to explore others that look interesting. See also Drinking p313, as many pubs also have full menus.

CAFES

When the sun shines, outdoor cafes sprout like mushrooms. A popular terrace is outside the Opera & Ballet Theatre (p314). There are also some good outdoor cafes opposite the main entrance to the university on Str A Mateevici and in the opposite courtyard leading to Parcul Valea Morilor. At the northern end of Str A Mateevici is another courtyard filled with outdoor cafes and chess fiends. The **chess club** (Map p306) is in the same courtyard.

Green Hills (Map p308; ☎ 220 451; B-dul Ştefan cel Mare 77; ⏰ 8.30am-10pm Mon-Sat, 10am-10pm Sun) Though the meals are delicious, most come here for a quick fix – great coffee, coffee cocktails or beer, and of course to people-watch while sitting on the city's main drag.

QUICK EATS

For the cheapest of cheap eats, there are some kiosks and small 'cafes' around the bus station and central market, where a dish of mystery meat or meat-filled pastries are less than $1. Most go there for beer and vodka shots.

Andy's Pizza (Map p306; ☎ 508 015; B-dul Ştefan cel Mare 169; mains $2-4; ⏰ 10am-11pm) This popular chain has locations all around Chişinău, but this is its slickest, most stylish branch, with a high-tech look that makes it popular with a young, on-the-move clientele. The thick and gooey pizzas, spaghetti and chicken wings keep clients happily purring.

Quickie (Map p308; ☎ 265 563; Str Ismail 46; mains $1-2; ⏰ 9am-11pm) The Turkish fast food isn't bad here, with şaşliks, other meat dishes and salads.

RESTAURANTS

La Taifas (Map p308; ☎ 227 692; www.lataifas.com; Str Bucureşti 67; mains $2-4; ⏰ 11am-midnight) Here you can sit and watch as bread is cooked the old-fashioned way in a wood-fired oven at the back of the restaurant while you're serenaded by a panpipe player. The menu, written in Romanian, French and English, includes the delicious *ciulama* (chicken in wine sauce) served with *mămăligă* as well as other traditional Moldovan fare.

Green Hills (Map p308; ☎ 220 451; Str 31 August 1989, 76; mains $2-4; 🕙 9am-midnight) What they saved on decor, they've passed on to you with their reasonably priced, excellent food. There's a large, extremely pleasant terrace (where they sell a good selection of foreign-language newspapers) that's perfect for a sit-down meal of a large selection of meat and vegetable dishes. This is run by the same bunch who operate the Green Hills cafe and supermarket.

Oraşul Vechi (Old City; Map p308; ☎ 225 063; Str Armenească 24; mains $2-7; 🕙 noon-midnight) One of your best bets is this stylish folk restaurant which doesn't overdo the folk thematic. Be sure to sit in the smaller of their two rooms, a cosy 22-seat old-style dining hall; the other one is formal and stuffy. Fish is their speciality with shark and octopus on the un-PC section of the menu.

Class (Map p308; ☎ 227 774; Str Vasile Alecsandri 121; mains $3-6; 🕙 11am-midnight) One of the country's rare Lebanese restaurants, Class doesn't disappoint with excellent starters, falafel and eggplant dishes. There are waterpipes for smoking from ($2.50), and Friday evening there's exotic dancing and a $10 all-you-can-eat buffet.

Symposium (Map p308; ☎ 211 318; Str 31 August 1989, 78; mains $4-8; 🕙 11am-midnight) Though not as expensive as some top-class restaurants in town, this can be called one of the city's top dining experiences in terms of elegance and refinement. In this cellar refitted with antiques, the French-style cuisine is succulent, with lamb dishes their speciality. There's a large selection of local wines.

El Paso (Map p308; ☎ 504 100; mains $3-11; Str Armenească 10) To get your Mexican fix, head to this excellent, comfortable place. The menu runs the gamut from quesadillas to salmon in chili sauce and pork with chocolate-almond sauce!

Mesogios (Map p308; ☎ 278 498; Str Armenească 23; mains $6-12; 🕙 12.30am-11pm) Seafood is the focus here, with fish imported from the Mediterranean. There are meat dishes and Moldovan specialities too in this elegant dining room which incorporates some Art Nouveau design elements to match the building's impressive exteriors.

SELF-CATERING

The **central market** (Map p308; Piaţa Centrală; 🕙 7am-5pm) has since 1825 been the place where Moldovans haggle over prices for fresh produce. It's well worth a visit for its choice of fresh food and lively ambience. It sprawls out around the central bus station on Str Bendery, and Str Armenească. There's always something going on here at all times of the day or night.

Slightly out of the center is **Green Hills Market** (Map p308; B-dul Decebal 139B; 🕙 9am-9pm) – one of the best-stocked supermarkets in town. Their B-dul Ştefan cel Mare 77 location has a good grocery section too, and is more convenient.

Drinking

Dublin Irish Pub (Map p308; ☎ 245 855; www.irish pub-md.com; Str Bulgară 27; mains $4-8; 🕙 10-1am) The atmosphere is always lively at this relatively expensive but popular Celtic-cum-Moldovan Irish pub. The bar section, which draws the biggest crowds, is truly cosy – that's where they've really got it going on. Yet the pricey restaurant is a temptation as well with tantalisingly named dishes such as Cock-a-leekie (leek with duck, chicken, prunes and veggies stewed in Guiness). A pint of the good stuff runs to about $3.

AUTHOR'S CHOICE

Cactus Café (Map p308; ☎ 504 094; www.cactus.md; Str Armenească 41; mains $1.50-4; 🕙 9am-10pm) This is a true winner. The eclectic interior decor (Wild West meets urban bohemian, but with grace and humour) is matched by the city's most creative menu. There are incredible breakfasts (a real rarity in these parts), lots of vegetarian meals (soy meat!), wild plates such as turkey with bananas and the country's most killer gazpacho. Even their web site's a gas.

Beer House (Map p308; ☎ 756 127; B-dul Negruzzi 6/2; mains $3-6; 🕙 11am-11pm) Of all Chişinău's hot dining places, you'll be returning to this brewery-cum-restaurant again and again – most likely for its four delicious home-brewed beers, but also for its excellent menu, which ranges from chicken wings and soups to rabbit and chicken grilled in cognac. Its relaxed ambience and impeccable service add to the charm.

MOLDOVA

Déjà Vu (Map p308; ☎ 227 693; Str Bucureşti 67; ✆ 11am-2am) This is a true cocktail bar, where the drinks menu is tantalising and where the bartenders twirl glasses with aplomb. There is also a small dining hall serving meals, but most come here to lounge about looking fabulous with multicoloured cocktails perched in their hands.

Robin Pub (Str Alexandru cel Bun 83; ✆ 11am-1am) A friendly local pub feel reigns supreme in this relaxed, tastefully decorated hang-out – an ideal place to forget about the world for hours in a down-to-earth, unpretentious atmosphere.

CLUBS

Chişinău rocks in all directions throughout the night, but in some of the larger clubs be prepared to have to walk through metal detectors and deal with tough-guy posturing from goonish doormen. To cut the pretension and bop with a college crowd, try the **university cultural house** (Str M Kogălniceanu 65A; ✆ after 8pm Fri-Sat).

Black Elephant: the Underground Club (Map p308; ☎ 234 715; Str G Bănulescu Bodoni 78a; ✆ 3pm-6am) You know you're in for something different when you see the bust of Frank Zappa in the entrance. A highlight of the club scene, this place mainly hosts jazz evenings, but something different goes on here every night. Film projections (often jazz-related) and performances are also on the menu. There are also billiard tables. Look for the black door with a large guitar perched above.

Soho (Map p306; ☎ 275 800; B-dul Negruzzi 2/4; ✆ 10pm-4am Tue-Sun) The best disco in town has lots of theme nights, special DJs and the occasional gay night. The doormen might try to lead male customers into their next-door strip club (though not on gay night!), but it's on the dance floor that the real action is; this is a slick, lively, fun club. The crowd is mainly early 20s, though 'middle-aged customers are also welcome'.

Star Track (Map p306; ☎ 496 207; Str Chievskaia 7; ✆ 10pm-4am Tue-Sun) The dark interior sports comfortable sofas and intimate booths where love-struck couples can smooch while keeping one eye open to catch the lacy dance performances in which scantily clad men and women prance around to techno tunes.

Entertainment

Posters listing what's on where are pasted on the *teatrul concerte* noticeboard outside the Opera & Ballet Theatre on B-dul Ştefan cel Mare. The English-language magazine *Welcome* runs a fortnightly calendar of cultural events.

CIRCUS

Itching to see the man in the flying trapeze? Head to the loftily titled **National Centre of Culture and Circus Art** (Map p306; ☎ 496 803; B-dul Renaşterii 33; box office ✆ 9am-6pm), across the river. Performances are held at 6.30pm Friday, and noon, 3pm and 6.30pm Saturday and Sunday. Bus No 27 from B-dul Ştefan cel Mare goes there.

LIVE MUSIC

Black Elephant (see Clubs, above) has nightly jazz music concerts. Classical concerts and organ recitals are held at the **Sala cu Orgă** (Organ Hall; Map p308; ☎ 225 404; B-dul Ştefan cel Mare 79) next to the Mihai Eminescu National Theatre. Performances start at 6 pm and tickets are sold at the box office in the Eminescu theatre.

Moldova's National Philharmonic is based at the **Philharmonic Concert Hall** (Map p308; ☎ 224 505; Str Mitropolit Varlaam 78).

SPECTATOR SPORTS

Moldovans are big football fans and they have two stadiums to prove it. The main **Republic Stadium** (Stadionul Republican), south of the centre, has floodlighting. The main entrance is on Str Ismail, with a smaller entrance at the southern end of Str Bucureşti. The entrance to the smaller **Dinamo Stadium** (Stadionul Dinamo) is north of the centre on the corner of Str Bucureşti and Str Lazo. In fact, Moldovans like football so much there's an American football team called the Chişinau Barbarians that holds occasional matches, in full gear.

THEATRE, OPERA & BALLET

The **Opera & Ballet Theatre** (Map p308; ☎ 244 163; B-dul Ştefan cel Mare 152; box office ✆ 10am-2pm & 5-7pm) is home to the esteemed national opera and ballet company. They mainly stage classics but some modern pieces are occasionally performed. Tickets costs upwards of $3.

If your Moldovan is up to snuff, you'll get a few belly laughs from the plays that are staged at the **Satirical Theatre** (Teatrul Satiricus; Map p308; ☎ 224 034; Str Mihai Eminescu 55). Contemporary Romanian productions can be seen at the **Mihai Eminescu National Theatre** (Map p308; ☎ 221 177; B-dul Ştefan cel Mare 79; ✆ box office 10am-1pm & 3-6pm) founded in 1933, while plays in Russian are performed at the **Chekhov Drama Theatre** (Teatrul Dramatic A Cehov; Map p308; ☎ 223 362; Str Pârcălab 75), situated where Chişinău's choral synagogue was until WWII.

The **Luceafărul Theatre** (Poetic Star Youth Theatre; Map p308; ☎ 224 121, Str Veronica Micle 7), stages more alternative productions. Productions in Moldovan and Russian are held at the **Licurici Puppet Theatre** (Map p308; ☎ 245 273; Str 31 August 1989, 121; box office ✆ 9am-2pm Tue-Sun). Performances the kids will enjoy despite the language barrier usually start at 11am daily.

Various cabarets, musicals and local theatre group productions take place at the **National Palace** (Map p308; ☎ 213 544; Str Puşkin 21; box office ✆ 11am-5pm).

Shopping

Cricova (Map p308; ☎ 222 775; B-dul Ştefan cel Mare 126; ✆ 10am-7pm Mon-Fri, 10am-6pm Sat, 10am-4pm Sun) Definitely worth a visit, especially if you won't be taking the Cricova tour, is this commercial outlet of the Cricova wine factory. It stocks many types of affordable Cricova wines and champagnes (only $2 to $5 each), and the crystal glasses to drink them in.

Ialoveni (Map p308; B-dul Ştefan cel Mare 128; ✆ 9am-6pm Mon-Fri, 10am-4pm Sat-Sun) This is the outlet for the Ialoveni sherry factory; staff will help you get loaded down with bottles of the good stuff.

Cosjuşna (Map p308; Str Tighina 53; ✆ 9am-6pm Mon-Sat 10am-4pm Sun) Get some of this winery's finest for as little as $1 per bottle!

Unic (Map p308; B-dul Ştefan cel Mare 8; ✆ 8am-7pm Mon-Sat) This main shopping centre is redolent of Soviet times but will have everything you need.

Galeria L (Map p308; ☎ 221 975; Str Bucureşti 64; ✆ 10am-7pm Mon-Fri, 10am-5pm Sat) This place holds temporary art exhibitions but also sells small works of art and souvenirs crafted by local artists.

Getting There & Away

AIR

Moldova's only airport is in Chişinău, 14.5km southeast of the centre. It has only international flights.

All international flights to Moldova use Chişinău (Kishinev) airport. Moldova has three national airlines:

Moldavian Airlines (Map p308; ☎ 549 339, B-dul Ştefan cel Mare 3, ☎ 525 506 airport; www.mdv .md) offers 12 weekly flights to Timişoara, and two daily flights to Budapest, from where it has connections to other European destinations.

Air Moldova (Map p308; ☎ 546 464, B-dul Negruzzi 8, ☎ 525 506 airport) is the state carrier for Moldova, with direct flights to Amsterdam, Istanbul, Larnaca, Minsk, Moscow, Paris, St Petersburg, Sofia and Yekaterinburg.

Transaero (Map p308; ☎ 542 454; www.transaero.md; B-dul Ştefan cel Mare 4, ☎ 525 413 airport) has three weekly flights to Amsterdam and Rome, two to Paris and Prague, one or two daily flights to Bucharest, Moscow and Istanbul, two daily flights to Budapest, and a daily flight to Vienna.

BUS

Chişinău has two bus stations. Most buses within Moldova depart from the **central bus station** (Autogară Centrală; Map p308; ☎ 542 185), behind the central market on Str Mitropolit Varlaam. Tickets cannot be bought in advance.

Buses and maxitaxis go to Tiraspol and Bendery every 20 to 35 minutes from 6.30am to 6.30pm, with reduced services until 10pm. Other services include 12 daily buses to Străşeni, and regular buses to Bălţi, Recea, Ediniţa and Briceni. There are buses every half-hour between 9.15am and 10pm to Orhei. At least seven daily buses or maxitaxis go to Bucharest ($14; 12 hours).

Bus services to/from Comrat, Hânceşti and other southern destinations use the less crowded southwestern bus station (Autogară Sud-vest; ☎ 723 983), 2km from the city centre on the corner of Şoseaua Hânceşti and Str Spicului. Above each ticket window is a list of destinations covered by that ticket-seller. Daily local services include five buses to Comrat ($2.95) in Gagauzia and six to Hânceşti.

Eurolines (☎ 549 813, 271 476; www.eurolines.md; offices at bus and train stations) has regular routes to Italy, Spain and Germany (usually around $140 return) as well as to Moscow, St Petersburg and Minsk.

Buses to Turkey depart from the train station. **Öz Gülen Turizm** (☎ 273 748), also at the

MOLDOVA

VISIT TO A MOLDOVAN FORTUNE TELLER

In the dusty, muddy village of Maximovca, some 15km east of Chişinău, lives an old woman named Maria whose fortune-telling skills are renowned throughout Moldova. On any day, you'll find the angel-topped blue gates to her house open and a small line of people waiting to see her. They come from all over, from young children to the elderly, to seek her advice or hear about their future; her powers are revered and spoken about in hushed tones. She even fields calls from England and Australia from past clients who need the occasional long-distance seer session.

We wait in the outer hall nervously, sitting on a wooden plank. Maria's daughter, a buxom woman in her 40s, dressed as if she'd just been gardening, opens the main door to let out a 'client' – an elderly lady whose eyes are darting about fretfully; she's just been told something horrific, no doubt – what's in store for me? The daughter looks sternly at me and says in Moldovan and Russian, 'You're next. Take off those shoes!' I remove them, stand up, bid farewell to my companions, enter the wooden house, and head down a corridor cluttered with boots, jackets and a sack of potatoes. I'm led into the main room where Maria is sitting at a table by the window, shuffling a deck of cards. She does not look at me, only nods continually with what seems to be a touch of Parkinsons.

I'm seated next to her. On the table is an old Nescafé tin stuffed with plastic Virgin Mary icons, some candles and various beads. Still without looking at me, and with slightly shaky hands, she shuffles then places some cards on the table (I don't get to pick any), her head bobbing up and down as if in a trance.

'Are you married?' she asks me in Russian. Her first question. My negative reply seems to momentarily cure her Parkinsons.

'Why not?' After I tell her that I just hadn't met anyone special yet, she turns to look at me full on for the first time. My heartbeat quickens.

'You looking for girls?' she asks. 'You like Moldovan girls?'

Her daughter, her interest piqued by the way the conversation's going, approaches the table and sits on the other side of me. 'Why, yes, they're quite nice, I guess,' I stammer. The daughter removes her headscarf and smiles plumply at me. She asks me what country I'm from, and starts fixing her hair when I say Canada.

'We have many pretty girls in Moldova! You should get married!' Maria continues, dealing the cards at a more furious pace. 'And you should have two children. Look!' She pushes the Seven of Spades to my face. 'Two children! You have broken your fate! You need to open your fate again! You need a wife very soon!'

I gasp. Broken my fate! 'How can I open it again?' I ask warily.

'We can help you!' mother and daughter reply in unison. Maria's now-steady hands reach for an empty Danone raspberry yoghurt cup, in which are stuffed dozens of typewritten pieces of paper in Russian. The blueberry cup has ones in Moldovan.

'Follow these instructions – you must collect water from two wells, pour it into a plate, tie a ribbon around a candle and look into a mirror…' It was all rather complicated, plus it would take seven days to perform these rituals, and I only have three left in Moldova. They look at each other and Maria decides, perhaps because I'm a speedy foreigner, 'You can do it in three. And for 250 lei we can show you how to do it.'

Shaking with the thought that I had broken the cycle of my fate, I thank her, give her the suggested 100 lei donation (it's against God to charge money for fortune telling, but if I felt grateful, she couldn't refuse a gift) and exit. After my companions emerge from their sessions, I feel comforted in knowing that I at least am not alone: they too are clutching the same pieces of paper as they, pale and distressed, tell me that they have broken their fate and need to open it up again.

Maria's house is near the extremity of the village. All the locals know where she lives. Look for the blue gates in front of the house that, oddly, looks quite well kept and richer compared to all the others.

train station, runs a daily bus to Istanbul at 6pm ($34, 27 hours).

TRAIN

The **train station** (Map p306; ☎ 252 737; Aleea Gării) is swelling with pride after major renovations have made it as modern as any in Western Europe. The 24-hour **left luggage** is 100m north of the main entrance alongside the platform. Ticket counter Nos 13, 14 and 15 are for international destinations; No 12 is for destinations within Moldova and the CIS.

International routes include three daily trains to Moscow ($36; 27 to 33 hours), 11 to Odesa ($3; five hours), one each to St Petersburg ($42; 37 hours), Bucharest ($26; 14 hours) and Lviv ($7; eight hours), and two a week to Minsk ($29; 25 hours). To get to Budapest, you must change in Bucharest.

Within Moldova, both Odesa-bound and two of the Moscow-bound trains stop at Bendery ($1; two hours) and Tiraspol ($1.50; 2½ hours). There are 11 extra trains to Bendery and 25 to Tiraspol. Five daily trains go to Comrat and four to Ungheni.

Getting Around

TO/FROM THE AIRPORT

Bus No 65 departs every 30 minutes between 5am and 10pm from the central bus station to the airport. Maxitaxi No 65 ($0.25) departs every 20 minutes from Str Ismail, near the corner of B-dul Ştefan cel Mare.

BUS & TROLLEYBUS

Bus No 45 (and maxitaxi No 45a) runs from the central bus station to the southwestern bus station. Bus No 1 goes from the train station to B-dul Ştefan cel Mare.

Trolleybus Nos 1, 4, 5, 8, 18 and 22 go to the train station from the city centre. Bus Nos 2, 10 and 16 go to Autogară Sud-vest. Tickets costing $0.15 for buses and $0.10 for trolleybuses are sold at kiosks or direct from the driver.

Most bus routes in town and to many outlying villages are served by nippy maxitaxis. These small buses are faster and more expensive than regular buses ($0.25 per trip, pay the driver). Route numbers, displayed on the front and side windows, are followed by the letter *a* or *t*. Those with

the letter *a* follow the same route as the bus of the same number. Those with a letter *t* follow the trolleybus routes. Maxitaxis run regularly between 6am and midnight.

CAR & MOTORCYCLE

Hertz (Map p306; ☎ 274 097; www.hertz.md; Hotel Cosmos & Airport; ⏲ 9am-7pm) Though a major chain, Hertz has excellent deals. A car with driver can be hired for $8 for four hours or $15 for eight hours (plus $0.15 per km), enough to see some sites around Chişinău; Opels start at $22 per day (plus mileage). There are many package deals.

There is a 24-hour petrol station, Zimbru, northeast of the central bus station on the corner of Str Sfântu Gheorghe and B-dul Avram Iancu.

TAXI

Drivers at official taxi stands often try to rip you off. Calling a **taxi** (☎ 746 565, 705, 706, 707) is cheaper. The official rate is $0.25 per kilometre.

WINE ROUTE

Though vineyards small and large are scattered throughout the country, the ones most often visited are in the vicinity of Chişinău. Each of these places makes for a pleasant (and woozy) day trip, and some can be combined into a fully-fledged wine-tasting adventure.

Getting Around

Private transport is really the way to get around in these parts. Sometimes it's essential (to get into Cricova, for example), other times extremely convenient. Buses of varying frequencies bring you to most of the villages, though not always near the wineries. If you aren't on an organised tour with a travel agency (p307), you can always rent a car and make the journey yourself, or more simply hire a private taxi in Chişinău and agree upon a price for the driver to drive you around for a day. Most will be happy to do it for $40 to $60 for a six- to eight-hour day.

Cricova

The **Cricova winery** (☎ 22-441 204; info@cricovawine .md; Str Ungureanu 1; ⏲ 8am-4pm) is the grand duke of Moldovan wineries – and it knows it. Its underground wine kingdom, 15km north of Chişinău in the village of Cricova, is one of Europe's biggest. It boasts 120km of labyrinthine roadways, 60 of which are used for wine storage. These avenues are lined with wall-to-wall bottles. Up to 100m underground, the 'cellars' are kept at a temperature of 12°C to 14°C, with humidity at 96% to 98% to best protect the 1.25 million bottles of rare and collectible wine plus the 30 million litres of wine the factory produces annually (during Soviet times, their output was two to three times this!). Tunnels have existed here since the 15th century, when limestone was dug out to help build Chişinău. They were converted into an underground wine emporium in the 1950s.

Cricova wines and champagnes have a high national and international reputation. Astronaut Yuri Gagarin spent a few days flying high in these cellars in 1966, and Russian president Vladimir Putin celebrated his 50th birthday here. Cricova's wines were among the top wines produced in the USSR. Its sparkling white wine was sold under the label 'Soviet Champagne'. Demand for its dry white sauvignon, muscadet and sweeter muscats remains high. Unique to the Cricova cellars is its sparkling red wine, kodrinskoie-sparkling, made from cabernet sauvignon stocks and marketed as having a rich velvet texture and a blackcurrant and cherry taste. The *champenoise* method used to make sparkling wines here is unique to Moldova, France, Ukraine and Russia.

The most interesting part of your obligatorily guided tour is a visit to their wineglass-shaped cellar of collectible bottles, including 19 bottles of Gerhing's wines, a 1902 bottle of Becherovka, a 1902 bottle of Evreiesc de Paşti from Jerusalem and pre-WWII French red wines.

You must have private transport and advance reservations to get into Cricova. It's most easily done through travel agencies in Chişinău, but you can call Cricova yourself and book a time. The four-hour tour ($27 per person) includes trips down streets with names such as Str Cabernet, Str Pinot etc; wine tasting; a light meal; and a few 'complimentary' bottles. Though the tour is worthwhile, most visitors find that Cricova is too big for its britches and that other wineries offer friendlier, less starchy formal tours.

Cojuşna

Cricova's competitors operate 12km northwest of Chişinău in the village of Cojuşna. This is a sad-looking place, moribund in comparison with Cricova or even Ialoveni. However, the tours given here are first-rate, down-to-earth and very friendly. What they lack in production they make up for with heart and charm. Sales have plummeted since its fabulous distribution network collapsed along with the USSR, and since most of its land was taken over and privatised (they reap the harvest of smaller wineries). Foreign investment will most likely be required to get the plant back up to its 12,000 bottle-per-hour capacity.

Cojuşna (☎ 22-744 820, 715 329; Str Lomtadze 4; 2-3hr tour $17 per person; ☯ 8am-6pm Mon-Fri), founded in 1908, is geared for tourists and is therefore very flexible – they will open their wine cellars and wine-tasting rooms for you day and night. Their cellars comprise six 'alleys', each 100m long. The wine tasting comes with a full meal, served in an impressive and seductively cosy hall decorated with wooden furniture carved by a local 17-year-old boy and his father.

It is easy to organise your own tour of Cojuşna – you needn't pay exorbitant fees at Chişinău travel agencies. They'll need advance warning if you require a tour in English. You can buy wines ($1 to $10 per bottle) from the Cojuşna shop in the complex.

GETTING THERE & AWAY
Bus No 2 runs every 15 minutes from Str Vasile Alecsandri in Chişinău towards Cricova. Get off at the Cojuşna stop. Ignore the turning on the left marked Cojuşna and walk or hitch the remaining 2km along the main road to the winery entrance, marked by a tall, totem pole-style pillar.

Străşeni, Recea & Romaneşti

Străşeni, 25km northwest of Chişinău, is renowned for its fine sparkling white wines, which have been produced in the village since the early 1970s. The **Străşeni Wine Factory** (☎ 237-22 756; Str Oreiului 36) produces around 1.25 million litres of wine a year, 80% of which is exported to CIS countries. Vineyards sprawl for 10,000 hectares around the town. Also here is **Zubresti winery** (☎ 237-79 225; Str Alexandru cel Bun 4), famous for its fruity white wines and aperitifs.

In the isolated village of **Căpriana**, 7km southwest of Strășeni, is a large 15th-century **monastery**, Moldova's second oldest. You can make this a stop during your wine tour to absolve your drinking sins – and give your liver a brief rest! First built in wood in 1429, the church was rebuilt in stone in 1545. Daily services have been held here since 1926, and some forty Orthodox monks live here today. Căpriana wasn one of the few monasteries in Moldova to survive the wrath of the Communist regime following WWII.

Recea, 9km north of Strășeni, is a small, family-run wine cellar, signposted along the main road. The 2000 decilitres of sauvignon wine it yields annually are bottled, labelled and prepared for export at the local cooperative.

Also in this area is **Romanești** (☎ 237-40 478, 40 230), one of the largest wineries in Moldova and once one of the USSR's leading wine producers. Organised tours flocked here in droves to taste the red Bordeaux-type wines drunk by Russian tsars. Romanești is 7km north of Recea.

You can visit all of these wineries on an organised tour. At Recea visitors are welcome all hours – just turn up. At Strășeni and Romanești you have to book a tour in advance.

GETTING THERE & AWAY

Buses and maxitaxis run regularly throughout the day from Chișinău's central bus station to Strășeni ($0.65; 30 minutes). There are 10 trains daily to/from Chișinău (30 minutes). Most Ungheni-bound trains stop at Strășeni, as do the daily Chișinău–Moscow and Chișinău–Odesa trains. From the bus stop at the northern end of the village, cross the footbridge over the Chișinău–Ungheni highway and continue for 1km until you reach a crossroad. Continue straight, following a dirt drive that leads to the factory. Strășeni train station is 200m south of the bus stop on the main road.

From Chișinău there's a daily bus to Recea ($0.85). From Strășeni, the only means of getting to Recea is by taxi ($3). Romanești is not served by public transport. Three buses leave daily, in the morning, from Chișinău to Căpriana. The bus makes its return journey immediately, making a day trip difficult. Forget hitching: few cars or carts pass by.

South of Chișinău

Moldova's wine road sprawls south of Chișinău, too. **Ialoveni**, 10km south of the capital, is home to the **Vinuri Ialoveni** (☎ 2-737 825; www.ialoveni.com; Str Alexandru cel Bun 4; 1-4hr tours $7.50-32; ☺ 8am-5pm Mon-Fri), known for its fine sherry called Heres. It's the only place in Moldova that makes this sweet drink. Their premises aren't as impressive as Cricova's though here you get to see enormous oak barrels (some holding over 20,000L of the good stuff) up close.

At their shop you can buy bottles of Heres and other wines for as little as $1. Their Gloria line of sherry is particularly good, though they pack a wallop at 33% alcohol. Most prefer the dry matured Heres, which has a slight walnut taste. They offer a range of tours, from a one-hour tour and tasting session to a four-hour excursion with a light meal and souvenir bottles.

The cellars at **Mileștii Mici** (☎ 268-22 241, 22-382 777; natalia_capmare@yahoo.com; tours $35-50 per person; ☺ 8am-5pm Mon-Fri), some 8km east of Ialoveni, specialise in white table wines, though their red cabernet and sauvignon wines have repeatedly won medals at national and international wine contests. Their premises are enormous and impressive. You'll need private transport to take a tour ($30), which includes, naturally, wine tasting. Tours can be arranged directly with the winery or via a travel agency. Only groups of 15 or more people can visit on Saturday and Sunday.

The area around **Hâncești**, 35km southwest of Chișinău, is also famed for its rich soil and excellent wines. **Hâncești winery** (☎ 269-22 349) produces some 1.3 million decilitres of white table wines a year and offers wine-tasting tours. The village of **Lăpușna**, 12km to the west of Hâncești, is home to **Vino Vitis** (☎ 22-234959; www.vinovitis.com), which produces a line of much-praised wines, including a particularly good Kagor (sweet red wine). They don't offer tours per se, but are open to visitors if contacted in advance.

GETTING THERE & AWAY

From Chișinău, take bus No 35 from Autogară Sud-vest to Ialoveni. There are no buses between Ialoveni and Mileștii Mici but a local driver will take you there for around $2. There is one direct bus from Chişinău's Autogară Sud-vest to Mileştii Mici ($1.20), and six buses daily to Hânceşti.

ORHEI

☎ 235 / pop 37,500

The modern town of Orhei, not to be confused with Orheiul Vechi, is 45km north of Chişinău. Almost decimated during WWII, Orhei is a depressed little town with little to offer tourists, but might be worth a brief detour on the way to or from Orheiul Vechi, even though coming from Chişinău, it's not on the way.

Information

The **telephone office** (Str Vasile Mahu 119; 24hr) is next to the former Catholic church. There is Internet access here too. The central **post office** (Str Vasile Mahu 129) is a few doors down. There are several banks and exchange offices on Str Vasile Lupu, including the **Banca Economii** (Str Vasile Lupu 50).

Sights

A **statue of Vasile Lupu**, reigning prince of Moldavia (ruled 1634–53), stands majestically at the entrance to the city in front of **St Dimitru Church** (1637). The main street, Str Vasile Lupu, is dominated by **St Nicholas' Church**.

Behind the impressive Catholic church on Str Vasile Mahu (two blocks north of Str Vasile Lupu) is a **monument** to the soldiers killed during the 1992 Moldovan-Transdniestran conflict in Bendery and Dubaşari. Some 200m further west on this street is a small **bust** of Pushkin.

Exhibits at the excellent **History & Ethnographic Museum** (☎ 20 298; Str Renaşterii Naţionale 23; 9am-5pm Tue-Sun), trace the city's history from Vasile Lupu's reign to Moldova's declaration of independence in 1989. The text is in Moldovan and Russian but is well illustrated with photographs.

Perhaps the most interesting place in this area lies 1.5km from Orhei's southern border on the main road to Chişinău. In the parking lot of the Café Safari restaurant is a supposed 'magnetic hill'. Nazis were reputed to have buried Jews alive here, and strange happenings are alleged to occur in the area. Motorists often park right in front of the cafe, facing the main road, and slip the car into neutral to see if it still advances, despite it going slightly uphill.

Sleeping & Eating

Hotel Codru (☎ 24 821; Str Vasile Lupu 36; s/d/ste $6/10/16) Not exactly your dream hotel – the unheated rooms with shared bathroom not only don't have hot water, they don't have any water at all. No fear, however – the staff are happy to bring up buckets of water to your room at no extra charge. Otherwise, the friendly staff are full of information on interesting sights in the Orhei region. The **Codru Restaurant** next door is open noon to midnight daily.

Getting There & Away

Daily buses depart every half-hour from Chişinău's Autogară Centrală to Orhei between 9am and 10pm ($0.80; two hours). All northbound buses from Chişinău stop in Orhei too, including daily buses to Bălţi, Ediniţa and Briceni. From Orhei there is one daily bus at 6am to Orheiul Vechi.

ORHEIUL VECHI

Ten kilometres to the southeast of Orhei lies Orheiul Vechi (Old Orhei; marked on maps as the village of Trebujeni), arguably Moldova's most fantastic sight. It's certainly among its most haunting places. The chimerical **Orheiul Vechi Monastery complex** (Complexul Muzeistic Orheiul Vechi; ☎ 235-34 242; admission $0.40; 9am-5pm Tue-Sun), carved into a massive limestone cliff in this wild, rocky, remote spot, draws visitors from around the globe. The **Cave Monastery** (Mănăstire în Peşteră), inside a cliff overlooking the gently meandering Răut River, was dug by Orthodox monks in the 13th century. It remained inhabited until the 18th century, and in 1996 a handful of monks returned to this secluded place of worship and are slowly restoring it.

You can enter the cave via an entrance on the cliff's plateau. A small, highly atmospheric chapel inside acts as the church for three neighbouring villages, as it did in the 13th century. You can visit the area where up to 13 monks lived for decades at a time, sleeping on pure bedrock, each occupying a tiny stone bunk (*keilies*) that opens into a central corridor. This leads to a stone terrace, from where views of the entire cliff and surrounding plains are nothing less than breathtaking. The cliff face is dotted with what appear to be holes; most of these are other caves and places of worship dug over the millennia, as this region was a place of worship for Geto-Dacian tribes from before Christ's time. In all, the huge cliff contains six complexes of interlocking caves, most of which are accessible only by experienced rock climbers and many of which are out of bounds for tourists.

Ștefan cel Mare built a fortress here in the 14th century but it was later destroyed by Tartars. Archaeologists since WWII have uncovered several layers of history in this region; some of their finds are on exhibit in Chișinău's National History Museum (p310). The area is rich in archaeological treasures.

In the 18th century the cave-church was taken over by villagers from neighbouring Butuceni. In 1905 they built a church above ground dedicated to the Ascension of St Mary. The church was shut down by the Soviets in 1944 and remained abandoned throughout the Communist regime. Services resumed in 1996, though it still looks abandoned. Archaeologists have uncovered remnants of a defence wall surrounding the monastery complex from the 15th century.

On the main road to the complex you'll find the headquarters where you purchase your entrance tickets. You can also visit a tiny **village museum** (☎ 235-34 242; 🕙 9am-5pm Tue-Sun) where several archaeological finds from the 15th and 16th centuries are presented. Here, you can also arrange guides and get general information. Shorts are forbidden and women must cover their heads inside the monastery.

For an amusingly over-enthusiastic description of Orheiul Vechi, as well as excellent photographs and many details of the site, see http://orhei.dnt.md.

Ten kilometres south of Orhei en route to Orheiul Vechi is **Ivancea**, with an excellent **ethnographic museum** (Muzeul meşte şugirilor populare; ☎ 235-43 320; admission $1; 🕙 10am 5pm Tue-Sun) housed in a 19th-century stately mansion. Its eight halls are filled with traditional Moldovan costumes, musical instruments, pottery and folk art.

Sleeping

Antrec-Moldova (Map p308; ☎ 22-237 823; antrec_ong@yahoo.com) Antrec, Romania's rural homestay network, is quite new in Moldova, but should be able to find you a place to stay near Orheiul Vechi for under $10 per person. They are located in Chișinău.

Satul Moldovenesc (☎ 248-36 136; http://moldovacc.md/satmoldovenesc; Hârtopul Mare; 1/2-room house $15-45/52) Only 30km northeast of Chișinau (head towards Dubăsari then north to Hârtopul Mare and follow the signs), this full-service complex in the middle of nature offers a very active programme of rest and relaxation! You can rent an island for $12 and enjoy a picnic there, have a sauna, go horse riding (children can be 'accompanied on their ride of the donkey'), and go swimming or fishing in one of the three lakes nearby.

Getting There & Away

Daily buses depart every half-hour from Chișinău's Autogară Centrală to Orhei ($1.20). From Orhei, a bus departs daily for Trebujeni at 6am. Ask to be dropped off by the signposted entrance to the complex. There is a daily afternoon bus (3pm) back to Orhei from Orheiul Vechi. A taxi from Orhei to Orheiul Vechi costs around $6.

BĂLȚI, REZINA & ȚIPOVA

Bălți (*balts*, from the Romanian word for 'swamp'; population 155,000), 150km northwest of Chișinău, is Moldova's fourth-largest city. A major industrial area, and predominantly Russian-speaking, it offers little beyond being a convenient stopover en route to Ukraine.

Some 60km east of Bălți on the western banks of the Dniestr River is the small town of Rezina. Seven kilometres south of the town is the Orthodox **Saharna Monastery**. Founded in 1495, the church used today dates from the 19th century and sits in a small valley. There are walking trails all around, some offering beautiful views of the entire monastery complex, and one leading to the Virgin Mary's footprint in rock (protected by a glass covering). There's also a lovely waterfall tumbling off an overhanging cliff. It celebrates the **Day of the Holy Trinity** (8 September), a good time to visit.

Some 12km further south is the marvellous **Țipova Monastery**, Eastern Europe's largest cave monastery, another of Moldova's memorable highlights. It dates from the 10th to the 12th centuries, and is famous as the place where Ștefan cel Mare got married. Embedded in a large cliff, the caves are more accessible here than at Orheiul Vechi, as footpaths lead up the cliff. Services resumed here in 1994 after the monastery was closed and partially ruined during the Soviet period. It's in a lovely area, and paths lead to a small, picturesque waterfall nearby.

Ţipova is in a remote corner of the country on the western banks of the Dniestr River. It's best accessed by car by following the turn-off to Horodişte. The monastery is 4km past Horodişte at the far end of the village.

Sleeping & Eating

Hotel Basarabia (☎ 231-61 219; Str M Sadoveanu 1; s/d $12/16) This 80-place 1960s holdout in central Balţi is slightly run-down as you might expect, but could be a convenient stopover while exploring northern Moldova.

Timoti (☎ 254-23 986; Str A Sciusev; mains $1-4; ☽ 8am-3am) Probably your best dining bet in Rezina is this complex of restaurant, bar, casino and discotheque.

Getting There & Away

Balţi is well served by buses. Daily services include five to Tiraspol, eight to Soroca and seven to Ungheni. There are buses every half-hour to/from Chişinău ($2.65). One daily bus goes to Iaşi, Romania. It's possible to get to Ţipova by taking a bus from Chişinău to Rezina, and getting off 20km before Rezina at the turn-off to Horodişte. It's a 12km hitchhike or just plain hike from there.

SOROCA

pop 39,600

Soroca is the Roma 'capital' of Moldova. The large Roma population here, even in Soviet times, were renowned for living at a much higher standard than most Moldovans; hence part of the reason for the palpable prejudice that exists against them. You can see a number of stately mansions that the richer Roma built for themselves on the hilltop facing the river and Ukraine on the other side of it.

Yet people come here to see the outstanding **Soroca fortress** (free admission). Visitors are thrown back to medieval times while wandering the grounds of this marvel, which gives a great impression of what life must have been like centuries ago in between the nearly intact walls. Part of a medieval chain

---

DIVINE COMMUNICATION

When Mircea Cerari, the king of Moldova's Roma community, died at the age of 59 in July 1998, it was not his death but his entrance into the afterlife that raised eyebrows. Determined to keep in contact with loved ones from beyond the grave, the king had made arrangements to be buried with his computer, fax and mobile phone.

The lavish funeral, held in Soroca in northern Moldova two weeks after his death, was attended by some 15,000 Roma who had gathered from the far reaches of Europe to pay their respects. Also in attendance was Mircea Cerari's son Arthur, who has since inherited Moldova's Roma crown.

The king's impressive white marble grave contained not only his communication equipment but also a bar stocked with – what else? – vodka!

Arthur is also now the main representative for the **Cultural Society of Roma of Moldova** (☎ 22-229 975) in Chişinău.

---

of military fortresses built by Moldavian princes between the 14th and 16th centuries to defend Moldavia's boundaries, it was founded by Ştefan cel Mare and rebuilt by his son Petru Rareş in 1543 to 1545. The walls (18m high on the inside, 21m high on the outside) are over 3m thick. Four towers plus a rectangular entrance tower still stand. Strategically placed at Moldavia's then most northeastern tip on the banks of the Dniestr River, Soroca (founded in 1502) was one of the key military strongholds.

The fortress is administered by the **Soroca Museum of History and Ethnography** (☎ 230-22 264; Str Independentei 68; admission $0.60; ☽ 10am-6pm Tue-Sun). This well-designed museum is a real treat: its 25,000 exhibits cover archaeological finds, weapons and ethnographic displays. From Balţi there are eight daily buses to Soroca.

LOWER DNIESTR NATIONAL PARK

The Parcul Naţional Nistrul Inferior has been set up in recent years by the nonprofit organisation **Biotica** (☎ 22-498 837; www.biotica -moldova.org), who will continue to oversee its gradual implementation over the following years. Comprising over 50,000 hectares of wetlands, forest and agricultural land, it encompasses some 40 sites of archaeological importance, observation points, many villages and some of Moldova's best vineyards (at Purcari and Tudora for example). Though not yet fully set up with a tourist infrastructure, excursions and rural homestays are possible via Biotica. Canoeing, hiking, wine tasting and camping are all possible in this lovely area which feels unexplored and shimmers with possibility. You can also visit private vineyards and village artisans to see them at work making wicker baskets or furniture.

Though Biotica can help arrange visits, one guesthouse that's been set up to accommodate tourists is **Meşter Faur** (☎ 242-35 259; Str Ştefan cel Mare 100) in the village of Cioburciu. Run by Pavel Taranu, they can guarantee a splendid time in remote Moldova countryside, with boat tours, visits to local village enterprises, wine tasting and relaxation galore. Only Moldovan and Russian are spoken, but after a few glasses of their home-made brew, everyone makes themselves understood.

TRANSDNIESTR

The self-declared republic of Transdniestr (Pridnestrovskaya Moldavskaya Respublika, or PMR in Russian; population 633,600) is one of the world's last surviving Communist bastions. At least that's what most people say. Yet despite the amusing everpresence of rousing slogans such as 'Bendery – Our Pride!' and monuments to Lenin and other Soviet heroes that adorn street corners, the sugary smell of capitalism is too pungent here to uphold illusions of any kind of worker's paradise. Expensive shops, hotels and stadiums are popping up around Tiraspol, reaffirming that money speaks louder than the cries of the simple folk, who are struggling to get by in a land that the rest of the world knows nothing about.

Transdniestr incorporates the narrow strip of land covering only 3567 sq km on the eastern bank of the Dniestr River. It was the scene of a bloody civil war in the early 1990s when the area declared independence from Moldova. Travellers will be stunned by a region that is very much an independent state in all but name. It has its own currency, police force, army and borders, which are controlled by Transdniestran border guards. Western travellers are allowed to travel in the region. Russian is the predominant language. Transdniestrans boycott the Moldovan Independence Day and celebrate their own independence day on 2 September.

See http://geo.ya.com/travelimages/transdniestr.html for some excellent photos of the region, and www.cbpmr.net for the 'official' account of Transdniestr.

GOVERNMENT & POLITICS

Igor Smirnov was elected president of Transdniestr in 1991 following the region's declaration of independence four months earlier. In 1994 the Moldovan Parliament ratified a new constitution providing substantial autonomy to Transdniestr in regional affairs, as it did for Gagauzia. Transdniestrans, however, refused to recognise this autonomy as it didn't go nearly as far as they wanted. They insist it's an independent country and a sovereign state within Moldova. Most of the time, they push for the creation of a Moldovan federation, with proportionate representation between Moldova, Transdniestr and Gagauzia. This on the condition, of course, that Smirnov would then become vice-president of Moldova.

Neither Smirnov's presidency nor the Transdniestran Parliament is recognised by the Moldovan – or any other – government, which has nonetheless been forced to engage in dialogue with the breakaway state, often brokered by Russian officials who still act as if the area is within their sphere of interests. The Russian 14th army, headquartered in Tiraspol since 1956, covertly supplied Transdniestran rebels with weapons during the 1992 civil war. The continued presence of the 5000-strong Russian 'operational group' in Transdniestr today is seen by local Russian-speakers as a guarantee of their security and are generally welcomed.

The Ministry of State Security (MGB), a modern-day KGB, has sweeping powers and has sponsored the creation of a youth wing called the Young Guard for 16- to 23-year-olds who want to be indoctrinated into the happy world of xenophobia and military games in the hopes of building a dedicated nationalistic future generation.

MOLDOVA

YOU CAN CHECK OUT ANYTIME YOU LIKE...

Foreign travellers have had great fun over the years getting in and out of Transdniestr. Border guards would often make up rules as they went along, scratch their heads while looking at a New Zealand passport then wonder how much to charge for an entrance 'visa', or accept payment in cigars and vodka in the rare cases when cash wasn't enough of a bribe.

There were joyously Kafkesque moments – the kind that make travel so memorable – when a tourist would get to the border, be told he/she didn't have the proper permits to enter the Republic of Transdniestr and would need to get a visa. The fact that there are no foreign consulates for a country that doesn't exist never seemed to hold sway on the stalwart defenders of this Communist enclave. Then, even if you had the proper permits, you had to have them registered – at first it was if you stayed in Transdniestr for three or more days; then the powers that be substituted 'days' for 'hours' without telling anyone and without telling travellers where they could get themselves registered. Tourists were told to go to Bendery or Chişinău to undisclosed locations and get whatever stamps were missing – until money or a sudden burst of down-to-earth human communication saved the day. Here's a letter from one of our readers who entered without a problem but six hours later was taken off the Tiraspol-Chişinău bus for not having a permit:

'After studying a huge tome, the border guard decided you had to register after three hours, not three days. I would have to pay a fine of $12 (worked out by the number of hours I'd overstayed) but they wouldn't take the money as they had no receipts. I should have got a permit from the Transdniestr Police in Chişinău. I pointed out that there were none. They decided that I should go back to Bendery for the permit. OK, what address do I go to? They didn't know. So what do I do now? They didn't know that either. Fortunately the English speaking one managed to glean that I was a customs officer by profession and made me draw him a picture of my shoulder epaulets (I added an extra stripe for effect). It worked, he jumped to his feet, saluted me of all things and suddenly it was handshakes and cigarettes all round! They flagged down the next Chişinău bus and waved me off. They even refunded my bus fare so I profited by 40 pence from this incident.'

Mike Wallace, Glasgow

Well, sadly times have changed and you're likely to have a very dull time at the border. You can purchase an entry permit at the border for $1 to $5 (depending on your nationality), and if you stay under 24 hours, you needn't register at all. If you enter with a Moldovan national, you can be listed on their entry permit (as several names can be inscribed on one) for a few pennies. All hotels will register you automatically, but if you're staying at a private home for over 24 hours, you'll need to register with the **Tiraspol Militia Passport office** (Map p328; ☎ 34 169; ulitsa Rosa Luxembourg 2). Who knows though, the fun may continue as long as laws keep changing faster than the inflation rate. Have fun!

To observers, they are more akin to disenchanted skinheads than anything else.

Alongside a number of agreements between Moldova and Transdniestr since 1991, there have been countless moves by both sides designed to antagonise or punish the other. In 2003 alone, Smirnov, reacting to one of his demands having been refused by Moldova, slapped exorbitant tariffs on all Moldovan imports, instantly halting trade over the 'border' and making life more difficult for common people on both sides. In September 2003, Smirnov even got so huffy he severed phone connections between the two, so that calls could not be made between the regions (this was only for a few weeks).

Smirnov is becoming increasingly disliked and mistrusted by his 'electorate' and few people here believe that slogans and Lenin statues will better their lives in any way. Everyone knows that returning to the USSR is impossible, even undesirable; people just want a piece of the pie, like everywhere else.

ECONOMY

As a self-declared republic, Transdniestr's economy is disastrous, despite the fact that 40% of Moldova's total potential industrial output is concentrated in Tiraspol. In mid-2000 the rebel republic owed $338 million to Russian gas company Gazprom.

Inflation is rampant and the local currency, the Transdniestran rouble, is worthless. The average monthly salary is $45 a month. State employers are often not able to pay their workers, forcing many to earn a living at the flea market.

So far, it has been widely speculated that the mainstays of the economy – and why the people in charge of Transdniestr are unfathomably rich – have included illegal arms trading (of old Soviet military machinery conveniently left on its territory), extortion of businessmen trying to open businesses on the territory, money laundering and reaping profits from state-owned currency exchange booths.

Things have been slowly improving, however, with some increased activity in metal production and light industry.

POPULATION
Two-thirds of Transdniestr's population is elderly and impoverished. Ethnic Russians comprise 29% of the population, ethnic Moldovans 34% and Ukrainians 29%. The populace is tired of living in an area where the average salary is less than that in neighbouring Moldova (itself often considered Europe's poorest country). They care less and less about the charade of upholding a supposed socialist paradise when they know that only their 'leaders' benefit economically from the pretence. People here tend to be more cautious and reserved than in the rest of Moldova, with the older generations uneasy about openly speaking their mind against the government.

LANGUAGE
The official state languages in Transdniestr are Russian, Moldovan and Ukrainian. Students in schools and universities are taught in Russian, and local government and most official institutions operate almost solely in Russian. All street signs are written in Russian, sometimes Moldovan and even Ukrainian.

MONEY
The days when it took a degree in mathematics to buy bread or when there were two versions of the same banknote, each a different value, are over. The only legal tender is the Transdniestran rouble (TR). There are 1, 5, 25, 50 and 100 rouble notes and 1, 5, 10 and 50 kopek coins. The notes are tiny, often

dirty and disintegrating. All notes sport the much-revered and famous 18th-century Russian military general Alexander Suvorov on the front, while the back features different places of 'national' importance, such as the Kvint brandy factory on the 5-rouble note. Not surprisingly, hard currency is desperately sought after by most taxi drivers, shopkeepers and market traders, who will gladly accept payment in US dollars – or even Moldovan lei or Ukrainian hryvnia.

Exchange Rates
For the latest exchange rates, check out www.cbpmr.net. At the time of writing, the exchange rates were:

country	unit		rouble
Moldova	1 Lei	=	TR0.55
Russia	R1	=	TR0.27
UK	£1	=	TR13.95
Ukraine	1 hv	=	TR1.41
US	$1	=	TR7.77
euro zone	€1	=	TR9.47

POST & TELEPHONE
Transdniestran stamps featuring Suvorov can only be used for letters sent within the Transdniestran republic and are not recognised anywhere else. For letters to Moldova, Romania and the West, you have to use Moldovan stamps (available here but less conveniently than in Moldova). If you bring your cell phone here, note that there is no roaming available on the territory save for Moldovan cell phones.

MEDIA
The predominantly Russian Transdniestran TV is broadcast in the republic between 9am and midnight. Transdniestran Radio is on air during the same hours.

The two local newspapers are in Russian. The *Transdniestra* is a purely nationalist affair advocating the virtues of an independent state; *N Pravda* is marginally more liberal.

BENDERY
☎ 282 / pop 133,000
Perhaps due to all the bloodshed in the city's history, Bendery (sometimes called Bender, and previously known as Tighina), on the western banks of the Dniestr River, is a decidedly unpleasant, sad town. More polite

MOLDOVA

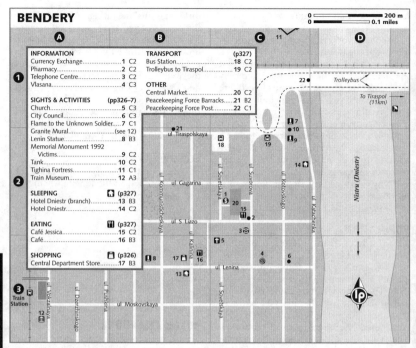

BENDERY

INFORMATION	
Currency Exchange	**1** C2
Pharmacy	**2** C2
Telephone Centre	**3** C2
Vlasana	**4** C3

SIGHTS & ACTIVITIES	(pp326–7)
Church	**5** C3
City Council	**6** C3
Flame to the Unknown Soldier	**7** C1
Granite Mural	(see 12)
Lenin Statue	**8** B3
Memorial Monument 1992 Victims	**9** C2
Tank	**10** C2
Tighina Fortress	**11** C1
Train Museum	**12** A3

SLEEPING	(p327)
Hotel Dniestr (branch)	**13** B3
Hotel Dniestr	**14** C2

EATING	(p327)
Café Jessica	**15** C2
Café	**16** B3

SHOPPING	(p326)
Central Department Store	**17** B3

TRANSPORT	(p327)
Bus Station	**18** C2
Trolleybus to Tiraspol	**19** C2

OTHER	
Central Market	**20** C2
Peacekeeping Force Barracks	**21** B2
Peacekeeping Force Post	**22** C1

observers might call it languid and peaceful, with blooming acacia trees giving it a delicate feel. Others would simply call it a depressed outpost whose fate is spiralling downwards.

During the 16th century, Moldavian prince Ştefan cel Mare built a large defensive fortress here on the ruins of a fortified Roman camp. In 1538 the Ottoman sultan Suleiman the Magnificent conquered the fortress and transformed it into a Turkish *raia* (colony), renaming the city Bendery, meaning 'belonging to the Turks'. During the 18th century, Bendery was seized from the Turks by Russian troops who then massacred Turkish Muslims in the city. In 1812 Bendery fell permanently into Russian hands. Russian peacekeeping forces remain here to this day. The bloodiest fighting during the 1992 military conflict took place in Bendery and many walls of buildings in the centre remain bullet-pocked.

Information

Change money at the **currency exchange** (ulitsa Sovetskaya next to Central Market; ⏲ 7am-5pm). Local maxitaxis (70 kopeks) leave from here. In-

ternational telephone calls can be booked from the **telephone office** (cnr ulitsa S Liazo & ulitsa Suvorova; ⏲ 8am-6pm Mon-Fri, 8am-4pm Sat). The **central department store** (cnr ulitsa Lenina & ulitsa Kalinina) is opposite Hotel Dniestr. You can log onto the Internet at **Vlasana** (☎ 29 477; ulitsa Lenina 29; per hr \$0.25; ⏲ 9am-9pm). There's also a **pharmacy** (cnr ulitsa Suvorova & ulitsa S Liazo; ⏲ 8am-8pm Mon-Sat, 8am-4pm Sun).

Sights

Bendery's main sight is paradoxically impossible to see. The great Turkish fortress, built in the 1530s to replace a 12th-century fortress built by the Genovese, is now being used by Transdniestran military as a training ground and is strictly off-limits. The best view of it is from the bridge going towards Tiraspol. At the entrance to the city, close to the famous **Bendery-Tiraspol bridge**, is a **memorial park** dedicated to local 1992 war victims. An eternal **flame** burns in front of an armoured tank, from which flies the Transdniestran flag. Haunting memorials to those shot dead during the civil war are evident throughout many of the main streets in the centre. The **City Council** building is at ulitsa Lenina 17.

Next to the train station is a **Train Museum** inside an old Russian CY 06-71 steam locomotive. The museum was closed at the time of writing. Alongside Bendery's only museum is a typically Soviet, oversized **granite mural** in memory of the train workers who died in the 1918 revolution.

Sleeping & Eating

A three-tier pricing system is intact here, with prices for the locals, Moldovans, Ukrainians and Belorussians, and all other foreigners.

Hotel Dniestr (☎ 29 478; ulitsa Katachenka 10; s/d $9/23) The single rooms occasionally don't have hot water, but can be shared by two people as long as they are of the opposite sex (no funny stuff going on here!). The pricier doubles have hot water, TV and fridge – these are permitted to be shared by two people of any sex. There's an adjacent restaurant and terrace cafe. They run another branch of the hotel at ulitsa Kalinina 50, with similar prices, but you must register at the main ulitsa Katachenka hotel first.

Café Jessica (☎ 23 540; ulitsa S Liazo; mains $1; ☺ 10am-midnight) The year-round Christmas lights and the glow from the one-armed bandits in this dingy cafe provide a surreal atmosphere. Don't bother reading the menu, just ask what's on that day and stick with the tried and true *pelmeni*. There's 'surpriz' on the menu but we caution against risking finding out what it is. For dessert, indulge in lemon slices sprinkled with sugar.

Café (cnr ulitsa Kalinina & ulitsa Lenina; mains $1-2; ☺ 9am-11pm) In the park across from the department store, this small restaurant has a popular, pleasant terrace where grilled meat dishes are the favourite. It also doubles as a hang-out and bar.

Getting There & Away

The train station is at Privokzalnaya ploschad. You might be charged $0.05 to ask a question here. At least 15 daily trains go to Chişinău, including ones coming from Moscow and Odesa. There are buses and maxitaxis every half-hour or so to Chişinău, and two daily to Comrat.

Trolleybus No 19 for Tiraspol ($0.10) departs from the bus stop next to the main roundabout at the entrance to Bendery. Maxitaxis regularly make the 20-minute journey ($0.15). There are two daily buses to Odesa and one to Kiev.

TIRASPOL

☎ 284 / pop 194,000

Tiraspol (from the Greek, meaning 'town on the Nistru'), 70km east of Chişinău, would be the second-largest city in Moldova if only it weren't the capital of a nonexistent country. Instead, it's no doubt the world's largest open-air museum of Soviet-style communism, only one that's been plunged into capitalism for years. Thus, the have/have-not divide is glaring, shocking and disturbing. Entering the city from Bendery, it's impossible not to notice the enormous series of gleaming, state-of-the-art football and sports stadiums and a five-star hotel on the city's outskirts (in construction at the time of writing). They were built at the cost of untold hundreds of million of dollars at the instigation of Tiras Sheriff, owner of the Tiraspol football team. A favourite pastime of people on the street, who are lucky to earn $40 a month, is wondering where all the money came from.

The city was founded in 1792 following Russian domination of the region. Its population is predominantly Russian (41%), with ethnic Ukrainians comprising 32% and ethnic Moldovans 18% of the population.

Orientation & Information

The train and bus stations are next to each other at the end of ulitsa Lenina. Exit the train station and walk down ulitsa Lenina, past Kirov Park, to ulitsa 25 Oktober (the main street).

The **post office** (ulitsa Lenina 17; ☺ 7.30am-7pm Mon-Fri) won't be of much use to you unless you want to send postcards to all your friends in Transdniestr (but if you do, be sure to bring your own postcards). At the **central telephone office** (cnr ulitsa 25 Oktober & ulitsa Kommunisticheskaya; ☺ 7-8.45pm), you can buy phonecards ($2.15 or $7.75) to use in the modern payphones (the old metal clunkers can only make local calls), send telegrams or make long-distance calls. Change money next door at the **Prisbank** (☺ 8.30am-4.30pm Mon-Sat). **Bunker** (pereulok Naberezhnyi 1; per hr $0.40; ☺ 9am-11pm) is a modern Internet club.

MOLDOVA

TIRASPOL

INFORMATION		EATING	(p329)	TRANSPORT	(pp329-30)
Beltsy	1 B3	Kafe 7	21 B3	Bus Station	26 D1
Bunker	2 B3	Kafe Chudesnitsa	22 C3		
Central Telephone Office	3 C3	Kafe Prieteniya	23 C3	OTHER	
Dom Knigi	4 C3			Kvint shop	27 B3
Militia Passport Office	5 C3	DRINKING	(p329)		
Post Office	6 C3	Prokhlada	24 A3		
Prisbank	7 C3				
		ENTERTAINMENT	(p329)		
SIGHTS & ACTIVITIES	(pp328-9)	Drama Theatre	25 D3		
Heroes' Cemetery	8 A3				
House of Soviets	9 D3				
Kirov Statue	10 C2				
Kvint Factory	11 C2				
Museum of Headquarters	12 C3				
Palace of the Republic	13 C3				
Presidential Palace	14 A3				
Suvorov Statue	15 A3				
Tiraspol National United Museum	16 A3				
University	17 D3				
SLEEPING	(p329)				
Hotel Aist	18 B3				
Hotel Drushba	19 D3				
Hotel Timothy	20 C2				

Beltsy (ulitsa 25 Oktober 74; ⏰ 9am-10pm) is a well-stocked supermarket and department store that has an exchange office as well. **Dom Knigi** (ulitsa 25 Oktober 85; ⏰ 9am-7pm Mon-Fri, 9am-4pm Sat) is a big bookstore with a limited selection of Russian-only books (good luck finding any maps here).

Sights

At the western end of ulitsa 25 Oktober stands a Soviet armoured **tank** from which the Transdniestran flag flies. Behind is the **Heroes' Cemetery** with its Tomb of the Unknown Soldier, flanked by an eternal flame in memory of those who died on 3 March 1992 during the first outbreak of fighting. The inscription in Russian reads 'You don't have a name but your deeds are eternal'. There's also an Afghan war memorial here. Other victims of the civil war are buried in the **city cemetery**, north of the centre, where a special alley has been allocated to the 1992 victims.

The **Tiraspol National United Museum** (ulitsa 25 Oktober 42; admission $0.30; ☎ 9am-5pm Sun-Fri) is the closest the city has to a local history museum, with an exhibit focusing on

poet Nikolai Dimitriovich Zelinskogo, who founded the first Soviet school of chemistry. Opposite is the **Presidential Palace**, from where Igor Smirnov rules his mini-empire. The enormous ploshchad Konstitutii backs up into a park-lined concrete promenade along the Dniestr, a popular strolling area.

Ulitsa 25 Oktober, Tiraspol's backbone, is also its commercial strip, with most of the shops and restaurants. Fancy new stores blend with photo studios displaying hand-coloured portraits from the 1970s in their windows – a surreal mix. Tree-lined and wide, there's a pleasant, carefree rhythm to the flow of life on this street.

The few Western foreigners who make it to Tiraspol love to shoot rolls of film of the city's Soviet-style buildings and monuments. A must-snap is the **Dvorets Respubliki** (Palace of the Republic), slightly recessed south of the main street between ulitsa Kotovskogo and ulitsa Kommunisticheskaya. On it is a glorious relief of young Communist men and women engaged in strange activities that surely have something to do with building a better world.

Change rolls before you get to the administration building, the neoclassical **House of Soviets** (Dom Sovetov), towering over the eastern end of ulitsa 25 Oktober. Lenin's angry-looking bust peers out from its prime location smack in front of the building. Inside the building is a memorial to those who died in the 1992 conflict. Close by is the military-themed **Museum of Headquarters** (ulitsa Kommunisticheskaya 34; admission $0.30; 9am-5pm Mon-Sat). The **Drama Theatre** is at ulitsa 25 Oktober, and close by is the **university**, founded in 1930.

The **Kvint factory** (37 333; www.kvint.com; ulitsa Lenina 38) is one of Transdniestr's pride and joys. Since 1897 it's been making some of Moldova's finest brandies. There are no excursions, but a gander at the factory might be of interest. Buy some of their products either near the front entrance of the plant or at their **town centre store** (ulitsa 25 Oktober 84; 24hr).

Further north along ulitsa Lenina towards the bus and train stations is **Kirov Park**, with a **statue** of the Leningrad boss who was assassinated in 1934, conveniently sparking off mass repressions throughout the USSR.

Sleeping

Hotel Drushba (34 266; ulitsa 25 Oktober 116; rooms $9-32) Several dozen categories of rooms are on offer at this massive place that has hopefully seen better days. Some have hot water, TV, fridge, larger beds, private bath or shower. Your check-in is guaranteed to be a memorable experience. The atmosphere is rather dour but the rooms are fine and the staff pleasant.

Hotel Aist (37 174; pereulok Naberezhnyi 3; d $16-27) The grass in the cement cracks outside give it a derelict feel, but this is a decent hotel. More expensive rooms have luxuries such as hot water, private toilet and TV.

Hotel Timothy (36 442; ulitsa K Liebknechta 395A; s/d $55/75;) The fanciest place in town is an ultra-modern, small hotel geared to businessmen (there's a business centre next-door). Posh rooms have spa baths. Yes, that framed portrait behind the check-in desk is of President Igor Smirnov, whose pals are probably the ones who use the hotel most.

Eating

Kafe Chudesnitsa (ulitsa 25 Oktober; mains $0.05-0.50; 8am-8pm) This one's a real blast – a

true Soviet-style cafeteria with dirt-cheap meals that are bland but hit the spot fine. Just hanging out with the waitresses can be a hoot.

Kafe 7 (32 311; ulitsa 25 Oktober 77; mains $0.35-1.50; 9am-11pm) A great selection of tasty Russian fast food like blini (stuffed pancakes) and Western imports like pizza, as well as salads are on offer at this modern, pleasant cafe.

Kafe Prieteniya (ulitsa 25 Oktober 112; 8am-11pm) This bar serves light snacks to customers whose eyes are glued to the gangster and action movies shown on the monitor. It has a great terrace out back.

Getting There & Away

BUS

Tickets for all buses are sold in the main ticket hall. You can only pay for tickets to other destinations in Transdniestr in the local currency, but you can pay in Moldovan lei or Ukrainian hryvnia for tickets to Moldova or Ukraine. You can usually pay the driver directly also.

From Tiraspol five daily buses go to Bălţi, 13 to Odesa, one to Kiev, and one a week to Berlin. Buses go to Chişinău nearly every half-hour from 5.50am to 8.50am, and maxitaxis run regularly from 6.30am to 6.10pm.

TRAIN

The train station is at the northern end of ulitsa Lenina. Tickets for same-day departures are sold in the main train station ticket hall. There is also an information booth – a question about national train services costs $0.05 and a question about services to CIS countries costs $0.10, though most tellers don't bother charging it. Buy advance tickets (24 hours or more before departure) in the ticket office on the 2nd floor.

Most eastbound trains from Chişinău to Ukraine and Russia stop in Tiraspol. Seven daily trains go to Chişinău ($0.90; 2½ hours), three to Odesa ($2; 2½ hours), two to Moscow ($31; 25 to 31 hours) and Minsk ($23; 23 hours) and one to St Petersburg ($28; 35 hours).

Getting Around
Bus No 1 and maxitaxi No 3 run between the bus and train stations and the city centre. Tickets for regular buses ($0.10) are sold by the driver. Tickets for maxitaxis cost $0.15. Trolleybus and maxitaxi No 19 cross the bridge over the Dniestr to Bendery.

GAGAUZIA

Compared to the violent events in Transdniestr, Gagauzia (Gagauz Yeri) won its autonomy relatively calmly. While subordinated to Moldova constitutionally and for foreign relations and defence, Gagauzia is an autonomous region covering 1832 sq km of noncontiguous land in southern Moldova. On a national level, Gagauzia is represented by the assembly's elected başkan (head, governor), a member of the Gagauz Halki political party who holds a safe seat in the Moldovan Parliament. Since 1995, this has been George Tabunshik.

Comrat is Gagauzia's capital. The republic is divided into three districts – Comrat, Ceadăr-Linga and Vulcăneşti. Wedged between these last two is the predominantly Bulgarian-populated district of Taraclia, which is not part of Gagauzia. Gagauz territory is further broken up by three Bulgarian villages in Ceadăr-Linga and a predominantly Moldovan village in Comrat district, all of which are part of 'mainland' Moldova too. Gagauzia comprises three towns and 27 villages.

The population of Gagauzia is 171,500, 78% of which are Gagauz nationals; an additional 25,000 Gagauz live in other areas of Moldova, and 20,000 more live in Greece and Bulgaria, and 32,000 in Ukraine. The Gagauz are a Turkic-speaking, Christian ethnic minority whose Muslim antecedents fled the Russo-Turkish wars in the 18th century. They were allowed to settle in the region in exchange for their conversion to Christianity. Their language is a dialect of Turkish, with its vocabulary influenced by Russian Orthodoxy as opposed to the Islamic influences inherent in Turkish. Gagauz look to Turkey for cultural inspiration and heritage.

The republic has its own flag (blue, white and red stripes with three white stars in the upper left corner), its own police force, its own newspapers (Sabaa Ildyzy, Gagauz Vesti and Guneshhik), and its own university. The official languages here are Gagauzi, Moldovan and Russian, though Russian is used almost everywhere, even in their university. Gagauzi is taught in 37 schools throughout Moldova.

Gagauz autonomy was officially recognised by the Moldovan government on 23 December 1994; that day is now celebrated annually as **Independence Day**. Unlike the more militant separatists in Transdniestr, the Gagauz forfeited independence for large-scale autonomy. Theirs is a predominantly agricultural region with little industry to sustain an independent economy. There are 12 vineyards on their territory, however, producing fine wines, the profits for which Gagauzia accuses Chişinău of reaping. Though the mainly calm relations between Moldova and this autonomous region have been praised as a model of rationality, there are many unfinished issues between them, including disputes over language and economic issues.

COMRAT
☎ 298 / pop 32,000
Gagauzia's capital, 92km south of Chişinău, is no more than a dusty, provincial town. In 1990 Comrat was the scene of clashes between Gagauz nationalists and Moldovan armed forces, pre-empted by calls from local leaders for the Moldovan government to hold a referendum on the issue of Gagauz sovereignty. Local protesters were joined by Transdniestran militia forces.

Comrat is home to the world's only Gagauz university – so what if nearly all courses are taught in Russian? Most street signs are in Russian; some older ones are in Gagauzi but in the Cyrillic script. Since

1989, Gagauzi, alongside Moldovan, has used the Latin alphabet.

Orientation & Information

From the bus station, walk south along the main street, Str Pobedy, past the market to ploshchad Pobedy (Victory Square). St John's Church stands on the western side of the square, behind which lies the central park. Prospekt Lenina runs parallel to Str Pobedy, west of the park.

Change money at the **Moldovan Agrobank** (Str Pobedy 52; 8am-2pm Mon-Fri). A small currency exchange is inside the entrance to the market. You can make international calls at the **post office** (Str Pobedy 55; 8am-6pm Mon-Fri, 8am-5pm Sat). Surf the Web at **IATP** (25 875; Str Lenina 160; per hr $0.40; 9am-6pm Mon-Fri).

Sights

The regional **başkani** (assembly) is on prospekt Lenina. The Gagauzi and Moldovan flags fly from the roof.

Next to the assembly is the **Gagauz Culture House**, in front of which stands a statue of Lenin. West of prospekt Lenina at Str Galatsăna 17 is **Gagauz University** (Komrat Devlet Üniversitesi), founded in 1990. Four faculties (national culture, agronomy, economics and law) serve 1500 students who learn in Russian and Gagauz. The main foreign languages taught are Romanian, English and Turkish. The university gets some funding from universities in Turkey.

Sleeping & Eating

Hotel Aina (22 572; Str Pobedy 127A; s/d $11/16) On the eastern side of ploshchad Pobedy, this is a fairly modern hotel. Its bar serves light meals, including delicious şaşlik and salads.

Eugenia (24 968; Str Pobedy 52; mains $1-3; 9am-midnight) This cafe/bar isn't a bad place to grab a meal or hang out for a few drinks.

Getting There & Away

Five daily return buses run from Chişinău to Comrat ($2.95). From Comrat there are two buses daily via Bendery to Tiraspol, and one only as far as Bendery.

MOLDOVA

Directory

CONTENTS

ACCOMMODATION

The choice of accommodation in Romania and Moldova runs the gamut from seedy camping grounds and train-station hotels to world-class luxury. In this book, we've listed places to stay classified as budget, including camping grounds, B&Bs, hostels, cabanas and inexpensive hotels costing under €20 per person ($20 in Moldova). Our mid-range choices are for hotels or villas with singles/doubles from €20 to €70, and top-end choices are business or luxury hotels with all the fixings you would expect anywhere from a four- or five-star hotel charging over €75 for a single room.

Unless otherwise noted, breakfast is included in the prices quoted. For budget accommodation, we have noted when a room is 'without toilet', meaning there are shared toilets in the corridor; when there is a toilet

---

PRACTICALITIES

- Video System: PAL
- Time: GMT/UTC+2; DST observed
- Electricity: 220V, 50Hz AC; European plugs required
- Weights & Measures: Metric system
- Photography & Video: Colour film, flash cards and video cassettes easily available in large centres; slide and black-and-white film hard to find

---

but no shower in the room, this has been noted. In mid-range and top end choices, rooms have both toilet and shower. Even the grottiest hotels supply towels and soap.

There is no uniformity about discounted rates and periods. Many hotels in resort towns such as Poiana Braşov and Mamaia raise their prices during ski or summer seasons, respectively, but not all. Some of the larger hotels in the mid-range or top-end categories have weekend specials; others lower prices slightly on weekdays. Where possible this has been noted, but your best bet is to contact them yourself.

Sometimes tourist information bureaus or travel agencies are privy to discounts on some hotels in town; consider contacting them before heading out. Hotels charge regular, posted rates when you just walk in off the street. Some are open to bargaining, however, especially for extended stays, so it always helps to ask if any special prices are available.

Even when hotel prices are listed in euros (in Romania) or dollars (in Moldova), you must pay in lei. You will be asked to briefly present your passport upon registration. In Moldova, they may keep it for several hours in order to register it. Floors are numbered counting the ground floor as the first floor.

A particularly helpful website where you can search in advance for a place to stay is www.rotravel.com.

Camping

While camping grounds (*popas turistic*) in Moldova are practically nonexistent, in

Romania they tend to be extremely grungy affairs; this book has recommended very few of them. Don't expect to find any Western-style camping grounds here. They usually comprise wooden huts *(căsuţe)* which fit two to four people. Bare mattresses are usually provided but you have to bring your own sleeping bag. Not very clean toilets and showers are shared, and hot water is a rarity. Not only are these places usually filled to the brim with local tourists who set up temporary homes for weeks or months on end, they tend to be dirty, cramped, poorly attended and unpleasant affairs, badly serviced by public transport and often situated on main roads. Moreover, a few of them double as poorly disguised houses of prostitution and single males will be propositioned.

The good news is that wild camping anywhere in Romania and Moldova is legal unless otherwise prohibited (in the Danube Delta there are allocated zones; along the Black Sea coast it is forbidden to camp on the beach; and obviously private property and areas in development are off limits), so if you have your own tent, there are much better places to spend the night than these places.

Homes & Farmstays

Someone's private home is the most down-to-earth type of accommodation anyone wanting to get to the roots of Romanian home life, tradition and cuisine can find. A paying guest you may well be, but that will not deter your host family from welcoming you with open arms. Evening meals cost extra.

Many families rent rooms *(cazare)* as a way of supplementing income, and so in almost every town and village in Romania, walking around will avail you of numerous choices. This practice is almost non-existent – so far – in Moldova.

The trick is finding a good place to stay. Families can be pushy, intrusive and noisy as often as they are respectful and delightful. Travellers arriving at train stations, and to a lesser extent bus stations, will be accosted by a gaggle of babushkas offering rooms (even teenagers are in on the act now, hoping to throw a modern spin on things). Make sure you understand exactly where the room is before you accept their offer, and don't part with cash until you've checked the room. Expect to pay €7 to €12 per person.

A more pleasing alternative is agrotourism (B&B in the countryside), which has blossomed in recent years. A superb website where you can see photos of rural homestay options in many regions of Romania is www.ruraltourism.ro. For comfortable places in the Apuseni Mountains, try www.greenmountains.ro. Local travel agents can also usually help find a private home.

The largest agro-tourism organisation in Romania is **Antrec** (National Association of Rural, Ecological and Cultural Tourism; www.antrec.iiruc.ro), which has branches or representatives in many regions. Depending on which branch you chance upon, they can either be helpful (as at Piatra Neamţ and Mangalia) or not even answer the door/phone. Travellers are frequently disappointed. We've listed the branches you're more or less likely to get some assistance from, but you can't expect much from an organisation that hasn't updated its website since 1997!

In Moldova, the nascent branch of **Antrec** (☎ 22-237 823; antrec_ong@yahoo.com; Str Serghei Lazo 13, Chişinău) is more helpful, but its choice of places to stay is so far small – the idea of rural homestays in Moldova is in its infancy.

Hostels

Romania currently has 17 accredited Hostelling International (HI) hostels and hotels in 12 cities, and more are opening all the time, as well as some independent ones. Some of the best and friendliest ones include the Retro Hostel (Cluj-Napoca; p152), the Kismet Dao Villa (Braşov; p91), the Class Hostel (Suceava; p287), Sighişoara's Burg Hostel (p128) and Elvis Villa (p128), and Bucharest's Elvis Villa (p68) and Vila 11 (p68). Others range from great to shabby would-be hostels in run-down student dorms. The going rate is about €7 to €13 per person in rooms for four to eight persons; some have private singles/doubles for higher prices. There are no hostels in Moldova.

At these places, you can count on Internet access, good breakfasts, clean accommodation, laundry, lively surroundings and super-friendly, helpful and knowledgeable staff. Some of them, like the Retro and Class, also offer reasonably priced and fun local excursions and organised activities.

Youth Hostels Romania (www.hihostels-romania.ro) is headquartered in Cluj-Napoca (p147) and can be contacted for information. On its website, you can see that several hotels are affiliated with YHR; these provide discounts on certain rooms upon presentation of your HI card.

Hotels

Romanian hotels are rated by a government star system, which should be used as a rough guide at best. The top end of the scale (four and five stars) nearly guarantees semiluxury with all the bells and whistles. The three-star category could be called 'anything goes'. There are some three-star hotels as comfortable as any four-star one, and others that seem to be two-star variants which found an extra star on the ground and posted it. You can at least be assured of hot water, a phone, private bathroom and cable TV.

Not much separates one- and two-star hotels. Hot water *(apă caldă)* is common but not a given. In rural towns, it can be restricted to a few hours in the morning and evening. In rare cases, cold water *(apă rece)* will be programmed too. You can usually choose between a more expensive room with private bathroom or a cheaper one with shared bathroom. In Bucharest and Chişinău you'll pay €25 to €40 per room, but outside the capitals singles will usually be €15 to €25 and doubles €20 to €30.

Mountain Huts

In most mountain areas there's a network of cabins or chalets (cabana) with restaurants and dormitories. Prices are much lower than those of hotels and no reservations are required, but arrive early if the cabana is in a popular location such as next to a cable-car terminus. Expect to find good companionship rather than cleanliness or comfort. Many are open year-round and cater for skiers in winter. Cabanas invariably close for renovations at some time or other and it is always wise to check with the local tourist office before heading off.

You will also come across unattended, empty wooden huts *(refuges)* in the mountains. These are intended as shelter for hikers and anyone can use them. It is possible to free camp in the mountains and most cabanas allow camping in their grounds.

BUSINESS HOURS

There is considerable variety throughout the two countries, but generally, banks can be expected to open from 9am to 3pm, with many closing for an hour around noon; most shops are open from 9am or 10am to 6pm or 7pm, some closing on Sundays; museums are usually open from 11am to 5pm, most closing on Monday; post offices are open from 8am to 7pm Monday to Friday, until 4pm Saturday and closed Sunday; most restaurants and cafés open from 8am or 9am and close at 11pm. Theatrical performances and concerts usually begin at 7pm. Where opening hours vary from standard, they are detailed in the regional chapters.

CHILDREN

Romania is a great destination for children as well as adults. The sights and things to do are endless – from climbing mountains by foot or cable car, to heading deep underground in salt mines or ice caves, to fun on the beach and in aqua parks, to horse-riding excursions and encounters with farm animals, to following Dracula's dastardly trail. Moldova offers fewer sights of interest to children, though visits to farms or orchards might help pass the time.

The main challenge will be having to rely on your own resources a bit more than you might in other countries, as there is very little infrastructure set up specifically for kids. Finding a highchair in a restaurant is next to impossible, children's menus are nearly unheard of, bathrooms are not equipped with nappy-change counters, shopping malls don't have play centres where you can drop the kids off, hotels aren't set up with video-game rooms.

That said, there's always room to improvise: accommodating restaurant staff can bring out smaller portions of food or a phone book to sit on; nappies can be changed elsewhere; malls and hotels are different enough in Romania to be fun to explore, and video games are available at nearly every Internet salon and café we list. Though childcare facilities are meager, your homestay hosts will likely be happy to do some baby-sitting for you. Many of the larger hotels have family rooms and most hotels will put an extra bed or cot in your room. Nappies and formula shouldn't be a problem to find as all cities and most towns have Western-style and well-stocked supermarkets.

While travelling with children over Romania's vast distances, be sure to bring items (toys, portable games, books) from home that they can use to pass the time; you're unlikely to find anything suitable (especially in your mother tongue) in Romania. That goes for food and drink too as none is available on buses and most trains. If you need to breast-feed, note that this is not something Romanians and Moldovans are used to seeing and doing in public; some discretion would be advised.

It would also be a good idea to have a talk with your children about the issue of orphans and child homelessness in Romania, as they are likely to see some street kids or child beggars and may be troubled by this. A visit to an orphanage might also be an eye-opening, life-changing experience for some children. In this case, bringing along a few extra toys or clothes to give away will make all involved feel good. Contact the **Information and Cooperation Centre for Homeless Children** (☎ 21-212 6176; http://members.tripod.com /cicfa) in Bucharest for any information about this grave social issue and related charities. For information about the situation in Moldova and how you can help, see **Save the Children Moldova** (http://scm.ngo.moldnet.md/index 1024.html).

For some good specific tips on places the kids will love, see p15 in the Itineraries chapter – an exhausting but fun route has been planned out for you and the kids (though you might need a vacation afterwards to recuperate!). See also Lonely Planet's *Travel with Children* for some useful tips.

CLIMATE CHARTS
Temperatures can vary greatly in Romania and Moldova, depending not only on when but also where you go. Even in the summer, don't count on the 30° to 35°C heat that has befallen the region in recent years; if you plan to include trips into the mountains, be prepared for cold winds at high altitudes and cool nights everywhere else. Winters are fairly temperate, especially near the coast, but again, in the unpredictable mountains be prepared for virtually any conditions.

See also p9 in the Getting Started chapter for more practical information.

CUSTOMS
Romania
Officially, you're allowed to import hard currency up to a maximum of US$10,000. Valuable goods and foreign currency over US$1000 should be declared upon arrival – this is not obligatory, but suggested. That way if any of your items get stolen (heaven forbid!), you can use that declaration to file a police report; this will ease insurance claims as well.

For foreigners, duty-free allowances are 4L of wine, 1L of spirits and 200 cigarettes.

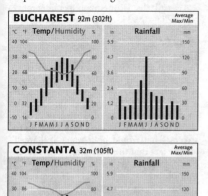

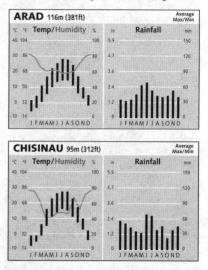

Moldova

Moldova has more complicated customs procedures (Soviet legacies die slowly), but generally there should be little problem bringing whatever you like into an out of the country. See www.turism.md for the latest changes in customs regulations.

There is no limit to the amount of foreign currency you can bring into or out of the country, but the amount must be declared upon entering on a customs declaration sheet you'll be given, and then again upon exiting the country; purportedly, this is to ensure you do not leave with more money than you arrived with (not without a good explanation anyway!). You might be asked to prove that you have at least $30 for each day of your stay.

You're allowed to cross the border either way with 1L of alcohol, 2L of beer and up to 200 cigarettes, though these rules are not strictly enforced (most tourist leave with several bottles of good, cheap wine!). Should you require official permission to take out antiques or large art pieces, the **customs office** (☎ 22-569 460; Str Columna 65) is in Chişinău.

DANGERS & ANNOYANCES

Every country has its annoyances, and every traveller has their particular dislike; not everyone will be happy all the time. Whether it's the summer heat, winter cold, mosquitoes, barking dogs, a shop closed for a lunch break, a long wait between buses, or the billows of smelly smoke from car exhausts or from the smoker next to you (and there will always be one), there's bound to be something to annoy everyone here. Yet what country can't you say that about? All in all, most travellers will not undergo particular difficulties in Romania and Moldova. Patience, especially when not everything on the menu is available, or when plans have to change at the last minute, or when there's just no hot water no matter how much you need a shower, will help inordinately.

See p56 for a list of some popular tourist scams in Romania, but realise that most of the ways people try to take advantage of tourists are relatively harmless: a security guard at Bucharest's Gara de Nord train station might offer to help you decipher the train schedules – for a fee; or a ticket conductor on a bus might try to make you believe your ticket has been improperly punched – so you can pay the fine, straight into his pocket. Take steps not to be taken advantage of, but remember too the social backdrop of poverty and need (and sometimes greed).

Street Crime

Despite its bad reputation, Bucharest is no more dangerous than any other European city of comparable size. Street crime has soared in the region since the collapse of communism, primarily because daily survival for many is so damn difficult. This most often takes the form of pickpocketing. Extreme vigilance should be exercised on crowded public transportation and even on the streets, where a purse or video camera slung around a shoulder can be gone in two seconds flat. Be on guard if walking late at night, keep to well-lit streets and look purposeful.

Outside the capital, street crime is not much of an issue. Vigilance is always called for, however, and common sense should tell you not to leave valuables unattended, including in hotel rooms, at camp sites and in the boot of your car. Motorists should lock their vehicles at night and leave not so much as a tourist map on the dashboard.

Moldova is a very safe country for travellers. Perhaps that's just due to the lack of potential crime victims (so few tourists!). Still, it pays to be alert and wary, as everywhere.

To call the (Romanian-speaking only) police dial ☎ 955. In Moldova, dial ☎ 902.

Stray Dogs

They say that the evident problem of stray dogs in Bucharest is a legacy of Ceauşescu's systemisation in the 1980s, when scores of city-centre and countryside homes were demolished. Replacement tower blocks proved so cramped that many dog-owners faced no alternative but to let their pets loose on the streets. That would hold water if it wasn't for the fact that there are stray dogs literally everywhere across Romania (relatively few in Moldova).

Most dogs roaming cities and towns are harmless – indeed most are deeply frightened of humans, who often beat them – but it only takes one to ruin a holiday. Bitches with puppies can be snappy. It's best to keep clear of all strays. At night, most dogs are a barking nuisance; earplugs are your best defence.

Should you be bitten by a dog, seek medical advice. See the Medical Services and Emergency sections in the regional chapters for places to call. See also p354 in the Health chapter.

Other Nuisances
Hay-fever sufferers will sneeze their way around the region in May and June when the pollen count is at its highest. Blood-sucking mosquitoes are rife in summer, particularly in the Danube Delta.

DISABLED TRAVELLERS
Disabled travellers will find it difficult, if not downright impossible, to conquer Romania. Street surfaces are woefully uneven, ramps are rare (though plentiful in Sibiu, thanks to local government initiatives) and specially equipped toilets and hotel rooms are virtually unheard of. Consider joining a package tour that will cater to your specific needs. Wheelchair-accessible hotels have been noted throughout this book; however, in many instances staff will be happy – if perhaps slightly awkward about – aiding wheelchair-bound visitors. Some hotels on the Black Sea coast have wheelchair access from the hotel to the beach.

Though there are laws providing for wheelchair access to public buildings, in reality little has been done. As the country is still economically and politically finding its footing, persons with disabilities and their problems have not been a priority. The **Romania Motivation Foundation** (☎ 21-420 8445; rommot@mail.sfos.ro) in Bucharest has worked incredibly hard since its foundation in 1995 to provide access to wheelchairs (and training on how to use them in urban settings) for locals in need. They may be able to provide information and assistance.

The situation for the disabled in Moldova is in even greater need of overhaul, and travellers will find obstacles all along their route. However, staff at hotels and restaurants will be obliging, and taking a wine tour at Cricova, for example, is entirely possible. For a good summary on the situation for disabled people in Moldova, see www.iatp .md/usmlaw/clinic.htm.

DISCOUNT CARDS
A Hostelling International (HI) card yields a token discount in some hostels. You can become a member by joining your own national Youth Hostel Association (YHA) or IYHF (International Youth Hostel Federation); see www.hihostels.com for details. Alternatively, you can buy an annual card for about €5 at one of Romania's HI-affiliated hostels (p333).

Holders of the International Student **Identity Card** (ISIC; www.isic.org) are privy to many discounts in Romania and in Moldova (though only in Chişinău), and the **Euro<26 card** (www.euro26.ro) entitles those under 26 years of age to some 600 discounts in Romania (none in Moldova). Helpful hints for student travellers in Romania can be found at www.studenttravel.ro, including a list of all ISIC's discounts.

Elderly foreigners may obtain discounted entry to some museums and on some long-distance bus and train journeys, but not much more.

EMBASSIES & CONSULATES
Romanian Embassies & Consulates
Romania has widespread diplomatic representation abroad.

Australia Canberra (☎ 02-6286 2343; www.roembau .org; 4 Dalman Crescent, O'Malley ACT, 2606)

Bulgaria Sofia (☎ 02-973 2858; ambsofro@exco.net; Sitnjakovo 4, Sofia)

Canada Ottawa (☎ 613-789 5345; www.cyberus.ca /~romania; 655 Rideau St, Ottawa, Ontario)

Consulates: Montreal (☎ 514-876 1792; romcon@videotron .ca; 1111 St Urbain, Suite M01-04, Montreal) Toronto (☎ 416-585 5802; cgrt@ca.inter.net; 111 Peter St, Suite 530, Toronto)

France Paris (☎ 01 47 05 10 46; www.amb-roumaine.fr; 5 rue de l'Exposition, Paris)

Germany Berlin (☎ 030-803 30 18; ro-amb.berlin@ t-online.de; Matterhornstrasse 79, Berlin)

Hungary Budapest (☎ 01-352 0271; roembbud@mail .datanet.hu; Thököly út 72, Budapest)

Ireland Dublin (☎ 031-269 2852; ambrom@eircom.net; 47 Ailesbury Rd, Ballsbridge, Dublin)

Moldova Chişinău (☎ 22-228 126; ambrom@ch.moldpac .md; Str Bucureşti 66/1, Chişinău)

Consulate: Chişinău (☎ 22-237 622; Str Vlaicu Parcalab 39, Chişinău)

UK London (☎ 020-7937 9666; www.roemb.co.uk; 4 Palace Green, Kensington Gardens, London)

Ukraine Kyiv (☎ 044-224 52 61; romania@iptelecom .net.ua; ulitsa Mihaia Kotziubinskogo 8, Kyiv)

USA New York (☎ 212-682 9120; www.romconsny.org; 200 East 38th St, New York); Washington DC (☎ 202-232 3694; www.roembus .org; 1607 23rd St NW, Washington DC)

Consulates: Los Angeles (☎ 310-444 0043; www.romanian
.org/consulat; 11766 Wilshire Blvd, Suite 1230, Los Angeles)
New York (☎ 212-682 9120; www.romconsny.org;
200 East 38th St, New York)
Yugoslavia Belgrade (☎ 011-646 151; ambelgro@infosky
.net; Kneza Miloša 70, Belgrade)

Embassies & Consulates in Romania

Unless stated otherwise, the following foreign embassies are in Bucharest (city code
☎ 21).

Australia *Consulate:* (☎ 320 9802; don.cairns@austrade
.gov.au; B-dul Unirii 74)
Bulgaria (☎ 230 2150; Str Rabat 5)
Canada (☎ 307 5000; bucst-im@dfait-maeci.gc.ca; Str
Nicolae Iorga 36)
France (☎ 312 0217; www.ambafrance.ro; Str Biserica
Amzei 13-15)
Consulate: (☎ 312 0991; Intrarea Cristian Tell 6)
Germany (☎ 202 9853; www.deutschebotschaft
-bukarest.org/ro/home; Str Rabat 21) Sibiu (☎ 269-211
133; Str Lucian Blaga 15-17, Sibiu) Timişoara (☎ 256-220
796; Hotel Continental, B-dul Revoluţiei 1989 3, Timişoara)
Consulates: Sibiu (☎ 269-214 442; Str Hegel 3, Sibiu)
Timişoara (☎ 256-190 495; B-dul Republicii 6, Timişoara)
Hungary (☎ 312 0073; hunembro@ines.ro; Str Jean
Louis Calderon 63-65)
Consulates: (☎ 312 0468; Str Henri Coandă 5) Cluj-Napoca
(☎ 264-596 300; huconkol@codec.ro; Piaţa Unirii 23,
Cluj-Napoca)
Ireland *Consulate:* (☎ 211 3967; Str Vasile Lascăr 42-44)
Moldova (☎ 230 0474; moldova@customers.dirigo.net;
Aleea Alexandru 40)
Consulate: (☎ 410 9827; B-dul Eroilor 8)
Russia (☎ 222 3170; Şoseaua Kiseleff 6)
Consulate: Constanţa (☎ 041-222 1389; Str Tuberozelor
4, Constanţa)
Turkey (☎ 210 0279; Calea Dorobanţilor 72)
Consulate: Constanţa (☎ 041-611 135; turkkons@fx.ro;
B-dul Ferdinand 82, Constanţa)
UK (☎ 201 7200; www.britain.ro; Str Jules Michelet 24)
Honorary Consulate: Constanţa (☎ 041-638 282; B-dul
Tomis 143A, Constanţa)
Ukraine (☎ 211 6986; Calea Dorobanţilor 16)
Consulate: (☎ 222 3162; Str Tuberozelor 5)
USA (☎ 210 4042; www.usembassy.ro; Str Tudor
Arghezi 7-9)
Consulate: (☎ 210 4042; Str Nicolae Filipescu 26)
Information Bureau: Cluj-Napoca (☎ 264-594 315; Str
Universităţii 7-9, Cluj-Napoca)
Yugoslavia (☎ 211 9871, consulate section ☎ 211 4980;
Calea Dorobanţilor 34)
Consulate: Timişoara (☎ 256-590 334; gktyug@mail.dnttm
.ro; Str Remus 4, Timişoara)

Moldovan Embassies & Consulates

Moldova has embassies and consulates in
the following countries:
Bulgaria (☎ 02-981 7370; moldova@www1.infotel.bg;
B-dul Patriarh Evtimii 17, Sofia)
France (☎ 01 40 67 11 20; ambassade.moldavie@free.fr;
1 rue Sfax, Paris)
Germany (☎ 069-52 78 08; mongenmold@aol.com;
Adelheidstrasse nr. 8, Frankfurt)
Hungary (☎ 1-209 1191; amrung@mail.elender.hu; Str
Kazinthy 17, fsz 5-6, Budapest)
Romania (☎ 01-230 0474; moldova@customers.digiro
.net; Aleea Alexandru 40, Bucharest)
Consulate: (☎ 01-410 9827; B-dul Eroilor 8, Sector 5,
Bucharest)
Russia (☎ 095-924 5353; moldemb@online.ru; 18
Kuznetskii most, Moscow)
Turkey (☎ 312-446 5527; ambmold@superonline.com;
Kaptanpasa Sok 49, Ankara)
Ukraine (☎ 044-290 7721; moldovak@sovam.com;
ulitsa Kutuzov 8, Kyiv)
USA (☎ 202-667 1130; moldova@dgs.dgsys.com; 2101 S
Street NW, Washington, DC)

Embassies & Consulates in Moldova

Countries with embassies or consulates in
Chişinău (city code ☎ 22) include:
Bulgaria (☎ 237 983; amb_bg@mdl.net; Str Bucuresti 92)
France (☎ 228 204; www.ambafrance.md; Str 31 August
1989, 101A)
Germany (☎ 234 607; www.ambasada-germana.org
.md; Str Maria Cibotari 35)
Hungary (☎ 227 786; huembkiv1@meganet.md; B-dul
Ştefan cel Mare 131)
Romania (☎ 228 126; ambrom@ch.moldpac.md; Str
Bucureşti 66/1)
Consulate: (☎ 237 622; Str Vlaicu Pircalab 39)
Russia (☎ 234 941; www.moldova.mid.ru; B-dul Ştefan
cel Mare 153)
Turkey (☎ 242 608; tremb@moldova.md; Str V Cupcea 60)
Ukraine (☎ 582 124; www.mfa.gov.ua; Str V Lupu 17)
UK (☎ 238 991; www.britishembassy.md; Str Banulescu-
Bodoni 57/1)
USA (☎ 233 772; www.usembassy.md; Str A
Mateevici 103A)

FESTIVALS & EVENTS

Moldova is not a festival-heavy country,
perhaps as its citizens find any excuse to
party anytime throughout the year. Their
major festival is the Wine Festival on the
second Sunday in October (and for several
wine-drenched days preceding and following it). The government has even instituted
a visa-free regime for this period (see p342

and p324 for more details). Chişinău's City Day is 14 October.

Romania has festivals going on year-round in all regions of the country. Our favourite 10 are listed on p11, and many others are listed in the regional chapters.

FOOD

In this book, we have listed the prices for main courses (mains); the price of a full-course meal will depend on whether you also add garnish, entree, dessert, beverage or alcoholic drink. As the cost of eating out in Romania and Moldova is relatively low, budget places include fast-food joints, kebab kiosks and inexpensive cafés, bistros or cafeterias where the mains might cost under €1.50 ($1.50 in Moldova). About the average are decent restaurants and cafés where you'll still pay only €1 to 3 ($1 to $3) for a main course. Top-end is pretty much anything over €4 ($4) per main course; except for some very expensive places, even 'fancy' restaurants are very affordable by Western European standards.

For more detail concerning cost and types of food and drink available in Romania and Moldova, see the Food chapter (p43).

GAY & LESBIAN TRAVELLERS
Romania

Romania's rather puritan attitude towards homosexuality was reflected by its laws: only in 2001, it became one of Europe's last countries to decriminalise homosexual activity (in 1994 the Constitutional Court repealed Communist-era laws against homosexuality but in 1996 it was reinstated as a criminal offence). Until then, people were prosecuted and jailed even for acts in private between consenting adults. Police harassment and brutality were common-place against homosexuals – human-rights groups in Romania and abroad have reams of reports of violence, extortion and entrapment, even in the 1990s.

Not surprisingly, few gay and lesbian Romanians show affection in public. The Orthodox Church still considers homosexuality a sin. The situation is slowly getting more relaxed, especially in urban centres with a high student population (there are gay bars and associations in Bucharest, and gay club nights in Cluj-Napoca, Transylvania; see those chapters for details), but in general, it's not a subject most are comfortable with. The age of consent is 15.

Romania's capital is the only place with an active gay and lesbian scene, represented by Bucharest-based **Accept** (www.accept-romania.ro). It provides education and support and hosts social events. Its site has links to other Romanian gay sites, but see also www.gayonline.ro and www.gay bucuresti .ro (in Romanian, but has a chat room).

Moldova

Before Moldova repealed its Soviet antigay law in 1995, it was one of only four European countries to still criminalise homosexuality. Now, Moldova has one of the most progressively liberal laws on the continent: homosexual activity is legal for both sexes at 14, the same age as for heterosexual sex. In 2003 the government adopted a National Human Rights Plan which would see the prohibition of discrimination against homosexuals enshrined in law. Gay Pride parades happen in Chişinău yearly in late April/early May. However, homosexuality is still a hushed topic, and politicians still get away with antigay rhetoric. While most people take a laissez-faire attitude towards the notion of homosexuality, being visibly out is likely to attract unwanted attention.

There are no officially gay nightclubs in Moldova, but at least one Chişinău club hosts gay nights (p314). Check out www.gay.md, run by GenderDoc-M (an information centre on gender studies), for the latest news.

HOLIDAYS

Public holidays in Romania are New Year (1 and 2 January), both Catholic and Orthodox Easter Mondays (in March/April), Labour Day (1 May), Romanian National Day (1 December) and Christmas (25 and 26 December).

Moldova's national holidays include New Year's Day (1 January), Orthodox Christmas (7 January), International Women's Day (8 March), Orthodox Easter (March or April), Memorial Day (27 April), Labour Day (1 May), Victory (1945) Day (9 May), Independence Day (27 August) and National Language Day (31 August).

INSURANCE

Though medical insurance is not compulsory in Romania and Moldova, a fully comprehensive travel-insurance policy to cover theft, loss and medical problems is strongly advisable, especially if you intend to do a lot of travelling. A policy which covers the costs of being flown out of the country for treatment is a definite bonus, given the still-limited local facilities. See also car insurance (p348) and health insurance (p353).

INTERNET ACCESS

Most hotels, except for the most expensive, will not have dial-up or cable connections available in the rooms, but there has been a proliferation of Internet cafés throughout Romania (even in smaller towns) such that it is never a problem to find somewhere to log on. The speeds are usually fast, and the price will rarely be over €0.60 per hour, though you may have to contend with legions of noisy video-game enthusiasts. Chişinău is also full of Internet cafés, though outside the capital access may be restricted to a booth at the local telephone centre.

For more information see p12.

LEGAL MATTERS

If you are arrested you can insist on seeing an embassy or consular officer straight away. It is not advisable to present your passport to people on the street unless you know for certain that they are authentic officials – cases of theft have been reported. Better still, carry a copy of your passport with you instead of the actual document while touring the city.

Romanians and Moldovans can legally drink, drive and vote (though not simultaneously!) at 18. The age of consent in Romania is 15, in Moldova 14.

Romania and Moldova have high rates of incarceration, and drug possession is a criminal offence in both countries, so getting caught with drugs here is really not a good idea.

MAPS

Good-quality maps are definitely in order for any form of travel throughout these countries. Details on which maps are best and where to buy them are found throughout the regional chapters under Maps and Publications.

MONEY

In both Romania and Moldova the only legal tender is the leu (plural: lei), though they are separate currencies and have different exchange rates (see Quick Reference inside the front cover). In Romania you'll see prices quoted in euros, while in Moldova people talk in US dollars. Consequently, this book quotes prices in euros for Romania, and in dollars for Moldova. After tumultuous times of inflation and devaluation in the 1990s, both currencies are showing signs of stability. For general costs, see p10.

Romanian lei come in denominations of 2000, 10,000, 50,000, 100,000 and 500,000. There are (heavy) coins for one, five, 10, 20, 50, 100, 500 and 1000 lei.

Moldovan lei come in denominations of one, five, 10, 20, 50, 100, 200 and 500. There are coins for one, five, 10, 25 and 50 bani (there are 100 bani in a leu).

Note that the breakaway Transdniestran republic in Moldova has its own currency, which is useless anywhere else in the world (see p325).

In order to change money in Romania (exchange bureaus are easy to find in any city and town; in villages you'll be out of luck) you'll need to present your passport (supposedly so tax officials can better control the moneychangers). Some places will do it 'unofficially' without one. Dollars and euros are easiest to exchange, though other major currencies such as the British pound are widely accepted and at larger exchange bureaus most major world currencies (and from neighbouring countries) can be changed.

Primarily due to the fact that so many citizens of both countries work abroad and support their families from there, Western Union works highly efficiently, and there are offices almost everywhere.

ATMs

ATM machines giving 24-hour advances (Cirrus, Plus, Visa, MasterCard, Eurocard) are rife in Romanian cities and towns. You can only make withdrawals in lei; however, Banca Comercială Română will give you cash advances on your credit card in your home currency. It's easy to find ATMs in Chişinău, but not in other towns in Moldova.

Black Market

This activity is not seen much in either country (except, for some reason, in Cluj-Napoca; see p146), but you may still be approached on the street or at train stations.

Wear a scowl and ignore them; black marketeers are pros at ripping off even the most street smart of travellers.

Travellers Cheques & Credit Cards

Travellers cheques offer protection against theft and are easy to cash at major banks, usually for a 1.5% to 3% commission. In Romania all branches of the Banca Comercială Română, among others, will do it; in Moldova, Eximbank will cash them. Both banks will also give cash advances on major credit cards. It is almost impossible to use travellers cheques in either country in stores or restaurants. However, while credit cards won't get you anywhere in rural areas, they are widely accepted in larger department stores, hotels and most restaurants in cities and towns. You'll need a credit card to rent a car, unless you're willing to pay a large deposit up front.

American Express is represented in Bucharest by **Marshal Travel Agency** (☎ 21-335 1224; B-dul Unirii 20; also B-dul Magheru 43), but has no representatives in Moldova.

POST

A postcard or letter under 20g to Europe from Romania costs €0.15 and takes seven to 10 days; to the rest of the world it costs €0.40 and takes 10-14 days. The postal system is reliable, if slow. Recommended mail (*poştală recomandată)* can be sent from any post office.

Poste-restante mail is held for one month (addressed c/o Poste Restante, Poşta Romană Oficiul Bucureşti 1, Str Matei Millo 10, RO-70700 Bucureşti, Romania) at Bucharest's main post office (p55).

From Moldova, it costs $0.35 to send a postcard or letter under 20g to Western Europe, Australia or the USA.

DHL (www.dhl.com) is the most popular international courier service in the region. It has offices in 21 Romanian cities; in Moldova there are offices in Chişinău, Balţi and Tiraspol. See the website for details.

SHOPPING

Pack light on your way to Romania and Moldova so you have room to fill it with bottles of the good stuff on your way out (not that we're encouraging you to break customs' rules in any way...see p335). From Moldova, local wine, sparkling wine

or a nice bottle of Kvint, a Transdniestrian brandy, make for nice souvenirs, and from Romania, you'll not want to forget to bring back some *ţuică* (clear fruit brandy).

Other traditional purchases include embroidered blouses, ceramics, wooden sculptures, tablecloths and hand-woven carpets. Some specific shopping suggestions are found in the appropriate sections in the regional chapters.

SOLO TRAVELLERS

If you're a solo traveller, you can expect Romanians to look at you with surprise, admiration and curiosity for your bravery and independence. Moldovans will just worry about you being lonely.

Generally Romania and Moldova are pretty safe countries to tour alone – taking all the normal precautions. Women travelling solo do have to be a bit more assertive than those travelling in a couple. At restaurants the waiters assume you are waiting for your other half and can ignore you for ages unless you make it clear you are alone. You will be regarded as somewhat of an oddity – it isn't normal practice here for a woman to do anything much by herself. People might fuss over your safety. Don't worry – it's only cultural differences and Romanians' generally caring disposition that causes this reaction.

TELEPHONE

Romania's international operator can be reached by dialling ☎ 971. For an English-speaking operator abroad, dial ☎ 01-800 4444 (British Telecom), ☎ 01-800 4288 (AT&T USA Direct), ☎ 01-800 1800 (MCI Worldwide) or ☎ 01-800 0877 (Sprint).

For national and international phone codes and dialing codes, see Quick Reference inside the front cover.

Mobile Phones

Any European cellphone with roaming will work inside Romania and Moldova, though reception inside Transdniestr is not a given.

Cellular phone service in Moldova is provided by Chişinău-based Moldcell (run by Moldtelecom) and **Voxtel** (☎ 22-575 757; www.voxtel.md; Str Alba Iulia 75).

Phonecards

In Romania, phonecards costing €2.15 or €4 can be bought at any telephone centre and

DIRECTORY

at many newspaper kiosks. International calls can also be made with these.

Moldtelecom, the state-run telephone company, sells pay cards which can be used to dial any number within Moldova only, for $2.25 or $3. These are sold at any telephone centre in the country. To make an international call using a prepaid card, you need to use a private company such as Treitelecom. Its cards cost from $3.75 to $35 at any Moldpressa newspaper stand (and can be used to make local calls too).

TIME

Both Romanian and Moldovan time is GMT/UTC plus two hours, and both countries observe daylight savings time. Both also use the 24-hour clock in telling time. Dates are listed with the month first, followed by the day and year, ie 03/08/04 refers to 8 March 2004.

TOILETS

Let's just say that public toilets in these countries won't be among your highlights. The ones at train and bus stations are often smelly holes in vile pits which will make you rush out gasping for fresh air. While the vast majority are quite usable, the fact that many do not have a toilet seat (or have a cracked or soiled one) can be annoying. Locals might be used to squatting, but most tourists aren't. Though you might be handed a coarse piece of toilet paper by a babushka at the entrance for a nominal fee, this is where having some extra tissues comes in handy.

Many toilets have a plastic bin by their side. This is intended for used toilet paper. Women's toilets are marked with the letter F (*femei*) or with an s. Men's are marked B (*bărbaţi*) or t.

In Moldova most toilets bear Russian signs: Ж for women and M for men.

TOURIST INFORMATION
Local Tourist Offices

Amazingly, Romania still has no national tourist office network, making information tough to track down. A handful of highly efficient, independently run tourist centres – such as those in Arad, Sinaia and Bistriţa – have sprung up in the past couple of years. Elsewhere, private travel agencies double as tourist offices, although

their quality, usefulness and attitude varies dramatically. In each city section, we have recommended the places you are most likely to get the best help from.

Tourist Offices Abroad

Contrary to the disheartening lack of information locally, Romania runs a string of efficient tourist offices abroad, coordinated by Romania's **National Authority for Tourism** (☎ 21-410 1262; www.turism.ro; Str Apolodor 17, Bucharest). The full list is available on the website.

France Paris (☎ 01 40 20 99 33; fax 01 40 20 99 43; roumanie@office-tourisme-roumanie.com; 12 rue des Pyramides, Paris)

Germany Berlin (☎ 030-241 9041; www.rumaenien-tourismus.de; Budapester Str 20A, Berlin) Munich (☎ 089-5156 7687; Dachauer Str 32-34, Munich)

Moldova Chişinău (☎ 22-222 354; B-dul Ştefan cel Mare 151-153, Chişinău)

UK London (☎ 020-7224 3692; romaniatravel@btconnect .com; 83A Marylebone High Street, London)

USA New York (☎ 212-545 8484; www.romaniatourism .com; 14 East 38th St, 12th Floor, New York, NY 10016)

VISAS
Romania

Your number one document is your passport. Its validity must extend to at least six months beyond the date you enter the country in order to obtain a visa.

Citizens of Canada, Japan and all EU countries may travel visa-free for 90 days in Romania. US citizens and those from many Eastern European countries can travel visa-free for 30 days. All other foreign visitors require a visa to enter. As visa requirements change frequently, check at the **Ministry of Foreign Affairs** (www.mae.ro) before departure.

Romania issues two types of visas to tourists: transit and single-entry. Transit visas (for those from countries other than the ones mentioned above) are for stays of no longer than three days, and cannot be bought at the border.

To apply for a visa you need a passport, one recent passport photograph and the completed visa application form accompanied by the appropriate fee. Citizens of some countries (mainly African) need a formal invitation from a person or company in order to apply for a visa; see the above-mentioned website of Romanian Foreign Affairs for details.

Regular single-entry visas (US$25) are valid for 60 days from the day you enter the country. Single-entry visas are usually issued within a week (depending on the consulate), but for an extra US$6 can be issued within 48 hours.

Transit visas can be either single-entry (US$15) – valid for three days and allowing you to enter Romania once – or double-entry (US$25), allowing you to enter the country twice and stay for three days each time.

VISA EXTENSIONS

In Romania, you can extend your tourist visa for another 60 days at any passport office, such as the one at Str Nicolae Iorga 2 in Bucharest. You must apply before your current visa expires. Travel agencies can help you with this.

VISAS FOR NEIGHBOURING COUNTRIES

Check your visa requirements for Yugoslavia, Hungary, Bulgaria and Ukraine if you plan on crossing those borders. Contact the relevant embassy in Bucharest for details. If you are taking the Bucharest–St Petersburg train you need Ukrainian and Belarusian transit visas on top of the Russian visa.

Moldova

All Western travellers need a visa to enter Moldova.

Citizens of the EU, Canada, the USA and Israel need only present their passports (valid for six months after the visa's expiration date) and one photo to the nearest Moldovan consulate to obtain a visa. All others require either a tourist voucher from an accredited travel agency or an invitation from a company, organisation or individual (difficult to get). Tourist vouchers ensure that you have a hotel prebooked and prepaid. Payments to the consulates are usually in the form of a bank deposit at a specified bank.

Citizens of the EU, Japan, the USA or Canada can buy visas on arrival at Chişinău airport or at the border-crossing points at Sculeni (north of Iaşi), Leuseni (main

Bucharest-Chişinău border) and Cahul if arriving by bus or car from Romania. No invitation is required, but you may be asked to prove that you have at least $30 per day for each day you plan on being in the country. Citizens of countries normally requiring an invitation must present one at the border if buying a visa there.

In 2002 Moldova generously started instituting a visa-free programme for all foreigners wishing to partake in the Wine Festival (2nd Sunday in October). The visa can last for 10 days.

An HIV/AIDS test is required for foreigners intending to stay in Moldova longer than three months. Certificates proving HIV-negative status have to be in Russian and English.

See www.moldovavisa.com/visas or www.turism.md/eng/content/66 to check for the latest changes on the visa rules.

COSTS & REGISTRATION

The price of a single/double-entry tourist visa valid for one month is $60/75. Single/double-entry transit visas valid for 72 hours cost $30/60. Special rates apply for tourist groups of more than 10 persons, and for children, disabled travellers and senior travellers.

Visas can be processed within a day at the **Moldovan consulate** (☎ 40-21-410 9827; B-dul Eroilor 8, Bucharest) in Romania. Applications must be made between 8.30am and 12.30pm weekdays. After paying for the visa at a specified bank in the city centre, you then collect your visa between 3pm and 4pm the same day.

Anyone staying longer than three days must have their visa registered by the local police. While this is an unfortunate Soviet holdover (and a good way of generating income), it's actually a simple process which is automatically done at hotels and apartment-rental firms. If you need to do it yourself, call the **Office for Visas and Registration** (☎ 22-213 078) to find out where to register; you're liable for a fine on the way out without registration.

Transport

GETTING THERE & AWAY

ENTERING ROMANIA & MOLDOVA

Travellers entering Romania should not experience any trouble at customs and immigration, particularly if they come from a country which does not require them to possess a Romanian visa (see p342). As a result of a Soviet legacy, travellers may experience more questioning or minor hassle entering Moldova, but, thanks to the same legacy, any potential complication is easy to resolve on the spot – most often by offering a few dollars. Still, though you and your luggage may be checked more thoroughly by the Moldovans than the Romanians, Moldovan border guards are generally friendly and down-to-earth (they may simply be curious about you as they see few foreign tourists); most travellers are breezed through with no problems.

Passport

Romanian nationals may have trouble entering Transdniestr.

AIR

Airports & Airlines

Tarom (Transporturile Aeriene Române; RO; ☎ 21-337 2037; www.tarom.ro) is Romania's state airline. Nearly all international flights to Romania arrive at Bucharest's **Otopeni International Airport** (OTP; ☎ 21-201 4050; www.otp-airport.ro). Moldova's only main airport is the **Chişinău International** (☎ 22-526 060; www.airport.md). **Voiaj Travel** (www.voiaj.md) in Chişinău publishes the latest airport schedules.

AIRLINES FLYING TO & FROM ROMANIA

Aeroflot (SU; ☎ 21-315 0314; www.aeroflot.org; Moscow SVO)
Air France (AF; ☎ 21-312 0086; www.airfrance.com; Paris CDG)
Air Moldova (RM; ☎ 21-312 1258; Chişinău KIV)
Alitalia (AZ; ☎ 21-210 4111; www.alitalia.it; Rome FCO)
Austrian Airlines (OS; ☎ 21-312 0545; www.austrian air.com; Vienna VIE)
British Airways (BA; ☎ 21-303 2222; www.british -airways.com; London LHR)
Czech Airlines (OK; ☎ 21-315 3205; www.csa.cz; Prague PRG)
El Al Israel Airlines (LY; ☎ 21-330 8760; www.elal.co.il; Tel Aviv TLV)
Hemus Air (DU; ☎ 21-211 3082; www.hemusair.bg; Sofia SOF)

THINGS CHANGE

The information in this chapter is particularly vulnerable to change: prices for international travel are volatile, routes are introduced and cancelled, schedules change and special deals come and go. Airlines and governments seem to take a perverse pleasure in making price structures and regulations as complicated as possible. You should check directly with the airline or a travel agent to make sure you understand how a fare (and ticket you may buy) works. In addition, the travel industry is highly competitive and there are many lurks and perks.

The details given in this chapter should be regarded as pointers and are not a substitute for your own careful, up-to-date research.

KLM (KL; ☎ 21-312 0149; www.klm.com; Amsterdam SPL)

LOT Polish Airlines (LO; ☎ 21-212 8365; www.lot.com; Warsaw WAW)

Lufthansa (LH; ☎ 21-312 9559; www.lufthansa.com; Frankfurt FRA)

Malev-Hungarian Airlines (MA; ☎ 21-312 0427; www .malev.hu; Budapest BUD)

Olympic Airways (OA; ☎ 21-210 7445; www.olympic -airways.gr; Athens ATH)

Swiss Airlines (LX; ☎ 21-312 0086; www.swiss.com; Zurich ZRH)

Syrian Arab Airlines (RB; ☎ 21-312 7673; www.syrian -airlines.com; Damascus DAM)

Turkish Airlines (TK; ☎ 21-311 2410; www.turkish airlines.com; Istanbul IST)

AIRLINES FLYING TO & FROM MOLDOVA

Austrian Airlines (OS; ☎ 22-244 083; www.austrianair .com; Vienna VIE)

Tarom (RO; ☎ 0992 541 254; www.tarom.ro; Bucharest OTP)

Turkish Airlines (TK; ☎ 22-527 078; www.turkishairlines .com; Istanbul IST)

Tickets

Better-known travel agents where you may pay slightly more than a rock-bottom fare in return for security and peace of mind include **Flight Centre** (☎ 131 600 in Australia, ☎ 09-309 6171 in New Zealand; www.flightcentre .com.au), **STA Travel** (www.sta-travel.com), **Nouvelles Frontières** (www.nouvelles-frontiere.fr) in France, Canada-based **Travel CUTS** (www.travelcuts.com), Ireland-based **USIT** (www.usit.ie) and the France/ Belgium-based **Wasteels** (www.voyages-wasteels.fr), which also has offices in Bucharest and Braşov.

Between Romania & Moldova

Air Moldova and Tarom together operate daily flights between Chişinău and Bucharest, and Moldova's Transaero also has flights on that route. Air Moldova also has daily flights to Timişoara.

From Australia & New Zealand

From Australia, expect to pay around A$1500 return during low season and upwards of A$1900 during high season. Swiss, Lauda Air and Qantas all have some good fare deals. From New Zealand, count on around NZ$2399 for a return low-season fare from Auckland with either Swiss or Qantas.

From Central & Eastern Europe

Bucharest is connected with regular flights to and from Prague, Budapest, Warsaw, Sofia and Moscow. See www.otp-airport.ro for the latest schedules. Chişinău is connected with regular flights to and from Sofia, Minsk, Moscow, Budapest and Prague. Expect to pay about €200 to €350 for a return flight between any of these capitals.

From Turkey

Tarom operates regular flights between Bucharest and Istanbul that sometimes stop in Constanţa from May to mid-September only. Return fares are about €175. Turkish Airlines also flies this route. See Istanbul's **Orion Tour** (www.oriontour.com) for any specials.

From Western Europe

Bucharest is well linked with all of the major European capitals (see the list of airlines flying to Romania, p344), while Chişinău has direct flights from Amsterdam, Rome and Paris. In addition, Tarom runs flights from Arad to Verona, from Timişoara to Milan, from Sibiu to Munich and Stuttgart, and from Cluj-Napoca to Vienna, Frankfurt and Munich. Tarom often has great specials – in 2003 a 12-month return ticket to London was €275. Prices will vary wildly for all of these more competitive routes, but expect to pay between €250 and €500 for a return fare, and usually around €300 to €350 for a sale price.

While most of Moldova's international flights are eastward, Air Moldova travels daily to Vienna, four times a week to Rome, three times a week to Athens and Amsterdam, and twice a week to Paris.

From the USA & Canada

Tarom has a flight at least once a week direct to/from New York. A sale price can be as low as US$500 return, but is usually around US$700.

LAND
Border Crossings

When crossing the border by car, expect long queues at Romanian checkpoints, particularly on weekends. Carry food and water for the wait. Don't try bribing a Romanian official and beware of unauthorised people charging dubious 'ecology', 'disinfectant' or other dodgy taxes at the border. Though this

TRANSPORT

is unlikely to happen, ask for a receipt if you are unsure. It is best to stick to major border crossings, as small ones may not always know how to process foreign visitors. Note that obtaining a Moldovan visa is only possible at three border crossings with Romania (see p342). To avoid potentially major hassles, avoid driving to Moldova from Ukraine via Transdniestr.

Bus

Romania and Moldova are well linked by bus lines to central and western Europe as well as Turkey. While not as comfortable as the train, usually, buses tend to be faster, though not always cheaper.

Car & Motorcycle

The best advice here, and it's worth repeating, is to make sure all your documents (personal ID, insurance, registration and visas, if required) are in order before crossing into Romania and Moldova. See p348 for some rules and regulations. The Green Card (a routine extension of domestic motor insurance to cover most European countries) is valid in both Romania and Moldova. Extra insurance can be bought at the borders.

Train

International train tickets are rarely sold at train stations, but rather at CFR (Romanian State Railways) offices in town (look for the Agenţie de Voiaj CFR signs) or at Wasteels offices. Tickets must be bought at least two hours prior to departure.

Those travelling on an Inter-Rail pass still need to make seat reservations (€2 to €3) on express trains within Romania. Even if you're not travelling with a rail pass, practically all international trains require a reservation (automatically included in tickets purchased in Romania). If you already have a ticket, you may be able to make reservations at the station an hour before departure, though it's preferable to do so at a CFR office at least one day in advance.

BETWEEN ROMANIA & MOLDOVA

There's an overnight train service between Bucharest and Chişinău; at 12 hours, the journey is longer than taking a bus or maxitaxi (the train heads north to Iaşi, then south again), but is more comfortable if you

want to sleep. It also lets you experience a unique bogie change at the border. The train lurches, vibrates and clanks while the undercarriages are changed; to slow down a potential invasion, the USSR changed all its train tracks to a wider gauge, and to this day, trains entering and exiting the ex-Soviet Union must undergo this bizarre operation. Each carriage is lifted 2m off the ground by cranes and the wheels are switched mechanically.

There are numerous maxitaxis and private cars making the trip daily between the two capitals; this is the quickest route (usually 10 to 12 hours). There are also at least four daily maxitaxis running between Chişinău and Iaşi.

FROM BULGARIA & TURKEY

The train service between Romania and Bulgaria is slow and crowded but cheap. Between Sofia and Bucharest (11 hours) there are two daily trains, both of which stop in Ruse. Sleepers are available only on the overnight train; buy your ticket well in advance to guarantee yourself a bunk for the night.

The *Bosfor* overnight train travels from Bucharest to Istanbul (803km, 17 to 19 hours). Buses galore trundle the 804km between Bucharest and Istanbul in 14 to 16 hours. There are also some leaving from Constanţa. There's a daily bus between Chişinău and Istanbul. All of these are modern, with air conditioning and refreshments.

FROM HUNGARY

The Budapest–Bucharest train journey (873km) takes around 12 hours. To or from Arad it is a mere 28km to the Hungarian border town of Lököshaza, from where it is a further 225km (4½ hours) to Budapest. There are five daily trains between Bucharest and Budapest (around €40 one way). A one-way ticket from Arad or Oradea to Budapest costs around €30. It's also possible to pick up the Budapest-bound train from other Romanian cities, including Constanţa, Braşov and Cluj-Napoca. From Chişinău, you must go to Bucharest, then catch a Budapest-bound train.

There are many daily buses from cities throughout Romania, including Bucharest, Arad, Braşov, Cluj-Napoca, Târgu Mureş, Miercurea Ciuc and Satu Mare, to Budapest with stops along the way. Eurolines and other private companies make these journeys. See those sections in the regional chapters for details. There are no buses from Moldova to Hungary.

FROM UKRAINE & BEYOND

Between Romania and Ukraine, there is a daily Bucharest–Moscow train which goes via Kyiv. A second train, the Sofia–Moscow *Bulgaria Expres*, takes a different route through western Ukraine to Chernivtsi (Cernăuţi in Romanian), and stops at Bucharest. Some wagons of this train continue to St Petersburg through Ukraine and Belarus (you'll need transit visas for these countries).

From Chişinău, there are 11 daily trains to Odesa, one to Lviv and three to Moscow. Buses between Chişinău and Kiev or Odesa run through Transdniestr and Tiraspol; even with a Moldovan visa, local authorities will most likely make you pay for an additional transit permit.

FROM WESTERN EUROPE

There's only a direct train service to Bucharest from Vienna (around €65 one-way).

Eurolines (www.eurolines.ro; www.eurolines.md) has a flurry of buses linking numerous cities in both Romania and Moldova with Western Europe; it has many offices in both countries. Buses to Germany from either country cost €45 to €60 one way, and as far as Spain can cost €95 to €110. Many routes offer a 10% to 15% discount for those aged under 26 or over 60. Children under 12 and under 4 years old receive additional discounts. Some passes, good for extended periods, are available. Eurolines offices are listed throughout the regional chapters; otherwise, see the websites for schedules.

RIVER

There are ferry crossings into Bulgaria from Calafat and Giurgiu in Romania (p196).

TOURS

It is usually – though not always – more expensive to travel from your home country on a prebooked tour. However, many travellers prefer the convenience prearrangement accords. Here are a few recommended international tour agencies who have specialised tours of Romania.

Adventures Abroad (☎ 09-273 9366; www.adventures-abroad.com) Based in Auckland, New Zealand.
Discover Transylvania (☎ 01377-200 118; www.enzia.com) Based in East Yorkshire, UK.
Explore Worldwide (☎ 01252-760 000; www.explore worldwide.com) Based in the UK.
Quest Tours (☎ 800-621 8687; www.romtour.com) Based in Oregon, USA.

GETTING AROUND

AIR
Airlines in Romania & Moldova

State-owned carrier **Tarom** (www.tarom.ro) is Romania's main carrier and in 2003 invested in new 747s and improved its already excellent on-board service. Smaller airlines such as **Angel Airlines** (www.angelairlines.ro) and **Carpatair** (www.carpatair.ro) run domestic flights. It makes economical sense to purchase return fares within Romania as they are only slightly more expensive than one-way fares. Most domestic flights are around €80 to €100 one-way, and €90 to €110 return.

BICYCLE

Cyclists are becoming a more frequent sight in Romania, particularly in Transylvania, Maramureş and Moldavia. But villagers will still stop and stare blankly at you as you roll by. Intercity roads are generally in decent condition (as opposed to hellish roads inside villages and towns), and biking offers an excellent way of seeing the country and meeting with locals. However, as so many places of interest require climbing steep roads, being in top shape is definitely a plus! Also, be aware that motorists are not as used to sharing roads with cyclists as in some western countries, and may drive accordingly. Be particularly vigilant in urban settings. Bikes are possible to rent or buy in most major towns, which also have bike-repair shops. Still, bringing a lot of spare parts with you will save you time and headaches. Two good towns to get bikes from are Sibiu and Braşov in Transylvania.

Bicycles can be taken on trains. Most trains have a baggage car (*vagon de bagaje*), marked by a suitcase symbol on train timetables. Bicycles stored here have to be labelled with your name, destination and the bicycle's weight. But it is easier and safer to simply take your bicycle on the train with you. On local and express trains there is plenty of room at either end of the carriage next to the toilet. Be sure not to block passageways. You might be charged a minimal 'bulky luggage' fee, and any conductor that appears to be giving you hassle will be placated by a pack of cigarettes or some cash.

The best source of advice and information is the Clubul de Cicloturism Napoca (p150), a friendly and English-speaking environmental group in Cluj-Napoca. There is also some excellent advice on biking in Romania at www.bikeromania.de/einfo, written in heavily Germanised English.

Bicycle theft, as everywhere, is common so take extra precautions.

Moldova, being flat as a board, makes cycling an excellent way of getting around. That is, if it weren't for the bad condition of most of its roads, and for a lack of infrastructure – outside of Chişinău, you'll have to rely on your own resources or sense of adventure (and trying to enlist help from friendly locals) if you run into mechanical trouble.

BOAT

Boat is the only way of getting around much of the Danube Delta. **Navrom** (www.navrom.ro), operates passenger ferries along the three main Danube channels from Tulcea (p217). You can easily hire private motorboats, rowing boats and kayaks in Tulcea and all the Delta villages to explore the smaller waterways. Local fishermen and boatmen double as guides.

BUS

In order to make the best of bus service in Romania and Moldova, you need a good sense of ironic humour and an appreciation of the surreal. Regular buses travel to most corners of the countries – slowly, clunkily, dustily, but surely. Endlessly better are the maxitaxis (also referred to as microbuses or minibuses) which have blanketed the countries in recent years. The size of an SUV that might be used to drive to the local mall in the US, these zippy machines hold eight to 12 passengers, drive at breakneck speeds between and within cities, and run regularly throughout the day.

Sounds good, but there's a catch – it requires a detective's skills and Job's patience to figure out the schedules. Timetables

for regular buses posted in bus stations (autogară) are often incomplete or out of date, so always ask at the ticket window for details. Buses in transit are written on the timetable in a different colour (usually red). Fares are cheap and calculated per kilometre: a 10km trip will cost €0.40, a 100km trip €2.40.

Maxitaxis are even more elusive creatures. Because routes are run by different private companies, which crop up all the time, there is no centralised system of information. Sometimes separate timetables are posted on scraps of paper in windows and/or metallic placards on the pavement or station platform; sometimes none are posted at all and are included in the timetable for regular buses – only the info kiosk knows for sure which are buses and which are maxitaxis, but getting the information can be like pulling teeth. On some popular routes, reservations are required or suggested – if you can find the number to call and try to make yourself understood! Fares on maxitaxis are higher than for regular buses.

All this, of course, is contingent upon you actually knowing where buses and maxitaxis depart – in many cities, departure points can be not only at the bus station but at any nearby parking lot. In short, getting around by bus and maxitaxi is possible, it just takes a sense of adventure!

CAR & MOTORCYCLE

Don't drive in Romania unless your car is in good shape and has been serviced recently. Repair shops are common but, unless you're driving a Renault (the same as Romania's Dacia) or a Citroën (the basis of Romania's Oltcit model), parts are hard to come by. Most Romanian roads are best suited to 4WD vehicles that can take child-sized potholes in their stride.

ROMANIA ON 500CCS

Motorcycling is still fairly marginal as a way of life in Romania, but if that's your thing, **Transylvania Motorcycle Tours** (www.tm tours.freeservers.com) is your way to see the country. Its six-day zoom across the Carpathians is a reasonable €300 per person, and it also offers a nine-day, 2000km expedition along the Black Sea coast.

ROAD DISTANCES (KM)

	Alba Iulia	Arad	Baia Mare	Bistrița	Brașov	Bucharest	Cluj-Napoca	Constanța	Deva	Iași	Miercurea Ciuc	Oradea	Piatra Neamț	Pitești	Ploiești	Satu Mare	Sibiu	Suceava	Târgu Mureș	Timișoara	Tulcea
Alba Iulia	---																				
Arad	236	---																			
Baia Mare	236	319	---																		
Bistrița	217	393	151	---																	
Brașov	229	429	392	267	---																
Bucharest	340	538	574	439	175	---															
Cluj-Napoca	94	270	142	123	281	432	---														
Constanța	581	809	781	648	383	243	662	---													
Deva	84	150	290	301	279	388	178	631	---												
Iași	458	686	508	355	380	428	432	432	586	---											
Miercurea Ciuc	288	522	349	209	99	272	261	486	378	258	---										
Oradea	247	117	202	276	434	528	153	815	190	581	411	---									
Piatra Neamț	358	620	383	244	236	342	310	425	422	118	140	463	---								
Pitești	231	431	467	375	147	107	325	349	281	454	246	478	383	---							
Ploiești	344	544	507	382	115	58	396	291	349	347	214	549	300	119	---						
Satu Mare	264	251	67	226	458	607	175	822	319	581	433	129	456	497	573	---					
Sibiu	73	274	322	271	156	265	167	538	126	413	255	320	295	188	271	343	---				
Suceava	408	588	318	191	328	434	300	562	492	140	247	467	107	475	392	403	406	---			
Târgu Mureș	137	378	227	93	174	347	106	554	221	321	151	260	201	282	289	282	124	284	---		
Timișoara	240	52	370	457	435	545	334	829	156	742	534	168	578	440	550	297	279	648	377	---	
Tulcea	600	813	777	591	384	304	665	147	666	335	406	817	345	401	262	846	540	437	558	825	---

Romania has only a few short stretches of motorway (*autostrada*). Some major roads (*drum național*) have been resurfaced, but many remain in a poor (understatement!), potholed condition. Secondary roads (*drum judeţean*) can become dirt tracks, and mountain and forestry roads (*drum forestier*) can be impassable after heavy rain. While roads are being repaved all the time and the government has made them a priority (especially the main roads which form sections of pan-European corridors), the costs involved are enormous: 1km of four-lane motorway costs between €3 million in flat areas and €10 million in mountainous areas. It's estimated that it would cost €29 billion to modernise all of Romania's roads; now, only some €600 million a year is invested.

While keeping your eyes peeled for cracks and potholes, also watch out for other obstacles, namely a flock of sheep appearing out of nowhere and wanting to cross the road with their shepherd, or the ubiquitous horse-drawn carts piled high with hay, playing children, drunkards, cows, pigs and other moving objects. Never a dull moment!

Western-style petrol stations are easy to come by (though don't embark on long journeys into mountainous regions or remote village areas without a full tank), and a litre of unleaded 95E in both countries is approximately €0.45. Most stations accept credit cards.

Road Rules

EC driving licences are accepted here; otherwise, bring both your home country's driver's licence and the International Driver's Permit, which is recognised in both Romania and Moldova. In Romania, there is a 0% blood-alcohol tolerance limit, seat belts are compulsory in the front and back seats (if fitted), and children under 12 are forbidden to sit in the front seat. Speed limits are indicated, but are usually 90km/h on major roads, 100–110km/h on motorways, and 50km/h inside cities. Having a standard first-aid kit is also compulsory. Honking unnecessarily is prohibited, and headlights need not be turned on in the daytime.

TRANSPORT

Romania's main automobile association is the **Automobil Clubul Român** (ACR; ☎ 21-222 1553; www.acr.ro), but while it might provide some information and assistance, it's mainly for Romanians to renew licences and is not geared to handle tourists. Its 24-hour emergency service number is ☎ 927.

In Moldova, the intercity speed limit is 90km/h and in built-up areas 60km/h; the legal blood-alcohol limit is 0.03%. For road rescue, dial ☎ 901. **The Automobile Club Moldova** (ACM; ☎ 22-292 703; www.acm.md) can inform you of all regulations and offer emergency assistance.

Hire

Avis, Budget, Hertz and Europcar have offices in most cities and at Otopeni airport in Bucharest. For a list of reliable car-rental agencies in Romania, see p75. In Chişinău, travel agencies can arrange car rental, and Hertz offers great deals (p317).

Consider renting a Dacia. Romania's national car might well be the butt of endless jokes but in the event of a breakdown you'll be glad you're not driving a Mercedes. Romanians are adept at dismantling and reassembling Dacia engines and take great pride in showing off their engineering skills. If you break down, flag down the first passing car. It will be a Dacia and its driver will be able to make yours go again. And they'll have all the necessary tools too.

HITCHING

Hitching is never entirely safe in any country in the world, and we don't recommend it. People who do choose to hitch will be safer if they travel in pairs and let someone know where they are planning to go. That said, hitching is very popular in both countries, where people usually stand along the main roads out of a city or town. It's common practice in Romania and Moldova to pay the equivalent of the bus fare to the driver. Many local motorists solicit business at bus and train stations as a way of covering their fuel costs.

LOCAL TRANSPORT
Bus, Tram & Trolleybus

Buses, trams and trolleybuses (buses run by electricity with wires overhead) provide transport within most towns and cities in Romania, although many are crowded. They usually run from about 5am to midnight, although services can get thin on the ground after 7pm in more remote areas. Purchase tickets at street kiosks marked *bilete* or *casă de bilete* before boarding, and validate them once aboard. Some tickets are good for one trip; others are for two trips, each end of the ticket being valid for one ride. Tickets cost from €0.20 to €0.40. Travellers staying any length of time in Bucharest or another large city should invest in a weekly or monthly travel pass.

If you travel without a validated ticket or with no ticket at all you risk a €6 on-the-spot fine. Spot checks are carried out on all modes of public transport by gruff, plain-clothed ticket inspectors. Some travellers report scams whereby inspectors will act as if your ticket has not been properly stamped (or invent some other infraction); if you're certain you've done nothing wrong, stand your ground and refuse to pay, or insist on the police being called. If you were trying to get away with a free ride, you'd best shut up and pay the fine.

In Moldova buses cost about $0.10, trolleybuses $0.05 and city maxitaxis $0.20.

Horse, Donkey & Wagon

In many rural parts, the only vehicle that passes will be horse-powered. Horse and cart is the most popular form of transport in Romania and you will see numerous carts, even in cities (although some downtown areas are off limits to them). Many carts will stop and give you a ride, the driver expecting no more than a cigarette in payment.

Metro

Bucharest is the only city to sport a metro; see p77 for details.

Taxi

Romanian taxi drivers, as in many places across the globe, are notorious rip-off merchants who have no scruples in charging you over the odds or driving you around in circles. It's always best (and cheaper) to call a reliable company – either recommended by your hotel or by us in the regional chapters.

In Bucharest, cabs with functioning meters and reasonably honest drivers – identifiable by the yellow pyramid attached to their roofs and visible phone numbers – do exist. Their fixed meter rate is €0.35 per kilometre, compared to €0.15 per kilometre in other cities and towns. If a taxi has no meter then bargain before roaring off.

In Moldova there are official metered taxis, but the more common way to get a lift is to follow the handy Russian-style practice of waving a private car down for a 'ride' with someone who just happens to be going your way (for a fee!). With both, you'll often need to agree upon a price before driving off; a drive to anywhere inside Chişinău is unlikely to cost more than $3. The going rate is about $0.10 to $0.15 per kilometre.

TOURS

It might seem that every travel agency in Romania offers a seemingly impressive array of guided tours around Romania, enabling visitors to see the prime sites in a minimum amount of time. Most do not cater to individuals or small groups of tourists who don't like being herded about with 20 other people. Aside from the fun hostels which organise their own tours (see p333), here are a few of the more imaginative organisations (see the appropriate locations in the regional chapters for details of what's on offer):

Aventours (p87; ☎ 0722 746 262; www.discoveromania.ro; Braşov)

Caliman Club Holidays (p161; ☎ 0744 600 140; www.caliman.ro; Bistriţa)

Contur Travel (p203; ☎ 619 777; www.contur.ro; Constanţa)

Corbet Transair (☎ 268 463; www.corbet-transair.ro; Târgu Mureş)

Green Mountain Holidays (p150; ☎ 257 142; www.greenmountainholidays.ro; Cluj-Napoca)

Mysterious Journeys (☎ 679 2881; www.mysteriousjourneys.com; Bucharest)

RoCultours/CTI (p56; ☎ 223 2619; cti@pcnet.ro; Bucharest)

Roving România (p87; ☎ 0744 212 065; www.roving-romania.co.uk; Braşov)

Voiaj (p308; ☎ 546 464; www.voiaj.md; Chişinău)

TRAIN

Rail has long been the most popular way of travelling around Romania. **Căile Ferate Române** (CFR; Romanian State Railways; www.cfr.ro) runs trains over 11,000km of track, providing services to most cities, towns and larger villages in the country. The national train

timetable *(mersul trenurilor)* is published as a little red book each May and is sold for €2 from CFR offices. It's also available on their Web site, though it takes a degree in engineering to use it.

Sosire means arrivals and *plecare* is departures. On posted timetables, the number of the platform from which each train departs is listed under *linia*.

Classes & Types of Trains

In Romania there are five different types of train, all of which travel at different speeds, offer varying levels of comfort and charge different fares for the same destination.

The cheapest trains are local personal trains. These trains are achingly slow – they're OK if you want to enjoy scenery or people watch, but unless you're a sociologist with lots of time on your hands, you'll avoid these like the plague. Seats are unnumbered, so it's a free-for-all when the train pulls into the station.

Accelerat trains are faster, hence a tad more expensive and less crowded. Seat reservations are obligatory and automatic when you buy your ticket. There's little difference between *rapid* and *expres* trains. Both travel at a fair speed and often have dining cars. Pricier InterCity trains are the most comfortable but aren't faster than *expres* trains.

Sleepers *(vagon de dormit)* are available between Bucharest and Arad, Cluj-Napoca, Oradea, Timişoara, Tulcea and other points, and are a good way to cut accommodation expenses. First-class sleeping compartments generally have two berths, 2nd-class sleepers generally have four berths and 2nd-class couchettes have six berths. Book these in advance at a CFR office.

Fares listed in this book generally indicate one-way, 1st-class seats on *rapid* or *accelerat* trains. Fares for all Romanian trains comprise three parts: the basic fare, calculated on the kilometres you are travelling; a speed/comfort supplement; and a seat reservation (automatic on all but the personal trains).

Travelling 100km 1st class costs €2 on a personal train, €5 on a *rapid* or *expres* and €5.40 on an InterCity train.

Buying Tickets

Tickets are sold in advance for all trains except local personal ones. Advance tickets are sold at an Agenţie de Voiaj CFR, a train-ticket office found in every city centre. When the ticket office is closed you have to buy your ticket immediately before departure at the station. Whenever possible, buy your ticket in advance. This saves time queuing at the train station and also guarantees you a seat.

Theoretically you can buy tickets at CFR offices up to two hours before departure. In reality many do not sell tickets for trains leaving the same day so try to buy your ticket at least the day before you intend to travel.

You can only buy tickets at train stations two hours – and in some cases just one hour – before departure. Get there early as queues can be horrendous. At major stations there are separate ticket lines for 1st and 2nd classes; you may opt for 1st class when you see how much shorter that line is. Your reservation ticket lists the code number of your train along with your assigned carriage *(vagon)* and seat *(locul)*.

If you have an international ticket right through Romania, you're allowed to make stops along the route but you must purchase a reservation ticket each time you reboard an *accelerat* or *rapid* train. If the international ticket was issued in Romania, you must also pay the *expres* train supplement each time.

Health

CONTENTS

Travel health depends on your predeparture preparations, your daily health care while travelling and how you handle any medical problem that does develop. Romania and Moldova will not provide any major challenges to visitors' health.

BEFORE YOU GO

Prevention is the key to staying healthy while abroad. A little planning before departure, particularly for pre-existing illnesses, will save trouble later. Carry a spare pair of contact lenses and glasses, and take your optical prescription with you. Bring extra medications in their original, clearly labelled, containers. A signed and dated letter from your physician describing your medical conditions and medications, including generic names, is also a good idea. If carrying syringes or needles, be sure to have a physician's letter documenting their medical necessity.

INSURANCE

If you're an EU citizen, an E111 form, available from health centres or, in the UK, post offices, covers you for most medical care. E111 will not cover you for nonemergencies or emergency repatriation. Citizens from other countries should find out if there is a reciprocal arrangement for free medical care between their country and the country visited. If you do need health insurance, strongly consider a policy that covers you for

---

HEALTH ADVISORIES

It's usually a good idea to consult your government's travel health website before departure, if one is available:

Australia: www.dfat.gov.au/travel/
Canada: www.travelhealth.gc.ca
United Kingdom: www.doh.gov.uk /traveladvice/
United States: www.cdc.gov/travel/

---

the worst possible scenario, such as an accident requiring an emergency flight home.

INTERNET RESOURCES

The WHO's publication *International Travel and Health* is revised annually and is available online at www.who.int/ith/. Other useful websites include www.mdtravelhealth .com (travel health recommendations for every country; updated daily), www.fitfor travel.scot.nhs.uk (general travel advice for the layperson), www.ageconcern.org.uk (advice on travel for the elderly) and www .mariestopes.org.uk (information on women's health and contraception).

IN ROMANIA & MOLDOVA

AVAILABILITY & COST OF HEALTH CARE

Medical care is not always readily available outside of major cities, but embassies, consulates and five-star hotels can usually recommend doctors or clinics. They can also recommend where to seek treatment in smaller towns or rural areas. In some cases, medical supplies required in hospital may need to be bought from a pharmacy and nursing care may be limited. Note that there can be an increased risk of Hepatitis B and HIV transmission via poorly sterilised equipment.

INFECTIOUS DISEASES
Tickborne encephalitis

This is spread by tick bites. It is a serious infection of the brain and vaccination is advised for those in risk areas who are unable to avoid tick bites (such as campers, forestry workers and walkers). Two doses of vaccine will give a year's protection, three doses up to three years'.

Typhoid & Hepatitis A

These diseases are spread through contaminated food (particularly shellfish) and water. Typhoid can cause septicaemia; Hepatitis A causes liver inflammation and jaundice. Neither is usually fatal but recovery can be prolonged. Hepatitis A and typhoid vaccines can be given as a single dose vaccine, Hepatyrix or Viatim.

Rabies

This is a potential concern considering the number of stray dogs running around Romania. If bitten by a homeless dog, seek medical attention immediately (most main hospitals will have a rabies clinic), but don't panic – while rabies is transmitted via the animal's saliva, the rabies virus is present in saliva only during the final stages of the disease in the animal, often only in the last week of the dog's life. It is therefore a relatively rarely transmitted disease. Still, do not take any chances and seek medical attention. Any bite, scratch or even lick from an unknown animal should be cleaned immediately and thoroughly. Scrub with soap and running water, and then apply alcohol or iodine solution.

TRAVELLER'S DIARRHOEA

If you develop diarrhoea, be sure to drink plenty of fluids, preferably an oral rehydration solution (eg Dioralyte). A few loose stools don't require treatment, but if you start having more than four or five stools a day, you should start taking an antibiotic (usually a quinolone drug) and an antidiarrhoeal agent (such as loperamide). If diarrhoea is bloody, persists for more than 72 hours or is accompanied by fever, shaking, chills or severe abdominal pain you should seek medical attention.

ENVIRONMENTAL HAZARDS
Hypothermia & Frostbite

Proper preparation will reduce the risks of getting hypothermia. Even on a hot day in the mountains, the weather can change rapidly, so carry waterproof garments and warm layers, and inform others of your route.

Acute hypothermia follows a sudden drop of temperature over a short time. Chronic hypothermia is caused by a gradual loss of temperature over hours.

Hypothermia starts with shivering, loss of judgment and clumsiness. Unless rewarming occurs, the sufferer deteriorates into apathy, confusion and coma. Prevent further heat loss by seeking shelter, warm dry clothing, hot sweet drinks and shared bodily warmth.

Frostbite is caused by freezing and subsequent damage to bodily extremities. It is dependent on wind-chill, temperature and length of exposure. Frostbite starts as frostnip (white, numb areas of skin) from which complete recovery is expected with rewarming. As frostbite develops, the skin blisters and then becomes black. Adequate clothing, staying dry, keeping well hydrated and ensuring adequate calorie intake best prevent frostbite. Treatment involves rapid rewarming.

Water

Tap water is generally considered safe to drink in Romania and Moldova. Beware only of drinking water from the polluted Danube River. Some travellers have reported upset stomachs after drinking tea or eating soup or fish prepared with the Danube's waters. In this case, get yourself some Ercefuryl (200mg), an antibiotic available at any pharmacy without prescription; it will stop you from doubling over.

Any water found in the mountains should be treated with suspicion – never drink it without purifying (with filters, iodine or chlorine) or boiling it first, unless assured that it's safe to drink by a guide or local authority. At high altitude water boils at a lower temperature, so germs are less likely to be killed. Boil it for longer in these environments.

WOMEN'S HEALTH

Emotional stress, exhaustion and travelling through different time zones can all contribute to an upset in the menstrual pattern. If using oral contraceptives, remember some antibiotics, diarrhoea and vomiting can stop the pill from working and lead to the risk of pregnancy – remember to take condoms with you just in case. Time zones, gastrointestinal upsets and antibiotics do not affect injectable contraception. Travelling during pregnancy is usually possible, but always consult your doctor before planning your trip. The most risky times for travel are during the first 12 weeks of pregnancy and after 30 weeks.

HEALTH

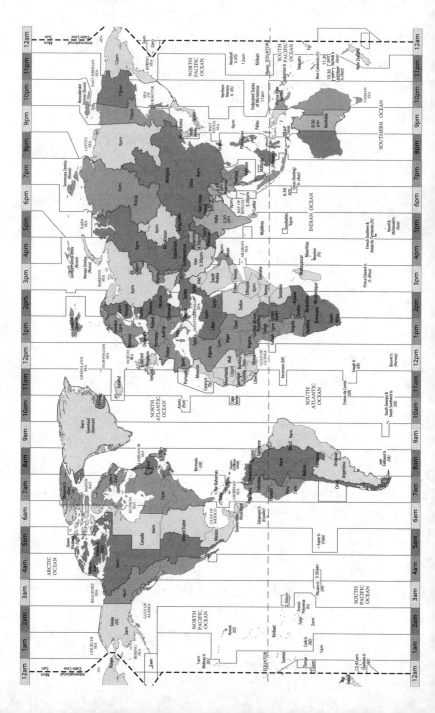

Language

CONTENTS

Romanian is a Romance language, along with the majority of western European languages such as French, Italian, Spanish and Portuguese. Its origins date back to the 2nd century AD when the Emperor Trajan founded the Roman province of Dacia in the south-west of present-day Transylvania. Romanian is much closer to classical Latin than the other Romance languages, and the grammatical structure and basic word stock of the parent language are well preserved.

Romanian has been influenced considerably by the Slavonic languages of neighbouring countries such as Poland, Bulgaria and Serbia, with many words finding their way into the language over the centuries.

Speakers of French, Italian and Spanish won't be able to understand much spoken Romanian but will find written Romanian more or less comprehensible. Moldovan is a very closely related dialect of Romanian.

For useful words and phrases for use when ordering food and trying to decipher menus, see the Food & Drink chapter on p43. For a more comprehensive look at the language, get a copy of Lonely Planet's *Eastern Europe Phrasebook*. If you wish to delve still further, James Augerot's comprehensive *Romanian/Limba Română – A Course in Modern Romanian* (2000) is a good resource. It's published by the Iaşi-based Center for Romanian Studies and is available either in Romania or via the Internet.

WRITING SYSTEM

Until the mid-19th century, Romanian was written in Cyrillic script. Once the decision was made to adopt a Latin-based alphabet, a long period of debate ensued over whether the alphabet should be phonetically-based or etymologically-based (ie reflecting the orthography of Classical Latin).

Between 1953 and 1994 elements of Slavic writing systems were introduced as part of the Russification of the country, under which the letter **â** was replaced by the Slavic **î**. In 1994, the Romanian Academy ruled out the 'Stalinist' **î** and reverted to the original **â** of the Latin orthography. A few words still use the **î**, and nearly all of these begin with it. In place names, old spellings such as Tîrgu Mureş (instead of Târgu Mureş) still lurk on the odd map – this book uses the correct **â** spellings for all place names.

The writing system today uses a Latin-based alphabet of 28 letters, some of which bear accents.

ROMANIANLY SPEAKING

Romanian	Pronunciation Guide	
a	a	as the 'u' in 'cut'
e	e	as in 'tell'
i	ee	as in 'meet'
ă	a	a neutral vowel; as the 'a' in 'ago'
â/î	i	as in 'river'
c	k/ch	as 'k' before **a**, **o** and **u**; as the 'ch' in 'church' before **e** and **i**
ch	k	as 'k' before **e** and **i**
g	g/j	as in 'go' before **a**, **o** and **u**; as the 'j' in 'jet' before **e** and **i**
gh	g	as in 'go'
ş	sh	as in 'ship'
ţ	ts	as in 'cats'

PRONUNCIATION

Written Romanian is more or less phonetically consistent, so once you learn a few simple rules you should have no trouble with pronunciation. In any case, you can always fall back on the pronunciation guides included with the words and phrases in this chapter (see the boxed text Romanianly Speaking on p357, which covers the more difficult sounds).

There are no long variants of vowels, but **e**, **i**, **o** and **u** form diphthongs or triphthongs (vowel combinations) with adjacent vowels. At the beginning of a word, **e** and **i** are pronounced as if there were a faint 'y' preceding them, while at the end of a word a single **i** is almost silent, and **ii** is pronounced 'ee'. Word stress generally falls on the penultimate syllable.

ACCOMMODATION

Where is a ... hotel?
Unde este un hotel ...?
oon·de es·te oon o·tel

cheap	*ieftin*	yef·teen
good	*bun*	boon
nearby	*apropiat*	a·pro·pee·at

youth hostel
cămin studenţesc
ka·meen stoo·den·tsesk
camping ground
camping
kam·peeng
What's the address?
Care-i adresa?
ka·ray a·dre·sa
Could you write the address, please?
Poţi să-mi scrii adresa, te rog?
po·tsee sa·mee skree a·dre·sa te rog
Can I make a reservation?
Pot face o rezervare?
pot fa·chay o re·zair·va·re

I'd like ...
Aş dori ...
ash do·ree
   a single room
   o cameră de o persoană o ka·me·ra de o pair·soa·na
   a double room
   o cameră dublă o ka·me·ra doo·bla
   a private room
   o cameră particulară o ka·me·ra par·tee·koo·la·ra
   a bed
   un pat oon pat

How much is it ...?
Cât costă ...?
kat kos·ta ...
   per night
   pe noapte pe no·ap·te

per person
de persoană de pair·soa·na

Is that the total price?
Acesta este preţul total?
a·ches·ta es·te pre·tsool to·tal
Does it include breakfast?
Include micul dejun?
een·kloo·de mee·kool de·joon
Are there any extra charges?
Mai este ceva de plătit?
ma·ee es·te che·va de pla·teet
May I see it?
Pot să văd?
pot sa vad
Are there any others?
Mai sunt şi altele?
ma·ee soont shee al·te·le
It's fine, I'll take it.
Este în regulă, îl (o) iau.
es·te een re·goo·la (o) yao
Where is the toilet?
Unde este toaleta?
oon·de es·te to·a·le·ta

CONVERSATION & ESSENTIALS
Hello.
   Bună. boo·na
Goodbye.
   La revedere. la re·ve·de·re
Good morning.
   Bună dimineaţa. boo·na dee·mee·ne·a·tsa
Good day.
   Bună ziua. boo·na zyoo·a
Good evening.
   Bună seara. boo·na sey·ra
Yes.
   Da. da
No.
   Nu. noo
Please.
   Vă rog. va rog
Thank you.
   Mulţumesc/Merci. mool·tsoo·mesk/mair·see
Excuse me.
   Scuzaţi-mă. skoo·za·tsee ma
I'm sorry/Forgive me.
   Iertaţi-mă. yer·ta·tsee ma
What's your name?
   Cum vă numiţi? koom va noo·mee·tsee
My name is ...
   Numele meu este ... noo·me·le me·oo es·te
Where are you from?
   De unde sunteţi? de oon·de soon·te·tsee
I'm from ...
   Sunt din ... soont deen ...

EMERGENCIES

Help!
Ajutor! a·joo·tor
I'm sick.
Sunt bolnav. soont bol·nav
Could you help me, please?
M-ați putea ajuta? m·a·tsee poo·te·a a·joo·ta
It's an emergency!
Este o urgență! es·te o·oor·jen·tsa!
There's been an accident.
A fost un accident. a fost oon oon ak·chee·dent

Call ...!	*Chemați ...!*	ke·ma·tsee ...
a doctor	*un doctor*	oon dok·tor
an ambulance	*o ambulanță/*	o am·boo·
	salvare	lan·tsa/
		sal·va·re
the police	*poliția*	po·lee·tsee·a

Go away!
Du-te/Pleacă! doo·te/ple·a·ka
I'm lost.
Sunt pierdut. soont pyer·doot
Where are the toilets?
Unde este toaleta? oon·de es·te to·a·le·ta

I have ...
Eu am ... e·oo am ...

constipation
constipație kons·tee·pa·tsee·ye
diarrhoea
diaree dee·a·re·e
a fever
febră fe·bra
a headache
o durere de cap o doo·re·re de kap
a stomachache
o durere de stomac o doo·re·re de sto·mak

antibiotics
antibiotice an·tee·bee·o·tee che
antiseptic
antiseptic an·tee·sep·teek
aspirin
aspirină as·pee·ree·na
high/low blood pressure
hipo-/hipertensiune hee·po/hee·pair
contraceptive
contraceptive kon·tra·chep·tee·ve
medicine
medicament me·dee·ka·ment
nausea
greață/rău de mare gre·a·tsa/ra·oo de ma·re

ENTERTAINMENT

Where can I hear live music?
Unde pot asculta muzică în concert?
oon·de pot as·kool·ta moo·zee·ka in kon·chairt
Where can I buy a ticket?
Unde pot cumpăra un bilet?
oon·de pot koom·pa·ra oon bee·let
I'm looking for a ticket.
Nu aveți un bilet în plus?
noo a·ve·te oon bee·let in ploos
Is this a good seat?
Este un loc bun?
es·te oon lok boon

at the front	*în primele*	in pree·me·le
	rânduri	rin·doo·ree
ticket	*bilet*	bee·let
cinema	*cinema*	chee·ne·ma
nightclub	*discotecă*	dees·ko·te·ka
theatre	*teatru*	te·a·troo

HEALTH

Where is the ...?	*Unde este ...?*	oon·de es·te ...
chemist	*farmacistul*	far·ma·chees·tool
dentist	*dentistul*	den·tees·tool
doctor	*doctorul*	dok·to·rool
hospital	*spitalul*	spee·ta·lool

LANGUAGE DIFFICULTIES

Do you speak English?
Vorbiți engleza? vor·bee·tsee en·gle·za
I understand.
Eu înțeleg. e·oo in·tse·leg
I don't understand.
Eu nu înțeleg. e·oo noo in·tse·leg
Could you write it down?
Puteți să notați? poo·te·tsee sa no·ta·tsee
How do you say ...?
Cum spuneți ...? koom spoo·ne tsee ...
What does ... mean?
Ce înseamnă ...? che in·se·am·na ...
What's it called?
Cum se cheamă? koom se kya·ma

NUMBERS

1	*unu*	oo·noo
2	*doi*	do·ee
3	*trei*	tre·ee
4	*patru*	pa·troo
5	*cinci*	cheen·chee
6	*șase*	sha·se
7	*șapte*	shap·te
8	*opt*	opt
9	*nouă*	no·oo·a
10	*zece*	ze·che

11	*unsprezece*	oons·pre·ze·che
12	*doisprezece*	do·ees·pre·ze·che
13	*treisprezece*	tre·ees·pre·ze·che
14	*paisprezece*	pa·ees·pre·ze·che
15	*cinsprezece*	chins·pre·ze·che
16	*şaisprezece*	sha·ees·pre·ze·che
17	*şaptesprezece*	shapt·es·pre·ze·che
18	*optsprezece*	opts·pre·ze·che
19	*nouăsprezece*	no·was·pre·ze·che
20	*douăzeci*	do·wa·ze·chee
21	*douăzeci şi unu*	do·wa·ze·chee shee oo·noo
22	*douăzeci şi doi*	do·wa·ze·chee shee do·wee
23	*douăzeci şi trei*	do·wa·ze·chee shee tre·ee
30	*treizeci*	tre·ee·ze·chee
40	*patruzeci*	pa·troo·ze·chee
50	*cincizeci*	cheen·chee·ze·chee
60	*şaizeci*	sha·ee·ze·chee
70	*şaptezeci*	shap·te·ze·chee
80	*optzeci*	op·te·ze·chee
90	*nouăzeci*	no·wa·ze·chee
100	*o sută*	o soo·ta
1000	*o mie*	o mee·ye
10,000	*zece mii*	ze·che mee·yee
one million	*un milion*	oon meel·yon

QUESTION WORDS

Who?	*Cine/Care?*	chee·ne/ka·re
Which?	*Care?*	ka·re
What?	*Ce?*	che
When?	*Cânde?*	kan·de
Where?	*Unde?*	oon·de
How?	*Cum?*	koom

SHOPPING & SERVICES

I'm looking for ...
Caut ... — ka·oot ...

Where is ...?
Unde este ...? — oon·de es·te ...

a bank
o banca — o ban·ka

the ... embassy
ambasada ... — am·ba·sa·da ...

the market
piaţa — pya·tsa

the museum
muzeu — moo·ze·oo

the police
poliţia — po·lee·tsya·

the post office
poşta — posh·ta

a public toilet
o toaetă publică — o to·wa·e·ta poob·lee·ka

the tourist office
informaţii pentru turism — in·for·ma·tsyee pen·troo too·rees·me

open	*deschis*	des·kees
closed	*închis*	in·kees

What time does it open/close?
La ce oră se deschide/închide?
la che o·ra se des·kee·de/in·kee·de

Do I need permission?
Am nevoie de aprobare?
am ne·vo·ye de a·pro·ba·re

Where is the nearest ...?
Unde e cel mai apropii at ...?
oon·de e chel ma·yee a·prop·yee at

bookshop
librărie — lee·bra·ree·ye

chemist
farmacie — far·ma·chee·ye

laundry
spălatorie — spa·la·to·ree·ye

market
piaţă — pya·tsa

newsagent
chioşc de ziare — kee·yosk de zya·re

There is.
Există. — eg·zee·sta

There isn't.
Nu există. — noo eg·zee·sta

Where can I buy one?
Unde aş putea — oon·de ash poo·te·ya
cumpăra? — koom·pa·ra

How much is it?
Cât costă? — kit kos·ta

That's (much) too expensive.
Este (mult) prea scump. — es·te (moolt) pre·ya skoomp

Is there a cheaper one?
Pot găsi ceva mai ieftin? — pot ga·see che·va ma·yee yef·teen

Do you accept credit cards?
Acceptaţi cărţi de — ak·chep·ta·tsee kar·tsee de
credit? — kre·deet

clothing
îmrăcăminte/haine — im·ra·ka·meen·te/hay·ne

condoms
prezervative — pre·zair·va·tee·ve

sanitary napkins
şerveţele igienice — shair·ve·tse·le ee·jye·nee·che

shampoo
şampon — sham·pon

soap
săpun — sa·poon

sunscreen
cremă de soare — kre·ma de so·wa·re

tampons
  tampoane tam·po·wa·ne
toilet paper
  hârtie igienică har·tye ee·jye·nee·ka

TIME & DATES
When?
  Când? kind
At what time?
  La ce oră? la che·o·ra
today
  azi a·zee
tonight
  diseară dee·se·ya·ra
tomorrow
  mâine ma·yee·ne
in the morning
  dimineaţa dee·mee·ne·ya·tsa
in the evening
  seara se·ya·ra
every day
  în fiecare zi in fye·ka·re zee
day after tomorrow
  poimâine poy·ma·yee·ne

Monday
  luni loo·nee
Tuesday
  marţi mar·tsee
Wednesday
  miercuri myer·koo·ree
Thursday
  joi jo·ee
Friday
  vineri vee·ne·ree
Saturday
  sâmbătă sim·ba·ta
Sunday
  duminică doo·mee·nee·ka

January
  ianuarie yan·wa·rye
February
  februarie fe·broo·wa·rye
March
  martie mar·tye
April
  aprilie a·pree·lye
May
  mai ma·yee
June
  iunie yoon·ye
July
  iulie yoo·lye

August
  august ow·goost
September
  septembrie sep·tem·bree·ye
October
  octombrie ok·tom·bree·ye
November
  noiembrie no·yem·bree·ye
December
  decembrie de·chem·bree·ye

TRANSPORT
What time does the ... leave/arrive?
  La ce oră pleacă/soseşte ...?
  la che o·ra ple·ya·ka/so·sesh·te
  boat
    vaporul va·po·rool
  bus
    autobuzul ow·to·boo·zool
  train
    trenul tre·noo

'STREET' ROMANIAN

A few useful terms for getting around are:

Aleea	a·lee·ya	avenue
Bulevardul	boo·le·var·dool	boulevard
Calea	ka·le·ya	road
Piaţa	pya·tsa	square
Şoseaua	sho·sya·wa	highway
Strada	stra·da	street

---

first
  primul pree·mool
las
  ultimul ool·tee·mool
next
  următorul oor·ma·to·rool
arrival
  sosire so·see·re
departure
  plecare ple·ka·re
bus timetable
  mersul autobuzelor mair·sool ow·to·boo·ze·lor
train timetable
  mersul trenurilor mair·sool tre·noo·ree·loor

How long does the trip take?
  Cât timp durează excursia?
  kat·timp doo·re·ya·za eks·koor·sya
Where is the bus stop?
  Unde este staţia de autobuz?
  oon·de es·te sta·tsya de ow·to·booz

Where is the train station?
Unde este gara?
oon·de es·te ga·ra

Where is the left-luggage room?
Unde este biroul pentru bagaje de mână?
oon·de·es·te bee·rool pen·troo ba·ga·je de ma·na

I want to go to ...
Vreau să merg la ...
vre·ow sa mairg la ...

I'd like a ... ticket.
Aş dori un bilet ...
ash do·ree oon bee·let ...

one-way	
dus	doos
return	
dus-întors	doos·in·toors
1st class	
clasa întâi	kla·sa in·ta·yee
2nd class	
clasa a doua	kla·sa a doo·wa

How do I get to ...?
Cum ajung la ...?
koom a joong la ...

Is it near here?
Este aproape de aici?
es·te a·pro·a·pe de a·ee·chee

Is it far from here?
Este departe de aici?
es·te de·par·te de a·ee·chee

Can I walk there?
Pot să merg pe jos până acolo?
pot sa mairg pe jos pa·na a·ko·lo

Can you show me (on the map)?
Puteţi să-mi arătaţi (pe hartă)?
poo·te·tsee·mee a·ra·ta·tsee (pe har·ta)

Go straight ahead.
Du-te drept înainte.
doo·te drept in·a·yeen·te

left	
stânga	stin·ga
right	
dreapta	dre·yap·ta
at the traffic lights	
la semafor	la se·ma·for
at the next corner	
la următorul colţ	la oor·ma to·rool kolts
behind	
în spatele	in spa·te·le
in front of	
în faţa	in fa·tsa
opposite	
opus	o·poos
north	
nord/miazănoape	nord/mya·za·no·wa·pe
south	
sud/miazăzi	sood/mya·za·zee
east	
est/răsărit/orient	est/ra·sa·reet/o·ryent
west	
vest/apus/occident	vest/a·poos/ok·see·dent

Glossary

These handy Romanian words can also be used in Moldova. Hungarian (Hun) is included for key words.

ACR – Automobil Clubul Român
Agenţia Teatrală – theatre ticket office (Hun: színház jegyiroda)
Agenţie de Voiaj CFR – train ticket office (Hun: vasúti jegyiroda)
alimentară – food shop
Antrec – National Association of Rural, Ecological & Cultural Tourism
apă caldă – hot water (Hun: meleg víz)
apă rece – cold water (Hun: hideg víz)
astăzi – today
autogară – bus station (Hun: távolsági autóbusz pályaudvar)
autostrada – highway

bagaje de mână – left-luggage office (Hun: csomagmegőrző)
bandă roşie – red stripe (hiking)
barcă cu motor – motor boat
barcă cu rame – rowing boat
berărie – beer house
biserică – church (Hun: templom)
biserică de lemn – wooden church

cabană – mountain cabin or chalet
cale ferată – railway
cameră cu apă curentă – room with running water
cameră matrimonală – double room with a double bed
casă de bilete – ticket office (Hun: jegyiroda)
cascadă – waterfall
căsuţe – wooden hut
cazare – accommodation
CFR – Romanian State Railways
cheile – gorge
Crăciun – Christmas
crap – carp
cruce albastră – blue cross (hiking)

de jos – at the bottom
deschis – open (Hun: nyitva)
de sus – at the top
dispecerat cazare – accommodation office
drum – road, trip

en detail – retail (shopping)
en gros – wholesale (shopping)

floare de colţ – edelweiss

gară – train station (Hun: vasútállomás)
grădină de vară – summer garden
grind – sand dune

închis – closed (Hun: zárva)
ieşire – exit (Hun: kijárat)
intrare – entrance (Hun: bejárat)
intrarea interzisă – no entry (Hun: tilos belépni)

jos – low, down

mănăstire – monastery (Hun: kolostor)
mâine – tomorrow
meniu – menu
metropolitan – the head of a province of the church
muzeu – museum (Hun: múzeum)

noapte – night
notă (de plată) – bill (Hun: számla)

orar – timetable (Hun: menetrend)

păduri – forest
pâine – bread
parter – ground floor
pensiune – usually denotes a modern building or refurbished home, privately owned, that's been turned into accommodation for tourists
peron – platform
piaţa – square or market (Hun: főtér or piac)
piatră – stone, rock
plecare – departure (Hun: indulás)
popas – camping ground (Hun: kemping)
primărie – town hall
punct galben – yellow circle (hiking)

sală de concert – concert hall (Hun: hangversenyterem)
scaun de WC – toilet (Hun: toalett)
schimb valutar – currency exchange
scrumbie de Dunăre – Danube herring
şosea – road
sosire – arrival (Hun: érkezés)

spălătorie – laundrette (Hun: patyolat)
spălătorie auto – car wash
stradă – street
stufăriş – reed bed
sus – up
Sistematizire – systemisation – Ceauşescu's scheme for bulldozing entire rural villages and shifting inhabitants into purpose-built agro-industrial complexes on city outskirts or into concrete-block buildings

ţară – land, country
telecabină – cable car
teleferic – cable car
telescaun – chairlift

teleski – drag lift
terasă – terrace
toaleta – bathroom
traseu – hiking trail
triunghi roşu – red triangle (hiking)

vamă – customs (Hun: vámkezelés)
vilă – denotes a 19th- or 20th-century two- or three-storey house; many have been refurbished and turned into dwellings for tourists
vin alba – white wine (Hun: bor fehér)
vin roşu – red wine (Hun: bor vörös)

zi – day

Behind the Scenes

THIS BOOK

The 1st edition of this guide was written by Nicola Williams. She was joined by Kim Williams for the 2nd edition. This 3rd edition was written by Steve Kokker and Cathryn Kemp.

THANKS from the Authors

Steve Kokker Heart-felt *mulţumescs* to all the lovely people in these fascinating countries who helped me in this head-explodingly big project. Above all, thanks to Alexandru ('The Bat') Dumitru, my most reliable (and hilariously cynical) source of information (he should write the next edition!). Also, my gratitude to the sweet, smiley and ever-helpful Radu Vadeanu in Cluj-Napoca; Angord Zsolt-Kerekes and the charming thief Claudiu in Cluj-Napoca; Tudor and Gabi Petraru in Iaşi; Colin, Laura and the delightful Ramona Cazacu in Braşov; the Soldan family in Tarcău; Akes ('Seby') Vaida in Doi Mai; Bogdan Croitoru and the wonderful, *palincă*-swigging gang in Mangalia; Cristian Lascu, Iurie Maxim and Emilian Burdusel in Bucharest; Ionuţ Tomoiaga between Tulcea and Brăila; the local sheriff and owners of Cabana Mai in Răşnari; Adriana Popa, Corina and the warm-souled Costina Fulga in Constanţa; the resourceful Edit Bartha in Odorheuil Secuiesc; and to Rob Livengood, living up to his family name in Paltiniş.

In Moldova, I'll always be ready to have *la botul calului* with Ruslan, Maksim, Inna and Silva; huge thanks to Alexei Andreev, Ilya Trombitsky and Igor Rotaru for generously showing me more than I could have imagined; Sasha, my prima driver; Sergiu Calmic and the rest of the Ministry staff; the Taranu family in Cioburciu; the Griu family in Tudora; the dazzling Slavic Vutcariov in Ialoveni; Sergiu Sarojka; the border guards who accepted my bribe and let me into the country; and Denis from Taraclia.

Also thanks to Oana Suteu for setting things into motion in Montreal; and at LP, my eternal respect to Imogen Franks, a lovely soul and great editor.

Cathryn Kemp There are way too many people to thank personally for their insight, help and attention in Romania so I have to say a big thank you overall. But my heartfelt gratitude for his contacts, tips and patience has to go to Steve Kokker who was fantastic at every level during the making of this tough book. In Bucharest I gratefully thank the InYourPocket team, Accord Travel and Cornelius, the guide who showed me every corner of this great city. Thanks to the Vadu Izei team at the Information Centre who were charming and friendly and who greeted me like I was one of the family. And last but not least, to Jo and her fab mates in Bucharest – you saved me in my hours of need with strong spirits and plenty of Romanian wine!

CREDITS

Romania & Moldova 3 was commissioned and developed in Lonely Planet's London Office by Imogen Franks with assistance from Fiona Christie. Cartography for this guide was developed by Mark Griffiths, and the Project Manager was Huw Fowles.

This book was coordinated by Craig Kilburn (editorial), Bonnie Wintle (cartography) and Tamsin Wilson (layout). Craig was assisted by Carolyn Boicos, Emma Koch, Elizabeth Swan, Stephanie Pearson, Adrienne Costanzo, Rebecca Lalor, Cathryn

---

THE LONELY PLANET STORY

The story begins with a classic travel adventure: Tony and Maureen Wheeler's 1972 journey across Europe and Asia to Australia. There was no useful information about the overland trail then, so Tony and Maureen published the first Lonely Planet guidebook to meet a growing need.

From a kitchen table, Lonely Planet has grown to become the largest independent travel publisher in the world, with offices in Melbourne (Australia), Oakland (USA), London (UK) and Paris (France).

Today Lonely Planet guidebooks cover the globe. There is an ever-growing list of books and information in a variety of media. Some things haven't changed. The main aim is still to make it possible for adventurous travellers to get out there – to explore and better understand the world.

At Lonely Planet we believe travellers can make a positive contribution to the countries they visit – if they respect their host communities and spend their money wisely.

Game, Carly Hall, Katie Lynch and Melissa Faulkner. Bonnie was assisted by Louise Klep, and Tass was supported by Cris Gibcus, Kate McDonald and Sally Darmody in layout. The cover was designed by Brendan Dempsey, and the language chapter was looked after by Quentin Frayne.

THANKS from Lonely Planet
Many thanks to the travellers who used the last edition and contacted us with helpful hints, advice and interesting anecdotes:

A Nick Adlam, Joe Allred, Sonja Andreotti, Alan Andrews, Suttipong Aramkun, Hilmir Ásgeirsson, John Atherton, Andrei Avram **B** Seth Baker, François Barbiche, Andrew Barton, Pierre Bayenet, Ed Bell, Kriss Bell, Agnès Bensussan, Ulrich Berge, Mandi Booth, Sean Bowden, Jane Boxall, Graham Boyd, Michael Bratan, Claire Briggs, Henry Briscoe, Dawson Brown, Cristu Budescu, Hans J Buhrmester, Eileen Burke, Megan Burkholder, Mihai Bursesc, Catalin Buzatu **C** Andrew Cameron, Fergy Campbell, Andrew Cerchez, Roger Charret, Erin Christman, Yoav Cohen, Edward Congdon, Elizabeth Connolly, Lucy Cooper, Kevin Cornish, D N Coutts, Todd Covalcine **D** Alix Daley, John Dargie, Frederic de Condappa, Han de Looper, Michel Delporte, Hans Dirkse, Sarah Dodson, Peter Duffy, Michelle Dumford, Alexandru Dumitru, Alison Duthie, Kim Duva **E** Moray Easdale, Jalba Eugen **F** Susannah Farnworth, Christoph Fehlandt, Amy Fletcher, Heather Fraser, Anne Froger, Charlotte Froomberg **G** Wes Galt, Dorin Garofeanu, Rose George, Gerard Godbaz **H** Mark Hambly, Clare Hamilton, T Handler, David Harrison, Jennie Hatchel, John Hawboldt, Sina Helbig, Coleman Higgins, Matthew Higgins, Nick & Anita Hillman, Michael Hiltscher, Paul Hoffman, Matthew Hossack, Josephine Hutton, P N Hutton **I** Molnar Ildiko, Dancea Ioana **J** Caroline Jackson, Rok Jarc, Richard Jensen, Frank Jenssen, Nicky Johnson, Thomas Neumark Jones **K** J Kalina, Antti Karjalainen, Andrew Keeley, Jacqueline Ketel, Bianca Kimber, Robyn Kinsey, Andrew Knight, Denis Koishi, Jaap J Komen, Nathan Korpela, John Korst, Les Kozel, Sari Kreitzer **L** Anja Landgraf, Flo Le Corff, Lee Leatham, Guillaume Lecup, Alessandro Ledda, Jonathan Legg, Jorg Lehnert, Clare Lester, Juha Levo, Ruth Lloyd, Karin M Loch, John Lorden, Tero Luomala **M** Frank MacDonald, Robin MacGregor Lane, Richard Madge, Malcolm Martin, Alina Matei, Jennifer & Bruce McCoy, Tom McElderry, Ian McElmoyle, John McKellar, William McVeigh, E R Mein, Agota Molnar-Veress, Ian Moseley, Rittick Tonmoy Mukherjee, Bill Myer **N** Mary Nagy, Rudy Narine, Gavin Nathan, Luca Navarra, Beryl Nicholson, Annelies Nijboer **O** Jutta Loiuse Oechler, Razvan Oltean, Rikke Ortved, Alistair Ozanne **P** Jean Perrette, Julie Pervan, Vanessa Phillips, Oksana Podolyak, Oliver Pogatsnik, Robert Pontnau, Oliver Progatsnik **R** Carla Rodriguez, Julian Ross, David Rowe, Melanie Rubenstein, David Rubinstein **S** Marta & Paolo Saggiorato, Rachel Samsonowitz, Stefan Samuelsson, Wilhelm Scherz, Alexander Schleich, Adam Schreck, Lothar Schumann, Larry Schwarz, William Scraggs, Fulko Sennrat, John Sherman, Alex Shore, Richard Shrader, Terry Sikora, Lincoln Siliakus, Marc Smeehuijzen, Teresa Smith, Georgeta Stefan, Julie Stenberg, Lisa Stone, Katharina Stupka, Ms Susan **T** Chester Tapley, Michelle Tayleur, Dan Tebbutt, Louis Tisne, Scott Turner **V** Peter van Oostrum, Timea Vass, Anton van Veen, Marco Veul, Susan Viner **W** Andrew Wallace, Mike Wallace, Samantha Wamer, Julian & Steve Warner, Aaron Watson, Dawn Watson, Julie Webb, Gloria Widger, Edina Winternitz, Kate Wrigley **Z** Monica Zavoianu

SEND US YOUR FEEDBACK

We love to hear from travellers – your comments keep us on our toes and help make our books better. Our well-travelled team reads every word on what you loved or loathed about this book. Although we cannot reply individually to postal submissions, we always guarantee that your feedback goes straight to the appropriate authors, in time for the next edition. Each person who sends us information is thanked in the next edition – and the most useful submissions are rewarded with a free book.

To send us your updates – and find out about LP events, newsletters and travel news – visit our award-winning website: **www.lonelyplanet.com**.

Note: We may edit, reproduce and incorporate your comments in Lonely Planet products such as guidebooks, websites and digital products, so let us know if you don't want your comments reproduced or your name acknowledged. For a copy of our privacy policy visit www.lonelyplanet.com/privacy.

Index

INDEX

000 Map pages
000 Location of colour photographs

000 Map pages
000 Location of colour photographs

INDEX

LEGEND

ROUTES

	Tollway		Walking Path
	Freeway		Unsealed Road
	Primary Road		Pedestrian Street
	Secondary Road		Stepped Street
	Tertiary Road		Tunnel
	Lane		One Way Street
	Walking Tour		Walking Tour Detour

TRANSPORT

	Ferry		Rail
	Metro		Rail (Underground)
	Monorail		Tram

HYDROGRAPHY

	River, Creek		Lake (Salt)
	Intermittent River		Mudflats
	Canal		Reef
	Glacier		Swamp
	Lake (Dry)		Water

BOUNDARIES

	International		Ancient Wall
	State, Provincial		Cliff
	Regional, Suburb		Marine Park

POPULATION

● CAPITAL (NATIONAL)	◉ CAPITAL (STATE)
● Large City	● Medium City
● Small City	● Town, Village

AREA FEATURES

	Area of Interest		Land
	Beach, Desert		Mall
	Building		Market
	Cemetery, Christian		Park
	Cemetery, Other		Sports
	Forest		Urban

SYMBOLS

SIGHTS/ACTIVITIES
	Beach
	Buddhist
	Castle, Fortress
	Christian
	Confucian
	Diving, Snorkeling
	Hindu
	Islamic
	Jain
	Jewish
	Monument
	Museum, Gallery
	Picnic Area
	Point of Interest
	Ruin
	Shinto
	Sikh
	Skiing
	Taoist
	Winery, Vineyard
	Zoo, Bird Sanctuary

INFORMATION
	Bank, ATM
	Embassy/Consulate
	Hospital, Medical
	Information
	Internet Facilities
	Parking Area
	Petrol Station
	Police Station
	Post Office, GPO
	Telephone
	Toilets

SLEEPING
	Sleeping
	Camping

EATING
	Eating

DRINKING
	Drinking
	Café

ENTERTAINMENT
	Entertainment

SHOPPING
	Shopping

TRANSPORT
	Airport, Airfield
	Border Crossing
	Bus Station
	Cycling, Bicycle Path
	General Transport
	Taxi Rank
	Trail Head

GEOGRAPHIC
	Hazard
	Lighthouse
	Lookout
	Mountain, Volcano
	National Park
	Oasis
	Pass, Canyon
	River Flow
	Shelter, Hut
	Spot Height
	Waterfall

NOTE: Not all symbols displayed above appear in this guide.

LONELY PLANET OFFICES

Australia
Head Office
Locked Bag 1, Footscray, Victoria 3011
☎ 03 8379 8000, fax 03 8379 8111
talk2us@lonelyplanet.com.au

USA
150 Linden St, Oakland, CA 94607
☎ 510 893 8555, toll free 800 275 8555
fax 510 893 8572, info@lonelyplanet.com

UK
72–82 Rosebery Ave,
Clerkenwell, London EC1R 4RW
☎ 020 7841 9000, fax 020 7841 9001
go@lonelyplanet.co.uk

France
1 rue du Dahomey, 75011 Paris
☎ 01 55 25 33 00, fax 01 55 25 33 01
bip@lonelyplanet.fr, www.lonelyplanet.fr

Published by Lonely Planet Publications Pty Ltd
ABN 36 005 607 983

© Lonely Planet 2004

© photographers as indicated 2004

Cover photographs by Lonely Planet Images: Rural countryside, Romania, Diana Mayfield (front); Beach life at Constanţa, on the Black Sea, Juliet Coombe (back). Many of the images in this guide are available for licensing from Lonely Planet Images: www.lonelyplanet images.com.